PROMISES TO KEEP

Stopping by Woods on a Snowy Evening

Whose woods these are I think I know.
His house is in the village though;
He will not see me stopping here
To watch his woods fill up with snow.

My little horse must think it queer
To stop without a farmhouse near
Between the woods and frozen lake
The darkest evening of the year.

He gives his harness bells a shake
To ask if there is some mistake.
The only other sound's the sweep
Of easy wind and downy flake.

The woods are lovely, dark and deep,
But I have promises to keep,
And miles to go before I sleep,
And miles to go before I sleep.

—Robert Frost, 1923

PROMISES TO KEEP

The United States Since World War II

SECOND EDITION

PAUL S. BOYER

University of Wisconsin, Madison

HOUGHTON MIFFLIN   BOSTON   NEW YORK

Senior Sponsoring Editor: Jean Woy
Assistant Editor: Leah Strauss
Senior Project Editor: Janet Young
Editorial Assistant: Nasya Laymon
Associate Production/Design Coordinator: Jodi O'Rourke
Assistant Manufacturing Coordinator: Andrea Wagner
Marketing Manager: Sandra McGuire

Cover design by Diana Coe.

Credits appear on page 533.

Printed in the U.S.A.

Library of Congress Catalog Card Number: 98-71991

ISBN: 0-395-90386-6

123456789-DH-02 01 00 99 98

CONTENTS

Chapter 15
THE CLINTON YEARS: THE SEARCH FOR NEW DIRECTIONS
AT CENTURY'S END   445

List of Charts
and Graphs

LIST OF MAPS

PREFACE

Promises to Keep seeks to make sense of a cycle of American history whose beginnings are fading from memory but whose totality continues to shape the world in which we live. The initial impetus behind the book was a personal one: I was ten years old when World War II ended, and the post-1945 era thus coincides with a span of U.S. history that I myself experienced. Researching this book helped me to understand more about a period still vividly present in my own consciousness. Indeed, I frequently found that my recollections were imprecise and distorted, and needed to be checked against the historical record and current scholarship. I hope that this effort at self-education will prove useful to others as well, including those whose personal memories stop far short of 1945.

No work of history—and especially none dealing with the recent past—can claim to be definitive and final. *Promises to Keep* is an interim assessment intended to stimulate further interpretive efforts. Yet enough time has now passed that we can see some of the past half-century's major contours and fault lines. Thus, although the book includes essential factual coverage, it is also selective and interpretive, interweaving four principal themes.

The first of these is the pervasive impact of the Cold War, the superpower struggle that touched all facets of U.S. history from nuclear strategy and international relations to the domestic economy and culture. A second theme is the sweeping effect of a series of broad social-protest movements—among African-Americans, women, and others—that by the 1990s had given rise to a society radically different from the America of 1945.

Third, *Promises to Keep* pays close attention to an interconnected set of economic, demographic, and cultural changes, including changes in the manufacturing system and in the nature of work in America; religion's ever-shifting role in American life; population movements and changes in immigration patterns; and, not least, the new technologies that have transformed the way in which Americans communicate and entertain themselves, from television to personal computers, CDs, and VCRs.

Finally, the book takes politics seriously. The study of traditional political history declined after 1960 as many young scholars rightly found it (as then practiced) sterile and boring. But we are now gaining an enlarged understanding of politics as the arena where vital issues are defined, debated, and (sometimes) resolved. Ongoing political wrangles over budget deficits, health care, education reform, and social-welfare policy, for example, are part of a process by which Americans are deciding what kind of society they wish to live in and want their children to inherit.

The structure and style of *Promises to Keep* reflect my commitment to narrative history. History began in heroic tales and epics, and historians abandon these roots at their peril. Although I offer analysis and interpretation and discuss broad themes and trends, I do so within a narrative framework firmly grounded in human action and in the unfolding of the story over time. Reflecting this approach, the chapters are organized chronologically within four major sections. These sections are not arbitrary but reflect historical turning points.

Part One, "The American Century," focuses on the aftermath of World War II—the years when the optimism of victory dissipated amidst the U.S.-Soviet confrontation; a new political generation defined a post–New Deal public agenda; and citizens spooked by depression, war, and fresh global menaces sought the security of 1950s-style material abundance, mass culture, and suburban living.

Part Two, "Dissent, Terror, Reform," considers another side of the 1950s and carries the story forward to the mid-1960s. While the Cold War ground on, bringing moments of frightening confrontation and all manner of home-front ramifications, a surge of reform inspired by the southern civil-rights struggle crested in 1964–65 with a wave of legislation that represented the high-water mark of postwar liberalism.

Part Three, "The Loss of Innocence," explores the breakdown of this liberal consensus. The late sixties and early seventies saw turmoil and white backlash on the racial front, conflicts over the Vietnam War, and a wrenching political crisis summed up in a single word: Watergate.

Part Four, "Uncertain Triumph," brings the narrative to the present. As Americans in the seventies coped with the triple traumas of defeat in Vietnam, presidential malfeasance, and runaway inflation, they struggled to chart new directions in public policy and social action. While this reorientation brought feminism and environmentalism to the fore, it also spawned a conservative reaction that propelled Ronald Reagan to the White House in 1980 and that George Bush perpetuated in 1988. Democrat Bill Clinton, elected president in 1992, confronted radically new realities as the twentieth century ended. Domestically, Clinton and the nation grappled with issues as diverse as welfare reform, health-care policy issues, a booming but volatile economy, the legal ramifications of the new computer technologies, and the regulation of the tobacco industry and its deadly products. Internationally, Americans confronted a post–Cold War world that seemed to combine promise and menace in equal measure.

But structure and thematic generalizations, while essential if we are to make sense of history, are no substitute for attention to the gritty reality of the past. Through the book's fifteen chapters flow the juices of living history: the quiet heroism of civil-rights marchers; the charisma and shocking deaths of John and Robert Kennedy and Martin Luther King, Jr.; the vitriolic rhetoric of George Wallace; the boldness of feminists who challenged entrenched gender stereotypes; the passionate voices of writers such as Rachel Carson, Ralph Nader, and Michael Harrington who changed the way in which Americans perceived their society; the media wizardry of actor-turned-politician Ronald Reagan; the boyish computer tycoon Bill Gates; the colorful revival preachers and televangelists; the anxiety of blue-collar workers who faced disruptive economic changes; the courage of marchers and activists who revitalized the American reform tradition. History has been made not only in Washington, D.C., or in corporate boardrooms but at the grass roots all across the land—a fact that I have tried to keep constantly in mind while writing *Promises to Keep.*

This, then, is not an authoritative, predigested, take-it-or-leave-it version of recent U.S. history but one perspective on that history presented in a way that I hope will stimulate discussion and reflection. Not only the text but also the charts and graphs, the "In Perspective" essays, and the works listed in the "Selected Readings" that close each chapter are all intended to encourage readers to probe facets of the story more deeply and to reach their own conclusions.

No historian works in a vacuum, and certainly not one who rashly attempts an interpretive overview of five decades of American history. In addition to my own research in the sources, I have profited from the books and essays of scores of historians and journalists who have written about specific movements and events. These works are acknowledged in the chapter bibliographies, but I also wish to thank their authors here. Without the wealth of specialized scholarship now in print on the postwar period, the writing of this book would have been vastly more daunting.

This second edition of *Promises to Keep* not only assesses the central public issues and key domestic and international developments of the Clinton years, but also offers fresh interpretive perspectives on earlier events and trends. Each chapter introduces new findings and analytic insights based on the most recently published scholarship or newly released documents. The "In Perspective" essays, now featured in each chapter, place important topics in a broader historical framework. At the same time, through careful editing and pruning, the book has been shortened by some 25 pages, making it more readable and accessible for students and general readers alike.

I am grateful to the scholars who reviewed the second edition: David Bernstein, California State University—Long Beach; Roger Biles, East Carolina University; John J. Broesamle, California State University—Northridge; Gary May, University of Delaware; Jonathan Nashel, Indiana University—South Bend; and Marcia G. Synnott, University of South Carolina. The finished product is much stronger because of their unsparing but constructive criticism.

Heartfelt thanks, also, to the reviewers of successive chapter drafts of the first edition: Wesley Bagby, West Virginia University; Numan Bartley, University of Georgia; Hyman Berman, University of Minnesota; Barton Bernstein, Stanford University; David Bernstein, California State University—Long Beach; William Burton, Western Illinois University; Vincent Capowski, Saint Anselm College; William Deverell, University of California—San Diego; Joseph Dowling, Lehigh University; Anthony Edmunds, Ball State University; John Fairfield, Xavier University; Paul Faler, University of Massachusetts—Boston; Elizabeth Faue, Wayne State University; James Ferreira, Western Michigan University; James Findlay, University of Rhode Island; Steven Gillon, Yale University; Thomas Greene, Villanova University; Theodore Grivas, Sonoma State University; George Herring, University of Kentucky—Lexington; Dean Duncan Jamieson, Ashland University; Glenn Jeansonne, University of Wisconsin—Milwaukee; John Jeffries, University of Maryland—Baltimore; Wilbur Johnson, Rock Valley College; Christopher Kimball, Augsburg College; Paul Mertz, University of Wisconsin—Stevens Point;

William Moore, University of Wyoming; Otis Pease, University of Washington; David Roller, Bowling Green State University; Carl Ryant, University of Louisville; Steven Schoenherr, University of San Diego; Bruce Schulman, Boston University; Richard Sherman, College of William and Mary; James Sorelle, Baylor University; Marcia Synnott, University of South Carolina; Matthew Taylor, Rice University; Francis Thompson, Western Kentucky University; Samuel Webb, University of Alabama at Birmingham; Robert Westbrook, University of Rochester; and Kathleen Xidis, Johnson County Community College.

I am pleased to express my warm appreciation to the superb and supportive editorial team at Houghton Mifflin's College Division, especially Leah Strauss and Janet Young, who played such a crucial role in shepherding this second edition of *Promises to Keep* through the revision, review, and production processes. And a nostalgic salute to Jim Miller, Sylvia Mallory, Lauren Johnson, and others who were "present at the creation" when the first edition was planned, written, and brought into existence.

Finally, I take pleasure in acknowledging the friendship and sustained intellectual stimulation of my colleagues in the University of Wisconsin—Madison history department and at the Institute for Research in the Humanities housed in the Washburn Observatory overlooking Lake Mendora on the Madison campus. This fine old structure, built when Rutherford B. Hayes occupied the White House, provided not only an ideal workplace but also a living architectural link with the past as *Promises to Keep* was researched and written.

P.B.

PROMISES TO KEEP

PART ONE

The American Century

This book is the story of three generations of Americans. The first came of age during the Great Depression, fought in World War II or worked in home-front defense plants, and in 1945 looked forward to a future of peace, security, and prosperity. The second generation—the baby boomers—grew up in the affluent yet anxiety-ridden 1950s and reached maturity in the turbulent 1960s. The baby boomers' children, the third generation, will lead the United States in the early twenty-first century. To tell the story of these three generations is to write the history of the United States over the past half-century.

Part One focuses on the generation shaped by World War II and the early postwar years. The events and trends of that era molded the diplomacy, the politics, the economic and social agenda—even the cultural climate—of the next fifty years. The vast upheavals of 1941–45 also set the stage for the Cold War. This confrontation would split the wartime Grand Alliance, pitting the Soviet Union (and China, after 1949) against the United States and its Western European allies. World War II had scarcely ended before the new all-consuming confrontation began to influence U.S. foreign policy and military planning. Initially focused on Europe and the Middle East, the Cold War soon spread to Asia and elsewhere, including the United States itself. As fear of communism seized the nation, opportunistic politicians stoked suspicions of domestic subversion and disloyalty. Intellectuals who had criticized capitalism in the depression-ridden 1930s now hailed America as humanity's last best hope against totalitarianism. These thinkers deplored the vulgarity and conformity of middle-class culture but rarely challenged the postwar order in more fundamental ways.

World War II ended the Great Depression, revived the tarnished reputation of big business, and stimulated an economic boom. Military technological developments and production innovations gave rise to a postwar cornucopia of consumer products that enabled millions of Americans to enjoy unprecedented affluence. Construction techniques devised to house war workers made possible the suburbs that burgeoned in the late 1940s and the 1950s. Television, which would revolutionize U.S. politics, marketing, and mass culture, burst on the scene just after the war.

Fought against racist regimes abroad, World War II also revealed the irony of racism at home, most notably in the internment of thousands of Japanese Americans in remote detention camps in the West. Yet the global conflict also stimulated social changes that ultimately would defy entrenched gender, racial, and ethnic hierarchies. Women poured into war plants, thousands of African Americans migrated to cities, and Mexicans immigrated in great numbers to work in agriculture and in urban jobs. These demographic trends fostered social movements that would transform America in the decades ahead.

Finally, the war and the early Cold War years engendered a cultural mood that would resonate for decades. The conflict and the sweeping victory in 1945 stimulated national unity and encouraged feelings of national omnipotence summed up in the phrase the "American Century," coined in 1941 by magazine mogul Henry Luce. To some extent, this spirit of unity and high resolve spilled over into the immediate postwar years, as Washington mobilized public opinion against the new adversary based in Moscow. The stark rhetorical polarities of the early Cold War—polarities that pitted the "Free World" against the dark menace of a global communist conspiracy—enhanced the sense of destiny and mission that had long undergirded the national self-image. Booming prosperity whipped up further optimism about American capitalism, as well as pride in the American way of life.

But beneath the surface, currents of fear and uneasiness eddied. The nuclear arms race—the war's grimmest legacy—yielded nightmares of global annihilation. And beyond the well-tended suburbs lay a very different America of rural poverty and inner-city slums. The political process occasionally addressed the racial dis-crimination and economic disparities plaguing American society, but this early postwar generation more often swept such matters under the carpet. The Fair Deal, President Harry Truman's domestic reform program of 1948–49, may have set the political agenda for the next generation, but at the time most of Truman's program languished.

As the Democrats' long hold on the White House loosened in the early 1950s before a resurgent Republicanism led by war hero Dwight Eisenhower, the impe-tus for reform slackened. Dissenters—most notably African Americans no longer willing to tolerate second-class citizenship—would challenge the status quo more insistently as the decade wore on. Nevertheless, for a brief postwar moment, all seemed bright in America, and the future shone with promise. To a prospering and powerful nation, the "American Century" was not journalistic hyperbole but unvarnished truth.

CHAPTER 1

Crucible of Change: World War II and the Forging of Modern America

Few American entertainers of the 1940s enjoyed greater popularity than the singer Kate Smith, famous for her soaring rendition of "God Bless America." Thus, when CBS radio executives planned "War Bond Day" for September 21, 1943, they invited Miss Smith to host it. From 8 A.M. until well past midnight she tirelessly urged listeners to buy bonds, raising nearly $40 million in support of the war. The overwhelming success of "War Bond Day," thanks in part to the promptings of a popular-culture celebrity, symbolizes the national mood during World War II. During these years, the American people, reinforced by official propaganda and media publicity, stood united to a degree rarely seen either before or since. Social tensions and partisan conflicts simmered beneath the surface, but the widely shared goal of defeating the United States' enemies muted these differences.

For those who lived through it, World War II remains etched in memory, one of those events by which people mark the stages of their lives and define their generation. For historians, the war presents multiple layers of significance that go beyond the conflict itself and the immediate objectives for which it was fought. Any serious effort to understand modern America must circle back to World War II.

The Grand Alliance, Globalist Dreams, Big Power Realities

World War II spawned a tangle of postwar issues. This great conflict brought together an alliance of nations committed to the defeat of Germany, Italy, and Japan, the so-called Axis powers ruled by militaristic, expansionist dictatorships. The United States, Great Britain, and the Soviet Union led the coalition that ultimately defeated the Axis powers, and some policymakers hoped that this "Grand Alliance" among the "Big Three" would continue after the war. But the Grand Alliance, forged in opposition to a common foe rather than from a broad range of common interests, proved highly unstable. Although the U.S.-British coalition held firm and became part of a larger postwar Atlantic alliance linking the United States with Western Europe, the Soviet Union soon moved from the status of ally to that of deeply mistrusted adversary.

As for the Axis powers, ironically, World War II laid the groundwork for the eventual emergence of Germany and Japan as world economic giants and major trading competitors. Their industrial infrastructure shattered by bombs, both nations built new factories and the latest equipment from scratch after the war. This retooling depended, in part, on massive aid supplied by the United States, the nation that had defeated them militarily.

During the war itself, some visionaries hoped that out of the struggle would emerge a harmonious new global system based on internationalist principles. This dream, eloquently articulated by Woodrow Wilson during World War I, had survived the disillusionments of the interwar years and remained alive in the early 1940s. Republican Wendell Willkie's *One World* (1943), a wartime bestseller, fervently preached postwar global cooperation. The United Nations Charter, adopted at a fifty-nation conference in San Francisco in June 1945, seemed a step toward realizing this lofty vision.

Some opinion molders envisioned the new international order as a Pax Americana, or peace imposed by America. As early as 1941, writing in his *Life* magazine, publisher Henry R. Luce had hailed the advent of the "American Century." U.S. goods and popular culture already dominated the globe, proclaimed Luce; now the task was to spread American values: democracy, capitalism, philanthropy, and benevolence. "We must undertake now to be the Good Samaritan of the entire world," Luce grandly asserted. Physically untouched by the war, its industrial infrastructure intact and powerful, a seemingly omnipotent United States could well contemplate establishing a benign world order—the American way of life writ large.

But World War II had unleashed forces that would shatter the Grand Alliance, overwhelm the fledgling United Nations, and mock Henry Luce's rose-tinted scenario. The conflict left Europe prostrate and intensified nationalist stirrings in one-time colonial regions of Asia and Africa. Moreover, it set the stage for confrontation between the United States and the Soviet Union.

Soviet dictator Joseph Stalin held a very different view of the postwar world from the one envisioned by the Pax Americana theorists. Certainly Stalin had gone to war against Hitler in the early summer of 1941, thereby joining the Grand Alliance. But earlier, in August 1939, Hitler and Stalin had signed a nonaggression pact dividing Poland between them. The Nazi-Soviet Pact had collapsed in June 1941, however, when the German *Wehrmacht* (army), rumbling across a 2,000-mile front, attacked the Soviet Union. The U.S.S.R. suffered ghastly losses in repelling Hitler's forces. One campaign alone—the terrible German siege of Stalingrad in 1942–43—cost a million casualties on both sides. The Soviets' experience in what they called the "Great Patriotic War" deepened an already strong determination to maintain absolute security around the perimeter of their vast but unstable empire.

By the summer of 1945, Soviet armed might stood unrivaled on much of the Eurasian land mass. That stark military fact would soon translate into political realities. Repelling the Nazi invaders, the Soviet army had swept across Eastern Europe and thrust deep into Germany in the war's final months. Stalin set out to build a buffer zone of Soviet-controlled satellite states in this region. Marxist-Leninist ideology, with its prediction of inevitable world revolution, neatly dovetailed with Russian concerns about border security. Stalin also sought a sphere of influence in Eastern Europe to match what he saw as Anglo-American dominance in Western Europe. Even as the war wound down, shrewd observers detected the contours of a new conflict in the diametrically opposed worldviews of the two emerging superpowers.

During the war, a series of Big Power conferences and pronouncements had glossed over these differences. At the final meeting of the wartime Big Three leaders, held at the Crimean resort of Yalta early in 1945, Stalin, President Franklin D. Roosevelt, and British prime minister Winston Churchill laid plans for pursuing the war in the Pacific and set the course for the early postwar era. Stalin agreed to join the planned United Nations after extracting a pledge from Roosevelt and Churchill to admit two Soviet republics, Ukraine and Byelorussia, as full UN members. The Soviet leader secretly pledged to declare war on Japan within "two or three months" of Germany's surrender, in return for an occupation zone in Korea and other concessions. The Americans viewed Stalin's promise as highly important, because Japan, although battered in the Pacific island campaign and running low on war materiel and fuel, still had more than 4 million troops under arms.

The shadow of Poland hung over Yalta. Germany's invasion of that nation in 1939 had triggered the war, and the Western powers felt a moral obligation to protect Poland's postwar interests. Furthermore, a large Polish-American community in the United States remained vitally interested in the homeland. Nevertheless, Roosevelt and Churchill were in a weak bargaining position, given the Soviets' physical hold on Poland. On the key question of Poland's postwar boundaries, Stalin demanded a slice of the eastern portion of the country. More important, to weaken hated Germany, he proposed moving Poland's western boundary so as to incorporate large chunks of eastern Germany. Playing a weak hand, Roosevelt and Churchill proposed deferring the Polish-border issue to a postwar "peace conference," which never convened. After the war, Stalin unilaterally rearranged Poland's borders as he had proposed at Yalta. In another Yalta agreement that proved meaningless, Stalin offered promises of free elections in postwar Eastern Europe. In reality, he imposed pro-Soviet regimes throughout the occupied lands where his armies held sway.

Yalta would play a key role in American domestic politics when in the 1950s, Republicans charged that President Roosevelt had "given away" Eastern Europe to Stalin. In fact, the realities of Soviet military control of Eastern Europe, hopes that the United Nations might indeed function as a force for peace and world order, and FDR's eagerness to secure Stalin's entry into the war against Japan all shaped the terms of the Yalta settlement. But the tenacious myth of a "great betrayal" at Yalta would for years be used by Republicans to portray Democrats as naive dupes, if not traitors, in their dealings with the Soviet Union.

Popular misconceptions of the wartime alliance helped shape Americans' postwar attitudes toward the Soviets. Behind the scenes, this coalition of wartime convenience crackled with tension, as Stalin made territorial demands and urgently called on the Allies to open a western front against the Nazis, a move that the Allies delayed until 1944. Despite Stalin's cooperation with the West against Germany, his brutal regime in many ways mirrored Hitler's. Indeed, as we have seen,

Stalin and Hitler in 1939 had cynically sliced up Poland between them. In 1940 Soviet forces had massacred twenty thousand Polish officers and subsequently blamed the Nazis for the crime.

Most Americans, however, remained largely unaware of these tensions. The media and official Washington pronouncements generally presented the Soviet Union as a heroic ally in a struggle for common ideals. One poster depicted a row of cannons bearing the flags of the United States, the Soviet Union, and the other Allies with the caption "UNITED We Will Win." Hollywood movies such as *Mission to Moscow* (1943), *North Star* (1943), and *Song of Russia* (1944), produced with the Roosevelt administration's blessing, offered idealized images of the brave Russian people struggling against the Nazi invaders. *Life* magazine portrayed pipe-puffing "Uncle Joe Stalin" as a benevolent, beloved leader.

Such propaganda encouraged the popular assumption that Soviet-American cooperation would endure into the postwar era. Yet within months of the war's end, as conflicts and power rivalries took shape, U.S. leaders began publicly to portray the Soviet Union in menacing terms. Americans soon came to view the Soviet Union with a deep hostility that was a mirror image of the simplistic and rose-tinted perceptions fostered during the war. Thus, as the war years' unrealistic expectations eroded under harsh postwar realities, disillusionment set in and a stark, black-and-white worldview emerged that would characterize Cold War America. In this, as in many other ways, World War II continued to influence events long after hostilities had ceased.

High Resolve and National Unity

Most of America's twentieth-century wars were far from universally popular. In 1917, a minority of socialists, pacifists, and some German Americans bitterly opposed President Woodrow Wilson's call for war. The Korean War (1950–53) initially won broad support, but many citizens soon turned against the frustrating, stalemated conflict. The Vietnam War proved deeply divisive in the 1960s.

World War II was different; it stirred near-universal feelings of patriotism and common purpose, and for good reason. Although the conflict actually started when Germany invaded Poland on September 1, 1939, for Americans it began on December 7, 1941, with Japan's sneak attack on the U.S. Pacific fleet at Pearl Harbor, which killed 2,400 U.S. servicemen. In his war message, President Roosevelt described December 7 as "a date which will live in infamy," and, indeed, "Remember Pearl Harbor" became a driving slogan of the war. Unlike the murky justifications offered for some other wars, the issues in 1941–45 seemed crystal clear: to avenge Pearl Harbor and to defeat the dictators and militarists in Germany, Italy, and Japan who threatened the world with their racism, totalitarianism, and brute strength. With enemies like these, the war took on overtones of a religious crusade. Americans "in their righteous might," Roosevelt proclaimed after Pearl Harbor, "will win through to . . . inevitable triumph." One top general, George C. Patton, reportedly assured a group of army chaplains that he went to church "every goddam Sunday."

If GIs at the front felt less enthusiasm than propagandists suggested, most nevertheless believed that they were fighting for a just cause and performing a necessary job. Families that sent a son or daughter into the service proudly displayed a blue star in their window. Those who received the dreaded War Department telegram that began "I regret to inform you . . ." substituted a gold star. Millions purchased war bonds, contributed to paper drives, and planted victory gardens. War workers shared in the sense of national purpose. As one recalled, Pearl Harbor brought "an immediate change in people's attitude toward their work—their sense of urgency, their dedication, their team work." Children chalked caricatures of Hitler and Japan's wartime military leader Hideki Tojo on walls and turned in pencil stubs so the graphite could be recycled as a lubricant. Gleefully, they passed along anti-German, anti-Japanese jokes overheard from adults. (The German *Messerschmidt* fighter, they told each other, savoring the naughty word, was a "mess o' shit.") When Japan formally surrendered on August 14, 1945, the nation erupted in celebration. Even toddlers sensed the excitement; one man recalled decades later: "I remember leading a parade of kids around our summer house, me with a potato masher."

To be sure, the war spirit was carefully orchestrated. The government's Office of War Information (OWI) ground out propaganda posters, magazine ads, and radio spots and worked with Hollywood studios to ensure that wartime movies promoted patriotism and reinforced U.S. war aims. Director Frank Capra's *Why We Fight* series offered troops the OWI version of the nation's objectives and the heinous nature of the enemy. By controlling the flow of photographs from the front, particularly images of U.S. dead, the OWI further molded popular perceptions of the conflict. The OWI also fostered myths of American GIs' wisecracking under fire, such as the one about the survivors of a bloody U.S. assault in the Pacific who supposedly radioed the jaunty message: "Send us more Japs."

Another government agency, the Office of Civilian Defense (OCD), offered an idealized version of the home-front mood. A 1942 OCD pamphlet reported, "The kids still play baseball in the corner lot—but they knock off early to weed the victory garden, cart scrap paper to the salvage center, carry home the groceries that used to be delivered." These manipulative techniques, however heavy-handed, had their desired effect: a nation already well aware of the stakes of the conflict solidified its support for the war.

Influential mass-culture organs—from movies, ads, cartoons, and popular songs to novels, essays, newspaper editorials, and political speeches—contributed to the martial mood. The association of music educators did its bit in 1943 by preparing a version of "The Star-Spangled Banner" that was pitched in A-flat, and thus easier to sing. The heroes of children's radio shows like *The Green Hornet* and *Captain Midnight* pursued enemy spies and saboteurs. *Dick Tracy* fans who promised to save scarce wartime commodities had their names inscribed on the show's "Victory Honor Roll." Over a million youthful listeners to *Jack Armstrong–All-American Boy* joined his "Write-a-Fighter Corps," pledging to write a soldier once a month. Even comic-strip characters, including the hero of "Terry and the Pirates," marched off to war. Of the major male comic-strip characters, only Superman and Li'l Abner (Al Capp's stereotypical southern hayseed) failed to don a U.S. military uniform. (Superman, of course, already had a uniform in which to fight for "truth, justice, and the American way.") War reporters such as Ernie Pyle, and battlefront cartoonists such as Bill Mauldin might underscore the grimmer aspects of war, but they never questioned the righteousness of the war itself.

Only rarely in 1941–45 did an American writer suggest that even a just war could involve official hypocrisy, routinized slaughter, and the denial of the essential humanity of those labeled "the enemy." Among the few who acknowledged this side of the story was the poet Randall Jarrell, whose 1945 poem "Losses" began:

> In bombers named for girls, we burned
> The cities we had learned about in school—
> Till our lives wore out; our bodies lay among
> The people we had killed and never seen.
> When we lasted long enough they gave us medals.
> When we died they said "Our casualties were low."

A few pacifists and religious leaders protested the Allies' terror-bombing of cities, a practice initiated by the Nazis that spread more widely as the war ground on. (In fact, the firebombing of Tokyo by an armada of U.S. B-29s on the night of March 10–11, 1945, killed more civilians than later died in the atomic bombing of Hiroshima.) The political writer Dwight Macdonald, anticipating a theme later expanded by opponents of the Vietnam War, warned of the anonymity of mass slaughter by modern technological means. In *Politics,* his one-man journal of opinion, Macdonald wrote in 1944:

> One of the things which makes it possible for a modern civilian to participate in war without more psychological resistance . . . is the fact that the murderous aspect of war is depersonalized. Most of the killing is done at such long range that the killers have no sense of the physical effects of their attack. . . . [I]t is one thing to know that one may be responsible for the death and mutilation of invisible people ten miles away or five miles down, and another to cut a man's throat with one's own hands.

But such reflections were rare as the nation mobilized for the struggle against totalitarianism.

Despite propaganda campaigns that channeled patriotism in specific directions, Americans' overwhelming support for the war was genuine. At the most elemental level, Americans saw the war as a fight for a perhaps semi-mythic but cherished way of life that the Axis powers threatened. Lumps swelled in throats when Kate Smith sang "God Bless America"; when Humphrey Bogart gave up Ingrid Bergman to Paul Henreid, a courageous Czech Resistance leader, in *Casablanca* (1943); when Bing Crosby crooned "I'm Dreaming of a White Christmas," the hit song of 1942; or when the hero of Nevil Shute's *Pied Piper* (1942) spirited a group of children out of France ahead of the advancing Nazis. A California girl later reminisced, recalling her family's victory garden, "[W]e all wanted to do our part for the war. You got caught up in the mesmerising spirit of patriotism."

Anticipating a major cultural theme of the 1950s, the propagandists of 1941–45 defined American war aims in terms of community life and family togetherness. One war-bond poster featured a little girl with a message written in a childish hand: "Please help bring my Daddy home." The war's most famous visual images, initially published as *Saturday Evening Post* covers, were Norman Rockwell's illustrations of the "Four Freedoms" enunciated by President Roosevelt in 1941. In Rockwell's version, a family Thanksgiving dinner embodied "Freedom from Want," a mom and dad lovingly looking at their sleeping children represented "Freedom from Fear," a man having his say at a New England town meeting stood for "Freedom of Speech," and parishioners in a little church portrayed "Freedom of Worship."

In contrast to the Vietnam era, World War II veterans came back as heroes. The Servicemen's Readjustment Act of 1944, popularly known as the GI Bill of Rights, gave veterans hiring preference, tuition and other educational benefits, and loan guarantees to purchase homes, farms, or small businesses. The measure staved off postwar unemployment and eased veterans' reentry into the labor force, although often displacing women workers. Driving college enrollments to record highs, the act hastened the growth of a college-trained middle class in postwar America. Finally, the program contributed to a surge of suburban housing construction.

Just as wartime unity and idealism affected Cold War attitudes toward the Soviet Union, so, too, did they influence the postwar domestic political climate. As the sense of common purpose gave way to political dissent and ideological differences—normal ferment in a democracy—some Americans responded by charging dissenters with disloyalty and even subversion. The climate of the war years thus contributed to the postwar drive for conformity, as patriots tried to impose on the nation the consensus and dedication to a common purpose that characterized the war era. As early as 1944, while the war still raged, the Republican vice-presidential candidate, Senator John W. Bricker of Ohio, ominously previewed the postwar air of suspicion when he warned that sinister and divisive forces were "worming their way into our national life."

The American Economy Goes to War

The war finally broke the back of the Great Depression and laid the foundation for sustained postwar economic growth. After Pearl Harbor, surging military spending and war production fueled an economic boom, and by June 1942, more than $100 billion in military contracts had poured out of Washington. By 1943–44, with war production in full swing, joblessness almost vanished. The Works Progress Administration (WPA), the New Deal's principal relief agency, distributed its final checks early in 1943.

The war brought unprecedented affluence for millions of Americans. From 1939 to 1945, average real wages for all employees (adjusted for inflation) increased 44 percent, and the gross national product soared from $90 billion to $212 billion. Farmers prospered as crop production rose by 50 percent and farm income by 200 percent in the period. Reviving prosperity stimulated an upturn in the birthrate. The 1943 birthrate, although below that of the fecund 1950s, was still more than 20 percent higher than the mid-1930s rate. Despite the absence of many males at the front, the "postwar baby boom" actually began during the war itself.

The heavy government spending of 1941–45 appeared to validate the theories of British economist John Maynard Keynes, who argued that to fight a depression, a government should stimulate consumer demand and buying power through massive spending, even if large budget deficits resulted in the short run. FDR, distrustful of unbalanced budgets, had rejected Keynesianism during the 1930s, but the war-induced spending of the early 1940s produced precisely the economic result that Keynes had predicted, although by means of military spending rather than government-encouraged consumer buying.

With the military absorbing much of the nation's industrial and agricultural production, numerous consumer goods and basic foodstuffs fell in short supply (coffee, sugar, butter, and meat) or disappeared entirely (new cars, household appliances). Many citizens, now benefiting from rising wages, apparently saw no contradiction between patriotic support for the war and turning to the black market to acquire and hoard scarce goods, thereby circumventing wartime rationing.

When the war began, a British observer, D. W. Brogan, predicted that the U.S. war effort, like the rest of American life, would be mechanized, and that victory would depend on the nation's "colossal business enterprises, often wastefully run in detail, but winning by their mere scale." Brogan was right. The war drove industrial production to new levels. Factories ran twenty-four hours a day, pouring out planes, tanks, jeeps, guns, and the vast array of support materials, from shoes to typewriters, needed by the military. The Ford bomber plant at Willow Run, Michigan, with a main building covering sixty-seven acres, employed more than forty thousand workers. One awed observer called it "a sort of Grand Canyon of the mechanized world." By 1944, total annual U.S. aircraft production reached a stag-

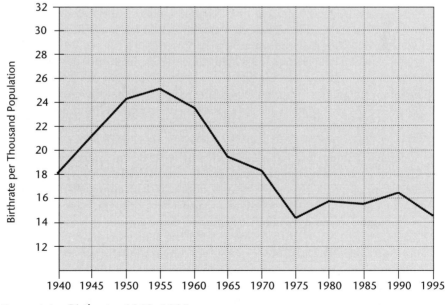

FIGURE 1.1   *Birthrate, 1940–1995*

SOURCE: National Center for Health Statistics, U.S. Dept. of Health and Human Services, as reported in *Statistical Abstract of the U.S., 1997* and *World Almanac, 1998.*

Homefront Patriotism. *Urged on by the U.S. government and by the advertising industry, citizens across America, such as these in New York City, contributed aluminum, graphite, and other materials to aid the war effort.* (Hulton Getty/Tony Stone Images)

gering 96,318. Dam builder Henry J. Kaiser, turning to ship construction during the war, cut the manufacturing time for a cargo carrier from 355 days to 14. Securing government loans to cover start-up costs, Kaiser by 1943 held $3 billion in war contracts and controlled 30 percent of U.S. shipbuilding. Even occasional embarrassments such as a ship that sank at the launching dock left intact Kaiser's reputation as a wizard of wartime production.*

Some feared that the Depression would come roaring back once the war ended, but in fact the groundwork was being laid for a postwar boom. Mass-production and prefabrication techniques perfected in wartime would soon be converted to peacetime purposes, and the accumulated savings and pent-up purchasing impulses of war workers would fuel a monumental postwar buying binge. Wartime productivity feats had ideological consequences as well, for the corporate contribution to victory reshaped popular attitudes toward business. After the 1929 stock-market crash, the reputation of businessmen had plummeted, and in 1936 President Roosevelt had denounced them as "malefactors of great wealth." As war approached, however, Washington portrayed giant corporations as partners in a common cause. A wartime Senate committee admiringly noted, "The hand that signs the war contract is the hand that shapes the future." Congress granted war industries tax breaks and exemption from antitrust laws. Many corporate executives served in Washington as unpaid administrators of wartime agencies. Factories proudly flew the "Army and Navy 'E'" banner (a War Department commendation), and a heavy gloss of patriotism overlay corporate advertising. Indeed, some business ads did not mention a product

---

* Kaiser also pioneered an employee medical plan that would later provide a model for health-care plans nationwide, another example of World War II's long historical reach.

at all but simply featured public-service messages urging Americans to buy bonds. "War Bonds Mean Bullets in the Bellies of Nazi Hordes," proclaimed one ad sponsored by a New York City banking association.

Businesses showed remarkable ingenuity in linking their products to the war effort. By building bottling plants wherever GIs went, the Coca-Cola Company cultivated a taste for Coke among the troops and developed a worldwide market. The Parker Pen Company boosted sales of its ink 800 percent with an ad campaign reminding Americans of their patriotic duty to write long and frequent letters to lonely GIs overseas. Tobacco companies hooked a new generation of smokers by distributing free cigarettes to soldiers, including those in military hospitals. As John Morton Blum notes in *V Was for Victory* (1976), Philip K. Wrigley persuaded the government to include his Wrigley's chewing gum in the "K-Rations" (food packs) distributed to servicemen in combat and urged war plant managers to give each worker five sticks daily to combat boredom, fatigue, nervous tension, and an insidious condition known as "false thirst."

The war influenced corporate attitudes toward government as well. In the 1930s, many corporate leaders had vehemently attacked the New Deal and the proliferation of regulatory agencies. Now the mood shifted. As FDR appointed businessmen to Washington posts and the shower of military contracts demonstrated the profitable possibilities in business-government cooperation, antigovernment hostility faded. In *America Unlimited* (1944), Eric Johnston of the U.S. Chamber of Commerce sought to solidify the heightened prestige of business and to reinforce corporate leaders' newly positive attitude toward government. "[C]redit for the most astounding production job in all human history," declared Johnston, "must go primarily to American capitalism." Calling for an end to the feud between corporate America and the Roosevelt administration, Johnston urged forward-looking capitalists to embrace "a middle way . . . of realistic adjustment between old-style laissez-faire capitalism and [the] current economy." Such conciliatory views decisively influenced postwar political thought. President Dwight Eisenhower's espousal of "moderate Republicanism" in the 1950s rested on the premise of cooperation between government and enlightened leaders from all sectors of society, including business. Thanks in part to memories of the wartime experience, this view won many adherents.

Organized labor, which had thrived in the later New Deal years, experienced further growth but also setbacks during the war. To head off strikes that could hurt war production and to control inflationary wage increases, the Roosevelt administration limited hourly wage raises during the war to no more than the rise in the cost of living. (Thanks to overtime hours at time-and-a-half pay, however, many war workers took home fat paychecks.) To enforce the labor unions' wartime "no-strike" pledge, the National War Labor Board (NWLB) focused on settling disputes by arbitration. In 1943 conservatives in Congress passed, over Roosevelt's veto, the Smith-Connally Anti-Strike Act. This law forbade political contributions by labor unions and expanded the president's powers to take over war plants threatened by labor disputes. When the nation's rail workers threatened a strike late in 1943, the U.S. Army at FDR's direction briefly seized the railroads. In another example of the war's aftereffects, these measures anticipated the Taft–Hartley Act of 1947, which further restricted labor unions.

Despite these constraints, the surge in wartime employment proved a boon to the labor movement. From 1941 to 1945, union membership soared from about

10.5 million to nearly 15 million. By the latter year, nearly 36 percent of the labor force was unionized, an all-time high. Moreover, the NWLB adopted a generally prounion stance. As one example, the board resisted corporate efforts to impose an open-shop rule, permitting workers in unionized plants to remain outside the union if they wished. The NWLB gave new employees in unionized plants fifteen days to resign from the union if they desired. After that, they were required to pay union dues as long as the plant remained unionized. Overall, the labor movement came of age during World War II, as the principle of collective bargaining gained wide acceptance. At the same time, the wartime boom and the favorable climate toward unions diluted the militance of the 1930s and led to a bureaucratization of the labor movement that would prove costly after the war.

Government and Politics in the War Years

The role of the federal government, already vastly enlarged in the New Deal era, expanded still more in 1941–45 as wartime agencies mobilized the economy and the American people for total war. The War Production Board oversaw resource allocation and industrial output. The National War Labor Board arbitrated labor disputes in defense industries. The Office of Price Administration (OPA) touched every American with its rent controls in cities with war plants and its price controls and ration coupons for butter, sugar, coffee, meat, tires, gasoline, and other products. Although merchants, landlords, and many consumers grumbled at the OPA's bureaucracy, it achieved its goal: from mid-1943 to mid-1945, consumer prices rose by less than 2 percent. These and other agencies brought home to Main Street the reality of Washington's expanded regulatory role. As one New Dealer observed in 1943, "The most important change wrought by the war has been the greatly increased participation of Government in our economic life." Even FDR's Republican predecessor, Herbert Hoover, declared in 1942, "To win total war, President Roosevelt must have many dictatorial economic powers. There must be no hesitation in giving them to him."

Overall, the ranks of civilian federal employees more than tripled from 1940 to 1945, growing from a little more than 1 million to nearly 3.4 million. The giant Pentagon building, erected in 1942 to house the War Department, symbolized the expansion of the executive branch. Celebrated as the world's largest office building, the Pentagon featured 17.5 miles of corridors.* This ballooning of the federal bureaucracy, coupled with Washington's enlarged wartime role, accelerated a long-term trend in twentieth-century U.S. history, one that would continue in the decades to come.

Wartime politics cast a long shadow on postwar political history. In 1940 President Roosevelt had won an unprecedented third term, defeating Republican candidate Wendell Willkie. As Roosevelt shifted roles from, as he put it, "Dr. New Deal" to "Dr. Win-the-War," his popularity remained high. In 1944, despite undisclosed failing health, he ran for a fourth term against New York governor Thomas E. Dewey and again won, garnering 53.4 percent of the vote. Despite voter frustra-

---

* The construction of the Pentagon was supervised by General Leslie R. Groves, later director of the Manhattan Project, the research effort that developed the atomic bomb.

tion with wartime regulation and Republican attacks on the administration's alleged radicalism and socialistic tendencies, the Rooseveltian magic and well-coordinated Democratic efforts to retain the Solid South while wooing blacks, union members, and big-city ethnics—all key components of the New Deal coalition—paid off. Roosevelt's wartime role as commander-in-chief, along with favorable news from the front, also served him well at the polls.

Nevertheless, the conservative shift already evident in the late 1930s and in the 1940 election was accelerating. In the midterm election of 1942, Republicans gained nine Senate and forty-four House seats. Farmers led the defection from the New Deal coalition. Their goal, however, was not to reduce the government's role in the economy but to enlarge it. Specifically, they wanted increased federal price supports for agricultural commodities. When the administration tried to fight inflation by capping escalating agricultural price supports, the farmers, especially the larger agribusinesses represented by the American Farm Bureau Federation, struck back at the polls.

Interpreting the 1942 election as a repudiation of the New Deal, a conservative coalition of Republicans and southern Democrats in Congress in 1943 passed the Smith–Connally Anti-Strike Act and slashed the funding of many New Deal agencies. That same year, the House Un-American Activities Committee, which in the 1950s would stoke the flames of a domestic Red Scare, issued a list of administration officials it considered dangerously radical. Observed the liberal *New Republic,* "The New Deal is being abandoned.... A new crowd is preparing to take over." The conservative coalition that solidified after the 1942 election would hold sway in Congress for years to come. In short, the shift to the right that would profoundly influence American politics in later decades had gathered steam in the war years.

The Republican party, while united in its desire to unseat Roosevelt, otherwise suffered from deep internal divisions. Across a broad swath of states from Ohio to Colorado, conservative GOP members denounced the New Deal and adopted isolationist stances in foreign policy. Influential legislators such as Senator Robert A. Taft of Ohio, son of former president William Howard Taft, led this wing of the party. The Republican party's eastern, New York–based wing, by contrast, was more internationalist in outlook and marginally more receptive to the fundamental contours of the welfare state. Thomas E. Dewey, for example, elected governor of New York in 1942 after winning fame as a racket-busting district attorney, accepted various New Deal programs, including social security. The 1940 Republican presidential candidate, Wendell Willkie, although a native of Indiana and a power-company executive, embodied this internationalist, somewhat more liberal wing of the Republican party. (His 1943 book, *One World,* written after a world tour undertaken with Roosevelt's blessing, underscored his global vision.) Midwestern conservatives deplored the maverick Willkie, and his campaign for the 1944 Republican presidential nomination had already failed before his death from a heart attack that fall. Yet despite Republican right-wingers' strength in the party, they could not control it, and the 1944 presidential nomination went to Dewey. Senator Taft and other archconservatives mistrusted Dewey, whom Taft called "arrogant and bossy." The New Yorker's skill at building alliances—he named Ohio's conservative senator John Bricker as his running mate, for example—brought the party a degree of unity. But Dewey's stiff manner alienated voters (one critic quipped that he was the only man who could strut sitting down), and he lost the election to FDR.

Roosevelt's 1944 decision to change running mates also helped the Democrats to hold the White House until 1952. Vice President Henry Wallace would have continued happily in that post, but his unabashed liberalism had antagonized the party's conservative wing, and Roosevelt dropped him. In choosing Senator Harry S Truman of Missouri from a large field of prospects, Roosevelt unwittingly bequeathed his final legacy to the American people. A protégé of Kansas City's corrupt Democratic political machine, Truman had won respect as an honest, hardworking senator but enjoyed little national reputation. "Who the hell is Harry Truman?" exploded a top navy official upon learning of the nomination.

The importance of Roosevelt's choice became apparent on April 12, 1945, when the vacationing sixty-three-year-old president died of a massive cerebral stroke. The administration and the media had largely concealed Roosevelt's worsening health, so the news came as a profound shock. The radio networks broke into regular programming for the bulletin; newspapers unfurled their blackest headlines; in the Solomon Islands halfway around the world, a U.S. Navy patrol boat received the message in Morse code beamed from a nearby island: "Y-E-S-T-E-R-D-A-Y P-R-E-S-I-D-E-N-T R-O-O-S-E-V-E-L-T D-I-E-D." On the eve of victory, the wartime leader had fallen. As the nation mourned, Truman assumed the presidency. The news of Roosevelt's death, he told reporters, made him feel as if "the moon, the stars, and all the planets had fallen on me." Over the next seven years, however, Truman would prove a far more capable chief executive than most would have predicted in April 1945.

A People in Wartime

World War II generated population movements, social changes, and ethnic tensions that deeply influenced postwar American life. Continuing a long-term trend, urbanization gained momentum. As war plants posted "Help Wanted" signs, workers flocked to the cities. An estimated 15 million Americans moved during the war to take advantage of job opportunities. Indiana farm girls, for example, ventured to Dayton, Ohio, to work as secretaries at Wright-Patterson Air Force Base. Cities in the mid-Atlantic region burgeoned, as did southeastern coastal regions that were home to shipyards and naval bases. The industrial belt around Detroit hummed as auto companies converted to war production. The West Coast, especially California, with its sprawling shipyards and aircraft plants, saw explosive growth. California's population spurted by 3.7 million in the 1940s. Many newcomers would remain in the cities, or more typically move to the suburbs, once the war ended. Indeed, the migration to the suburbs that reached flood tide in the 1950s was already well under way during the war.

Population movements on such a scale produced severe housing shortages and overcrowding, with families doubling up in beds or even sleeping in garages. Some landlords devised the "hot bunk" system, renting the same bed to three different tenants working successive eight-hour shifts. In 1942 Roosevelt set up the

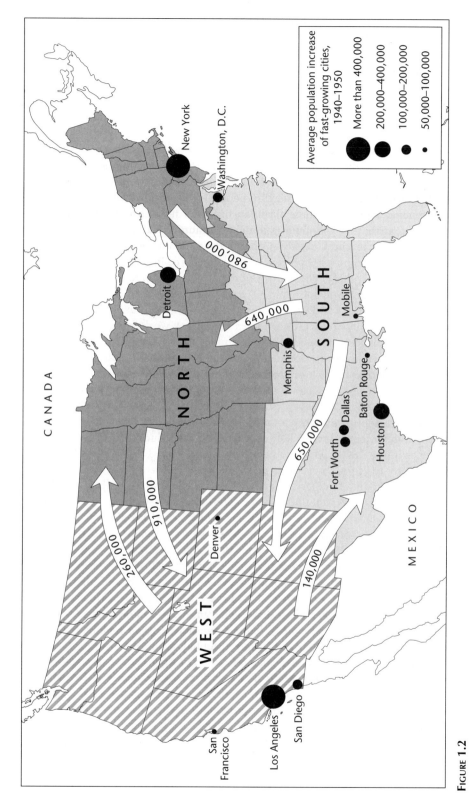

Legend (map key):

Average population increase
of fast-growing cities,
1940–1950

- More than 400,000
- 200,000–400,000
- 100,000–200,000
- 50,000–100,000

Map labels:

CANADA

New York
Washington, D.C.
Detroit
Memphis
Mobile
Dallas
Fort Worth
Baton Rouge
Houston
Denver
San Francisco
Los Angeles
San Diego

NORTH
SOUTH
WEST

MEXICO

Migration flow figures:

980,000
640,000
650,000
910,000
790,000
140,000

FIGURE 1.2
Internal Migration in the United States During World War II

17

Federal Housing Agency to respond to this shortage. By the war's end, a combination of federal and private construction had built more than 1.8 million new housing units. Construction firms such as Abraham Levitt and Sons of Long Island developed prefabrication techniques that would make possible the boom in suburban housing construction in the postwar period.

For the nation's African-American population, the war brought changes heavy with implications for the future. Although the military services remained segregated, for some of the 1 million blacks in uniform,* the experience provided a glimpse of European societies less rigidly racist than the United States. Moreover, military service in some cases gave blacks training in skills transferable to the postwar civilian labor market. Continuing a migration under way for decades, blacks joined the trek to the cities, seeking jobs in the booming war plants. By 1945 African Americans composed 9 percent of the labor force in war production.

Many of these workers relocated in northern factory centers. Detroit's black population grew from fewer than 150,000 in 1940 to more than 350,000 in 1950. Others moved to the new industrial cities of the South, such as the shipbuilding center of Mobile on Alabama's Gulf coast. In 1944 black workers in a Mobile shipyard set a yard record for the speed with which they built a merchant ship. Even in the war emergency, however, some major employers initially confined African Americans to low-paying jobs or excluded them altogether. The giant Douglas Aircraft plant in Los Angeles, for example, had an overwhelmingly white work force.

The surge in the urban black population sparked social tensions that sometimes erupted in violence. Unrest tore at America's cities during World War II, as it would later in the 1960s. Three days of racial conflict in Detroit during the hot summer of 1943, triggered by rumors that whites had pushed a black woman and her baby into a lake in a city park, left twenty-five blacks and nine whites dead before federal troops could quell the violence. Thurgood Marshall, the chief counsel of the National Association for the Advancement of Colored People (NAACP), bitterly criticized the Detroit police for using excessive force against blacks. The police handled the riot and previous racial incidents like "the Nazi gestapo," he declared. A racial explosion in Harlem that same summer, set off by stories of racist abuse of African-American soldiers, caused five deaths, hundreds of injuries, and the looting and burning of white-owned shops and businesses. Ignoring the obvious, a secret 1943 report to President Roosevelt by J. Edgar Hoover, director of the Federal Bureau of Investigation (FBI), blamed the pervasive "unrest and dissatisfaction" in black America on "Foreign-Inspired Agitation."

But the war also prepared the way for the civil-rights activism that would sweep America in the 1950s and 1960s. The paradox of a nation's fighting tyranny abroad while tolerating racism at home did not escape African Americans. Lillian Smith, a white Georgia writer who toured the South in the summer of 1942, commented on "a quiet ... resentment, running like a deep stream through [young blacks'] minds and hearts." A white Virginia newspaper editor wrote of Virginia's

---

* Blacks made up 16 percent of the total armed forces, higher than their proportion (10 percent) of the population as a whole.

African Americans, "The war and its slogans have roused . . . hopes, aspirations and desires which they formerly did not entertain, except in the rarest instances." NAACP membership soared. At its 1942 convention, the NAACP denounced segregation and discrimination against black voters and called for a "double victory": over America's enemies abroad and over racism at home. In *What the Negro Wants* (1944), a group of prominent African-American leaders set forth an uncompromising agenda for the postwar civil-rights struggle.

Anticipating tactics that civil-rights demonstrators of the 1960s would employ, black students at Howard University entered a segregated Washington, D.C., restaurant in 1944 while others marched outside with signs bearing the emotion-laden slogan: "We Die Together. Let's Eat Together." The Congress of Racial Equality (CORE), a biracial organization founded in 1942, organized similar demonstrations at segregated theaters and restaurants in a number of cities.

The Roosevelt administration and the courts responded to this rising discontent. In 1941 FDR issued Executive Order 8802, which barred racial discrimination in defense plants and created the Fair Employment Practices Committee (FEPC) to investigate discrimination in the defense industry and labor unions. The president's immediate goal was to avert a massive protest march in Washington, D.C., threatened by A. Philip Randolph, head of the Brotherhood of Sleeping Car Porters. In a 1944 decision that sent shivers of apprehension through the white South, the U.S. Supreme Court declared the Texas Democratic party's all-white primary unconstitutional. But these few gestures against domestic racism were primarily cosmetic. The FEPC, beset by a minuscule budget, bureaucratic infighting, and hostility from racists, accomplished little. One bigoted southern journalist ridiculed it as "dat cummittee fer de perteckshun of Rastus & Sambo." Because sustaining war production outranked racial justice in Washington's and the nation's priorities, the FEPC could use only moral suasion to combat racial discrimination in war plants. Although the war raised the consciousness of black America and brought a few steps toward equality, the great struggles for civil rights lay in the future.

For Hispanic Americans, too, the years 1941–45 brought fresh reminders of the ugly reality of prejudice. When an undertaker in Three Rivers, Texas, refused to bury Felix Longoria, a Mexican-American war hero, young congressman Lyndon B. Johnson arranged for his burial in Arlington National Cemetery with full military honors. Despite urgent labor needs, war plants discriminated against Mexican Americans and denied them promotions. Of ten thousand employees at giant Kelley Air Base in Texas in 1944, for example, not one Mexican American held a post above the level of laborer or mechanic's assistant. The vast Los Angeles Shipbuilding and Dry Dock Company employed only three hundred Chicanos among its twelve thousand workers. When Mexican-American war workers in Hanford, Washington, protested their exclusion from the dormitory occupied by other workers, the FBI investigated them.

Mexican Americans played a key role, however, in western agriculture, where labor needs intensified after the internment of Japanese Americans (see p. 21). Many Mexicans entered the United States under the so-called *braceros* ("helping arms") agreement negotiated by the U.S. and Mexican governments in 1942. For the United States, the program met urgent farm needs; for Mexico, it alleviated the desperate poverty of a rapidly growing population.* The *braceros* contracts guaranteed temporary agricultural workers a minimum wage of thirty cents per hour and exemption from the draft. Under the agreement, 220,000 Mexicans entered the United States between 1942 and 1947, laboring in Texas cotton fields, California truck farms, and Northwest sugar-beet fields. Some 67,000 *braceros* worked on U.S. railroads as well. These laborers often endured racism and discrimination, graphically illustrated by signs reading "No Mexicans. White Trade Only," posted in saloons and pool halls in Washington and Oregon. Texas cotton growers, too, unhappy with the protections and wage guarantees of the *braceros* program, pressured Washington to leave the border open, in violation of the 1942 agreement. Thus, many thousands more Mexicans flooded north to work in the agricultural harvest as undocumented laborers.

The Chicano population of West Coast cities grew rapidly amid the wartime employment boom. By 1942 Los Angeles' Mexican population stood at more than three hundred thousand. Anti-Mexican prejudice intensified with this growth and erupted in the so-called Sleepy Lagoon case. In August 1942, after a young Mexican American died in a Los Angeles gang fight, twenty-three male Chicanos were arrested and charged with the murder. Tried before an openly prejudiced judge in a hostile climate fanned by sensational press stories, three of them were convicted of first-degree murder and nine of second-degree murder. A defense committee gained a reversal of the convictions on appeal, but the case exacerbated anti-Mexican feeling. The Los Angeles Police Department, with only 22 Mexican-American officers in a force of 2,547, systematically harassed the Mexican-American community.

Hostility also broke out in the Los Angeles "zoot suit" riots of 1943. During the war, some young men, including Mexican Americans, favored a flamboyant outfit that featured widely draped trousers pegged at the ankle, a broad-rimmed hat, a long double-breasted jacket, and a long gold watch chain. The popularity of this so-called zoot suit with Mexican-American street gangs, or *pachucos,* led the Los Angeles City Council to outlaw the clothes, but with little success. In June 1943, sailors on leave in Los Angeles rampaged against zoot suiters for their alleged lack of patriotism, beating them and pulling off their garb. These flashes of racism and urban ethnic conflict in wartime warned of social tensions that would erupt repeatedly in succeeding decades.

The persistence of racist attitudes in wartime emerged starkly in anti-Japanese propaganda. In ads, political cartoons, and animated cartoons produced by the Disney organization, the "Japs" figured as grotesque, buck-toothed caricatures, subhuman primates, or even insects. "Probably in all our history," wrote historian Allan Nevins in 1946, "no foe has been so detested as were the Japanese." (The Japanese, in equally crude racist propaganda, portrayed Americans as greedy, predatory monsters.) In later years, when Japanese automobiles, TVs, and other products flooded the American market, echoes of this wartime anti-Japanese propaganda would reverberate.

Racist attitudes toward the Japanese were echoed in the treatment of the West Coast's Japanese-American population, consisting of some 47,000 Issei (foreign-

---

* From 1940 to 1950, Mexico's population swelled by 16.5 million, some 30 percent.

born aliens) and 80,000 Nisei (Japanese Americans born in the United States and thus U.S. citizens). This minority had long faced hostility, sometimes rooted in economic rivalry, and after Pearl Harbor, it broke into the open. Powerful groups in California demanded the detention of all Japanese Americans, citizens and aliens alike, for the duration of the war. California's attorney general, Earl Warren (later chief justice of the Supreme Court), told a congressional committee early in 1942 that "something should be done and done immediately" about the threat of sabotage by Japanese Americans. Warren invoked dire images of another Pearl Harbor, this time in California. That no evidence of sabotage or planning for sabotage had been uncovered, he explained, proved the diabolical cleverness of the potential perpetrators. Japanese-American leaders protested. "Is citizenship such a light and transient thing that [it] . . . can be torn from us in times of war?" asked one.

But their pleas fell on deaf ears. In February 1942, President Roosevelt authorized the army to designate any area a military zone from which persons might be excluded. Under this order, the War Relocation Authority (WRA) rounded up 110,000 Japanese Americans in California, Oregon, and Washington and sent them to primitive detention camps hastily built in remote parts of the West. In many cases, the internees' property was confiscated and sold. One young internee recalled that her house was ransacked by investigators who took "everything we had, all the old Japanese suitcases filled with parents' old kimonos, my parents' past life. . . . Everything." Seeking to maintain morale under trying conditions, the internees held religious services, conducted schools, and organized baseball teams and Boy Scout troops. Some talented artists recorded camp life in watercolors and oil paintings. Nevertheless, such activities could not erase the emotional distress that internees suffered at being held in the camps virtually as prisoners. In April 1943, a guard at a Utah internment camp shot and killed a 63-year-old internee when he approached the camp fence.

The constitutionality of the Japanese-American internment was upheld by the U.S. Supreme Court in the 1944 case *Korematsu* v. *United States.* The WRA gradually released internees who could prove their loyalty (by enlisting in the military, for example) or who were willing to take jobs elsewhere in the country, but as late as 1945 nearly twenty thousand remained in custody. As a side effect of internment, parental authority in Japanese-American families weakened, a phenomenon occurring throughout American society in the war years. One young internee, Ben Yorita, later recalled:

> [In Japanese-American families] the father was the traditional breadwinner and in total command of the family. But after going into the camps, fathers were no longer the breadwinners; the young sons and daughters were. Most of them couldn't even communicate in English, so all the burdens fell on the second generation. . . . Consequently there was a big turnover of responsibility and authority. . . . When we returned to the cities after the war, it was the second generation again that had to make the decisions and do all the negotiating with landlords, attorneys, and the like.

Only years later, in the 1980s, would Congress at last partially redress the injustice by compensating surviving internees.

Although racism stained America's home-front record during World War II, the Nazi foe far more openly pursued a deadly program aimed at wiping out European Jewry. German persecution of the Jews, which during the war became genocide, met with a somewhat ambiguous response in the United States. Many Jewish scholars, scientists, psychiatrists, artists, writers, and musicians escaping Nazism found a haven in the United States, where they would profoundly influence postwar American cultural life. But anti-Semitism and anti-immigrant sentiments also influenced the U.S. reaction to the crisis. While Roosevelt and other national leaders routinely condemned Nazi anti-Semitism, proposals to admit large numbers of Jewish refugees faced legislative roadblocks, bureaucratic stonewalling, and public opposition as expressed in opinion polls. As word of the magnitude of the Holocaust filtered out of wartime Europe, the story received only muted and fragmentary coverage in the American press. Military planners vetoed proposals to bomb the death camps at Auschwitz and elsewhere, or even the railroads leading to the camps. The best way to help the Jews, they argued, was to win the war.

Only after the war, as accounts and photographs of the death camps, gas chambers, crematory ovens, mountains of corpses, and emaciated survivors received wide publicity, did the Holocaust's full horror penetrate the American consciousness. In 1940 the American author John Dos Passos had written that the only hope of preserving a sense of humanity as the tide of atrocities mounted lay in "the frail web of understanding of one person for the pain of another." During the years when the Nazis and their collaborators systematically tried to exterminate Europe's Jews, that web of understanding, tragically, failed to develop in America.

Finally, American women experienced profound, if sometimes short-lived, changes in their lives during the war. Approximately 350,000 women, black and white, became army nurses or went directly into the military, serving in noncombat roles in the female branches of the Army Air Corps (WACS), Navy (WAVES), Coast Guard (SPARS), and Marine Corps Women's Reserve. The number of women government workers, mostly in clerical positions, also increased sharply. After initial reluctance, war-plant managers hired armies of women to replace male workers, now at the front. During the Great Depression of the 1930s, government policy and popular attitudes had strongly opposed working women because so many men lacked jobs. In wartime, views changed markedly. "Longing won't bring him back sooner . . . GET A WAR JOB!" one government poster exhorted women. With the War Department's urging employers to draw upon "the vast resources of womanpower," the female labor force jumped from 14.6 million in 1941 to 19.4 million in 1944. In some plants, including the giant Boeing aircraft factory in Seattle, women composed half the work force. A particularly high rate of married women, many of them servicemen's wives, went to work; by 1945, 25 percent of married women held jobs outside the home.

Women encountered resentment from male coworkers and the stereotype that they were suited only for simple, repetitive tasks, and few rose to managerial ranks. But in general, a highly favorable public response prevailed. To encourage women to join the work force, the mass magazines featured photos and cover art of strong-armed women assembling warplanes, stitching parachutes, or working in munitions plants. "Rosie the Riveter," a muscular, confident female worker pictured in a Norman Rockwell *Saturday Evening Post* cover in 1943, also became the subject of a popular song of the day. A photo of an eighteen-year-old California airplane-plant employee, Norma Jean Dougherty, adorned a *Yank* magazine article on women war workers. Later she would win fame as Marilyn Monroe.

But one must not exaggerate the change. The increase in women workers reflected a gradual, long-term trend associated with industrialization. The upsurge of female employment in 1942–45 represented not an awakening of feminism but a response to the war emergency. Government propaganda and the media made clear that traditional notions of women's roles remained intact and treated females' entrance into the work force as strictly temporary. Indeed, wartime concerns about the divorce rate, extramarital sex, child neglect, and juvenile delinquency testify to the uneasiness that the notion of working women aroused. As one worried commentator observed: "The hand that holds the pneumatic riveter cannot rock the cradle—at the same time." The federal government belatedly funded daycare centers for the children of working mothers in 1943 but met a mere 10 percent of the need. In Seattle, for example, only seven publicly funded and three private facilities, accommodating a total of 350 children, served the city's 75,000 working women. In some cases, working mothers themselves opposed government daycare facilities as a form of welfare and left children with friends and relatives instead.

How did these millions of new women workers assess their situation? In wartime surveys, many described their jobs as more interesting than housework, and a majority, especially older women with grown children, consistently expressed a desire to continue working. But most admitted that they probably would return to the home when peace came. "My husband wants a wife, not a career woman," said a female naval worker in Washington State. Whatever their wish, women workers had little choice about keeping their jobs: they were fired in droves as veterans returned. Daycare centers closed, and the media's celebration of working women abruptly fell silent. But even during the heyday of domesticity in the 1950s, many women who had found employment during the war would remain in the labor force or return to work. Memories of the war years, when barriers to female employment had temporarily fallen, remained vivid, a precedent for the dramatic changes to come.

On several fronts, then, a war that united the nation against a foreign foe also exposed fissures in American society and darker realities about American attitudes. The racism, prejudice, and mixed messages about the role of women that surfaced during the war—along with the great capacity of millions for self-sacrifice in a common cause—would help to sculpt the nation's social agenda after peace returned.

Technology, Oil, and the Atomic Bomb

War-spawned technological innovations played their part, too, in shaping postwar America. The Office of Scientific Research and Development (OSRD), set up in 1941, sponsored studies on defense-related projects. The computer emerged from wartime research aimed at improving Great Britain's antiaircraft defenses against the German *Luftwaffe*. These early calculating machines were massive. The Mark I, completed in 1944 by Harvard physicist Howard Aiken, stretched 50 feet in length, stood 8 feet high, and required 765,299 separate parts. Another prototype

IN PERSPECTIVE: *Government and Science—*
❖❖ ──────── *An Uneasy Partnership*

[Note: These "In Perspective" features will trace the shifting historical impact of certain major themes through the entire time span of this study, from World War II to the end of the twentieth century.]

Of all the long-range consequences of World War II, one of the most momentous was the emergence of the federal government as a patron of scientific research and development (R&D). Cooperation between government and science persisted after the war. The Atomic Energy Act of 1946, for example, set up the Atomic Energy Commission to fund nuclear research, especially in the field of weaponry. The National Science Foundation (1950), the National Institutes of Health, and other federal agencies also funneled taxpayers' dollars into R&D.

This partnership, which helped to establish the United States as the world leader in science, also catalyzed criticism and uneasy doubts over the years. As the Cold War deepened in the 1950s, Washington's role in underwriting scientific research grew increasingly politicized. The National Defense Education Act of 1958, passed after the Soviet Union launched its *Sputnik* satellite in 1957, appropriated an initial $621 million for college student loans and programs to upgrade scientific and foreign-language instruction. In 1961, pushing the Cold War competition with the Soviets into space, President Kennedy called for a race to rocket an American to the moon by 1970. Amid superpower tensions, one historian of science wrote in 1966, "The prospect of peace breaking out, though unlikely, posed a real threat" to federally financed scientific work. During the Vietnam War, protesters often targeted the Pentagon's funding of secret research on the nation's campuses. Indeed, a 1970 bombing at the University of Wisconsin targeted the Army Mathematics Research Center, a federally funded facility.

The politicization and militarization of science continued into the 1980s and beyond. President Reagan, emulating President Kennedy, set a new high-tech goal for the nation: a permanent space station. The space-shuttle program of the National Aeronautics and Space Administration (NASA), having begun modestly in the early 1970s, was budgeted at over $4 billion in 1987. In 1983 Reagan proposed the Strategic Defense Initiative, a controversial missile-defense shield using futuristic laser and computer technology. As the years passed, the lion's share of federal R&D money ended up in

───────────────────────────

computer, the ENIAC (Electronic Numerical Integrator and Calculator), built by John Mauchly and John Eckert, Jr., at the University of Pennsylvania, boasted eighteen thousand vacuum tubes. These wartime behemoths laid the groundwork for a revolution that in future years would transform information processing and revolutionize American life.

Many aeronautical advances, including helicopters and radar (developed with OSRD funding), date from World War II. U.S. pilots tested the first jet planes in the military's hands. Of a total federal R&D budget of $48.6 billion in 1990, some $36 billion, or 74 percent, found its way to the Pentagon.

By 1990 Washington had become a major player in U.S. science, and American higher education depended heavily on federal R&D funds. In 1989 Johns Hopkins University received over $400 million in such research support, Stanford nearly $250 million, the Massachusetts Institute of Technology more than $200 million, and on down the list. Yet even as scientists benefited from Washington's largesse, they worried that it compromised their autonomy. The Cold War did more than shake loose billions of dollars in R&D support; it also shaped—and perverted, some argued—that research. The secrecy and destructive purposes of military research, critics charged, mocked the spirit of science. The skeptics worried, as had a physician working for the Army Medical Corps in 1886, lest their knowledge "prove a firebrand and destroy more than it illuminates."

Even the more modest nonmilitary R&D budget has generated controversy. Medical research, for example, funded by Washington to the tune of over $8 billion in 1990, roused passionate debate over such issues as the genetic altering of plants and animals, the experimental use of tissue from aborted fetuses, funding levels for AIDS research, and the speed with which experimental drugs become available.

As the federal deficit mushroomed in the 1970s and 1980s, big-ticket scientific programs such as NASA's space station attracted critical scrutiny. One disillusioned scientist called the space-station project "an orbiting pork barrel." Yet communities that had grown to depend economically on government R&D programs fought for their survival. The Cold War's end at the close of the 1980s brought deep cuts in military spending, including R&D funding, and many communities felt the pinch. Slashes in these funds in California in the early 1990s contributed to that state's devastating economic tailspin. As the Soviet threat evaporated and governmental red ink spread, expensive research projects faced the ax. The superconductor supercollider, a costly project favored by theoretical physicists and scheduled to be built in Texas, succumbed to congressional budget slashers in 1993.

But although President Clinton would criticize some aspects of federal patronage of science and technology, he did not advocate ending it. Indeed, quite the reverse. In the 1992 presidential campaign, Clinton called for a federal "industrial policy" to identify and finance cutting-edge technologies in which the United States could become a world leader.

As the twentieth century closes, the marriage of politics and science faces strains, but neither partner shows any interest in a divorce or even a trial separation. The link forged during World War II, when Washington enlisted scientists in the struggle against fascism, proved not only more enduring but also more complex and problematic than anyone imagined in 1945.

1942. The German V-1 rockets that fell on British cities evolved after the war into intercontinental missiles and space-launch vehicles. Synthetic rubber filled in for the scarce real article in automobile tires and other products. Synthetic fabrics such as nylon, introduced by the Du Pont Corporation in 1938, did duty as wartime substitutes for silk and other natural fabrics in short supply. Department stores that advertised "nylons" during the war faced deluges of eager buyers. In the postwar years, a shimmering array of synthetic fabrics would find many varied uses.

The war, ironically, also produced notable advances in the saving of human lives. Research on blood-plasma technology and on antibacterial sulfa drugs progressed rapidly. Production of penicillin, discovered in England in 1929, moved to America when the war began. Funded by the War Production Board, researchers developed new techniques for vastly increasing the output of this lifesaving antibiotic. Wartime research led to the development of other substances of value to peacetime medicine, including streptomycin, another key antibiotic. The insecticide DDT, developed in the 1930s, first received wide use during the war to protect GIs from typhus, malaria, and other insect-borne diseases.

The role of science and technology in ensuring victory over the nation's enemies solidified a pro-technology mindset that in later decades would come under heavy challenge. In particular, the government's large-scale funding of research would generate ambivalence in the future, especially for its environmental implications. DDT, hailed as a lifesaver during the war, later would spark controversy as an ecological menace. During the war, however, compelling military objectives overrode all other considerations.

Of the war's technological aspects, none held more portents for the future than the struggle for oil. Indeed, oil oozes its way through the history of World War II. Japan's efforts to reduce its dependence on Western oil spurred the expansionist policies in Asia that led President Roosevelt in July 1941 to freeze all Japanese funds in the United States and in effect to embargo oil exports to Japan. The Japanese attack on Pearl Harbor would have been even more catastrophic had the Japanese also destroyed the 4.5 million barrels of oil stored there in surface tanks.

During the initial stages of the war, Japan met its energy needs by seizing British and Dutch refineries in Borneo and Sumatra. But as U.S. forces advanced across the Pacific and sank more and more Japanese tankers en route to the home islands, Japan's oil reserves dwindled to practically nothing, crippling its warmaking capacity. Toward the end, Japan resorted to desperate measures to save fuel, sending pilots on *kamikaze* suicide missions against U.S. ships carrying just enough gasoline to reach their targets.

Hitler frantically sought fuel for his war machine, too. He invaded the Soviet Union in part to capture a vast Soviet oil refinery in the Caucasus and to prevent the Soviets from seizing the rich oilfield in Romania, a German ally. Hitler also channeled enormous resources into developing synthetic fuels. But fuel shortages ultimately doomed Germany just as they did Japan. Stalin's counteroffensive denied Hitler the oilfields he desperately needed, and Allied bombing slashed the synthetic-fuel output of the German chemical giant I. G. Farben. The Nazi's North African campaign faltered for want of gasoline, and by the end of the war, the German armies had run dry. In the spring of 1945, German military vehicles in Italy were being towed by oxen.

For the Allies, too, oil was critical. U.S. oil shipments to Great Britain under the wartime Lend Lease program helped the British to repel the Nazi *Luftwaffe* during the 1941 Battle of Britain. Once the United States entered the war, Interior Secretary Harold Ickes, doubling as petroleum administrator, stimulated domestic oil exploration and vastly expanded production. Two major pipelines, the "Big Inch" and the "Little Inch," built in 1943–1944, carried gasoline and other petroleum products from the Southwest to the East Coast. Strict rationing coupled with tire shortages, a moratorium on auto production, and a 35-mile-per-hour speed limit cut civilian oil and gasoline consumption by 30 percent. By such means, the United States met nearly 90 percent of the Allies' wartime oil needs.

Meanwhile, the shape of the future emerged on another front when U.S. geologists on a government mission in 1943 conservatively assessed the oil potential of Saudi Arabia and other Middle East nations at 25 billion barrels. "The oil in this region," the mission reported, "is the greatest single prize in all history." A behind-the-scenes struggle unfolded between the United States and Great Britain for control of this find. Early in 1945, following Yalta, President Roosevelt met with King Ibn Saud of Saudi Arabia for a conference that included intense discussions of oil.*

In August 1944, meanwhile, the United States and Great Britain signed the Anglo-American Petroleum Agreement creating an eight-member International Petroleum Commission (IPC) charged with shaping postwar oil policy, allocating quotas, and recommending production levels. Domestic producers in the United States rebelled, however, fearing that the new agency would set oil prices. A 1945 revision of the agreement ensured that the IPC had no authority over U.S. production. The postwar American economic boom would roar forward on a tide of oil, untrammeled by limits or restraints.

Oil, then, was never far from the mind of any world leader during World War II and by 1945 had emerged as a key issue in postwar diplomacy. The war demonstrated the industrialized world's utter dependence on this limited resource and showed that, in an emergency, America could radically cut its consumption. The conflict also made crystal clear the Middle East's critical role in postwar geopolitics.

Of all the scientific breakthroughs of World War II, none had a more immediate impact on the consciousness of ordinary citizens than the atomic bomb. In August 1939, a few weeks before Hitler invaded Poland and plunged Europe into war, Albert Einstein, a world-famous émigré German-Jewish physicist, sent President Roosevelt a message sketching the implications of current work in his field. Einstein wrote the letter at the initiative of Leo Szilard, a refugee Hungarian physicist worried about German research in atomic energy. Recent research by Szilard and the Italian physicist Enrico Fermi, wrote Einstein,

> leads me to expect that the element uranium may be turned into a new and important source of energy in the immediate future. . . . This new phenomenon would also lead to the construction of bombs, and it is conceivable—though much less certain—that extremely powerful bombs of a new type may thus be constructed.

Heeding Einstein's suggestion that the government support further research, Roosevelt approved a modest grant. The army took over the project in 1942 and code-named it the Manhattan Project. In 1943, bomb construction began at Los Alamos, New Mexico, under the direction of physicist J. Robert Oppenheimer.

---

* The American president and the Mideast monarch got along famously. When Ibn Saud, who limped severely from old war injuries, admired Roosevelt's wheelchair, Roosevelt promptly gave him a duplicate, which the Saudi ruler thereafter highly prized.

Before dawn on July 16, 1945, a group of scientists huddling in the darkness at the Alamogordo Bombing Range in New Mexico detonated the world's first atomic bomb. Physicist Philip Morrison, watching from ten miles away, later wrote, "You felt the morning had come, although it was still night, because there your face felt the glow of this daylight—this desert sun in the midst of night." A few minutes after the blast (code-named Trinity), test director Kenneth Bainbridge approached Oppenheimer, shook his hand, and said, "Oppie, now we're all sons of bitches."

The Alamogordo test that propelled humankind into a new era also presented Roosevelt's successor, President Truman, with a fateful decision. Eager to end the war, Truman ordered use of the atomic bomb against Japan as soon as technically possible and without explicit warning. Leo Szilard and other Manhattan Project scientists proposed a demonstration, but neither the president nor Secretary of War Henry Stimson appear to have considered this option.

Later, Truman and Stimson would claim that the atomic bomb offered the only sure alternative to a land invasion of Japan that might have cost thousands of American lives. Indeed, War Department contingency plans called for an invasion of Japan's southernmost island late in 1945 and of the main island, Honshu, early in 1946 if the war continued. Thousands of GIs never doubted that Truman's decision spared them from death on Japanese soil. But other factors may have figured in Truman's decision. Although some Japanese military leaders were prepared to fight on, a new Japanese government that came to power in April 1945 soon began maneuvering to end the war on the Allied terms, and Washington knew of this. (U.S. and British cryptologists had broken the Japanese diplomatic code, and all official communications out of Tokyo were monitored.) After postwar research in Japan, the U.S. Strategic Bombing Survey concluded in 1946 that Japan would have surrendered "certainly prior to 31 December 1945, and in all probability prior to 1 November 1945 . . . even if the atomic bombs had not been dropped, even if Russia had not entered the war, and even if no invasion had been planned or contemplated." Moreover, at the July 1945 Potsdam Conference, when Stalin renewed his pledge to declare war on Japan in mid-August (and before Truman learned of the atomic bomb test in New Mexico), Truman noted exultantly in a hasty diary jotting: "[Stalin] will be in Jap War on August 15 . . . Fini Japs when that comes about."

It was not, then, the nightmare of a bloody land invasion months in the future that loomed large in Truman's mind as he made his decision to drop the atomic bomb but rather the precise means by which Japan's imminent surrender would be achieved. If Japan's surrender were perceived to be a response to the Soviet declaration of war (which came on August 8, 1945), Stalin would have won substantial claim to a role in postwar Japan. But if the U.S. atomic bomb appeared to be the major factor in Japan's capitulation, America would hold the upper hand in postwar Japan—indeed, in the entire postwar world. British prime minister Winston Churchill later described U.S. leaders' thinking in late July 1945: "It was now no longer necessary for the Russians to come into the Japanese war; the new explosive alone was sufficient to settle the matter."

The Manhattan Project's enormous cost may have been another influence. How could Truman justify to Congress and to U.S. taxpayers spending $2 billion on a weapon and then not using it? The president himself later insisted that he made up

Hiroshima, September 1945. *A survivor pushes his possessions along a path amid the rubble of what had been a bustling city. Images such as this offered Americans a grim preview of what a future atomic war might bring.* (UPI—Corbin/Bettmann)

his mind without the slightest qualm: "Let there be no mistake about it. I regarded the bomb as a military weapon and never had any doubt that it should be used."

Whatever his precise reasoning (and we may never know for sure), Truman issued his order. The first bomb, nicknamed *Little Boy,* utilizing uranium-235, fell on Hiroshima at 8:15 A.M. on August 6, destroying the city and killing upwards of a hundred thousand people. The second, *Fat Man,* a plutonium bomb, dropped on Nagasaki on August 9, leaving more than forty thousand dead. The atomic bomb gave the final push to a Japanese government already on the verge of surrender, but at a terrible cost: a horrendous weapon unleashed on the world, under circumstances that vastly complicated efforts at international control. Within a few years, the United States and the Soviet Union would become locked in a dangerous nuclear arms race, and nuclear weaponry would spread to other nations as well.

Conclusion

The final chapter of World War II, then, also served as the opening chapter of the nuclear age. Americans swiftly realized that their world had changed forever. Dreams of a technological utopia formed one strand of the nation's initial response to the atomic bomb. President Truman hailed atomic energy as "the greatest achievement of organized science in history" and stressed its peacetime promise. Magazine writers and radio commentators conjured up visions of atomic cars, atomic power too cheap to meter, atomic agriculture that would solve the world's food problems, and atomic medicine that would conquer death itself. But Americans soon recognized that the force that had demolished two Japanese cities could be turned against themselves. Radio newscasters compared Hiroshima with U.S. cities of similar size, such as New Haven and Denver; newspapers printed maps of their own communities overlaid by concentric circles showing the pattern of devastation at Hiroshima. The life expectancy of the human species, commented the *Washington Post* on August 26, 1945, had "dwindled immeasurably in the course of two brief weeks." Even President Truman, in the privacy of his diary, expressed grave misgivings about the new weapon. After the Alamogordo test, he called the atomic bomb "the most terrible thing ever discovered" and resorted to apocalyptic biblical imagery: "It may be the fire destruction prophesied . . . after Noah and his fabulous Ark." Fear of nuclear holocaust sank deep into the American consciousness in August 1945, where it would linger for decades, rising and falling with the ebb and flow of Cold War hostilities.

Japan surrendered on August 14, 1945, three months after the collapse of Nazi power in Europe. The long-awaited V-J (Victory over Japan) Day had arrived; World War II was over. At a cost of 407,000 dead and 672,000 wounded, the United States had contributed its share to the defeat of powerful foes. The radio news flash set off frantic celebrations. Crowds swarmed the streets, horns honked, whistles blared, screaming headlines confirmed the initial reports. Photographers captured scenes of delirious joy. As the shouting subsided, however, sober thoughts set in. What kind of world would peace bring? What would life be like in the postwar United States? With a mixed sense of their nation's vast power and sudden vulnerability, Americans faced the postwar age.

Despite America's losses, the war touched it less heavily than some other nations. Historians conservatively estimate that the conflict cost the lives of some 17 million soldiers and 20 million civilians, plus millions more who were injured or made refugees. Germany lost more than 3 million soldiers, Japan and China around 2 million each. The Soviet Union suffered the heaviest casualties, including the death of more than 6 million soldiers and as many as 20 million civilians; the precise number will never be known. After the war, Stalin would say that Great Britain paid for the war in time, the United States in materials, and the Soviet Union in blood. The war brought massive physical devastation and shattered the industrial infrastructure of Germany, the Soviet Union, Japan, and other nations. By contrast, the United States in 1945—its factories intact, its economy booming, and its occupying armies triumphant in Western Europe and Asia—stood at the pinnacle of world power. What would it do with that power?

"The past is never dead. It's not even past"—so observes a character in William Faulkner's 1948 novel *Intruder in the Dust.* This observation certainly applies to World War II. In countless ways, the history of the United States since 1945 has its roots in the years 1941–45. Nearly every important strand of early postwar American history—the booming prosperity, the Cold War, the civil-rights revolution, the nuclear arms race, the cultural conservatism and business-oriented government of the Eisenhower years, the rise of computers, the space program, even social trends such as suburbanization, the growth of the middle class, and the climbing birthrate—can be understood only if one pays careful attention to World War II. When Franklin Roosevelt led the nation into war on December 8, 1941, he little realized how profound would be the long-range consequences of the conflict whose end he did not live to see.

SELECTED READINGS

The War and Wartime Diplomacy

Gar Alperovitz, *The Decision to Use the Atomic Bomb and the Architecture of an American Myth* (1995); Edward M. Bennett, *Franklin D. Roosevelt and the Search for Victory: American-Soviet Relations, 1939–1945* (1990); Russell D. Buhite, *Decision at Yalta* (1986); Robert Dallek, *Franklin D. Roosevelt and American Foreign Policy, 1932–1945* (1979); John Lewis Gaddis, *The United States and the Origins of the Cold War, 1941–1947* (1972); Patrick Hearndon, *Roosevelt Confronts Hitler: American Entry into World War II* (1987); Walter LaFeber, *America, Russia, and the Cold War* (rev. ed., 1985); Warren Kimball, *The Juggler: Franklin Roosevelt as Wartime Statesman* (1991); Robert James Maddox, *The United States and World War II* (1992); Eric Markusen and David Kopf, *The Holocaust and Strategic Bombing: Genocide and Total War in the Twentieth Century* (1995); Michael S. Sherry, *The Rise of American Air Power* (1987); Martin Sherwin, *A World Destroyed: The Atomic Bomb and the Grand Alliance* (1975); Christopher Thorne, *Allies of a Kind: The United States, Britain and the War Against Japan, 1941–1945* (1978); Gerhard L. Weinberg, *A World at Arms: A Global History of World War II* (1994); David Wyman, *The Abandonment of the Jews: America and the Holocaust, 1941–1945* (1984); Daniel Yergin, *The Prize: The Epic Quest for Oil, Money, and Power* (1991).

Domestic Social Trends During World War II

Rodolfo Acuña, *Occupied America: A History of Chicanos* (1981); Allan Berube, *Coming Out Under Fire: The History of Gay Men and Women in World War Two* (1990); Dominic J. Capeci, *The Harlem Riot of 1943* (1977); John Costello, *Virtue Under Fire: How World War II Changed Our Social and Sexual Attitudes* (1985); Richard M. Dalfiume, *Desegregation of the United States Armed Forces: Fighting on Two Fronts, 1939–1953* (1969); Clete Daniel, *Chicano Workers and the Politics of Fairness: The Fair Employment Practices Committee in the Southwest, 1941–1945* (1991); Roger Daniels, *Concentration Camps USA: Japanese Americans and World War II* (1981); Philip J. Funigiello, *The Challenge to Urban Liberalism: Federal-City Relations During World War II* (1978); Mario T. Garcia, *Mexican-Americans: Leadership, Ideology, and Identity, 1930–1960* (1989); Susan M. Hartmann, *The Home Front and Beyond: American Women in the 1940s* (1982); Robert A. Hill, ed., *The FBI's RACON: Racial Conditions in the United States During World War II* (1995); Peter Irons, *Justice at War: The Inside Story of the Japanese-American Internment* (1983); Kristine C. Kuramitsu, "Internment and Identity in Japanese American Art," *American Quarterly,* December 1995; Ruth Milkman, *Gender at Work: The Dynamics of Job Discrimination by Sex During World War II* (1987); Gerald D. Nash, *The American West Transformed: The Impact of the Second World War* (1985); Kenneth Paul O'Brien and Lynn Hudson Parsons, eds., *The Home-Front War: World War II and American Society* (1995); Gary Y. Okihiro, *Whispered Silences: Japanese Americans and World War II* (1996); William L. O'Neill, *A Democracy at War: America's Fight at Home and Abroad in World War II* (1993); Paula E. Pfeffer, *A. Philip Randolph: Pioneer of the Civil Rights Movement* (1990); Merl E. Reed, *Seedtime for the Modern Civil Rights Movement: The President's Committee on Fair Employment Practices, 1941–1946* (1991); Robert Shogan and Tom Craig, *The Detroit Race Riot: A Study in Vio-*

lence (1964); Sandra C. Taylor, *Jewel of the Desert: Japanese American Internment at Topaz* [Utah] (1993); William M. Tuttle, *Daddy's Gone to War: The Second World War in the Lives of America's Children* (1993); Allan M. Winkler, *Home Front U.S.A.: America During World War II* (1986); Jenel Virden, *Goodbye, Piccadilly: British War Brides in America* (1996).

Cultural Trends and Wartime Propaganda

Jeanine Basinger, *The World War II Combat Film: Anatomy of a Genre* (1986); John Morton Blum, *V Was for Victory: Politics and American Culture During World War II* (1976); John Dower, *War Without Mercy: Race and Power in the Pacific War* (1986); Lee Finkle, *Forum for Protest: The Black Press During World War II* (1975); William S. Graebner, *The Age of Doubt: American Thought and Culture in the 1940s* (1991); Clayton R. Koppes and Gregory D. Black, *Hollywood Goes to War: How Politics, Profits and Propaganda Shaped World War II Movies* (1987); Clayton D. Laurie, *The Propaganda Warriors: America's Crusade Against Nazi Germany* (1996); Mark H. Leff, "The Politics of Sacrifice on the American Home Front in World War II, *Journal of American History*, 77, no. 4 (1991); Richard R. Lingeman, *Don't You Know There's a War On? The American Home Front: 1941–1945* (1970); George H. Roeder, Jr., *The Censored War: American Visual Experience During World War II* (1993); Leila J. Rupp, *Mobilizing Women for War: German and American Propaganda, 1939–1945* (1978); Lawrence R. Samuel, *Pledging Allegiance: American Identity and the Bond Drive of World War II* (1997); Holly Cowan Shulman, *The Voice of America: Propaganda and Democracy, 1941–1945* (1990); Studs Terkel, *"The Good War": An Oral History of World War II* (1984); Alan M. Winkler, *The Politics of Propaganda: The Office of War Information, 1942–1945* (1978); Robert B. Westbrook, "Fighting for the American Family: Private Interests and Political Obligation in World War II," in Richard Wightman Fox and T. J. Jackson Lears, eds., *The Power of Culture: Critical Essays in American History* (1993).

The War's Impact on the Economy, Labor, and Technology

Gerard H. Clarfield and William M. Wiecek, *Nuclear America: Military and Civilian Power in the United States, 1940–1980* (1984); Alan Clive, *State of War: Michigan in World War II* (1979); James W. Cortada, *The Computer in the United States: From Laboratory to Market, 1930–1960* (1993); Donald W. Cox, *America's New Policy Makers: The Scientists' Rise to Power* (1964); Richard G. Hewlett and Oscar E. Anderson, Jr., *The New World, 1939–1946* [atomic-bomb project] (1972); Gregory Michael Hooks, *Forging the Military-Industrial Complex: World War II's Battle of the Potomoc* (1991); Daniel J. Kevles, *The Physicists: The History of a Scientific Community in Modern America* (1979); Paul A. C. Koistenen, *The Military-Industrial Complex: A Historical Perspective* (1980); Nelson Lichtenstein, *Labor's War at Home: The CIO in World War II* (1982); Alan I. Marcus and Howard P. Segal, *Technology in America: A Brief History* (1989); Richard Rhodes, *The Making of the Atomic Bomb* (1986).

CHAPTER 2

"Not Since Rome and Carthage":
Into the Cold War

As World War II wound down and Germany's defeat was near, staff at the American embassy in Moscow seemed more worried than joyous. Conflict simmered between Washington and Moscow over a number of issues, including Stalin's apparent unwillingness to honor his Yalta pledge to permit free elections in Poland. On March 8, 1945, young Kathleen Harriman, whose father, W. Averell Harriman, served as U.S. ambassador to the Soviet Union, wrote from Moscow to her sister back in the States, "The war is going wonderfully well again now. But the news is slightly dampened here by our gallant allies who at the moment are being most bastard-like."

The climate in Washington mirrored the dark mood at the embassy in Moscow. Throughout the war, President Roosevelt had uneasily hoped for postwar cooperation with the Soviets, but he fully understood a somber wartime warning given him by diplomat William C. Bullitt: "To win the peace at the close of this war will be at least as difficult as to win the war." By March 1945, FDR's fragile hopes had faded: "Averell is right," he sighed. "We can't do business with Stalin. He has broken every one of the promises he made at Yalta." Worries about the future, rooted in disturbing Soviet actions and amplified by the news media and political writers, soon rippled across America. C. L. Sulzberger of the *New York Times* wrote shortly after Japan's surrender:

> The most important political development during the last ten years of localized and finally global warfare has been the emergence of [the Soviet Union] as the greatest dynamic and diplomatic force on the vast Eurasian land mass.

From some perspectives, of course, America in 1945 had reason for exuberant confidence. Triumphant in war, it stood at the pinnacle of power. The demands of war had so expanded U.S. productive capacity that by 1945 the United States accounted for 60 percent of the world's industrial output. However, America faced not only friction with the Soviet Union but also rancorous domestic politics, the task of converting to a peacetime economy, and the looming threat of the new weapon that U.S. military research had unleashed—the atomic bomb. Confronted with these challenges was a new and untested president, Harry Truman. Treasury Secretary Henry Morgenthau, Jr., offered a cautious preliminary assessment: "[Truman] has a lot of nervous energy, and seems to be inclined to make very quick decisions. But, after all, he is a politician, and what is going on in his head only time will tell."

The postwar moment that Americans had hoped would bring a respite from worry instead gave rise to tension and crises. A series of confrontations with America's erstwhile ally, the Soviet Union, produced a powerful and well-grounded conviction, transmitted from Washington and the media to the grassroots, that Moscow's course profoundly threatened U.S. national-security interests. From this firm belief arose the long political, economic, and military struggle that pundits soon would label the Cold War.

Roots of the Cold War

The conflict that erupted after World War II between the Soviet Union and the West, most notably the United States, had deep roots in ideology and history. A belief in the New World's divine commission to redeem and uplift humanity had influenced thought in America since the days of the Puritans. Gradually secularized, this sense of mission had, by Woodrow Wilson's day, evolved into a vision of spreading democracy and a liberal capitalist order around the globe.

In Russia, meanwhile, under a succession of tsars, an elaborate centralized bureaucracy had ruled a growing empire comprising an array of peoples and languages. Only a firm controlling hand, the tsars believed, could hold this vast domain together. As in America, many Russians viewed their nation as specially favored by God. Memories of Napoleon's failed invasion in 1812, when Russia's armies and its people had heroically thrown back the foreign foe, evoked patriotic pride. Yet while displaying strong expansionist tendencies, Russia also endured nagging self-doubt, a backward economy, and chronic feelings of insecurity. These problems worsened in the nineteenth and early twentieth centuries as a series of reactionary tsars subjected the realm to despotic rule.

When Europe plunged into World War I in 1914, Russia under Tsar Nicholas II joined the Allies and declared war on Germany. But after the Bolshevik Revolution of 1917, the communist rulers of the new Soviet Union headed by V. I. Lenin denounced the conflict as a struggle among imperialists. Signing a separate peace with Germany, they proclaimed their primary goal: the overthrow of world capitalism. In 1918 President Woodrow Wilson ordered some ten thousand U.S. troops to the Soviet Union as part of an Allied force charged with protecting Allied war materiel and preventing Germany from occupying the Soviet Union's Baltic ports. The Western troops, which remained until 1920, also aided Russian groups seeking to overthrow the Bolsheviks. Later, Soviet propagandists would hark back to the events of 1918–1920 as proof of the capitalist powers' malicious intentions.

Between World Wars I and II, most Americans, including Washington officialdom, viewed the Soviet regime, with its announced enmity to capitalism, as a clear threat to U.S. security. The United States did not even grant diplomatic recognition to the Soviet Union until 1933.

American aversion to Moscow and its revolutionary program diminished during World War II, when the two nations joined forces against Nazi Germany. President Roosevelt, although cautiously hoping for postwar accord, never forgot that "a dictatorship as absolute as any . . . in the world" ruled in Moscow. He hid from the Soviets the war's supreme secret, the atomic-bomb project, but Stalin learned of the Manhattan Project anyway through espionage and secretly began his own program to develop the bomb. British prime minister Winston Churchill, for his part, never doubted Stalin's duplicity and urged Roosevelt to beware of the Soviet dictator. The cynicism of the Nazi-Soviet Pact, not to mention Stalin's wartime massacre of thousands of Polish officers and subsequent effort to pin the blame on the Nazis, lent powerful credence to Churchill's suspicions.

The Soviet Union's postwar outlook reflected its ghastly wartime losses: more than 6 million soldiers dead and 14 million injured. The toll in the Battle of Stalingrad alone exceeded U.S. combat casualties for the entire war. Civilian deaths mounted to incalculable levels as Russia battled the Nazi invaders. Enormous physical destruction, homelessness, and malnutrition deepened the Soviets' fierce concern with border security and roused a grim determination that their wartime enemies would never again pose a threat. As Ambassador Harriman cabled the State Department early in 1945, "The overriding consideration in Soviet foreign policy is . . . 'security' as Moscow sees it." Moscow's wartime foes included not only Germany but nearby Finland, Hungary, and Romania, which had joined the Nazis in attacking the Soviet Union. Bulgaria, too, had allied with Hitler. As the war ended and Soviet forces rolled across Eastern Europe and into Germany, Moscow expressed its determination to establish a buffer zone in the territories it was occupying. Western allies protested, then watched nervously.

World War II roused other tensions as well. As the Red Army had grappled with the invading Nazis, Stalin had repeatedly called on his Western partners to open a second front—that is, launch an invasion that would compel Hitler to divert his forces westward. When the United States and Great Britain waited until 1944 to act, the delay became a source of festering resentment and deepened the Soviet dictator's suspicions of the Western democracies.

Sources of conflict were thus already in place when World War II ended in August 1945. Yet Americans were investing great faith in a new international organization, the United Nations. After World War I, the United States had spurned the League of Nations despite Woodrow Wilson's pleas, but now it would remedy that mistake. The Senate quickly ratified the UN Charter adopted at the San Francisco conference of June 1945. "We have learned from experience," Secretary of State James F. Byrnes told the UN in January 1946, pledging America's "wholehearted cooperation."

Internationalist dreams withered, however, with a series of confrontations. The first of these focused on Eastern Europe. Americans—many of whom traced their ethnic roots to this region—had long supported the aspirations of Eastern Europeans for independence and freedom from domination by their powerful neighbors. These hopes had briefly flowered after World War I, but the coming of World War II had squelched them. As the war in Europe ended, U.S., British, and other Western leaders, already seeking to rebuff Soviet expansionism, deemed independence for the nations of Eastern Europe a prime strategic objective. The

West viewed Stalin's determination to control Eastern Europe, reinforced by an ideology of world revolution, as clear evidence of imperialist intent. From Moscow's perspective, the United States and Great Britain, now possessing the atomic bomb, seemed poised to pursue the quest for raw materials and markets that, according to Marxist doctrine, the capitalist world required. Age-old Russian fears of encirclement helped to shape—and to skew—Moscow's view of postwar realities. Soviet control of Eastern Europe, Stalin insisted, would help counter America's overwhelming economic and military superiority.

Attention initially centered on Poland. The Allies had a strong emotional investment in restoring freedom to that country, which Stalin and Hitler had callously divided between them in 1939 and which had suffered first under the Nazis and then under the advancing Red Army. The Soviet army had even deliberately halted on the outskirts of Warsaw in the late summer of 1944, just as an uprising by Polish insurgents engulfed the city, allowing the Nazis to kill the maximum number of Poles before retreating to Germany. Furthermore, throughout the war, a Polish government-in-exile had functioned in London. When Roosevelt and Churchill insisted at Yalta that Stalin permit free elections in Poland, he retorted, "The Prime Minister has said that for Great Britain the question of Poland is a question of honor. For Russia it is not only a question of honor, but of security. . . . During the last thirty years our German enemy has passed through this corridor twice." Despite Stalin's vague pledge of free elections, the Soviets installed a pro-Soviet puppet government in Warsaw.

Stalin then moved to tighten his grip elsewhere in Eastern Europe. Within weeks of the Yalta Conference, the Soviets installed a communist-led government in Romania and reoccupied Latvia, Estonia, and Lithuania, Baltic nations they had annexed in 1940 and then lost to Hitler's armies. In mid-1945, Prime Minister Churchill, foreshadowing his famous "iron curtain" speech of 1946, complained to Stalin that an "iron fence" was rising across Europe. Moscow tolerated a degree of political autonomy in Hungary and Czechoslovakia until 1948, but the prospects for freedom in Eastern Europe looked bleak in 1945–1946.

Any assessment of the Soviet Union's postwar actions and the West's response must begin with the fact that the U.S.S.R. was a one-party state under the absolute rule of one man, Joseph Stalin. Born Josif Visarionovich Dzhugashvili in 1879, the son of a Georgian shoemaker, he studied for the priesthood but in his mid-twenties, joined the communist cause, and adopted the name "Stalin" ("Man of Steel"). He rose in the party and entered the cabinet after the 1917 revolution. Part of the triumvirate that ruled after Lenin's death in 1924, he soon gained sole power. In the Moscow purge trials of the later 1930s, he ruthlessly eliminated former comrades and potential rivals. No Russian tsar ever wielded power more absolutely or more brutally. Millions of peasants died under Stalin's program of forced collectivization. As the symbol of resistance against the German invaders, Stalin achieved almost mythic status during World War II. After 1945, a cult of personality, promoted by a vast propaganda machine, grew up around him. Despite his power, paranoid fears assailed him before his death in 1953. "He saw enemies everywhere," his daughter Svetlana later wrote. This, then, was the ruler and the state that Western leaders confronted in the early Cold War years. Soviet foreign policy cannot be separated from Stalin's absolutist rule. As diplomatic historian

Robert H. Ferrell has written, "Stalin almost needed a foreign enemy in order to tighten his control upon the Russian people."

Communist ideology, too, influenced Moscow's postwar strategy. Karl Marx's prediction of communism's inevitable triumph lent a certain rhetorical coherence to Soviet policy. However, balance-of-power calculations, territorial ambitions, and security fears (legitimate or not) took top priority. Stalin's postwar course, although cautiously executed, followed a long tradition of Russian imperialism, but an imperialism whose limits remained imprecise. Shrouded in secrecy and suspicion, Stalin seemed unable to delimit Russia's legitimate security concerns. With maddening inconsistency, he clamped down on some countries while leaving others relatively free. Imposing absolute rule on Eastern Europe, he sought to expand Soviet influence in Western Europe and elsewhere. It was this ill-defined expansionist impulse, not Moscow's justifiable security objectives, that alarmed and alienated the West.

In Washington, the challenge of responding to Stalin's postwar probes and feints fell to President Truman, a novice in foreign policy. After twelve years of FDR's patrician accent and larger-than-life image, Americans only slowly adjusted to Truman's flat Missouri twang and folksy style. A farm lad whose poor eyesight had excluded him from boyhood games and from West Point, Truman had served in World War I and operated a Kansas City men's store before winning election as a county executive in 1922. His political rise—chief county administrator in 1926, U.S. senator in 1934—had hardly been meteoric. "I look just like any other fifty

The Big Three. *President Truman with Prime Minister Winston Churchill and Premier Joseph Stalin, July 1945. Barely three months after becoming president, Truman traveled to the Berlin suburb of Potsdam for the last of the Allied leaders' wartime conferences. The smiles and handshakes masked deepening differences.* (Imperial War Museum)

people you meet in the street," he once observed. An omnivorous reader with a love of American history, he had won respect, although not fame, as chair of a Senate committee investigating waste in wartime military procurement. Now he was a world leader.

In diplomatic exchanges, Truman tended toward cocky self-assurance and snap judgments, comparing Stalin to Boss Tom Pendergast of Kansas City, his early political mentor, and he concluded early that Stalin understood only force and blunt language. Soviet expansionism, coupled with Truman's short-fuse temper, led to volatile early encounters. Outraged by Stalin's failure to hold free elections in Poland, Truman in April 1945, only a few days after becoming president, delivered such a tongue-lashing to visiting Soviet foreign minister V. I. Molotov that, according to Truman, Molotov sputtered, "I have never been talked to like that in my life!" Truman allegedly retorted, "Carry out your agreements and you won't get talked to like that."

Stalin responded with equal vehemence, asserting his plan to impose a pro-Soviet communist regime on the Poles despite his earlier promises. "Poland borders ... the Soviet Union," he cabled Truman sarcastically, "[which] cannot be said of Great Britain and the United States." Stalin's stonewalling on Poland convinced Truman that only an equally tough Western response would deter Moscow's aggression.

A few Washington voices, including Secretary of War Henry Stimson and Army Chief of Staff George C. Marshall, urged a patient search for common interests with the Soviets. Stalin's actions were understandable, argued Stimson, in view of Soviet security concerns. This minority view, however, largely vanished from Truman's inner circle when Stimson retired in September 1945 and when Marshall left Washington in November on an extended mission to China.

1946: The Iron Curtain, Iran, Atomic Energy

In 1946 the dispute over Poland widened into a conflict that spilled across Eastern Europe, the Middle East, and the United Nations. *Pravda,* the propaganda voice of the Soviet regime, grew virulently anti-American, and from the White House to Main Street, American hostility toward the Soviets deepened. Early in the year, *Time* published a map portraying "Communist Contagion" as a global epidemic. Iran, Turkey, and China were already "infected," warned *Time;* Saudi Arabia, Egypt, Afghanistan, and India had been "exposed" and might sicken at any moment.

Two speeches underscored the chasm opening between the wartime allies. In the first, on February 9, 1946, Stalin belligerently blamed the capitalist nations for World War II and reaffirmed Moscow's determination to lead the struggle against Western imperialism. The war-weary Soviet people, Stalin announced, must achieve new feats of military production. The speech reverberated through Western capitals. Supreme Court justice William O. Douglas, a New Deal liberal, called it "the Declaration of World War III." One month later, on March 5, 1946, Great Britain's wartime prime minister, Winston Churchill, traveled to Fulton, Missouri—Truman's home state—to speak at tiny Westminster College. As Truman sat behind him on the stage, Churchill bluntly warned of Soviet aggression, declaring:

From Stettin in the Baltic to Trieste in the Adriatic, an iron curtain has descended across the continent. Behind that line lie all the capitals of the ancient states of central and eastern Europe. Warsaw, Berlin, Prague, Vienna, Budapest, Belgrade, Bucharest, and Sofia, all the famous cities and the populations around them lie in the Soviet sphere and all are subject, in one form or another, not only to Soviet influence but to a very high and increasing measure of control from Moscow.

The Soviets did not want war, advised Churchill; "What they desire is the fruits of war and the indefinite expansion of their power and doctrines." The response, he insisted, had to be unflinching resistance: "There is nothing [the Russians] admire so much as strength, and there is nothing for which they have less respect than military weakness." Eager to continue London's wartime partnership with Washington, especially in developing nuclear weapons, Churchill called for Anglo-American cooperation to resist this latest threat to Western civilization.

Americans revered Churchill, symbol of Britain's resistance to the Nazis, and his words carried great weight. Moreover, events lent his claims credence: Stalin had unleashed his blast only a few weeks earlier, Poland and much of Eastern Europe lay under Moscow's heel, and a mood of crisis hung over Iran, as we shall see. Repeated and amplified by public leaders and the media, the "iron curtain" image and Churchill's larger themes entered the ideological arsenal of the early Cold War.

As a response to threatening events and to Churchill's eloquence, a new ideological consensus coalesced across the United States. Republican senator Arthur Vandenberg of Michigan, head of the Senate Foreign Relations Committee and once a well-known isolationist, wrote in May 1946, "I am more than ever convinced that communism is on the march on a world-wide scale which only America can stop."

One prominent dissenter from this view was Truman's secretary of commerce, Henry Wallace. A New Dealer who had served President Roosevelt as secretary of agriculture and then as vice president, Wallace criticized what he saw as the needless stridency of Western leaders' anti-Soviet pronouncements. In a July 1946 memo to Truman, Wallace deplored "the irrational fear of Russia . . . being built up in the American people by certain individuals and publications." That September he went public with his ideas in an address at New York's Madison Square Garden, triggering a behind-the-scenes uproar in the administration. Secretary of State James Byrnes, in Paris for a conference, cabled Truman: "You and I spent fifteen months building a bipartisan policy. We did a fine job convincing the world that it was a permanent policy upon which the world could rely. Wallace destroyed it in a day." Truman had approved Wallace's speech (although without reading it carefully, he claimed), but faced with Byrnes's fury, he demanded Wallace's resignation.

Against this backdrop of belligerent speechmaking and wrangling over Eastern Europe, conflict flared in Iran, long a cockpit of Big Power rivalry. For nearly 150 years, Russian leaders had coveted the warm-water ports of the Mediterranean and the Persian Gulf. In 1940 Soviet foreign minister Molotov had told the Nazi leaders candidly that Iran—rich in oil and a gateway to the Persian Gulf—was a major target of Soviet aspiration. During World War II, the British and Soviets had occupied Iran jointly, agreeing to withdraw six months after Germany's defeat. But Soviet troops remained into 1946, well beyond the six-month deadline, while Stalin sought to force from Tehran an agreement for joint Soviet-Iranian oil exploration in northern Iran.

The Soviet Army's failure to leave Iran posed a major security threat to the West and further convinced Truman of Stalin's perfidy. "I'm tired of babying the Soviets," he complained to Secretary of State Byrnes in January 1946. In March, Byrnes sent Moscow a strongly worded note demanding immediate Soviet withdrawal. The administration also brought the matter before the fledgling UN Security Council. By May, having extracted from Tehran a pledge of a joint oil-exploration treaty, the Soviets had departed. With the U.S.S.R.'s troops safely gone, Iran's parliament rejected the proposed treaty.

The Iranian crisis resolved, Western oil companies moved swiftly to secure Middle Eastern oil. In September 1947, the British-owned Anglo-Iranian Oil Company and two U.S. companies, Socony and Standard Oil of New Jersey, signed a twenty-year agreement to drill and market Iranian oil. The next year, following up on FDR's 1945 meeting with King Ibn Saud, a consortium of four U.S. oil companies organized as Aramco (Arab-American Oil Company) concluded an oil agreement with Saudi Arabia. At the same time, the American-owned Gulf Oil Company, in partnership with Royal Dutch Shell, arranged to refine Kuwaiti oil and market it in Europe. In short, by 1948 the corporate structure was in place for a massive flow of oil from the Middle East to Western Europe, the United States, and elsewhere in the noncommunist world. The Iran crisis thus not only helped to define the early Cold War but also figured in the continued jockeying among the industrialized powers for access to the region's precious resource.

A newer form of energy, derived from the splitting of the atom, molded early postwar diplomacy as well. Indeed, the beginnings of the Cold War coincided with the United States' four-year atomic monopoly, from 1945 to 1949. Wartime planners such as Secretary of War Stimson had realized the bomb's profound implications for postwar Soviet-American relations. When Truman learned of the successful Alamogordo test while at the Potsdam Conference in July 1945, he was, noted Stimson, "tremendously pepped up," showing an "entirely new feeling of confidence" in his dealings with Stalin. In meetings late in 1945 among Soviet, American, and British officials in London and Moscow, Secretary of State Byrnes attempted to use U.S. atomic supremacy as a lever to influence Soviet behavior in Eastern Europe and elsewhere, but with disappointing results. Stimson, for one, warned against this heavy-handed atomic diplomacy. As early as September 1945, he wrote to Truman:

> [T]he problem of our satisfactory relations with Russia [is] not merely connected with but . . . virtually dominated by the problem of the atomic bomb. . . . These relations may be perhaps irretrievably embittered by the way in which we approach the solution of the bomb with Russia. For if we fail to approach them now and merely continue to negotiate with them, having this weapon rather ostentatiously on our hip, their suspicions and their distrust of our purposes and motives will increase.

Stalin instantly grasped the bomb's importance for balance-of-power politics. Soon after Hiroshima, he directed Soviet scientists, "Provide us with atomic weapons in the shortest possible time. . . . The equilibrium has been destroyed. Provide the bomb. It will remove a great danger from us." The atomic weapon in American hands fed the generalized fear of encirclement that lurked just beneath the surface in Moscow. The bomb, wrote Ambassador Harriman late in 1945, had "revived [the Soviets'] feeling of insecurity. . . . The Russian people have been aroused to feel that they must again face an antagonistic world. American imperialism is included as a threat to Russia." Secretary of State Byrnes' veiled atomic threats lent substance to these fears.

A combination of internationalist idealism and suspicion of Soviet intentions drove Washington's abortive efforts to devise a system of international control of atomic energy. Early in 1946, a State Department committee chaired by Undersecretary of State Dean Acheson and including David Lilienthal, head of the Tennessee Valley Authority in the New Deal, unveiled a plan for atomic-energy control under UN auspices. The Acheson–Lilienthal plan won praise in the American press, although a few critics saw it as a formula for a continued U.S. atomic monopoly. Under the proposal's terms, the United States reserved the right to build and stockpile atomic bombs until full implementation of a control plan acceptable to Washington. Doubts about U.S. intentions intensified when Truman named the vain and fiercely anti-Soviet Bernard Baruch to conduct the atomic-energy negotiations at the UN.

Amid much publicity and hope, Baruch presented the U.S. plan, which he had revised and toughened, to the UN in June 1946. It called for creation of an international atomic development authority, free of the veto power of any nation, that would license and supervise the mining of uranium and the manufacture of fissionable material. Nations would be encouraged to explore the atom's peaceful uses but forbidden to make nuclear weapons. Any nation violating this ban would be subject to "condign [appropriate] punishment" under UN authority.

The Soviet Union's UN delegate, Andrei Gromyko, rejected the Baruch Plan as a scheme to serve U.S. interests. Talks ground on, but hopes for control of atomic energy soon faded. Some U.S. military planners quietly welcomed this outcome, viewing the bomb as America's "winning weapon" in the emerging conflict with the U.S.S.R. General Dwight Eisenhower, writing Baruch in June 1946, cautioned against any plan that limited America's capacity to build atomic bombs, which he saw as "a deterrent . . . to aggression in the world."

In the summer of 1946, during the UN debate, the United States conducted a series of atomic tests at Bikini Atoll in the Pacific. (A French designer, introducing a new line of women's swimwear, named one scanty number "the Bikini.") The Bikini tests' timing actually reflected interservice rivalries between the navy and the air force rather than intentional atomic diplomacy, but the Soviets angrily denounced them as proof of America's lack of seriousness about international control.

Later that year, in a memo to Truman, presidential adviser Clark Clifford warned against disarmament negotiations "as long as the possibility of Soviet aggression exists" and called for an urgent military buildup, including readiness for "atomic and biological warfare." Truman heeded this advice, which came from many other quarters as well. By 1949, before the Soviets had exploded a single nuclear weapon, the U.S. arsenal included about 150 atomic bombs, together with a growing number of nuclear-capable bombers.

Thus, with victory celebrations still a vivid memory, the Cold War already dominated U.S. diplomacy by the end of 1946. The first half of the 1940s had witnessed the bloodiest war in human history; as the second half unfolded, many sober observers feared the breakout of another full-scale conflict.

1947: The Truman Doctrine, Containment, and the Marshall Plan

The year 1947 brought influential statements of America's Cold War purposes as well as major initiatives aimed at blunting Soviet influence in war-torn Europe. The first of the policy pronouncements, the Truman Doctrine, emerged from a crisis in Greece. An insurgency backed by Marshall Josip Broz Tito, the communist ruler of neighboring Yugoslavia, and by the pro-Soviet puppet regimes of Albania and Bulgaria was battling Greece's corrupt, right-wing monarchy. Great Britain, historically a key player in the region, had restored Greece's monarchy in 1944 after expelling German, Bulgarian, and Italian occupation forces. But in February 1947, the economically strapped British informed Washington that they could no longer finance the Greek government's fight. The Soviet Union, while tacitly backing the Greek insurgents, was also menacing Turkey's Dardanelles strait, the waterway linking the Black Sea and the Mediterranean. Tsarist Russia had long sought access to the Mediterranean for its Black Sea fleet. In pressuring Turkey to share control of the Dardanelles, Stalin had revived this long-term goal.

Alarmed U.S. and British strategists agreed that keeping Greece and Turkey in the Western camp and the Soviet fleet out of the Mediterranean merited the highest priority. President Truman favored military and economic aid to the two nations, but congressional approval appeared far from certain. Opponents raised various objections. Leftists such as Henry Wallace, now a private citizen, denounced the administration's bellicose tone toward the Soviet Union. Greece and Turkey, they pointed out, hardly shone as beacons of freedom and democracy. The strongest opposition, however, came from conservatives. Republican senator Robert A. Taft of Ohio warned against new global involvements. Some fiscal conservatives deplored the cost; others invoked traditional anti-British sentiments or predicted that aid to Greece and Turkey would lead to deeper foreign entanglements. Senator Walter George of Georgia, a respected Democratic elder statesman, cautioned against starting down a road whose end no one could predict.

At this delicate junction, Truman called congressional leaders to a White House meeting. Dean Acheson presented the administration's case in somber and sweeping terms. Greece, he intoned, was merely a bit player in a much larger drama: "Like apples in a barrel infected by the corruption of one rotten one, the corruption of Greece would infect Iran and all to the East . . . , Africa . . . , Italy, and France." "Not since Rome and Carthage," he concluded in clipped, assured accents, had there been "such a polarization of power on this earth." Senator Vandenberg, even more convinced that only America could halt communism's world-wide march, assured Truman that if he followed Acheson's lead and "scare[d] hell out of the country," Congress would surely support the aid request.

Adopting Vandenberg's advice, Truman addressed Congress on March 12, 1947. Requesting $400 million in aid to Greece and Turkey, he couched the issue in global terms that soon came to be called the Truman Doctrine. The world, he pronounced, must choose between two "alternative ways of life": democracy and freedom or totalitarianism, terror, and oppression. The implication was clear: The United States and the Soviet Union exemplified these two opposed philosophies. Wherever this struggle erupted, the president declared, America must "support free peoples who are resisting attempted subjugation by armed minorities or by outside pressures." Rewarding Truman with a standing ovation, both houses of Congress passed the aid bill by solid majorities. Public-opinion polls strongly supported the aid request, and Truman's poll ratings shot up. Democratic congressman Sam Rayburn of Texas, the House minority leader, declared:

> People who love liberty and cry for a fair chance want us to . . . lead the world. . . . If we do not accept our responsibility, if we do not . . . extend a helping hand to people . . . , who do not want to be smothered by communism, . . . [then] God help this world.

The aid program to resist Moscow's probes in the eastern Mediterranean succeeded. Soviet pressure on Turkey eased, and by 1949 the undemocratic Greek government, with U.S. help and the defection of Tito from the Soviet camp, had quashed the insurgents. Equally important, the Truman Doctrine contributed to a process by which Americans came to view specific confrontations with Soviet power as parts of an all-encompassing, primarily ideological global struggle.

The most influential summation of early Cold War thinking was an essay, "The Sources of Soviet Conduct," in the July 1947 issue of the journal *Foreign Affairs*. The author, identified only as "X," soon became known: George Kennan, director of the State Department's policy-planning staff. The essay had a lengthy history. Early in 1946, Kennan, then a foreign-service officer in Moscow, had sent to Washington a secret "Long Telegram" summarizing his views of Soviet foreign policy. Amid a crescendo of ominous developments—the Iran crisis, Moscow's tightening grip on Eastern Europe, Stalin's alarming speech insisting on the inevitability of war with the capitalist powers—the scholarly Kennan had placed U.S.-Soviet relations in a broad historical and philosophical perspective. The telegram had deeply impressed Navy Secretary James V. Forrestal, who in 1947 became the nation's first secretary of defense.* One of the most passionate of the early Cold Warriors, Forrestal circulated Kennan's telegram widely and became his loyal ally when Kennan moved from Moscow to the State Department.

Kennan's *Foreign Affairs* article, written at Forrestal's urging, expanded the 1946 "Long Telegram." In this more public forum, the essay proved highly influential in swaying opinion about the Soviet Union and the nature of the Cold War

---

* Prior to 1947, the Department of Defense was known as the War Department, and the cabinet officer who ran it bore the title of Secretary of War.

IN PERSPECTIVE: *Presidential Persuasion on Foreign Policy Issues*

When President Truman in 1947 asked Congress to invest millions of dollars to buttress Greece and Turkey against feared Soviet expansionism, he joined a long line of presidents who sought with varied success to win backing for major foreign-policy initiatives from an often reluctant nation. The Constitution puts the president in charge of foreign affairs, but it also sets up an elaborate system of governmental checks and balances, so presidents from George Washington on have had to struggle to exercise that power.

In 1846, President James K. Polk called for war with Mexico because (among other reasons) the Mexicans had shed "American blood on American soil." In fact, the circumstances were highly ambiguous: The bloodshed had occurred during a U.S. Army foray into territory that was in fact claimed by Mexico. Antiwar Whig congressmen, including Abraham Lincoln, challenged Polk's claims. Lincoln, for example, introduced his "spot resolutions" insisting that Polk identify the precise spot on which American blood had been shed "on American soil." But expansionist sentiment prevailed, and the war came.

President William McKinley, by contrast, only reluctantly backed war with Spain in 1898. Pressured by tabloid newspapers like William Randolph Hearst's *New York World* that trumpeted Spain's misdeeds in Cuba, McKinley eventually called for war. Most Americans rallied behind what promised to be a quick and one-sided contest (one U.S. statesman declared it a "splendid little war"). But influential opponents including the philosopher William James and the steel magnate Andrew Carnegie denounced the war and challenged McKinley's justifications. The controversy deepened when the Spanish-American War evolved into a bloody, drawn-out campaign to suppress an independence movement in the Philippines. McKinley's justification for this action—reached, he said, after an anguished night of prayer—was that the Filipinos, left on their own, would soon fall prey to European imperial rivalries, and thus it was in the interests of "our little brown brothers" to be under the benign oversight of Christian America. But despite McKinley's rationale, the fighting in the Philippines stirred congressional opposition. Senate hearings publicized shocking atrocities committed by U.S. soldiers in the Philippines.

President Woodrow Wilson's eloquent summons to war in April 1917 anticipated Truman's 1947 call for aid to Greece and Turkey. Wilson, too, framed the issue in

struggle. Soviet rhetoric, Kennan suggested, arose from "a traditional and instinctive Russian sense of insecurity." For historical and ideological reasons, Kennan argued, the Soviets were waging "a patient but deadly struggle" to expand their influence worldwide and to crush all rivals. The U.S. objective must be "a long-term, patient, but firm and vigilant containment of Russian expansive tendencies," a waiting game in which negotiation over specific issues would play little role.

cosmic terms: This would be a war to defend American ideals, make the world safe for democracy, elevate the conduct of international relations, and create a new world order based on justice, not brute power. Americans embraced the war on gusts of Wilsonian rhetoric, but such exalted idealism could not possibly be sustained, and by 1919 a reaction had set in. Congress repudiated Wilson's beloved League of Nations, and Wilson left the White House in 1921 broken and embittered.

President Franklin Roosevelt trod a careful line from the late 1930s through 1941 as he tried to maneuver a reluctant Congress and nation into supporting U.S. efforts to resist Hitler and aid a beleaguered Great Britain. Isolationist and pacifist sentiment was strong, and Roosevelt faced bitter opposition at every step. FDR's task eased immeasurably after December 7, 1941. With the Japanese surprise attack on Pearl Harbor, an outraged Congress and nation rallied behind Roosevelt's call for war. The force of that outrage, and the sense that the nation's cause was righteous, sustained U.S. support for the war, and for Roosevelt as war leader, up to the moment of FDR's death in April 1945, and on to the final victory that August.

When North Korea invaded South Korea in 1950, President Truman initially enjoyed strong support as he portrayed the invasion as a test of U.S. will that had to be bravely met. Americans also backed Truman's plan to fight under the United Nations flag as a multinational "police action" authorized by UN resolutions rather than by a congressional declaration of war. As the Korean War dragged on, however, support for Truman eroded. By 1952 the war had become deeply unpopular, and Truman's defense of it was no longer sufficient to rally national support.

Vietnam, of course, offers the classic instance of a president's failure to rally the nation behind a foreign war. Initially, Johnson and his advisers marshaled support for the war with apparent success. The 1964 Gulf of Tonkin Resolution, passed overwhelmingly by Congress after a supposed attack on U.S. Navy ships by North Vietnamese gunboats, provided Johnson with the congressional support he wanted for an expanded war. But Johnson's escalation of the war in early 1965 brought the first ominous stirrings of opposition. Initially Congress and most Americans supported the war, but the support was reluctant and uneasy, and as the war dragged on, it steadily eroded. Johnson never succeeded in finding a coherent and persuasive rationale for the war that would rally undivided support for the expenditure of American life and treasure. Like Wilson, he, too, left office under a cloud, successful domestically but a failure in his role as shaper of the nation's foreign policy.

Given this mixed record, Truman's ability early in 1947 to rally a war-weary nation for yet another major foreign-policy initiative, and the administration's campaign for the Marshall Plan a few months later, must count as notable successes in the long history of presidential efforts to exert constitutional power as leader of the United States in its relations with the rest of the world.

Kennan's summation of America's mission distantly echoed nineteenth-century prophecies of the United States' manifest destiny. Americans should be grateful, he maintained, to "a Providence which, by providing [them] with this implacable challenge, has made their entire security as a nation dependent on their pulling themselves together and accepting the responsibilities of moral and political leadership that history plainly intended them to bear."

Kennan's "containment" doctrine crystallized Washington's Soviet policy. He urged the Truman administration to deploy its economic and military resources to prevent the Soviets from expanding beyond Russia's historic Eurasian sphere of influence. (A traditional balance-of-power diplomat, Kennan accepted spheres of influence but saw their undue expansion as dangerous.) In many respects, Kennan offered a prudent response to the threat posed by a nation ruled by a paranoid and unpredictable dictator. As head of the policy-planning staff until 1949, Kennan applied his strategic vision to specific areas of U.S.-Soviet confrontation. However, as Kennan himself soon recognized, some Cold Warriors, at least in their public pronouncements, ignored his emphasis on the cautious side of Soviet behavior. They also overlooked his call for patience and restraint—along with military strength—in dealings with the Soviets. Instead, they focused on the belligerent and aggressive aspect of Moscow's complex approach to the external world. James Forrestal himself went far beyond Kennan in his obsession with the global communist menace. The navy secretary saw revolutionary conspiracies everywhere and offered nightmarish visions of "Russians swarming over Europe."* Forrestal's apocalyptic anticommunism demonstrated that Kennan's limited, cautious doctrine easily could mutate into a far more aggressive formulation of the nation's Cold War mission.

As Washington debated containment doctrine, Western Europe's postwar suffering persisted. The Truman administration's response led to the single most important initiative of the early Cold War era: the Marshall Plan. In early 1947, two years after hostilities ended, Europe still struggled in the grip of inflation, crippled industry, and near-famine conditions. A particularly fierce winter in 1946–1947 deepened the suffering. Train cars froze to the tracks; government workers shivered in unheated offices; misery was everywhere.

The political situation looked equally alarming. European Marxist parties seemed poised to exploit the crisis, with the goal of dragging the whole region into the Soviet orbit. The powerful French Communist party, for example, was quite Stalinist and doggedly loyal to Moscow. The grave problems plaguing Europe, wrote a *New York Times* reporter from Paris in February 1947, proved "how battered and shaken are the old strongholds of democracy in Europe, and how few these strongholds are. . . . [I]f freedom as we understand it is to survive it's up to the United States to save it." While U.S. strategists did not seriously fear a Soviet invasion of Western Europe, they did worry that desperate voters, especially in France, might bring communist regimes to power via the ballot box.

Against this ominous backdrop, the Truman administration offered a program of massive U.S. economic assistance to Western Europe. Drafted in the State Department, the plan was unveiled in a June 1947 commencement address at Harvard University by George C. Marshall, an aloof, self-disciplined, and highly respected former soldier who had replaced James Byrnes as secretary of state the preceding January. A graduate of Virginia Military Institute and a career army officer, Marshall had served as army chief of staff during World War II.

---

* Forrestal's demons eventually mastered him; he committed suicide in May 1949 while a patient at Bethesda Naval Hospital.

While appealing to humanitarian impulses, Marshall also stressed the political issues at stake: "Our policy is directed not against any country or doctrine but against hunger, poverty, desperation, and chaos. Its purpose should be the revival of a working economy in the world so as to permit the emergence of political and social conditions in which free institutions can exist."

Beyond economic recovery, the administration harbored a larger political objective for the Marshall Plan: European unity. Only a united Europe, Marshall believed, could present a strong front against Soviet expansionism. To further this aim, (and to win acceptance for the inclusion of Germany in the program), the Washington architects of the Marshall Plan insisted that aid not be distributed on a piecemeal, nation-by-nation basis but collectively as part of a unified Europe-wide recovery strategy drafted collaboratively by the European nations themselves. In effect, the Marshall Plan's architects envisioned an American-style liberal capitalist order in Europe, where consumer abundance, economic integration, and a federative political system would dilute national conflicts and ideological differences and inoculate the masses against radical appeals from the Right or Left.

Marshall's proposal set off feverish political activity at home and in Europe. In Washington, despite Republican grumbling about "an international WPA" and renewed warnings from the Left about the "Martial Plan's" anti-Soviet subtext, Congress by 1951 had funded no less than $13 billion in aid to Europe. On the Continent, the plan stimulated economic cooperation with profound long-term significance. In the summer of 1947, sixteen European foreign ministers gathered at the Grand Palais in Paris to draft the European Recovery Plan (ERP). From these beginnings evolved the European Coal and Steel Community in 1952 and the European Economic Community (the Common Market) in 1958. By the late 1990s, Western Europe had integrated its economic and trade policies and was moving toward a common currency, the Euro; a United States of Europe seemed a distinct possibility. The Marshall Plan played a crucial role in stimulating this development.

Washington initially proposed the inclusion of the Soviet Union and Eastern Europe in the Marshall Plan, mainly as a public-relations gesture. The Truman administration assumed that the Soviet bloc would remain aloof, but somewhat to its surprise, Poland and Czechoslovakia tried to join the 1947 Paris talks. Stalin objected, however. American plans for revitalizing Western Europe directly challenged the Soviet ruler's hope of expanded influence in the region, and the prospect of a thriving West Germany touched an always raw nerve. The Soviet embassy in Washington denounced the plan as a U.S. plot to restore Germany and Japan as major powers, only this time "subordinated to [the] interest of American capital." When Stalin personally ordered Poland and Czechoslovakia to leave the Paris talks, the Czech prime minister Klement Gottwald obeyed, visibly shaken by Stalin's rage. The moment symbolized Europe's deepening division.

In September 1947, Andrei Vyshinsky, the Soviet deputy minister for foreign affairs, blasted the Marshall Plan in a UN address. He complained that the plan bypassed the United Nations; would "split Europe into two camps"; denied European nations the right "to plan their national economy in their own way"; and would subordinate Western Europe to "the interest of American monopolies, which are

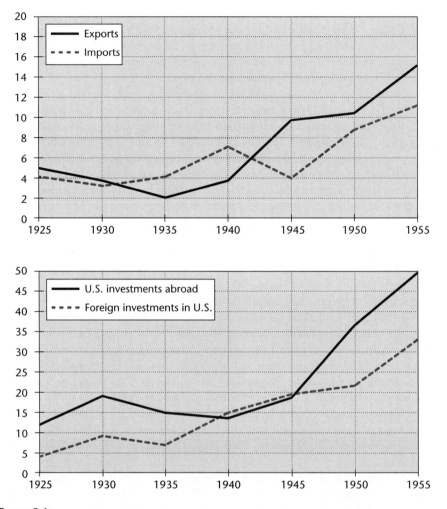

FIGURE 2.1

(a) U.S. Foreign Trade, 1925–1955, (b) Investments, 1925–1955

SOURCE: Adapted from *Historical Statistics of the United States* (Washington, D.C., 1975), pp. 537, 542, 564.

striving to avert the approaching depression by an accelerated export of commodities and capital to Europe."

Although Vyshinsky's analysis of the Marshall Plan's economic effect reflected his Marxist assumptions, he had a valid point. Along with its humanitarian and strategic purposes, the plan benefited American business. In 1947 U.S. exports to Europe neared $16 billion, whereas European exports to America totaled barely half as much. One immediate goal of the Marshall Plan was to provide the credit that would enable Europe to buy more U.S. goods. This goal was candidly acknowledged by a key architect of the Marshall Plan, William L. Clayton, the undersecretary of state for economic affairs and a millionaire Mississippi cotton investor. "Let us admit right off," said Clayton in 1947, "that our objective has as its background the needs and interests of the people of the United States. We need markets—big markets—in which to buy and sell." The journal *Foreign Affairs,* in a fiftieth-anniversary retrospective on the Marshall Plan in 1997, commented: "The American initiative is remembered for its altruism, but it was neither naive nor devoid of self-interest. . . . [T]his was clearly a policy to benefit the United States." Indeed, U.S. trade and investment in Western Europe quickened sharply with economic recovery, and millions of dollars in Marshall Plan aid returned to America in the form of orders for industrial machinery, farm equipment, and other goods.

This trade stimulus influenced a larger pattern of rising U.S. exports. From 1946 to 1952, U.S. merchandise exports jumped from $9.5 billion to $15 billion. These years also saw growing corporate investment abroad as U.S. businesses developed multinational operations, pursued foreign markets, and built factories and distribution facilities overseas. By 1950 foreign investment by U.S. corporations approached $12 billion. A decade later it would total some $32 billion.

The Marshall Plan was part of a larger American effort to rebuild a world financial structure shattered by depression and war and to ease an acute postwar dollar shortage throughout the industrialized world. In 1944, a twenty-eight-nation monetary conference at an elegant old mountain-resort hotel at Bretton Woods, New Hampshire, had laid the groundwork for two important agencies: the International Bank for Reconstruction and Development, or World Bank, and the International Monetary Fund (IMF). The World Bank arranged long-term capital transfers to help poor nations develop their transportation, health, and education systems. The IMF promoted trade, monetary cooperation, and exchange-rate stability among the industrialized nations by creating a pool of currency reserves convertible at agreed-upon rates. The IMF started with thirty-nine member nations; the Soviet Union, despite repeated invitations, refused to join. (In 1992, after the Cold War's end, Russia and other former Soviet republics would at last become members.)

The international monetary order that arose in 1944–1946, coupled with the Marshall Plan and U.S. foreign investment, helped to rebuild Europe's economy, create jobs, and better the living conditions of millions of people. It also served the interests of U.S. business by laying the foundation for a revival of world trade and the eventual emergence of a network of multinational corporations. These new financial structures strengthened the capitalist system, expanded world markets, and forestalled the economic chaos that would have provided fertile breeding ground for social unrest and communist gains. As such, they represented another front in the Cold War.

The Marshall Plan, officially called the European Recovery Plan (ERP), was not solely responsible for European recovery, which was already under way when U.S. aid reached Europe in 1948. But cash grants, loans, farm commodities, and construction projects to rebuild and modernize harbors, factories, mines, and refineries played a central role. Historian Charles Maier has compared the plan to "the lubricant in an engine—not the fuel—allowing a machine to run that would otherwise buck and bind." By 1951, Europe's aggregate production exceeded the 1948 figure by 32 percent, and its industrial output far surpassed even prewar levels. The twenty-five years after 1948 saw the highest rates of economic growth in

Europe's history. West Germans spoke of the *Wirtschaftwunder* (economic miracle) in their country.

The deepening Cold War raised the stakes in the traditional rivalry among the American military services. This jockeying for resources and power played a key role in military and strategic planning in the early postwar years. The air force, in particular, felt in danger of being shunted to the sidelines. To address the problem, Congress in July 1947 passed the National Security Act. This measure combined the old army and navy departments, together with a newly independent air force, into the cabinet-level Department of Defense headed by a civilian secretary of defense and unified the military services under the Joint Chiefs of Staff. Interservice struggles persisted, but under the pressure of the Cold War, the government had introduced greater coordination into the military establishment. The National Security Act also created a new, high-level strategic planning body, the National Security Council (NSC), and set up the Central Intelligence Agency (CIA) to carry on the espionage operations of the wartime Office of Strategic Services (OSS). These reforms hastened the shift of foreign-policy formation from the State Department to the White House, a development that by the late 1960s and early 1970s would enable President Richard Nixon and National Security Adviser Henry Kissinger to ignore their secretary of state as they took sweeping foreign-policy initiatives.

By 1947 the wartime Grand Alliance lay in ruins. That August, Charles E. Bohlen, a Soviet specialist in the State Department, gloomily assessed the new world order and sketched a scenario for U.S. foreign policy:

> Instead of unity among the great powers—both political and economic—after the war, there is complete disunity between the Soviet Union and the satellites on one side and the rest of the world on the other. There are, in short, two worlds instead of one.... Faced with this disagreeable fact, ... the United States ... must re-examine its major policy objectives.... [T]he non-Soviet world ... [must] draw closer together politically, economically, financially, and, in the last analysis, militarily. ... Only in this way can a free and non-Soviet world hope to survive in the face of the centralized and ruthless direction of the Soviet group.

In the months ahead, the fundamental policy reorientation that Bohlen advised would proceed with breathtaking speed.

1948–1949: The Prague Coup, the Berlin Airlift, and NATO

Moscow's grip on Eastern Europe tightened in February 1948, when Czech and Slovak communists overthrew Prague's fragile coalition government and installed a pro-Soviet communist regime. Soon after, Czechoslovak foreign minister Jan Masaryk, a national hero, died in a plunge from a foreign-ministry window. The country's new rulers rendered a verdict of suicide, but many in the West suspected murder. The Prague coup rang alarm bells in Western Europe and struck Washington as further proof of Stalin's treachery.

The sense of crisis deepened that summer, with Germany the focus of attention. At the war's end, the Allies had divided Germany into four occupation zones: the Soviets in the east and the British, French, and Americans in the west. These zones, supposedly temporary, rapidly hardened into long-term political divisions as Moscow clamped down on eastern Germany and the Western powers combined their zones. The introduction of currency reform in early 1948, coupled with U.S. Marshall Plan aid, stimulated a dramatic economic recovery in West Germany. These moves formed part of a larger plan for making West Germany, which contained most of Germany's population and industry, into an independent nation linked to the West.

Stalin, determined to stop this process, took Berlin hostage. Although the former German capital lay deep in the Soviet zone, the four powers governed it jointly and kept it open to access from the West. But on June 24, 1948, as the Western occupiers prepared to extend the currency reform to Berlin, the Soviets abruptly blocked all highway routes to the city. This action posed a major dilemma for President Truman: To smash through the Red Army's highway barricades could bring war, yet to abandon Berlin would make a mockery of the containment doctrine—and weaken Truman's chances in the forthcoming presidential election.

Treading a careful middle path, Truman ordered the U.S. Air Force to maintain a lifeline to Berlin. For the next 321 days, an armada of U.S. and British aircraft flew around the clock into Berlin's Templehof Airport, ferrying food, coal, and other necessities into the beleaguered city. Conceding defeat in May 1949, the Soviets reopened land access to Berlin. Within days, a new constitution launched the Federal Republic of Germany as a parliamentary democracy. In October, Soviet authorities set up the German Democratic Republic in the east.

The communist coup in Czechoslovakia and the Berlin crisis hastened plans for a Western military alliance. In the early postwar years, Washington planners had viewed the contest with the Soviet Union as primarily political and economic. But in Europe itself, especially Great Britain, fears of a military showdown mounted. Early in 1948, British foreign secretary Ernest Bevin warned Washington of an encroaching "Soviet tide" and urged a military alliance between the United States and Western Europe for "the defense of Western civilization." With twenty-five Soviet divisions in Central Europe facing twelve underequipped divisions in Western Europe, these fears seemed well grounded.

Working behind the scenes, the Truman administration built bipartisan support for an alliance linking the United States and Western Europe. In June 1948, Congress adopted, 64–4, a resolution that in principle approved U.S. security alliances with other nations. In April 1949, a treaty-signing ceremony in Washington launched the North Atlantic Treaty Organization (NATO) joining the United States, Canada, and ten nations of Western Europe in a mutual defense arrangement: An attack on any member would be an attack on all. The Senate ratified the treaty in July, 82–13. In September—the Soviets having exploded an atomic bomb in the interim—Congress voted $1.5 billion in military aid for Western Europe.

The ancient U.S. policy dating to the 1780s against peacetime foreign alliances had evaporated in the worsening international climate. NATO marked a key step in America's postwar emergence on the world stage and for the next four decades would symbolize Western resolve in the Cold War. Like the Marshall Plan, NATO

FIGURE 2.2
Cold War Europe, 1950

was intended to prevent a political fragmentation in Europe that would serve Moscow's interests. As Dean Acheson observed, "[Without] the continuing association and support of the United States . . . , free Europe would split apart."

As NATO took shape, President Truman signaled a still greater expansion of America's global commitments. In his 1949 State of the Union message, he announced a new program of U.S. foreign aid to help undeveloped regions. Like the Marshall Plan, this Point Four program (it was the fourth point of the foreign-policy section of Truman's address) combined humanitarian, anticommunist, and economic objectives. By the early 1970s, the Agency for International Development (AID) had channeled over $100 billion in economic assistance to Latin America, Asia, Africa, and the Middle East to promote economic development and political stability, and so forestall the spread of communism. Point Four assistance, together with other federal agencies such as the Export-Import Bank,* also promoted U.S. exports and foreign investment. Indeed, aid was sometimes tied directly to the recipients' purchase of U.S. manufactured goods or farm commodities.

The close of 1949 found the basic framework of the Cold War firmly in place. In Moscow, fears of encirclement by "capitalist imperialism" were almost palpable; in some U.S. circles, the conviction that the Soviets harbored a grand design for world conquest had become an article of faith. "There is only one language [the Soviets] understand, force," declared Truman to an associate in 1949. George Kennan, leaving the State Department to return to private life, deplored the neglect of diplomacy amid a "general preoccupation with military affairs" and lamented the rhetorical excesses and "flamboyant anti-communism" by which the administration sought congressional and public support for its foreign-policy initiatives.

Kennan's critics insisted that the picture of the world presented in Churchill's iron-curtain address, in the Truman Doctrine, and in countless speeches and editorials accurately reflected postwar realities. The Soviet Union *was* a brutal dictatorship; its military forces *did* prop up pro-Soviet regimes across Eastern Europe. Mao Zedong's triumph in China in 1949 (see p. 54) further confirmed communism's global march. Compared to the Soviet sphere, the United States and many of its allies displayed an incomparably greater adherence to democratic values and human freedom.

Nevertheless, Kennan had a point. The black-and-white globe portrayed by many early Cold War ideologists obscured the fact that many states of the "Free World"—Greece, Spain, Iran, South Africa, various military dictatorships in Latin America, and authoritarian regimes in the Middle East, for example—fell far short of the democratic ideal. Furthermore, several leading nations of the Western Alliance still held colonies in Africa and Asia. More important, the Truman administration's penchant for highlighting the ideological differences between the two systems, to the neglect of strategic and economic considerations, made it hard for diplomats to isolate specific, limited issues. The hypnotic allusions to the Soviets' alleged master plan of world rule obscured in a fog of verbiage the diplomatic

---

* The Export-Import Bank, a New Deal agency created in 1934, encouraged U.S. foreign trade by granting loans and credits to U.S. companies seeking to export farm commodities or manufactured goods.

processes by which Washington and Moscow might have reached accommodation on concrete issues in which each side had legitimate and conflicting interests.

In its internal strategic assessments, the White House understood that "the communist world" was not monolithic and that it faced varied stresses and tensions. (This fact had become clear in 1948 when Marshall Tito, the communist ruler of Yugoslavia, broke with Moscow.) Still, some early Cold Warriors proved better at portraying the Soviet menace luridly than at pursuing the art of negotiation. In 1947, amid the crisis over Greece and Turkey, Dean Acheson had written, "[I]t is a mistake to believe that you can, at any time, sit down with the Russians and solve questions. I do not think that is the way that our problems are going to be worked out with the Russians." How would differences be resolved other than by negotiation? Acheson did not provide an answer.

Thus, in these early Cold War years, the nation that had invented pragmatism threatened to succumb to a rigidly ideological mindset that impeded the practical resolution of specific issues. Some Cold War rhetoric resembled theological disputation more than diplomatic exchange. The Truman administration's effort to build support for its national-security program by exaggerated and simplistic representations of world realities succeeded in its immediate purpose but impeded the longer-term goal of finding ways to ease tensions. With Soviet diplomacy proving even more inflexible under a dictator increasingly mired in paranoia, the conflict wore on.

Deeper into the Cold War:
China, the H-Bomb, Korea

The rhetorical portrayals of a monolithic communist threat under Moscow's absolute control especially hobbled Washington's ability to understand and respond to developments in Asia. Late in 1949, after years of civil war, a communist government came to power in China. China's long struggle, dating to the 1920s, had pitted the communist forces of Mao Zedong (Mao Tse-tung) against the pro-Western government of Jiang Jieshi (Chiang Kai-shek). The conflict had abated during World War II as both sides focused on expelling the Japanese invaders, but full-scale civil war had erupted again in 1945.

Jiang's regime was corrupt, inefficient, and unpopular. Rampant inflation further eroded its support. Meanwhile, communist organizers, heeding Mao's advice to move among the people like fish in a stream, built a base among China's peasants, who made up 80 percent of the population. Jiang's position steadily weakened, and in 1949 the communists claimed victory. Jiang and what remained of his army withdrew to the offshore island of Taiwan and established a regime that for the next quarter-century the United States would recognize as China's legitimate government.

Mao's triumph sent shock waves across the United States. America's long and somewhat paternalistic interest in China, a legacy of the early New England China trade, had intensified with the activities of Christian missionaries to China. (Henry Luce, the publisher of *Time* and *Life* magazines, which espoused the Chinese Nationalist cause, was the son of missionaries to China.) China's role as a victim of Japanese aggression in the 1930s had strongly appealed to American sympathies.

In the Chinese civil war, the United States had backed Jiang Jieshi. President Roosevelt, hoping that a noncommunist China could replace Japan as a stabilizing force in postwar Asia, had superficially treated Jiang Jieshi as a coequal during wartime meetings of the so-called Big Four. As the Nationalists' power crumbled, however, Washington's ties to Jiang became a growing liability. Unqualified U.S. support for him, a State Department Far Eastern specialist predicted, would bring "only trouble, trouble, trouble." The victorious Mao Zedong established a new government, the People's Republic of China, and early in 1950 signed a trade and mutual-assistance treaty with the Soviet Union.

To the casual observer, the Eurasian land mass from the Elbe River in Germany to the China Sea seemed one vast domain of communist power. In reality, as Washington officials well understood, deep differences rooted in history and geography divided Moscow and Beijing. Stalin and Mao distrusted one another profoundly, and the Soviet leader had given Mao virtually no help in the Chinese civil war. Even as he negotiated the 1950 treaty, Stalin had angled behind the scenes to restore Moscow's influence in Manchuria and Mongolia, long-time objects of Russian imperialist ambition. But for most Americans, "the world communist conspiracy" seemed all too real. U.S. politics blazed with accusations over who had "lost" China.

On September 3, 1949, as climactic events unfolded in China, the Soviet Union tested its first atomic bomb. The United States' brief reign as the world's only nuclear power had ended. "This is now a different world," Senator Vandenberg wrote gloomily. The Soviet test triggered an intense debate in the Truman administration's inner circles. Some advisers advocated a crash program to build the hydrogen bomb, an awesome weapon a thousand times more powerful than the atomic bomb. Physicist Edward Teller, long an advocate of the "Super," the H-bomb's nickname, urged this course. Opponents included the chairman of the Atomic Energy Commission (AEC), David Lilienthal, and most of the AEC's scientific advisory committee, chaired by physicist J. Robert Oppenheimer, head of the wartime Los Alamos project. These critics argued for a new effort at international control of atomic energy. But Truman rejected their advice and in January 1950 ordered full-scale research on the hydrogen bomb. In a public-opinion poll, 78 percent of Americans endorsed the decision. The post-Hiroshima fear of atomic war and support for international control had given way to a grim determination to maintain U.S. nuclear supremacy.*

The ominous developments of 1949 gave rise to NSC-68, an important formulation of Cold War strategy drawn up by the National Security Council. NSC-68 began as a planning document drafted in April 1950 by, among others, Paul Nitze, a hard-liner who had replaced George Kennan in the State Department's policy-planning office. Discerning in postwar events a Soviet master plan for global domination, NSC-68 envisioned "an indefinite period of tension and danger." "The Kremlin is inescapably militant," the document declared,

> because it possesses and is possessed by a worldwide revolutionary movement, because it is the inheritor of Russian imperialism and because it is a totalitarian

---

* The United States exploded its first hydrogen device in November 1952, and the Soviet Union soon followed suit. By the mid-1950s, both sides were testing full-scale hydrogen bombs. For discussion of the nuclear arms race in the 1950s, see Chapter 4.

dictatorship. Persistent crisis, conflict and expansion are the essence of the Kremlin's militancy. . . . [The American people] in the ascendancy of their strength stand in their deepest peril.

A few months later, as the Korean War raged, President Truman approved NSC-68 as official U.S. policy.

Setting the nation's strategic agenda for the 1950s and beyond, NSC-68 summed up a view of the Cold War as an all-consuming global struggle. Although much evidence buttressed its scenario of a worldwide communist advance directed from Moscow, the document paid little heed to weaknesses or sources of division within the communist world, to strategies for reaching accommodation with the Soviets, or to world trends that did not fit its bipolar model. Foreseeing indefinite military confrontation between two nuclear-armed superpowers, NSC-68 called for massive increases in military spending to build up America's conventional and nuclear arsenal and to rearm NATO. The document offered few hints for constructive steps that the United States might take to reduce hostilities.

Mao's victory helped to inspire NSC-68; it also focused U.S. attention on Asia. In Indochina, the French were fighting to maintain their colonial power against a nationalist insurgency led by the communist Ho Chi Minh. Ho had courted U.S. support, but the Truman administration, eager to ensure France's entrance into NATO, had rejected his overtures. In May 1950, Dean Acheson, who had replaced George Marshall as secretary of state in 1949, announced a small program of U.S. aid and military assistance to the French in Indochina. This decision initiated an involvement that fifteen years later would suck the United States into the maelstrom of Vietnam.

It was Korea, however, not Vietnam, that soon dominated U.S. newspaper headlines. In 1945, ending forty years of Japanese rule, the United States and the Soviet Union had jointly occupied this country, with the 38th parallel demarking the two occupation zones. Both powers had withdrawn most of their troops by 1949, but, as in Germany, each continued to dominate its respective sector. In 1948, with U.S. support, the autocratic Syngman Rhee, elected South Korea's president that year, proclaimed the Republic of Korea, with its capital in Seoul. In the north, the Soviets set up their own client government in Pyongyang, headed by Kim Il Sung. Each regime was armed by its respective Big Power sponsor, and each claimed sovereignty over all Korea. The stage was set for confrontation.

Late in 1949, according to the memoirs of Nikita Khrushchev, later premier of the Soviet Union, Stalin approved Kim Il Sung's request to invade South Korea. Recent scholarship on the Korean War, based on newly available Soviet archives, makes clear Stalin's central role in planning North Korea's initial invasion and in all stages of the war thereafter. Stalin may have hoped that Pyongyang could win control over all Korea, and provide a counterweight not only to the United States and Japan but also to Mao's China. Statements emanating from Washington that downgraded Korea's importance may also have encouraged Kim and Stalin. In a January 1950 speech, Secretary of State Acheson defined the U.S. defense perimeter in Asia in a way that excluded South Korea.* In May, Texas senator Tom Con-

---

* The defense of parts of Asia outside this perimeter, asserted Acheson, rested with "the entire civilized world," acting through the United Nations.

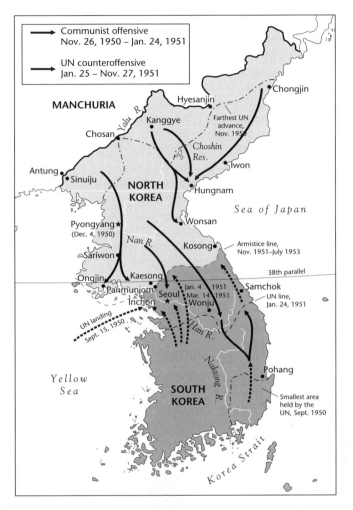

FIGURE 2.3
The Korean War, 1950–1953

nally, chair of the Senate Foreign Relations Committee, dismissed Korea as of little importance given the United States' strong line of defense in Asia extending from the Philippines through Okinawa and Japan. America's rapid postwar demobilization and subsequent emphasis on nuclear rather than conventional military strength probably figured in Kim Il Sung's calculations that a move against South Korea was a risk worth taking.

On June 25, 1950, Soviet-armed North Korean troops stormed across the 38th parallel. Capturing Seoul and pushing southward, they soon pinned the South Korean defenders and a few U.S. troops within a small defensive perimeter around the southern port of Pusan. President Truman responded by ordering full-scale U.S. military action to expel the invaders. Korea was the Greece of Asia, he argued—a further test of America's will to contain Soviet-sponsored communist aggression. The United States also rushed the case to the UN Security Council. With the U.S.S.R.'s delegate absent because of a Soviet boycott, the council passed U.S. resolutions calling on member nations to aid South Korea. The conflict was thus fought under UN auspices, and the Truman administration dubbed it a "police action" rather than a war. Congress never formally declared war, as required by the Constitution, an additional example of the expansion of executive power in these early Cold War years. Under whatever flag, though, Americans, Koreans, and eventually the Chinese did most of the fighting.

General Douglas MacArthur, the World War II hero who had directed the U.S. occupation of postwar Japan, commanded the UN forces in Korea. On September 15, 1950, MacArthur led a daring amphibious landing behind the enemy lines at Inchon, near Seoul. Simultaneously breaking out of the Pusan perimeter, MacArthur's forces swept across the 38th parallel and by the end of October had captured Pyongyang and were nearing the Yalu River, the boundary between Korea and the Chinese province of Manchuria. Washington now began to consider not merely repelling the invaders but overthrowing Kim Il Sung and uniting Korea under a noncommunist government. When China warned MacArthur against approaching the Yalu River, he dismissed this statement as "hot air" and promised to have "the boys home by Christmas." He also made the tactical error of dividing his strongest forces, with a weaker South Korean contingent in the middle.

On November 26, thirty-three Chinese divisions poured across the Yalu. Once more, the North Koreans, now massively reinforced by the Chinese, drove down the peninsula. Viewing the Korean fighting as a prelude to a larger struggle against communism in Asia, MacArthur urgently asked permission to widen the war by bombing Chinese bases in Manchuria and "unleashing" Jiang Jieshi for an invasion of the Chinese mainland.

Korea, Winter 1950. *U.S. marines retreating from North Korea's Changjin Reservoir after Chinese Communist forces entered the war in massive numbers.* (UPI/Corbis-Bettmann)

A Last Hurrah. *General Douglas MacArthur, every inch the war hero, greets adoring crowds in San Francisco after being dismissed from his command in Korea by President Truman.* (Wayne Miller/Magnum Photos, Inc.)

President Truman and his military advisers rejected the general's request. With the Sino-Soviet alliance still in force, they feared that MacArthur's aggressive plan would trigger a third world war. Further, Washington strategists feared that a wider war in Asia would weaken the U.S. ability to respond to hostile Soviet moves in Europe. Truman also vetoed using atomic bombs in Korea, a course favored by about half the American people in public-opinion polls. He did, however, toy with the idea of giving the Soviets a nuclear ultimatum. In December 1950, an alarmed British prime minister Clement Atlee flew to Washington, fearful that nuclear weapons in Korea might provoke Moscow to attack Western Europe and even drop atomic bombs on Great Britain.

General MacArthur, meanwhile, pushing his proposals to the point of insubordination, gave media interviews and wrote a leading Republican congressman complaining of the restraints imposed on him by the White House. "Here in Asia is where the communist conspirators have elected to make their play for global conquest," MacArthur stormed. "Here we fight Europe's war with arms while the diplomats there fight it with words." In war, he summed up, "there is no substitute for victory." *Time* magazine and some leading Republican politicians endorsed MacArthur's call for a wider war.

Furious over MacArthur's open defiance, Truman relieved him of his command on April 10, 1951. Despite his insubordination, the seventy-one-year-old general returned to a hero's welcome. His reception reflected not only enthusiasm for a legendary warrior but public frustration with the Korean stalemate and an apparently endless Cold War struggle. Sixty-six percent of Americans initially opposed Truman's firing of MacArthur. On the day that New York City gave the general a ticker-tape parade, fans booed Truman when he threw out the first ball on opening day of the baseball season at Washington's Griffith Stadium.* A cartoon in the Republican *Chicago Tribune* portrayed Truman as a little boy in short pants, gazing up enviously at the larger-than-life profile of a heroic MacArthur, his trademark corncob pipe clamped firmly between his teeth.

To a joint session of Congress, MacArthur delivered an emotional address that ended with the words of a barracks ballad: "Old soldiers never die, they just fade away." His congressional fans held hearings to air his views, but Truman countered with General Omar Bradley, chairman of the Joint Chiefs of Staff, who testified that MacArthur's strategy would "involve us in the wrong war, at the wrong place, at the wrong time, and with the wrong enemy." As Americans had sober second thoughts about the issues at stake, the general soon faded away, as predicted.

In Korea, armistice talks began in July 1951, but the fighting dragged on for two more years. When the conflict finally ended in 1953, it had taken the lives of 54,000 Americans and some 3,000 soliders from other nations who fought under the UN command—a tragic toll that nevertheless paled in comparison to the estimated 3 million Koreans (one-tenth of the population) and 1 million Chinese who died. Historian William Stueck, author of a recent history of the war, leaves no doubt that North Korea, abetted by Stalin, bore responsibility for starting the war, but adds that after the Inchon landing and MacArthur's drive northward, "the burden shifted squarely to the U.S. side for escalating the battle to the brink of Armageddon." The U.S. defense budget, fueled by Korean War spending as well as by the military build-up outlined in NSC-68, surged to $44 billion by 1952 and $50 billion in 1953, up sharply from the 1946–1949 levels of about $13 billion annually.

Even as the Korean War raged, Cold War strategists never lost sight of Europe. In April 1950, the administration had begun to plan the rearmament of West Germany within a NATO framework. The aim was less to repel a Soviet invasion, which few expected, than to ensure West Germany's integration into the European community. To overcome the protests of Great Britain, France, and other NATO members whose war memories were still fresh, Truman in December appointed General Dwight Eisenhower commander of NATO's new integrated command structure. Truman also pledged to send four more U.S. divisions to Europe, joining the two already there.

The NATO ministers in December 1950 agreed in principle to the integration of German forces in a joint defense force. Not until 1955, however, over die-hard French resistance, did West Germany formally join NATO. In March 1952, the Soviet Union called for a Big Power conference to discuss German reunification. Whether this request was a propaganda ploy or a serious proposal aimed at preventing West German rearmament may never be known; Dean Acheson rejected the proposal out of hand.

As more U.S. divisions flew to Europe, NATO military strategizing proliferated, including plans for a nuclear response if the Soviets attacked. Greece and

---

* In 1951 the nation's capital still had a big-league baseball team, the Washington Senators.

Turkey entered NATO in 1952. Turkey, on the Soviet Union's border, bristled with an armada of U.S.-supplied air power, including 180 F-47 fighter planes and 30 B-26 bombers.

Cold War ideology, somewhat open to debate in the late 1940s, rigidified after Korea. Beset by Republicans who smelled victory in '52, the administration redoubled its efforts to prove itself "tough on communism." A similar intransigence gripped Moscow, where the aging, fear-ridden Stalin still ruled. George Kennan, appointed ambassador to the Soviet Union in 1952, found vitriolic anti-Americanism among Soviet leaders. In his memoirs he would later write, "I began to ask myself whether . . . we had not contributed . . .—by the overmilitarization of our policies and statements—to a belief in Moscow that it was war we were after." Kennan understated the Soviet Union's own responsibility for the frigid climate of 1952, but his assessment of the dismal state of relations between Washington and Moscow was on the mark. The wartime allies had become bitter enemies.

Conclusion

For years, diplomatic historians hotly debated the origins of the Cold War, some placing the blame entirely on Moscow, others, glossing over the dark side of Stalin's regime, finding the United States almost wholly culpable and the Soviet Union essentially blameless. Viewing history through the reductionist prism of economic determinism, some Marxist historians portrayed American Cold War policies as dictated solely by capitalism's global search for raw materials, markets, and investment opportunities.

Gradually, however, a consensus emerged that reemphasized the grave challenges the United States and Western Europe faced after the war and the merits of the responses devised by statesmen of the era. John Lewis Gaddis's thoughtful *The Long Peace: Inquiries into the History of the Cold War* (1987), although far from uncritical of U.S. Cold War policy, stresses the remarkable stability in U.S.-Soviet relations through their long confrontation. Writing before the Cold War's end, Gaddis observed: "Given all the conceivable reasons for having had a major war in the past four decades . . . it seems worthy of comment that there has not in fact been one. . . . The Cold War, with all of its rivalries, anxieties, and unquestionable dangers, has produced the longest period of stability in relations among the great powers that the world has known in this century." Although the "stability" of this "long peace" saw bloody conflict in Korea, Vietnam, and elsewhere and a potentially deadly nuclear arms race, the point merits recognition in any assessment of U.S. Cold War policy.

Melvyn Leffler's *A Preponderance of Power: National Security, the Truman Administration, and the Cold War* (1992) argues that what most troubled Cold War strategists was not the risk of global war or even of a Soviet invasion of Western Europe but the prospect of Moscow's extending its influence through subversion, economic means, or electoral victories by local communist parties. Leffler credits Washington for shaping a diplomacy that ensured Western Europe's recovery and the emergence of Germany and Japan as healthy democracies allied to the West while containing the Soviet threat. Rejecting the caricature of U.S policymakers as warmongering imperialists, Leffler portrays them for the most part as prudent, responsible leaders intent on protecting American security interests as they understood those interests.

But Leffler, like George Kennan, also finds misjudgments and lost opportunities in U.S. postwar policy, including a persistent tendency to denigrate the value of diplomacy in resolving conflicts, to exaggerate the danger of all-out Soviet attack, and to downplay the caution that often characterized Soviet policy. He also documents simplistic, inflated views of Moscow's global power and a consequent inattention to the indigenous social unrest, anticolonialism, and nationalistic fervor seething in many parts of the world. This myopia, he suggests, ultimately led to America's disastrous intervention in Vietnam.

While historians continue to analyze the origins of the Cold War, few question the degree to which the conflict became all-consuming for both sides or the risks it posed for humanity. That the Cold War arose just as nuclear weapons entered the world sharply heightened those risks. Indeed, the existence of the ultimate weapon may have encouraged both sides' tendency to identify the Cold War adversary as the ultimate enemy.

Yet the specter of nuclear holocaust and the fear of reprisal may in fact have helped to prevent the Cold War from escalating into world war. As the Soviets maneuvered menacingly in Iran and Eastern Europe in late 1945, an adviser tried to lift President Truman's spirits by commenting, "Mr. President, you have an atomic bomb up your sleeve." Truman replied, "Yes, but I'm not sure it can ever be used." John Lewis Gaddis, exploring the reasons for "the long peace," claimed in 1987, "It seems inescapable that what has really made the difference . . . has been the workings of the nuclear deterrent. . . . [T]he development of nuclear weapons has had, on balance, a stabilizing effect on the postwar international system."

Whatever its deterrent effect, the risk of nuclear war nevertheless terrified many Americans in these years. In 1947, General H. H. ("Hap") Arnold, chief of the U.S. Army Air Force, warned that the combination of atomic bombs and guided missiles (another legacy of World War II) had made the United States infinitely more vulnerable than at any point in its history. "Without warning," wrote Arnold, nuclear-armed missiles could "pass over all . . . barriers or 'lines of defense' and . . . deliver devastating blows at our population centers and our industrial, economic, or governmental heart." Reiterated time and again, Arnold's somber warning deeply penetrated the American psyche and shaped American culture in the Cold War era.

Quite apart from the nuclear arms race, the Cold War by the early 1950s had led to an arms buildup of unprecedented peacetime magnitude. One of the Truman administration's principal legacies, military historian Walter Millis observed in 1951, was "an enormously expanded military establishment, beyond anything we had ever contemplated in time of peace." This expansion, he continued, had called forth "a huge and apparently permanent armament industry now wholly dependent . . . on government contracts." Yet, Millis reflected, the administration seemed unsure about the long-term objectives of its heavily militarized strategy or how the Cold War might be brought to closure.

Nuclear fear and the rise of a vast peacetime military establishment were only two of many ways by which the Cold War seeped into the fabric of U.S. society and into the lives of an entire generation of Americans. The Cold War, whose beginnings young Kathleen Harriman had watched during those bleak March days of 1945 in Moscow, had America in its grip.

SELECTED READINGS

The Early Cold War: General Studies

Terry H. Anderson, *The United States, Great Britain, and the Cold War, 1944–1947* (1981); Richard Crockatt, *The Fifty Years War: The United States and the Soviet Union in World Politics, 1941–1991* (1995); Thomas H. Etzold and John L. Gaddis, eds., *Containment: Documents on American Policy and Strategy, 1945–1950* (1978); John L. Gaddis, *The United States and the Origins of the Cold War, 1941–1947* (1972), *Strategies of Containment: A Critical Appraisal of Postwar American National Security Policy* (1982), *The Long Peace: Inquiries into the History of the Cold War* (1987), and *We Now Know: Rethinking Cold War History* (1997); Lloyd C. Gardner, *Architects of Illusion: Men and Ideas in American Foreign Policy, 1941–1949* (1970); James L. Gormly, *The Collapse of the Grand Alliance, 1945–1948* (1987); Walter LaFeber, *America, Russia, and the Cold War, 1945–1984* (1985); Melvyn Leffler, *A Preponderance of Power: National Security, the Truman Administration, and the Cold War* (1992); Melvyn Leffler and David S. Painter, eds., *The Origins of the Cold War: An International History* (1994); Martin Walker, *The Cold War: A History* (1994); Samuel Walker, *Henry A. Wallace and American Foreign Policy* (1976); Daniel Yergin, *Shattered Peace: The Origins of the Cold War and the National Security State* (1977).

Nuclear Policy; Postwar Diplomacy in Europe and the Middle East

Barton J. Bernstein, "Truman and the H-Bomb," *Bulletin of the Atomic Scientists* (March 1984); Michael J. Cohen, *Truman and Israel* (1990); Lawrence Freedman, *The Evolution of Nuclear Strategy* (1981); James F. Good, *The United States and Iran, 1946–1951* (1989); Fraser J. Harbutt, *The Iron Curtain: Churchill, America and the Origins of the Cold War* (1986); Gregg Herken, *The Winning Weapon: The Atomic Bomb in the Cold War, 1945–1950* (1980); Michael Hogan, *The Marshall Plan* (1987); Timothy P. Ireland, *Creating the Entangling Alliance: The Origins of NATO* (1981); Ethan B. Kapstein, *Insecure Alliance: Energy Crises and Western Politics Since 1944* (1989); Jon V. Kofas, *Intervention and Underdevelopment: Greece During the Cold War* (1989); Bruce R. Kuniholm, *The Origins of the Cold War in the Near East* (1980); "The Marshall Plan and Its Legacy," *Foreign Affairs* (May/June 1997); David S. Painter, *Oil and the American Century: The Political Economy of U.S. Foreign Oil Policy, 1941–1954* (1986); Robert A. Pollard, *Economic Security and the Origins of the Cold War, 1945–1950* (1985); David Alan Rosenberg, "American Atomic Strategy and the Hydrogen Bomb Decision," *Journal of American History* (June 1979); Georg Schild, *Bretton Woods and Dumbarton Oaks: American Economic and Political Postwar Planning in the Summer of 1944* (1995); Avi Shlaim, *The United States and the Berlin Blockade* (1983); Lawrence L. Wittner, *American Intervention in Greece, 1943–1949* (1982).

The Korean War and the Cold War in Asia

Barton J. Bernstein, "New Light on the Korean War," *International History Review* (April 1981); Russell D. Buhite, *Soviet-American Relations in Asia, 1945–1954* (1982); Ronald J. Caridi, *The Korean War and American Politics: The Republican Party as a Case Study* (1969); Bruce Cumings, *Child of Conflict: The Korean-American Relationship, 1943–1953* (1983); Roger Dingman, "Atomic Diplomacy During the Korean War," *International Security*

(Winter 1988–89); Lloyd C. Gardner, *Approaching Vietnam: From World War II Through Dienbienphu* (1988); June Grasso, *Harry Truman's Two-China Policy* (1987); Jon Halliday and Bruce Cumings, *Korea: The Unknown War* (1988); Gary Hess, *The U.S. Emergence as a Southeast Asian Power* (1986); D. Clayton James, *The Years of MacArthur* (3 vols., 1970–1985); Burton I. Kaufman, *The Korean War: Challenges in Crisis, Credibility, and Command* (1986); Geoffrey Perret, *Old Soldiers Never Die: The Life of Douglas MacArthur* (1996); Andrew J. Rotter, *The Path to Vietnam: Origins of the American Commitment to Southeast Asia* (1987); Howard Schonberger, *After the War: Americans and the Remaking of Japan* (1989); William W. Stueck, Jr., *The Road to Confrontation: American Policy Toward China and Korea, 1947–1950* (1981) and *The Korean War: An International History* (1995); Kathryn Weathersby, "From the Russian Archives: New Findings on the Korean War," *Cold War International History Project Bulletin* [Woodrow Wilson International Center for Scholars], 3 (Fall 1993); Odd Arne Westad, *Cold War and Revolution: Soviet-American Rivalry and the Origins of the Chinese Civil War, 1944–1946* (1993).

CHAPTER 3

Uneasiness at Dawn: Domestic Trends in the Early Postwar Years

N ew York City, September 1945. As the writer James Agee watched a victory parade, his pleasure was edged with apprehension: "The whole city has a kind of love-feast warmth of thousands of great and small homecomings," he wrote a friend. But immediately he added, "God, what most of the homecomers, and those they come home to, are in for!"

Agee had reason to worry. Even as they welcomed the end of World War II, Americans eyed the future with concern. The mushroom cloud that had risen over the New Mexico desert in July 1945 seemed to hover over the entire culture as Americans contemplated the atomic era. "The Age of Anxiety," the title of a 1948 poem by the Anglo-American poet W. H. Auden, summed up at least a part of the postwar mood. Less apocalyptic sources of concern also shadowed the victory celebrations. Without the stimulus of military production, would hard times return? In fact, demobilization proceeded remarkably smoothly. The economy absorbed the returning veterans as industry switched promptly to peacetime production. These years launched an economic boom that with periodic interruptions would last for several decades.

Nevertheless, as peace returned, so did the political cleavages of the 1930s. Truman and his liberal supporters sought to expand the New Deal, but conservatives in both parties doggedly hacked away at its "socialistic" excesses, and business groups gained a greater voice in shaping public policy. Although Truman won an upset electoral victory in 1948, disputes over the the postwar domestic order raged on.

The war had stirred unsettling changes. Women had donned uniforms or worked in war plants. African Americans had served in the military or moved northward and cityward to seek work. Mexican workers had immigrated to the United States in great numbers. Poverty and economic inequities pervaded America. Yet the early postwar era generally failed to address the social and political implications of these developments. President Truman's reform program, offered in the 1948 campaign, made little headway. Indeed, in contrast to the New Deal years, the late 1940s brought a conservative drift in U.S. politics and social thought. In celebrating the good life of suburbia and an idealized domesticity, mass culture, including television, the newest medium, sought to contain the forces of social change, much as Cold War planners worked to contain communism abroad. Just as Cold War calculations drove U.S. foreign policy, so, too, in this crucial transitional era, did the anticommunist struggle influence domestic politics and culture.

Demobilization and the Limits of Liberalism at Home

Fears of a new depression as military contracts dried up and veterans reentered the labor market hung heavily in many minds in August 1945. Producer Sam Goldwyn's bleak movie about veterans' problems, sardonically titled *The Best Years of Our Lives,* won the Academy Award for best picture of 1946. In fact, demobilization was accomplished successfully as industries retooled to meet pent-up demands for consumer goods. "From tanks to Cadillacs in two months," boasted General Motors. Unemployment remained mostly under 4 percent from 1946 to 1952. These figures in part resulted from millions of veterans who, taking advantage of the GI Bill's educational benefits, enrolled in school rather than entering the labor market.* Many women workers, fired to make room for veterans, chose not to seek other employment. Other women left the workplace voluntarily for the domestic sphere. The female labor force fell from 35.8 million in 1945 to 30.8 million in 1946; not until 1956 would it regain its 1945 level.

Demobilization was not entirely painless. Housing shortages and inflation plagued postwar America. Addressing the latter issue, Truman in June 1946 asked Congress to extend the authority of the wartime Office of Price Administration (OPA), which had controlled prices and rents. But conservative legislators, ill disposed toward this reminder of wartime regulations, radically cut the OPA's powers. Within two weeks, prices shot up 25 percent. A Tulsa grocer even advised customers not to buy his shrimp, so outrageous was the cost. By the end of 1946, price controls on all but a few items had ended, and inflation had set in. Coffee prices rose by 54 percent from 1945 to 1947; the cost of meat nearly doubled.

Galloping inflation sparked a rash of strikes for higher wages. In late 1945 and early 1946, nearly five thousand walkouts idled some 4.6 million workers. President Truman reacted firmly to stoppages that he believed threatened the national welfare. When railway workers struck early in 1946, he told the union leaders, "If you think I'm going to sit here and let you tie up this whole country, you're crazy as hell." As Truman prepared to ask Congress for powers to resolve the crisis, the workers returned to the job. When four hundred thousand coal miners belonging to John L. Lewis's United Mineworkers union walked out on April 1, 1946, Truman ordered the army to seize the mines. Lewis finally called off the strike late in 1947, after a long court battle. Truman took these conflicts as personal challenges; when the miners went back to work, he wrote his mother, "Well, John L. had to fold up. He couldn't take the gaff. No bully can."

---

* By 1956, 7.8 million veterans had attended college or technical schools with federal support.

Image and Reality. *Left: Union leaders in 1941 adopted a "No Strike" policy for the duration of the war. Government propaganda such as this 1942 War Production Board poster urged patriotic workers to stay on the job. With the war's end, however, pent-up frustration produced a wave of strikes. (War Manpower Commission, 1942) Right: Labor unrest, February 1946. Philadelphia police struggle to seize a flag carried by striking electrical workers, many of them World War II veterans. (Temple University)*

The Republicans, capitalizing on labor unrest and consumer anger over high prices, adopted a simple slogan for the 1946 midterm elections: "Had enough? Vote Republican." The strategy worked: Republicans won control of both houses of Congress for the first time since 1928. Among the newcomers, reported *Time* magazine, were Joseph McCarthy of Wisconsin, elected on the slogan "Washington Needs a Tail-Gunner"; a "dark, lank, Quaker attorney" from California, Richard M. Nixon; and a Democrat, "boyish, raw-boned, Harvard-bred" John Kennedy of Massachusetts.

The strains of demobilization intensified the ongoing debate over America's political course. FDR's Depression-spawned New Deal had sketched the preliminary outlines of a welfare state. The legacy of the 1930s to postwar America was a federal government committed to maintaining prosperity, regulating capitalism, and ensuring a minimal level of well-being for all. For liberal ideologists, the reforms of the 1930s offered an admirable long-term blueprint that they wished to extend to include other objectives such as full employment. Others, in both parties, accepted basic New Deal reforms such as social security and found merit in the goal of full employment but believed that the nation needed breathing space. They urged consolidation, not more reform. Sometimes Truman himself shared this view. "I don't want any experiments," he told an adviser in 1945. "The American people want a rest." The president and his administration, steering a cautious middle course, kept their eye on a more mundane goal as well: electoral victory in 1948.

Further right on the political spectrum gathered those who thought that the New Deal had undermined individualism and free enterprise. Down with government regulation and welfare programs, they urged; up with laissez faire. This camp much admired the émigré Austrian economist Friedrich Hayek, whose *The Road to Serfdom* (1944) portrayed the welfare state as a step down the slippery slope to socialism and, eventually, totalitarianism. Hayek's work propelled a resurgent conservative ideology that a generation later would loom large in American public life.

The reputation of corporate America, tarnished in the 1930s, had taken on fresh lustre during the war, and business groups such as the National Association of Manufacturers and the U.S. Chamber of Commerce sought to use this new prestige to influence domestic policy. As one business leader wrote in 1944, corporations in the postwar era should work together to "rid the economy of injurious or unnecessary regulation, as well as administration that is hostile or harmful," and to create a political climate "in which a private enterprise system can flourish." The Advertising Council, founded during World War II by ad agencies and corporate advertisers to publish public-service ads in support of the war effort, led this campaign. After the war, the council supplemented its ads for driver safety and charitable giving with pitches aimed at "selling" the free-enterprise system and the "economic miracle" of modern capitalism.

For a while after the war, advocates of expanding the New Deal appeared to hold the political high ground. In September 1945, President Truman proposed to Congress a sweeping reform program that included an extension of social security, slum clearance, public housing, and a federal commission to combat racism in employment. Most of these proposals extended New Deal programs or initiatives undertaken by the Roosevelt administration. But much of Truman's program languished in a Congress veering rightward. One exception, the Employment Act of 1946, enacted with bipartisan support, committed the government to a policy of "maximum employment, production, and purchasing power." To this end, the law required the president to submit an annual economic report to Congress, with recommended programs to promote economic growth. It also created a three-person Council of Economic Advisers (CEA) to advise the president on economic policy.

The Employment Act of 1946 reflected the ideas of the British economist John Maynard Keynes, who advocated using the government's tax, credit, and spending powers to stimulate economic growth. But the law also illustrated the business community's mounting influence. The initial drafts had a distinctly "New Dealish" tone, calling for government spending on health, education, public works, rural electrification, urban renewal, and so on, to promote full employment. Intense lobbying by business groups blunted this activist thrust, however, and in its final form, the bill called for such measures as tax cuts to stimulate investment and business-government cooperation in achieving economic growth.

The Employment Act of 1946 reveals the multiplying links between foreign affairs and domestic policy. At the 1944 Bretton Woods Conference, the British had insisted that if the dollar were to become the world's monetary standard, Washington would have to ensure economic stability at home. This pressure from abroad proved a major impetus behind the passage of the 1946 legislation committing the government to an expanded economic role.

The Atomic Energy Act of 1946 further highlights the political crosscurrents of the period. The law mandated public control of atomic energy under the civilian Atomic Energy Commission (AEC) and called for research on peacetime uses of the atom. The appointment of David E. Lilienthal, head of the New Deal's Tennessee Valley Authority (TVA), as the AEC's first chairman strengthened the act's link to the liberal tradition. In reality, the AEC mainly supplied nuclear weapons to the military. Although Lilienthal maintained an optimistic public facade about the peacetime benefits of atomic energy, he privately deplored his agency's focus on bomb production. Deeply discouraged, Lilienthal resigned in 1950, after losing his battle against development of the hydrogen bomb.

Although basic New Deal measures such as social security remained firmly in place, Republicans and many southern Democrats loathed other reforms of the Franklin Roosevelt era. Business leaders and their political allies had long chafed at the expansion of union power in the 1930s. The 1935 Wagner Act, they insisted, with its guarantees of union rights, had gone too far in a prolabor direction. The Taft-Hartley Act of 1947 evidenced this hostility with particular clarity.* This law, passed over Truman's veto, outlawed the closed shop, wherein hiring must be done through a union hall; permitted states to pass so-called right-to-work laws barring the exclusion of nonunion workers from unionized plants; permitted employers to sue unions on various grounds; and authorized federal injunctions against strikes that jeopardized public health or safety. Finally, reflecting the nation's growing antiradical mood, Taft-Hartley required union leaders to swear that they were not communists.

The Taft-Hartley Act symbolized the conservative, probusiness climate of late-1940s America. It directly undercut union leaders eager to make organized labor a forceful voice in shaping public policy. One bitter Congress of Industrial Organizations official complained, "When you think of [the Taft-Hartley Act] as merely a combination of individual provisions, you are losing entirely the full impact of the program, the sinister conspiracy that has been hatched."

For organized labor, the postwar era eroded the substantial gains of the 1930s. For African Americans, different circumstances prevailed. Largely ignored during the New Deal, millions of blacks emerged from the war determined to force the nation to live up to its egalitarian ideals.

African Americans and the Liberal Agenda

The growing political clout of northern urban blacks, the surge of black activism during World War II, and the court challenges to segregation by the National Association for the Advancement of Colored People (NAACP) gave racial issues high

---

* Named for its sponsors, Senator Robert Taft of Ohio and New Jersey congressman Fred Hartley, the bill's official title was the Labor-Management Relations Act.

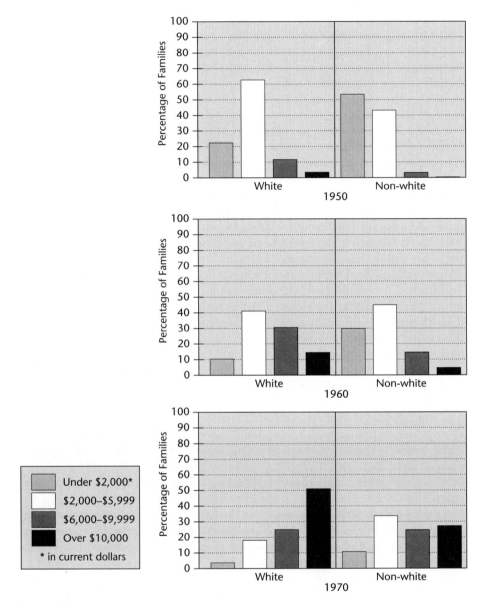

FIGURE 3.1

Family Income by Race, 1950–1970

SOURCE: Adapted from *Statistical Abstract of the United States, 1974* (Washington, D.C., 1973), p. 382.

priority in the Truman years. So, too, did the logic of America's wartime struggle against fascism. This point was underscored in *An American Dilemma: The Negro Problem and American Democracy* (1944), by the Swedish economist Gunnar Myrdal: "This war is an ideological war fought in defense of democracy.... Fascism and nazism are based on a racial superiority dogma.... In fighting [them], America had to stand before the whole world in favor of racial tolerance and cooperation and of racial equality." Similarly, Myrdal continued, the United States would confront the issue even more directly in the internationalist climate of the postwar era:

> America has now joined the world and is tremendously dependent upon the support and good-will of other countries. . . . The treatment of the Negro is America's greatest and most conspicuous scandal. . . . For the colored people all over the world, whose rising influence is axiomatic, this scandal is salt in their wounds.

Racial segregation, agreed the African-American Leader A. Philip Randolph, was "the greatest single propaganda and political weapon in the hands of Russia and International Communism today."

Myrdal and Randolph were right. As the Cold War became global, American racism proved a growing embarrassment. When U.S. hotels and restaurants refused service to dark-skinned diplomats from developing nations, the insults received worldwide publicity. As foreign-policy considerations propelled race onto President Truman's agenda, once again the line between domestic and international issues in the Cold War era blurred.

For Truman, civil rights posed a dilemma both personally and politically. The grandchild of slaveowners, he grew up in an era when blatant racism pervaded American life. While a senator, he had supported a federal antilynching bill while privately assuring southern colleagues that he did so only because of blacks' voting power in Kansas City and St. Louis. But Truman showed capacity for growth during his White House years, and his sense of decency eventually responded to injustice when it was made plain to him. As a politician, Truman realized that the Democratic coalition included northern blacks and liberal whites as well as southern whites who clung to racial segregation. As president, he confronted powerful southern Democrats in Congress, but as "leader of the Free World," he realized that racism represented a painful liability in America's ideological war with communism.

Amid this welter of contradictory impulses and calculations, Truman cautiously embraced the black cause. Late in 1946, after heavy Democratic losses in that year's midterm elections, Truman set up the presidential Committee on Civil Rights, dominated by liberal activists. Its 1947 report, *To Secure These Rights,* called for vigorous action against racism, including an end to school segregation. That year Truman delivered a strong address to the NAACP, and early in 1948 (by no coincidence, an election year) he sent Congress a civil-rights message proposing a federal antilynching law and a permanent Fair Employment Practices Commission patterned on FDR's temporary wartime agency. Southern Democrats easily buried Truman's proposals, but the message gave racial issues visibility at the highest political level for the first time.

Truman's major civil-rights achievement came in July 1948, when he ordered an end to racial segregation in the military. Although not fully implemented until the Korean War, Truman's order hastened the process of breaking down structures of institutionalized racism built up over many decades. The *Chicago Defender,* a black newspaper, euphorically called it "unprecedented since the time of Lincoln."

Despite Truman's civil-rights proposals, a broad-based movement still lay in the future. Instead, attention focused on individual black achievers: diplomat

Ralph Bunche, boxer Sugar Ray Robinson, and baseball player Jackie Robinson, who broke the major-league color barrier in 1947. In 1949, playing second base for the Brooklyn Dodgers, Robinson led the National League in batting and was the league's most valuable player. After years of segregation in the separate Negro League, black baseball stars could now compete on the same fields with whites.

Despite notable individual achievements, racism held a relentless grip on America. Jackie Robinson stayed in segregated hotels when the Dodgers traveled. Black jazz musicians, however famous, still faced the humiliation of racial segregation. In 1946 a security guard pistol-whipped bandleader Cab Calloway as he tried to enter Kansas City's all-white Pla-Mor Ballroom. Despite gradual gains, blacks lagged far behind the white majority economically and educationally. In 1950, when some 39 percent of white families earned annual incomes under $3,000, the figure for black families was an appalling 77 percent. Black high-school graduates attended college in the early 1950s at less than half the rate of whites.

Postwar antiradical obsessions discouraged racial protest. African-American leaders such as Paul Robeson and W. E. B. Du Bois, because of their ties to the Communist party, encountered ostracism even by black organizations like the NAACP. The absence of grassroots civil-rights activism also reflected the NAACP's preference for litigation over marches and protests. In 1947, when two small civil-rights organizations, the Fellowship of Reconciliation and the Congress of Racial Equality (CORE), organized an interracial "Journey of Reconciliation" on segregated interstate buses operating in the South, the NAACP stayed on the sidelines.

Yet changes were astir. As President Truman's election-year attention to civil rights made plain, blacks' political clout was growing. Even in the South, bastion of white supremacy, where election boards still used various devices to bar blacks, the number of African-American voters rose from 250,000 to more than 1 million between 1940 and 1950. The NAACP's patient legal approach, too, although undramatic, showed signs of paying off. In three landmark cases of 1950—all argued by NAACP lawyer Thurgood Marshall—the Supreme Court outlawed segregated railroad dining cars and narrowed the scope of *Plessy* v. *Ferguson,* the 1896 decision upholding the constitutionality of segregated schools and other public facilities. While these decisions did not overturn *Plessy*—that would not occur until 1954— they did weaken segregation's legal underpinnings. As the NAACP observed, "Some might call these [rulings] mere straws in the wind, but they do indicate the direction in which the wind is blowing."

While black discontent mounted and pressure for change intensified, white America for the most part remained oblivious. As journalist John Gunther wrote in 1947, the fact that America was 10 percent black was "known to everybody and ignored by almost everybody—except maybe the ten percent."

A Growing Mexican-American Community
Faces Postwar Challenges

The postwar years saw a continued influx of Mexican-American immigrants, both legal and illegal. Through the influence of agribusiness owners, the wartime *braceros* program—which admitted Mexicans for low-paid seasonal farm labor, mainly in California and Texas—was renewed after the war, bringing in some 300,000 Mexicans annually. The program was terminated in 1964, amid mounting evidence of exploitation of workers. Many *braceros* remained in the United States legally, either by securing temporary work permits ("green cards") or by marrying Mexican-American women who were U.S. citizens. Many thousands of poor Mexicans also crossed the border illegally each year, seeking work. These *mojados,* or "wetbacks," often performed the unskilled and low-paid—but essential—labor that other workers scorned. In 1953, the Immigration and Naturalization Service (INS) returned 865,000 *mojados* to Mexico. Under "Operation Wetback," a major INS program launched in 1954, over 1 million illegal immigrants were arrested and returned.

This massive influx of newcomers profoundly affected the Mexican-American community. It reinforced the Spanish language and Mexican culture in the barrios (urban Mexican-American neighborhoods), and also produced tension between the new arrivals and second- or third-generation Mexican Americans. The flow of newcomers represented a large pool of unskilled workers desperate for even low-wage jobs. While some Mexican Americans became entrepreneurs, professionals, or skilled workers, most worked at unskilled or semiskilled jobs. The median level of schooling for Mexican Americans in the 1950s was 8.1 years, well below the national median. While the more overt forms of discrimination were fading, in many subtle ways Mexican Americans, and Latin American immigrants, faced prejudice and discrimination.

The postwar years saw the beginnings of organization among Mexican Americans to address these problems. In East Los Angeles (the largest concentration of Mexican Americans in the United States) the Community Service Organization focused on civil-rights and police-abuse issues, promoted community improvement projects, and in 1949 elected the first Mexican American to the Los Angeles city council. The Associación Nacional México Americana (National Mexican American Association), founded in Albuquerque, New Mexico, in 1949 by left-wing labor union leaders, sought to play a similar role in the larger Mexican-American community, but it was weakened by attacks on it as a communist front.

The Cold War at Home and the 1948 Election

The ideological fallout of the early Cold War had a chilling effect on home-front politics. The 1946 dismissal of Commerce Secretary Henry Wallace (see Chapter 2) signaled a more general stifling of dissident opinion. Politicians and conservative groups eager to further their own goals responded to the drumfire of warnings about the red menace by raising the specter of domestic disloyalty. The socialist leader Norman Thomas, visiting California in 1947, expressed shock at the "hysterical anticommunism" sweeping the state.

To be sure, fears of subversion had a basis in fact. The tiny American Communist party did promote Moscow's interests, and the Soviets, like most other nations, did conduct espionage. In March 1945, OSS security officials found three hundred secret OSS reports, State Department memos, and other government documents in the office of a left-wing journal of Asian affairs, *Amerasia.* One file bore the cryptic

Anticommunism in Los Angeles, July 1950. *Autoworkers attack a fellow employee for refusing to tell them whether he is a communist.* (AP/Wide World Photos)

label "'A' Bomb." Six persons were arrested on espionage charges, but the government dropped the case, rousing suspicions of a cover-up. In 1946 Canadian authorities uncovered a Soviet spy ring. And in 1948, amid newspaper stories about a "Beautiful Blonde Spy Queen," the House Un-American Activities Committee (HUAC) questioned Elizabeth Bentley, a former government employee who had confessed to the Federal Bureau of Investigation (FBI) that during the war she had transmitted secret documents to a Soviet agent who was then her lover.

But the spreading hysteria about domestic subversion bore little relation to specific security lapses. In fact, it was a wholly predictable byproduct of the fear of communism that the Truman administration, J. Edgar Hoover's FBI, and media voices such as Henry Luce's *Life* and *Time* magazines fanned to build support for the Cold War. As *Life* put it, "The fellow traveler [communist sympathizer] is everywhere, in Hollywood, on college faculties, in government bureaus, in publishing companies, even on the editorial staffs of eminently capitalist journals." Conservatives who cried "communist subversion" to attack dissidents of all kinds and politicians who hammered at the same theme for partisan purposes exploited an opening that the Democrats in the White House had already provided them.

Attuned to the rising clamor, Truman in March 1947, soon after enunciating the Truman Doctrine, launched the domestic corollary of his global anticommunist struggle: a federal loyalty-review program. By 1952 the FBI had investigated some twenty thousand government employees, of whom about four hundred were fired and twenty-five hundred resigned "voluntarily." Although Truman warned against "witch hunts," his loyalty program invited abuse. Persons accused of subversive associations or sympathies could appeal, but they received only summaries of derogatory material in their FBI files and could not confront their anonymous accusers. The attorney general compiled a list of "subversive" organizations. Some of these had expired years before, but even past membership drew suspicion. Employees faced questions about their opinion of Henry Wallace or the Truman Doctrine, or whether they owned recordings by Paul Robeson. Persons active in civil-rights causes endured special scrutiny. Homosexuals, considered vulnerable to blackmail, were targeted by the loyalty investigators. Following Washington's lead, local groups launched their own loyalty-review programs. Although the postwar paranoia about domestic subversion crested in the McCarthyite witch hunts of the early 1950s, the Truman administration's loyalty program nurtured it.

Meanwhile, as the 1948 election approached, Truman's chances looked bleak. The Republicans had done well in 1946 and still seemed on the rise. Inflation fed voter discontent. Henry Wallace, running for president on a third-party Progressive ticket, seemed likely to siphon votes from the Democratic ticket. Worse, the Democratic convention in Philadelphia that nominated Truman also saw a major party split. Following a plan adopted by administration strategists and big-city Democratic leaders, the convention featured a ringing civil-rights speech by the young mayor of Minneapolis, Hubert Humphrey. "The time has come," declaimed Humphrey, "to walk out of the shadow of states' rights and into the sunlight of human rights." Prodded by northern liberals, the convention not only applauded Humphrey's speech but adopted a strong civil-rights plank—not part of the White House game plan. Southern delegates who tried to protest found their microphones dead. Outraged delegates from Mississippi and Alabama walked out. Soon after, six thousand cheering whites in Birmingham, Alabama, formed the States' Rights Democratic party (known as the Dixiecrats) and nominated Governor Strom Thurmond of South Carolina for president. The Democrats' prospects appeared bleaker still. "Send up a bottle of embalming fluid," a roomful of thirsty Democrats in Philadelphia told room service. "If we're going to hold a wake, we might as well do it right."

By contrast, the Republicans oozed confidence. Their candidate, New York governor Thomas Dewey, had run well against Roosevelt in 1944 and appeared certain to beat the lackluster Truman. "How long is Dewey going to tolerate Truman's interference in the government?" mused one reporter as the campaign unfolded. Dewey's running mate, California's popular governor Earl Warren, strengthened the ticket in the rapidly growing West Coast states.

In fact, however, Truman's adviser Clark Clifford had devised a potent campaign strategy. The plan, embodied in a 1947 memo, called for appeals to the old Roosevelt coalition, notably blacks and union members, and aimed to deflect anger over inflation and other problems from the White House to Congress. Clifford also urged Truman to stress the anticommunist theme. The "battle with the Kremlin," he noted, offered "considerable political advantage to the Administration." Implementing Clifford's plan, Truman peppered Congress with reform proposals, including repeal of the Taft-Hartley Act, a housing bill, and a civil-rights program. Most of these proposals predictably died, but they projected the image of Truman as a reformer in the FDR tradition and of a reactionary Congress deaf to social issues. Truman called a special session of Congress for late July 1948, supposedly to enable the Republicans to pass all the measures that they had promised in their platform. As Truman anticipated, this two-week session accomplished little.

The president undertook a grueling national campaign by rail, traveling 22,000 miles and delivering 271 speeches. He spoke tirelessly, lambasting the "gluttons of privilege," the "economic tapeworms of big business," and, above all, "the do-nothing Eightieth Congress," shrewdly shifting attention from the bland Dewey to the Republican Congress. The drama of the Berlin airlift that summer helped Truman as well. The crowds grew larger and the shouts of "Give 'em hell, Harry" more exuberant. The confident Dewey, meanwhile, spoke in vague generalities. ("Your future is still ahead of you," he informed one audience.) With his short height, stiff manner, and trim black mustache, Dewey reminded one commentator of "the little man on top of the wedding cake." But still the polls predicted a Dewey landslide. The vast illusion continued into the early balloting. The *Chicago Tribune,* in an instantly famous election-night headline, proclaimed, "DEWEY DEFEATS TRUMAN!"

The polling had stopped too soon, missing a crucial last-minute swing to Truman. In a stunning upset, Truman amassed 24.2 million votes to Dewey's 22 mil-

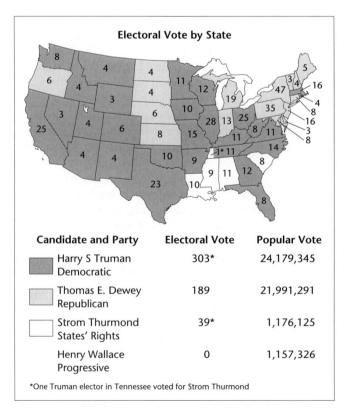

Candidate and Party	Electoral Vote	Popular Vote
Harry S Truman Democratic	303*	24,179,345
Thomas E. Dewey Republican	189	21,991,291
Strom Thurmond States' Rights	39*	1,176,125
Henry Wallace Progressive	0	1,157,326

*One Truman elector in Tennessee voted for Strom Thurmond

FIGURE 3.2
Presidential Election of 1948

lion, and the Democrats regained both houses of Congress. The day after the election, a Kentucky store offered framed portraits of Truman with the sign, "Were $1.98, Now $10.00."

Accounts of the '48 campaign understandably focus on Truman's feisty personality, but his victory also owed much to a brilliant campaign strategy and tireless speechmaking by his running mate, Senator Alben Barkley of Kentucky, and by various cabinet members. Appealing to key voting blocs and demonizing the Republican Congress, Truman ran as the leader of the battle against communism abroad and reaction at home. "The issues in this campaign are not hard to define," he told voters in Rock Island, Illinois. "The issue is the people against the special interests." He struck an array of themes that touched millions of Americans, including, historian Donald McCoy writes, "housing, federal aid to education, health care, higher minimum wage and Social Security benefits, flood control, public power, civil rights, labor, conservation, agriculture, and regulation of business, among others."

The splinter parties fared less well than expected. Most voters rejected Wallace's attacks on the administration's foreign policy and objected to the Communist party's role in his campaign. Wallace, who garnered just over a million votes, may even have helped Truman by validating the president's anticommunist credentials and shielding him from Republican redbaiting. The States' Rights party, criticized in the media for its racism, raised little campaign money. The Democrats' civil-rights plank that triggered the Dixiecrats' defection also produced a tide of northern black votes for Truman. Governor Thurmond, however, with 1.7 million votes, carried four Deep South states, portending long-term problems for the Democrats in a no longer Solid South.

Truman did well among farmers, urban ethnics, and union members irked by the Taft-Hartley Act. Although it was eroding, the battered New Deal coalition still held. Having emerged from Roosevelt's giant shadow to win the presidency in his own right, Harry Truman stood at the pinnacle of his career. His final four years in the White House, however, would bring mostly frustration and setbacks.

The Fair Deal and McCarthyism

While mobilizing for the Cold War abroad, the Truman administration struggled to chart a domestic agenda in an increasingly venomous political climate. In his January 1949 State of the Union address, Truman proposed a far-reaching domestic program soon labeled the Fair Deal. Building on existing programs, the president recommended broader social security coverage, an increase in the minimum wage from forty to seventy-five cents an hour, and development programs for the nation's river systems modeled on the TVA. Truman addressed organized labor's big grievance by urging repeal of the Taft-Hartley Act. He proposed aid to education, a cabinet-level department of welfare, and an expanded public housing program. Pleas for a national health-insurance system funded by a combination of federal payments and employer and employee contributions capped Truman's program. To finance all this, and to combat inflation, the president recommended a $4 billion tax increase. On the civil-rights front, Truman once more asked for a

Fair Employment Practices Commission (FEPC) and, in later messages, federal laws against lynching and the poll tax, a stratagem used to exclude black voters in the South.

Representing the consensus of advanced liberal thinking on domestic issues, the Fair Deal assumed an expansive economy and an array of federal programs and agencies to promote the public welfare, combat racial discrimination, maintain prosperity, and ensure fair play in the marketplace. It is not surprising that most of the Fair Deal got nowhere, since it came at a time of growing conservatism and retreat from reform. Lacking the broad public support that FDR had rallied behind the New Deal, Truman's program also faced strong legislative opposition. The president's party nominally controlled Congress, but in practice a coalition of Republicans and conservative Democrats held sway. Furthermore, Truman was unwilling to weaken bipartisan support for the Cold War—especially after the outbreak of the Korean War in June 1950—by pushing his domestic program. When conservative Democrats opposed his Fair Deal proposals, he took no steps to curb their power. Finally, Truman's health-insurance plan met a firestorm of opposition from the American Medical Association (AMA), which denounced it as "socialized medicine." Fearful of federal regulation and lower physicians' income, the AMA posted billboards that showed a worried doctor at a patient's bedside and warned, KEEP THE GOVERNMENT OUT OF THIS PICTURE.

Truman's farm program also ran into strong opposition—from farmers. The New Deal's strategy for raising farm income had included buying and storing the "surplus" production of basic commodities. By the late 1940s a glut of wheat, corn, and other products choked government warehouses. To cope with this headache, Secretary of Agriculture Charles Brannan in 1949 proposed a complicated plan whereby the government would stop buying surpluses of perishable commodities and simply allow the total output to be sold on the open market. Because this strategy would depress farm prices, Brannan proposed cash subsidies to compensate farmers for their losses. Labor and consumer groups welcomed the Brannan Plan for its promise of lower food prices, but the Farm Bureau Federation, speaking for the nation's largest farmers, charged that the scheme would cut farm income. When the Marshall Plan and other foreign-aid programs depleted the overflowing farm surpluses, the administration quietly shelved the Brannan Plan, once again demonstrating the Cold War's pervasive influence on domestic politics.

The president's civil-rights program fared no better, as southern Democrats, joined by conservative Republicans, blocked his proposals. Even a bill to grant self-government to the heavily black District of Columbia failed in the Senate. The only governmental progress on the civil-rights front came through executive action. Truman integrated the military (as we have seen), named several African Americans to midlevel federal posts, and in 1951 moved to deny government contracts to firms practicing racial discrimination.

A few items on Truman's Fair Deal agenda won Congress's approval. The National Housing Act of 1949, supported by the construction industry, authorized federal subsidies for eight hundred thousand low-income housing units. But the postwar housing shortage had eased, and only half the authorized units were built. In 1950, as Truman had urged, Congress raised the minimum wage and expanded the coverage of social security, a program whose retirement benefits appealed to middle-class and working-class Americans.

Overall, Truman's domestic record proved thin. A conservative postwar climate, assertive opposition, the distractions of the antiradical campaign, and the weakened voice of Left-liberal social thinkers amid the intellectually repressive early Cold War climate all undermined the postwar reform effort. Nevertheless, the Fair Deal remains historically significant. On civil rights, education and national health care, it set the liberal domestic agenda for years to come.

As Truman's second term wore on, charges of corruption beset his administration. Journalist I. F. Stone had earlier described the president's cronies as "the kind of men one was accustomed to meet in county courthouses . . . big-bellied, good natured guys who knew a lot of dirty jokes [and] spent as little time in their office as possible." The seedy aura spread. GOP orators denounced the "mess in Washington," especially corruption in the Internal Revenue Service and the Reconstruction Finance Corporation (RFC), a New Deal agency that lent large sums to banks and corporations. The "mess" also included "five percenters"—officials who took payoffs for helping favored corporations secure government contracts.

The scandals offer a revealing glimpse into postwar consumer society. One Truman aide allegedly accepted no fewer than seven freezers, which he gave to friends, including Mrs. Truman; a White House secretary received a mink coat from a corporation seeking an RFC loan; the Lustron Corporation got millions in RFC funds, never repaid, to build pastel-tinted prefabricated houses of a new plasticlike material. Although not personally implicated in wrongdoing, Truman drew criticism for his lax judgment in friends and advisers. But while his opinion ratings fell and anti-Truman jokes proliferated, the president remained in good spirits; perhaps he sensed that his historical reputation would outdistance his contemporary standings in the polls.

Rivaling the accusations of corruption, charges of domestic subversion rooted in the anticommunist preoccupations of the era increasingly poisoned national politics. The administration, continuing to display its toughness on domestic radicals, in January 1949 put on trial eleven Communist party leaders under the 1940 Alien Registration Act (also known as the Smith Act), which made advocating the forcible overthrow of the government illegal. The eleven were convicted in a decision upheld by the Supreme Court in 1951.

Along with the Elizabeth Bentley case, two other highly publicized spy cases surfaced in these years. The first began in August 1948 when ex-communist Whittaker Chambers, an editor at *Time,* told HUAC that as a spy for the Soviets in the 1930s he had received secret government documents from Alger Hiss, a State Department official who had later become head of the Carnegie Foundation for International Peace. With a flair for drama, Chambers hid microfilms of documents allegedly given him by Hiss in a hollowed-out pumpkin on his Maryland farm. The urbane and self-assured Hiss denied Chambers's charges. But Congressman Richard Nixon doggedly pursued the case. In a major break, HUAC investigators traced a typewriter once owned by Hiss and found that it matched the typing on Chambers's documents. Convicted of perjury (the statute of limitation on treason having expired), Hiss served five years in prison.

The second of these sensational espionage cases began in England in 1950 when Klaus Fuchs, an émigré German physicist who had worked in the wartime atomic-bomb project at Los Alamos, was arrested as a Soviet spy. Fuchs fingered David Greenglass, a serviceman assigned to the Los Alamos machine shop. Greenglass in turn charged that his sister and brother-in-law, Ethel and Julius Rosenberg, had recruited him for Soviet espionage. The Rosenbergs were arrested, convicted of spying for the Soviets, and sentenced to death. Despite worldwide protests, they went to the electric chair in 1953.

The Hiss and Rosenberg cases long stirred impassioned debate. Recent scholarship suggests that all three were guilty but that the Rosenbergs to some extent were victims of Cold War hysteria. Ronald Radosh and Joyce Milton argue in *The Rosenberg File: A Search for the Truth* (1983) that prosecutors sought the death sentence for Ethel Rosenberg, despite her minor role, hoping—in vain, as it turned out—that Julius Rosenberg would name other spies to save his wife. E. L. Doctorow's novel *The Book of Daniel* (1971) explored the psychological and political dimensions of the Rosenberg case. Doctorow linked the shrill anticommunism of the early Cold War to the passions of World War II: "Enemies must continue to be found. The mind and heart cannot be demobilized as quickly as the platoon. . . . [L]ike a fiery furnace at white heat, it takes a considerable time to cool."

The Hiss and Rosenberg cases worsened an already rancorous political climate. From 1945 to 1952, HUAC conducted some eighty probes of atomic scientists, black activists, Hollywood writers, and others. Ten directors and screenwriters who refused to discuss their political beliefs or to implicate others before the committee went to prison. In 1951 the chairman of HUAC, J. Parnell Thomas, convicted of fraud, found himself in the same federal prison with Ring Lardner, Jr., one of the "Hollywood Ten." One day, Thomas was working in the prison chicken yard while Lardner cut grass with a sickle nearby. "Hey Lardner," Thomas called out, "I see you've got part of your old communist emblem. Where's the hammer to go with the sickle?" Lardner replied, "I see you're up to your old tricks, Congressman, shoveling chicken shit."

HUAC's circuslike investigations left a trail of shattered reputations and broken lives. When a former State Department official committed suicide by leaping from a building, a HUAC committee member announced that HUAC had been investigating him and added jovially, "We will give out the other names as they jump out of windows." The FBI's bulging files on alleged radicals, included rumor, gossip, and material gathered by illegal wiretaps.

The anticommunist hysteria underlay two laws passed over Truman's veto. The Internal Security Act of 1950 required communist and "communist-front" organizations to register with the government. The McCarran-Walter Immigration Act of 1952 set up procedures to keep out "subversives" and mandated the deportation of immigrants, even those who had become citizens, who belonged to suspect organizations. Echoing the wartime confinement of Japanese Americans, the law provided for the imprisonment of suspected security risks in the event of a national emergency.

Of all the politicians to capitalize on the communist scare, none gained greater notoriety than Senator Joseph McCarthy of Wisconsin. In February 1950, McCarthy burst from obscurity with a Lincoln Day speech in West Virginia. Waving a piece of paper, he claimed to have a list of 205 communists in the State Department. In what would become a typical pattern, McCarthy soon reduced the number to fifty-seven, and eventually to one. Refusing to release his "list," he hedged on whether he meant actual communists or more vaguely defined "policy risks." But the public responded avidly, and for five years McCarthy basked in the limelight as the media reported his endless charges, countercharges, and sensational revelations. In a rambling four-hour Senate speech fueled by swigs from a bottle of "cough medicine," McCarthy in May 1950 smeared the reputation of Owen Lattimore, an Asian specialist at Johns Hopkins University and occasional State Department adviser. "Ask almost any schoolchild who the architect of our Far Eastern policy is," McCarthy declared inanely at one point, "and he will say 'Owen Lattimore.'"

Lattimore was one of many Asian specialists who had viewed Mao Zedong's revolution as a complex phenomenon rooted in China's history and politics, not simply a manifestation of a "world communist conspiracy" controlled from the Kremlin. No evidence supported McCarthy's claims that Lattimore was "the top Russian spy in America." At worst, Lattimore was "guilty" of possessing a prickly personality and of having written naively upbeat assessments of Stalin and the Soviet system in the 1930s and the war years. But Lattimore's challenge to Cold War oversimplifications in his view of China made him vulnerable. By their smear tactics, McCarthy and those who took his charges seriously blighted the careers of a generation of Asian specialists whose wisdom would be sorely missed.

In the summer of 1950, a Senate committee chaired by Millard Tydings of Maryland found McCarthy's charges "a fraud and a hoax," but this failed to silence him. When McCarthy campaigned against several Democratic senators that fall and four of them lost, including Tydings, the potency of the "communist issue" became chillingly clear. At first, Republican leaders, hoping to regain the White House in 1952, embraced McCarthy. Senator Taft advised, "Keep talking and if one case doesn't work out, proceed with another." McCarthy, invariably lugging a briefcase crammed with "documents," became a fixture on the right-wing lecture circuit.

"McCarthyism," however, was not the creation of a lone senator. Many others in Congress and the nation joined in the frantic search for subversives. Crusty Senator Pat McCarran of Nevada, chair of the Senate Internal Security Subcommittee, although less publicity-mad than McCarthy, grimly pursued security risks. Senators from both parties—Democrat James Eastland of Mississippi and Republican William Jenner of Indiana, for example—joined in. Blacklists circulated by shadowy organizations of superpatriots called for boycotts of suspected actors and performers; one influential list was called *Red Channels*. An American Legion post in Syracuse set up its own Un-American Activities Committee. To a blitz of media attention, the American Legion post of Mosinee, Wisconsin, in 1950 illustrated the menace facing America by staging a one-day "communist takeover" of the town.

Radio and television performers, labor organizers, public-school teachers, college professors, ministers, civil-rights activists, and librarians faced charges of disloyalty. Methodist bishop G. Bromley Oxnam, folksinger Pete Seeger, playwright Arthur Miller, and actors Charlie Chaplin, John Garfield, and Zero Mostel ranked among the targets. Some three hundred New York City school teachers were fired

IN PERSPECTIVE: *The National-Security State*

It was in the early Cold War that Congress, fearful of communist subversion at home and abroad, created what came to be called the national-security state. In 1947 Congress transformed the wartime Office of Strategic Services into the Central Intelligence Agency (CIA) and set up the high-level National Security Council to advise the president on security matters. The Internal Security Act of 1950 restricted the civil rights of communists and alleged "fellow-travelers." In these years, too, the Justice Department's Federal Bureau of Investigation, headed since 1924 by J. Edgar Hoover, expanded its national-security role, gathering files on individuals and organizations stigmatized as subversive or disloyal. There were 890 FBI agents in 1940 and 10,000 by 1970.

Initially, the public paid little heed to these agencies' activities. When security operations did impinge on Americans' awareness, the response was generally favorable. "The FBI in Peace and War," a popular radio show of the 1950s, presented Hoover's agency in a heroic light, as did the 1959 movie *The FBI Story.* Tourists flocked to FBI headquarters in Washington, where exciting exhibits showed how the G-men had cracked tough cases.

The heyday of the national-security state came in the 1950s and 1960s. The CIA, operating largely outside congressional oversight, plotted assassinations, overthrew hostile governments, and conducted clandestine operations all over the world. It promoted anticommunism by secretly funding Radio Free Europe, the Congress of Cultural Freedom, and other front organizations. In addition, CIA money financed activities of the National Student Association, the largest student organization in the 1960s. At home, the FBI pursued its antiradical activities, even conducting illegal break-ins and tapping telephones to spy on what it considered extremist groups. Reflecting Hoover's hostility to the civil-rights movement, the FBI, with the approval of Attorney General Robert Kennedy, tapped the telephones and hotel rooms of Martin Luther King, Jr., in 1963. America's national-security apparatus, created to protect U.S. freedom, began to threaten that freedom.

The CIA's botched Bay of Pigs invasion of Cuba in 1961 had stimulated some criticism of national-security agencies, but far harsher attacks came in the mid-1970s in

as security risks. University of Michigan mathematician Chandler Davis went to jail for six months for refusing to tell HUAC whether he was a communist. Witnesses before investigative committees who invoked their constitutional right not to testify were smeared as "Fifth Amendment Communists." Soviet spies were not a figment of the Right's imagination, but the peddlers of hysteria and ideological conformity spread their nets widely and destructively, ruining lives and shattering careers.

the wake of the Watergate scandal. In 1974 the *New York Times* reported that the CIA, although legally banned from domestic activities, had assembled dossiers on thousands of American citizens and organizations. In 1976 President Ford's attorney general, Edward Levi, revealed that J. Edgar Hoover, who had died in 1972, had secretly kept derogatory files on presidents and legislators as a way of protecting his vast power. Responding to the shifting mood, Congress expanded the 1966 Freedom of Information Act ensuring citizens' access to their government files and restricted the CIA's power to carry out clandestine operations.

But abuses continued. The National Security Council became the focus of controversy in 1986–1987 with revelations that staffer Oliver North, operating out of the White House, had funneled millions of dollars to a CIA-backed army fighting Nicaragua's leftist government. Congress had explicitly banned such funding. Much evidence linked CIA director William Casey to these illegalities, but Casey died before his role could be fully explored.

In 1986, Congress at last reined in the FBI, requiring that all future FBI directors be approved by Congress and limited to ten-year terms. (Hoover had enjoyed a forty-eight-year tenure.) At the same time, historians and journalists began to chip away at the FBI's carefully burnished image. Books such as Athan Theoharis's and John Stuart Cox's *The Boss* (1988) and Curt Gentry's *J. Edgar Hoover: The Man and the Secrets* (1991) revealed shocking details about the FBI and its director. As Americans requested their FBI files under the Freedom of Information Act, the scope of the agency's snooping emerged. Even Walt Disney was exposed as an FBI informant. (Disney gave FBI agents free admission to Disneyland, and Hoover permitted Disney to film an episode of TV's "Mickey Mouse Club" at FBI headquarters after Disney assured him that the show would portray the FBI in a laudatory light. Questions about the FBI's shadowy relations with a succession of presidential administrations from Roosevelt's to Nixon's remain unanswered.

The end of the Cold War further eroded the national-security state, as the CIA struggled to redefine its role in a political culture no longer obsessed by the Soviet menace. In 1993, fending off calls for deep cuts in the agency's budget, CIA director R. James Woolsey portrayed the post–Cold War world as a jungle in which a dragon had been killed but where deadly snakes still abounded. Reflecting the shift from military to economic issues, the agency turned its sleuthing skills to ferreting out the positions of America's economic rivals in sensitive trade negotiations.

The period from the mid-1970s through the 1990s, in short, proved trying for the national-security state. Having enjoyed high public esteem earlier as leaders in the crusade against communism abroad and subversion at home, these agencies now confronted an uphill battle to reshape their mission and rebuild their tarnished reputations.

Unions, film studios, school boards, professional societies, and even the American Civil Liberties Union purged alleged radicals and affirmed their patriotism. The president of the American Historical Association declared in 1949: "Total war, whether it be hot or cold, enlists everyone and calls upon everyone to assume his part. The historian is no freer from this obligation than the physicist." Universities imposed loyalty oaths to placate outside investigators. With politicians, patriotic groups, and right-wing broadcasters such as Fulton Lewis, Jr., fanning the anticommunist flames, it is hardly surprising that many organizations failed to take a courageous stand.

Eventually Congress and the nation would turn against McCarthy (see Chapter 4), but in the early fifties, he reigned as one of the most powerful and feared men in America. For all his apparent zealotry, though, McCarthy was primarily an opportunist, who cared about little beyond tomorrow's headlines. Nevertheless, the fears that he rubbed raw in the American psyche represented the Cold War's principal domestic legacy. A climate of suspicion and ideological conformity pervaded the nation as the 1952 election approached.

Boom Times

In August 1945, just as the war ended, a group of marketing experts gathered to plan postwar selling strategies. An official of the Du Pont Corporation offered a bright vision of coming prosperity as corporate America met the "great backlog of unfilled wants" left by fifteen years of consumer deprivation. Marketers' task, he said, was to stimulate consumer demand and "see to it that Americans are never satisfied . . . ; a satisfied people is a stagnant people." If marketers did their job well, he predicted, the postwar era would bring "an upward spiral of productivity, raising the standard of living, increasing the national income, [and] making more jobs." To a remarkable degree, this rosy vision was realized.

The same years that saw the deepening Cold War, the coming of the Korean War, and acrid political controversies at home also brought a long-term economic boom of impressive proportions. By late 1948 unemployment stood at an amazingly low 2 percent. The gross national product, which had surged to $211 billion during the war, dipped briefly afterward but soon resumed its upward climb, hitting $346 billion by 1952. Their savings accounts bulging with wartime earnings, Americans binged on a buying spree. *Holiday* magazine, founded in 1946 to capitalize on the wanderlust of newly affluent Americans, embodied the new culture of consumption. *Holiday,* proclaimed the editors, borrowing Thomas Jefferson's ringing phrase, was "dedicated to the pursuit of happiness."

As consumer spending exploded, businesses expanded, modernized, and retooled to meet the demand. When young Henry Ford II took over Ford Motor Company from his aging grandfather in 1945, the moment seemed to symbolize a new era for American capitalism. The goods that gushed from U.S. factories in 1950 included 6.2 million refrigerators, 14.6 million radios, and 6.2 million automobiles. Nearly 5 million new housing units sprang up between 1945 and 1950. Corporate America prospered as never before. By 1952 the United States boasted fifty-nine companies with more than $1 billion in assets.

The military demands of the Korean War did cut civilian output somewhat and contributed to an inflationary uptick in 1951 and 1952, but overall the conflict stimulated the economy. In addition to its own defense build-up, the United States sold large quantities of military equipment to its Cold War allies. U.S. military exports reached $2.1 billion by 1952, translating into jobs and profits for defense industries. As we saw in Chapter 2, nonmilitary foreign aid also drove exports of farm commodities and industrial goods. Unemployment, which had crept up to 5 percent in the spring of 1950, fell to less than half that level by autumn. To sustain the economic boom during the Korean War, the government permitted corporations to depreciate capital investment in five years rather than the usual twenty-five, spurring a wave of plant construction and modernization.

A baby boom fueled postwar prosperity. From a 1930s low of fewer than twenty births per thousand population, the U.S. birthrate climbed steadily during and after the war to more than twenty-five per thousand in 1947, as young couples looked to the future with hope.* Home building thrived, along with school construction and sales of baby food, diapers, strollers, children's clothes, and play equipment. With a surging birthrate added to ample raw materials and energy, pent-up demand, a mature corporate structure, and well-established systems for advertising and distributing goods, the economy took off.

Yet not all Americans enjoyed prosperity. As we shall see in Chapter 4, poverty remained a fact of life for millions, especially the rural poor and inner-city minorities. In 1950 over a third of U.S. families earned under $3,000 annually. Although the buying power of the 1950 dollar was about five times what it would be in the 1990s, these figures suggest the precarious situation of many families. For those at the lower end of the scale, the new cars and appliances in showrooms, department stores, and magazine ads remained distant dreams. This underside of the economic picture, however, attracted little notice as the consumer boom roared on.

A parade of new products, from ballpoint pens and televisions to transistor radios and Polaroid cameras, contributed to the boom. In 1947 a small company in Rochester, New York, bought the rights to a machine that could reproduce print copy by means of "xerography," a technique patented by Chester Carlson in 1940. Soon the company would become the Xerox Corporation. Photocopying machines, spreading from corporate offices, government bureaus, and academia into the larger society, launched a revolution in communications.

Computer technology, spurred by wartime antiaircraft research (see pp. 23–24), also burgeoned after the war. In 1946 University of Pennsylvania engineers formed a company to produce and market a computer they called UNIVAC (Universal Automatic Computer), one of which became the first government computer, delivered to the Census Bureau in 1951. International Business Machines (IBM), already a leader in office equipment, marketed its first computer in 1953.

The computer age still lay ahead, but its theoretical and technical foundations were in place by the early fifties. Norbert Weiner, a professor of mathematics at the Massachusetts Institute of Technology, speculated on the computer's social and intellectual implications. A child prodigy who had earned his Ph.D. from Harvard at age nineteen, Weiner in a 1940 memo to the U.S. government's Office of Scientific Research and Development had set forth key theoretical elements of the modern computer. In *Cybernetics* (1947) and *The Human Uses of Human Beings* (1950), Weiner explored the computer's implications for American society. Although conceding the new technology's promise—in medical research, for example—Weiner remained apprehensive. As computers took over routine production functions, he warned, "the average human being . . . [will have] nothing to sell that is worth any-

---

* By contrast, the 1996 birthrate was 14.8 per 1,000 population.

one's money to buy." Weiner also foresaw a time when the computer's ability to process data would vastly extend the power of governments, the military, and corporate giants.

Of all the new products, none better captured the postwar sense of newness and promise than plastic. Celluloid and Bakelite had been around for years, but it was after World War II that plastic exploded into the consumer marketplace. In 1946 a "National Plastics Exposition" in New York City drew thousands of excited visitors, Earl Tupper introduced his line of Tupperware kitchen and household products marketed through suburban "Tupperware parties," and an entrepreneur in Leominster, Massachusetts, began to market plastic pink flamingos for suburban lawns. Plastic production by 1960 surpassed six billion pounds. Almost everything, it seemed, could be made of plastic, from furniture, countertops, and luggage to dolls, shower curtains, garden hoses, and Christmas trees. Kids in the fifties twirled plastic hula hoops. By the mid-fifties, writes historian Jeffrey Meikle, plastic products "had penetrated so far into the material fabric of everyday life that their presence could not be denied no matter how many people considered them second-rate substitutes or a sad commentary on modern times."

Beyond "Rosie the Riveter": Women in Postwar America

For American women, the post-1945 era brought uncertainty as strong cultural and social forces buttressed the status quo in the face of incipient pressures for change. At first glance, postwar employment data suggest major changes in women's lives. The drop in female employment immediately after the war soon reversed itself. By 1950, 29 percent of U.S. women held jobs, higher than in 1940 although still below the wartime peak. As during the war, women who entered the labor force in this period—especially middle-class married women—seemed more interested in contributing to the family income than in pursuing feminist goals or breaking new ground professionally. Discriminatory hiring practices and subtle cultural pressures channeled most of them into traditional "women's jobs" as secretaries, salespersons, or clerks.

A few old-line feminist organizations fought on for women's rights, but efforts to better women's lot through legislation fared badly. When the Senate in 1946 failed to muster the necessary two-thirds vote to pass an equal rights amendment, the *New York Times* intoned approvingly, "Motherhood cannot be amended." That same year, an equal-pay bill for women workers failed in the Senate. The conservative mood, revealing a longing for stability after years of upheaval, recoiled against even moderate challenges to traditional gender roles.

Perhaps in delayed reaction to the upsurge of female workers during the war, many writers in the late 1940s and the 1950s urged women to embrace the domestic role that they said nature intended. Dr. Benjamin Spock's bestselling *Baby and Child Care* (1946) assumed the mother's presence at home. In a 1950 *Atlantic Monthly* article, "Women Aren't Men," the female author exclaimed, "God protect us from the efficient go-getter business woman whose feminine instincts have been completely stifled." In *Modern Woman: The Lost Sex* (1947), Freudian analyst Mary-

Mixed Messages. *Left: Government propaganda such as this poster urged women to take jobs in industry. When the war ended, the message suddenly changed.* (War Manpower Commission) *Right: Reinforcing several female stereotypes, this 1952 beer ad portrayed the typical wife as a fashion-conscious consumer devoted to making her husband happy, yet manipulative as well.* (Courtesy The Stroh Brewery Company)

nia Farnham and sociologist Ferdinand Lundberg warned that women who resisted the domestic and maternal roles would suffer emotional disorders and social difficulties.

The mass culture drove home the message. Lucille Ball, star of the early TV comedy *I Love Lucy,* invariably met disaster when she sought a job or pursued interests beyond the home. (She never stopped trying, however, revealing the underlying tension in the cult of domesticity.) In the 1950 film *All About Eve,* Ann Baxter played a coldly ambitious career woman whose charming manner masked her drive to succeed, hardly an admirable role model for young women in postwar America. While Tennessee Williams's play *A Streetcar Named Desire* (1947) and Mickey Spillane's murder mysteries such as *I, the Jury* (1947) featured violent, macho protagonists, the mass media increasingly domesticated the American woman. Predictably, this theme pervaded the *Ladies Home Journal, Woman's Home Companion,* and other leading women's magazines.

The day of the WACS, the WAVES, "Rosie the Riveter," and "Wonder Woman," a comic-book character introduced in 1941, seemed remote by the late 1940s. The idealized domesticity that loomed so large in the 1950s had roots in a long tradition of American social thought, but it received strong reinforcement from the early postwar reaction to the unsettling changes in women's roles during World War II. Just as the anticommunist crusaders responded to global threats by trying to enforce political conformity at home, so the celebrators of the domestic ideal coped with the threat of shifting gender roles by seeking to reimpose the imagined stability and clear-cut distinctions of an earlier era.

Diversion and Doubt:
Culture in the Early Postwar Years

Early postwar popular culture reflected the ambivalence of a nation powerful and prospering yet unnerved by Cold War anxiety and nuclear fears. Movies like *The Sands of Iwo Jima* (1949), starring John Wayne and featuring the famous flag-raising over Mount Suribachi, evoked the patriotism and sense of purpose of the war years. The vastly popular 1954 TV documentary *Victory at Sea,* with a rousing musical score by Richard Rodgers, celebrated the navy's role in the war in carefully edited highlights. But uneasiness about the atomic bomb shadowed Americans' satisfaction about the triumph of 1945. John Hersey's *Hiroshima* (1946), initially published in the *New Yorker* magazine, offered a horrifying account of what a single atomic bomb could do to a major city. Nuclear anxieties were reflected in movies like *The Day the Earth Stood Still* (1951), in which highly evolved aliens arrived in a spaceship to urge earthlings to stop their foolish quarrels before they self-destructed. Mass magazines such as *Reader's Digest* and *Life* offered dire warnings of the communist menace and occasional lurid scenarios of World War III. A few Hollywood movies presented heavy-handed anticommunist sermons, but the mass culture offered escape more frequently than overt propaganda. A series of Broadway musicals—*Guys and Dolls* (1949), *South Pacific* (1950), *The King and I* (1951)—with their movie and record spinoffs, provided diversion as well.

America's radio stations, whose numbers nearly tripled from 1945 to 1950, remained important mass culture outlets. In the late 1940s, millions of housewives tuned in daily for teary soap operas such as *Stella Dallas* and *When a Girl Marries.* World issues rarely intruded into these sagas of romance and domestic crisis. (How could so many listen so long to so little? marveled one critic.) To adolescents, radio continued to offer a series of mostly male role models and stereotypes: *Sergeant Preston of the Yukon,* or *The Lone Ranger* with his faithful Indian companion, Tonto. The whole family gathered for the evening comedy shows of vaudeville veterans Jack Benny, Bob Hope, and Fred Allen.

Radio's preeminence soon ended, however. The first commercial television broadcast dated from 1939, when NBC televised Franklin Roosevelt's opening the New York World's Fair. Soon after the war's end, TV sets with tiny screens attracted fascinated crowds to store windows even when transmitting only a greenish test pattern. By 1952, more than a third of U.S. households had television. Indeed, the resulting mass-culture explosion went hand-in-glove with the postwar economic boom. Corporate spending on TV advertising promoting an array of consumer goods, from cars to toothpaste, surged from $171 million in 1950 to $454 million by 1952; by mid-decade it would surpass $1 billion.

Early TV shows often copied radio programming. *Faraway Hill,* the first TV soap opera, debuted in 1946, as did two durable variety shows: Ed Sullivan's *Toast of the Town* and Arthur Godfrey's *Talent Scouts.* Some shows such as *The Life of Riley* and *The Lone Ranger* moved directly from radio to TV. Live drama began in 1947 with *Kraft Television Theater;* that year also launched the popular children's show *Howdy Doody*. One mother remarked, "The hours between play and bed used to be the most hectic part of the day. Now I know where the children are. The television set is the best nurse in the world."

At first, many local channels did their own programming with home-grown talent—one Atlanta station spotlighted "Morgus, the Crazy Weatherman"—but television soon went national. NBC put together the first television network in 1949. CBS, under hard-driving William Paley, soon passed NBC in the ratings. Paley perfected the concept of "audience flow," luring the audience for one show to stay tuned for the programs that followed.

Although Hollywood and TV eventually formed a profitable alliance, movie moguls initially viewed the new medium as a threat, and with good reason: Movie attendance fell by 14 percent between 1946 and 1949. In movie-industry circles, the *New York Times* reported in 1949, "The very mention of television . . . evokes only icy silence." Politicians, on the other hand, loved TV, trimming their long-winded speeches to fit its demands. Planners of the 1948 Democratic convention warned delegates to behave, for the proceedings would now be seen as well as heard. When television covered Truman's 1949 inaugural, *Time* magazine exclaimed: "Ten million televiewers from the Atlantic coast to the Mississippi felt that they had truly been there with Washington's cheering thousands."

Some held high hopes for the new medium's cultural promise. A media executive in 1945 proclaimed: "[T]elevision . . . is going to make every city, town, and village in the United States a more democratic, more progressive, more closely knit community." For a time, intelligent, well-written dramatic shows like *Playhouse 90* and *Studio One* and light-classical musical programs such as *The Bell Telephone Hour* and *The Voice of Firestone* seemed to fulfill such hopes.

But advertisers' demands for ever-larger audiences quickly doomed such quality fare. Scriptwriters for the popular show "Men Against Crime," which premiered in 1949, were instructed, "[W]e retain audience interest best when our story is concerned with murder. Therefore, . . . somebody must be murdered, preferably early, with the threat of more violence to come." (The cigarette-company sponsor of *Men Against Crime* also insisted that no actor ever cough on the show.) Hand-wringing over the medium's banality replaced the early enthusiasm; Fred Allen called TV "chewing gum for the eyes." Television did sometimes give viewers a window on the world—the UN debates when the Korean War broke out were carried live, for example—but mediocrity and the trivial predominated.

The marketing of goods drove the entertainment media, hastening the emergence of a standardized mass culture organized around consumerism. As in the rest of corporate America, large companies dominated. Three networks—CBS, NBC, and ABC—controlled early television. Four periodicals—*Life, Collier's, Saturday Evening Post,* and *Reader's Digest*—ruled the magazine world. Five major studios—MGM, Paramount, Warner Brothers, RKO, and 20th Century Fox—produced nearly all U.S. movies and controlled a network of big-city theaters. Under pressure not only from corporate advertisers but also from powerful institutions and interest groups, the mass culture turned bland. The Catholic Church's Legion of Decency and Hollywood's own Production Code Authority monitored movie morals. (The Legion of Decency condemned the 1953 film *The Moon Is Blue,* for example, because the word *virgin* was used in dialogue.) The Cold War climate of intellectual conformity intensified what a 1948 critic called the movies' "retreat into apathy" and "ideological fatigue." The mass media thus helped to create a national culture shaped by market calculations and a quest for the lowest-common-denominator level of diversion. Innovation, creativity, or the thoughtful exploration of public issues had little part.

Beneath the popular culture's bland, escapist surface eddied currents of apprehension vaguely connected with the nuclear threat, Cold War alarms, and fears of domestic subversion. A rash of "flying saucer" sightings began in 1947. (Soviet diplomat Andrei Gromyko, in a rare flash of humor, quipped that they came from his nation's discus throwers practicing for the Olympics.) Postwar movies of the "film noir" genre, such as *He Walked by Night* (1949), featured betrayal, sinister shadows, and menacing dangers lurking in familiar settings. The mystified hero of one such film complained, "I'm backed up in a dark corner and I don't know who's hitting me!"

The nervousness revealed in these movies affected American religion as well. Thousands of young people flocked to the Saturday night rallies of a newly founded evangelical Protestant movement, Youth for Christ. Evangelist Billy Graham rocketed to fame on the strength of a Los Angeles tent revival in September 1949, just as the Soviet Union exploded its first atomic bomb. Graham thundered, "An arms race unprecedented in the history of the world is driving us madly toward destruction! ... Time is desperately short. ... [P]repare to meet thy God!" Other religious leaders offered less apocalyptic remedies for nuclear worries. In *A Guide to Confident Living* (1948) and *Faith Is the Answer* (1950), the Reverend Norman Vincent Peale advised anxious Americans to "say confidently to yourself: 'Through God's help and the application of simple techniques, I will be free from fear.' Believe that—practice it, and it will be so." Pharmaceuticals offered a chemical means to the same end; the year that witnessed the advent of hydrogen-bomb research, the outbreak of the Korean War, and the beginning of Senator McCarthy's anticommunist rampage (1950) also brought the first commercially available tranquilizer, called Miltown.

While popular culture offered its mix of diversion, escape, and foreboding, several young writers probed the stresses and fault lines of American culture. (In all four books, interestingly, women are either absent or serve as ineffectual background figures.) Norman Mailer's cynical war novel *The Naked and the Dead* (1948), set in the South Pacific, offered a view of the coarse and mechanical behavior of men in combat that differed strikingly from wartime propaganda images of cheerful, idealistic GIs. Arthur Miller's play *Death of a Salesman* (1949) searingly portrayed a bewildered loser caught up in fantasies of success pathetically at odds with the realities of his defeated life. Kurt Vonnegut's *Player Piano* (1952) presented a bleak fantasy of a totally automated America in which the masters of the machines rule society. The novel's influences included Vonnegut's unhappy experience as an employee of the General Electric Company and earlier dystopian novels such as Aldous Huxley's *Brave New World* (1932) and George Orwell's *1984* of 1949.

J. D. Salinger's *The Catcher in the Rye* (1951) sardonically viewed middle-class pretenses through the eyes of seventeen-year-old Holden Caulfield. An atomic-age Huck Finn, Holden clings to his innocence—trying, for example, to erase "Fuck You" graffiti so his kid sister won't see it—in a grown-up world shadowed by the bomb. A classic coming-of-age novel, *Catcher* captured the historical moment when the moral clarity and national unity of the war dissolved into postwar ambiguities. Salinger uses Holden's youthful naiveté to judge a "phony" society troubled by Cold War obsessions, nuclear angst, and an inconclusive war in Korea, a society that determinedly insists that all is well because the economy is thriving. Huck heads west at the end of Mark Twain's novel; Holden, after a nervous breakdown, narrates his story from a psychiatric institution.

A few postwar writers explored specific social problems that roiled beneath the surface of American life. Nelson Algren's *Man with the Golden Arm* (1949) looked at drug addiction, gambling, and crime in Chicago's inner city, subjects largely ignored in the 1940s. Laura Hobson's *Gentlemen's Agreement* (1946), written in the shadow of the Jewish holocaust, whose horror emerged in shocking photographs of the Nazi death camps, exposed anti-Semitism in American society. Hobson began her novel in 1944 when Mississippi congressman John Rankin called radio newsman Walter Winchell "the little Kike" on the House floor and not a single legislator rebuked him. Both as a novel and a 1947 movie starring Gregory Peck, *Gentlemen's Agreement* spotlighted a hitherto-neglected social issue.

Ralph Ellison's *Invisible Man* (1952) explored the theme of race in America from a black perspective. In a succession of often surreal, almost hallucinatory episodes of great imaginative power, the action moves from the turn-of-the-century rural South to the urban North of World War II. The nameless narrator seeks his identity ("When I discover who I am, I'll be free") and probes the psychological experience of African Americans living in a society that is simultaneously racist and blind to their existence. He joins "The Brotherhood," a thinly fictionalized Communist party, but finds that it, too, exploits him, and quits in disillusionment. Apart from its anticommunist theme, *Invisible Man* did not take an overtly political stand. Ellison rejected both the radical politics and the naturalistic style of Richard Wright's *Native Son* (1940), with its stark picture of life in Chicago's black ghetto. "This is not an attack upon white society," Ellison insisted. "[The hero] must assert and achieve his own humanity." *Invisible Man,* a work of stunning psychological clarity, avoided politics and any hint of collective protest in ways that spoke volumes about the early Cold War cultural climate in which it was written.

Postwar social critics, too, employed the neutral vocabulary of psychology and sociology rather than of radical politics. In *The Lonely Crowd* (1950), sociologist David Riesman looked at the psychological effects of mass society and consumer abundance. Exploring changes in "the American character" (that is, the white, middle-class character), Riesman discerned a progression from "inner directedness" to "other directedness." Americans, he claimed, lacked a firm sense of self in the new consumerist age and thus placed a high premium on social acceptance and "fitting in." *The Lonely Crowd,* as we shall see, opened a floodgate of books lamenting the conformism and cultural insipidity of 1950s America.

All Aboard the Freedom Train:
Rallying Against Communism

Early postwar culture mobilized behind the Cold War. A red, white, and blue "Freedom Train," its gleaming engine named "The Spirit of 1776," toured America in the late 1940s, bringing replicas of the Declaration of Independence, the Constitution, and other icons of American freedom to hundreds of cities and towns. Hollywood, having idealized the heroic Soviet people during the war, quickly shifted gears after 1945. *Red Danube* (1949) chronicled Eastern Europe's fall to Soviet imperialism. In *I Married a Communist* (1950) and *My Son John* (1952), patriots find the communist taint in their own families. *Big Jim McClain* (1952) starred John Wayne as a HUAC investigator tracking communist spies in Hawaii.

The art world, too, reflected Cold War preoccupations. When abstract-expressionist artist Jackson Pollock began to drip paint on canvas to produce his swirling "action paintings" in the late 1940s, Henry Luce's *Life* magazine promoted him as a symbol of New York's rise to artistic supremacy that paralleled America's global dominance in other spheres. *Life* also pointed to avant-garde artists like Pollock as heartening proof of U.S. cultural freedom in contrast to the repression found behind the Iron Curtain.

Intellectuals who wrote about politics in the Truman years, many of them disillusioned Marxists, called for a toughened liberalism purged of the naiveté of the 1930s, more appreciative of American democracy, and more alert to the communist menace. The era brought a stream of confessional literature—the 1950 anthology *The God That Failed* and Whittaker Chambers's *Witness* (1952), for example—in which intellectuals and writers repented of their flirtation with communism.

The critic Lionel Trilling, professor of English literature at Columbia University, was part of a cadre of New York intellectuals who influenced early Cold War political thought. In his 1947 novel *The Middle of the Journey* and 1950 collection of essays entitled *The Liberal Imagination,* Trilling repudiated Marxism and criticized liberals' naive faith in reform and their optimism about human nature. Although he insisted on the morally ambiguous nature of all political systems, Trilling argued passionately that a democratic, culturally diverse society was far preferable to an absolutist one (such as Stalinist Russia), whatever its ideological pretensions.

In *The Vital Center* (1949), Arthur Schlesinger, Jr., who taught American history at Harvard, offered a chastened liberalism—sternly anticommunist yet committed to the New Deal's social-welfare agenda—as the fighting faith that could fortify America against totalitarianism. Schlesinger carefully distinguished his anticommunism from HUAC's redbaiting, yet his own discussion of communism was fairly monolithic. The Soviet Union could never be negotiated with, only defeated, Schlesinger implied, if not in war then through the West's superior "technological dynamism." Like NSC-68, *The Vital Center* largely ignored legitimate Soviet security interests and world realities that did not fit the book's starkly bipolar analytical framework.

The Protestant theologian Reinhold Niebuhr profoundly influenced Trilling, Schlesinger, George Kennan, and many other Cold War intellectuals. A Missourian of German immigrant stock, Niebuhr attended Yale Divinity School, held a parish in Detroit, and after 1928 taught at New York's Union Theological Seminary. Initially drawn to the reform-minded Social Gospel, Niebuhr had embraced Marxism in the early 1930s. But disillusionment soon set in, and in a stream of books and essays, he exhorted Americans to abandon their idealism and sentimental optimism, and to recognize the power calculations that underlie international relations and the sinfulness inherent in the behavior of all nations and social groups.

Communists were especially fearsome, Niebuhr warned in *The Irony of American History* (1952), because in their absolutist zeal they tried to achieve by force the social ideal that Western liberals only fitfully pursued. Indeed, Niebuhr found communism more sinister than Nazism, because its gloss of idealism made its evil less obvious. Although skeptical of American political thought, Niebuhr, like Trilling, argued that the United States, with its pragmatism, freedom of expression, and relatively open politics, offered far greater promise of a reasonably just social order than did the communist world.

Niebuhr translated these generalities into avid support for the Cold War. The Soviets would not stop with swallowing Eastern Europe, he predicted in 1946, but would try to "extend their power over the whole of Europe." To avoid war, he advised, do not be too afraid of it. He praised the apocalyptic tone of the Truman Doctrine. That the governments of Greece and Turkey were undemocratic was irrelevant, he insisted. "What is at stake is not the internal structure of these nations, but the peace of Europe, which cannot be preserved if the communist tide inundates it."

Niebuhr exerted enormous influence in the early Cold War era. One journalist called him "the official Establishment theologian." Opinion molders cited his authority, and popularized versions of his message appeared in *Time, Life,* and *Reader's Digest.* His somber, world-weary visage on the March 8, 1948, cover of *Time* seemed to personify the desperate nature of the Cold War struggle. Under Niebuhr's influence, anticommunism became the one absolute for Cold War liberals otherwise wary of absolutist thinking.

In 1947 Niebuhr, Schlesinger, and others founded Americans for Democratic Action (ADA) to rally New Deal liberals who were also staunchly anticommunist. In 1948, after toying with the idea of an Eisenhower candidacy, the ADA endorsed Truman and denounced Henry Wallace's Progressive party as a communist front.

These Truman-era liberals formulated their anticommunist dogma at a time when Joseph Stalin ruled the Soviet Union as absolute dictator, when the Soviet grip on Eastern Europe seemed unconditional, and when Mao Zedong's communists were triumphant in China. The changes triggered by Stalin's death in 1953, the breakup of the Sino-Soviet alliance, and Moscow's more moderate stance in the era of détente all lay ahead in the late 1940s and early 1950s.

These liberal intellectuals' worldview merits respect, yet such thinkers served as cheerleaders for the Cold War in its period of maximum rhetorical excess. Their broad generalizations about the essential nature of communist ideology tended to ignore the Soviet Union's actual history and legitimate interests and to blur the nuances of specific issues. Despite their caveats, the logic of their position led to an unquestioning embrace of "the West" and of the Truman administration's version of Cold War issues. The oversimplification became even cruder as the media packaged their message for mass consumption. When the *New York Times Magazine* in

April 1948 published an article by Schlesinger entitled "Not Left, Not Right, But a Vital Center," the magazine's cover illustration, reminiscent of the propaganda posters of the 1930s, showed the armies of "the Left" and "the Right" frantically retreating as a giant Statue of Liberty hand bearing the Torch of Freedom smashes a wedge between them.

As liberals enlisted for the Cold War, they tended to dismiss the conservatives at the other end of the ideological spectrum who shared their fervent anticommunism. Indeed, in *The Liberal Imagination,* Lionel Trilling insisted that the Right had no ideas, only "irritable mental gestures which seek to resemble ideas." Even as he wrote, however, a conservative ideological resurgence could be discerned, not only in the popularity of Hayek's *Road to Serfdom* but elsewhere. In 1951, for example, young William F. Buckley, Jr., entered the polemical wars with *God and Man at Yale,* a caustic attack on the secular rot eating away at the soul of his alma mater. Soon Buckley's magazine, the *National Review,* would arise as a witty and vigorous conservative voice challenging the assumptions of Marxists, democratic socialists, and New Deal liberals alike.

Whereas liberals like Trilling, Schlesinger, and Niebuhr contributed to a Cold War consensus on international issues, the social-welfare themes of their domestic program stirred far less enthusiasm. White, middle-class Americans, including many business leaders, may have come to terms with the New Deal, but they were in no mood for further reforms such as those espoused by Left-liberal intellectuals and embodied in Truman's Fair Deal. Advocating an aggressive, confrontational foreign policy, they sought a politics of stability on the domestic front.

Conclusion

What underlying themes emerge from the welter of events, foreign and domestic, chronicled in the last two chapters? First, of course, these years gave rise to the Cold War, with all its ramifications. President Truman's handling of the early postwar differences with the Soviets and his presentation of the issues to the American people set a course that would influence U.S. history for decades. But many voices contributed to the molding of Cold War ideology, from Washington politicians to theologians, historians, literary critics, magazine editors, and moviemakers. In their sweeping rhetorical portrayals of the communist menace, the ideologists of 1945–52 introduced powerful and enduring themes into American public discourse. Despite the quest for consensus on the domestic front as well as on international issues, the comparative unity of World War II soon gave way to heated political controversies and dark suspicions that pitted American against American.

The nuclear arms race dates from these years as well. Truman's fateful decision of August 1945, the failure of the postwar international-control effort, and critical actions in Washington and Moscow in the late 1940s and early 1950s launched a struggle for nuclear supremacy that for four decades would shadow the world with fears of thermonuclear annihilation.

The postwar boom dramatically molded American history as well. Building on the production feats of the war years, the U.S. economy in the late 1940s and early 1950s achieved new levels of consumer abundance. Corporate America, taking credit for this cornucopia of consumer goods, moved to translate economic achievement into political influence. Although not directly attacking the New Deal, business organizations redefined some of its basic premises on their own terms. The rhetoric of "business-government partnership" that would pervade the politics of the 1950s took shape in this period. Organized labor, highly influential in the 1930s, found itself increasingly marginalized in debates over public policy.

The paradoxically upbeat and escapist, yet occasionally ominous, tone of post-war mass culture and the bleak outlook of some writers and social critics also held important implications for the future. During the war, most Americans had stood together in support of the common cause. This unity continued after 1945 in the foreign-policy arena, as the nation's political, intellectual, and media elites promulgated a broadly supported Cold War consensus. But the story differed on the domestic front. Amidst the postwar boom, millions remained outside looking in. Regardless of the social changes transforming the lives of African Americans, institutionalized racism persisted. And in contrast to the culture's celebration of domesticity, the constraints that early postwar society imposed on women in its quest for stability would prove ultimately unsustainable. The elements of future conflict and unrest, in short, were already evident in the early 1950s.

While redbaiters flung their charges of "subversion" and "disloyalty," novelists, playwrights, and social thinkers criticized the hypocrisies and evasions of postwar America. The America of Hobson, Salinger, Mailer, Ellison, and Riesman was not the America of the TV shows, the mass magazines, and the glossy ads. The alienation of an articulate minority of intellectuals would intensify as the 1950s wore on.

The Truman years thus marked an uneasy transition from an era of depression and global war to one of economic abundance tempered by Cold War fears, nuclear menace, divisions in the body politic, and only fitful attention to troubling social issues. The apprehensions that James Agee had felt as he watched the victory celebrators in September 1945 were all too well founded.

By 1952 war memories were fading; Americans no longer self-consciously perceived themselves as living in a "postwar" era. In that year, Harry Truman, the residual legatee of a reform movement that had started twenty years before, neared the end of a remarkable political career. In electing a new president, Americans turned to a war hero known more for his generalship than for his political views. The Eisenhower era was about to dawn.

SELECTED READINGS

Demobilization and Early Postwar Politics

Jack S. Ballard, *The Shock of Peace: Military and Economic Demobilization After World War II* (1983); William C. Berman, *The Politics of Civil Rights in the Truman Administration* (1970); Richard O. Davies, *Housing Reform During the Truman Administration* (1966); Robert Donovan's two-volume history of the Truman presidency, *Conflict and Crisis* (1977) and *Tumultuous Years* (1982); Andrew Dunar, *The Truman Scandals and the Politics of Morality* (1984); John Ehrman, *The Rise of Neoconservatism: Intellectuals and Foreign*

Affairs, 1945–1994 (1995); Robert H. Ferrell, *Harry S. Truman and the Modern American Presidency* (1983); Elizabeth A. Fones-Wolf, *Selling Free Enterprise: The Business Assault on Labor and Liberalism, 1945–60* (1994); Alonzo L. Hamby, *Beyond the New Deal: Harry S. Truman and American Liberalism* (1973); Richard G. Hewlett and Oscar E. Anderson, Jr., *Atomic Shield, 1947–1952* [Atomic Energy Commission] (1989); Michael J. Lacey, ed., *The Truman Presidency* (1989), Part I, "Domestic Politics and Issues"; Stephen Lawson, *Running for Freedom: Civil Rights and Black Politics in America Since 1941* (1977); Donald McCoy, *The Presidency of Harry S. Truman (1984);* George T. Mazuzan and J. Samuel Walker, *Controlling the Atom: The Beginnings of Nuclear Regulation, 1946–1962* (1984); William L. O'Neill, *A Better World: The Great Schism: Stalinism and the Intellectuals* (1982); Herbert Parmet, *The Democrats: The Years After FDR* (1976); Monte S. Poen, *Harry S. Truman Versus the Medical Lobby: The Genesis of Medicare* (1979); Irwin Ross, *The Loneliest Campaign: The Truman Victory of 1948* (1968); Alice Kimball Smith, *A Peril and a Hope: The Scientists' Movement in America* (1965); Athan Theoharis, *The Truman Presidency: The Origins of the Imperial Presidency and the National Security State* (1979); Allen Yarnell, *Democrats and Progressives: The 1948 Presidential Election as a Test of Postwar Liberalism* (1974).

Postwar Society, Economy, and Culture

Erik Barnouw, *Tube of Plenty* [television] (1982); Paul Boyer, *By the Bomb's Early Light: American Thought and Culture at the Dawn of the Atomic Age* (1985); Albert Camarillo, *Chicanos in California* (1984); Mary Ann Doane, *The Desire to Desire: The Woman's Film of the 1940s* (1987); Chester E. Eisinger, *Fiction of the Forties* (1963); Ernesto Galarza, *Merchants of Labor: The Mexican Bracero Story* (1964); Mario T. García, *Mexican-Americans: Leadership, Ideology and Identity, 1930–1960* (1989); Carol George, *God's Salesman: Norman Vincent Peale and the Power of Positive Thinking* (1993); David Goldfield, *Black, White, and Southern: Race Relations and Southern Culture* (1990); William S. Graebner, *The Age of Doubt: American Thought and Culture in the 1940s* (1991); Richard A. Griswold del Castillo, *La Familia: Chicano Families in the Urban Southwest, 1848 to the Present* (1984); Susan Hartman, *The Homefront and Beyond* [women in the war and early postwar era] (1984); Wendy Kozol, *Life's America: Family and Nation in Postwar Photojournalism* (1994); Nelson Lichtenstein, "From Corporatism to Collective Bargaining: Organized Labor and the Eclipse of Social Democracy in the Postwar Era," in Steve Fraser and Gary Gerstle, eds., *The Rise and Fall of the New Deal Order, 1930–1980* (1989); Karal Ann Marling, *As Seen on TV: The Visual Culture of Everyday Life in the 1950s* (1994); Martin E. Marty, *Modern American Religion*, Vol. 3 [1941–1960] (1996); Lary May, ed., *Recasting America: Culture and Politics in the Age of the Cold War* (1989); Jeffrey L. Meikle, *American Plastic: A Cultural History* (1995); Geoffrey Perrett, *A Dream of Greatness: The American People, 1945–1963* (1979); Leila J. Rupp and Verta Taylor, *Survival in the Doldrums: The American Women's Rights Movement, 1945 to the 1960s* (1987); Julian Samora, *Los Mojados: The Wetback Story* (1971); Herbert Stein, *Presidential Economics: The Making of Economic Policy from Roosevelt to Reagan and Beyond* (1984); Allan M. Winkler, *Life Under a Cloud: American Anxiety About the Atom* (1993).

Anticommunism and the Early Cold War at Home

Michael Belknap, *Cold War Political Justice: The Smith Act, the Communist Party, and American Civil Liberties* (1977); H. W. Brands, *The Devil We Knew: Americans and the Cold War* (1993); Virginia Carmichael, *Framing History: The Rosenberg Story and the Cold War* (1993); David Caute, *The Great Fear: The Anti-Communist Purges Under Truman and Eisenhower* (1978); James K. Davis, *Spying on America: The FBI's Domestic Counterintelligence*

Program (1992); Sigmund Diamond, *Compromised Campus: The Collaboration of Universities with the Intelligence Community, 1945–1955* (1988); Bernard F. Dick, *Radical Innocence: A Critical Study of the Hollywood Ten* (1988); Richard Freeland, *The Truman Doctrine and the Origins of McCarthyism* (1972); Richard M. Fried, *Nightmare in Red: The McCarthy Era in Perspective* (1990); Harvey Klehr and Ronald Radosh, *The* Amerasia *Spy Case: Prelude to McCarthyism* (1996); Earl Latham, *The Communist Controversy in Washington* (1966); Mary McAuliffe, *Crisis of the Left: Cold-War Politics and American Liberals, 1947–1954* (1978); Gary May, *Unamerican Activities: The Trials of William Remington* (1994); David M. Oshinsky, *A Conspiracy So Immense: The World of Joe McCarthy* (1983); Richard Gid Powers, *Not Without Honor: The History of American Anticommunism* (1995); Ronald Radosh and Joyce Milton, *The Rosenberg File* (1983); Thomas C. Reeves, *The Life and Times of Joe McCarthy* (1982); Natalie Robins, *Alien Ink: The FBI's War on Freedom of Expression* (1992); Ellen W. Schrecker, *No Ivory Tower: McCarthyism and the Universities* (1986); Athan Theoharis, *Seeds of Repression: Harry S Truman and the Origins of McCarthyism* (1971); Allen Weinstein, *Perjury: The Hiss-Chambers Case* (1978); Stephen J. Whitfield, *The Culture of the Cold War* (1991).

CHAPTER *4*

Modern Republicanism and Suburban Togetherness in the 1950s

I n the 1955 movie *Strategic Air Command,* World War II Air Force ace Dutch Holland is recalled to active duty. Dutch (James Stewart) grumbles at first; he and his pregnant wife, Sally (June Allyson), have just redecorated their home and are settling into cozy domesticity. But when a giant bomber flies overhead, Dutch recalls the lure of the skies and gladly joins the new Strategic Air Command (SAC). Sally gamely supports Dutch as he defends the nation. "Anything you do is fine with me," she assures him, "just as long as you don't leave me behind."

The movie reflected several key realities of the 1950s: SAC embodied the new emphasis on nuclear readiness in U.S. defense policy; SAC's complex organizational hierarchy, into which Dutch smoothly fits, paralleled that of corporate America; and Sally's loyal support of her husband echoed the idealization of domesticity at a time of rising birthrates and migration to the suburbs. Indeed, the movie repeatedly equates real-life families with the SAC "family" of pilots and crews and "the new family of nuclear weapons" that the bombers are designed to deliver.

As the public flocked to view *Strategic Air Command* with its blend of menacing and upbeat themes, the Cold War and the postwar economic boom surged on. Americans, prosperous yet worried about nuclear war and communist subversion, had little patience with social critics or political dissidents. Ready enough to endorse Washington's pursuit of the Cold War overseas, most people turned away from public concerns at home. The media presented the burgeoning suburbs as a microcosm of an affluent America, downplaying such social problems as poverty and ignoring the citizens excluded from the charmed circle of economic abundance. In the White House, a new president, Dwight D. Eisenhower, mirrored the nation's cautious, conservative, inward-turning mood.

The Politics of Moderation

Dwight Eisenhower, in Paris as supreme commander of NATO forces, faced a stream of visitors in 1951 and early 1952 as top Republicans flew in from the States to implore him to run for president. He seemed a sure winner, although few knew anything about his politics. Indeed, Harry Truman, who had decided not to be a candidate in 1952, had earlier urged him to run as a Democrat.

Born in Texas in 1890, Eisenhower had graduated from West Point and won fame during World War II as commander of the North African invasion in 1943 and the Normandy landing in 1944. After serving for a time as president of Columbia University, he had returned to Europe to head NATO's military forces. Americans weary of the Korean War and of Truman administration scandals saw in Ike a refreshing political outsider and delighted in his easy smile and avuncular manner.

To compete in the election, Eisenhower would have to grapple with a divided Republican party. Republicans from the party's eastern, moderate, internationalist wing who now wooed him mistrusted the more conservative and isolationist midwestern wing, headed by Ohio's senator Robert Taft. More progressive Republican leaders feared that if Taft won the 1952 party nomination, he would either lose the election (the more likely prospect) or win and turn the party sharply to the right. Behind Taft, too, loomed Senator Joseph McCarthy. For the moment, McCarthy served GOP interests by attacking Democrats, but a strong Republican was needed in the White House to curb his excesses. All of these reasons—plus the overriding desire to regain the White House—led moderate Republicans to woo Eisenhower. As Thomas Dewey put it, "We must look around for someone of great popularity . . . [who can] lead us back to safe channels and paths."

Ending the suspense early in 1952, Eisenhower proclaimed himself a Republican and threw his hat in the ring. He won several state primaries, but Taft loyalists

They Liked Ike. *Although he was no silver-tongued orator, Dwight Eisenhower's infectious grin and status as a World War II military hero drew adoring throngs during the 1952 presidential campaign. (Joe Scherschel* Life Magazine, *© Time Inc.)*

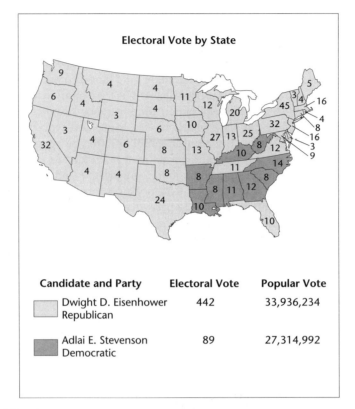

FIGURE 4.1

Presidential Election of 1952

controlled other states' delegations. However, Eisenhower's floor managers at the GOP convention in Chicago won a battle over disputed delegates, and the general was nominated on the first ballot. As his running mate, Eisenhower tapped Senator Richard Nixon of California, famed for his dogged pursuit of accused spy Alger Hiss.

The Democrats nominated Illinois governor Adlai Stevenson. Stevenson's witty speeches charmed liberals, but given Eisenhower's appeal, plus the Republicans' potent themes—Korea, China, communism, and corruption (summed up in the formula K_1C_3)—few oddsmakers bet on a Democratic upset as campaign crowds chanted "I like Ike."

Yet two campaign incidents illuminated McCarthy's power and Richard Nixon's political style, both of which would pose dilemmas for Eisenhower. In McCarthy's home state of Wisconsin, Eisenhower dropped from a prepared speech a passage implicitly criticizing the senator for his attacks on General George Marshall. Marshall had served as Eisenhower's superior in World War II, yet Ike dared not challenge McCarthy's smear even of his old comrade-in-arms and benefactor.

When the press revealed a secret Nixon fund set up by rich California businessmen, Eisenhower declined to defend his running mate, the first of many indications that Ike neither trusted nor much liked Nixon. Nixon fought back with a

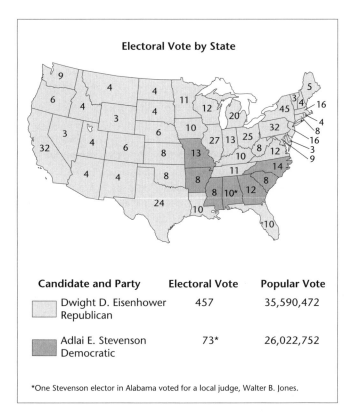

Electoral Vote by State

Candidate and Party	Electoral Vote	Popular Vote
Dwight D. Eisenhower Republican	457	35,590,472
Adlai E. Stevenson Democratic	73*	26,022,752

*One Stevenson elector in Alabama voted for a local judge, Walter B. Jones.

Figure 4.2
Presidential Election of 1956

cloying television speech, potently demonstrating the political clout of this new medium, that included a reference to his daughters' little dog, Checkers, another campaign gift. An outpouring of support ensured Nixon's place on the ticket and a long run in U.S. politics. For decades, connoisseurs of political demagoguery would cherish the "Checkers speech."

That November, Eisenhower garnered 55 percent of the popular vote. Foreshadowing later Republican successes, he even did well in the once solidly Democratic South, winning 49 percent of the vote and carrying Virginia, Florida, Tennessee, Texas, and Oklahoma. He would score another firm victory in 1956, once again over Adlai Stevenson, and extend his presidency to two terms.

Hardly a sophisticated thinker, Eisenhower was on firmer ground on foreign affairs than on domestic issues. Nevertheless, he possessed a well-formulated and fairly coherent set of political views. He deplored, for example, the politicizing of class conflict. All Americans had "areas of common interest," he believed, and the political process should identify and further these shared concerns. In this cooperative process, he hoped that public-spirited business leaders would play a key role.

The "drift toward statism" troubled him as well. Like many conservatives, he chafed at the growth of the federal government and the consequent weakening of both the private sphere and the power of the states. On the other hand, he was no knee-jerk enemy of "big government" or cheerleader for laissez faire. As had Theodore Roosevelt, Eisenhower espoused a capitalism moderated by regulatory laws and a concern for social welfare, and he advocated a government strictly limited yet strong enough to promote the national interest, including economic growth, productivity, and foreign trade. His outlook reflected that of the more sophisticated and liberal corporate leaders of these years. Rejecting the backward-looking politics of people like Taft who still fought the New Deal, this corporate elite accepted the main outlines of FDR's reforms, including social security, the rights of organized labor, and a central role for government in the economy. A partnership of government, business, and "responsible" labor leaders, they argued, could lead the country in progressive paths.

Yet Eisenhower Republicans also believed that the New Dealers had created a bloated federal bureaucracy and had pushed America in a "socialistic" direction. One task of moderate Republicans, then, was to rectify the "excesses" of the 1930s while preserving New Deal gains. Accordingly, Eisenhower always balanced his calls for governmental and fiscal restraint with a concern for the general welfare. The Republican party must be "progressive," he insisted, "or it is sunk." The party should avoid the political extremes, he advised, and hew to the center of the road "where the traction is best and where you can bring the most people along with you." This was "the middle way," and he embraced it devoutly. To Eisenhower's admirers, his moderation provided a needed respite after the traumas of depression and war. His liberal critics, a small band in the 1950s, charged that his cautious approach to politics muffled fundamental social issues and conflicts in the bland rhetoric of cooperation and shared interests.

Eisenhower's personal popularity only briefly propelled his party to majority status. The Republicans narrowly won both houses of Congress in 1952, but in the 1954 midterm election, despite general prosperity, the end of the Korean War, and McCarthyite attacks on Democrats' disloyalty, the Democrats regained control of both houses and retained it for the rest of the decade. To Eisenhower, this proved that the GOP must purge its reactionary elements and broaden its base.

In Congress, Ike thus faced not only a hard core of reactionary Republicans but also a powerful Democratic delegation led by Sam Rayburn and Lyndon Johnson, two wily Texans who served after 1955 as speaker of the House and Senate majority leader. The decade's legislation thus emerged from complex three-way negotiation among the White House, various stripes of congressional Republicans, and congressional Democrats.

Several crucial measures reflected the Republican belief that twenty years of Democratic rule had concentrated too much power in Washington. In 1953, reversing the policy of the Truman administration, Eisenhower transferred control of offshore oil rights, and the lucrative tax revenues from such rights, from the federal government to the states. This change opened the door to private drilling and fulfilled a long-sought objective of U.S. oil companies. In 1954 the administration supported a private power company's challenge to the Tennessee Valley Authority, a New Deal showpiece.* Finally, in 1955 the Federal Power Commission re-

---

* Eisenhower later reversed himself on this issue when evidence surfaced of legal improprieties by the private-power interests.

jected congressional calls for a TVA-like public-power project on Idaho's Snake River and instead authorized privately financed hydroelectric dams on the river. All of these measures testified to Eisenhower's suspicions of statism and his wish to encourage private entrepreneurial energies.

Further venting their hostility to FDR and the New Deal, conservative Republicans in Congress killed the Reconstruction Finance Corporation (RFC), a once-powerful New Deal agency. (Ironically, the RFC actually arose in 1932, when the Republican Herbert Hoover was still president.) They changed the name of Boulder Dam to Hoover Dam and nearly passed the Bricker Amendment. Introduced by Senator John Bricker of Ohio, this constitutional amendment would have restricted the president's treatymaking powers and subjected presidential "executive agreements" with foreign nations to the same Senate ratification requirement established by the Constitution for treaties. The amendment, a belated attack on Roosevelt's alleged giveaway of Eastern Europe to Stalin at the 1945 Yalta Conference, fell one vote short of the necessary two-thirds majority in the Senate in 1954.

In other respects, the Eisenhower administration lived up to its progressive claims. To build his record in this area, Eisenhower relied on the Democratic leadership in Congress, especially Lyndon Johnson. The wheeling-dealing Texan dominated the Senate and no important legislation passed without his approval. Most notably, Johnson played a critical role in passage of the landmark Civil Rights Act of 1957 (see pp. 159–160). Eisenhower much admired Johnson, whom he privately called "the best Democrat of them all," and appreciated his cooperation on measures favored by the administration.

Of course, Johnson never lost sight of his party's interest in building its own liberal record. On housing and school construction bills, for example, the Democrats voted more money than Eisenhower requested. However, except for election time, Johnson, with his House counterpart Sam Rayburn, worked so closely with the White House that more partisan Democrats criticized them. To a later generation who would forever identify Johnson with the disastrous Vietnam War, his outstanding legislative record in the 1950s sank into undeserved obscurity.

This close relationship between the White House and Congress led to the creation of the Department of Health, Education and Welfare; an increase in the minimum wage from seventy-five cents to a dollar an hour; and the extension of social security to more than 7 million workers, most of them farmers. In 1954, with White House support, Congress approved construction of the Saint Lawrence Seaway, which gave oceangoing freighters access to Great Lakes ports. That year Eisenhower signed a housing act that expanded the Truman housing program. This and later measures provided large sums for slum clearance and urban renewal and guaranteed housing loans and low-cost mortages to Korean War veterans.

Eisenhower's belief that government should promote economic growth also sustained the prosperity of the 1950s. As government spending rose both in absolute terms and as a percentage of the GNP, federal outlays for housing, highways, and, above all, defense yielded many thousands of jobs. The Saint Lawrence Seaway Project alone revitalized the economies of the Northeast and the Great Lakes.

The Eisenhower era's most enduring monument, a vast highway program, rivaled the New Deal's public-works projects. The Federal Highway Act (1956) allocated more than $30 billion for a 41,000-mile interstate-highway system. Soon ribbons of concrete and asphalt were winding through prairies, cornfields, and urban districts. The program stimulated the economy and eventually allowed Americans to drive cross-country without encountering a single stop sign or traffic light. One rationale for the interstate system illustrated again the Cold War's effect on domestic policy: Highways would provide easy escape from cities in a nuclear war.

This vast highway program spawned what historian Kenneth Jackson calls the 1950s "drive-in culture." Motels proliferated, and fast-food franchises mushroomed along the new interstates, offering identical fare to travelers nationwide. In 1954 salesman Ray Kroc bought a locally popular hamburger restaurant from the McDonald brothers of San Bernardino, California. Soon McDonald's golden arches would rise across America. The downside of this orgy of highway building emerged only gradually: a decayed rail system, profligate gasoline consumption, air pollution, and a degraded landscape. Countless poor and vulnerable city neighborhoods were shattered by the tangle of overpasses, concrete pylons, and access ramps.

The highway program proved a gold mine for the construction industry, illustrating how Eisenhower's policies and the ideology of modern Republicanism, in this case with strong bipartisan support, nurtured a probusiness climate in Washington. Ike's cabinet, drawn mainly from the corporate world, revealed this orientation as well. A much-quoted comment by Secretary of Defense Charles E. Wilson summed up the prevalent view. Asked about possible conflict of interest between his public duties and his former role as head of GM, Wilson replied, "I have always assumed that what was good for the United States was good for General Motors, and vice versa."

Meanwhile, Senator Joseph McCarthy, little interested in such mundane topics as housing or highways, continued to exploit the obsession with communism that the Truman administration had aroused. Even Eisenhower himself was blind to the red danger, McCarthy hinted. In 1953 McCarthy warned of communist infiltration of the U.S. Army, focusing on an obscure left-wing army dentist. During the so-called Army-McCarthy hearings, televised live in the spring of 1954, a riveted nation watched as McCarthy badgered witnesses, including a timid secretary of the army.

Still on a rampage, McCarthy and other witch-hunters ruined reputations and trampled constitutional rights in the early Eisenhower years as they had in the Truman era. Citizens were pressured not only to "confess" their own radical pasts but to implicate others. Filmmaker Elia Kazan, hauled before the House Un-American Activities Committee, agreed to "name names." In his next movie, *On the Waterfront* (1954), Kazan justified his action by making a hero of a dockworker (Marlon Brando) who informs on the mobsters who control his union. "I'm glad what I done—you hear me?—glad what I done!" Brando stridently insists.

McCarthy, a Roman Catholic, won support from influential parts of the Catholic community. The Knights of Columbus, a 920,000-member Catholic fraternal organization, strongly backed the crusading senator. Francis Cardinal Spellman of New York endorsed him, asserting, "[McCarthy] is against communism and he . . . is doing something about it. He is making America aware of the dangers."

Under McCarthyite pressure, the State Department in 1953 ordered books or artworks by "Communists, fellow travelers, etc." removed from United States Information Agency libraries abroad. Eisenhower condemned "bookburners," but when asked whether he meant McCarthy, he characteristically backed off. Indeed, the president consistently avoided challenging McCarthy. In 1953 he even agreed to Senator Taft's demand that McCarthy, in effect, be given a veto over all diplomatic nominations. This concession came after a bruising Senate battle over the White House's nominee as ambassador to the Soviet Union, whom McCarthy, typically, had found soft on communism. In a 1953 diary entry, Eisenhower rationalized his policy of silence: "Nothing will be so effective in combatting [McCarthy] . . . as to ignore him. This he cannot stand."

But the McCarthyite taint infected the administration itself. In 1953 Eisenhower issued an executive order revoking the safeguards built into President Truman's internal-security program. Now it became easier to fire radicals or suspected "security risks." Indeed, both parties played the politics of anticommunism. In 1954, congressional Democrats passed the Communist Control Act. Toughening the 1950 McCarran Act, this law limited the legal rights of "Communist-infiltrated" organizations and required them to register with the government. All the same, Vice President Nixon that fall accused Democrats of being "blind to the Communist conspiracy."

Fame offered no protection against the spreading paranoia. In 1954 Eisenhower approved the Atomic Energy Commission's decision to cancel the security clearance of physicist J. Robert Oppenheimer. This action, ostensibly based on old charges that Oppenheimer had had communist friends in the 1930s, in reality grew out of his opposition to the H-bomb. "The impossible search for 'absolute security' is incompatible with a free and healthy society," journalist I. F. Stone wrote of the Oppenheimer case. "If this is to be national policy, why should anyone be trusted?"

The miasma of suspicion prevented the vigorous debate over the precise nature of the Soviet threat that might have moderated the rhetorical excess and tendency to oversimplify, and left the Cold War assumptions that had solidified in the late 1940s and early 1950s largely unexamined. Leading Democrats, terrified of the "soft on communism" label, outdid each other in denouncing the Soviet Union. Even liberal senator Hubert Humphrey endorsed the Communist Control Act. Young Robert Kennedy, brother of the future Democratic president John F. Kennedy, served on Senator McCarthy's staff.

But the four-year McCarthy melodrama was wearing thin. To most television viewers, the Wisconsin senator came across as a barroom bully. Joseph Welch, a lawyer representing witnesses in the Army-McCarthy hearings, shrewdly heightened this impression. When McCarthy attacked one of Welch's young assistants, Welch burst out, "At long last, Senator, have you no decency?" A damning TV documentary on McCarthy by CBS newsman Edward R. Murrow in 1954 hastened the senator's decline while underscoring TV's growing influence.

Key Republican senators concluded that "Joe Must Go." A motion to censure him, introduced by GOP senator Ralph Flanders of Vermont in June 1954, passed in December by a 67–22 vote. McCarthy responded predictably, accusing his foes of abetting world communism, but he was finished. Drinking more heavily, he died in 1957.

IN PERSPECTIVE: *Highways and America's Car Culture*

The Federal Highway Act of 1956 defined the decade. It set off a surge of highway construction that reshaped American life and brought Americans' long love affair with the automobile to its pinnacle of besotted infatuation.

In fact, however, transportation issues had loomed large in American history from the beginning. The National Road (1811–38), stretching westward from Maryland to Illinois, was one of the new nation's major public-works projects, linking the coast and the interior. President Jackson's 1830 veto of federal support for a Kentucky road project favored by his political rival Henry Clay enlivened the politics of the era. The *Charles River Bridge Case* (1837), involving two rival bridges in Boston, produced a notable Supreme Court decision defining the rights of publicly chartered corporations.

After 1900, highway-construction issues became interconnected with the automobile. The first automobiles were playthings of the rich, but thanks to Henry Ford and mass production, they soon came within reach of the masses. The automobile's rural cousin the tractor transformed U.S. agriculture, and its big brother the truck revolutionized transportation. Popular culture embraced the automobile. "Come away with me, Lucille, in my merry Oldsmobile," went a pop song of 1906. George F. Babbitt, the conformist hero of Sinclair Lewis's 1922 novel *Babbitt,* idolizes his new car with its array of gadgets. Laurel and Hardy starred in a 1924 comedy about a traffic jam—an experience familiar to many moviegoers.

The first wave of interstate highway construction in the automobile era was a series of two-lane roads stretching westward to the Pacific. Most famous of all was Route 66, linking St. Louis and Los Angeles, and featured in John Steinbeck's Depression-era classic *The Grapes of Wrath.* "You'll get your kicks, on Route 66," went a popular song of 1946.

"Futurama," the General Motors exhibit at the 1939 New York World's Fair, previewed America's postwar car culture. Visitors watched mesmerized as a miniature landscape unfolded, crisscrossed by ribbons of limited-access highways with gracefully curving ramps and cloverleafs, carrying thousands of cars smoothly and effortlessly, with no accidents, stop signs, or traffic jams. A brilliant piece of corporate propaganda, "Futurama" helped convince Americans that the future of transportation lay with the automobile, not with light-rail systems or mass transit. This propaganda subtly ap-

---

Eisenhower had remained nearly mute as the McCarthyites assaulted the fundamental values of an open society. He also failed to exert strong leadership on the most profound moral issue to emerge in the 1950s: racism and civil rights. As we shall see, the politics of moderation proved ill-adapted to cope with this volatile, divisive issue that stirred strong passions and challenged deep-rooted beliefs.

And what of Eisenhower's overall domestic record? Although leery of federal power, he endorsed measures that buttressed and even extended the New

pealed to something deep in the American soul that cherished freedom and individual-
ity and resisted constraint. Of course, the cars were mass produced, and the dream
highways were crowded with drivers all headed in the same direction, but the illusion
of freedom remained. Mass transit was for conformist societies; the car and the open
road embodied America.

With the coming of peace in 1945, the nation set about translating "Futurama"
from dream to reality. By the 1950s, the magazines and TV commercials were full of
alluring ads for Chevrolets, Mercurys, and Plymouths. "See the USA in your Chevrolet,"
warbled singer Dinah Shore on her TV show. The introduction of new models brought
moments of high drama, heightened by Detroit hype. The models usually differed only
superficially from their predecessors, but the excitement remained. In 1958 came the
Pontiac Bonneville Custom Sport Coupe, with "Tri-Power Engine," three "two-barrel
carburetors," and a body design that—like the Russian *Sputnik* launched the year before—seemed poised for space travel.

With the car culture came the postwar wave of interstate highway construction,
anticipated in the 1930s by Pennsylvania's "Super Highway," modeled on Adolph
Hitler's Autobahn. Drivers loved the new high-speed highways, as did the construction
companies that built them and the trucking companies that relied on them. Civil-
defense experts emphasized their value for quick evacuation in a nuclear war.

U.S. business embraced the interstate highways as well. Holiday resorts and
theme parks catered to car-driving vacationers. Standardized chains of motels (an
American coinage, dating from 1925) replaced the spartan, unpredictable tourist cabins of the 1930s. The fast-food chains grew up with the automobile and the new highway systems. A&W Root Beer and White Castle hamburger stands started it all in the
1920s and the 1930s. But it was in the 1950s, the heyday of America's love affair with
the automobile, that the fast-food franchises soon to spread around the world—
Howard Johnson, McDonald's, Burger King, Kentucky Fried Chicken, and the others—
became icons of the American road.

Like most romances, this one eventually cooled. After the 1950s came the second
thoughts. Not only did highways eat up thousands of acres of farmland, but their voracious space demands and spaghetti-like interchanges destroyed hundreds of urban
neighborhoods—usually the poorest and politically weakest. As the public mood
changed, some highway projects were abandoned, leaving interstates dead-ending in
cornfields and access ramps soaring off to nowhere. With the 1970s energy crisis, Detroit's gas guzzlers gave way to smaller, more energy-efficient cars, often Japanese imports. Environmental awareness intensified, and automobile emissions faced strict regulation. Mass transit and electric cars stirred new interest. But if the romance with the
automobile had lost its glow, few spoke of divorce. In the car ads, highway projects,
and glittery dealer showrooms of the 1950s, the careful observer would have seen the
shape of the future.

Deal reforms. Some of his measures benefited corporate interests, but others
responded to the needs of a broader spectrum of the population. The extension
of social security, for example, helped farmers and other self-employed persons.
Construction workers prospered thanks to public housing and highway projects.
The pitfalls of urban renewal would later loom large, but the administration's
support for aid to cities impressed many at the time as enlightened public
policy.

Ike's reputation has shifted radically over the years. At first, historians echoed 1950s critics such as I. F. Stone, who saw him in 1953 as an amiable cipher "who enjoys his bridge and his golf, . . . [leaving] a sort of political vacuum in the White House." He often struck observers as unsure of himself when thrust from the military planning room into the political arena. Ike's rambling answers to reporters' questions confirmed skeptics' doubts. His press conferences, observed humorist Jules Feiffer, were "headlong leaps into verbal gridlock." At one he observed: "Great Britain has a hard row to hoe to keep its economic head above water." Eisenhower also slowed down noticeably during his two terms, partly as a result of a heart attack in 1955 and intestinal surgery in 1956. An aide noted privately in 1958, "He can sprint a few yards, but he tires quickly. . . . [H]e can become momentarily fascinated by individual pieces of the international jigsaw puzzle, [but] he does not seem to be able to see what the picture would look like when all the pieces were put together."

Eventually, however, a more nuanced picture of Ike emerged. Eisenhower's letters and diaries and his associates' memoirs reveal a thoughtful man who actively, if unobtrusively, pursued his political goals. One historian has described his administration as "the hidden hand presidency." Ike's talent for compromise and staff coordination served him well as both general and president. In his own words, he was "pragmatic . . . by inclination." But he was no bloodless manager. Behind the easy smile lay a hot temper capable of explosive rages and barracks-room language. And the puzzling verbal gridlock was often deliberate. He once told his press secretary, who worried about how his boss would handle a complex issue in a news conference, "Don't worry, I'll just confuse them."

1953–1956: Nuclear Strategy and Global Containment

Seeking to fulfill a campaign pledge to end the Korean War, Eisenhower flew to Korea soon after the election to prod the cease-fire talks. He also dropped hints to China through diplomatic channels of his readiness to use nuclear weapons in Korea. In July 1953, negotiators signed a cease-fire that restored the line between North and South Korea more or less at the 38th parallel, where it had stood when hostilities began in 1950.

In shaping its overall strategic policy, the Eisenhower administration faced a dilemma. The primary planning document of the Truman years, NSC-68, had called for an across-the-board military buildup to prepare for everything from local conflict to nuclear war. The resulting expansion, coupled with the costs of the Korean War, drove up military spending nearly fourfold from 1950 to 1953 and produced a whopping budget deficit in fiscal 1952–53.

Eisenhower's enthusiasm for the Cold War was tempered by his belief in limited government and balanced budgets. Whereas the military services called for ever-greater defense spending, the budget balancers—led by Treasury Secretary George Humphrey, the Council of Economic Advisers, and Eisenhower himself—warned that uncontrolled defense outlays could undermine the United States from within as surely as communist expansion abroad. The tension between these conflicting perspectives significantly influenced military policy in the Eisenhower years.

The deterrent threat of nuclear weapons offered one path of compromise. Far cheaper than large armies and a full panoply of conventional weaponry, nuclear armaments promised to maintain U.S. military might at less cost, or, in the blunt phrase of Defense Secretary Wilson, to give "more bang for the buck." Such reasoning underlay what became the Eisenhower administration's rhetoric of "massive retaliation." John Foster Dulles, who soon would become secretary of state, coined a variant of the phrase in a 1952 *Life* article. In the event of war, declared an NSC document that Eisenhower approved in October 1953, "the United States will consider nuclear weapons to be as available for use as other munitions." In the future, warned Dulles in January 1954, U.S. defenses would "depend primarily upon a great capacity to retaliate, instantly, by means and at places of our own choosing."

To be effective, the massive-retaliation doctrine had to be believable. Dulles observed in a 1953 NSC meeting, "Somehow or other we must . . . remove the taboo from the use of these [nuclear] weapons." To increase the credibility of its threat, the United States stepped up construction of hydrogen bombs and planes capable of dropping them on the Soviet Union. By 1956, SAC possessed an armada of 1,400 such aircraft. The Soviets, in contrast, had no more than 150 strategic bombers.

This so-called New Look defense policy (a term borrowed from the fashion world), coupled with the end of the Korean War, enabled Eisenhower to slash defense spending by some 20 percent by 1955 (over protests from the Pentagon and military contractors) and to produce a budget surplus in 1956. The cuts were imposed selectively, however; while army appropriations fell, the air force budget soared.

Massive-retaliation strategy came under fire from analysts at think tanks such as California's RAND Corporation who charged that it lacked credibility. Did anyone truly believe that the United States would obliterate Moscow or Vladivostok in response to a localized Soviet move in Asia, Africa, or the Middle East? Some ethicists and religious leaders attacked the doctrine on moral grounds. Furthermore, the strategy assumed decisive U.S. nuclear superiority, but Moscow was balancing the scales. The Soviets tested a hydrogen device in 1953, and May Day air shows in Moscow in 1954 and 1955 featured overflights by strategic bombers capable of delivering nuclear bombs to North America. (The Soviets apparently flew the same ten planes repeatedly over Red Square, convincing U.S. observers that they possessed hundreds of nuclear bombers.) In Eisenhower's second term, as we shall see in Chapter 6, the nuclear balance of terror would grow more precarious still.

As in the Truman years, the Eisenhower administration in its public pronouncements focused on the ideological sources of Soviet behavior and the all-or-nothing nature of the conflict. As Eisenhower warned in his first inaugural address, "Forces of good and evil are massed and armed and opposed as rarely before in history."

Under Eisenhower and especially Secretary of State Dulles, U.S. Cold War policy, while essentially continuous with that of the Truman years, became more ideologically charged. A Presbyterian lay leader and Wall Street lawyer, Dulles brought to diplomacy a rigid moralism; a single-minded preoccupation with the "vast, monolithic system" of "world communism"; and a passion for encircling the Soviet Union with a network of treaties and military alliances. By 1960, the United States was treaty-bound to defend no fewer than forty-three different nations against "communist aggression." The secretary of state delivered sanctimonious harangues that even his supporters found tedious. "Dull, duller, Dulles," went one Washington joke. Eisenhower himself occasionally lost patience, calling Dulles in a 1958 diary entry "a sort of international prosecuting attorney."

A shrewd negotiator behind closed doors, Dulles also had a penchant for scary public rhetoric. In 1956 he boasted of his readiness to go to "the brink of war" to defeat communism. Rejecting George Kennan's containment doctrine, he insisted that the United States not only contain communism but aggressively challenge its influence everywhere. To this end, he asserted America's readiness to help the people of Eastern Europe liberate themselves from Soviet rule. "You can count on us," he assured them in 1953 on a Radio Free Europe broadcast.

Such talk was largely intended to stir unrest behind the Iron Curtain and to win ethnic East European voters to the Republican camp. In practice, U.S. policy toward Eastern Europe proved cautious. When Soviet and East German troops in 1953 put down uprisings in East Berlin and elsewhere in East Germany, the United States did nothing. Similarly, when Russian tanks crushed an anti-Soviet revolt in Hungary in 1956, the United States verbally supported the insurgents but refrained from intervention. Dulles's rhetoric gradually grew more muted, particularly with reference to Eastern Europe. The terrible logic of nuclear stalemate, plus the realities of Soviet conventional military might, limited U.S. options in this part of the world. After the Hungarian incident, President Eisenhower explicitly disavowed any interest in stirring rebellion in Russia's European satellites.

The death of Joseph Stalin in 1953 and the rise of Nikita Khrushchev to power in Moscow further moderated U.S. posturing. Khrushchev was no democrat, but neither was he another Stalin. He softened some brutal features of Stalinist rule and in 1956, at a Communist party congress, emotionally denounced the "crimes of the Stalin era." These signs of change in the Soviet Union encouraged a more temperate U.S. stance.

Eisenhower even saw merit in a Big Power "summit"—a term coined by Winston Churchill in 1953—despite Dulles's doubts. In July 1955, Eisenhower and Khrushchev, with their British and French counterparts, met in Geneva for the first top-level conference of the wartime allies since 1945. The gathering failed to settle such issues as European disarmament and German reunification, and Khrushchev rejected Eisenhower's "Open Skies" proposal that the two sides permit aerial surveillance of their territories. (When the Soviets spurned this idea, Eisenhower authorized a CIA plan for high-altitude photographic spying on the Soviet Union, a decision that would return to plague him.) But the somewhat nebulous "Spirit of Geneva" suggested an easing of Cold War tensions. Ignoring advice by the grim-faced Dulles that he maintain an "austere countenance" in all photographs taken at Geneva, Ike repeatedly flashed his famous grin. In 1956 the Soviets contributed to the thaw by proclaiming a policy of "peaceful coexistence" with the capitalist world.

Although the power balance in Europe somewhat stabilized, a series of regional conflicts kept Cold War antagonisms raw. These situations had complex origins, but Washington viewed them as aspects of the U.S.-Soviet struggle. This tendency is evident, for example, in U.S. policy toward the oil-rich Middle East. The formation of the new nation of Israel with U.S. backing in 1948 had produced a tide of Palestinian Arab refugees and generated bitter opposition among Arab countries deeply opposed to a Jewish state. Vowing destruction, the Arab countries launched a war against the fledgling nation.

The Eisenhower administration, like its predecessor, backed Israel diplomatically and economically, in part as a bastion against Soviet penetration in the Middle East. At the same time, Washington worked to weld the divided Arab nations into an anticommunist alliance. In 1955, pursuing his strategy of encircling the

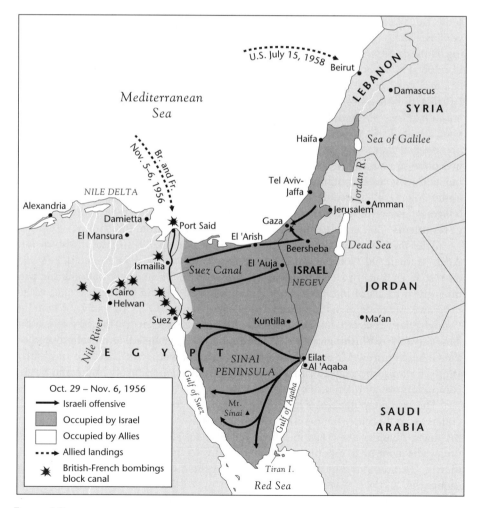

FIGURE 4.3

The Suez Crisis, 1956

Soviet Union with military treaties, Dulles masterminded the Baghdad Pact, a mutual-defense treaty linking Turkey, Pakistan, Iran, and Iraq. Although Washington did not officially join the pact (in a futile effort to avoid antagonizing Iraq's rival Egypt) it cooperated closely with the members on security matters. Furious over U.S.-Iraqi military cooperation, Egyptian leader Gamal Abdel Nasser late in 1955 allied with Moscow and stockpiled Soviet arms for the struggle against Israel. The crisis worsened in the summer of 1956, when Dulles, angered by Nasser's actions, abruptly withdrew promised U.S. aid for the construction of the Aswan Dam on the Nile, a major Egyptian development project. In retaliation, Nasser nationalized the Anglo-French-owned Suez Canal.

This sparked another war in the Middle East. As Soviet tanks rumbled through Budapest in October 1956, Israel, France, and Great Britain attacked Egypt. The Israeli army rolled across the Sinai Peninsula, while the British and French bombed Egyptian military targets and seized the canal in a paratroop assault. But the new giants on the world stage quickly squelched this imperialistic venture. The Soviet Union threatened to come to Egypt's defense and, appropriating Dulles's "massive retaliation" threat, hinted at nuclear attacks on Paris and London. The Eisenhower administration, unwilling to be sucked into war by its allies and concerned about the flow of oil, refused to support the British-French-Israeli action. A cease-fire soon followed, and the invading forces pulled back. The episode left a residue of bad feeling among the NATO allies, but a larger war had been avoided.

Rather than resorting to direct military intervention, as the British and French had done so clumsily in the Suez crisis, the Eisenhower administration more often pursued its goals through alliances, foreign aid, and clandestine action. The CIA under Allen Dulles, brother of the secretary of state, expanded its role beyond intelligence gathering to secret political activities, including the overthrow of foreign governments. CIA activities in Iran and Guatemala illustrate the pattern.

After the Soviets withdrew from Iran in 1946 (see pp. 39–40), the British-owned Anglo-Iranian Oil Company gained monopolistic control over the country's vast oil resources. But by 1951 Mohammed Mossadegh, an intensely nationalistic premier given to fits of histrionic weeping, dominated Iranian politics. As part of his program, Mossadegh nationalized the Anglo-Iranian Oil Company. When the United States rejected his aid requests, Mossadegh turned to the Soviet Union. This galvanized Washington. A 1953 coup, planned, financed, and orchestrated by the CIA, overthrew Mossadegh and consolidated power in the hands of Iran's pro-Western monarch, Shah Reza Pahlavi, who kept his nation firmly in the anti-Soviet camp for more than a quarter of a century.

The Iran coup illustrates how anticommunism could mesh with more practical concerns, in this case, the need to preserve the flow of oil. As Eisenhower noted in his diary, "Unless the areas in which these materials [such as oil] are found are under the control of people who are friendly to us and want to trade with us, then . . . we are bound in the long run to suffer the most disastrous and doleful consequences."

A similar mix of economics and ideology shaped U.S. policy toward Guatemala, a nation dominated by the United Fruit Company, a U.S. corporation with close links to the Eisenhower administration. John Foster Dulles's former law firm represented United Fruit, the assistant secretary of state for Latin American affairs held a large block of stock in the company, and the husband of Eisenhower's personal secretary headed the firm's public-relations department. In the early 1950s, United Fruit found itself less concerned with bananas and avocados than with Guatemala's leftist president, Jacob Arbenz Guzmán. Launching a land-reform program, in a country where 2 percent of the people owned 70 percent of the land, the Arbenz government appropriated more than 200,000 undeveloped acres controlled by United Fruit, at a price that the corporation considered unfair.

When a small shipment of arms from Czechoslovakia reached Guatemala in May 1954, John Foster Dulles warned that the country could become an outpost of communist power in Latin America. The Senate passed, 69–1, a resolution denouncing "Soviet interference" in Guatemala. The CIA, meanwhile, in collaboration with United Fruit, organized and financed an anti-Arbenz coup. In June, right-wing conspirators overthrew Arbenz and installed a military government headed by the CIA's handpicked man, Carlos Castillo Armas, who restored the appropriated lands to United Fruit and abandoned efforts to tax the corporation's profits. Millions in U.S. aid poured into Guatemala, and in 1956 the two nations signed a military pact.

In 1956, when the Senate rejected a proposal to tighten oversight of the CIA, Senator Richard Russell of Georgia declared, "If there is one agency of the Government in which we must take some matters on faith without a constant examination of its methods and sources, I believe this agency is the Central Intelligence Agency." This see-no-evil, hear-no-evil attitude would haunt the nation in future years.

Deepening Entanglements in Asia

The Cold War unfolded in a world also torn by resistance to European colonialism. The ambiguities to which this combination could lead emerged starkly in Vietnam, where the Vietnamese Communist party under Ho Chi Minh led the fight against the French colonial power and its puppet government in Saigon. Confronted with a choice between anticommunism and anticolonialism, the United States supported the colonial power against nationalists who were also communists. By 1954 Washington was paying 80 percent of the cost of France's war against the Vietminh, the military arm of the Vietnamese Communist party.

A crisis arose early in 1954 when the Vietminh besieged a large French garrison at Dienbienphu in northern Vietnam. Facing defeat, the French urgently requested U.S. military intervention. Some top U.S. officials favored this course. The chairman of the Joint Chiefs of Staff proposed an air strike by sixty B-29s, including the dropping of three atomic bombs. Eisenhower vetoed this operation as too risky, however, and the French garrison surrendered on May 7, 1954.

That July, the French and the Vietminh signed an armistice in Geneva that temporarily divided Vietnam at the 17th parallel, gave Ho Chi Minh control of the north, and provided for elections throughout Vietnam in 1956. Ho's negotiators left Geneva confident that all of Vietnam would soon be theirs. The United States kept its distance from the agreement and did not sign it. In fact, Washington had already decided on a major effort to foil Ho Chi Minh's plans. Drawing an analogy to a row of dominoes, Eisenhower made his position clear: If Vietnam fell to communism, the rest of Southeast Asia would inevitably follow.

The administration realized, as Eisenhower conceded in his memoirs, that the popular Ho Chi Minh would win a free election. The challenge was to find an alternative leader. Pushing aside France's puppet emperor, Washington installed as head of state in Saigon Ngo Dinh Diem, a Vietnamese nationalist and devout Catholic living a monastic existence in a New Jersey seminary. The CIA's top agent in Vietnam, Edward Lansdale; Senator John Kennedy; and Francis Cardinal Spellman all voiced confidence that Diem could rally Vietnam against communism. U.S. aid flowed to South Vietnam, and the first U.S. military advisers arrived in February 1955. Energetic, idealistic Americans, the White House thought, could certainly succeed where the French had failed.

As he pursued the Cold War in Asia, Dulles in 1954 set up yet another military alliance, the Southeast Asia Treaty Organization (SEATO). Under this agreement, the United States pledged to defend Australia, New Zealand, Thailand, Pakistan, and the Philippines against communist aggression. The treaty also extended U.S. military protection to Vietnam, Laos, and Cambodia. SEATO, an extension of Dulles's strategy of ringing the Soviet Union and China with military alliances, would provide a legalistic basis for U.S. intervention in Vietnam.

Elsewhere in Asia, relations with the People's Republic of China (PRC) remained frigid. When China's foreign minister, Zhou Enlai (Chou En-lai), offered to shake hands with John Foster Dulles at the 1954 Geneva Conference, Dulles rebuffed him. Refusing to recognize the PRC or to permit travel between China and the United States, Washington continued to recognize the nationalist regime of Jiang Jieshi on Taiwan as China's legitimate government. Eisenhower in 1953 ordered the U.S. 7th fleet out of the straits of Taiwan, supposedly unleashing Jiang to renew the war against the PRC. Privately Eisenhower and Dulles hoped for an eventual Sino-Soviet split and considered strategies for promoting such a break. But in the face of a powerful pro-Jiang "China Lobby" in Congress and the press, including the magazine publisher Henry Luce, Eisenhower publicly remained unbendingly hostile toward Mao Zedong's communist government.

Washington also supported Jiang in a long-simmering territorial dispute with the PRC. In late 1954, when the PRC began shelling two nationalist-held islands, Washington signed a treaty with Jiang pledging to resist any PRC attack on Taiwan and at least some of the disputed islands. (The treaty was deliberately vague on details.) With Lyndon Johnson providing crucial support, both houses of Congress passed resolutions authorizing Eisenhower to defend Taiwan and certain disputed islands by any means necessary. For a time, war between the United States and China—perhaps even the "massive retaliation" invoked by Dulles—over a few tiny specks of real estate seemed likely. In a March 1955 memo to Eisenhower, Dulles saw "at least an even chance that the United States will have to go to war." When the PRC made conciliatory gestures, announcing its shelling schedule in advance, for example, the crisis eased. But the deep freeze in U.S.-Chinese relations continued.

Overall, Eisenhower's first-term foreign-policy record was mixed. He ended the Korean War and showed restraint in the Suez crisis; additionally, U.S.-Soviet relations improved somewhat. Yet his public inflexibility toward China set a pattern that would continue for two decades, and decisions made in 1954 laid the groundwork for the Vietnam War.

The administration lavished attention on global issues that fit its Cold War mindset but paid scant attention to the upsurge of nationalism, as well as the poverty, illiteracy, disease, and overpopulation that plagued much of the world. The image of a globe divided between good and evil that Eisenhower evoked in his first inaugural address limited his administration's ability to respond to complex global realities. As John Lewis Gaddis has observed, this ideological rigidity represented "a fundamental failure of strategic vision."

Moreover, although Eisenhower's New Look defense policy held down military spending, it contributed to an accelerated nuclear arms race and a disconcerting willingness to consider a nuclear response in a variety of Cold War confrontations, some of them, in retrospect, quite minor. These years also saw the expansion of shadowy Cold War agencies epitomized by the CIA, with its far-flung clandestine operations. Thus, despite Eisenhower's loathing of statism, the Cold War's home-front ramifications included a significant extension of government power.

Indeed, Congress's abdication of responsibility under Cold War pressures emerged not only in its failure to rein in the CIA but also in a readiness to grant the White House broad powers to pursue almost any action that could be construed as advancing the struggle against communism. The 1955 resolution granting Eisenhower a free military hand against the Chinese in the offshore-islands dispute, in which Senator Johnson played a central role, uncannily anticipated the 1964 Gulf of Tonkin resolution (see p. 280) that would give Johnson as president a virtual blank check in Vietnam.

While embracing Truman's militantly anti-Soviet policy, the Eisenhower-Dulles team infused it with a quasi-religious fervor and extended it globally. Yet despite the apocalyptic rhetoric and the nuclear buildup, Eisenhower at crucial junctures refrained from the military response that some urged—and from any nuclear response. This restraint averted an irrevocable turn to open hostilities and gave diplomacy a chance to work toward an easing of tensions. In Eisenhower's second term, however, discussed in Chapter 6, a series of crises would wither the hopeful spirit of the mid-fifties and propel the Cold War to new levels of intensity.

While presidents must handle specific crises, they also shape the national discourse on issues of war and peace, and here, too, Eisenhower compiled a mixed record. Following the logic of the massive-retaliation strategy, he occasionally spoke of nuclear weapons as simply another arrow in the quiver. Asked in 1955 whether he would use atomic bombs if the crisis with China escalated to war, he replied, "I see no reason why they shouldn't be used just exactly as you would use a bullet or anything."

On the other hand, Eisenhower revealed a profound insight into war's toll and the social cost of military spending. A career soldier, he had been reared in a small Mennonite-related pacifist church, the Brethren in Christ, whose values remained close to him. For the cost of one modern bomber, he noted in a 1953 speech, the nation could build thirty schools or two hospitals. "Every gun made, every warship that is launched, every rocket fired," he asserted, "signifies, in the final sense, a theft from those who hunger and are not fed, those who are cold and are not clothed."

The best remembered of Eisenhower's presidential pronouncements was his 1960 farewell address, in which he reflected on the wastefulness of the arms race and warned of the growing influence, "economic, political, and even spiritual," of the "military-industrial complex" in Cold War America. This phrase referred to the large and politically influential sector of the U.S. economy, including labor unions and entire regions, that relied heavily on Pentagon contracts for research, development, and production of military weaponry.

The importance of rhetorical calls for peace can easily be exaggerated. Eisenhower presided over a major nuclear buildup, authorized unsavory CIA operations, and contributed to the expansion of the military-industrial complex even as he deplored its political and social ramifications. The irony in this complex picture is that Eisenhower, a towering twentieth-century military leader, left as his principal legacy somber warnings of an increasingly militarized American society.

The Economic Boom Rolls On

As the administration pursued the Cold War, the nation's economy continued to flourish. President Eisenhower saw a close link between these two realities. "[There is] a direct connection," he observed to Dulles in 1953, "between a prosperous and happy America and the execution of an intelligent foreign policy." A thriving United States, he believed, demonstrated the superiority of the free-enterprise system over the Soviet Union's state-run economy. The president thus had several reasons to take pleasure in the economic abundance. The business cycle underwent periodic downturns, and many Americans still lived in want, but a booming economy overall provided an upbeat accompaniment to 1950s politics and culture. In *People of Plenty* (1954), historian David Potter even argued that America's material well-being explained much of U.S. history and "the American character." Economist Walt Rostow's 1960 study, *The Stages of Economic Growth,* contended that the United States had reached the ultimate stage: "high mass consumption." With 75 percent of adult Americans owning automobiles and 87 percent of households boasting TV sets, Rostow's analysis seemed justified.

Not all was rosy. Mild recessions slowed growth in 1953–1954, 1957–1958, and 1960–1961. The first dip stemmed in part from defense-spending cuts after the Korean War. The 1957–1958 slowdown, triggered by plant overexpansion and a drop in exports, stirred uneasy memories. As unemployment rose to 7.5 percent, one Democratic wag wrote, "Eisenhower is my shepherd, I am in want. . . . He leadeth me through still factories. He restoreth my doubt in the Republican Party." Ike's popularity fell below 60 percent for the first and only time, and the Democrats won big in the 1958 midterm elections. Still, joblessness in the 1950s averaged a modest 4.6 percent, and when Ike left office, a record 73 million Americans held jobs, in contrast to 66.5 million when he took office. Per-capita income, in constant dollars, grew by about 10 percent in the 1952–1960 period.

In the midst of prosperity, poverty persisted. As in the Truman years, many Americans—including older citizens, inner-city blacks, small farmers, displaced New England millworkers, female-headed households, and rural southerners both white and black—did not share in the decade's abundance. A 1957 study by

Robert Lampman of the University of Wisconsin found that more than 32 million Americans, nearly one person in four, fell below the government's poverty line. Furthermore, although overall wealth increased, its distribution remained very uneven. In 1950 the bottom one-fifth of American families received only 4 percent of the total national income, whereas the top fifth garnered 43 percent. Ten years later, these figures remained practically unchanged.

But despite recession, pockets of poverty, and uneven income distribution, prosperity in the 1950s was real and widespread. Encouraged by federal spending and measures promoting economic growth, the GNP increased 25 percent between 1953 and 1961. Stock prices in 1954 at last regained the level that they had reached before the 1929 crash. General Motors in 1955 posted a profit of $1 billion, a first for a U.S. corporation. By 1960, on the basis of income levels, demographers defined 60 percent of Americans as "middle class." And unlike other boom times, runaway prices did not eat up rising income: inflation averaged only 1.5 percent annually in the 1950s.

Canny entrepreneurs catered to a newly affluent and mobile clientele seeking leisure-time diversion. Walt Disney, canniest of all, opened Disneyland in Anaheim, California, in 1955. An instant success, it eventually spawned an even larger version in Florida, Disneyworld.

Home construction boomed as millions of Americans purchased suburban tract houses. Many such buyers, newcomers to the middle class, spent freely on new household goods, from bedroom sets and dishwashers to TVs, power mowers, and lawn furniture. The rising birthrate stimulated sales of products for infants and children, as well as school construction. Suburban families needed transportation, and auto sales soared. Car models changed yearly amid great hoopla, and two-car households became common. To entice buyers, the typical 1950s auto flashed some 180 separate pieces of chrome or stainless steel "brightwork."

New products poured into the marketplace. The postwar vogue for plastic continued. The number of TV sets in U.S. living rooms zoomed from 1 million in 1950 to 50 million in 1960. Americans snapped up goods ranging from freezers to 45-RPM record players to electric knives to ballpoint pens. Trix, the world's first multicolored breakfast cereal, made its debut in the 1950s. Westinghouse introduced all-color refrigerators in 1956. Du Pont and other chemical companies offered a rainbow of new synthetic fabrics with such futuristic names as Orlon, Dacron, and Acrilan.

Advertising, a $12-billion-a-year industry by 1960, fueled the boom. TV screens and the pages of *Life, Collier's,* and *Saturday Evening Post* glittered with ads. "Home Means More with a Carpet on the Floor," proclaimed the Carpet Institute. "Drive More . . . It Gets Cheaper by the Mile," advised the Ethyl Corporation. "Be Happy, Go Lucky," chirped the makers of Lucky Strike cigarettes. "I Dreamed I Went Shopping in My Maidenform Bra" launched a series of fantasy ads in which lovely women cavorted in a variety of public places in their brassieres.

Credit buying spread as Americans rushed to acquire the new consumer products. The first credit card, Diner's Club, debuted in 1950; American Express cards soon followed. When Sears, Roebuck offered its own credit card, 10 million customers signed up. Signalling a long-term trend, aggregate consumer debt neared $200 billion by 1960.

The glorification of American business, rooted in the war years, continued in the 1950s. "The $9 billion-a-year chemical industry has transformed American life," gushed *Life* in 1953. "It has scrubbed the modern world with detergents, doctored it with synthetic drugs, dressed it in synthetic textiles, cushioned it with synthetic rubber and adorned it from head to toe with gaudy plastic." What the media trumpeted, scholars echoed. Economist John Kenneth Galbraith, in titling his 1958 book *The Affluent Society,* also named the era. Although critical of the way Americans expended their abundance, Galbraith did not question its reality. For him, as for many other social scientists in the 1950s, poverty scarcely existed. The typical American, Galbraith wrote, "has access to amenities—foods, entertainment, personal transportation, and plumbing—in which not even the rich rejoiced a century ago."

America's global economic situation looked bright as well. U.S. exports—mainly machinery, cars and trucks, grain, metals, and manufactured goods—nearly doubled during the decade, reaching just under $20 billion by 1960. Imports rose also, but most of what Americans bought still bore the "Made in the USA" label. In contrast to the massive trade deficits of future decades, the United States enjoyed a trade surplus of nearly $5 billion in 1960.

The rise of the multinational corporations accelerated in the 1950s, as U.S. companies built plants and distribution centers near their foreign markets. As early as 1951, twenty-three General Motors factories in seven foreign countries were producing 176,000 cars and trucks annually. By 1960 the value of such corporate investment abroad stood at nearly three times the 1950 level. This trend meshed neatly with the ideology of the Cold War, for Washington viewed corporate America's global operations as a key bulwark against communism. As U.S. capital and productive skills brought jobs and consumer goods to a waiting world, U.S. leaders thought, the lure of Marxism would surely evaporate. The State Department, the Commerce Department, and the Agency for International Development all promoted U.S. business expansion abroad.

The globalization of American capital emerged with particular clarity in the Middle East, as the postwar boom demanded more and more oil. In a little-noted turning point, the United States in 1953 for the first time imported more oil than it exported. As access to petroleum fields in the Middle East grew more vital, U.S. companies muscled aside the British firms that dominated the region. In 1950 a U.S. consortium led by Texaco, Socony (now Mobil), and Standard Oil of New Jersey (now Exxon) built a thousand-mile pipeline from Saudi Arabia to Lebanon, from which tankers shipped oil to European refineries. These developments required vast investments, not only in the Middle East but also in European production and distribution facilities. By 1960, thanks to favorable U.S. tax laws and other government policies, five of the world's seven largest oil companies (quaintly nicknamed the Seven Sisters) were American owned. Ironically, the centralized, tightly controlled structure of oil production and distribution developed by U.S. and other Western oil companies in the 1950s was imitated by the oil-producing nations themselves when they set up their own cartel, the Organization of Petroleum Exporting Countries (OPEC), in 1960.

While the flow of consumer goods was the most visible characteristic of the postwar economy, deeper structural changes were occurring as well. Business consolidation, a long-term trend, continued. In 1960 the top 5 percent of U.S. corporations earned nearly 90 percent of all corporate income. The ranks of the self-employed dwindled from 26 percent of the work force in 1940 to 11 percent in 1960. With fewer individual entrepreneurs and small-scale businesses, the American economy increasingly featured giant conglomerates that controlled an ever larger share of the market.

Other economic changes hinted at trouble ahead. As one example, the German-made Volkswagen, nicknamed the "Bug" or the "Beetle" for its rounded body, became a familiar sight on U.S. highways. Although Detroit still dominated domestic sales, the popularity of the cheap and fuel-efficient VW foretold the day when American car buyers would increasingly turn to foreign imports. In another portentous development, the number of industrial workers dropped from 39 to 36 percent of the labor force in the fifties, and the ranks of professional and service workers crept up from 40 to 46 percent. GM alone employed about one hundred thousand salaried white-collar workers by the mid-1950s. Some analysts saw this shift as an inevitable result of automation and the rise of a consumer-oriented economy, but others worried about the decline of a labor force celebrated for its feats of productivity. Home to only 6 percent of the world's population, the United States in the 1950s produced about half the globe's manufactured goods, yet the trend of labor statistics suggested that this dominance might not last. The long decline in the farm population continued as well, as mechanization and the rise of agribusinesses rendered the family farm an endangered species.

The growth of the "professional and service workers" census category attracted the notice of social observers. As early as 1951, in his study *White Collar,* sociologist C. Wright Mills speculated that the rise of a new class that shuffled paper rather than tilled the soil or ran machines would transform the very "tang and feel of the American experience." A society shaped by the farm, frontier, and factory, wrote Mills, had to rethink its fundamental identity. Seeking metaphors to convey that new identity, Mills envisioned 1950s America as "a great salesroom, an enormous file, an incorporated brain, a new universe of management and manipulation." To a nation nurtured on an image of itself as a land of free enterprise and individual opportunity, Mills offered a darker vision in which repetitive paperwork performed for large bureaucracies would become the lot of millions.

Even the feats of productivity and consumption celebrated by 1950s publicists look different from a later perspective. The statistics on energy use and raw-materials consumption cited at the time as proof of a thriving economy suggest heedlessness to a generation worried about the environment and dwindling resources. When *Life* in the 1950s gloated over foreign visitors' awe at the shelves of pet food in U.S. supermarkets, or photographed housewives posed on suburban lawns flanked by mountains of foodstuffs, detergents, and other goods representing the typical middle-class family's annual consumption, it all seemed wonderfully reassuring. In retrospect, these images evoke a society wallowing in material bounty, oblivious to the limits of the earth's resources, the ecological costs of unchecked consumption, and the chasm separating the world's rich and poor societies.

A few observers criticized the consumerist binge on aesthetic grounds—one journalist complained that "the loudest sound in the land has been the oink-and-grunt of private hoggishness"—but more typically praise for capitalism replaced the criticism of the 1930s. Columbia University professor Adolph A. Berle, who in the 1930s had warned against corporate power, now exulted that American business had "left every other system in recorded history far behind" as a mechanism for supplying consumer goods to the masses. *Life* summed up the prevailing mood by quoting a steelworker: "In the 1930s I worried about how I could eat. Now I'm worrying about where to park." Such cheery assessments resonated powerfully with the millions for whom the 1950s brought unprecedented prosperity.

The determinedly upbeat tone of this economic and social commentary was clearly linked to Cold War fears and anxieties about subversion that pervaded 1950s political culture. At a time when Americans longed for a respite to enjoy the good life that the marketers so tantalizingly promised, the menace of communism seemed especially intolerable. The conviction that America, having survived depression and war, at last stood on the threshold of a millennium of material abundance reinforced the Cold War image, shared by Democrats and Republicans alike, of a world in which the forces of good and evil grappled in deadly combat.

Walt Disney, technologically brilliant and politically conservative, both celebrated America and upheld traditional values in the 1950s. Films such as *The Lady and the Tramp* (1956), in which a scruffy male street dog and a dainty pedigreed female dog achieve a canine version of suburban domesticity, and *Sleeping Beauty* (1959), an animated version of the fairy tale of the dreaming princess at last awakened by her prince, affirmed domestic values and traditional gender stereotypes. Disneyland offered visitors an upbeat, mythic version of America as the ideal society past, present, and future, beginning with a nostalgic stroll down "Main Street U.S.A." and ending with the technological utopia of "Tomorrowland U.S.A."

The prosperity of the fifties forms the essential context of the cultural and social conflicts explored in Chapter 5. As millions of middle-class citizens—or aspirants to middle-class status—pursued their versions of the American dream, they grew puzzled and angry at those who challenged Eisenhower's America. Cultural criticism, youthful rebelliousness, and racial protest seemed so out of step with the abundance and optimism suffusing the consumer culture of the 1950s that, to many upwardly mobile white citizens, these disruptions appeared to emanate from some altogether alien realm. When Michael Harrington in 1962 published *The Other America,* a study of poverty in the United States, his title could have described the reality of a deeply divided nation as well as the economic fact of want amid plenty.

Suburban Living and Family Togetherness

As in the movie *Strategic Air Command,* the family loomed large in 1950s American culture. After two decades of depression, war, and postwar deconversion, America longed for social stability and traditional values, and no institution better embodied these virtues than the nuclear family.

The focus on the family was rooted in demography. Along with economic data, the statistics that most compelled attention in these years were those tracking marriages and births. Young people had delayed marriage in the Depression-ridden 1930s and the war-torn 1940s; now they rushed to the altar. The median age at first marriage for both men and women dropped nearly a full year between

Welcome to Suburbia! *Hundreds of would-be buyers turned out in 1951 to view the model homes planned for Levittown in Bucks County, Pennsylvania. By 1958, this de- velopment boasted more than 17,000 nearly identical houses.* (Temple University)

1947 and 1957, and these young couples had children in record numbers. The birthrate, which had hovered at around eighteen per thousand population during the 1930s, stood at more than twenty-five per thousand through most of the 1950s, a spurt of nearly 40 percent. This "baby boom" generation would influence U.S. social history throughout their lives. In the 1950s, they fueled the economic boom. In the 1960s, many would protest racism and the Vietnam War. In the seventies and eighties, many would become Yuppies—affluent young urban professionals. In the 1990s, female baby boomers would snap up books about menopause. In the twenty-first century, the toddlers of the 1950s will swamp the nation's health-care facilities and retirement homes.

As an immediate consequence of soaring marriage and birthrates, suburban growth exploded. Of course, throughout history, people have left cities to settle on the outskirts. One cuneiform letter written to the ruler of Persia in 539 B.C. boasted, "Our property . . . is so close to Babylon that we enjoy all the advantages of the city, and yet when we come home we are away from all the noise and dust." Sub- urban growth, a U.S. social trend throughout the early twentieth century, pro- ceeded at a sizzling pace in the 1950s. Aided in many cases by low-cost govern- ment loans for veterans, young couples and many older families flocked to the single-family housing developments that sprang up around America's cities. From 1950 to 1960, the suburban population surged from 21 million to 37 million. As whites abandoned the cities, low income or discriminatory real-estate policies forced most blacks and Hispanics to remain behind, a development that exacerbated the nation's racial and ethnic stratification and laid the groundwork for future problems.

The first wave of suburban construction had come in response to the severe postwar housing shortage. New housing starts had plummeted during the Depression, and the wartime migrations of workers seeking defense jobs had worsened the problem. The 2 million young married couples forced to crowd in with relatives in the early postwar years found the housing shortage especially galling.

The postwar builders who eased the shortage used techniques pioneered by Abraham Levitt and Sons. In the late 1940s, the Levitts had transformed four thousand acres of Long Island potato farms into Levittown, a community of seventeen thousand houses. Similar projects followed in Pennsylvania and New Jersey. The Levitts standardized every stage of the process, from laying out streets and hooking up utilities to pouring concrete-slab foundations and erecting as many as thirty houses a day from components assembled elsewhere. Thanks to mass-production wizardry and nonunion labor, the Levitts sold their standard two-bedroom house for less than $8,000. The average new house elsewhere cost more—about $14,500—but easy credit made these dwellings accessible to millions. The year 1955 alone saw 1.65 million new housing starts, mostly one-family residences. Farmland and rolling hills on the outskirts of the nation's cities sprouted rows of tract houses. If the gaunt-eyed sharecropper was the quintessential visual image of 1930s, the sprawling suburban housing development became the central symbol of the 1950s.

The more capacious of the new suburban residences were called "ranch houses," but despite the evocation of the Old West, the design, as historian Clifford Clark has pointed out, originated in postwar California. Many of them, in fact, had sprung up in California, the fastest-growing state in these years. "Picture windows" showcased the material goods within and opened the family to neighbors' scrutiny. The interior design expressed the occupants' aspirations to affluence, offering, for example, not one but two bathrooms, the second attached to the "master bedroom." Two-car garages sheltered what one writer called the "insolent chariots" that became another icon of the decade. Family togetherness found expression in designs that combined kitchen, dining room, and living room into one large space, plunging occupants and visitors alike into a swirl of family activity. In larger houses, a separate "family room" provided space for TV, pool table, and board games, testifying to the proliferation of leisure time.

As we shall see, these suburban communities attracted the attention of critics who deplored their alleged cultural aridity and lockstep conformity. The naysayers often overstated their case, but the suburban migration did produce communities that were relatively homogeneous economically, racially, and demographically. The Levittowners' newsletter noted: "Our lives are held closely together because most of us are within the same age bracket, in similar income groups, live in almost identical houses, and have common problems." Cut off from the extended families and social networks of the small town or the close-knit urban immigrant neighborhood, the new suburbanites turned for emotional support to the nuclear family and sometimes to their new neighbors, uprooted like themselves. The conformity and cloying family togetherness that some social observers lamented in the 1950s stemmed in part from such isolation and disorientation.

While the critics carped, the suburbs soared. Levittown, nicknamed Fertility Valley, epitomized a process that was transforming America. For millions, suburban life was a dream come true. "Houses are for people, not critics," declared Abraham Levitt's son William. "We who produce lots of houses do what is possible—no more—and the people for whom we do it think it's pretty good." When asked, suburbanites vehemently denied that they were mindless conformists. Objected one, "We're not peas in a pod. I thought it would be like that, especially because incomes are nearly the same. But it's amazing how different and varied people are."

Suburbia played an important metaphorical role in the cultural discourse of the fifties. For some, it proved the vitality of the U.S. free-enterprise system; for a vocal minority, it summed up all that they disliked about Eisenhower's America. The truth lay somewhere in between. Suburbia was not utopia, but neither was it the social disaster conjured up by some. The rise of the suburbs and their accompanying network of highways unquestionably promoted middle-class homogeneity (a category that included many blue-collar workers) and cut off millions of whites from the poor and minorities of the inner cities. Yet it also provided affordable, safe, and pleasant housing and a crucial boost up the ladder for these same millions. For them, as cultural historian Warren Susman has put it, a house in the suburbs symbolized "the world of new possibilities" that the postwar era seemed to promise.

Icon of the Eisenhower Era. *The ubiquitous jukeboxes of the 1950s initially featured syrupy love ballads, but the rock-and-roll revolution soon changed that.* (Library of Congress)

Advertisers zeroed in on the suburban market of young marrieds, children, and teenagers. As *Life* pointed out in 1959, the typical teenager, possessing phonograph, camera, sports gear, and bulging clothes closet, was a "big-time consumer." The ads' images of young parents and excited children hovering worshipfully around the new Chevrolet automobile, Zenith television set, or Kelvinator refrigerator conveyed a potent unspoken message: consumption itself gave sufficient meaning to life. Sages such as Benjamin Franklin had once urged frugality: "A penny saved is a penny earned." In an era of abundance, advertisers proclaimed, everyone had a right to share the bounty.

Targeting consumers, advertisers offered endless variations on a single image: the clean-cut nuclear family—young, white, and middle class—in a spanking new suburban house, puttering about the weed-free lawn, or gliding along in a shiny new car. Blacks, Hispanics, and Asian Americans; manual laborers; apartment dwellers; and single-parent or multigenerational families rarely appeared. To people who vaguely fit the image, the ads confirmed their vision of America. Those outside the scenario also hungered for the good life portrayed in the ads, but they knew firsthand about the vast national diversity, as well as the discrimination and deprivation, that the ads ignored.

The movies reinforced this fantasy of the United States as one big carefree suburb. Many movies, despite undercurrents of unease and menace, offered upbeat family entertainment. Five of the ten films that captured the best-picture Oscars of the 1950s were lighthearted musicals or escapist epics, including *An American in Paris* (1951), *Around the World in Eighty Days* (1956), and *Ben Hur* (1959). *Bedtime for Bonzo* (1951), featuring Ronald Reagan and Diana Lynn as the long-suffering "parents" of a chimpanzee, typified the 1950s frothy domestic comedy. In *Room for One More* (1952), a heartwarming tribute to domesticity, Cary Grant and Betsy Drake played a kindly couple who can't resist adopting children to add to their ever growing family.

TV producers loved suburbia. The few dramatic shows of the early 1950s that addressed contemporary social issues soon vanished as the sponsors demanded larger audiences. TV turned into what a later chairman of the Federal Communications Commission would call a "vast wasteland" of game shows, formulaic westerns, and vapid comedies. Shows like *Ozzie and Harriet, Father Knows Best,* and *Leave It to Beaver* peddled a standard image of middle-class family life and gender roles: supportive wives and mothers who rarely remove their aprons, benign fathers who materialize at dinnertime to resolve the petty crises of the day, wise-cracking kids who get into amusing scrapes but who ultimately recognize their parents' authority. In *I Love Lucy,* immensely popular from its debut in 1951, Lucille Ball's bandleader husband, played by Desi Arnaz, her real-life spouse, treated her like a lovable but irresponsible child. Reality and make-believe blended when the producers incorporated Ball's pregnancy and the birth of her child into the show. (Ball and Arnaz later divorced, but off camera.) Only a few shows—such as *Our Miss Brooks,* with Eve Arden as a tart-tongued, unmarried schoolteacher, and *The Honeymooners,* with Jackie Gleason and Audrey Meadows as a childless working-class couple living in a bleak apartment—broke free of gender stereotypes or hinted at the world beyond suburbia.

The "America" portrayed in 1950s mass culture masked the full reality: The nation was not all white, few teenagers fit the bland and docile stereotype of the TV sitcoms, white-collar workers did not dominate the labor force as completely as they did the media, and not all women spent their days happily in the kitchen. Nevertheless, the idealized image captured part of fifties social reality and affected the way Americans at the time and since perceived the decade.

Suburbs also influenced 1950s religious life. Church membership soared from 64 million in 1940 to 114 million in 1960. When Congress added "under God" to the Pledge of Allegiance and "In God We Trust" to the nation's coinage in 1954, religion gained an official imprimatur. Many of the newly devout were sincere in their faith, but other factors played a part as well. Church membership represented a way to overcome isolation and to embrace community norms. Indeed, as church-going increased, specific theological belief seemed to fade for some. As a vogue for ecumenical mergers swept liberal Protestantism, the media celebrated the virtue of "belief" for its own sake, regardless of substantive content. A series of Religion in American Life public-service messages sponsored by the Advertising Council ignored theological details and instead stressed the family closeness and sense of belonging that church attendance provided. One church advertised in 1955, "Lots of acquaintances, not many friends? . . . Meet future friends in church next Sunday."

Religion's social utility emerged in *The Organization Man* (1956), William H. Whyte's study of the white-collar suburb of Park Forest, Illinois. Most Park Forest residents, Whyte found, considered a church's ability to provide a sense of community more important than its creed. "This is the basic need—the need to belong to a group," one minister told him. "In a community like Park Forest, when young people see how many other people are going to church regularly, they feel they ought to."

Churchgoing also highlighted the contrast between America and the officially atheistic Soviet Union. "Against the force of Communism," *Life* observed, "we still have faith that the force of Christendom, arrayed with the other great religions of the world, will prevail." The staunchly anticommunist Catholic bishop Fulton J. Sheen became a TV celebrity of the 1950s. (Accepting an award for his show *Life Is Worth Living,* Sheen modestly thanked his writers, "Matthew, Mark, Luke, and John.") Evangelist Billy Graham, his popularity growing throughout the decade, endlessly wove the latest alarming escalation of the nuclear arms race into his sermons. Theologian Reinhold Niebuhr remained influential among intellectuals as he defined the issues of the Cold War in a series of incisive books and essays.

Like much else about the 1950s, the religious reality was complex. Despite the bland ecumenicity and suburban "social religion" of mainstream Protestantism, traditional evangelicalism remained strong. "Youth for Christ" rallies continued to draw young people, the faith healer Oral Roberts attracted throngs to his evangelistic tent, and Charles E. Fuller's *Old Fashioned Revival Hour* reached a vast radio audience each week. Evangelical bodies such as the Assemblies of God and the Southern Baptist Convention grew rapidly. The ranks of Southern Baptists increased by 2.7 million in the decade. The National Association of Evangelicals provided an organizational haven for conservative Protestant denominations. Billy Graham might use sophisticated technology and techniques in his "crusades," but the message that he sent forth in his riveting voice, Bible in hand, was the age-old one of human sinfulness and God's grace. Underestimated at the time, evangelicalism would surge to prominence in the 1970s.

Suburban culture and the rites of family togetherness had obvious implications for women, as 1950s mass media celebrated domesticity and the womanly virtues. Young housewives uncertain of their kitchen skills could rely on prepared cake mixes, Swanson's frozen TV dinners (introduced in 1953), or *Betty Crocker's Picture Cook Book* (1950). Offering the novice suburban cook a kind of surrogate mother or grandmother, General Mills Corporation gave "Betty Crocker" a makeover in the mid-fifties, graying her hair and endowing her with a wiser, more mature look. Another iconic fifties female, Mamie Eisenhower, with her perky bangs, benign if rather vague smile, and matronly "New Look" fashions, hovering charmingly in the background while her husband led the Free World, epitomized at least one version of the decade's feminine ideal.

In *A Man Called Peter* (1953), Catherine Marshall eulogized her recently deceased husband, the minister Peter Marshall, and regretted the wifely rebelliousness that she had felt living in his shadow. Adlai Stevenson told the 1955 graduates of Smith College that "the humble role of housewife" was vital to the Cold War. Wives, he advised, refurbishing an argument mossy with age, must keep their busy husbands sensitive to the finer things of life. "Keeping your man straight on the difference between Botticelli and Chianti," he suggested, was challenge enough for any woman.

Movies and television programs preached the same message of male dominance and female subordination. In *The French Line* (1954), a feisty, buxom Jane Russell was literally carried away in the final scene by a Frenchman with whom she had a shipboard romance. The lighthearted 1954 musical *Seven Brides for Seven Brothers* offered an updated and much-diluted version of the rape of the Sabine women, an ancient Roman myth of forcible abduction and male power. In 1950s ads, women invariably played subordinate roles. Ads for one household cleanser, Mr. Clean, featured a brawny superman performing tough chores for pitifully grateful housewives.

Assumptions about the subordinate role of women pervaded the business world. In a 1951 study of corporate executives, William H. Whyte found that most businessmen viewed the ideal wife as one who devoted herself to her husband's career, conversed wittily at parties while never saying anything controversial, accepted his work transfers cheerfully, soothed and satisfied her man at night, and ran the household so domestic worries need not intrude on his professional concerns. As one corporate leader put it, the business wife should maintain a "constructive attitude . . . that will liberate her husband's total energies for the job." Most corporate wives accepted this role, Whyte insisted, having concluded that "nurturing the male ego . . . is not only a pretty good fulfillment of their own ego, but a form of therapy [for the husband] made increasingly necessary by the corporation way of life."

These stereotypes distorted the actual situation of many women. The late 1940s rise in female employment continued in the 1950s, and by 1960, some 40 percent of American women held jobs. Even in this heyday of culturally promoted domesticity, millions of these working women were also wives and mothers. By mid-decade, one-quarter of all mothers with young children were wage earners as well.

Largely confined to specific sectors of the labor market and paid less than men performing the same or comparable tasks, working women continued to face discrimination. Few held political office, rose to the executive ranks in business, or became doctors, lawyers, or professors. Even a strong-willed and independent woman such as playwright Clare Booth Luce, who served as U.S. ambassador to Italy in the 1950s, owed her influence mainly to her marriage to the publisher Henry Luce. African-American, Hispanic, and other minority women faced dual discrimination on gender and racial grounds.

The rise in female employment was not accompanied by an organized women's movement, and social observers of the time downplayed its long-term significance. Frederick Lewis Allen, for example, compared "the strident suffragettes" of earlier days with the married working women of the 1950s who, he insisted, did not work as a result of feminist impulses or dissatisfaction with domesticity but only "for the double paycheck that makes it possible to buy a TV set, a car, or in many cases simply to make ends meet." As soon as the family's economic needs were satisfied, Allen implied, women would return to the kitchen, and the natural order would return.

Indeed, many housewives professed to find their lives fulfilling. As one told a psychologist in 1955, "[Marriage has given me] my place in life. I feel I am doing exactly as I am fitted—with an occasional spurt of independence growing less all the time." And Allen was doubtless correct that many women worked for practical economic reasons. The cultural climate of the 1950s did not encourage feminist theorizing or challenges to gender stereotypes. But change lay ahead, and the working women of the 1950s laid the groundwork. If they did not themselves become feminists, social researchers found, their daughters looked to them as role models and came to question the status quo.

Conclusion

Working women represented only one of many groups that did not fit the 1950s picture of America as a society of placid, prosperous, lily-white suburbs populated by happy nuclear families led by hard-working dads and contented, homebody moms. The stereotype never offered more than a blurred approximation of one slice of 1950s social reality, and forces astir in America would soon undermine it further. Nevertheless it wielded enormous power. As historian Elaine Tyler May argues, this image intersected in complex ways with the ideology of the Cold War. Policymakers' obsession with containing communism abroad paralleled a strong compulsion to contain threatening social pressures at home with a rhetoric of domesticity, consumption, and clear gender roles. The conviction that "the American way of life" faced heavy ideological assault from abroad intensified pressures to defend the status quo at home, and suburbia was one of the ideological battlegrounds. As homebuilder William Levitt put it, "No man who owns his own house and lot can be a Communist. He has too much to do."

Richard Nixon's famed 1959 "kitchen debate" with Nikita Khrushchev at a U.S. exhibit in Moscow, conducted as the two leaders gazed earnestly at automatic dishwashers and boxes of laundry detergent, epitomized the interconnectedness of global anticommunism and the home-front ideology of domesticity. It was as though the essential meaning of America resided in the suburban kitchen and its panoply of consumer products. One of capitalism's finest achievements, boasted Nixon, was to ease women's domestic labor. Khrushchev, by contrast, insisted that Soviet women were valued as workers, not just as housewives. Ridiculing U.S. kitchen technology, the Soviet leader jeered, "Don't you have a machine that puts food into the mouth and pushes it down?"

Like Nixon in Moscow, many powerful cultural voices insisted throughout the 1950s that the postwar American social order approached perfection. "Looking ahead 10 years, 25 years, there is nothing to hold us back," exulted *Life* in 1954. But *Life's* crystal ball was clouded. The twenty-five-year time frame that the magazine evoked in 1954 in fact would bring struggles against racism, ghetto riots, bitter divisions over an unpopular war, a resurgent women's movement, and deep worries about economic decline and limited resources. Indeed, the decade of the fifties itself offered ample evidence that beneath the deceptively placid surface of American life roiled powerful currents of anxiety, unease, and protest.

SELECTED READINGS

Politics in the Eisenhower Era

Charles C. Alexander, *Holding the Line: The Eisenhower Era, 1952–1961* (1975); Craig Allen, *Eisenhower and the Mass Media: Peace, Prosperity and Prime-Time TV* (1993); Stephen E. Ambrose, *Eisenhower: The President* (2 vols., 1983–1984); Jean H. Baker, *The Stevensons: A Biography of an American Family* (1996); Jeff Broadwater, *Eisenhower and the Anti-Communist Crusade* (1992) and *Adlai Stevenson and American Politics* (1994); Robert F. Burk, *Dwight D. Eisenhower* (1986); Blance Wiesen Cook, *The Declassified Eisenhower: A Divided Legacy* (1981); Fred L. Greenstein, *The Hidden-Hand Presidency: Eisenhower as Leader* (1982); Robert Griffith, *The Politics of Fear: Joseph McCarthy and the Senate* (1970) and "Dwight D. Eisenhower and the Corporate Commonwealth," *American Historical Review* (February 1982); Robert P. Newan, *Owen Lattimore and the "Loss" of China* (1992); Herbert Parmet, *Eisenhower and the American Crusades* (1972); Gary W. Reichard, *Politics as Usual: The Age of Truman and Eisenhower* (1988); David W. Reinhard, *The Republican Right Since 1945* (1983); Mark H. Rose, *Interstate Express Highway Politics, 1939–1989* (1991).

Foreign Policy and Nuclear Strategy in the 1950s

Stephen E. Ambrose with Richard H. Immerman, *Ike's Spies: Eisenhower and the Espionage Establishment* (1981); James R. Arnold, *The First Domino: Eisenhower, the Military, and America's Intervention in Vietnam* (1991); Scott D. Breckinridge, *The CIA and the Cold War: A Memoir* (1993); Robert Divine, *Eisenhower and the Cold War* (1981); Saki Dockrill, *Eisenhower's New Look National Security Policy* (1996); Norman Graebner, ed., *The National Security: Its Theory and Practice, 1945–1960* (1986); George C. Herring and Richard H. Immerman, "Eisenhower, Dulles, and Dienbienphu," *Journal of American History* (September 1984); Richard G. Hewlett and Jack M. Holl, *Atoms for Peace and War, 1953–1962: Eisenhower and the Atomic Energy Commission* (1989); Richard H. Immerman, *The CIA in Guatemala: The Foreign Policy of Intervention* (1982); Loch K. Johnson, *America's*

Secret Power: The CIA in a Free Society (1989); Burton Kaufman, *Trade and Aid: Eisenhower's Foreign Economic Policy* (1982) and *The Arab Middle East and the United States* (1996); Cole E. Kingseed, *Eisenhower and the Suez Crisis of 1956* (1995); Michael Mandelbaum, *The Nuclear Question: The United States and Nuclear Weapons, 1946–1976* (1979); Richard A. Melanson and David Mayers, eds., *Reevaluating Eisenhower: American Foreign Policy in the 1950s* (1987); Donald Neff, *Warriors at Suez: Eisenhower Takes America into the Middle East* (1981); William B. Pickett, *Dwight David Eisenhower and American Power* (1995); Ronald E. Powaski, *March to Armageddon: The United States and the Nuclear Arms Race, 1939 to the Present* (1987); John Ranelagh, *The Agency: The Rise and Decline of the CIA* (1986); Andrew Rotter, *The Path to Vietnam: Origins of the American Commitment to South East Asia* (1987); Evan Thomas, *The Very Best Men* (1995) [the early CIA].

Economic and Social Trends in the 1950s

John F. Bauman, *Public Housing, Race, and Renewal: Urban Planning in Philadelphia, 1920–1974* (1987); David P. Calleo, *The Imperious Economy* (1982); Clifford E. Clark, Jr., "Ranch-House Suburbia: Ideals and Realities," in Lary May, ed., *Recasting America: Culture and Politics in the Age of the Cold War* (1989); John Kenneth Galbraith, *The New Industrial State* (1971); Mark I. Gelfand, *A Nation of Cities* (1975); Claudia Dale Goldin, *The Great Compression: The Wage Structure in the United States at Mid-Century* (1991); Jeffrey Hart, *When the Going Was Good: American Life in the Fifties* (1982); Delores Hayden, *Redesigning the American Dream* (1984); Kenneth T. Jackson, *Crabgrass Frontier: The Suburbanization of the United States* (1985); Landon Y. Jones, *Great Expectations: America and the Baby Boom Generation* (1980); Elaine Tyler May, *Homeward Bound: American Families in the Cold War Era* (1988); Douglas T. Miller and Marion Nowak, *The Fifties: The Way We Really Were* (1977); Zane I. Miller, *Suburb: Neighborhood and Community in Forest Park, Ohio, 1935–1976* (1981); William L. O'Neill, *American High: The Years of Confidence, 1945–1960* (1986); Richard Polenberg, *One Nation Divisible: Class, Race, and Ethnicity in the United States Since 1938* (1981); Herbert Stein, *Presidential Economics: The Making of Economic Policy from Roosevelt to Reagan and Beyond* (1984).

Women in the Fifties

Wini Breines, *Young, White and Miserable: Growing Up Female in the Fifties* (1992); Ruth Schwartz Cowan, *More Work for Mother: The Ironies of Household Technology from the Open Hearth to the Microwave* (1983); Benita Eisler, *Private Lives: Men and Women of the Fifties* (1986); Cynthia Harrison, *On Account of Sex: The Politics of Women's Issues, 1945–1968* (1988); Brett Harvey, ed., *The Fifties: A Women's Oral History* (1993); Eugenia Kaledin, *Mothers and More: American Women in the 1950s* (1984); Susan Estabrook Kennedy, *If All We Did Was to Weep at Home: A History of White Working-Class Women in America* (1979); Leila Rupp and Verta Taylor, *Survival in the Doldrums: The American Women's Rights Movement, 1945 to the 1960s* (1990).

Mass Culture and Popular Religion

Glenn T. Altschuler and David I. Grossvogel, *Changing Channels: America in* T.V. Guide (1992); James L. Baughman, *The Republic of Mass Culture: Journalism, Filmmaking and Broadcasting in America Since 1941* (1992); Peter Biskind, *Seeing Is Believing: How Hollywood Taught Us to Stop Worrying and Love the Fifties* (1983); William Boddy, *Fifties Television: The Industry and Its Critics* (1990); Stephanie Coontz, *The Way We Never Were: American Families and the Nostalgia Trap* (1992); James Hudnut-Beumler, *Looking for God in the Suburbs: The Religion of the American Dream and Its Critics, 1945–1965* (1994); George

Lipsitz, *Class and Culture in Cold War America* (1981) and *Time Passages: Collective Memory and American Popular Culture* (1990); David Marc, *Democratic Vistas: Television in American Culture* (1984) and *Prime Time/Prime Movers: From* I Love Lucy *to* L.A. Law: *America's Greatest T.V. Shows and the People Who Created Them* (1992); William Martin, *A Prophet with Honor: The Billy Graham Story* (1991); Karal Ann Marling, *As Seen on TV: The Visual Culture of Everyday Life in the 1950s* (1994); Martin E. Marty, *Modern American Religion,* Vol. 3 [1941–1960] (1996); Donald Meyer, *The Positive Thinkers: Religion as Pop Psychology from Mary Baker Eddy to Oral Roberts* (1980); Nora Sayre, *Running Time: Films of the Cold War* (1982); Lynn Spiegel, *Make Room for TV: Television and the Family Ideal in Postwar America* (1992); Robert Wuthnow, *The Restructuring of American Religion: Society and Faith Since World War II* (1988).

❖ ❖ ❖

PART TWO

Dissent, Terror, Reform

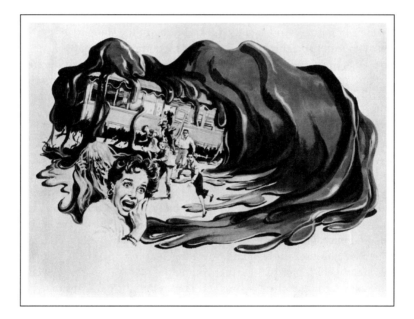

131

From some perspectives, the United States in the mid-1950s radiated confidence. Ike presided benignly in the White House, the Cold War consensus enjoyed broad support, and the media offered reassuring images of an affluent society typified by TV sitcoms' cheery white suburban families.

But no society, and certainly not Eisenhower's America, is wholly homogeneous or uncomplicated. America in the 1950s concealed more turbulence and tension than a casual observer might have guessed. This darker, more ambiguous side of the picture emerged with growing starkness as the decade wore on, coming to the light most graphically in the popular culture. Anxieties about nuclear war, alien menace, and social-conformist pressures all surfaced intriguingly in the Hollywood films of the fifties. As the baby-boom generation reached adolescence, the bland world of pop music found itself shaken and rattled by rock-and-roll. Indeed, the gyrating Elvis Presley and other new rock-and-roll icons won a fanatically loyal following among the young. The Beats sounded a jarring, assertive new note in the decade's literature. And social critics, although they stepped gingerly around fundamental issues of social injustice and class inequities in capitalist America, offered sharp-edged critiques of middle-class conformity and mass-culture insipidity.

Regarding race, the Supreme Court in 1954 thrust a profoundly important issue onto the national agenda by outlawing segregation in public schools. This ruling, reflecting years of legal effort by the National Association for the Advancement of Colored People (NAACP) and other groups, launched a civil-rights movement that would transform America. In 1955–56, African Americans in Montgomery, Alabama, organized a successful, year-long boycott of the city's segregated buses that radically challenged the political passivity of the decade. From the Montgomery movement emerged Martin Luther King, Jr., who raised a powerful moral voice against racism and on behalf of Americans' common humanity.

As the nation confronted the ugly reality of racism, a new menace materialized: radioactive fallout from U.S. and Soviet nuclear tests that posed alarming environmental and health hazards. Further roiling the political waters, citizens organized campaigns to ban nuclear testing and rein in the nuclear arms race. Moviemakers, television producers, and science-fiction writers explored the not-so-hidden terror of nuclear holocaust underlying the surface optimism of the fifties.

A further shock came in 1957 when the Soviet Union launched its space satellite, *Sputnik*. Sharply eroding the sense of invincibility in which Americans had gloried since World War II, *Sputnik* unleashed an orgy of self-doubt. Continued Cold War jousting only worsened the national attack of the jitters. Despite a partial thaw in East-West relations after Stalin's death in 1953, tensions remained high as the fifties ended.

This intensifying sense of unease contributed to the Democratic victory of 1960 that put John F. Kennedy into the White House. The "Eisenhower generation" that had led the nation during World War II now yielded to the generation that had been only in their twenties during the war. JFK, however, pursued the Cold War as relentlessly as had his predecessors. His activist, liberal foreign policy espoused economic development, social programs, and nation building as strategies for winning over the Third World. Convinced that the United States must stand firm against the Soviets, Kennedy set out to prove his toughness to the Kremlin leaders. In this spirit he presided over an expanded military budget, a nuclear-weapons buildup, an abortive invasion of Castro's Cuba, and a terrifying missile crisis. He also edged cautiously toward a deeper engagement in Vietnam. In contrast to these aggressive strategies, however, Kennedy's foreign-policy legacy also included the Peace Corps and the 1963 limited nuclear-test ban treaty.

At home, Kennedy brought the cool, pragmatic, and liberal outlook of his generation to domestic policy. In the later 1950s, congressional Democrats led by liberals such as Senator Hubert Humphrey and Senate majority leader Lyndon Johnson had helped the Eisenhower administration to pass a landmark civil-rights bill over conservative opposition. In the early sixties, with the Democrats now in control of both the White House and the Congress, the momentum for reform gained strength. President Kennedy proposed various measures but did not live to see many of them enacted. His successor, Lyndon Johnson, used the nation's grief over Kennedy's assassination and his own political genius to push through Congress a remarkable array of reforms, from civil-rights legislation to antipoverty, education, and urban measures to environmental-protection laws. The result was a surge of reform matched in the twentieth century only in the Progressive era and in Franklin D. Roosevelt's New Deal. In 1964, Johnson won one of the great landslide victories of U.S. political history.

The years 1964–65 represented the high-water mark of postwar liberalism. The civil-rights campaign lay at the heart of the reformist wave that crested in the mid-1960s. Since its beginnings in the 1950s, the movement had broadened and deepened into a full-scale assault on the South's deeply entrenched racial caste system. The moment of liberal ascendancy would prove brief. The electorate veered rightward as early as the 1966 midterm election, and by the later 1960s a troubled economy, racial divisions, and civil turmoil over the war in Vietnam had shattered the fragile consensus over which Johnson had presided in the bright noonday of his presidency.

CHAPTER 5

The Other Side of the Picture Window: Outsiders, Dissidents, and Critics in the 1950s

The year is 1954, and in movie houses and drive-ins across America, wide-eyed audiences are watching *Them!*, an early entrant in a deluge of "mutant" movies. The film depicts a storybook family—father, mother, and daughter—vacationing in New Mexico. But even before the action begins, disaster has struck: Monstrous creatures have ripped apart the family's camper and brutally murdered the parents. Only the daughter survives, so traumatized that she cannot speak except to scream, "*THEM!!!*" Soon we learn that the killers are giant ants, hatched from the radioactive soil of the atomic-bomb test site at Alamogordo, who spread death and destruction in their insatiable search for sugar. The army finally exterminates the last of the loathsome mutants in the Los Angeles storm sewers.

In its bizarre fashion, *Them!* epitomized a central paradox of the 1950s. Americans should have been happy and confident. They had won a terrible war, and a booming economy, cheap suburban housing, and abundant consumer products placed the good life within reach of millions. Hollywood, television, and mass magazines provided diversion. But an undercurrent of anxiety reflected in movies, youthful rebelliousness, introspection by troubled intellectuals, fear of nuclear tests, and rising waves of protest against racial segregation all belied the upbeat mood. The United States in the 1950s was not as trouble-free as a quick visit to suburbia or a glance at television might have suggested. Yet the decade's ill-defined social issues made their presence felt only sporadically and indirectly.

Domestically, prosperity's byproducts—rampant materialism, a homogenized mass culture, and the enormous growth of a desk-bound white-collar class—roused dissident artists, writers, and intellectuals. Was a nation noted for its individualism becoming timid and conformist? Alexis de Tocqueville had raised the question in the 1830s, and it resurfaced with fresh urgency in the 1950s. Furthermore, although John Kenneth Galbraith's *The Affluent Society* focused on the persistence of want amid abundance, many people misunderstood its ironic title as a celebration of U.S. prosperity. In 1959 economist Robert Lampman of the University of Wisconsin estimated the size of the American underclass at a whopping 32 million.

Journalist Michael Harrington published several articles in small-circulation magazines between 1950 and 1960 with titles such as "Our Fifty Million Poor." At the time, these reports attracted little notice. Untold numbers of poor Americans struggled in rural regions and inner cities, but the realities of poverty and wide economic inequities remained relegated to the periphery of the nation's consciousness.

Globally, the nuclear arms race and Cold War anxieties about Moscow's alleged drive for world domination constantly undercut efforts to sustain a positive cultural tone. Nevertheless, in this arena, too, tensions rarely found political voice except in McCarthyite hysteria about domestic subversives.

With two notable exceptions—the movement to halt nuclear testing and an emerging civil-rights campaign—protest impulses stood little chance against the stand-pat outlook expressed in Eisenhower's two electoral victories. Suburban complacency and Cold War clichés were too powerful. And despite the increasing tempo of civil-rights activism in the South, awareness of racism as a *national* issue penetrated white America only slowly and fitfully.

In contrast to the 1930s or the 1960s, reform currents flowed sluggishly in Eisenhower's America. Rather than coalescing into a single movement, discontent with the status quo found a variety of outlets, from the writings of critics and novelists to the world of jazz and folk-music clubs, drive-in theaters, coffee houses, rock-and-roll concerts, antinuclear marches, and southern black churches.

Films of the Fifties: Undercurrents of Menace

The Hollywood dream factory both shapes and reflects American hopes and fears, and the films of the fifties are no exception. They mirrored the decade's ambiguities, with some offering escapist fare and endorsing conventional social values but others revealing the anxieties of the era and laying bare more about the fifties than moviemakers may have intended.

The messages of these films were rarely obvious. Producers, their eye on box-office receipts, crafted movies that appealed to the largest possible audiences. Many films of the decade therefore can be interpreted in a variety of ways. In Howard Hawks's *The Thing* (1951), for example, the alien blob buried in the Arctic ice may represent communist subversion, repressed sexuality, modern science—or simply an alien blob. The popular western *High Noon* (1952) invites a similar array of interpretations. As the movie opens, badman Frank Miller rides into town to kill former marshal Will Kane (Gary Cooper), who had sent him to prison years before. Kane expects the townspeople to rally to his aid, but they are a cowardly lot and abandon Will to confront Miller and his two equally unsavory brothers alone. Once the Miller boys lie dead in the street, the townspeople rush out to congratulate Kane, but in disgust he throws his badge in the dust and rides out of town.

High Noon's director and scriptwriter, opponents of McCarthyism, intended the film as a critique of those who remained silent in the face of McCarthy's demagoguery. Did moviegoers catch this subtle political message, or did they view the film as a traditional western extolling individualism, a classic American theme? Kane's Quaker bride (Grace Kelly) is portrayed as naive in her efforts to persuade him to avoid the showdown. Thus, the film could also be read as a Cold War tract preaching the inevitability of an H-bomb "shootout" with the Russians.

Despite the ambiguity in many 1950s movies, an underlying pattern emerges. Typically, a menace lurks beneath a tranquil surface. The films begin with cheerful, everyday scenes in an ordinary community, followed by mounting tension as inexplicable events shatter the routine. The giant ants of *Them!* spawned a lurid progeny of shrinking men, towering women, prehistoric monsters jolted from their long slumber, and unclassifiable creatures from black lagoons.

The Invasion of the Body Snatchers (1956) is particularly terrifying because the monsters appear in human guise. As the movie opens, Dr. Miles Bennell (Kevin McCarthy) gradually realizes that all is not well in his California town. People look the same, but they are different. As Miles's girlfriend Becky says of her Uncle Ira, "There's something missing. Always when he talked to me there was a certain look in his eyes. Now it's gone. There's no emotion." Uncle Ira is actually a robotlike clone, hatched from a pod brought from outer space by aliens. The pod people are zombies, carrying out the malevolent wishes of their alien masters.

Like many other 1950s movies, *Invasion of the Body Snatchers* played on different anxieties. Most obvious is the Cold War obsession with subversion, the suspicion that alien ideologies menaced America, and that one's best friend or neighbor could be a traitor. Unlike earlier stereotypical enemies such as the "redskins" of countless westerns or the "Japs" of World War II propaganda, the communists *looked* like everyone else, yet they threatened everything Americans held dear.

As pod people take over the town, Becky and Miles flee for their lives. Finally Becky herself falls victim to the pods. In the film's original ending, Miles stares wild-eyed at the camera and screams, "You're next!" In the more upbeat ending actually released, a police official telephones Washington and shouts, "Get me the FBI!" Even so paranoid a film as *The Invasion of the Body Snatchers* had to offer assurance of some center of stability and authority.

Other movies exposed the fragility of the middle-class family ideal. In William Wyler's *The Desperate Hours* (1955), an escaped convict terrorizes a storybook suburban family. In the 1958 potboiler *I Married a Monster from Outer Space*—a knockoff of *Invasion of the Body Snatchers*—a housewife discovers that her model husband is not what he seems. Whatever the specific danger in these films, the pervasive mood was one of impalpable menace lurking just beyond the campfire. In *The Thing*, the scientist who wants to communicate with the mysterious entity rather than destroy it is portrayed as dangerously naive. As he approaches the blob, calling out, "I am your friend," the malicious creature zaps him. This sense of encroaching horror—of amorphous but nevertheless deadly forces that cannot be understood, only destroyed—captured a powerful undercurrent in the national mood.

Rebellious Youth

Movies of the fifties often featured alienated or ominous teenagers very different from the cheery juveniles of the TV sitcoms. In *Rebel Without a Cause* (1955), James Dean, Natalie Wood, and Sal Mineo play a trio of disturbed youths from affluent homes who are frustrated with their privileged lives and hell-bent on trouble.

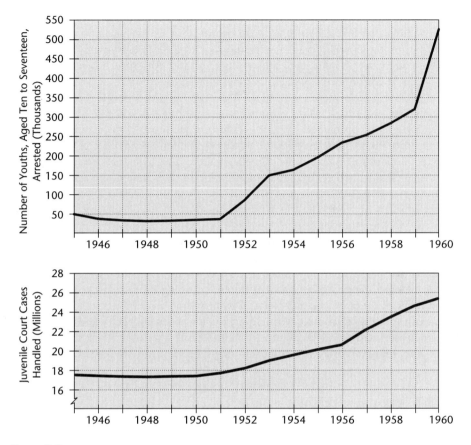

FIGURE 5.1

(a) *Number of Youths, Aged Ten to Seventeen, Arrested, 1945–1960*
(b) *Juvenile Court Cases Handled, 1945–1960*

SOURCE: *Historical Statistics of the United States: Colonial Times to 1970,* U.S. Department of Commerce, Bureau of the Census.

Dean's character races hot rods and pretends to be tough. Actually, he is unsure of his masculinity because his father is a poor role model; Dad wears aprons and helps with the housework. Natalie Wood's character, troubled by her uptight father's inability to deal with her budding sexuality, has turned to promiscuity.

 Rebel Without a Cause pictured a suburbia awash in psychopathology. The social order as a whole is presented favorably, however, and by the end, Dean and Wood have fallen in love (with Mineo as a kind of surrogate child) and have begun to accept middle-class values. *Rebel Without a Cause* was thus a fundamentally conservative film, idealizing Dean's juvenile-court officer and other therapeutic experts. In the 1930s, experts had blamed delinquency on poverty. In the 1950s, film portrayals of the affluent middle class faulted psychosexual problems instead.

 Far more sinister were *The Wild One* (1953) and *Blackboard Jungle* (1955). In *The Wild One,* based on an actual incident, Marlon Brando and Lee Marvin play the leaders of rival motorcycle gangs that invade a California town. When a waitress asks Brando what he's rebelling against, Brando sneers, "What have you got?" A message after the opening credits made the movie's point frighteningly clear: "This is a shocking story. It could never take place in most American towns—but it did in this one. It is a public challenge not to let it happen again."

Blackboard Jungle offered a sanitized look at inner-city schools, a subject rarely examined in the 1950s. After various scenes of violence and mayhem at North Manual High, accompanied by a rock-and-roll soundtrack, an idealistic teacher (Glenn Ford) finally wins over his tough class and even persuades one bright black student (Sidney Poitier) to apply to college. Like *The Wild One, Blackboard Jungle* treats its unsettling subject matter cautiously. Not only is the ending optimistic, but the movie insists that schools like North Manual are rare. When Ford visits an orderly suburban high school, a teacher assures him, "For every school like [North Manual] there are thousands like this one." To prove it, he takes Ford to an assembly where rows of well-groomed youths are fervently singing the national anthem.

The free-floating discontent of many 1950s youth found expression above all in music. The early-fifties pop-music scene was numbingly bland, with singers such as Perry Como, Bing Crosby, and Pat Boone crooning insipid love ballads devoid of authentic emotion. Rock-and-roll and its first superstar, Elvis Presley, defied all that. Born in 1935 in Tupelo, Mississippi, Elvis was a nineteen-year-old truck driver when he recorded demo tapes for Sun Records, a small Memphis label, in 1954. The young entertainer crafted his singing style from rhythm and blues. Indebted to legendary black singers such as Robert Johnson of Mississippi, R&B, with its powerful rhythms and raw sexual energy, was popular with African Americans but largely unknown to whites. Elvis blended R&B with country music and the gospel songs of his boyhood Assemblies of God church, concocting a potent formula that scored an instant hit. Midway through Eisenhower's first term, teenagers thrilled deliriously to his version of such R&B standards as "That's All Right Mama."

The new star enthralled screaming audiences, his records sold phenomenally, and youth-oriented radio stations programmed hours of rock-and-roll. Elvis's "Heartbreak Hotel" topped the charts in 1956 in three categories: pop, country, and R&B. Songs such as "I'm All Shook Up" and "Don't Be Cruel" sustained his popularity. Ultimately, he would be credited with twenty-one-million-record sellers. Some male fans even adopted his glistening pompadour hairstyle. As the dulcet tones of the crooners gave way to the shouts, moans, percussive beat, and open eroticism of rock-and-roll, teenagers' record hops became loud, rocking affairs, the antithesis of the well-chaperoned high-school dances of a few years earlier.

Elvis was king, but other rock stars won fame as well. Bill Haley and the Comets won fame with "Rock Around the Clock," heard on the soundtrack of *Blackboard Jungle.* Out of Georgia burst the black R&B singer Little Richard (Richard Wayne Penniman) with such hits as "Tutti Frutti" (1955) and "Long Tall Sally" (1956). Chuck Berry, the product of a lower-middle-class black neighborhood in St. Louis, was a reform-school veteran and autoworker when he formed an R&B band in 1953. His first big hit, "Maybelline," came in 1955. In Texas, teenager Charles "Buddy" Holly assembled a band and achieved stardom before his death in a plane crash in 1959. In the barrio of East Los Angeles, Ritchie

Valens (his surname shortened from Valenzuela) headed a popular Chicano rock-and-roll group until he perished in the same plane crash.

The mainstream culture recoiled from this multiethnic explosion of raucous music making. Church leaders denounced rock-and-roll as indecent and attacked Elvis's lyrics and the suggestive hip thrusting that earned him the nickname Elvis the Pelvis. In a 1955 Florida concert, police insisted that Presley sing without moving his midsection. "Elvis is a symbol, of course, but a dangerous one," wrote one worried parent. "The gangster of tomorrow is the Elvis Presley type of today."

Indeed, fears of "juvenile delinquency," comparable to a later generation's concern about drugs, swept America. Movies like *Rock All Night* (1957), *Dragstrip Girl* (1957), and *High School Hellcats* (1958) fed the fantasy of an entire generation sliding into anarchy. Stories of rebellious youth filled the newspapers. In 1953 a U.S. Senate subcommittee investigated the problem. Under Senator Estes Kefauver of Tennessee, the group called a parade of expert witnesses and received a flood of mail from concerned parents.

Leonard Bernstein elevated gang warfare to the status of Shakespearean tragedy in his 1957 hit musical, *West Side Story,* but anxieties about the younger generation continued. These fears had a basis in fact: The number of young people arrested on charges from petty vandalism to murder rose sharply in the fifties. In New York City, historian James Gilbert notes, arrests of youths under the age of sixteen more than tripled in the decade. But the "juvenile delinquency" hysteria also expressed more intangible concerns about the youthful subculture emerging in 1950s America, often linked to broader Cold War fears. Moral rot from within and the communist menace from without, many believed, represented two facets of the same danger. As the head of the Chicago Crime Prevention Bureau put it, "The obscene material that is flooding the Nation today is another cunning device of our enemies, deliberately calculated to destroy the decency and morality which are the bulwarks of society." The communists' alleged skill at "brainwashing" the innocent into accepting their doctrines thus dovetailed psychologically with fears about the power of the mass media to sabotage parental authority and to peddle alternative cultural values to the young.

In *Seduction of the Innocent* (1954), psychiatrist Frederic Wertham attacked comic books that glorified crime and violence. Other pretended experts on teenage rebelliousness indicted not just the comics but the mass media in general. Harvard sociologist Pitirim Sorokin warned in *The American Sexual Revolution* (1956) of a "sexualized" youth culture and exhorted parents to protect their children from rock-and-roll, suggestive movies, and violent, crime-ridden radio shows.

Radio disc jockeys adored by the young struck frightened elders as demonic Pied Pipers luring children away from their parents' influence. DJ Alan Freed, using the name Moondog, popularized rock-and-roll on his radio shows, first in Cleveland and then, after 1954, in New York City. In 1955 a Buffalo DJ caused a massive traffic jam by broadcasting his show from atop a large downtown billboard. He urged youthful drivers in the cars below to blow their horns if they liked "Rock Around the Clock," the song that he was playing. Hundreds obeyed, creating a deafening cacophony. The DJ spent six hours in jail.

Generational conflict that in the sixties would erupt in campus protests and street marches took the form in the fifties of angry quarrels over music, dress, and hairstyles. A Texas school board, reported *Cosmopolitan* magazine in 1957, banned from high schools "tight blue jeans worn low, or ducktail haircuts," citing the connection between "undisciplined dress and undisciplined behavior." The rock revolution responded to such pronouncements in the title of one hit song: "Yakkety Yak."

This distinct youth culture had its roots in larger social changes of the postwar period. With young people remaining in school through their teens, the American high school became a cultural bazaar where youth of diverse backgrounds shared tastes and fads. As early as 1950, a White House Conference on Children noted with alarm that "the standards of the lowest class" of youth threatened to infect "the boys and girls of other social groups." Furthermore, the economic boom gave young people new discretionary income, reducing their dependence on parents. Many high school students held part-time jobs, boosting their buying power even more. Increasingly, too, teenagers had access to a family car or owned one of their own. Hot rods, congregated at drive-in hamburger shops or other oases, became a ubiquitous symbol of teenage autonomy.

The rock-and-roll revolution gave youth a way to protest the blandness and superficiality of 1950s mass culture. Although the decade's artists and their fans did not evolve into a politically conscious counterculture, they laid the groundwork for a distinctive style among the baby-boom generation's advance guard. In the 1960s, that style would take an overtly political turn.

Ironically, the youth subculture rested on the same affluence that underlay the middle-class suburban culture that it challenged. The phenomenon spread, for example, via the radios and 45-RPM record players in countless teenagers' bedrooms. Indeed, corporate America profited hugely as it supplied the records, movies, fashions, foods, automobile accessories, and reading matter by which the younger generation defined itself. In a further irony, the dominant culture partially absorbed and tamed rock-and-roll and youthful unrest. As early as 1956, Elvis signed a movie contract and appeared (from the waist up) on Ed Sullivan's TV variety show. The Presley movies and soundtrack albums of the late fifties and early sixties proved bland and forgettable. The mass-entertainment industry neutralized Presley's iconoclastic energy and turned him, with his full cooperation, into a conventional romantic idol and pop star. Ceasing to produce innovative music, he became merely a celebrity. Toward the end of his life (he died in 1977), even an admirer observed, "Elvis transcends his talent to the point of dispensing with it altogether." Unsurprisingly, the older Presley kept his distance from the musical and cultural revolution of the sixties that he had helped spawn. He even volunteered his services as an FBI informant; J. Edgar Hoover tactfully declined the offer.

As the mainstream culture absorbed and co-opted the rock-and-roll revolution, the public's obsession with juvenile delinquency faded. By 1959 a movie such as *Teenagers from Outer Space* could celebrate the virtues of suburban togetherness as perceived by a familyless time traveler from the future. The alien mourns, "I have learned how it once was: families, brothers, and sisters. There was happiness; there was love." *Blue Denim* (1959), starring Brandon De Wilde as the new James Dean (Dean had died in an auto crash in 1955), offered a similarly reassuring message. At the film's end, teenage rebel De Wilde sees his error and joins the family for dinner as his father says grace. But the waning of generational conflict proved short-lived. Both the strength of youthful dissent, and society's ability to absorb that dissent, would be tested again in the late 1960s, with the stakes incomparably higher.

Cultural Resistance: The Arts and Social Criticism in Cold War America

Some artists and social critics also expressed doubts about Eisenhower's America. But in contrast to the Depression-ridden 1930s and the politicized 1960s, the dissidents of the 1950s rarely took political stands. They focused on the psychological and cultural toll of affluence, not on poverty, economic inequities, or the unequal diffusion of power across the lines of class, race, and gender. Rather than proposing structural changes in society, they looked for ways whereby the individual could achieve a more authentic existence in a materialistic, conformist age. The existentialist credo of French intellectuals Jean-Paul Sartre and Albert Camus, with its focus on the dilemma of individuals' seeking meaning in a meaningless universe, enjoyed a vogue on U.S. college campuses in these years.

In the realm of jazz, the postwar cultural crosscurrents encouraged the decline of swing and the rise of bebop. Swing, popular in the 1930s and the war years, had evolved from its African-American roots to reach a mass audience through the big bands of Benny Goodman, Tommy Dorsey, and others. Bebop, featuring long, introspective solos, found favor with small jazz ensembles instead. Whereas swing offered jazz adaptations of familiar melodies, bebop involved complex improvisation. Demanding close concentration by the listener, bebop arose outside a profit-driven music industry that, in the view of bebop artists, had diluted the authentic jazz tradition. Tense and edgy, bebop expressed the anxious underside of the fifties. Bebop musicians, turning their backs on the suburban middle class, shared their highly personal vision with small audiences of rapt fans in smoky jazz clubs.

White bandleaders and musicians had dominated swing; bebop's high priests were African American, including trumpeter Dizzy Gillespie, drummer Max Roach, pianist Thelonious Monk, and saxophonists Charlie Parker and Lester Young. Although bebop musicians avoided direct political engagement, they saw their music as an expression of black consciousness and thus politically significant. Bebop stood "in the vanguard of social change," Gillespie later wrote: "We didn't . . . make speeches or say 'Let's play eight bars of protest.' We just played our music. . . . The music proclaimed our identity."

In the visual arts, abstract expressionism remained the most vital movement of the 1950s. Like bebop, this trend represented an intensely individual art form rather than overt social or political commentary. Jackson Pollock's career illustrates the shift. Pollack began in the late 1930s as a student of Thomas Hart Benton, who had portrayed workers, farmers, and cowboys in realistic canvases and murals. After World War II, however, Pollack began to drip and swirl paints directly onto large canvases stretched on the floor. Initially, the new style aroused much ridicule. The magazine illustrator Norman Rockwell produced a drip painting in imitation of Pollack (as if to say: "Anybody can do it") but as part of a larger realistic painting in which a middle-aged museumgoer scratches his head in be-mused wonderment at the abstract style.

Like the beboppers, leading abstract expressionists such as Pollack, Robert Motherwell, and Mark Rothko viewed their innovations as a response to the post-war world. "Modern art to me is nothing more than the expression of . . . the age that we're living in," Pollack commented in 1950. "The modern painter cannot ex-press this age, the airplane, the atom bomb, the radio, in the old forms. . . . Each age finds its own technique." But abstract expressionism's relationship to the larger world of 1950s political culture remains complex. Unquestionably, these artists abandoned the realism and overt social engagement that had characterized U.S. art in the 1930s. Indeed, they rejected an entire tradition of literal representation. Whether this break with the past and turn to pure self-expression represented a re-action to the atomic bomb and the mass media, as Pollack implied, it did suggest skepticism about the political relevance of art. To this extent, abstract expression-ism mirrored the decade's move away from political engagement. Yet that same turning inward also implicitly mocked those who were summoning the nation to mobilize for the Cold War struggle. To this extent, abstract expressionism could be seen as a protest against intellectual conformity.

But like rock-and-roll, both bebop and abstract expressionism experienced the dominant culture's capacity to adapt even incipiently subversive cultural manifes-tations to its own purposes. Indeed, the line between "mainstream" and "dissident" in 1950s culture is hazy at best. Musicians such as Gillespie and artists like Pollack may have felt alienated from the postwar consensus, but the government and the media promoted their art as weapons in the ideological Cold War. Gillespie, for example, gave concerts in Europe for the State Department in the late 1950s, im-plicitly countering allegations of racism in America and underscoring Western cul-tural freedom at a time when Moscow forbade jazz and even kept classical com-posers like Dmitri Shostakovitch on a tight rein. Similarly, an abstract expressionist exhibit toured Europe in the 1950s with a State Department subsidy, offering pointed contrast to the communist world's heavy-handed "socialist realism." *Life* magazine promoted Pollack and abstract expressionism as proof not only of New York's postwar artistic dominance but also of the Free World's cultural openness.

Yet the Cold War's cultural ramifications could cut both ways. While Wash-ington patronized some artists and writers, radicals and leftists suffered. Folksinger Pete Seeger, an unabashed leftist and Cold War critic, found his career stymied. The black singer Paul Robeson, long identified with communist causes, left the country in 1958.

On the literary front, a group of younger writers cast a jaundiced eye on the suburbs and material abundance. John Cheever's *The Wapshot Chronicle* (1957) dis-sected the lives of contemporary New Englanders cut off from their ancestral roots. Cheever's short stories in the *New Yorker,* peopled with white-collar workers who commute from unrewarding jobs in New York City to bland Connecticut suburbs, commented even more pointedly on alienation in the midst of prosperity.

If Cheever offered a bleak picture of the upper middle class, John Updike pre-sented a mordant view of its lower fringes. Updike's *Rabbit Run* (1960) features Harry "Rabbit" Angstrom, a high-school basketball hero who as a young family man in the fifties senses that his best years are already behind him. "He feels underwater," Updike wrote, "caught in chains of transparent slime." Bored by his job as a vacuum-cleaner salesman and lacking inner resources, Harry finds illicit sex his only anodyne to despair. Things get worse: His alcoholic wife, Janice, accidentally lets their baby drown in its bath. In typical 1950s fashion, Angstrom has no real understanding of his malaise, its larger social context, or steps that he might take to alleviate his troubles.

A few writers commented more directly on the political and cultural realities of the 1950s. Arthur Miller's *The Crucible* (1953), a play ostensibly about Salem witchcraft, was widely and correctly read as an attack on McCarthyism. Ray Bradbury's science-fiction story *Fahrenheit 451* (1953) projected the Cold War, McCarthyism, and mass culture into the future. In Bradbury's dystopia, the state has outlawed books entirely; any volumes discovered are burned by the authorities. (Four hundred fifty-one degrees Fahrenheit is the temperature at which paper ignites.) The masses are narcotized by a state-run TV network whose propaganda and mindless entertainment dominate giant wall screens that surround the living room. Only a handful of dissidents, who have memorized the classics and recite them to each other in remote hideaways, preserve humanity's cultural heritage. Bradbury's novel powerfully evoked the sense of a radical minority's struggle to preserve both its own independence of thought and a vanishing cultural tradition.

Expressing the cultural coming of age of immigrants who had arrived several decades earlier, young Jewish writers produced notable novels in the fifties. Philip Roth's *Goodbye Columbus* (1959), a collection of stories about urban middle-class Jewish life, conveyed the same claustrophobia that pervades the stories of Cheever and Updike. Saul Bellow's *The Adventures of Augie March* (1953) told of a young Chicago Jew's quest for authenticity and meaning, the classic theme of the fifties. (Augie's search eventually brings him to Mexico on a bizarre but perhaps symbolic project: He trains American eagles to capture iguanas.) Bellow's *Henderson the Rain King* (1959) takes its hero even farther afield, as he abandons wife, family, and stifling daily routine to immerse himself in African tribal culture.

Some novelists criticized 1950s culture implicitly; the Beats challenged it frontally.* The Beat movement began after World War II when Allen Ginsberg, a Columbia University undergraduate, befriended Jack Kerouac, a Columbia dropout of working-class origins. Both men were influenced by William S. Burroughs, who chronicled his heroin addiction in the pseudonymous 1953 novel *Junky* and in *Naked Lunch* (1959). The Beat movement coalesced in 1955 during a gathering at San Francisco's City Lights Bookstore, where Ginsberg read *Howl,* a hallucinatory, drug-influenced poem excoriating America as a ravenous beast sacrificing its young on the altars of commerce and technology.

Kerouac's *On the Road* (1957), a sprawling autobiographical novel, recounts the adventures of two central characters, one based on Kerouac himself and the other on Neil Cassady, a figure on the fringes of the Beat movement, as they crisscross the country by car and bus. *On the Road,* together with *Howl,* launched the Beats' brief celebrity and notoriety.

---

* The origin of the term *Beat* is unclear. Jack Kerouac, asserting the movement's fundamentally religious impetus, claimed that it was short for "beatitude."

The Beat movement streaked like a Fourth of July rocket across the grey skies of Eisenhower's America. College students, young people, and the minority dissatisfied with the blandness of mass-media pap, welcomed its outrageous assertiveness. *On the Road* sold half a million copies, and *Howl* (published in 1956) became a campus favorite, its cachet heightened by efforts to suppress it as obscene. Like the satirical songs of Tom Lehrer and the mordant humor of coffeehouse comics Lenny Bruce and Mort Sahl, the Beats appealed to those seeking alternatives to banality. In common with Elvis and other luminaries of rock-and-roll, Ginsberg, Kerouac, and lesser Beats became cultural heroes of the disaffected, their literary iconoclasm underscored by their readiness to flout middle-class taboos. Asked at a poetry reading what his work meant, Ginsberg responded, "Nakedness," and proceeded to remove all his clothes.

Repudiating the middle-class propriety of Levittown and *Life,* the Beats substituted a cult of spontaneity, immediate sensation, and "transcendent" perceptions induced by various mind-altering substances. In a decade that idolized family life and domesticity, they cultivated frenetic movement, fleeting relationships, and casual sex. *On the Road,* which begins with the breakup of the narrator's marriage, is a classic tale of footloose males seeking freedom outside the constricting bonds of familial obligation. In the male-centered and often homoerotic world of the Beats, women provided diversion but otherwise played little role.

The Beats idealized outsiders—criminals, addicts, inner-city blacks, the truckers whose sixteen-wheelers rumble through the night—as more vibrant than the washed-out middle class. In the famous opening of *Howl,* Ginsberg wrote:

> I saw the best minds of my generation destroyed by madness,
> starving hysterical naked,
> dragging themselves through the negro streets at dawn
> looking for an angry fix

Novelist Norman Mailer, although not part of the movement, shared the Beats' fascination with the underclass. In his essay "The White Negro" (1957), Mailer romanticized the intense and dangerous world of "hipsters"—criminals, juvenile delinquents, and streetwise blacks—as an alternative to white middle-class America. This romanticizing of outside groups, however, was tainted not only by misogyny but also on occasion by ethnic prejudice. Describing the efforts of his fictional alter ego to persuade a young Hispanic woman to have sex with him in a Los Angeles hotel room, Kerouac writes, "How I moaned and pleaded, and then I got mad and realized I was pleading with a dumb little Mexican wench, and I told her so."

Anticipating a vogue for Eastern religions that would crest in the 1970s, the Beats sprinkled their writings with knowing references to *Satori, Karma,* and Zen Buddhism. But for all their cultural exoticism, they were solidly in the American grain. Their quest for inner awareness recalled Ralph Waldo Emerson and the transcendentalists. Ginsberg's summons to "return to nature and . . . revolt against the machine" echoed early-nineteenth-century Romantic poets and painters. Kerouac's *On the Road* evoked Huckleberry Finn's preference for freedom over civilization and Walt Whitman's exuberant patriotism. Looking eastward from San Francisco Bay, the narrator exults in "the great raw bulge and bulk of my American continent."

In typical fifties fashion, the mass media soon took up and exploited the Beats. *Life* ran a feature on the movement in 1957, and Kerouac, looking remarkably like James Dean, read from his work on a network television talk show. The "Beatnik" or "Hipster"—bearded, lascivious, and unkempt—became for the middle class a symbol of social and sexual menace. A 1950s potboiler, *Pads Are for Passion,* bore the alarming caption, "Anita Was a Virgin—Till the Hipsters Got Hold of Her."

The Beat movement, like rock-and-roll, anticipated the more politicized counterculture of the 1960s. Indeed, Ginsberg would become a campus guru in the Vietnam War era. Kerouac's gushy patriotism soon turned rancid, however, and he, like Presley, ended up denouncing the young radicals of the 1960s. But however they viewed their progeny, the Beats' role as fomenters of cultural change ensures their place in the history of the Eisenhower era.

On the whole, the literature of the 1950s, like the art, was more introspective than political or socially engaged. Yet this work had political implications, for in focusing on the individual search for authenticity, authors challenged the conformism and standardization of thought that they saw as dangerous consequences of the Cold War, mass culture, and consumer capitalism.

Amid this cultural ferment, social and cultural critics offered their own dissections of postwar America. William H. Whyte's already mentioned *The Organization Man,* for example, offered a wide-ranging exploration, rich in anecdotal detail, of middle-management business culture. An editor of the business magazine *Fortune,* Whyte saw much to praise in U.S. capitalism. But he deplored its psychological effects. The modern corporation, he argued, bred conformity while discouraging originality, risk taking, and any behavior that might be labeled eccentric or offbeat.

Dwight Macdonald, in a series of essays reprinted in his 1962 book *Against the American Grain,* acerbically criticized both mass culture and what he called midcult, or the watering down of high culture to expand its commercial appeal. Skewering a whole herd of sacred cows, Macdonald lambasted the Book-of-the-Month Club, the *Encyclopedia Britannica*'s "Great Books" program, and the Revised Standard Version of the Bible (1952), which, he charged, reduced the King James Bible's majestic English to the level of prose produced by a committee.

Historian Daniel Boorstin in *The Image* (1961) criticized the mass-produced culture made possible by modern technology. Americans, he argued, were settling for secondhand experience. They listened to Muzak instead of going to concerts, bought Van Gogh prints instead of visiting museums, took vacations prepackaged by travel agents, skimmed *Reader's Digest* condensed books instead of reading the original works, and accepted television's ersatz version of reality, including "news conferences" that generated no news and "pseudo-events" staged for the media by public-relations flacks. Like Bradbury, Boorstin feared a world of brain-dead men and women wholly dependent on the version of reality spoon-fed to them by the state or by the mass media.

The journalist Vance Packard, functioning as a kind of national conscience, criticized 1950s culture in several best-selling books: *The Hidden Persuaders* (1957) exposed the machinations of advertisers; *Status Seekers* (1959) deplored social climbing through the accumulation of high-status products; and *The Waste Makers* (1960) lamented that older virtues such as frugality and concern for the larger good were being swept away in the orgy of consumption.

❖❖ IN PERSPECTIVE: *The Mass-Culture Debate*

The culture critics of the 1950s drew on a long tradition in American thought. A century earlier, writer Nathaniel Hawthorne had attacked the fickle, novel-devouring public for slighting him in favor of a "damn'd mob of scribbling women." Movies, radio, and television gave the critics a succession of new targets.

Postwar mass-culture critics fell into three broad camps. Conservatives such as Dwight Macdonald dismissed popular culture as *kitsch*—German for "rubbish." The avidity with which the vulgar hordes consumed it, they declared, proved the low state of American culture and the need to defend elite standards. This dismissive view often, although not always, reflected a deeper bias against democracy itself.

Marxists treated mass culture as another form of capitalist exploitation, a view most fully articulated at the University of Frankfurt's Institute for Social Research, founded in 1923. With Hitler's rise in the 1930s, the leaders of the Frankfurt school fled to America, where, traumatized by European fascism, they cast a critical eye on U.S. mass culture. In *The Eclipse of Reason* (1947), Max Horkheimer probed the mass media's totalitarian potential. In "Television and Patterns of Mass Culture" (1954), Theodor Adorno portrayed television as a weapon of class manipulation, numbing the masses to their own alienation. Horkheimer and Adorno charged in a coauthored essay that radio and the movies left "no room for imagination or reflection on the part of the audience. . . . [T]hey react automatically [and] fall helpless victims to what is offered them." The Italian Marxist Antonio Gramsci, who died in a fascist prison in 1937, elaborated his theory of cultural hegemony in a series of influential essays in the 1920s and 1930s. Elites employ mass culture, Gramsci argued, to achieve hegemonic control, thereby persuading the rest of society willingly to embrace the existing social order, with all its inequities, as wholly desirable and "natural."

Others, including the Canadian medievalist Marshall McLuhan, viewed mass culture more positively. In *Understanding Media* (1964) and other works, McLuhan hailed the new electronic media, especially TV, as a quantum leap in human communications as profound as that introduced by Gutenberg. McLuhan's aphorism, "The

John Keats, meanwhile, lambasted suburbia in *The Crack in the Picture Window* (1956). The jacket blurb of Keats's book reads like a caricature of 1950s cultural criticism:

> Even while you read this, whole square miles of identical boxes are spreading like gangrene. . . . In any one of these new neighborhoods you can be sure all other houses will be precisely like yours, inhabited by people whose age, income, number of children, problems, habits, conversation, dress, possessions, and perhaps even blood types are precisely like yours.

To understand 1950s social thought, one must place it in historical context. Many of these critics had come of age in the intensely political 1930s. FDR's New medium is the message," summed up his belief that the technology of television itself, apart from program content, would change the world by transforming human perception of reality. In place of the linear medium of print, television's ceaseless flow of images would bring the world into the living room with compelling immediacy.

As the mass-culture debate wore on into the 1980s and 1990s, all three viewpoints found adherents. In *The Closing of the American Mind* (1987), the elitist Alan Bloom railed against rock music as "junk food for the soul" that ruins the young for serious intellectual pursuits. Bloom placed his hope in an elite who would carry on the great traditions of Western civilization. The religious Right, meanwhile, like earlier moral reformers, attacked the media for promulgating sex and violence. The American Family Asssociation of Tupelo, Mississippi, for example, founded by the Reverend Donald Wildmon, organized boycotts of the sponsors of television programs that it considered indecent or immoral. The radical critique of mass culture continued to find champions as well. Historian T. J. Jackson Lears, in "The Concept of Cultural Hegemony" (*American Historical Review*, June 1985), restated the Gramscian view of mass culture as a means by which capitalist elites market goods, mute class tensions, and in general legitimate the status quo.

Other mass-culture observers remained more upbeat. In *The Global Village* (1989), Marshall McLuhan envisioned a world united electronically—an image that would resurface in President Bill Clinton's dream of America linked by an "electronic highway." A more positive outlook emerged, too, in historian Lawrence Levine's studies of popular culture. Rejecting the view that moviegoers, radio listeners, and TV viewers are an inert mass that can be manipulated at will, Levine in *The Unpredictable Past: Explorations in American Cultural History* (1993) emphasized the active role of mass-culture consumers. They not only choose which movies and television shows to watch, but they imaginatively adapt these products to their own purposes. Indeed, in a 1992 *American Historical Review* essay, Levine portrayed mass culture as an arena of dynamic interaction between producers and consumers that creates a kind of TV-age folk culture. He cited research documenting how listeners and viewers continually criticize and comment on radio and TV programs rather than passively absorbing them. In a sharp rebuttal, Jackson Lears rejected this view as a romantically sentimental view of America's "culture industry."

This was hardly the last word. The mass-culture debate that flared so vigorously in the 1950s shows no signs of abating. And as the controversy rolls on, so does American mass culture, playing an ever larger global role.

Deal had won the passionate allegiance of many; others had embraced Marxism in response to the Great Depression and looked to the Soviet Union as a model. By the 1950s, however, the New Deal was history, Depression-era misery had given way to prosperity, and Stalin's brutalities had shattered communism's appeal, turning the intellectuals' youthful radicalism into a matter of embarrassment rather than pride. Sociologist Daniel Bell, having abandoned his own prewar radicalism, applied the definitive label to the 1950s in the title of his 1960 book about postwar America: *The End of Ideology.*

Postwar capitalism's feats of productivity, the declining influence of organized labor, the stifling effects of McCarthyism—all these factors served to mute political debates in Eisenhower's America. So, too, did the Cold War consensus that was the domestic corollary of the U.S.-Soviet confrontation. Promulgated by politicians, public intellectuals, and the mass media, this consensus celebrated America's political, economic, and social systems as bulwarks against the red menace. American democracy might involve media manipulation and the jostling of powerful interest groups, but it was clearly superior to totalitarianism. The capitalist system might be dominated by vast corporations and faceless managers, but it was preferable to the lumbering state-run economies behind the Iron Curtain. The ethic of consumption and endless growth could be faulted for encouraging materialistic excess, but it moderated the class conflict that Marxists saw as inevitable. Such simplistic observations, while true enough, dumbed down public debate and discouraged incisive social or political analysis. Historian Christopher Lasch, who grew up in the 1950s, later complained that his generation "lacked a political education."

In this climate, many intellectuals concluded that the safe course lay in working at the margins, criticizing certain aspects of American society but not challenging its basic structure or ideological premises. One observer wrote in 1957, "Almost all the problems that were once called 'political' now belong to a different context, psychological, sociological, and cultural."

Perceptive as they sometimes were, critics such as Packard, Whyte, Macdonald, and Boorstin focused on a narrow sector of 1950s America, the white middle class, and largely ignored minorities and the poor. Anyone reading their commentary might well conclude that all Americans were corporate executives or comfortable suburbanites. Sharing the prevailing view that U.S. capitalism had ensured abundance for all and that the remaining pockets of poverty would quickly vanish, these intellectuals concentrated on the cultural and emotional lives of the newly affluent.

The critics paid scant attention to the economic system that underlay the mass culture they deplored. In *Vance Packard and American Social Criticism* (1994), historian Daniel Horowitz makes clear that while Packard deplored aspects of the consumerist culture of the 1950s, he fundamentally believed in the system and avoided any call for structural changes in the capitalist order or public regulation of the marketing process. William Whyte offered no structural analysis of modern U.S. capitalism even as he criticized its social effects. Macdonald and Boorstin deplored mass culture and midcult while ignoring questions of social class, social power, or the nature of postwar consumer capitalism. Nor did these critics suggest how the problems they identified might be solved. Like 1950s novelists, they aimed not to mobilize collective political action but to heighten individual consciousness and sensibility. Through books such as *The Lonely Crowd, The Organization Man, The Image,* and *The Hidden Persuaders,* readers could become more conscious of and perhaps somewhat resistant to the cultural pressures that victimized the less knowing. The jacket blurb for *The Crack in the Picture Window* ended breathlessly, "The shaken reader puts down the book, stares for a moment, and then screams, 'Somebody do something! Quick!'" Such a response, however, would have been alien to the mood of the 1950s, when criticism rarely led to action.

American historians in the 1950s similarly downplayed social and economic conflict and instead stressed consensus and continuity as the central themes of U.S. history. In *The Genius of American Politics* (1953), Daniel Boorstin, another 1930s radical turned conservative, praised Americans' freedom from ideological debate and the pragmatic way they had fashioned their social and political institutions. Other scholars, while agreeing that U.S. history featured a lack of ideological conflict, felt less convinced than Boorstin that this trait was good. Historian Richard Hofstadter in *The Age of Reform* (1955) viewed with a skeptical eye the anti-intellectualism and self-serving individualism that he found at the core of the American political tradition. Political scientist Louis Hartz argued in *The Liberal Tradition in America* (1955) that Americans' ideological naiveté and their lack of exposure to class conflict made it hard for them to understand the allure of Marxism in large parts of the world.

An important exception to the prevailing emphasis on consensus and to the lack of a strong political edge in 1950s intellectual life was Columbia sociologist C. Wright Mills. A product of Depression-era Texas and the University of Wisconsin, where a tradition of radical social thought survived, Mills produced two books in the 1950s that challenged the dominant tenor of social thought. In *White Collar* (1951), as we have seen, he offered a picture of middle-class futility and discontent. But he surpassed other critics who were making similar points by linking his insights to a structural analysis of the political and economic order. The impotence felt by low- and midlevel functionaries in the new technocratic order was well founded, he insisted; these people had little voice in the political or corporate decisions that shaped their lives. In a memorable phrase evocative of the 1930s, Mills called them "sharecroppers in the dustbowl of business."

Mills extended his argument in *The Power Elite* (1956). The reins of power in contemporary America, he argued, lay in the hands of a shifting but basically stable group, concentrated at the upper levels of the corporate, political, and military elites. Mills went on to explore the social and cultural apparatus—family, schools, clubs—by which this elite perpetuated itself and recruited new members. Liberal democratic theorists who celebrated the power of the ballot box, argued Mills, ignored the many ways voters could be bamboozled and the electoral process perverted. Similarly, Mills rejected the theory advanced by economist John Kenneth Galbraith in *American Capitalism* (1951) that various competing and countervailing interest groups divided power among them. This argument, he protested, obscured the enormous concentration of power at the top and the commonalities of interest among "the Ones Who Decide."

Mills's books drew much criticism, even though his analysis anticipated President Eisenhower's 1961 farewell address, with its warning about the military-industrial complex. His polemical style, his casual methodology, the imprecision of his "power elite" model, and even his unconventional ways (he built his own house and rode a motorcycle to work) heightened his vulnerability to criticism. But in a decade when most intellectuals avoided radical analysis of the basic structure of American society, Mills's impassioned, highly readable books expressed what most Americans knew in their bones: that some groups and individuals wielded enormous power and influence, while most did not. To understand the culture and psyche of the middle class, Mills insisted, one must look at the economic and political framework within which that class functioned.

In the 1960s, young radicals seeking intellectual tools for understanding and changing American society rediscovered Mills and claimed him as their own.

Mills's period of greatest influence came posthumously, however; he died of a heart attack in 1962 at the age of forty-five.

Mills's vigorous dissidence found few echoes in the 1950s. When reformist energies and even radical attacks on the capitalist system revived in the 1960s under the New Left rubric, the movement's leaders lost little time repudiating what they saw as the tepid, ennervating liberalism of 1950s intellectuals. Those intellectuals, 1960s critics justifiably charged, had offered the bark of cultural criticism without the bite of political action.

Despite the political lassitude and diminished social activism of the Eisenhower years, two issues of profound importance stirred organized protest: the nuclear threat and racial discrimination. Each would continue to arouse passionate attention long after the fifties had become a memory.

Fallout Fears and Test-Ban Activism

By the early 1950s, the fear of atomic war that had gripped America after Hiroshima was less openly expressed. President Truman's 1950 decision to build the hydrogen bomb won overwhelming public approval. Under a steady barrage of Cold War propaganda, the dreaded destroyer of 1945 had become the cornerstone of the nation's security.

But public acquiescence in the nuclear arms race proved highly vulnerable to the unsettling news that began to seep into the popular consciousness in the mid-1950s as scientists reported deadly radioactive fallout from hydrogen-bomb tests conducted in the South Pacific. The U.S. test series of 1954 set off the first alarm, spreading radioactive ash over a vast area and causing illness and death to a Japanese fishing crew. In 1955 radioactive rain fell on Chicago, and meteorologists began to plot the diffusion of high-level radioactive clouds over North America. Medical specialists warned of the health hazards of fallout, including leukemia, bone cancer, and long-term genetic damage. Strontium-90, an especially horrifying byproduct of thermonuclear tests, accumulated in human bone marrow and teeth, particularly in infants and children. Despite efforts by the Eisenhower administration to downplay the danger, a full-blown fallout scare gripped the nation. Even the staid and conservative *Saturday Evening Post* ran a feature called "Fallout: The Silent Killer."

Fallout fear permeated the culture. The monster and mutant movies that poured out of Hollywood in these years usually blamed the scary creatures on nuclear tests. A 1954 rock-and-roll song by Bill Haley and the Comets, "Thirteen Women (and Only One Man in Town)," offered a male fantasy of endless sex in the aftermath of an H-bomb attack. Tom Lehrer won fans on college campuses by extracting black humor from the prospect of nuclear annihilation with such songs as "We'll All Go Together When We Go." *Mad* magazine, a favorite with teenage cognoscenti, some of whom would become sixties rebels, fantasized a postnuclear war Hit Parade of songs that young lovers would sing as they "walk down moonlit lanes arm in arm in arm."

Novels like Nevil Shute's *On the Beach* (1957) and Walter Miller's *A Canticle for Leibowitz* (1959) imagined apocalyptic scenarios of human extinction. In Mordecai

Roshwald's *Level 7* (1959), the inhabitants of a vast underground shelter die, level by level, as radiation seeps deeper into the earth. As the last survivors await their end, they create a new religion in which strontium-90 substitutes for Satan as the ultimate embodiment of evil. Even on television, rarely a bearer of bad news in the fifties, the science-fiction series *Outer Limits* and Rod Serling's *Twilight Zone* occasionally offered post–nuclear war plots or explored the psychological effect of atomic terror.

In an *Outer Limits* program, bees that have been genetically altered by radioactive fallout decide to infiltrate the human race. They transmute their queen into a sexually alluring young female humanoid who takes employment in the home of a cozy suburban couple and sets out to seduce the weak-willed husband. But the wife grows suspicious when she sees the newcomer in the yard one night pollinating flowers. As a swarm of bees stings the wife to death, the bee-woman offers herself seductively to the distraught husband. In his revulsion he kills her, foiling, for the moment, insect-world challenges to middle-class propriety. Laden with multiple cultural messages, this episode reflected not only fallout fears but also

Atomic-Age Domesticity. *In this posed* Life *magazine photo of 1961, family members embody gender stereotypes as they await the end: Dad ready to dig through the rubble, Mom with kitchen gear, son in charge of flashlight and radio, and daughters with blankets and board games. (Dmitri Kessel/Life Magazine, © Time Inc.)*

uneasiness about threats to suburban domesticity posed by the youth culture's brazen sexuality.

The resurgence of nuclear fear brought a spate of conferences and symposia pondering the larger implications of living with the bomb. A sense of personal helplessness in the face of the global nuclear threat, some writers speculated, contributed to the political passivity of the decade.

The federal government, ironically, intensified nuclear anxiety with a civil-defense program of school drills, propaganda films, and a fallout-shelter campaign. In a civil-defense test in Washington in 1956, ten thousand federal workers scattered to secret relocation centers, and President Eisenhower was helicoptered to an underground command post in Maryland. In 1959, *Life* persuaded a newlywed couple to honeymoon in a cramped underground shelter, publishing photographs of them kissing as they descended for their two weeks of subterranean marital bliss. "Fallout can be fun," quipped *Life*. Schoolchildren crouched under desks in nuclear-war drills and watched civil-defense films such as *Duck and Cover,* in which Burt the Turtle explained what to do when the nuclear flash came.

From the fallout scare arose a national movement to stop nuclear tests. When Adlai Stevenson called for a test ban in the 1956 presidential campaign, the Republicans accused him of aiding the enemy, but the issue would not fade. Groups with names like the Council for a Livable World, Physicians for Social Responsibility, and the National Committee for a Sane Nuclear Policy (SANE) took up the cause. One memorable SANE ad featured baby doctor Benjamin Spock gazing with furrowed brow at a little girl under the caption, Dr. Spock Is Worried. In New York, antinuclear activists went to jail for refusing to take shelter during a civil-defense drill. In the early 1960s, the test-ban movement attracted thousands of college students. An antinuclear group called Women's Strike for Peace organized marches in several big cities. Often led by religious pacifists, long-time political activists, or well-known public figures, these movements nevertheless attracted thousands of ordinary citizens terrified by the nuclear threat.

Responding to scientific warnings and world opinion, the superpowers halted nuclear testing in 1958. This moratorium broke down in 1961, however, as the Soviet Union and then the United States resumed atmospheric assays. But in 1963, after the Cuban missile crisis (see Chapter 6), the United States, the Soviet Union, and Great Britain signed a treaty banning such tests. The 1950s test-ban movement thus partially achieved its objective; it also provided a rare avenue of political engagement for thousands of Americans during a mostly passive decade.

Brown and Beyond: The Civil-Rights Movement in Eisenhower's America

Even more dramatic evidence of reviving political activism in an otherwise lethargic decade was the drive for racial justice that gathered momentum as the decade wore on. Focused initially on segregation in the South, this movement gradually broadened in scope, building the foundation for a revolution in race relations whose full implications would continue to unfold a generation later. The civil-rights campaign radically undermined the stereotyped image of 1950s America as

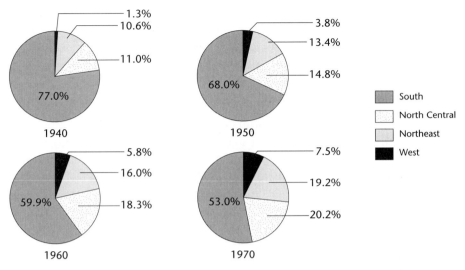

FIGURE 5.2

Regional Distribution of the Black Population, 1940–1970

NOTE: The Northeast consists of New England and the Middle Atlantic states of New York, Pennsylvania, and New Jersey. The North Central region consists of the Great Lakes states along with Missouri, Kansas, Iowa, Nebraska, and the Dakotas. The South is made up of all states south of the Mason-Dixon line (including the border states of Delaware, West Virginia, and Kentucky) and extends as far west as Texas and Oklahoma. The remaining states are in the West.

SOURCE: *The Negro Almanac: A Reference Work on the African American* (5th Edition, Detroit, Gale Research Inc., 1989).

one big, happy suburb. This chapter looks at the early stages of the drive for racial justice; Chapter 8 explores the changes that overtook this effort in the late 1950s and beyond, propelling it in far more radical directions.

Throughout the South, and in parts of the North as well, blacks attended segregated schools as the fifties began, a practice upheld in 1896 by the U.S. Supreme Court in *Plessy v. Ferguson*. The high court in *Plessy* had specified that the facilities provided for blacks and whites must be equal, thus providing the legal underpinnings of the South's so-called "separate but equal" public-school system. In reality, funding for black education fell far below that for whites, and the facilities provided for black students proved appallingly inferior.

But segregated schools formed only one piece in a vast mosaic of institutionalized racism. Although some of its cruder and more brutal manifestations had faded since the early years of the century, prejudice and discrimination infected every national institution from schools and churches to the media and the workplace. Wherever one looked in early postwar America, blacks were treated as second-class citizens.

A convergence of social and ideological trends challenged this pervasive reality. World War II had changed the lives of many blacks. Thousands served in the military, and thousands more flocked to the North and West where they took jobs in war plants, joined labor unions, and swelled the voting ranks. The narrator of

Invisible Man (1952), Ralph Ellison's novel exploring the modern African-American experience, comes North during the war to find work. (Ellison, writing on the symbolic as well as the realistic plane, gives his narrator a job at the Liberty Paint Company, a factory that specializes in an eye-dazzling paint called Optic White. The few drops of black added to each batch totally disappear.)

At the same time, industrialization and urbanization were straining the South's racial caste system. As blacks poured into southern cities and factories, and as the urban black middle class grew, segregation proved increasingly difficult to enforce. In the civil-rights activism that would soon sweep the South, white corporate and financial leaders, worried that protests would threaten the region's economy, often worked behind the scenes to moderate the more extreme forms of racial segregation. The affluence of the 1950s, although unevenly distributed, played a role as well, increasing the urban black work force, adding to the ranks of middle-class black churches and colleges, and fattening contributions to civil-rights organizations. The mass media, meanwhile—especially television—spotlighted civil-rights activism and violent white resistance in southern communities that might otherwise have gone largely unnoticed.

At the ideological level, long-held racial attitudes no longer commanded unthinking assent. Hitler's anti-Semitism and the Holocaust to which it led discredited a once quasi-respectable body of racial thought that had long undergirded the southern caste system and American racism in general. As we have seen, Gunnar Myrdal's *An American Dilemma* of 1944 helped accelerate this change in the intellectual climate.

Cold War realities further undermined ingrained patterns of racism. As Washington denounced the Soviets for their betrayal of human rights and courted allies among newly independent nations in Asia and Africa, the reality of racism at home became highly embarrassing. The worldwide revolutionary upsurge against colonialism stirred U.S. blacks as well. Thus economic, demographic, ideological, and strategic trends converged in the early postwar years to erode the foundations of racial segregation.

The immediate impetus for change came from the National Association for the Advancement of Colored People (NAACP), which for years had mounted court challenges to racism, including segregated schools. As early as 1938, the Supreme Court had ordered the University of Missouri Law School to admit a black applicant on the grounds that because Missouri had no law school for blacks, the separate-but-equal standard obviously could not be met. Supreme Court decisions in 1950, in cases brought by the NAACP (see p. 72), had further eroded *Plessy* v. *Ferguson*. Particularly important were *McLaurin* v. *Oklahoma State Regents* and *Sweatt* v. *Painter,* in which the high court outlawed segregated professional schools that were not fully equal to those available to whites.

The years of painstaking legal activity paid off on May 17, 1954, when a unanimous Supreme Court under Chief Justice Earl Warren, in the case of *Brown* v. *Board of Education of Topeka,* ruled that racially segregated public schools violated the constitutional principle of equal treatment for all citizens. The NAACP brief, presented by Thurgood Marshall, who later would become the first black Supreme Court justice, relied heavily on studies showing the effects of segregation on children. Particularly influential was the work of the black psychologist Kenneth

Clark. Clark found, for example, that black children as young as three years old, when presented with otherwise identical brown-skinned and white-skinned dolls, usually chose the white doll. Clark attributed this behavior to cultural conditioning: "The fact that young Negro children would prefer to be white," he wrote, "reflects their knowledge that society prefers white people."

Citing the work of Clark, Myrdal, and others, the justices declared:

> [s]egregation of children in public schools solely on the basis of race, even though the physical facilities . . . may be equal, deprive[s] the children of the minority group of equal educational opportunities[.] . . . To separate them from others of similar age and qualifications solely because of their race generates a feeling of inferiority . . . that may affect their hearts and minds in a way unlikely ever to be undone. . . . [I]n the field of public education the doctrine of "separate but equal" has no place. Separate educational facilities are inherently unequal.

Although the Court declared in a follow-up ruling of 1955 that school segregation should end "with all deliberate speed" and instructed the federal courts to ensure "a prompt and reasonable start toward full compliance," southern white segregationists organized a campaign of massive resistance. White "Citizens' Councils"—more "respectable" versions of the Ku Klux Klan—sprang up across the region to fight integration. Early in 1956, echoing the states-rights battles of the pre–Civil War era, the Virginia legislature proclaimed the right of a state to "interpose its sovereignty" to stop enforcement of the *Brown* ruling. In March 1956, one hundred southern senators and congressmen announced their intent to use "all lawful means" to overthrow the *Brown* decision. When Clinton, Tennessee, integrated its high school, segregationist mobs shouted "Kill the niggers!" at the black students. Soon after, a dynamite blast demolished the school.

President Eisenhower played a muted role in the controversy. Criticizing the Supreme Court's ruling in private, he later described his choice of Earl Warren as chief justice as "the biggest damnfool mistake I ever made." Citing Prohibition as an example, Eisenhower insisted to friends that deep-seated social mores could not be changed by legal fiat or by force. Political calculations reinforced Ike's distaste for the *Brown* decision. He had won four southern states in 1952 and five in 1956, and the Republican party's long-term southern strategy assumed growing white support in the once solidly Democratic stronghold.

Eisenhower's grudging response to the profound moral issue of racial equality constitutes his greatest failure as president. Instead of using his enormous prestige to help white America to confront the reality of racial injustice, he held back, tacitly encouraging those fighting to preserve white supremacy. The cabinet rarely discussed civil-rights issues, and White House meetings with black leaders were rare and tense. When the one black in the Eisenhower White House, E. Frederick Morrow, a special assistant in foreign affairs, alerted Eisenhower to rising racial tensions, Ike replied, "Oh Fred, you're an alarmist." When pressed, Eisenhower claimed that his was the path of moderation, as though racism and a determination to fight racism were equally deplorable extremist positions.

Eisenhower conceded, however, that the law must be obeyed. In a press conference after the *Brown* decision, he insisted, "The Supreme Court has spoken, and I am sworn to uphold the constitutional processes in this country; and I will obey."

It was this commitment to the rule of law, not enthusiasm for the substance of the *Brown* decision, that finally forced Eisenhower to take a decisive stand.

The flashpoint came in Little Rock, Arkansas, a moderate city whose school board, in cooperation with local black leaders, had worked out a plan for gradual integration. But the politics of race intervened. When Alabama's George Wallace lost a gubernatorial primary campaign to an outspoken segregationist in 1958, he commented, "They out-segged me that time, but they'll never do it again." Arkansas governor Orval Faubus, hitherto something of a moderate on racial issues, took the same demagogic low road as he sought a third term in 1956. As school opening approached that September, Faubus called out the Arkansas National Guard to prevent nine black students from enrolling at Little Rock's all-white Central High School. In a radio address the night before the fall term began, Faubus peddled alarmist rumors about caravans of white racists converging on Little Rock from all over the South. "Blood will flow in the streets" if the integration of Central High went forward, he intoned.

After Faubus's speech, black leaders decided to delay the nine teenagers' appearance at the school, fearful for their safety. However, one of the nine, Elizabeth Eckford, did not get the word. Showing up at the school the next morning, she encountered ranks of stony-faced national guardsmen and a screaming, spitting mob. "Lynch her! Lynch her!" they shouted. "No nigger bitch is going to get into our school. Get out of here!" Befriended by two sympathetic whites, she barely managed to escape.

A meeting between Faubus and President Eisenhower failed to heal the impasse; Eisenhower and his staff had treated him like a child, fumed the governor. Faubus obeyed a federal court order to withdraw the national guard, but when the black students tried to enroll at Central High, segregationist mobs again blocked their way.

At last, Eisenhower acted. In a national television address on September 24, he denounced the Little Rock mob as "disgraceful" and vowed to enforce the law. Responding to a request for help from Little Rock's mayor, he ordered a thousand U.S. paratroopers to the city and federalized the Arkansas National Guard. Protected by federal troops, the black students enrolled. When racists bombed the home of one student, Carlotta Walls, she went to school as usual. "Nothing has changed," she told reporters. Although local school boards raised roadblocks to integration and the white Citizens' Councils opened private schools for whites only across the South, school segregation in the South slowly eroded in the later 1950s and the 1960s under the pressure of demonstrations, court orders, and the glare of media publicity.

The sociological and psychological assumptions on which the Supreme Court relied in *Brown* v. *Board of Education* were not universally accepted at the time, and they later came into even greater question. In *Forced Justice: School Desegregation and the Law* (1995), for example, David J. Armor marshalls social-science studies that challenge the argument that self-esteem and academic performance are linked to segregated or integrated education. Similarly, the process of school integration proved far more complex, and its social benefits more elusive, than the Supreme Court assumed in 1954. Faced with court-ordered integration, many whites simply moved, so that school desegregation, ironically, may have furthered de facto hous-

Montgomery, 1956. *In a charcoal drawing sketched from life, New York City artist Harvey Dinnerstein captured the unity and quiet determination that propelled the Montgomery bus boycott to success.* (Walking Together, Montgomery, *by Harvey Dinnerstein, 1956. Charcoal on paper. Gift of the Artist, The Parrish Art Museum, Southampton, NY. Photo by Studio Nine, NY)*

ing segregation. What has remained unchallenged, however, is the recognition that officially sanctioned, legally enforced racial segregation has no place in a society claiming to embrace principles of democracy and equality. The Warren Court grasped that essential fact, and acted accordingly, with profound implications for American history.

Meanwhile, the revolution spread from the courts to the streets and churches as years of suppressed anger and aspirations for equality burst forth. Attention focused early on Montgomery, Alabama, the self-proclaimed "cradle of the Confederacy." As in much of the South, Montgomery had a segregated public transit system: blacks sat in the back of the bus, whites in the front. When a bus filled, blacks had to yield their seats to whites on demand. On December 1, 1955, Mrs. Rosa Parks, secretary of the state NAACP and a long-time activist, riding home after a day's work as a department-store seamstress, refused the driver's order to give up her seat to a white man. "I felt it was just something I had to do," Parks would later recall of a simple act of defiance that challenged an entire structure of racial injustice. With Parks's arrest, the state NAACP led by E. D. Nixon, a railroad porter, proposed that Montgomery's blacks organize a bus boycott, a technique that had been briefly tried in 1953 in Baton Rouge, Louisiana. Volunteers stayed up all night mimeographing leaflets announcing the boycott.

The boycott planners recruited as their leader the Reverend Martin Luther King, Jr., the newly appointed twenty-six-year-old pastor of a middle-class black Baptist church in Montgomery. King, the son and namesake of a prominent

Atlanta minister, had just received his Ph.D. in theology from Boston University. King gained inspiration not only from Christian thought but also from Henry David Thoreau, who had gone to jail rather than pay taxes to support the Mexican War, and from Mohandas Gandhi, whose nonviolent tactics had helped to end British rule in India.

From the outset, King underscored the ethical issues at stake and drew on appeals to conscience. Although he preached nonviolence, he never advocated passive acquiescence in oppression. Rather, he promoted strategies that would dramatize patterns of racism and generate a "creative tension" between the principle of equality and the fact of injustice. Charismatic and eloquent, heir to a rich tradition of black pulpit oratory, King would ultimately win a vast following of blacks and whites. A skillful tactician, he knew how to translate principles into actions.

King and his associates set three goals for the bus boycott: more courteous treatment of blacks, additional black drivers, and seating on a first-come, first-served basis. (In this cautious early stage of the civil-rights movement, the boycott leaders did not initially challenge the custom that relegated blacks to the rear of the bus.) For nearly a year, by walking or sharing rides, blacks stayed off the buses. "I'm not walking for myself," reflected one boycotter, "I'm walking for my children and my grandchildren." A bomb shattered the front of King's house in January 1956, and in February he and the other boycott leaders briefly went to jail, but they held firm. In weekly mass meetings at his church, King and the other leaders placed the boycott in a broader context. King promised his followers in December 1955:

> When the history books are written in the future, somebody will have to say, "There lived a race of people . . . who had the marvelous courage to stand up for their rights and thereby they injected a new meaning into the being of history and of civilization." And we are going to do that.

At last, in November 1956, a federal court ruled unconstitutional all state and local laws upholding segregated buses in Alabama. Beyond the legal victory, the Montgomery boycott had energized the black community and replaced resignation with hope. When an auto caravan of Ku Klux Klan members prowled through Montgomery's black neighborhood the night after the court ruling, expecting to inspire terror, a crowd of blacks trailed it exuberantly through the streets. And rather than huddling in the dark, as in the past, the residents flung their shades up and left their lights blazing.

For Martin Luther King, Jr., the Montgomery bus boycott launched a career that would propel him to world fame and end with an assassin's bullet. But in 1956, all that lay ahead. Moving back to Atlanta to become copastor of his father's church, King with other black ministers in 1957 started the Southern Christian Leadership Conference (SCLC) to guide the burgeoning movement. In *Stride Toward Freedom* (1958), he told the story of the bus boycott and provided a blueprint for similar actions elsewhere.

Black writers helped shape the new consciousness spreading among African Americans. While Ralph Ellison's *Invisible Man* was concerned less with immediate political action than with heightened individual consciousness (see p. 91), Ellison, like jazz artist Dizzy Gillespie, viewed his work as a step on the path to organized action. Any work by a black writer or artist, he insisted, inevitably represented a political act. "The consciousness of a race is the gift of its individuals who see, evaluate, record...," observes his narrator. "We create the race by creating ourselves." No less than the Montgomery bus boycott, *Invisible Man* heralded a growing resistance to decades of subordination and humiliation, a resistance that had both internal psychological and external activist manifestations.

Writer James Baldwin, born in Harlem in 1924, drew even more direct influence from the spirit of the civil-rights movement. Baldwin's first novel, *Go Tell It on the Mountain* (1953), incorporated his own experience as the son of an embittered, often abusive black preacher in a Harlem mission. In a series of penetrating essays in the 1950s and early 1960s—collected in *Notes of a Native Son* (1955) and *Nobody Knows My Name* (1961)—Baldwin considered the role of black intellectuals and writers and explored how racism penetrated both the nation's institutions and the consciousness of whites and blacks alike. Echoing psychologist Kenneth Clark, Baldwin emphasized racism's effects on the self-image of black children, "taught from the moment their eyes open on the world that their color was a badge of inferiority."

The Montgomery bus boycott also drew upon a long tradition of African-American protest. In the 1930s, black activists in Harlem had organized boycotts of white-owned businesses that refused to hire black salespersons. Various southern communities had witnessed black activism against segregated institutions well before World War II. But Montgomery was unique in scope and visibility, and it propelled black protest to unprecedented new levels.

The surge of civil-rights activism posed problems for both major political parties. Republicans sought to enlarge their traditional appeal to black voters while retaining their base in the white South. The Democratic party was torn between its northern and southern wings. The former included a strong black and white-liberal component but also many conservative white ethnics. The lily-white southern wing was overwhelmingly segregationist, with a small contingent of liberals on racial and other issues, mostly concentrated in university centers.

Out of this political minefield emerged the historic Civil Rights Act of 1957, the first such federal law since the 1870s. Attorney General Herbert Brownell had convinced Eisenhower that by introducing a civil-rights bill, Republicans could deepen the split in the Democratic party and win back northern blacks who had been voting Democratic since the New Deal. Blacks, Brownell calculated, held the balance of power in seven states and sixty congressional districts. The administration's civil-rights bill, first introduced in the election year 1956, passed the House but died in the Senate Judiciary Committee, where it was bottled up by Chairman James Eastland of Mississippi, a dyed-in-the-wool segregationist.

Senate majority leader Lyndon Johnson opposed the 1956 bill, aware of the risks it posed for the Democrats. But when Eisenhower again sent Congress a civil-rights bill in 1957, Johnson, eager for the 1960 Democratic presidential nomination and seeking to shed his purely regional image, supported it and cajoled his fellow southern Democrats to do the same.

The compromise bill that emerged was much watered down by southern legislators yet established certain important precedents. The measure focused entirely on voting rights. Although only part of the larger struggle, this issue was vital, for the disfranchisement of southern blacks by a variety of subterfuges posed a massive roadblock to the civil-rights cause. The 1957 Civil Rights Act authorized the attorney general to seek court injunctions to stop local electoral officials from interfering with any citizen's voting rights. It created a civil-rights division within the Justice Department and a new federal agency, the U.S. Civil Rights Commission, to monitor racial issues. A follow-up measure, the Civil Rights Act of 1960, authorized federal courts to appoint referees to ensure local compliance with the voting-rights laws.

Important as it was, this early phase of the civil-rights movement illustrated the limits of the nation's understanding of racism's grip. Liberal whites and even the middle-class leaders of the NAACP saw the problem as primarily a legal one involving racial segregation in the South. If Congress and the Supreme Court outlawed the more blatant forms of legalized racism and Americans of goodwill united against southern segregation and outspoken racists like Orval Faubus and George Wallace, they believed, the problem would ease.

Considerable evidence encouraged this reassuring view, including the Supreme Court's unanimity in the *Brown* decision, the enactment of the Civil Rights Act of 1957 with bipartisan support, the eloquence of Martin Luther King's appeals to Americans' better selves, and the successful Montgomery bus boycott. In short, in the 1950s the system seemed able to accommodate the racial grievances of African Americans by a series of moderate actions, without radical upheaval or undue social turmoil. In the next decade, this comfortable assumption would shatter as new strategies, new leaders, and new issues radically transformed the fight for racial equality.

Conclusion

The baby boomers who were children and teenagers in the 1950s later tended to bathe the decade in a warm glow of nostalgia. A 1989 TV promotion for a collection of fifties pop hits evoked those "warm, wonderful years, filled with magical memories." A 1980s television comedy series about teenage life in the 1950s was called *Happy Days*. In some ways, this nostalgia is justified. The prosperous, comparatively tranquil decade of the 1950s does seem almost idyllic. In these years, the economy hummed, joblessness remained low, Americans by the millions bought new homes in the suburbs, and many young couples looked confidently to the future after an era of depression and war.

Viewed more comprehensively, however, the "warm, wonderful" Eisenhower years take on a complex and more foreboding aura, shadowed by the nuclear arms race. As the Cold War became institutionalized, it narrowed political debate and cultural expression, forcing dissidents to the periphery. Nineteen-fifties conservatism stemmed from both Cold War anticommunism and from a reaction against the turbulence and upheavals of the recent past. Yet it also reflected a somewhat smug self-satisfaction in capitalism's capacity to produce unrivaled levels of material well-being for unprecedented numbers of people. And while the Eisenhower years produced a turn to the right and the further rehabilitation of American business, these shifts remained within the basic framework of welfare liberalism that was the New Deal's continuing legacy.

On the cultural front, the decade witnessed the emergence of television as the dominant new medium. A potent instrument for marketing and entertaining, TV rarely offered a critical perspective on the consumerist culture to which it contributed or acknowledged the America that lay outside the affluent suburbs. Television occasionally riveted the nation's attention on issues of public significance, but in the 1950s it served mainly to further the political apathy and privatization of American life so deplored by critics.

Yet this decade, so disparaged for its passivity, also spawned a campaign against nuclear testing, a historic Supreme Court school-desegregation ruling, an important if limited civil-rights bill, and the moral drama of the Montgomery bus boycott. What finally impresses one most about the fifties is less its bland uniformity than its vibrant diversity. The decade of Dwight Eisenhower, Norman Vincent Peale, Lucille Ball, and Ed Sullivan also gave rise to James Dean, C. Wright Mills, Allan Ginsberg, Jack Kerouac, Little Richard, Elvis Presley, Martin Luther King, Jr., Ralph Ellison, and James Baldwin. Any ten-year period that can accommodate such a range of voices, viewpoints, and causes clearly defies easy categorization.

Amid cultural ferment and rising waves of social protest, politicians in 1960 again geared up for the quadrennial race for the White House. The election that brought the Eisenhower era to a close highlighted what many feared was a dangerous erosion of America's position in the Cold War. This anxiety arose from a series of events in Eisenhower's second term that suggested alarming Soviet gains, from Cuba to outer space. Although the United States still possessed the strongest military, the later fifties and early sixties brought an ominous deterioration in superpower relations. Cold War tensions, which had briefly thawed in the mid-1950s, abruptly froze again as the decade closed.

SELECTED READINGS

Outsiders and Cultural Innovators

Rodolfo Acuna, *Occupied America: A History of Chicanos* (1981); Christopher Anderson, *Hollywood TV: The Studio System in the Fifties* (1994); Annette Cox, *Art-as-Politics: The Abstract Expressionist Avant-Garde and Society* (1982); Erika Doss, "The Art of Cultural Politics: From Regionalism to Abstract Expressionism," in Lary May, ed, *Recasting America: Culture and Politics in the Age of the Cold War* (1989); Colin Escott, *Good Rockin' Tonight: Sun Records and the Birth of Rock 'n' Roll* (1991); Simon Frith, *Sound Effects: Youth, Leisure, and the Politics of Rock and Roll* (1981); Mario T. Garcia, *Mexican Americans: Leadership, Ideology, and Identity, 1930–1960* (1989); James Gilbert, *A Cycle of Outrage: America's Reaction to the Juvenile Delinquent in the 1950s* (1986); William Graebner, *Coming of Age in Buffalo: Youth and Authority in the Postwar Era* (1990); Serge Guilbaut, *How New York Stole the Idea of Modern Art: Abstract Expressionism, Freedom, and the Cold War* (1983); John A. Jackson, *Big Beat Heat: Alan Freed and the Early Years of Rock and Roll* (1991); Jacqueline Jones, *The Dispossessed: America's Underclasses from the Civil War to the Present* (1992); W. T. Lhamon, Jr., *Deliberate Speed: The Origins of a Cultural Style in the American 1950s* (1990); Mark Thomas McGee and R. J. Robertson, *The J. D. Films: Juvenile Delinquency in the Movies* (1982); Greil Marcus, *Mystery Train: Images of America in Rock 'n' Roll Music* (1982); Douglas S. Massey, *American Apartheid: Segregation and the Making of the Underclass* (1993); Jane deHart Mathews, "Art and Politics in Cold War America," *American*

Historical Review (October 1976); Maria Reidelbach, *Completely Mad: A History of the Comic Book and Magazine* (1991); Ross Russell, "Bebop," in Martin T. Williams, ed., *The Art of Jazz* (1959); David P. Szatmary, *Rockin' in Time: A Social History of Rock and Roll* (1991).

Literature and Social Thought in Eisenhower's America

Alexander Bloom, *Prodigal Sons: The New York Intellectuals and Their World* (1986); William Chace, *Lionel Trilling: Criticism and Politics* (1980); Michael Davidson, *The San Francisco Renaissance: Poetics and Community at Mid-Century* (1989); Robert Booth Fowler, *Believing Skeptics: American Political Intellectuals, 1945–1964* (1978); Sam B. Girgus, *The New Covenant: Jewish Writers and the American Idea* (1984); Daniel Horowitz, *Vance Packard & American Social Criticism* (1994); Irving Louis Horowitz, *C. Wright Mills: American Utopian* (1983); Neil Jumonville, *Critical Crossings: The New York Intellectuals in Postwar America* (1991); Nathan Liebowitz, *Daniel Bell and the Agony of Modern Liberalism* (1985); George Lipsitz, *Class and Culture in Cold War America* (1981); Barry Miles, *Ginsberg: A Biography* (1989); Richard H. Pells, *The Liberal Mind in a Conservative Age: American Intellectuals in the 1940s and 1950s* (1984); Sanford Pinsker, *Jewish-American Fiction, 1917–1987* (1992); Thomas Hill Schaub, *American Fiction in the Cold War* (1991); John Tytell, *Naked Angels: The Lives and Literature of the Beat Generation* (1976); Alan M. Wald, *The New York Intellectuals* (1987); Chaim I. Waxman, ed., *The End of Ideology Debate* (1968); Stephen Whitfield, *The Culture of the Cold War* (1991).

1950s Protest: Nuclear Testing and Racial Segregation

David L. Armor, *Forced Justice: School Desegregation and the Law* (1995); Taylor Branch, *Parting the Waters: America in the King Years, 1954–63* (1988); Robert Frederick Burk, *The Eisenhower Administration and Black Civil Rights* (1984); Clayborne Carson et al., eds., *The Eyes on the Prize Civil Rights Reader* (1991); Robert Divine, *Blowing on the Wind: The Nuclear Test Ban Debate, 1954–1960* (1978); Charles W. Eagles, ed., *The Civil Rights Movement in America* (1986); David Garrow, *Bearing the Cross: Martin Luther King, Jr., and the Southern Christian Leadership Conference* (1986); Elizabeth Huckaby, *Crisis at Central High: Little Rock, 1957–1958* (1980); Susan Lyan, *Progressive Women in Conservative Times: Racial Justice, Peace and Feminism, 1945 to the 1960s* (1992); Guy Oakes, *The Imaginary War: Civil Defense and American Cold War Culture* (1994); Howard L. Rosenberg, *Atomic Soldiers: American Victims of Nuclear Experiments* (1980); Bernard Schwartz and Stephen Lesker, *Inside the Warren Court, 1953–1959* (1983); Jack G. Shaheen, ed., *Nuclear War Films* (1978); Harvard Sitkoff, *The Struggle for Black Equality, 1954–1992* (1992); Mark Tushnet, ed., *The Warren Court in Historical Perspective* (1993); Mark V. Tushnet, *Making Civil Rights Law: Thurgood Marshall and the Supreme Court, 1936–1961* (1994); Robert Weisbrot, *Freedom Bound: A History of America's Civil Rights Movement* (1990); Andreas Wenger, *Living with Peril: Eisenhower, Kennedy, and Nuclear Weapons* (1997); J. H. Wilkinson, *From Brown to Bakke: The Supreme Court and School Integration, 1954–1978* (1979).

CHAPTER 6

The Cold War Heats Up:
From Sputnik to Vietnam

Washington, D.C., was cold and blustery and blanketed in snow on January 20, 1961, Inauguration Day, but the newly elected president, John Fitzgerald Kennedy, stood coatless and hatless, tousled hair blowing, as he took the oath of office from Chief Justice Earl Warren. An aged, frail Dwight Eisenhower huddled behind him. For a brief moment, the flow of history seemed to pause, suspended between past and future. JFK's short inaugural address, delivered in high-pitched, staccato bursts, offered a series of ringing assertions. The most memorable passage came near the end: "And so, my fellow Americans, ask not what your country can do for you; ask what you can do for your country."

Rose Kennedy, the president's mother, later described her emotions at the moment: "I felt that Joe [her husband, Joseph P. Kennedy] and I had given our country a young President whose words, manner, ideas, character, everything about him bespoke future greatness."

Kennedy took office at a time of deepening global tension. The late 1950s had seen a deterioration in Cold War relations and rising fears that the United States was lagging militarily. Kennedy had struck an alarmist note in the 1960 campaign, and as president he displayed a tough aggressiveness in the Caribbean, Europe, Africa, and Southeast Asia. In the Cuban missile crisis of October 1962, the world came perilously close to nuclear war.

Nevertheless, the 1960s opened on a note of fresh beginnings reflecting Kennedy's youthful confidence. In March 1961, in one of his most popular actions, Kennedy created the Peace Corps. Young people by the thousands volunteered for two years of service in educational, agricultural, and technical assistance projects in developing countries around the globe. The Peace Corps and the 1963 Test Ban Treaty halting atmospheric nuclear tests represented the best of the Kennedy legacy. Overall, however, Kennedy's record in international affairs remained sketchy and inconclusive when the Kennedy era ended prematurely in violence on November 22, 1963, leaving as its major legacy an idealized image of the fallen leader and bleak speculation about what might have been.

Cold War Alarms in the Late Fifties

Americans awoke to unsettling news on October 4, 1957: The Soviet Union had launched a 184-pound space satellite, called *Sputnik,* or "Little Traveler." One month later came a second satellite, this one carrying a dog, the first living creature to leave Earth's atmosphere. The next May came *Sputnik III,* weighing nearly three thousand pounds. More Soviet space probes followed, including one in 1959 that photographed the never-before-seen back side of the moon.

Initially, the Eisenhower administration had pooh-poohed the Soviet Union's achievement as a mere stunt. But in reality, *Sputnik* and its successors jolted Americans' smug assumptions about U.S. scientific superiority and stimulated a fierce debate over American public education. In *The American High School Today* (1959), former Harvard president James B. Conant found America woefully behind the Soviet Union in science, math, and foreign-language education.

In direct response to *Sputnik,* Congress in 1958 passed the National Defense Education Act, appropriating $800 million for loans to college and university students and to the states to beef up science and foreign-language instruction. The measure illustrates both the persistence of social-activist liberalism in the Eisenhower era and the importance of Cold War calculations in shaping domestic policy. But whatever the motives, colleges and universities welcomed federal help in serving a crush of students. From 1952 to 1960, enrollment in America's institutions of higher learning surged from 2.1 million to 3.6 million.

Sputnik sent the United States a still more chilling message: The Soviets now had the technology to deploy intercontinental ballistic missiles (ICBMs) that could whisk nuclear warheads to U.S. targets in minutes. Late in 1957, spooked by *Sputnik* and radioactive fallout, 64 percent of Americans cited the nuclear threat as the nation's top problem. For strategists, the more realistic threat was that the Soviets would use their edge in rocketry to advance their broader foreign-policy goals. Policy analyst Herbert Dinerstein developed this point in a January 1958 article in *Foreign Affairs:*

> If the Soviet Union should continue to gain technologically . . . [and] acquire . . . preponderant military strength, they would have policy alternatives even more attractive than the initiation of nuclear war. By flaunting presumably invincible strength, the Soviet Union could compel piecemeal capitulation of the democracies. This prospect must indeed seem glittering to the Soviet leaders.

As the Russians evened the nuclear balance, John Foster Dulles's doctrine of influencing Soviet behavior by the threat of massive retaliation lost credibility. Dulles himself, speaking at the Pentagon in 1958, acknowledged as much. Although the United States clung to massive-retaliation doctrine, the policy's underlying assumptions began to crumble.

Although U.S. intelligence reported no evidence of an operational Soviet ICBM system, Congress, columnists, and Pentagon officials warned of a "missile gap" and called upon the United States to deploy its own ICBM force. Eisenhower resisted on several grounds. Uncontrolled military spending, he continued to caution, would bring inflation and the governmental expansion that he so abhorred.

Strategically, he adhered to the doctrine of "sufficiency": the idea that beyond a certain point, ever-larger nuclear arsenals made no sense.

Eisenhower only partially succeeded in slowing the nuclear arms race. The first U.S. ICBM, the Atlas, became operational in 1959. By the end of his term, vaulting the nuclear competition to new levels of sophistication and menace, the president had authorized some eleven hundred nuclear missiles for deployment in the United States, intermediate-range missiles to be based in Europe, and nineteen nuclear-powered Polaris submarines, each carrying sixteen nuclear missiles. Ike battled with similarly mixed results to control military spending. As his term ended, military spending rebounded to Korean War levels, contributing to the 1959 budget deficit of $12.5 billion, the largest peacetime deficit up to that time.

In his 1995 study *Eisenhower and the Missile Gap,* historian Peter J. Roman shows that intelligence estimates by the CIA and the military consistently inflated the Soviet Union's strength in missiles and delivery systems. These inflated estimates then became the basis of competing demands by the U.S. military services, leading to a proliferation of land-, sea-, and air-based nuclear delivery systems. Eisenhower understood what was happening and tried to resist it, but given his behind-the-scenes approach to the presidency, he never effectively mobilized public opinion against the upwardly spiraling nuclear arms race. Nevertheless, his emphasis on cost control had some effect: Military spending was a smaller percentage of the GNP in 1960 than in 1957.

Given the bipartisan support for the Cold War and the economic benefits of Pentagon contracts, the Democrats rarely challenged military spending levels in these years; indeed, in 1957 the liberal Americans for Democratic Action argued for *more* military spending, especially on conventional forces. Only a few mavericks criticized wasteful Pentagon procurement practices such as the "cost-plus" contracts that guaranteed a fixed profit regardless of cost overruns. The radical journalist I. F. Stone wrote in 1957, "How can there possibly be wise and adequate expenditure in the field of social welfare if the military are allowed a blank check . . . [that] they fill in every year with ever larger amounts?"

Although Stalin's death and the 1955 Geneva summit conference temporarily had eased U.S.-Soviet relations, a string of crises in the later 1950s brought the tension to new heights. First, in the aftermath of *Sputnik,* the Soviet Union agreed to assist the Chinese in building an atomic bomb. Chinese Communist leader Mao Zedong declared on a Moscow visit in November 1957, "The East wind is prevailing over the West wind. . . . The forces of socialism are overwhelmingly superior to the forces of imperialism."

A year later, in November 1958, Stalin's successor Nikita Khrushchev, seeking to force recognition of communist East Germany, set a six-month deadline after which, he insisted, the Western powers would have to deal directly with East Germany, not with Moscow, on matters relating to Berlin. Thoughts of another Berlin blockade haunted many minds when NATO rejected Khrushchev's ultimatum. Fortunately, the mercurial Soviet leader, unwilling to jeopardize a U.S. trip scheduled for 1959, allowed his deadline to pass. Racing through his American tour, Khrushchev plied his heavy-handed folksiness on visits to Hollywood and an Iowa farm and met with Eisenhower at Camp David, the presidential retreat in Maryland. The two leaders scheduled another summit meeting for Paris in 1960. Soon

Vice President Nixon visited Moscow and engaged in his impromptu "kitchen de-bate" with Khrushchev.

The promise of a further thaw in U.S.-Soviet relations proved illusory, how-ever. On the eve of the Paris summit, the Soviets shot down a U.S. U-2 spy plane and captured the pilot, Francis Gary Powers.* Washington initially called the flight a weather-data-gathering mission that had wandered off course, but when the Sovi-ets produced Powers, Eisenhower admitted responsibility for the U-2 flight, citing U.S. security needs. Khrushchev stormed back to Moscow. Although a setback for détente, the incident solidified Eisenhower's popularity at home. Thousands turned out to welcome his return to Washington after the failed summit.

In the Middle East, the United States remained highly concerned about Soviet influence. In 1957, following a speech by Eisenhower before a joint session of Con-gress, both houses passed a resolution that came to be called the Eisenhower Doc-trine. It authorized the administration to provide economic and military aid and even to intervene militarily to defend any Middle East nation from "international communism." In the background loomed a fundamental objective: protecting the oil vital to the economies of the industrialized West and Japan. From 1948 to 1972, Middle East oil production gushed from 1.1 million to 18.2 million barrels per day, and the region's proved reserves grew more than sixteenfold. As Middle East pe-troleum gained importance in the world market, keeping the region securely in the Western camp became a foundation stone of U.S. foreign policy.

A major test of the Eisenhower Doctrine came in 1958 when Iraq, after a leftist coup engineered by Egyptian leader Gamal Abdal Nasser, left the Baghdad Pact (see p. 112). Dreading similar coups elsewhere, Eisenhower ordered fifteen thou-sand U.S. Marines to nearby Lebanon. British troops, meanwhile, landed in Jor-dan, whose pro-Western government faced threats by Nasser supporters. The troops soon withdrew as the immediate danger faded, but Washington's somewhat contradictory goals in the Middle East—to quarantine the area against Soviet pene-tration, to secure the flow of Arab oil to the West, and to maintain close ties with Israel—guaranteed that the United States would remain enmeshed in the struggles and intrigues of this region torn by deep-seated hatreds and rivalries.

In Cuba, meanwhile, guerrilla leader Fidel Castro overthrew pro-U.S. dictator Fulgencio Batista in 1959. Castro's insurgency, initially received favorable U.S. press coverage, but as he allied Cuba with the Soviet Union, Castro mounted a Marxist revolution, imprisoned his opponents, expelled U.S. businesses, including gambling casinos operated by organized-crime figures, and seized U.S.-owned oil refineries. Relations with Washington soured. After persuading the Organization of American States to pass anti-Castro resolutions, the administration halted U.S. im-ports of Cuban sugar, vital to the island's economy. In this context, the CIA planned and Eisenhower approved an anti-Castro invasion of Cuba to take place in 1961, after Eisenhower left office.

Foreshadowing the 1960s, the later Eisenhower administration paid more at-tention to Southeast Asia. Having managed successful coups in Iran and Guate-mala, the CIA in 1957 planned a similar operation in Indonesia, financing and

---

* Powers was tried in the Soviet Union and convicted of espionage but eventually was released. Ironically, he later died in a helicopter crash while employed as a radio traffic reporter.

organizing a guerrilla movement to overthrow the country's ruler, Sukarno, who was suspected of communist leanings. This secret effort failed, however. Sukarno maneuvered cleverly, and by the end of 1958, Washington had shifted policy and was giving him aid.

In Vietnam, an increasingly autocratic Ngo Dinh Diem, a Catholic in a largely Buddhist country, ignored the political and economic reforms urged on him by Washington (see p. 114). Declaring South Vietnam independent, he canceled the elections promised by the Geneva Accords. As his regime lost support, communist military action intensified. So, too, did American involvement; by 1960, the United States had sent some seven hundred military advisers to South Vietnam.

Campaign 1960: Variations on the Cold War Theme

The 1960 presidential race pitted Massachusetts senator John F. Kennedy against Vice President Richard Nixon, two men from opposite coasts and vastly different backgrounds. Kennedy was shaped from boyhood by his family's great wealth, Irish-Catholic roots, and immersion in politics going back to his maternal grandfather, a Boston saloonkeeper who became mayor. Young Kennedy graduated from Harvard in 1940. Nixon was born in Whittier, California, to lower-middle-class Quaker parents who operated a small grocery store. He attended tiny Whittier College during the depths of the Depression, graduating in 1934.

These two very different men had followed curiously parallel paths to the political summit. Both had served as naval officers in World War II, and both entered Congress in 1946. Whereas Kennedy's congressional years proved undistinguished, Nixon had achieved visibility, if not universal admiration, for his dogged service on the House Un-American Activities Committee and had been tapped to run with Eisenhower in 1952. His eight years as vice president had brought mostly frustration, as Eisenhower had kept him at arm's length. Prodded at a press conference in 1960 to name a major policy decision that Nixon had participated in, Ike laughed and asked the reporter to give him a week to think about it.

The most important force in John Kennedy's life was his father, Joseph P. Kennedy, who had made a fortune in the stock market and in the movie business. An ambitious Democrat, the elder Kennedy was appointed U.S. ambassador to Great Britain by President Roosevelt in 1938. His isolationism and belief in the inevitability of a Nazi victory thwarted his political plans, however, and he groomed his sons for high office. When his eldest son, Joseph, Jr., was killed in World War II, Joseph, Sr., turned to the next in line, John, a handsome, decorated navy veteran. Pressured by his father, John Kennedy ran for Congress in 1946. In 1952, only thirty-four years old, he moved up to the Senate. In 1953 he married Jacqueline Bouvier, a Rhode Island socialite twelve years his junior.

After testing the waters with a bid for the vice-presidential nomination in 1956 (and losing to Estes Kefauver), Kennedy in 1960 joined a crowded field seeking the Democratic presidential nomination. Senator Hubert Humphrey dropped out after Kennedy, aided by his father's heavy spending, won primary victories in Wisconsin and West Virginia. His most formidable opponent, Senate majority leader

The First Family of Camelot. *John F. Kennedy, Jacqueline Bouvier Kennedy, and daughter Caroline. The president's dashing good looks and his wife's cool sophistication underlay a carefully cultivated image that helped Kennedy win the presidency.* (AP/Wide World Photos)

Lyndon Johnson, avoided the primaries and entered the race only five days before the party convention. By then, Kennedy had the votes and won a first-ballot nomination. Despite a high level of animosity between the two ambitious men, Kennedy offered the vice-presidential slot to Johnson, who accepted.

Launching what would become a tradition in presidential races, Kennedy and Nixon participated in four televised debates. In the first, on September 26, the awkward, defensive, and sweaty Nixon, his makeup failing to mask his heavy five o'clock shadow, struggled to make a good impression. Kennedy, charismatic, smiling, and spewing facts like a machine-gun, dominated the event. His promises to bring fresh ideas and vigorous leadership to the White House and to "get America moving again" captured the public's attention. A recession that pushed joblessness to a postwar high in 1960 also increased voters' readiness for change.

Taking nothing for granted, Democratic strategists turned to securing the critical African-American vote. The 1960 Democratic platform included a vigorous civil-rights plank and promised strong presidential leadership on this front. On October 26, Kennedy phoned Coretta Scott King to express support for her husband Martin Luther King, Jr., in jail on trumped-up charges involving a minor traffic violation. Through the intervention of the candidate's younger brother, Robert F. Kennedy, King was released. Although he stopped short of an actual endorsement,

King praised Kennedy extravagantly. King's father, a Republican, switched his support to the Democratic candidate.

Playing on Cold War fears, Kennedy warned of a dangerous missile gap separating the United States and the Soviet Union, a gap that after the election would prove illusory. In the TV debate on foreign policy, the two candidates vied in portraying themselves as staunch Cold Warriors. Kennedy, however, argued that Eisenhower should have apologized for the U-2 flight to keep the Paris summit on track. He also took the position that the small islands claimed by both the Chinese nationalists and the Chinese communists were not worth the risk of war with China (see p. 114).

Kennedy's primary victory in overwhelmingly Protestant West Virginia helped to rebut the claim that a Catholic could not win, but concerns persisted. No Catholic had ever been elected president, and the only other one ever nominated, Governor Al Smith of New York in 1928, had suffered resounding defeat. When queried about the religion issue in the primary campaigns, Kennedy shot back, "Nobody asked if I was a Catholic when I joined the United States Navy. . . . Nobody asked my brother if he was a Catholic or a Protestant before he climbed into an American bomber to fly his last mission." When 150 prominent Protestants led

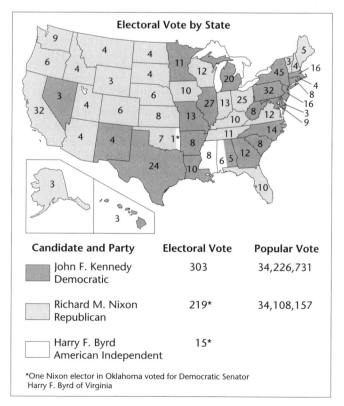

FIGURE 6.1

Presidential Election of 1960

by Reverend Norman Vincent Peale warned that a Catholic president inevitably would be influenced by the church hierarchy, Kennedy flew to Houston and assured a convention of Protestant ministers that, although proud of his religion, as president he would not allow Catholic doctrine or official pronouncements to dictate his decisions.

In an extremely close election, Nixon carried all but four states west of the Mississippi and won Tennessee, Kentucky, Virginia, and Florida in the South. Kennedy did well in the industrial belt and the big cities. Seventy percent of blacks voted Democratic, providing Kennedy's margin of victory in Pennsylvania, Michigan, Texas, and South Carolina. Illinois and Texas provided Kennedy's razor-thin 120,000-vote victory margin. Native-son Johnson helped the ticket in Texas, and in Illinois the powerful Democratic machine run by Chicago mayor Richard J. Daley threw its formidable resources behind Kennedy. When Kennedy phoned Daley on election night, as Illinois teetered in the balance, the mayor promised him, "Mr. President, with a bit of luck and the help of a few close friends, you're going to carry Illinois." Kennedy's coattails were short, however. Although the Democrats retained control of both houses of Congress, the Republicans gained twenty-one seats in the House.

For Richard Nixon, the 1960 defeat, followed by a loss in a California gubernatorial race two years later was a bitter setback. "You won't have Nixon to kick around anymore," he told reporters after the 1962 defeat. His self-pitying prediction proved decidedly premature.

Kennedy, remarkably boyish looking at forty-three, launched his presidency on a tide of popular support. His inaugural address invoked a "new frontier" of social progress and underscored the theme of generational change:

> [T]he torch has been passed to a new generation of Americans—born in this century, tempered by war, disciplined by a hard and bitter peace, proud of our ancient heritage—and unwilling to witness or permit the slow undoing of those human rights . . . to which we are committed today at home and around the world.

The Cold War, Kennedy-Style

Kennedy's approach to Cold War leadership differed markedly from Eisenhower's. Shaped by an intensely competitive family and a hard-driving father whom he both admired and feared, he eagerly sought to prove his toughness to the Soviet adversary. America, he declared in a particularly strident passage of his inaugural address, would "pay any price, bear any burden, meet any hardship, support any friend, oppose any foes, in order to assure the survival and success of liberty." Few expected that the nation would soon be asked to fulfill that grandiose pledge in the jungles and rice paddies of Vietnam.

In addition to his personal character traits, the new president brought the outlook of Democratic liberals to the Cold War. Rooted in New Deal activism, the liberal tradition had been toughened in the early years of the Cold War when Democrats such as Harry Truman, Dean Acheson, and George Kennan had first committed the nation to the anticommunist cause.

Cold War liberalism sprang from the belief, grounded in years of domestic re-form activism, that through intelligent, planned effort, the federal government could serve as an instrument of social betterment. Kennedy-style liberals such as White House speechwriter Arthur Schlesinger, Jr., a historian of the New Deal, ap-plied this commitment globally. The United States under liberal leadership could pursue the Cold War more effectively than the Republicans, they believed, by working for social and democratic change worldwide as an alternative to the siren song of Marxist revolutionaries. Repudiating what they caricatured as Eisen-hower's policy of drift, Cold War liberals called for energetic, aggressive tackling of foreign as well as domestic challenges. In the 1930s, Franklin Roosevelt had por-trayed the fight against the Depression as a great national crusade, and liberal Cold Warriors infused the anticommunist cause with the same high rhetoric. As Under-secretary of Defense John McNaughton put it in a 1961 memo to the White House, "The United States needs a *Grand Objective. . . .* [W]e behave as if . . . our real objec-tive is to sit by our pools and contemplate the spare tires around our middles."

The Kennedy administration's sense of new possibilities in foreign policy in-tensified as old rivalries and border conflicts between Moscow and Beijing re-asserted themselves. The CIA reported in 1963, "The U.S.S.R. and China are now two separate powers whose interests conflict on almost every issue." Washington did not fully exploit this division until the 1970s, but awareness of its possibilities hovered in the background of U.S. Cold War strategy from the early 1960s onward.

Kennedy's secretary of state, Dean Rusk, a soft-spoken, moon-faced Georgian, epitomized Cold War liberalism. As a liberal southerner, Rusk had worked for civil rights. As a political scientist specializing in Asian affairs, he had served in the Truman years as assistant secretary of state for Far Eastern affairs. In the 1950s, as president of the Rockefeller Foundation he had initiated health-care programs and other social reforms in the vast region of the globe that was coming to be called the Third World. But Rusk also proved a tough-minded Cold Warrior who had long urged a hard line toward communist China.

Rusk's influence in the Kennedy administration was muted, however. Quiet and self-effacing, he often maintained a Buddha-like silence in high-level meetings, allowing others to control the debate. On foreign-policy issues, Kennedy relied mainly on a team of advisers recruited from academia and corporate America, who prided themselves on being "hard-nosed realists." Secretary of Defense Robert McNamara, formerly president of Ford Motor Company, specialized in sta-tistical analysis of policy options. McNamara's no-nonsense manner and fondness for charts and graphs epitomized the Kennedy team's approach to foreign policy. Barry Goldwater called him a computer with legs. National security adviser Mc-George Bundy had served as dean of Harvard College. Kennedy's deputy, Walt Rostow, later head of the State Department's Policy Planning Staff, had taught gov-ernment at the Massachusetts Institute of Technology.

The grand strategist was Rostow, a facile synthesizer of big ideas. "Walt can write faster than I can read," Kennedy joked. His *Stages of Economic Growth: A Non-Communist Manifesto* (1960) had argued that the United States could win the Cold War by supplying aid and technical assistance to turn Third World nations into modern industrial democracies. Don't rely on entrenched elites in Asia, Africa, and Latin America, Rostow advised, but seek out noncommunist groups that can resist Marxism's lure while serving as agents of economic modernization within a democratic framework. Too often, he warned, communists in these countries, backed by Moscow, presented themselves as the only force that could rescue the masses from poverty. In Rostow's view, an intelligently crafted U.S. foreign policy could change all this by strengthening democratic alternatives.

Rostow summed up his ideas in a long policy document presented to Kennedy in mid-1961. Rather than continuing the Eisenhower-Dulles habit of backing entrenched conservative regimes as long as they opposed communism, Rostow argued, the United States should identify and support progressive, noncommunist forces in the developing world. Such action-oriented liberalism led Rostow to favor the idea of a highly interventionist U.S. role in nations threatened by leftist uprisings.

This emphasis on social and economic development as a Cold War strategy had the added advantage of downplaying direct nuclear confrontation with the Soviets. Indeed, one way Kennedy liberals distinguished themselves from Republican Cold Warriors was in repudiating the latter's overreliance on nuclear weapons in military planning. Kennedy's favorite general, Maxwell Taylor, who became chairman of the Joint Chiefs of Staff in 1962, in his 1959 book *The Uncertain Trumpet* had called for supplementing nuclear weapons with a wide range of conventional armaments and strategies capable of meeting all kinds of foreign challenges. Summing up the goal of Taylor's "flexible-response" doctrine in 1961, Kennedy declared: "We intend to have a wider choice than humiliation or all-out nuclear war."

Focusing initially on Latin America with its reactionary elites and yawning social inequities, Kennedy in March 1961 announced the Alliance for Progress, which pledged $20 billion in new foreign aid for the region. This aid, however, hinged on the recipients' committing themselves to radical social change, including reforms in their land-tenure and tax policies. The Alliance for Progress expressed the Rostow doctrine of encouraging fundamental social changes in societies threatened by communist insurgency. As one U.S. official put it, "A revolution is inevitable in Latin America. If you don't do it peacefully, you'll end up with blood." Soon, however, the idealism of the Alliance for Progress was mocked by a debacle that, although not of Kennedy's doing, had consequences that fell at his doorstep.

Disaster at Bahía de Cochinos

Upon taking office, Kennedy learned from CIA director Allen Dulles* of the plan to invade Cuba. The plot ignored the vast differences between the Cuban situation and that in other countries where CIA coups had succeeded, such as Iran and Guatemala, but it was far advanced when the new administration took office. Anti-Castro Cuban refugees being trained in Guatemala to carry out the attack joked that "CIA" stood for Cuban Invasion Authority. With misgivings, Kennedy approved the invasion.

---

* The younger brother of John Foster Dulles, who had died in 1959.

The plan assumed that the Cuban masses would rise up and overthrow Castro. But when the sixteen hundred invaders landed on April 17, 1961, at Bahía de Cochinos (the Bay of Pigs), the local populace showed no interest in joining them. Castro, who often vacationed at Bay of Pigs, enjoyed great popularity in the region. Furthermore, the Escambray Mountains that the CIA planners had envisioned as a hiding place for the invaders lay *eighty miles* away through swamps and jungles.

In a disaster that delivered a sobering dash of reality to both the CIA and Kennedy, Castro's forces killed more than 100 invaders and captured 1,189. Eventually the administration ransomed them for $10 million in medical supplies. Even had the plan worked, the United States might have been saddled with a protracted military occupation of Cuba amid a hostile population, evocative of the imperialistic days of the Spanish-American War.

Furious at his humiliation, Kennedy ordered the CIA to disrupt Cuba's economy and discredit its government. The intelligence agency responded with Project Mongoose, under which CIA operatives burned cane fields, blew up factories and power plants, and persuaded European industries to ship Castro defective equipment. CIA planners also devised numerous schemes for embarrassing or even killing Castro, including lacing his cigars with poison, exploding giant clamshells near where he snorkeled, and even trying to make his beard fall out by sprinkling depilatory powder into his shoes. In this campaign, the CIA recruited various organized crime figures eager to regain control of their Havana operations. All this scheming helped lay the background for the 1962 Cuban missile crisis.

Meanwhile, Moscow and Beijing feuded and China's nuclear-weapons program forged ahead. China did not test its first atomic bomb until October 1964, but Kennedy knew from intelligence sources that a Chinese bomb was imminent. The president hoped to exploit these circumstances to improve U.S.-Soviet relations, but initially this hope went unfulfilled. Kennedy and Khrushchev first met in Vienna in June 1961. The discussion, as so often in the past, centered on Germany. Testing the new administration in Washington, Khrushchev again made a pawn of Berlin as part of his larger strategy of forcing the West to accept the Soviet-backed East German regime. The continual flow of East German refugees seeking asylum in the West by way of Berlin posed another thorny problem for Moscow.

The Vienna meeting, convened amid this atmosphere of crisis, fared badly. The sixty-seven-year-old Soviet leader treated the new president like an immature youth whom he could intimidate through bullying and bluster. Kennedy left Vienna convinced that danger lay ahead. He called for increased military spending, tripled the draft call, activated thousands of reserves, and delivered a frightening television address warning that nuclear war could break out at any time. Echoing John Foster Dulles's language of brinksmanship, Kennedy cautioned the Soviets not to make the "dangerous mistake" of assuming that the West was "too soft" to go to war if necessary. Once again, he declared, evoking the crises of 1948 and 1959, Berlin had become "the great testing place of Western courage and will."

As part of his war of nerves with Moscow, Kennedy urged a crash program of fallout-shelter construction. Civil-defense planning included a program called NEAR (National Emergency Alarm Repeater) for installing alarms in every home and apartment. Nuclear fear, muted since 1958 when the superpowers had temporarily halted atmospheric tests, reawakened.

❖❖   ## IN PERSPECTIVE: *The Ironies of Civil Defense*

Federal civil-defense preparations for nuclear attack shaped millions of Americans' Cold War experience. The civil-defense program of the 1950s (see Chapter 5) crested in the early 1960s as President Kennedy proved his toughness in dealing with the Russians by somberly warning the American people of the threat of nuclear war and calling for an urgent program of fallout-shelter construction.

Kennedy's 1961 warning was part of a long history of civil-defense activity that began in 1945 and lasted into the 1980s. In the first anxious months after Hiroshima, a variety of survival schemes were proposed, including vast underground complexes to which people could retreat in the event of attack. The Federal Civil Defense Administration (1950) put matters on a more systematic basis. The motives were complex. Of course, the desire to save lives should nuclear war come was important. But civil-defense preparation also made Washington's nuclear threat more credible: It signaled to the Russians that America would go to the nuclear brink and beyond if necessary. Further, civil-defense planners sought to reassure nervous Americans that nuclear war need not be a death warrant: With advance planning, it was survivable. An upbeat 1950 civil-defense handbook was titled *You Can Survive an Atomic Bomb.* It advised worried readers to rake the leaves away from their houses (to reduce fire risks in a nuclear attack); keep a full tank of gas in the car for quick evacuation; and always wear hats (for men) and long-sleeved blouses (for women), as protection from the atomic flash.

Civil defense planners in the 1950s sought to make civil defense a national priority. Radio stations broadcast practice nuclear alerts. Schoolchildren watched civil-defense films and hid under desks in nuclear-attack drills; some were issued metal name tags. In a 1956 federal civil-defense movie, *Operation Alert,* Manhattan is evacuated calmly and quickly before a hypothetical missile attack, with no confusion, panic, or traffic jams. Yellow "Fallout Shelter" signs appeared on public buildings, and metal drums containing emergency water were placed in the basements of designated buildings. (When empty, the instructions advised, the drums could double as emergency toilets.) The medical profession was mobilized. Physicians received training in how to treat nuclear-attack victims. Psychologists discussed strategies for counseling the dis-

Khrushchev chose an unexpected route out of the impasse. On August 13, 1961, the Soviets erected a barrier across divided Berlin. The Berlin Wall blocked all movement between the two halves of the city, and would-be East German refugees challenged it at peril of their lives. General Lucius Clay, Kennedy's special representative in Berlin, advocated a military challenge to the Berlin Wall, but Kennedy rejected this advice. Although the wall caused anguish for divided families and hardened the division of Europe, it ended the cycle of confrontation over Berlin. It in fact was a retreat by Khrushchev disguised as a bold initiative. As

traught after the bombs fell. Entire cities organized emergency drills in which everyone was supposed to seek shelter when the alarm sounded. The federal government even held a drill in 1958 in which government workers retreated to fallout shelters and President Eisenhower was flown to a secret command center away from Washington.

The home fallout-shelter program was part of this larger effort. Some people constructed reinforced shelters in their basements. Others built backyard shelters and stocked them with emergency supplies. Theologians debated the morality of shooting outsiders who tried to break into one's family shelter in a nuclear emergency.

With the Limited Nuclear Test Ban Treaty of 1963 and the gradual easing of Cold War tensions, fear of nuclear war and the preoccupation with civil defense diminished. The Vietnam War, Watergate, and the 1970s energy crises focused attention on other matters.

But civil defense returned to center stage in the early 1980s, as the Reagan administration, pursuing its larger agenda of ideological and military confrontation with Moscow, aggressively pushed new civil-defense programs. The emphasis now was not on fallout shelters, but on "crisis relocation." Should nuclear war threaten, the plan went, city dwellers would evacuate to nearby rural areas and small towns, leaving the targeted cities empty when the missiles fell. Some questioned the practicality of crisis relocation. Given the typical rush-hour traffic jam, they wondered, what would happen when entire cities tried to evacuate simultaneously?

The skepticism about crisis relocation underscored a continuing irony and paradox of the entire civil-defense effort. The American people were never really convinced that civil defense offered genuine hope in the nuclear age, or that they would want to survive in a postnuclear world. Indeed, the main effect of the entire civil-defense effort seems not to have been to reassure the public, but to heighten nuclear fear by forcing Americans to confront a scary reality many would have preferred to ignore.

During the great waves of civil-defense activity, first in the fifties and early sixties, and again in the early eighties, critics dismissed and ridiculed the entire effort as deceptive and cynical. Science fiction stories like Walter Miller's *A Canticle for Leibowitz* (1954), movies such as *On the Beach* (1959), episodes on TV programs like *The Twilight Zone,* and TV specials such as *The Day After* (1984) offered a very different view of nuclear war than the reassuring pronouncements of civil-defense officials. Challenging the government's theme of safety through civil defense, antiwar activists presented an alternative message: that the best defense against nuclear war was to work for peace and nuclear disarmament, to make sure the attack never came.

By the late 1990s, as the Cold War receded into the past, so, too, did the era when fallout shelters, radio alerts, school drills, and Bert the Turtle had been an everyday part of American life. Only those who had lived through the era were left with the memories of what it was like.

Kennedy told an adviser, "This is his way out of his predicament. It's not a very nice solution, but a wall is a hell of a lot better than war." Visiting Berlin in June 1963, Kennedy denounced the barricade as proof of communism's failure and crowed to the cheering throng, *"Ich bin ein Berliner"* ("I am a Berliner").*

---

* Directly translated, Kennedy's phrase was an idiom that meant "I am a jelly doughnut," causing some initial confusion in his German-speaking audience. What the president should have said was, "Ich bin Berliner."

Divided City, Divided World. *The Berlin Wall, erected in 1961, not only bisected a city but also symbolized a world divided by Cold War hostilities.* (U.S. Army Photograph)

    The Cold War erupted also in Central Africa, where the former Belgian Congo, now independent, was led by Patrice Lumumba, who had received training in Moscow. Western leaders feared that Lumumba would halt the export to the West of copper, uranium, and other minerals from the southern province of Katanga. When Katangan leader Moise Tshombe announced the province's independence, the United States supported the move. Lumumba's assassination in January 1961 was widely blamed on the CIA. As civil war raged in the Congo, the Kennedy administration gave aid and air support to Lumumba's right-wing successor, Joseph Kasavubu, whom it viewed as a bulwark against Soviet expansion in Africa. This policy of orchestrating the downfall and possibly the assassination of a nationalist leader who tilted toward Moscow stirred ill will against the United States in Third World states struggling against colonialism.

October 1962: To the Brink

Heightened Cold War tension turned to terror during the Cuban missile crisis of October 1962. The incident began when the CIA informed President Kennedy that high-altitude photos by U-2 spy planes had confirmed earlier reports from a spy operating in Cuba: The Soviet Union had deployed in Cuba SS-4 intermediate-range ballistic missiles (IRBMs) designed to carry one- to three-megaton nuclear warheads.* With a range of 1,020 nautical miles, the SS-4s could reach targets in the eastern United States, including New York City and Washington, D.C., in eight minutes. Further, some of the missile sites were designed to house SS-5 mis-

---

* A megaton, the standard unit for measuring nuclear bombs, is the explosive force of one million tons of TNT. The bomb that destroyed Hiroshima in August 1945 had the explosive force of twenty thousand tons of TNT.

siles, which carried even larger warheads and had a range of more than two thousand nautical miles. Washington's precise knowledge of the capacity of the SS-4s
and SS-5s rested on information provided by a Soviet spy who had microfilmed
and transmitted to the CIA a key Soviet missile manual. Whether the missiles in
Cuba had actually been armed with nuclear warheads remained uncertain at the
time. Years later, when the Cold War was over, Russian military men would reveal
that the U.S.S.R. had installed nuclear weapons in Cuba and that the local Soviet
commander had the authority to use them in the event of a U.S. invasion. Thus,
the crisis was even graver, and the risks of nuclear war even higher, than Washington realized at the time.

Why did Khrushchev take this dangerous step? No evidence suggests that he
planned an actual nuclear attack, but he surely sought to increase Moscow's bargaining power on a range of Cold War issues by achieving nuclear parity. Overall,
despite Kennedy's talk in the 1960 campaign about a missile gap, the United States
possessed many more nuclear missiles than the Soviets. As the Soviet ambassador
to Cuba in 1962 later recalled, "[Khrushchev] was looking for any way to talk to
the Americans equally." Furthermore, in July 1962, the Kennedy administration
had deployed fifteen U.S. Jupiter missiles in Turkey, placing much of the Soviet
Union within a few minutes' striking time. Finally, Fidel Castro, justifiably alarmed
by the Bay of Pigs attack and by subsequent CIA plots against him, had begged for
a stronger Soviet military presence in Cuba.

To Khrushchev, putting SS-4s and SS-5s in Cuba offered a quick way to please
Castro, counter the Jupiter missiles in Turkey, and redress the larger strategic imbalance. The Bay of Pigs fiasco, and the poor impression that Kennedy had made
on Khrushchev in Vienna, also may have encouraged the Soviet leader to believe
that Kennedy would not dare challenge this provocation, especially in the midst of
the 1962 midterm electoral campaign.

Khrushchev's move sparked an urgent, top-secret policy debate within the
Kennedy administration. The Cuban missiles did not actually change the balance
of power, which remained overwhelmingly in America's favor, but they gave the
impression of a dramatic Soviet gain, and this Kennedy could not tolerate. The
Cuban missile deployment, he complained to his advisers, "makes [the Soviets]
look like they're co-equal with us." In short, as historian Stephen Ambrose has
observed, "The most serious crisis in the history of mankind . . . turned on a question of appearances. The world came close to total destruction over a matter of
prestige."

Kennedy secretly assembled a team of advisers called the Executive Committee, or EXCOM. Some members—former Secretary of State Dean Acheson; General Maxwell Taylor, chairman of the Joint Chiefs of Staff; and air force general
Curtis LeMay—favored a preemptive air strike, followed by an invasion if necessary. Several top congressional Democrats also urged this course. Others, notably
Undersecretary of State George Ball, advocated a blockade of Cuba, with the option of a military strike later. Kennedy, rejecting a surprise attack as too risky and
too reminiscent of Japan's attack on Pearl Harbor in 1941, chose the blockade.

In a TV address on Monday evening, October 22, the president revealed the
existence of the missiles in Cuba, demanded their withdrawal, and announced a
naval blockade of Cuba to begin at 10 A.M. Tuesday. The next morning, when

several Soviet ships turned back, tensions eased. Dean Rusk commented, "We're eyeball to eyeball and I think the other fellow just blinked." But the crisis continued. Fear ran high over the next few days as EXCOM—and the world—awaited the Soviet response. The Strategic Air Command moved to DEFCON 2, a high state of readiness. Presidential speechwriter Theodore Sorensen recalled, "Our little group seated around the Cabinet table in continuous session . . . felt nuclear war to be closer . . . than at any time in the nuclear age." Kennedy summoned his wife and children, who were traveling, back to the White House so that they could escape to a presidential nuclear shelter if necessary.

Millions of Americans watched helplessly as their fate hung in the balance. Through much of the Cold War, the nuclear threat loomed as a disturbing but somewhat abstract menace; in October 1962 it suddenly became starkly immediate, and chronic anxiety spiked into heart-throbbing terror.

Behind the scenes, urgent communications were passing between Washington and Moscow. On October 26, Khrushchev sent a rambling but essentially conciliatory message that expressed his own dread of nuclear war and offered to remove the IRBMs in exchange for a U.S. pledge not to invade Cuba. A second message on the 27th took a harder line: The United States must also remove its missiles from Turkey. Again the Joint Chiefs and some EXCOM members clamored for an invasion. Still the president held back. At the suggestion of his brother, Attorney General Robert Kennedy, JFK answered Khrushchev's more accommodating first message, pledging not to invade Cuba if the missiles were withdrawn. Robert Kennedy met secretly with Soviet ambassador Anatoly Dobrynin and assured him that once the Cuban crisis was resolved, the administration would soon remove the Turkish missiles. With these promises, Khrushchev agreed to remove the IRBMs. On Sunday, October 28, Kennedy announced the news, to universal relief. The Soviets removed the missiles, and Kennedy lifted the blockade. In April 1963, the U.S. Jupiter missiles quietly disappeared from Turkey, as well as from Great Britain and Italy, to be replaced by seaborne missiles aboard Polaris submarines.

John Foster Dulles had talked of going to the nuclear brink; Kennedy and Khrushchev had actually peered into the abyss and pulled back. Even for two such fiercely competitive Cold Warriors, the deadly logic of nuclear stalement served as a powerful constraint.

Viewed at the time as a victory for U.S. firmness and a personal triumph for Kennedy, the Cuban missile crisis had several unexpected ramifications. It undermined Khrushchev's position with his Kremlin colleagues, who perceived him as having buckled under U.S. pressure, and within two years he had fallen from power. French leader Charles de Gaulle, convinced that in a crisis the United States would pursue its own interests without consulting NATO, accelerated France's nuclear-weapons research, ordered NATO's headquarters out of Paris, and eventually withdrew from NATO's military command structure.

Most important, the crisis underscored the risk of global war. As John Kenneth Galbraith commented, "We were in luck. But success in lotteries is no argument for lotteries." After the crisis, Kennedy moderated his Cold War rhetoric and stepped up efforts to bring the nuclear arms race under control. In August 1961, confronted with a major U.S. nuclear-weapons buildup, the Soviets had resumed nuclear testing, including the detonation of a blockbuster fifty-eight-megaton bomb, the equivalent of three thousand Hiroshima-type bombs. Kennedy reluctantly ordered another round of U.S. tests, but he understood the fallout danger and genuinely desired a test ban. In addition, China's nuclear-weapons program raised the specter of nuclear proliferation. Indeed, the prospect of a Chinese bomb so worried Kennedy that he proposed a joint U.S.-Soviet military strike against China's nuclear facilities, an idea Khrushchev rejected.

In an address on June 10, 1963, Kennedy spoke of the "nuclear sword of Damocles" hanging over the earth and exhorted world leaders to diminish the danger. "Our most basic common link," the president declared, "is the fact that we all inhabit this planet. We all breathe the same air. We all cherish our children's future. And we are all mortal." In August 1963, the United States, the Soviet Union, and Great Britain signed a treaty banning nuclear testing in the atmosphere or underwater. On September 24, the Senate ratified the treaty by an overwhelming margin, 80–19. Important as an environmental and public-health measure and as a gesture of goodwill, the test-ban treaty nevertheless did not halt the nuclear arms race. Underground testing continued, and France and China carried on their atmospheric testing.

In a step to reduce the risk of nuclear war, the United States and the Soviet Union also set up a direct telecommunications system, or hot line, between the White House and the Kremlin. One cartoonist pictured a frustrated Khrushchev reaching Kennedy's daughter, Caroline, on the hot line and sputtering in exasperation, "No, I don't want your *dolly,* I want your *daddy!*" In still another effort toward improved relations, Kennedy in October 1963 authorized U.S. wheat sales to the Soviet Union.

Kennedy also, however, initiated a nuclear buildup that by 1967 gave the United States 41 Polaris subs armed with more than 650 missiles; 600 strategic bombers; and 1,000 intercontinental ballistic missiles (ICBMs)—a fivefold increase over the 200 inherited from the Eisenhower administration. The Soviet Union strove to keep pace. By 1967 even Defense Secretary McNamara conceded that the nuclear escalation had increased tensions and risks without strengthening U.S security.

Why did Kennedy authorize this expansion when strategists were downplaying nuclear missiles in favor of a flexible-response approach stressing nonnuclear weaponry? Essentially, nuclear weapons had become the symbol of world power. Kennedy had no intention of launching a nuclear war, and apart from the nerve-wracking days of the Cuban missile crisis, he little expected the Soviets to start one. But in the post-Hiroshima world, status required nuclear power. Paul Nitze, assistant secretary of defense, noted in a 1961 speech, "We believe this [nuclear] superiority, particularly when viewed from the Soviet side, to be strategically important in the equation of deterrence and strategy." The Soviets naturally held the same view, and the nuclear arms race proceeded at full tilt.

Southeast Asia and Vietnam: Deeper into the Tunnel

Although the nuclear competition continued, more conventional patterns of conflict preoccupied Washington strategists, especially when they turned to Southeast Asia. The map of this region presented a complex mosaic of poor and developing nations, many emerging from a colonial past, in which rival and often shadowy

GERMANY

August 1961:
Berlin Wall erected

AUSTRIA

1961: Kennedy-Khrushchev
Vienna meeting

1959: Castro
overthrows Batista

CUBA

April 1961:
Bay of Pigs fiasco

October 1962:
Cuban missile crisis

ATLANTIC OCEAN

1961: "Alliance for Progress"
aid to Latin America

1961: U.S. intervention
in the Congo

PACIFIC OCEAN

FIGURE 6.2
The Cold War Heats Up

groups vied for dominance. Viewing this confusing reality through a Cold War lens, Kennedy-era policymakers tended to see new arenas of East-West confrontation that their predecessors had dangerously neglected. "If you don't pay attention to the periphery," Dean Rusk warned in a May 1961 news conference, ". . . the first thing you know the periphery is the center. . . . [W]hat happens in one place cannot help but affect what happens in another."

This shift in focus responded to changes in Soviet policy, which in the Kennedy years oscillated between conciliation and belligerence. In their belligerent mode, the Soviets revealed a readiness to foment revolution in the Third

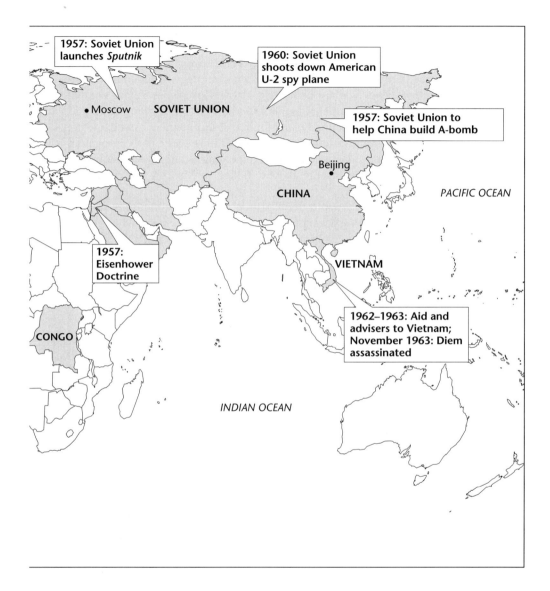

1957: Soviet Union launches *Sputnik*

1960: Soviet Union shoots down American U-2 spy plane

•Moscow   SOVIET UNION

1957: Soviet Union to help China build A-bomb

Beijing

CHINA

PACIFIC OCEAN

1957: Eisenhower Doctrine

VIETNAM

CONGO

1962–1963: Aid and advisers to Vietnam; November 1963: Diem assassinated

INDIAN OCEAN

World. In a January 1961 speech, just as Kennedy took office, Nikita Khrushchev made clear that Moscow, despite still seeking peaceful coexistence with the West, would happily sponsor "wars of national liberation" in Africa, Latin America, and Southeast Asia. Washington planners in turn focused on strategies for containing this new threat. Walt Rostow, as we have seen, emphasized social and economic development. In September 1961, Congress created the Agency for International Development (AID) to coordinate all U.S. foreign-aid programs. Throughout the 1960s, AID funneled $47 billion to development programs worldwide. The Food for Peace program, another Kennedy initiative in the area of social and economic development, had the dual function of easing hunger in poor nations while reducing U.S. farm surpluses.

But the liberal Cold Warriors saw the Third World struggle in military as well as economic terms. Maxwell Taylor's flexible-response strategy included new techniques of counterinsurgency warfare designed to show Moscow, as Taylor argued, that its fomenting of "wars of national liberation" would be "costly, dangerous, and doomed to failure." President Kennedy, an admirer of Ian Fleming's debonair fictional hero James Bond, found counterinsurgency planning particularly intriguing. Even Walt Rostow had no qualms about supplementing economic development with military measures against insurgents who looked to Moscow rather than to Washington.

The shift of focus from Europe to the Third World did not diminish the tendency of Washington Cold Warriors to view the world in black-and-white terms. In an April 1961 speech to newspaper publishers, Kennedy described the struggle in phrases that John Foster Dulles would have found wholly familiar, updating the analysis to convey the new emphasis on developing regions. As the president declared, "We are opposed around the world by a monolithic and ruthless conspiracy that relies primarily on covert means for expanding its sphere of influence."

In Southeast Asia, attention initially focused on Laos, where a three-way civil war raged among an American-supported right-wing general, a neutralist prince, and a communist prince backed by the Soviet Union. This small, poverty-stricken nation had little strategic significance, but it possessed symbolic importance for Kennedy. He told a columnist early in 1961, "We cannot and will not accept any visible humiliation over Laos." Victory was not worth a war, however. While some advised a military stand, Kennedy chose negotiation instead. At the 1962 Geneva Conference, in which the United States participated, the warring factions agreed to a neutral Laos. This decision encouraged Kennedy; negotiations had staved off a communist takeover in an Asian nation. At least one small region of the world had been withdrawn from the arena of U.S.-Soviet conflict.

As it turned out, the unstable truce in Laos proved short-lived. As part of America's deepening involvement in Vietnam, the CIA organized an army of Laotian Hmongs, an indigenous upland people, to attack North Vietnamese supply routes along the Vietnamese-Laotian border. The result was political and social chaos in Laos.

In neighboring South Vietnam, conditions were deteriorating. As a senator, John Kennedy had supported the Eisenhower administration's handpicked ruler, Ngo Dinh Diem. But Diem's autocratic and corrupt regime never won popular support. The Vietminh, the procommunist force that remained in South Vietnam after the 1956 Geneva Accords, worsened the situation by systematically killing village leaders and local officials. In 1960 an anti-Diem coalition of communists and Buddhists (the latter made up 80 percent of the population) established the National Liberation Front (NLF) in South Vietnam, which, with its military arm, the Vietcong, began operations against Diem's forces.

The United States had pledged in the 1954 SEATO pact to defend South Vietnam against external aggression, and Kennedy determined to stand firm. In May 1961 he warned that the United States would not tolerate the military overthrow of the Diem regime. After the Vienna meeting with Khrushchev, Kennedy told James

Reston of the *New York Times* that the United States must prove its resolve to the Soviets and that the place to do so was Vietnam.

This interview revealed a series of key assumptions guiding Kennedy's thought: that the Vietnam conflict was simply one front in a larger Cold War struggle; that the Vietnamese communist leader, Ho Chi Minh, was little more than a pliant tool of Moscow or Beijing; that South Vietnam was a distinct nation subject to aggression from abroad (that is, from North Vietnam). Though simplistic and misguided, these assumptions would underlie U.S. policy in Vietnam for years.

Moreover, South Vietnam seemed the ideal laboratory to test antiguerrilla strategies. While U.S. Green Berets, a counterinsurgency unit, advised the South Vietnamese army, U.S. civilian specialists introduced medical programs, technical aid, and economic and political reforms designed to win "the hearts and minds" of Vietnamese peasants. One reform measure, the Strategic Hamlet program, uprooted peasants from lands that their ancestors had occupied for generations and concentrated them in settlements supposedly secure from communist infiltration. The program only deepened the peasants' hatred of the Diem regime.

Administration leaders nearly unanimously viewed Vietnam as a vital Cold War battlefield. After touring South Vietnam early in 1961, Vice President Johnson advised, "The basic decision in Southeast Asia is here. We must decide whether to help these countries to the best of our ability or throw in the towel in the area and pull back our defense to San Francisco and a 'fortress America' concept." After visiting Saigon that fall, General Maxwell Taylor, who soon would become chairman of the Joint Chiefs of Staff, called for eight thousand U.S. combat troops, plus heavy U.S. air support. "As an area for the operations of U.S. troops," Taylor declared, "[South Vietnam] is not . . . excessively difficult or unpleasant." Secretary of Defense McNamara, visiting in 1962, concluded that "every quantitative measurement we have shows we're winning this war."

A rare cautionary note came from Undersecretary of State George Ball, who warned Kennedy in November 1961, "Within five years we'll have three hundred thousand men in the paddies and jungles and never find them again. That was the French experience. Vietnam is the worst possible terrain both from a physical and political point of view." Kennedy replied, "George, I always thought you were one of the brightest guys in town, but you're just crazier than hell." In fact, within five years, U.S. troop strength in Vietnam would reach nearly four hundred thousand.

Amid the calls for escalation, Kennedy proceeded cautiously. He initially rejected General Taylor's recommendation for a modest infusion of combat units, sensing that the ante would inevitably rise. "It's like taking a drink," he reflected. "The effect wears off and you have to take another." Nevertheless, Kennedy continued to sip. In his public statements, he echoed Eisenhower's domino theory and insisted on his determination to prevent a communist victory in Vietnam. He dreaded a 1964 presidential race dominated by Republican cries of "Who lost Vietnam?" as Democrats of the 1950s had faced the accusatory question, "Who lost China?" By mid-1962 Kennedy had increased the number of U.S. military "advisers" in Vietnam from seven hundred to twelve thousand. He added another five thousand in 1963. As more American blood spilled in Vietnam—U.S. casualties rose to more than four hundred in 1963—withdrawing became progressively more difficult.

In May 1963, a Buddhist monk in the ancient religious city of Hué burned himself to death to protest the Diem regime; Diem's sister-in-law, the powerful Madame Nhu, joked that she would "supply the mustard for the monks' next barbecue." But Diem's position eroded as Buddhist resistance grew, and Kennedy gave the green light for an anti-Diem coup. On November 1, South Vietnamese military officers working in coordination with the U.S. embassy in Saigon arrested and shot Diem and his brother and set up a new military government.*

Had Kennedy lived, what course might he have taken in Vietnam? Some argue that he planned to withdraw, but the evidence for such speculation is slim. Kennedy had little doubt that U.S. toughness and military might, coupled with the techniques of counterinsurgency and nation building, could contain communism anywhere. Had he survived, he would have received the same advice, from the same hawkish advisers, that determined Lyndon Johnson's course. Indeed, Kennedy's authorization of a substantial buildup of U.S. "advisers" in Vietnam, and his role in the overthrow of the Diem regime in Saigon and its replacement with a military government, limited significantly the options of his successor, Lyndon Johnson.

In one of his last comments on the war, Kennedy conceded that the United States could not control the outcome of a civil struggle in a small, distant country. "In the final analysis," he mused, "it is their war." But he added, "For the United States to withdraw . . . would mean a collapse not only of South Vietnam but [of] Southeast Asia. So we are going to stay there." The *New York Times,* a voice of the eastern liberal establishment, agreed. Chiding Kennedy for his "it is their war" comment, the *Times* editorialized that Vietnam was America's war, "a war . . . we dare not lose." The dilemma summed up in Kennedy's ambivalent comments would continue to haunt American policymakers for years after his death.

The Kennedy Cold War: A Summary

The six years from *Sputnik* in 1957 to the assassination of Diem in 1963 saw the management of the Cold War pass from moderate Republicans to liberal Democrats who defined the Cold War in terms that reflected the idealism and activism of the FDR/New Deal tradition. The blend of anticommunist militance and social-reform zeal, combined with a drive to systematize and rationalize the policy-formation process, that one finds in New Frontiersmen such as Walt Rostow and Robert McNamara epitomizes the distinctive quality of Kennedy-style liberalism applied to world affairs.

This approach to the Cold War would come in for sharp attack in later years. In *The Kennedy Promise* (1973), British journalist Henry Fairlie deplored JFK's craving for empty displays of energy and his compulsive competitiveness. The Kennedy-era shift of focus from Western Europe to the murkier terrain of Third

---

* Ambassador Henry Cabot Lodge and other U.S. officials who set the coup in motion apparently did not anticipate Diem's assassination; they had advised that he and his family be flown into exile. On the other hand, neither the U.S. embassy nor the coup leaders had made any plans for such an evacuation.

World struggles, Fairlie suggested, robbed Washington's Cold War leadership of some of its legitimacy and moral clarity and led directly to the debacle in Vietnam that finally would shatter the liberal consensus. Garry Wills in *The Kennedy Imprisonment* (1982) argued that Kennedy's attraction to tests of will and to power struggles for their own sake, rooted in his father's strong influence, found expression in his campaign to destroy Castro, in his alarmist response to Khrushchev's maneuvering over Berlin, and in the deepening engagement in Vietnam. The appeal that these traits held for liberals determined to move beyond Eisenhower's alleged inertia, Wills concluded, exerted a dangerous impact on the conduct of foreign policy.

The Kennedy years solidified an uneasy nuclear stalemate as the United States and the Soviet Union piled up ever more destructive missiles and warheads. Nuclear fears eased after the Cuban missile crisis of October 1962, although the inherently unstable balance of terror hardly inspired long-term confidence. Still, with a rough nuclear balance in place and the Big Power confrontation in Europe stabilized, Cold War attention shifted to the Third World. From the days of President Truman's Point Four program, Washington strategists had recognized that developing nations represented an important arena of ideological, economic, and potentially military competition. In the later 1950s and early 1960s, this arena moved from the periphery to the center of strategists' thinking.

When applied to South Vietnam, this shift of emphasis set the stage for a war that would leave its stamp on American history. In Chapter 9, after further exploring domestic politics and social movements in the 1960s, we return to the Vietnam story as it unfolded following the shocking end of the Kennedy presidency.

Tragedy in Dallas

On November 21, 1963, President Kennedy flew to Texas, a state he had barely carried in 1960, to patch up a quarrel among Texas Democrats that threatened his 1964 reelection hopes. Jackie Kennedy accompanied her husband, something she rarely did. At 12:30 P.M. on Friday, November 22, the presidential motorcade wound through Dallas. The Kennedys rode in the back of an open car, with Texas governor John Connally and his wife seated in front. Three shots rang out. The first bullet struck the president in the neck; the second tore a gaping hole in his head, killing him almost instantly.

The presidential car sped to Parkland Hospital, where priests administered last rites and Kennedy was pronounced dead. For the rest of their lives, Americans would remember where they heard the news. One young historian, working in the reading room of Baltimore's public library, received word from a trembling librarian that the library was closing: President Kennedy had been shot.

Lyndon Johnson took the oath of office aboard Air Force One as the jet waited at Dallas's Love Field, ready to carry the dead and living presidents back to Washington. An anguished Jacqueline Kennedy, a coat covering her blood-spattered dress, looked on hollowly.

The nation mourned as a horse-drawn caisson, the same that had borne Abraham Lincoln's body in 1865, carried Kennedy's remains from the White House to the Capitol. The young historian, down from Baltimore for the day, watched as the

November 1963. *In a tradition-shaped ritual, President Kennedy's flag-draped coffin leaves the White House. A press photographer captured the scene framed by the leafless trees of early winter and the starkly etched shadows of saluting soldiers.* (Flip Schulke/Black Star)

cortege moved along Pennsylvania Avenue, followed by the closed black limousines carrying the bereaved family and the Johnsons. Armed Secret Service agents manned the rooftops of nearby government buildings. The burial took place in Arlington National Cemetery, the grave marked by a perpetual flame.

Within hours of the assassination, Dallas police arrested Lee Harvey Oswald, a twenty-four-year-old ex-marine. Two days later, as police transferred Oswald to another prison, Dallas nightclub owner Jack Ruby shot and killed him. The circumstances surrounding these events aroused much speculation. Oswald, with a record of mental instability and threats against other public figures, had moved to the U.S.S.R., married a Russian woman, and belonged to a pro-Castro group, Fair Play for Cuba Committee. To many, these circumstances hinted at a larger conspiracy.

To quell rising rumors, President Johnson appointed a blue-ribbon commission chaired by Chief Justice Earl Warren. After research by legal and forensic experts and interviews with 552 witnesses, the Warren Commission reported in September 1964 that Oswald had acted alone in shooting the president. But rumors of a conspiracy—by Cubans, by the Mafia, by Lyndon Johnson, by a right-wing cabal within the government—persisted. Despite the Warren Commission's insistence on the fullness of its research, critics at the time and later insisted that the commission had failed to pursue all leads thoroughly. The political motive of reassuring the public, rather than the larger task of sifting all the evidence, these critics argued, had led the commission to assert an overly confident lone-assassin conclusion.

Although no credible evidence ever surfaced to disprove the Warren Commission report, the guesswork and theorizing continued, fed by a rash of books such as Mark Lane's *Rush to Judgment* (1966). Later revelations of actual high-level conspiracies—from the Watergate cover-up to the Iran-contra affair, further encouraged those who doubted the official version of the assassination. By 1993, two thousand books had been written on Kennedy's death, many of them proposing various conspiracy theories. Oliver Stone's 1992 film *JFK,* interspersed invented dialogue, fictional "witnesses," and imagined scenes with actual newsreel footage, to portray an elaborate conspiracy involving Vice President Johnson, the FBI, the CIA, the Pentagon, defense contractors, and assorted other officials and agencies.

Why have these conspiracy theories endured in the absence of any hard evidence to support them? When the Warren Commission report appeared in 1964, Harrison Salisbury of the *New York Times* offered an explanation:

> The evidence of Oswald's single-handed guilt is overwhelming. Yet, few Americans will feel that this is the final word. . . . [T]here is in each of our hearts some feeling, however small, of responsibility; some feeling that each of us had some share in the crime because we had a role in a society which made it possible; which gave birth to a young man who by a long, dreary, painful path became distorted into an assassin. Thus, there remains in each of us some communal share of guilt . . . , some feeling of a step not taken; an act not completed; a word not spoken; a thought not carried into life which would have spared us so great a tragedy.
>
> And it is this secret gnawing at our conscience that not all . . . the millions of words in the many volumes of the Warren findings will ever still.

Conclusion

Popular in life, Kennedy assumed mythic proportions in death. Later, a reaction would set in. Historians would point out that for all Kennedy's glitz and hype, his achievements proved modest. On the international front, they would praise the Peace Corps and the Test Ban Treaty but deplore the strident Cold War rhetoric, the nuclear buildup, and the escalation in Vietnam. On the personal side, the Kennedy myth would be tarnished by revelations of his ruthless behavior, his use of amphetamines, and his compulsive promiscuity both before and during the White House years, including affairs with the actress Marilyn Monroe, whom he shared with his brother Robert, and with the mistress of a Chicago mobster. Critics also questioned his concealment of serious physical ills, including Addison's disease, a failure of adrenal function that required heavy cortisone medication.

Three decades after Kennedy's death, the myth had lost its magic for many, but remained potent for others. It had always revealed more about the needs and hopes of the American people than about Kennedy himself. A flawed man, Kennedy's surface charm brought him such easy success that he had little need to develop the more complex qualities that make for character. In *The Kennedy Persuasion: The Politics of Style Since JFK* (1995), Paul R. Henggeler finds Kennedy's political legacy generally negative, as post-Kennedy politicians increasingly substituted style for substance, mouthing high-sounding rhetoric instead of seriously grappling with issues, to the debasement of American public life. For historian Thomas Reeves, the author of a critical biography of Kennedy, *A Question of Character* (1991), the lesson of his presidency was sobering:

> In the early 1960s, we became involved in a sort of mindless worship of celebrity; it was a love affair largely with images. That could happen again. . . . And the target of our affection might be much worse than Jack Kennedy.

Nevertheless, after the mystique had faded, and in awareness of Kennedy's flaws, many still remembered the finer moments of his presidency. For a fleeting instant, the New Frontier—not as it was, perhaps, but as Americans wished it to be—offered a chance to bring the American reality closer to the imagined ideal.

The violent shattering of the Kennedy presidency was only one of a series of events that fragmented the liberal consensus. Rooted in the 1930s, World War II, and the early Cold War, this consensus underlay the Democratic party's activist, reform-minded approach to domestic problems and to global challenges. Lyndon Johnson, making shrewd political use of Kennedy's memory, sustained that consensus briefly during a remarkable season of reform in 1964–65. But the shining liberal hour that Kennedy had personified would ultimately lose its lustre, darken, and pass into history.

SELECTED READINGS

Foreign Affairs and Defense Policy in the Later 1950s

Richard Aliano, *American Defense Policy from Eisenhower to Kennedy* (1975); Michael R. Beschloss, *Mayday: Eisenhower, Khrushchev, and the U-2 Affair* (1986); H. W. Brands, "The Age of Vulnerability: Eisenhower and the National Security State," *American Historical Review* (October 1989); Michael E. Brown, *Flying Blind: The Politics of the U.S. Strategic Bomber Program* (1992); Barbara B. Clowse, *Brainpower for the Cold War: The Sputnik Crisis and the National Defense Education Act of 1958* (1981); Lawerence Freedman, *The Evolution of Nuclear Strategy* (1985); Lloyd C. Gardner, *Approaching Vietnam: From World War II Through Dienbienphu* (1988); Audrey R. Kahin and George McT. Kahin, *Subversion as Foreign Policy: The Secret Eisenhower and Dulles Debacle in Indonesia* (1995); James R. Killian, Jr., *Sputnik, Scientists, and Eisenhower* (1977); Walter A. McDougall, . . . *The Heavens and the Earth: A Political History of the Space Age* (1985); Donald Neff, *Warriors at Suez* (1981); Stephen G. Rabe, *Eisenhower and Latin America* (1988); Peter J. Roman, *Eisenhower and the Missile Gap* (1995); Tad Szulc, *Fidel: A Critical Portrait* (1986); Richard E. Welch, Jr., *Responses to Revolution: The United States and the Cuban Revolution, 1959–1961* (1985); David Wise and Thomas B. Ross, *The U-2 Affair* (1962). See also the Selected Readings for Chapter 4.

Kennedy, Nixon, and the 1960 Election

David Burner and Thomas R. West, *The Torch Is Passed: The Kennedy Brothers and American Liberalism* (1984); Doris Kearns Goodwin, *The Fitzgeralds and the Kennedys: An American Saga* (1986); Paul R. Henggeler, *The Kennedy Persuasion: The Politics of Style Since JFK* (1995); Donald Lord, *John F. Kennedy: The Politics of Confrontation and Conciliation* (1977); Allen J. Matusow, *The Unraveling of America: A History of Liberalism in the 1960s* (1984), Chap. 1, "The Liberals, the Candidate, and the Election of 1960"; Richard M. Nixon, *Six Crises* (1962); Herbert S. Parmet, *JFK* (1981); Gerald Posner, *Case Closed: Lee Harvey Oswald and the Assassination of JFK* (1993); Thomas Reeves, *A Question of Character: The Life of John F. Kennedy in Image and Reality* (1991); Theodore White, *The Making of the President 1960* (1961); Garry Wills, *Nixon Agonistes* (1969) and *The Kennedy Imprisonment* (1983).

Kennedy and the Cold War

John C. Ausland, *Kennedy, Khrushchev, and the Berlin-Cuba Crisis* (1996); Desmond Ball, *Politics and Force Levels* (1981); Michael Beschloss, *The Crisis Years: Kennedy and Khrushchev, 1960–1963* (1990); H. W. Brands, *The Devil We Knew: Americans and the Cold War* (1994); Herbert Dinerstein, *The Making of a Missile Crisis: October 1962* (1976); William J. Duiker, *U.S. Containment Policy and the Conflict in Indochina* (1994); Henry Fairlie, *The Kennedy Promise* (1973); John Girling, *America and the Third World* (1980); David Halberstam, *The Best and the Brightest* (1972); George Herring, *America's Longest War: The United States and Vietnam* (rev. ed., 1985); Trumbull Higgins, *The Perfect Failure: Kennedy, Eisenhower, and the Bay of Pigs* (1987); George McT. Kahin, *Intervention: How America Became Involved in Vietnam* (1986); Stanley Karnow, *Vietnam: A History* (1983); Robert Kennedy, *Thirteen Days* [Cuban missile crisis] (1969); Diane B. Kunz, ed., *The Diplomacy of the Crucial Decade* (1994); Walter LaFeber, *Inevitable Revolutions: The United States in Central America* (1985); Sir Bernard Lovell, "The Great Competition in Space," *Foreign Affairs* (October 1971); Richard D. Mahoney, *JFK: Ordeal in Africa* (1983); Bruce Miroff, *Pragmatic Illusions: The Presidential Politics of John F. Kennedy* (1976); John M. Newman, *JFK and Vietnam: Deception, Intrigue and the Struggle for Power* (1992); Thomas G. Paterson, ed., *Kennedy's Quest for Victory: American Foreign Policy, 1961–1963* (1989) and "Bearing the Burden: A Critical Look at JFK's Foreign Policy," *Virginia Quarterly Review* (Spring 1978); Thomas G. Paterson and William J. Brophy, "October Missiles and November Elections: The Cuban Missile Crisis and American Politics, 1962," *Journal of American History* (June 1986); Marifeli Pérez-Stable, *The Cuban Revolution: Origins, Course, and Legacy* (1993); Glenn T. Seaborg, *Kennedy, Khrushchev, and the Test Ban* (1981); Roger Warner, *Back Fire: The CIA's Secret War in Laos and Its Link to the Vietnam War* (1995); Andreas Wenger, *Living with Peril: Eisenhower, Kennedy, and Nuclear Weapons* (1997); Peter Wyden, *Bay of Pigs* (1980).

CHAPTER 7

The Liberal Hour

In October 1967, Lady Bird Johnson, the wife of President Lyndon Johnson, received an honorary degree from Williams College in Williamstown, Massachusetts, and spoke on her favorite subject: the need to preserve and enhance America's natural beauty. Amid the autumn foliage of a picture-book New England college town, the setting and the theme meshed perfectly. But the sylvan tranquility shattered when hecklers protested a war raging in distant Vietnam. The scene was repeated the next day at Yale University in Connecticut. While an audience of eight hundred listened attentively to Mrs. Johnson's speech inside the hall, an equal number of antiwar protesters milled outside, shouting and waving placards.

Her New England visit, wrote an aide, left the First Lady "very disheartened." During the preceding four years, she had emerged as a strong environmental advocate. Yet her audience seemed to be drifting away as the Vietnam War muscled its way into the public discourse. Soon, she feared, she would be unable to travel freely to promote the cause that she cared about so deeply.

Mrs. Johnson's dilemma reflected a deep tension within the administration and indeed in the nation. The Johnson years had begun on a note of high resolve, as the new president pushed an ambitious reform agenda. Four years later, the mood had soured. The protests that greeted Lady Bird Johnson soon would mushroom, forcing President Johnson to abandon any hope of reelection in 1968.

Johnson's downfall followed a period of apparent political invincibility. Thrust into the presidency by an assassin's bullets, Johnson seized the reins adroitly. After pushing Kennedy's stalled program through Congress, he went on to win passage of a far-reaching reform agenda. Johnson's domestic achievements surely would place him among the greatest of reform presidents.

Having examined how the liberal political tradition shaped U.S. foreign policy in the Kennedy years, we trace in this chapter liberalism's influence on domestic policy: the revival of liberals' confidence in the late 1950s, the domestic initiatives of John Kennedy's presidency, and the flood of reform legislation in 1964–65—the high noon of postwar liberalism. Chapter 8 offers a close look at the civil-rights movement in the 1960s, from the confident early years to the fragmenting of the civil-rights consensus at mid-decade. By the end of Johnson's term, the liberal consensus would collapse under the battering of domestic turmoil, urban unrest, and the divisive war in Vietnam.

Shaping a Liberal Agenda: The 1950s

Through much of the 1950s, the once-powerful trumpet of New Deal liberalism sounded only feebly. As liberal intellectuals rallied behind the Cold War, criticism of the United States' social and economic order grew cautious and restrained. Economic issues that had preoccupied reformers in the 1930s attracted little notice. "[T]he jobless, distracted, and bewildered men of 1933," wrote historian Richard Hofstadter reassuringly in 1955, "have in the course of the years . . . become homeowners, suburbanites, and solid citizens." In this climate, politics held scant interest for intellectuals. To them, the provocative issues lay in the cultural arena. Liberal ideological discourse, so vigorous in the 1930s, grew tepid. In 1957 Arthur Schlesinger, Jr., lamented, "[L]iberalism in America has not for thirty years been so homeless, baffled, irrelevant, and impotent as it is today."

Toward the end of the prosperous fifties, however, some liberals concluded that the nation's priorities in the allocation of its vast wealth merited criticism. Inspired by John Kenneth Galbraith's *The Affluent Society* (1958), liberals called for increased investment in the public sector—schools, hospitals, roads, civic services, and so on. Schlesinger proposed this "qualitative liberalism," inspired by the "quantitative liberalism" of FDR's era, as a liberal agenda for the 1960s. Schlesinger's three-volume eulogy to the New Deal, *The Age of Roosevelt* (1957–60), presented Roosevelt's first term in glowing language calculated to inspire a new generation of liberals.*

Other liberals argued that the issues of the 1930s still lived. In a biting review of *The Affluent Society,* Leon Keyserling, chair of the Council of Economic Advisers under President Truman, rejected Galbraith's assumption that modern America enjoyed near-universal affluence. Despite the spread of middle-class suburbs, he insisted, the postwar boom had left millions of Americans behind. To fight poverty and want, Keyserling argued, liberals should work for government policies designed to promote economic growth. Further to the left, socialists criticized Cold War liberals who turned a blind eye to domestic economic injustice while attacking the nation's cultural flaws. Amid all the cultural criticism, wondered Irving Howe in the journal *Dissent* in 1955, why did liberals ignore the plight of southern sharecroppers, displaced New England textile workers, or Puerto Rican immigrants in New York City? As a sign of rising ferment on the Left, the socialists' elder statesman, Norman Thomas, became increasingly popular on the college lecture circuit.

Although the liberal agenda that took shape by the end of the 1950s did not include the radical restructuring advocated by socialists, liberal academics and journals of opinion stressed greater investment in the public sector, as Galbraith urged, and government stimuli to promote economic growth, as Keyserling advocated. Indeed, the decade's end found the public increasingly receptive to liberals' calls for renewed governmental activism. The civil-rights movement spotlighted an urgent social issue in which government could play an important role. Globally, *Sputnik* and other events fed the growing conviction that America had lost ground.

---

* Significantly, perhaps, Schlesinger never continued his history into the years after 1936, when the New Deal stalled and ultimately failed to end the Great Depression.

As anxious discussions of "the national purpose" broke out in the media, liberals' spirits rose. The election of a group of young, reform-minded Democrats to the Senate in 1956 and 1958 further roused the liberals' sense of anticipation.

Liberals did not automatically rally to John Kennedy's candidacy for president. Many remained loyal to Adlai Stevenson or supported Senator Hubert Humphrey of Minnesota, whose liberal credentials outshone Kennedy's. The Kennedy family had openly admired Senator Joseph McCarthy, and Kennedy's choice of the Texan Lyndon Johnson as his running mate further alienated liberals, for Johnson had a reputation as a conservative from a conservative state. As late as August 1960, Arthur Schlesinger, Jr., warned Kennedy that the liberal Americans for Democratic Action backed him only with the "utmost tepidity."

Kennedy avidly courted reformist intellectuals, and his campaign speeches stressed the liberal themes of economic growth and renewal of the public sector. "[T]he American people are tired of the drift in our national course . . . ," he asserted in one speech. "[T]hey are ready to move again."

Richard Nixon, of course, pointed proudly to the 1950s economic boom and denied that the country had stagnated. At an Oregon shopping mall, Nixon declared, "If you think the United States has stood still, who built the largest shopping center in the world, the Lloyd Shopping Center right here?" But Nixon's gloating over a shopping mall simply confirmed another liberal complaint: that the public sector had atrophied amid a self-indulgent consumerist orgy.

Despite Kennedy's razor-thin victory margin, liberals felt a thrill of expectancy. Political scientist Michael Walzer found "an openness to new ideas probably unlike anything since the 1930s." Still, Walzer noted, Kennedy's goals remained hazy. A vote for Kennedy, he observed, was more an act of faith than an endorsement of a fully formed liberal agenda. Liberals thus watched nervously to see whether events would justify their faith.

Implementing a Liberal Agenda: The Kennedy Years

Although civil-rights marches, confrontations, and Freedom Rides during the early sixties captured the nation's attention (see Chapter 8), President Kennedy turned his energies to other domestic economic and social issues. His approach, reflecting a liberal, social-activist orientation, yielded at best mixed results. In the economic sphere, JFK's advisers embraced the interventionist New Deal model of federal activism. The most powerful figure in shaping economic policy was Walter Heller, a University of Minnesota economist and chairman of the Council of Economic Advisers (CEA). Heller and the CEA argued that the government should use its full fiscal powers to fight recessions, control inflation, and stimulate economic growth. Heller endorsed John Maynard Keynes' activist model of government intervention, and even more than most Keynesians he was prepared to accept federal budget deficits as a price of economic growth.

As a senator, Kennedy had generally opposed governmental intervention in the economy. Heller converted him to Keynesian thinking: the promotion of economic growth through federal tax and spending policies. The Roosevelt administration had adopted a de facto Keynesian approach with its heavy spending during World War II, and in the Truman era, Leon Keyserling, CEA head, had pushed Keynesian strategies. But it was in 1961–63, when Kennedy made economic growth a top priority, that Keynesianism won broad acceptance in the White House. Guided by Heller, Kennedy fought the recession of 1960–61 with increased federal spending. At his request, Congress extended eligibility for unemployment compensation, raised the minimum wage, broadened social security benefits, increased the military budget by almost 20 percent, and approved over $4 billion in long-term spending on federally financed housing. The Area Redevelopment Act authorized the secretary of labor to identify economically "distressed areas," making them eligible for federal aid. As these programs kicked in, the recovery that had started in early 1961 gained momentum.

Three measures of 1962 further stimulated the economy. The Trade Expansion Act granted the White House broad powers to cut tariffs on imported goods. The Manpower Retraining Act provided some $435 million in matching grants to the states for programs to retrain workers who had lost their jobs to automation. Finally, the administration-sponsored Revenue Act of 1962 granted $1 billion in tax breaks to business, in the form of investment credits and broadened depreciation allowances, to stimulate corporate spending on new machinery, factories, and equipment.

Kennedy's stimulus measures, including the increase in defense spending, gave the economy a jolt. From 1961 to 1964, the GNP grew by an annual average of 5.3 percent, a rise in productivity significantly above the annual average of the 1950s. The unemployment rate, which stood at 6.7 percent in 1961, declined to 5.2 percent by 1964. But with recovery came rising prices, and by 1962 inflation loomed. The power of labor unions and giant corporations over wages and prices posed a major inflationary threat, as a face-off between the administration and the steel industry in 1962 dramatically underscored. That March, Kennedy and Labor Secretary Arthur Goldberg helped avert a steel strike and encouraged the steelworkers and management to negotiate a noninflationary contract. A few weeks later, however, Roger Blough, the head of United States Steel, coolly informed Kennedy of a $6-a-ton price increase. The other big steel companies quickly followed suit. This inflationary action infuriated the president. "My father always told me that all businessmen were sons-of-bitches," he fumed, "but I never believed it until now." When the Defense Department announced that no contracts would go to steel companies that raised their prices, the industry giants backed down.

The showdown with the steel industry, together with lawsuits against the General Electric Company for price fixing, turned most business leaders against Kennedy. In a 1962 survey of six thousand business executives, 52 percent rated the administration "strongly anti-business." In fact, the administration had compiled a probusiness record, with its tax-credit plan to promote investment, its trade-reform bill, and its support for a private communications-satellite corporation, a plan backed by the American Telephone and Telegraph Company.

Despite some important initiatives, Kennedy's domestic record reflected more promise than achievement. Democrats controlled both houses of Congress, but a working alliance of Republicans and conservative southern Democrats stymied many of JFK's proposals. The Democratic congressional leadership, weakened by

Lyndon Johnson's elevation to the vice presidency, eroded further in 1961 with the death of Sam Rayburn, who had served as speaker of the House almost uninterruptedly since 1940.

Of twenty-three bills that Kennedy submitted in his early months in office, only seven were enacted. The administration's health-care plan for the elderly, for example, roused the ire of the American Medical Association (AMA). Having battled Truman over this issue, the AMA now fought Kennedy's proposals. As key congressional Democrats also opposed the bill, it languished.

A White House proposal for federal aid to education, introduced in 1961 and again in 1962, met the same fate. Catholic leaders argued that such aid should go to parochial schools as well as to public schools, but Kennedy, unwilling to appear as yielding to church pressure, refused to concede this point. Southern legislators, meanwhile, saw the education bill as a tactic to force integration, and some civil-rights leaders refused to support any bill that did not explicitly exclude segregated schools.

Other administration proposals, including medical-education assistance, immigration reform, help for migrant workers, federal aid to mass transit, and a department of urban and housing affairs, received an equally cool reception. Like President Truman, Kennedy placed many reform ideas on the national agenda but saw few of them translated into law.

In a rare domestic success, JFK did stimulate the space program. The technological race with the Soviets stirred the president's competitive juices, particularly when Moscow orbited a cosmonaut around the earth in 1961. Casting the space program in the familiar rhetorical form of intrepid pioneers conquering a new frontier, the administration and the media built support in Congress and the public for this multimillion-dollar scientific/technical project with important Cold War implications. Congress doubled the budget of the National Aeronautics and Space Administration (NASA) and approved a plan to put an American on the moon by 1970. The program received a boost in February 1962 when astronaut John Glenn became the first American to orbit the earth. On July 20, 1969, beating Kennedy's deadline by five months, Neil Armstrong became the first human being to set foot on the moon. In a related 1962 program, Congress passed Kennedy's Communications Satellite Act, which set up a private corporation to develop and operate a system of telecommunications satellites. The first Telstar satellite, orbited by the American Telephone and Telegraph Company in 1962 using a government-furnished rocket, proved the forerunner of a global system of instantaneous telephone and TV transmissions. The space program rebuilt confidence in U.S. technological know-how and opened a new arena for the arms race. As satellites sent back breathtaking images of Earth, they also dramatized humanity's common fate. Some critics charged, however, that the billions spent on space research would be better channeled to urgent social needs.

The space program, the economic recovery, the successful outcome of the Cuban missile crisis, and Kennedy's continued popularity all aided the Democrats in the 1962 midterm elections. Reversing the usual midterm pattern, the Democrats increased their Senate margin by four seats and held their House losses to a minimum. In 1963, looking ahead to 1964, Kennedy pushed his domestic program enthusiastically but again with scant results.

The Romance of Space. *Astronaut John Glenn, the first American to orbit the globe, gives a thumbs-up before liftoff on February 20, 1962. Reflected in his suit is back-up astronaut Scott Carpenter.* (NASA)

Kennedy's most innovative fiscal-policy initiative, which he would not live to see enacted, came early in 1963. Troubled by a dip in the economy's annual growth rate in the summer of 1962 and by hints of another recession, Walter Heller and the CEA urged a major tax cut to stimulate business investment and productivity. In August JFK announced that in January 1963 he would ask the new Congress for a $10 billion, two-year cut without a corresponding slash in spending. Kennedy used charts to show how a tax cut would promote economic growth. The resulting boom would increase tax revenues despite lower rates, he insisted. In 1980, when President Ronald Reagan argued for a big tax cut, and minimized its effects on the federal deficit, on precisely the same grounds, Democrats ridiculed "Reaganomics." Yet it was a liberal Democrat, John Kennedy, who first proposed to jump-start the economy by this means.

Powerful Democrats in Congress proved skeptical, however, and influential figures in the administration favored higher government spending rather than reduced revenues. Leon Keyserling criticized the proposed cut as unfairly tilted toward the well-to-do. Worse, the CEA soon projected deficits far higher than those that Kennedy had anticipated in his August 1962 speech. The president nevertheless introduced the bill as promised in January 1963, although he spread the cut over three years rather than two. The measure finally passed the House in September 1963 but stalled in the Senate. The speech that JFK was scheduled to deliver on November 22, 1963, to a Dallas business group was intended to argue again for his tax-cut bill.

Kennedy's domestic program stood largely unrealized at his death. He had offered the outlines of a new liberal agenda but never brought it to fruition. His major achievement centered on economic policy, especially his open embrace of

Keynesian principles. Thanks in part to JFK's initiatives, even a conservative president such as Richard Nixon later could assert, "We are all Keynesians now."

Kennedy's failure to cultivate relations with Congress, even during his years on Capitol Hill, had hampered his efforts. In this respect, his successor, a master of manipulating the levers of congressional power, would prove far more effective.

LBJ: The Making of a President

Lyndon Baines Johnson was born in 1908 in Stonewall, Texas, the eldest child of Sam and Rebecca Baines Johnson. Sam worked at various pursuits, from ranching to real estate, with little success, and served several terms in the Texas state legislature. Rebecca, whose grandfather had founded Baylor University, harbored great hopes for Lyndon; through her encouragement he graduated from Southwest Texas State Teachers' College in nearby San Marcos, where he excelled as a campus debater and student politician. After a stint of schoolteaching, he took a job in Washington, D.C., in 1931 as clerk to a Texas congressman. Except for brief intervals, he would remain in Washington for the next thirty-eight years.

In 1935 Johnson became Texas director of the National Youth Administration, a New Deal agency. Two years later, he won a special election to Congress when the incumbent died in office. Johnson enormously admired Franklin Roosevelt, whom he described as "like a daddy to me." For Johnson, the New Deal became the model of activist, reform government at its best. He styled himself "LBJ," in imitation of Roosevelt's "FDR." He lost a Senate race in 1941, served as a lieutenant commander in the navy, and in 1948 went to the Senate in an election so close that it earned him the derisive nickname "Landslide Lyndon." Ballot-box stuffing by Johnson operatives had put him over the top by eighty-seven votes.

In 1953, Johnson's Democratic colleagues chose him as minority leader; two years later he became majority leader. He worked closely with the Eisenhower administration while remaining a highly partisan Democrat. Indeed, as a central figure in shaping the Highway Act of 1956, the Civil Rights Act of 1957, the 1958 National Defense Education Act, and other measures, he helped to set the liberal agenda in the era of the Cold War. He once summed up the art of political bargaining this way: "Before you do anything, your last thought ought to be 'I've got to live with the son-of-a-bitch.'" Surviving a near-fatal heart attack in 1955, Johnson sought the Democratic nomination in 1960 and grudgingly took second place on the ticket when Kennedy offered it.

A tall, physically imposing man characterized by a large nose and ears, earthy language, and a vast capacity for scotch whisky, Johnson overwhelmed those from whom he wanted a favor; no one who experienced the "Johnson treatment" ever forgot it. He charmed, bullied, made promises, called in debts, and scratched backs with a master's touch, wearing down opposition by the sheer force of his personality. Images of tornados and volcanos came to mind when associates described his style. He often met with aides in his bedroom, while seated on the toilet, or even while swimming naked in the White House pool.

LBJ often resorted to crass manipulation. In 1965, eager to put his friend Abe Fortas on the Supreme Court, he persuaded Arthur Goldberg, a Kennedy appointee, to leave the Court, offering vague promises of future preferment that went largely unfulfilled. Johnson's many petty slights toward Hubert Humphrey, his vice president from 1965 on, left Humphrey deeply embittered. After LBJ's death in 1973, journalist Robert Caro in a massive, multivolume biography portrayed him as virtually a monster of ego. Johnson, Caro concluded, "displayed a genius for discerning a path to power, an utter ruthlessness in destroying obstacles in that path, and a seemingly bottomless capacity for deceit, deception and betrayal." Johnson's press secretary, George Reedy, similarly portrayed LBJ as selfish, insensitive, and exploitive. "There was no sense in which he could be described as a pleasant man," Reedy wrote. "His manners were atrocious—not just slovenly but frequently *calculated* to give offense."

These accounts capture part of the truth but fail to explain how Johnson managed, over a long career, to inspire loyalty in scores of people who willingly overlooked his faults. A comment by George Reedy provides one clue. Conceding all of Johnson's flaws, Reedy also noted that LBJ at times would "do something so magnificent that all of his nasty characteristics would fade. . . . He was a tremendous figure—a combination of complexities and simplicities that bewildered all observers."

Johnson's wife, Claudia, known from childhood as Lady Bird, was crucial to his career. An accomplished woman with a journalism degree from the University of Texas, Mrs. Johnson promoted her husband's efforts while pursuing her own interests. With piercing eyes, jet black hair, and a wide Texas smile, Lady Bird Johnson had political instincts equal to her husband's and a commitment to public service that outmatched his. She managed his congressional office during his navy service and oversaw the family's financial interests in Texas, which eventually included real estate, ranch lands, and an Austin radio station and TV channel.

A somber and shaken Johnson exhibited a quiet dignity in the traumatic days following Kennedy's assassination. Addressing Congress on November 26, 1963, he pledged to carry on the slain president's agenda. Echoing JFK's clipped inaugural exhortation "Let us begin," Johnson intoned in his Texas twang, "Let us contin-yah."

The Apex of a Liberal Agenda:
The War on Poverty

As Johnson took office, he stressed continuity, asking the Kennedy cabinet and top advisers to stay on. Most did, although many resented him as a usurper. Johnson channeled the nation's grief into support for Kennedy's program. He pushed through a civil-rights bill that JFK had introduced (see Chapter 8) and the Kennedy tax-cut plan. A steady economic boom seemed to validate the wisdom of this pump-priming measure. Indeed, the nation's GNP rose from $591 billion in 1963 to $977 billion in 1970.

Not content merely to complete the Kennedy agenda, however, Johnson sought a program that would bear his personal brand. He found it initially in the War on Poverty.

The Other America. *President Johnson's ambitious War on Poverty reminded Americans of the persistence of want amidst abundance. Images such as this, of a poor family in Kentucky, reinforced the message.* (Inge Morath/Magnum Photos, Inc.)

Even liberal social thinkers of the 1950s had downplayed poverty as a social issue. Galbraith in *The Affluent Society* saw it "more nearly as an afterthought" than as a "massive affliction." Michael Harrington's angry *The Other America: Poverty in the United States* (1962) radically challenged such perceptions. Harrington documented the hardship in inner cities and rural backwaters and among the elderly, minorities, migrant laborers, and unskilled workers. Estimating the ranks of the poor at 40 to 50 million, Harrington argued that the problem was not simply isolated pockets of poverty but long-term, structural destitution—a vast subculture of poverty. Introducing his study, Harrington wrote, "I would ask the reader to respond critically to every assertion, but not allow statistical quibbling to obscure the huge, enormous, and intolerable fact of poverty in America. For, when all is said and done, that fact is unmistakable, . . . and the truly human reaction can only be outrage."

Prodded by Harrington's work and by Walter Heller, John Kennedy had planned to make this issue a major theme of his legislative program in 1964. At a meeting on November 19, 1963, Kennedy had authorized Heller to draw up a set of legislative proposals to fight poverty. President Johnson, meeting with Heller on November 23, enthusiastically endorsed this initiative. He knew poverty from his Texas boyhood, and he responded instinctively to the program. Furthermore, civil-rights activists were increasingly focusing on economic issues. With more than 40 percent of African-American families earning under $3,000 a year, a program to fight poverty clearly would have major implications for black America. Similarly, for the nation's growing Hispanic population—migrants from Mexico, Puerto Rico, Haiti, and other Latin American countries living in barrios in cities in the Southwest, the upper Midwest, and the two coasts—joblessness and lack of money posed major problems. An antipoverty initiative, Johnson realized, provided a way to address the unrest stirring in the inner cities, but as part of a larger program. Legislators hesitant to appropriate massive funds to aid urban minorities might support a broadly focused "war on poverty." Americans were accustomed to uniting in wartime, and Johnson, as he would recall in his memoirs, hoped to use the rhetoric of war to "sound a call to arms which would stir people."

Cold War considerations also may have shaped Johnson's calculations. The contest with the Soviet Union increasingly had taken on economic as well as military tones. Improving the skills and employment rate of the inner-city jobless would stimulate the nation's overall economic health and demonstrate capitalism's ability to benefit all ranks of society. Johnson's embrace of the antipoverty cause arose, too, from his exuberant, can-do personality. America was rich enough and resourceful enough, he believed, to uplift the poor without seriously inconveniencing the well-to-do. To a British journalist, the antipoverty campaign was "the archetypal liberal program . . . , inspired by a characteristic blend of benevolence, optimism, innocence and chauvinism." As LBJ grandly put it, "We know what must be done, and this nation of abundance can surely afford it."

On January 8, 1964, Johnson called on Congress to declare an "unconditional war on poverty. . . . [W]e shall not rest until that war is won. . . . We cannot afford to lose it." In this election year, he proposed a battery of programs and approaches to attack poverty head-on. For Kennedy's lofty rhetoric, he implied, he would substitute action and achievement. And in the remarkable political climate of 1964–65, he chalked up a striking string of successes.

The antipoverty package had taken shape in discussions late in 1963 at Johnson's Texas ranch by a team including Walter Heller; Wilbur Cohen, secretary of the Department of Health, Education and Welfare; Francis Keppel, the U.S. commissioner of education; and other top advisers. The program that emerged incorporated poverty-fighting ideas dating from the Truman and Eisenhower eras, Kennedy-era proposals, and programs initiated by private philanthropies such as the Rockefeller Brothers Fund and the Ford Foundation.

Johnson's omnibus antipoverty bill, the Economic Opportunity Act, passed in August 1964 after extensive hearings but with little critical scrutiny. As one Republican complained, to criticize the program was to put oneself "under the suspicion of being in favor of poverty." In a shrewd move, Johnson chose a southern conservative, Phil Landrum of Georgia, as the bill's House floor manager, thereby blunting southern opposition. Nevertheless, many conservative Republicans and southern Democrats remained unconvinced. The final vote on the measure—226–185 in the House, 61–34 in the Senate—reflected this uncertainty.

The Economic Opportunity Act had ten major components. One section expanded the 1962 Manpower Development and Training Act and focused it on job training of the poor. Other sections created the Job Corps to teach marketable skills to unemployed inner-city youth, and Volunteers in Service to America (VISTA), a domestic parallel of the Peace Corps. The most innovative of the antipoverty measures, Head Start, offered basic-skills training to preschool young-sters. The Upward Bound program helped gifted students from poor families to go to college. Other components funded public-works projects in poor areas and loans for small businesses and needy small farmers. The law created the Office of Economic Opportunity (OEO) as command center of the antipoverty battle. To head OEO, Johnson chose Peace Corps director R. Sargent Shriver, the husband of John Kennedy's sister Eunice.

Despite the ambitious scope of the antipoverty war, the first-year funding proved modest: $500 million in new money and $462 million from funds already budgeted. Later appropriations increased somewhat but never really matched the program's sweeping goals. Furthermore, the funds were divided among numerous programs, diminishing their effect even more.

The program's fundamental approach proved far from radical. Its framers never proposed to alter the nation's basic socioeconomic structure by redistribut-ing wealth and power on a major scale. Nor did the architects of the War on Poverty propose direct income transfers—payments to bring all Americans up to a minimal income level. Instead, they chose a different strategy. Their approach, im-plicit in the title Economic *Opportunity* Act, aimed to provide education, skills train-ing, employment opportunities, and an aura of hope and motivation, so that every-one who wished a decent job could get one. In the phrase of the day, they favored "a 'hand up,' not a 'hand-out.'" Despite later criticism to the contrary, the aim was not welfare but helping the poor to become self-sufficient. As Johnson asserted on signing the bill, "The days of the dole in this country are numbered." This broad objective gave an underlying coherence to the War on Poverty's diverse programs.

The Economic Opportunity Act's most controversial section was the Commu-nity Action Program (CAP), a plan based on a Ford Foundation project. It allo-cated $300 million for local antipoverty programs involving the "maximum feasi-ble participation" of local community members. The CAP initiative reflected the view of some analysts that social-policy formulation had become top-heavy with experts and bureaucrats and needed grassroots input. As a 1965 *Community Action Workbook* issued by Shriver's office stated, the CAP program sought to empower the poor so they could challenge the more "politically effective sectors of society."

Advocates of the CAP approach hoped that it would stimulate political ac-tivism, collective effort, and local antipoverty initiatives by the poor themselves. And indeed, by 1966 more than a thousand CAPs were functioning in cities across the country. In many African-American and Mexican-American inner-city neigh-borhoods, locally run antipoverty programs funded by OEO provided an avenue of community activism and organizational experience for local residents. This proved particularly important in the rapidly growing Hispanic districts of urban America, which prior to the 1960s had remained largely "invisible" in terms of grassroots organization or political activism, with nothing comparable to the African-American civil-rights movement. The census of 1960 reported 4.5 million Spanish-surnamed persons, overwhelmingly Mexican Americans living in cities of California, Texas, Arizona, New Mexico, and Colorado, an increase of some 25 percent over 1950. These urban barrios had high rates of joblessness and poverty, with a small but growing professional class. The War on Poverty, and especially the CAP program, provided an opportunity for political organization and community development in these settings. When the program functioned as it was meant to, CAP funds went for legal services, medical clinics, educational services, and other worthy purposes in poor neighborhoods.

But the program did not always work as planned. In Chicago, for example, Mayor Daley's lieutenants simply commandeered it and operated it as an adjunct of the Daley machine. In some big-city ghettos, radical black activists dominated the CAPs. Often, however, local CAPs were led neither by the poor nor by machine politicians but by middle-class, college-trained advocates skilled at the politics of poverty. These CAP activists typically decried the local power structure—city government, welfare agencies, school boards, the police, private charities—which they dismissed as more interested in keeping the poor pacified than in real reform. They formed tenant unions, used public funds to bail out demonstrators arrested in protest actions, and organized voter-registration campaigns aimed at throwing out elected city officials.

The OEO's apparent call to class conflict alarmed the establishment. Local Democratic officials groused that a Democratic-sponsored program was muscling them aside. Baltimore's mayor complained to President Johnson about CAP hotheads "who do not understand the problems and operations of local governments." When Johnson learned that a CAP group in Washington, D.C., was attacking local Democratic leaders, he instructed his aide Bill Moyers: "For God's sake get on top of this and put a stop to it at once." But the turmoil persisted. At a 1966 Washington conference of the Citizens Crusade Against Poverty, a major advocacy group, Sargent Shriver was shouted off the stage, and militants took the platform to denounce one aspect or another of the antipoverty program.

CAP became a prime target of critics of the War on Poverty. In *Maximum Feasible Misunderstanding* (1969), President Nixon's urban affairs adviser, Daniel Moynihan, attacked LBJ's plan and singled out the CAP initiative for special scorn, dismissing it as the brainchild of befuddled liberals ignorant of the real world of politics and power. CAPs, he charged, had functioned mainly as a welfare program for the middle-class activists who ran them. Moynihan summed up views that were widely held by the end of the 1960s, when the political climate had turned chilly toward reform. The War on Poverty, emphasizing expanded individual opportunity through job training and education, had been carefully devised to appeal to moderates. The Community Action Programs, however, in encouraging collective action by the poor themselves, ultimately roused warning bells and threatened the entire effort. As the 1964 election neared, however, few anticipated the intensity of the reaction that lay ahead.

Election 1964: Liberalism Triumphant

Riding a wave of liberal support for the War on Poverty and bathed in JFK's lingering aura, Johnson seemed a shoo-in for the 1964 Democratic nomination. At the party's Atlantic City convention, after a dispute over the makeup of the Mississippi delegation (see Chapter 8), Johnson won the nomination by acclamation. As his running mate, he chose Hubert Humphrey, the party's most outspoken champion of civil rights and of old-fashioned, New Deal liberalism.

LBJ's giant presence dominated the proceedings. Journalist Loudon Wainwright, who covered the event for *Life,* marveled:

> I had the feeling . . . that this was not a convention at all, [but] rather a party being thrown by the President in celebration of himself. The delegates, the visitors in the hall, the press, the television audience—we were all *his* guests. The convention wasn't giving him anything; he was giving the delegates the opportunity to share his wholehearted enthusiasm for his leadership and his vision. Like a good host, or perhaps more correctly a good emperor, he thanked his subjects for coming, praised their little acts of fealty, and then said how things were going to be.

The Republicans, meanwhile, had lurched sharply rightward. The party's moderate eastern wing failed to produce a candidate who had the appeal of an Eisenhower. With Richard Nixon biding his time, the party's right wing reasserted its power. Abetted by William Buckley's conservative journal, *National Review,* conservative radio commentators, and Far-Right organizations such as the John Birch Society, the Republican Right had steadily gained strength among conservatives disturbed by the welfare state and by the civil-rights movement and intent on escalating the global crusade against communism.

Right-wing activists rallied around Senator Barry Goldwater of Arizona, an air-force reservist and heir to a department-store fortune. Goldwater's 1960 book, *The Conscience of a Conservative,* though ghostwritten, summed up his creed: aggressive pursuit of the Cold War, untrammeled free enterprise, and a dismantling of

President Johnson Presses the Flesh. *LBJ's War on Poverty and Great Society programs, together with his strong support for civil rights, seemed to assure him a stunningly successful presidency. Unfortunately, the Vietnam War would soon intervene.* (Frank Wolfe/LBJ Library Collection)

character-sapping welfare programs such as social security. As a senator, Goldwater had praised Joe McCarthy, and now in 1964 he again hurled the tired "soft on communism" charge at the Democrats.

Defeating New York governor Nelson Rockefeller, the moderates' hope, in the crucial California primary, Goldwater handily won the nomination at the party convention in San Francisco. Welcoming the "extremist" label, he declared: "Extremism in the defense of liberty is no vice. Moderation in the pursuit of justice is no virtue." GOP campaign posters asserted of Goldwater, "In Your Heart You Know He's Right." Democrats retorted, "In Your Guts You Know He's Nuts."

Capitalizing on Goldwater's narrow appeal, LBJ cast his campaign as a big tent and invited all Americans to gather inside. Downplaying divisive issues, he sought votes from business and labor, farmers and city dwellers, and all racial and ethnic constituencies. "[O]ne of the great tasks of political leadership," Johnson asserted, "[is] to make people aware . . . that they share a fundamental unity of interest, purpose and belief." This unity theme takes on special poignancy as one reflects on the conflict and polarization that would plague the end of Johnson's term.

The 1964 presidential race, far more than in 1960, highlighted domestic issues. Nevertheless, America's deepening military engagement in Vietnam colored the contest. Whereas Goldwater advocated bombing North Vietnam and using tactical

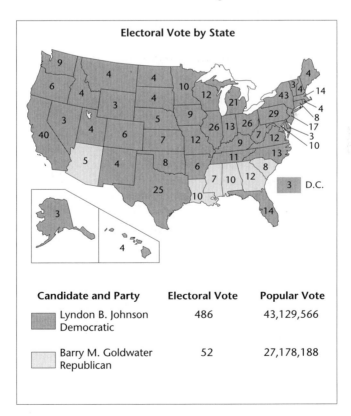

Candidate and Party	Electoral Vote	Popular Vote
Lyndon B. Johnson Democratic	486	43,129,566
Barry M. Goldwater Republican	52	27,178,188

FIGURE 7.1

Presidential Election of 1964

nuclear weapons on the battlefield, and even spoke cavalierly of "lobbing [a nuclear bomb] into the men's room of the Kremlin," LBJ held himself up as the peace candidate. He would not send American boys into any foreign war, he pledged. A *Time* cover story focused on "The Nuclear Issue," and a Democratic TV commercial came close to predicting nuclear holocaust if Goldwater prevailed.

Johnson scored a landslide victory. His role as Kennedy's heir and his advocacy of civil rights and domestic reform, together with fear of Goldwater, brought him an overwhelming 61 percent of the vote, more than even Franklin Roosevelt captured in 1936. No longer the accidental president, LBJ had won a tremendous personal endorsement. The Democrats' margin in the House widened by thirty-eight seats and in the Senate by two seats. The southern political realignment launched by Dwight Eisenhower continued, however: Of the six states that Goldwater carried, all except for Arizona lay in the Deep South. He might have made even greater southern inroads had not Mrs. Johnson, evoking memories of Harry Truman in 1948, toured the region by rail on the "Lady Bird Special." But if some southern whites abandoned LBJ because of his identification with civil rights, black votes more than balanced the defections. Six million African Americans cast ballots in 1964—a third more than in 1960—and an astounding 94 percent of them voted for the Johnson-Humphrey ticket. Blacks provided the victory margin in Arkansas, Florida, Tennessee, and Virginia.

The Politics of Hope: Johnson's Great Society

While pursuing Kennedy's legislative program, promoting the War on Poverty, and shepherding a civil-rights bill through Congress, President Johnson had also laid out a still more grandiose reform agenda. As early as May 1964, speaking at the University of Michigan, LBJ had limned an inspiring picture of America as a "Great Society." To waves of applause, he had poured out a cornucopia of social goals. Better schools, better health, better cities, safer highways, a more beautiful nation, support for the arts—Johnson's dream for America knew few bounds.

Fleshing out his Great Society vision in his State of the Union message on January 4, 1965, and again in his inaugural address on January 20, Johnson proposed a list of reforms drawn from Truman's Fair Deal, earlier Kennedy proposals, and ideas current among social reformers. "Hurry, boys," he urged his aides. "Get that legislation up to the Hill and out. Eighteen months from now, Ol' Landslide Lyndon will be lame-duck Lyndon." The heavily Democratic Congress passed a dizzying array of laws intended to improve the lives of millions of Americans. Congress doubled funding for the antipoverty program and appropriated $1.1 billion for public-works projects, rural health centers, and other programs in the chronically depressed Appalachian region.

Yet the heart of the Great Society program lay in measures to improve cities, education, and health care. In his "Message on the Cities," Johnson observed:

> Within the borders of our urban centers can be found the most impressive examples of man's skill . . . as well as the worst examples of degradation and cruelty and misery. . . . The modern city can be the most ruthless enemy of the good life, or it can be its servant.

Congress responded. The Housing and Urban Development Act of 1965 offered reduced interest rates to builders of housing for the poor and elderly. It also allocated funds for urban beautification, health programs, recreation centers, repairs on inner-city housing, and a rent-supplement program for the poor. To promote coordinated urban development, this law mandated that all applications for federal aid to cities be approved by citywide or regional planning agencies. Enacting a proposal first advanced by JFK, Congress also created a new cabinet-level agency, the Department of Housing and Urban Development, to administer the new programs.

Attention to cities meant attention to transportation. The 1950s highway program, for all its benefits, had weakened public-transit systems, worsened urban traffic congestion, and destroyed inner-city neighborhoods. In 1964, conceding these problems, Congress granted some $375 million for urban mass-transit planning. In 1966 Congress allocated more funds for this purpose and created a new agency, the Department of Transportation, to administer them.

Another important urban-development measure, the Model Cities Act of 1966, granted $1.2 billion for slum clearance and renewal. The aim was to revitalize all aspects of inner-city life, from housing and schools to health care, job training, and recreation. The law provided funds for new model communities, reflecting the deep-rooted utopian strand in American social thought. This sweeping measure represented the Great Society vision at its loftiest.

Convening a White House Conference on Education in 1965, LBJ proclaimed that every child in America "must have the best education our nation can provide." In this spirit, the 1965 Elementary and Secondary Education Act (ESEA) directed over $1 billion for programs to aid "educationally deprived children." Much of this money went to schools in poor districts, but the bill also targeted bilingual education for Hispanic children and education of persons with disabilities. With this infusion of federal dollars, inner-city and rural schools and institutions serving children with special needs hired more teachers and aides and developed new programs. Demonstrating his flair for the dramatic, Johnson in 1966, under the adoring gaze of an aged former teacher, delivered an education speech in the Texas schoolhouse he had attended as a lad.

Although billed as part of the War on Poverty, ESEA also channeled federal sums to general public-education programs and facilities. In securing its passage, LBJ, again demonstrating his political genius, overcame the divisive issues of race, region, religion, and constitutional scruples that had long blocked federal support for education.

The Higher Education Act, also passed in 1965, created a federal scholarship and loan program for needy college students and provided library grants to colleges and universities. Public-education funding, as well as policymaking, once exclusively a state and local matter, grew increasingly dependent on Washington. In 1965 federal spending on all levels of education topped $4 billion. Liberals hailed this trend as a national investment in the younger generation; conservatives worried that with expanded federal funding would come growing federal control.

The "big tent" motif of LBJ's 1964 electoral campaign found legislative expression in the Immigration Act of 1965. This measure eliminated the discriminatory quotas against certain national groups that had been written into the nation's

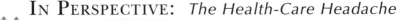

IN PERSPECTIVE: *The Health-Care Headache*

The Medicare law of 1965 was a major step—but only a step—in a long and acrimonious process of defining Washington's role in the U.S. health-care system. This process began after the Civil War, when Congress authorized a network of hospitals for disabled Union veterans. The system of federally funded medical facilities steadily expanded in the twentieth century to serve veterans of World War I, World War II, and later conflicts.

Efforts to extend the government's health-care role further met bitter opposition from the medical profession. The Sheppard-Towner Act of 1921 appropriated $1.2 million for rural prenatal and infant-care centers run by public-health nurses. However, the male-dominated American Medical Association (AMA) objected to this infringement on its monopoly, and Congress killed the program in 1929. Efforts to include health insurance in the Social Security Act of 1935 failed in the face of opposition from the AMA and private insurers. President Truman proposed a comprehensive medical-insurance plan to Congress in 1945, but the AMA again fought back, stigmatizing the plan as an encroaching wedge of "socialized medicine."

Medicare and Medicaid, which provide health insurance for the elderly, disabled, and poor, broke this logjam. Nevertheless, lobbyists for the AMA, hospitals, and private insurance companies succeeded in limiting Washington's function to that of bill-payer, with no role in shaping the health-care system or, most important, in containing costs. The new programs assured millions of Americans better health care, but they proved very expensive. From 1970 to 1990, Medicare costs ballooned from $7.6 billion to $111 billion, and Medicaid from $6.3 billion to $79 billion. As the population aged, long-term care for the elderly became an especially pricey component.

Rising costs made up only part of a larger tangle of problems. While America boasted the world's best health care, its benefits were unevenly distributed. Inner-city minorities and rural communities often lacked adequate care. Life expectancy, infant mortality, and other health indexes varied significantly along racial, regional, and income lines. The 1989 infant-mortality rate, for example, stood at 8.2 per 1,000 live births for whites and 17.7 for blacks. Although many workers belonged to prepaid health systems, millions of Americans lacked health insurance.

Despite such inequities, soaring costs remained at the center of the debate. The proportion of the GNP spent on health care jumped from 5.3 percent in 1960 to 14 percent in 1993. In the 1980s, health costs rose twice as fast as the general price index. A resentful public blamed "greedy doctors," but the problem had complex sources.

---

immigration law in 1924 and reaffirmed in the McCarran-Walter Act of 1952. The new law opened the door to an increased flow of immigrants from Asia and Latin America that would profoundly affect American life in the decades ahead.

In a historic health-care achievement, Congress in 1965 enacted Johnson's Medicare bill providing health insurance for all Americans over age sixty-five. Initially funded with a $6.5 billion appropriation, Medicare's long-range funding came from increased social security payroll deductions. The plan covered most

Breakthrough scientific discoveries; exotic new drugs such as tacrine, which improves cognition in some Alzheimer's patients; and new procedures such as angioplasty, kidney dialysis, hip replacement, organ transplants, coronary bypass, and magnetic resonance imagining scanners could work medical wonders but at a staggering cost. Indeed, some analysts saw the alleged "cost crisis" in U.S. medicine as stemming from a rational choice by a rich society to absorb the massive expense of new technologies and basic research. The AIDS epidemic, further straining an already floundering health-care system, exacerbated the sense of crisis.

While technology advanced, the human side of health care seemed to wither. Patient dissatisfaction contributed to an epidemic of malpractice suits, which pushed medical costs still higher. The modern physician, observed a medical sociologist in 1991, was no longer typically perceived as a dedicated healer but as "uncaring, uncommunicative, self-interested, and ambitious."

Bill Clinton highlighted this complex "health crisis" in his 1992 campaign, stressing cost containment as crucial to reducing the federal deficit. Once elected, Clinton named his wife, Hillary Rodham Clinton, to head a task force on health policy. As in the past, sharp differences divided the key players: the AMA, hospitals, drug firms, nursing homes, insurance companies, consumer advocates, retirees, spokespersons for the poor, and private prepaid systems. Whereas some participants in the debate favored allowing market forces broad latitude under a system of "managed competition," others advocated strict cost controls and a closely regulated system. Still others warned that regulating costs would inhibit research. Physicians in private practice balked at the income loss that they foresaw if they joined a prepaid plan. Oregon health officials proposed to "prioritize" (that is, ration) expensive medical procedures for Medicaid recipients, but many recoiled from such a concept. Still others favored less emphasis on technology and eleventh-hour heroics and more on preventive measures such as exercise, diet, and regular checkups and on factors such as tobacco, alcohol, pollution, and poverty that clearly impinge on health.

The health-care debate swirls around fundamental issues of ethics and public policy. Modern medicine achieves results unthinkable a few decades ago, curing once-lethal illnesses and granting men and women vigorous life into their eighties and even their nineties. In coming years, the number and effectiveness of such tests, procedures, and technologies will surely multiply. Yet at what cost? Is everyone to have access to all available treatment, regardless of the expense or the odds of success? Clearly one doesn't weigh the life of one's child or aged parent by the same cost-benefit calculations that one uses to decide whether to repair an old car. Yet as health care becomes an entitlement, funded by resources allocated by the political process, some system for making heart-wrenching decisions will have to be devised.

In short, the launching of Medicare and Medicaid in 1965, important as they were, represented only a breathing space in an ongoing national debate. As Americans focus on domestic issues in the 1990s, health care promises to remain high on the agenda.

hospital expenses, diagnostic tests, home visits, and some nursing-home costs. To supply the additional personnel needed for this expanded health-care program, Congress voted funds for nursing schools, medical schools, and medical-student scholarships. Medicaid, a key section of the law little noticed at the time, provided grants to the states to cover medical care for the poor of all ages. The American Medical Association's dire warnings against "socialized medicine," potent in the conservative 1950s, proved less effective in the reform climate of 1965. LBJ signed the Medicare bill in Independence, Missouri, as a beaming eighty-one-year-old Harry Truman, who had proposed such a measure twenty years earlier, looked on.

The influx of federal dollars stimulated by this legislation generated explosive growth in the health-care and nursing-home industries. By the 1990s, soaring Medicare and Medicaid costs would contribute mightily to a staggering burden of public debt. In the optimistic summer of 1965, however, questions of long-range cost rarely shadowed liberal reformers' triumphant mood.

While President Johnson rallied the forces of liberalism from the Oval Office, the Supreme Court contributed to the renewal and reassertion of liberalism by maintaining the activist course set by Chief Justice Earl Warren. The Court in a series of landmark rulings in the 1960s broke new ground in the areas of individual rights, electoral reform, and equal protection under the law, despite some warnings that the Court was moving into areas more properly left to the legislative process.*

Seeking to give all citizens an equal voice at the polls, the Court in *Baker* v. *Carr* (1962) held that states must, "as nearly as practicable," maintain population balance in setting the bounds of congressional and state-legislature electoral dis-

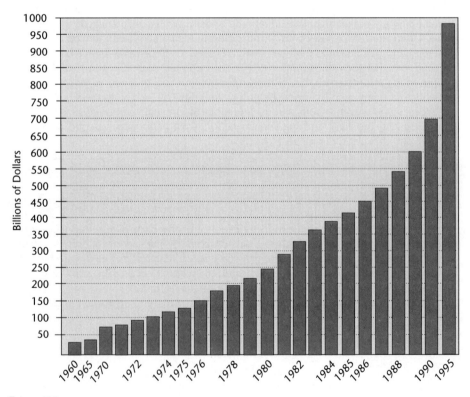

FIGURE 7.2

Total Spending on Health Care, 1960–1995

SOURCE: National Center for Health Statistics, U.S. Dept. of Health and Human Services, reprinted in *World Almanac, 1988.*

---

* Warren's closest allies in these endeavors were two FDR appointees, Hugo Black and William O. Douglas, and William J. Brennan, Jr., appointed by Dwight Eisenhower in 1956.

tricts. In *Gideon* v. *Wainwright* (1963), the Supreme Court extended to the state courts the right of poor people to court-appointed counsel. In *Miranda* v. *Arizona* (1966), the justices mandated that all prisoners must be informed of their legal rights at the time of their arrest.

Expanding freedom of the press, the Court in *New York Times* v. *Sullivan* (1964) protected newspapers from libel suits by public officials except when actual malice could be proved. In 1966, the Court reversed a Massachusetts ban on John Cleland's erotic classic *Fanny Hill,* reaffirming a 1957 ruling (*Roth* v. *United States*) that only works "utterly without redeeming social value" could be denied First Amendment protection. In other personal-freedom cases, the Court banned school prayer as a violation of the constitutional prohibition against an establishment of religion (*Engel* v. *Vitale,* 1962) and struck down a Connecticut law prohibiting the use of contraceptives or providing contraceptive information (*Griswold* v. *Connecticut,* 1964).

These decisions reflected the outlook of an activist Court majority committed to democratic principles and to upholding individual rights. When Warren retired in 1969, he left a harvest of decisions that for decades would make the Warren Court a target of both praise and denunciation. The same activism that liberals applauded dismayed conservatives, who warned of the Court's growing power and its penchant for plunging into highly controversial social issues.

The New Environmentalism

Environmental issues were central to Johnson's Great Society vision. "Once our national splendor is destroyed," the president cautioned in his May 1964 Ann Arbor speech, "it can never be recaptured." Indeed, he proclaimed, "The desire for beauty and the hunger for community" were the twin impulses driving his reformist campaign.

Most at home on his ranch in the rolling Texas hill country, Johnson loved the land. Lady Bird Johnson and Interior Secretary Stewart Udall helped to translate that emotion into policy. The environmentalism that emerged in the 1960s, however, reflected not merely a few individuals' efforts but a growing national awareness that a century of industrialization had taken a dire toll: shrinking wilderness areas, vanishing wildlife species, and health-threatening pollution.

The roots of modern environmentalism extended far into the past. As early as the Progressive era, when some reformers had campaigned to conserve natural resources for their economic benefit, others had worked to preserve scenic beauty in national parks and wilderness areas. John Muir's Sierra Club (1889), for example, lobbied to save California's Yosemite Valley and other areas of great natural beauty. Still other Progressive-era reformers had battled the environmental hazards of factory smoke, tainted milk, and filthy slaughterhouses and worked for urban beautification by establishing city parks, boulevards, and civic statuary. After fading during the 1920s, environmental concerns had revived during the New Deal, only to diminish in the booming, expansionist postwar years. Aldo Leopold's *Sand County Almanac* (1948), with its ecological focus and its call for "a new land ethic," later hailed as a classic, at the time attracted little notice.

With the resurgence of liberalism in the 1960s, environmental concerns again found a voice. President Kennedy sent a message to Congress in February 1961

addressing environmental issues and in May 1962 convened a White House conference on the subject. Kennedy and Udall pushed for more parks, especially along
the crowded eastern seaboard. The Cape Cod National Seashore was one result.
But once again, it was Johnson who scored the major achievements. From 1963 to
1968, Congress at LBJ's initiative passed nearly three hundred measures relating to
conservation, beautification, and pollution and appropriated some $12 billion for
these purposes.

Downplaying the conservation of natural resources, the great cause of many
Progressive-era reformers, the environmentalists of the 1960s emphasized the aesthetic and social benefits of natural beauty and the public-health hazards posed by
pollution. More broadly, they insisted that environmentalism was not a fringe issue
but central to the quality of human life and social well-being.

Interior secretary Stewart Udall did much to foster this new environmental
awareness. A friend of John Kennedy's from their days together in Congress, Udall
played a central role in delivering Arizona to Kennedy at the 1960 Democratic
convention. Appointed secretary of the interior, he crafted Kennedy's conservation
message of 1961, planned the 1962 White House conference, and set forth his environmental views in an influential 1963 book, *The Quiet Crisis:*

> America today stands poised on a pinnacle of wealth and power, yet we live in a
> land of vanishing beauty, of increasing ugliness, of shrinking open space, and of an
> overall environment that is diminishing daily by pollution and noise and blight.
> This, in brief, is the quiet conservation crisis of the 1960s.

From the intersection of these personal and historical factors emerged a remarkable body of environmental law. The Wilderness Act of 1964 echoed Udall's
warning that the American wilderness, once seemingly boundless, was at risk from
the advance of highways, tourism, and corporate exploitation. The culmination of
a campaign launched in the 1950s by the Sierra Club and the Wilderness Society,
this law set aside over 9 million acres of national forest for preservation. The Wild
and Scenic Rivers Act of 1968 similarly protected sections of eight rivers from de-
velopers. Other legislation responded to the threat to wildlife posed by the vanishing wilderness. The Endangered Species Act of 1966 for the first time set biodiversity as a national goal. A second measure, enacted seven years later, proved
considerably stricter and more precise, defining endangered species and the procedures for protecting them.

The 1960s also focused attention on the pollution of water, air, and land by the
toxic byproducts of an urban-industrial society. This concern, first voiced by
Progressive-era reformers, had faded in the intervening years, but it revived in the
1960s, thanks in large part to Rachel Carson's *Silent Spring,* published in 1963. Just
as Harrington's *The Other America* spotlighted poverty, so Carson's work thrust environmental pollution onto the national agenda.

A marine biologist with the U.S. Fish and Wildlife Service, Carson had grown
alarmed by the environmental impact of DDT, the postwar wonder chemical, and
other pesticides and herbicides pouring into the nation's water system. Several
magazines rejected her carefully researched article on the dangers of pesticides because their food advertisers, particularly baby-food manufacturers, worried that it
would cause "unwarranted fear" among consumers. The *New Yorker* eventually se-

rialized the work, and it appeared as a book soon after. Citing the mounting evidence of the ecological dangers of DDT and other chemicals, Carson concluded somberly:

> It is not my contention that chemical insecticides must never be used. I do contend that we have put poisonous and biologically potent chemicals indiscriminately into the hands of persons largely or wholly ignorant of their potentials for harm . . . [and] subjected enormous numbers of people to contact with these poisons, without their consent and often without their knowledge.

Carson also offered broader reflections that would make *Silent Spring* a key text of the emerging ecology movement.* The vogue for DDT and similar products, she warned, was only one manifestation of a larger heedlessness regarding the environmental consequences of modern technology:

> The "control of nature" is a phrase conceived in arrogance, born of the . . . age . . . when it was supposed that nature exists for the convenience of man. The concepts and practices of . . . [the chemical eradication of unwanted insects] for the most part date from the Stone Age of science. It is our alarming misfortune that so primitive a science has armed itelf with the most modern and terrible weapons, and that in turning them against the insects it has also turned them against the earth.

Pesticide manufacturers mounted a massive campaign to discredit Carson, but her scientific credentials and elaborate scholarly documentation gave *Silent Spring* impressive credibility.

Like Upton Sinclair's *The Jungle,* a 1906 exposé of Chicago packinghouses, *Silent Spring* exerted a dramatic impact. Carson's account of the effects of polluted water on marine life and of the way pesticides and herbicides entered the food chain roused national calls for regulation. The *Chicago Daily News* called Carson's work "one of the great and towering books of our time."

Responding to the furor, President Kennedy had appointed a scientific advisory committee on pesticides. Under President Johnson's prodding, Congress accelerated the pace of action. The Water Quality Act of 1965 toughened earlier water-pollution laws. It provided that if states failed to enforce water-quality standards for interstate waters within their borders, the federal government would step in. The Clean Waters Restoration Act of 1966 expanded water-quality regulations and authorized over $3.5 billion to clean up the nation's waterways and to halt further pollution of them by sewage or industrial waste.

The concerns about water pollution roused by Rachel Carson's work, following nearly a decade of intense publicity about radioactive fallout from nuclear tests, contributed to a larger awareness of environmental risks. The Task Force on Environmental Pollution, created by President Johnson in 1964, addressed not only pesticides but also emissions from coal-burning factories and auto exhaust systems. In a 1965 press release, the president placed the issue in a larger context:

---

* The science of ecology, central to the modern environmental movement, views all life forms of a given region, plants and animals alike, including human beings, as part of a single, complex, interdependent biological unit, or ecosystem.

Ours is a nation of affluence. But the technology that has permitted our affluence spews out vast quantities of wastes . . . that pollute our air, poison our waters, and even impair our ability to feed ourselves. At the same time, we have crowded together into dense metropolitan areas where concentration of wastes intensifies the problem.

A series of clean-air laws culminating in the Air Quality Act of 1967 set progressively stricter standards, covered a broader spectrum of pollution sources, including auto exhaust emissions, and appropriated large sums for air-pollution abatement programs. These laws, and similar ones dealing with water pollution, clearly identified environmental protection as a national issue requiring national action. Two major environmental disasters—the 1967 sinking of the giant oil tanker *Torrey Canyon* at the entrance to the English Channel that spilled 30,000 tons of crude oil and damaged 175 miles of British and French coastline, and a 1969 oil drilling accident off Santa Barbara, California, that befouled beaches and devastated marine life—accelerated concern about pollution.

This cycle of environmental legislation culminated in the National Environmental Policy Act of 1969. Among other provisions, the law required federal agencies to file environmental-impact statements for all major activities or proposed legislation. In 1970, Congress created the Environmental Protection Agency to enforce the growing body of federal environmental law. Environmental issues would loom still larger in the 1970s, but the surge of legislation and publicity in the Johnson years laid the groundwork for later growth.

Lady Bird Johnson inspired another major component of LBJ's environmental program: the campaign for national beautification. Although some ridiculed its advocates as "the daffodil and dogwood set," the beautification campaign of the 1960s provided a bridge to the ecological concerns of the 1970s and beyond. The beautification and preservation movements had deep roots in American history. As early as 1791, Pierre L'Enfant had drafted a visionary plan for Washington, D.C. The turn-of-the-century City Beautiful movement had focused on urban beautification projects, including the completion of the L'Enfant plan.

Lady Bird Johnson gave the theme new impetus in the 1960s. As early as the 1930s, while her husband had headed the National Youth Administration in Texas, Lady Bird had promoted the movement to create roadside parks. During the White House years, Mrs. Johnson devoted her time and considerable talents to the beautification cause. In the process she became the most influential presidential spouse since Eleanor Roosevelt. She worked behind the scenes, lobbied the media, and gave dozens of speeches encouraging support of efforts, as she put it in a 1965 magazine interview, "to make our cities and country more beautiful for all the people."

Through Lady Bird's influence, LBJ in 1965 sent Congress a message on "Conservation and the Restoration of Natural Beauty" and laid out a legislative agenda. That May, opening the White House Conference on Natural Beauty, Mrs. Johnson challenged the delegates: "Can a great democratic society generate . . . and execute great projects of beauty?" With LBJ's domestic reform program at flood tide, that rhetorical question could have but one answer.

Much of Lady Bird Johnson's campaign focused on Washington, D.C., reflecting the dual objectives of making the capital more attractive for the city's residents and visitors and of making Washington a model for other communities to emulate. In 1965 she invited a group of socially prominent and civic-minded citizens to a White House conference on beautifying Washington. From this meeting emerged the First Lady's Committee for a More Beautiful National Capital. Utilizing resources of the National Park Service, Mrs. Johnson's committee transformed the city's appearance by planting trees and flowers, establishing parks, sprucing up Pennsylvania Avenue, and other measures. Secretary of the Interior Udall enthusiastically backed the First Lady's interest in Washington, recognizing its value in raising environmental awareness. (Once, when LBJ found Udall and Lady Bird crouched over a large set of plans for the renewal of Pennsylvania Avenue, he burst out in mock rage: "Udall, what in hell are you doing down there on the floor with my wife?")

Another of Mrs. Johnson's interests—and hence another item on LBJ's environmental agenda—was highway beautification. During many auto trips between Texas and Washington in the 1930s and 1940s, Mrs. Johnson had had ample opportunity to observe the billboards and commercial clutter lining the nation's roadways. The Billboard Bonus Act of 1955 had offered increased federal highway funds to states that regulated billboards, but the offer had found few takers. Through Mrs. Johnson's efforts, Congress passed the Highway Beautification Act of 1965 despite powerful opposition from the Outdoor Advertising Association. The act banned or strictly regulated highway billboards outside commercial and industrial districts and required that roadside junkyards be concealed by fences. Proponents and opponents alike recognized Mrs. Johnson's key role. In the West billboards appeared demanding: "IMPEACH LADY BIRD JOHNSON."

The beautification campaign reflected Mrs. Johnson's particular concerns, but it also served the interests of the administration at a time of growing divisiveness. Beautification built consensus, and Mrs. Johnson emphasized this theme in all her speeches. At Yale in 1967, as protesters marched outside, she insisted almost plaintively that a concern for the environment was "one thing that we all share." Nevertheless, the divisions tearing at America's social fabric intruded even here. Advocates for Washington, D.C.'s large black community, for example, attacked the elitist tinge of the First Lady's beautification campaign in the nation's capital. "How many rats can you kill with a tulip?" sneered one critic. Mrs. Johnson vigorously rejected the notion that her efforts solely concerned rich do-gooders, maintaining that "beauty cannot be reserved 'for nice neighborhoods only.'" She set up a special committee directed by Walter Washington, a black leader, to initiate projects in the city's black districts, including vest-pocket parks and beautification efforts geared to schoolchildren and local residents. Mrs. Johnson took an avid interest in the committee's efforts and visited neighborhoods that most government leaders rarely saw.

Lady Bird Johnson's efforts, like the War on Poverty and the Great Society reforms, ultimately faded in the face of rising controversy over Vietnam. At the 1966 National Youth Conference on Natural Beauty and Conservation, the First Lady urged the delegates to "consider making America's beauty a full-time vocation." By then, however, the younger generation had less interest in Lady Bird's home-front campaign than in the war her husband was waging abroad.

The War on Poverty and the Great Society: A Postmortem

With an awesome roster of reforms to his credit and more in the pipeline during 1964–65, LBJ won approval ratings that hovered close to 70 percent. Indeed, a history of the domestic side of the Johnson presidency written as 1965 ended, and including the commitment to racial justice explored in the next chapter, would have told of soaring aspirations and impressive achievement.

Yet by 1968 the spirit of reform would evaporate. In that year, presidential candidate Richard Nixon declared, "For the past five years we have been deluged by government programs for the unemployed, programs for cities, programs for the poor, and we have reaped from these programs an ugly harvest of frustration, violence and failure." The political constituency for the War on Poverty had already collapsed when Nixon took office, and as president he would slash the program with impunity; in 1974 he shut down OEO altogether. The U.S. political landscape altered so rapidly that Americans found it difficult to recall the reformist zeal of 1964–65.

What lay behind this wave of reform, and what significance did it ultimately hold for American society? Why did it decline so rapidly? The causes are easiest to analyze. Kennedy's death, a series of books exposing problems in American life, and the idealism of the civil-rights movement encouraged a revival of liberal activism. Lyndon Johnson, with his New Deal background, political skills, and determination to build a memorable presidential record, translated that mood into tangible achievement.

The long-term ramifications of LBJ's domestic record are more difficult to evaluate. Certainly the Civil Rights Act of 1964 and the Voting Rights Act of 1965, discussed in Chapter 8, left lasting legacies. Similarly, the major Great Society measures—Medicare, aid to education, urban development and mass transit, environmental legislation—had long-term positive significance, especially for the middle class. Yet, as often in politics, efforts to grapple with one set of issues only exacerbated others—including, as we have seen, soaring federal deficits related to the Medicare and Medicaid programs.

By some measures, the War on Poverty succeeded. The proportion of Americans below the federal poverty line fell from 20 percent in 1963 to 13 percent in 1968.* For African Americans, who faced the harshest conditions, the statistics are even more impressive. In 1960 some 40 percent of blacks lived in poverty. By 1968, according to some data, this figure had been halved. In 1960 only 13 percent of black families enjoyed annual incomes of more than $10,000; by the end of the decade, the figure approached one-third. However, a booming economy contributed to these statistics as much as did the antipoverty program. The years of

---

* In 1964 the Council of Economic Advisers had set the poverty line at $3,000 annual income for a family of four—about one-half the median family income in America at the time.

maximum antipoverty expenditures also saw a big increase in federal spending related to the Vietnam War. The 1968–69 unemployment rate of about 3.4 percent, the lowest since the Korean War, reflected the increased draft calls, military spending, and war-related job opportunities of the Vietnam era as much as it did domestic economic policies. Similarly, another Vietnam byproduct, surging inflation, soon eroded many of the economic gains. All this complicates the task of isolating the effects of the War on Poverty.

The larger goal that LBJ at least rhetorically embraced—poverty's eradication—remained a dream. The tangle of social ills that the antipoverty warriors set out to cure, especially in the inner cities, proved more intractable than they had imagined. Despite the billions spent on social programs in 1964–67, inner-city joblessness, housing decay, educational problems, and social disorganization stubbornly persisted. The unemployment rate among black males aged sixteen to twenty-four actually rose in the late 1960s, just as various federal job-training programs peaked. The assumption that educational opportunities, job training, and a climate of hope would break the cycle of poverty was naive. In later years, President Ronald Reagan would joke cynically, "We fought a war on poverty, and poverty won."

The same enthusiasm that made Sargent Shriver an effective head of OEO inhibited objective assessment of the antipoverty program. A mood of boosterism, not critical self-scrutiny, prevailed. Like the reports from Vietnam that would soon tout "body counts" and other statistics to prove that America was "winning" the war, the well-intentioned cheerleading for the War on Poverty tended to dwell on its good intentions, overstate its successes, and sweep its failures under the rug.

As the high hopes faded, a backlash set in. Early evidence of the shift came in the 1966 midterm election, when Republicans gained three Senate seats and forty-seven House seats. On the ideological plane, the backlash revitalized the old view that blamed the poor themselves for their plight. In *The Unheavenly City* (1970), Edward Banfield argued that poverty stemmed from poor people's inability to grasp the concept of delayed gratification. The backlash was also connected with the racial politics of the 1960s. As white America increasingly identified poverty as a problem of blacks and Hispanics in the inner cities, the antipoverty program came to be seen as simply a means of shoveling federal dollars to minorities. The racial backlash that would splinter the civil-rights movement in the later 1960s thus also hastened the collapse of the liberal consensus and eroded backing for the War on Poverty.

One telling assault on the ideology undergirding Johnson's social agenda came in Theodore Lowi's *The End of Liberalism* (1969). A Cornell University political scientist, Lowi granted the need for government welfare policies to moderate capitalism's social effects. But 1960s-style liberalism, he contended, differed sharply from New Deal liberalism as embodied in the Social Security Act of 1935. Whereas Social Security specified its rules of operation and its criteria for eligibility, Lowi charged, the War on Poverty had a far looser structure, a "grab bag" of programs, and vaguely identified target groups. Rather than encouraging a sense of the common good, the government merely threw money at the inner cities, letting local bodies referee the resulting free-for-all among clashing interest groups. Lowi also accused the antipoverty crusade of defining social problems, especially racial ones, in economic terms when in fact they had complex cultural and historical roots.

The War on Poverty, he believed, drained the civil-rights movement of its momentum and moral authority. Lowi minced no words about his purpose: "[This book's] principal target is the modern liberal state itself, its outmoded ideology, and its self-defeating policies." Johnson-style liberalism, he charged, was "sincere humanitarianism gone cockeyed."

The debate continued into the 1980s. Critics on the Left dismissed the War on Poverty as a typical halfway palliative that offered superficial remedies without addressing underlying power realities. In *The Unraveling of America* (1984), Allan J. Matusow attacked the War on Poverty as a misdirected effort by a liberal political establishment wedded to the status quo. Only a radical redistribution of income and power, argued Matusow, offered hope of eradicating want in capitalist America. The War on Poverty's epitaph, he concluded, should be, "Declared But Never Fought." Although convincing on its own terms, Matusow's work gave little attention to the actual political realities of 1960s America, when the electorate's moderate-to-conservative tendencies put severe constraints on radical reform.

Conservatives, meanwhile, blamed the War on Poverty for encouraging welfare dependency. Charles Murray's *Losing Ground: American Social Policy, 1950–1980* (1984) argued that by portraying the poor as victims and by blaming poverty on social maladjustments that the government must correct, Johnson-era policymakers weakened the stigma associated with welfare. Despite LBJ's announced goal of ending welfare dependence, he suggested, 1960s social policy actually encouraged the poor to accept the dole as a way of life. New York City's welfare rolls did double between 1965 and 1975, with similar trends in other cities. By extending benefits to all whose income fell below a specified cutoff point, Murray contended, the War on Poverty and other well-intentioned programs reduced incentives to self-help. Reformers thereby slowed and eventually reversed what Murray claims was a long-term decline in poverty rates since World War II.

Murray paid scant attention to programs such as Head Start, the Job Corps, and Upward Bound that did encourage individual initiative and inculcate "middle-class" values of hard work and personal responsibility. Furthermore, if the problem was a growing dependence on federal largess, the poor were hardly alone. Defense industries boomed as Pentagon dollars showered down after 1965. Under Medicare and Medicaid, physicians and nursing homes set their own fees, and many profited vastly as Uncle Sam picked up the tab. Too, countless academics, lawyers, administrators, planners, builders, and "advocates for the poor" prospered from their participation in various War on Poverty programs. The funds designated for community action programs, urban betterment, and job training often landed in the hands of the middle-class staffers who ran the agencies, programs, and centers.

Liberals—a dwindling breed—generally praised the War on Poverty, although they, too, criticized its scattershot approach and inflated rhetoric. They argued as well that the antipoverty campaign, for all the money spent, still suffered from underfunding. One called it "a classic instance of the American habit of substituting good intentions for cold hard cash." Finally, liberals and conservatives alike generally agreed that by raising expectations in the inner cities and then only partially following through, the War on Poverty left a legacy of bitterness.

Why did support for reform fade so rapidly after 1965? Urban riots offer one reason. Initially, observers cited inner-city unrest such as hit Birmingham in 1963 and the Watts district of Los Angeles in 1965 (see pp. 231, 254) as evidence of the urgency of antipoverty efforts. But as more cities erupted, skepticism about Johnson's programs intensified. As urban turmoil worsened and black activists grew more radical, the white middle class turned hostile. Not poverty but the poor now seemed the enemy.

LBJ launched his domestic reforms amid an economic boom, confident that the nation could divert large sums to social problems without suffering deficit problems, raising taxes, or jeopardizing middle-class living standards. Little sense of bounds or limits inhibited the architects of reform. As Johnson burst out to a speechwriter, "I'm sick of all the people who talk about the things we can't do. Hell, we're the richest country in the world, the most powerful. We can do it all, if we're not too greedy; that's our job: to persuade people to give a little so everyone can be better off." In the 1970s, as the boom faded and inflation worsened while spending on various entitlement programs soared,* expansiveness gave way to resentment. Richard Nixon anticipated the shift in the 1968 campaign when he championed the middle class as the "Forgotten Americans."

In terms of economic theory, Kennedy had adopted the stimulus component of Keynesianism, using popular tax cuts, investment credits, and federal spending increases to spur economic growth. But Johnson resisted the more politically risky side of Keynesianism, which called for tax increases and spending cuts to cool an overheated economy. As inflation raged, Johnson did little. The resulting economic slowdown and erosion of consumer buying power ate away at the liberal consensus.

Above all, the Great Society succumbed to the Vietnam War, a cause that Johnson pursued with his left hand while championing domestic reform with his right. From 1965 to 1973, when Washington spent about $15 billion combating poverty, funding for the war reached $120 billion. Vietnam diverted attention from home-front issues and undermined LBJ's moral authority as a champion of reform. In the summer of 1966, a Johnson aide traveled to New York City to discuss new domestic-policy initiatives with a group of liberal academics. Afterward, one of the participants, historian William Leuchtenberg, wrote a postmortem of the event. "Like Banquo's ghost," he observed, "Vietnam was the unwelcome guest at the feast." As long as the war continued, he concluded "there is no hope at all for expanding the Great Society." The domestic challenge that Johnson set for the nation would have been daunting under the best of circumstances; after 1965 it proved hopeless, and the reform consensus evaporated. By the 1990s, when a Democrat could win the presidency on a pledge to "end welfare as we know it," and Democrats and Republicans alike could unite to dismantle vast parts of the federal human-services apparatus, the reaction against both the idealism and the ideology of the War on Poverty was complete.

---

* An entitlement benefit is one that the recipient is entitled to receive simply by virtue of being in a designated class of people: over age sixty-five or under a certain income level, for example.

Conclusion

Yet much remains admirable in Johnson's domestic record. All the major issues that he tackled—racism, poverty, the cities, education, health care, the environment—stayed on the nation's agenda long after his presidency had ended. Thanks to him, the nation not only confronted these problems but for a time granted them priority. Like FDR, Johnson on domestic issues may not have had all the right answers, but he asked the right questions. The mid-1960s remains the most productive era in U.S. domestic reform since the New Deal, and the credit largely goes to Lyndon Johnson. The tragedy is not that the War on Poverty and the Great Society fell short but that the impulse behind them faded so quickly.

Americans are still coming to terms with the crude, profane, arm-twisting Texan who figured so prominently in all the events that defined the 1960s. As we begin to grasp how Lyndon Johnson could with equal fervor espouse the rights of African Americans, the cause of the poor, educational and health reform, environmental protection and beautification, and a brutal and divisive war in Asia, we will begin to understand not only Johnson but also post–World War II American liberalism.

SELECTED READINGS

The Liberal Agenda in the 1950s and Early 1960s

Irving Bernstein, *Promises Kept: John F. Kennedy's New Frontier* (1991); Wayne Flynt, *Dixie's Forgotten People: The South's Poor Whites* (1979); Robert Booth Fowler, *Believing Skeptics: American Political Intellectuals, 1945–1964* (1978); Patrick M. Garry, *Liberalism and American Identity* (1992); Alonzo L. Hamby, *Liberalism and Its Challengers: From F.D.R. to Bush* (2d ed., 1992); Jim F. Heath, *John F. Kennedy and the Business Community* (1969); Walter Heller, *Fiscal Policy for a Balanced Economy: Experience, Problems and Prospects* (1968); Hubert H. Humphrey, *The Education of a Public Man* (1976); James L. Kauffman, *Selling Outer Space: Kennedy, the Media, and Funding for Project Apollo, 1961–1963* (1994); Daniel Knapp and Kenneth Polk, *Scouting the War on Poverty: Social Reform Politics in the Kennedy Administration* (1971); Arthur Larson, *A Republican Looks at His Party* (1956); Robert Lekachman, *The Age of Keynes* (1968); Richard H. Pells, *The Liberal Mind in a Conservative Age: American Intellectuals in the 1940s and 1950s* (1985); Edward Purcell, *The Crisis of Democratic Theory* (1973); Hobart Rowan, *The Free Enterprisers: Kennedy, Johnson and the Business Establishment* (1964); Arthur M. Schlesinger, Jr., *A Thousand Days* (1965); Alan Shank, *Presidential Policy Leadership: Kennedy and Social Welfare* (1980); Barbie Zelizer, *Covering the Body: The Kennedy Assassination, the Media and the Shaping of Collective Memory* (1992).

Johnson, the War on Poverty, and the Great Society

Henry J. Aaron, *Politics and the Professors: The Great Society in Perspective* (1978); Vaughn Davis Bornet, *The Presidency of Lyndon B. Johnson* (1983); Robert Caro, *The Years of Lyndon Johnson: The Path to Power* (1982) and *Means of Ascent* (1990); Richard Cloward and Frances Fox Piven, *Poor People's Movements* (1978); Robert Dallek, *Lone Star Rising: Lyndon Johnson and His Times, 1908–1960* (1991); Mark I. Gelfand, "The War on Poverty," in Robert A. Divine, ed., *The Johnson Years,* Vol. 1 (1987); Robert A. Gorman, *Michael Harrington: Speaking American* (1995); Hugh Davis Graham, *The Uncertain Trumpet: Federal Education Policy in the Kennedy and Johnson Years* (1984); Robert H. Haveman, ed., *A Decade of Federal Antipoverty Programs* (1977); Lyndon Johnson, *The Vantage Point: Perspectives of the Presidency 1963–1969* (1971); Doris Kearns, *Lyndon Johnson and the American Dream* (1977); Sar A. Levitan, *The Great Society's Poor Law* (1969); Theodore Marmor, *The Politics of Medicare* (1973); Peter Marris and Martin Rein, *Dilemmas of Social Reform: Poverty and Community Action in the United States* (1973); Alan Matusow, *The Unraveling of America: A History of Liberalism in the 1960s* (1984); Daniel Patrick Moynihan, *Maximum Feasible Misunderstanding* (1969); Charles Murray, *Losing Ground: American Social Policy, 1950–1980* (1984); James T. Patterson, *America's Struggle Against Poverty, 1900–1980* (1981); Frances Fox Piven and Richard A. Cloward, *Regulating the Poor: The Functions of Public Welfare* (1971); Diane Ravitch, *The Troubled Crusade: American Education, 1945–1980* (1983); David Zarefsky, *President Johnson's War on Poverty: Rhetoric and History* (1986).

Environmentalism

Craig W. Allin, *The Politics of Wilderness Preservation* (1982); Thomas R. Dunlap, *DDT: Scientists, Citizens, and Public Policy* (1981); Lewis L. Gould, "Lady Bird Johnson and Beautification," in Robert A. Divine, ed., *The Johnson Years,* Vol. 1 (1987); Samuel P. Hays and Barbara D. Hays, *Beauty, Health, and Permanence: Environmental Politics in the United States, 1955–1985* (1987); Lady Bird Johnson, *A White House Diary* (1970); Martin V. Melosi, "Lyndon Johnson and Environmental Policy," in Divine, ed., *The Johnson Years,* Vol. 2; Vera L. Norwood, "The Nature of Knowing: Rachel Carson and the American Environment," *Signs* (Summer 1987); Carroll W. Pursell, Jr., ed., *From Conservation to Ecology: The Development of Environmental Concern* (1973); Elmo Richardson, *Dams, Parks and Politics: Resource Development and Preservation in the Truman-Eisenhower Era* (1973); Walter A. Rosenbaum, *The Politics of Environmental Concern* (1973); Victor B. Scheffer, *The Shaping of Environmentalism in America* (1991).

❖ ❖ ❖

CHAPTER 8

The Civil-Rights Movement
at Flood Tide

O n Monday, February 1, 1960, four black freshmen from the North Carolina
  Agricultural and Technical College in Greensboro entered the local Woolworth's store, bought school supplies, and then sat down at the lunch counter and
ordered coffee. When the white waitress uttered the familiar formula, "We don't
serve Negroes here," they gave an unfamiliar response:

> We just beg to disagree with you. We've in fact already been served. . . . We won-
> der why you'd invite us in to serve us at one counter and deny service at another.
> If this is a private club or private concern, then we believe you ought to sell mem-
> bership cards.

The four remained seated and waited—all day. Years later, one of the four,
Franklin McCain, would look back on that Monday:

> If it's possible to know what it means to have your soul cleansed—I felt pretty clean
> at that time. . . . I felt as though I had gained my manhood. . . . Not Franklin Mc-
> Cain only as an individual, but I felt as though the manhood of a number of other
> black persons had been restored.

By Friday, more than three hundred protesters jammed the store and the
nearby Kress's five-and-dime. The movement rapidly spread to Fisk University in
Nashville, Atlanta University, and other black colleges and universities across the
South.

The sit-ins signaled fundamental changes in the civil-rights movement. From
the early twentieth century to the 1950s, two organizations had spearheaded the
African-American cause: the National Association for the Advancement of Colored People (NAACP) and the National Urban League. Led by educated, middle-
class blacks, both groups worked quietly through established channels. The
NAACP fought discrimination in the courts; the Urban League sought to improve
black employment opportunities by negotiations with corporate leaders. Neither
encouraged mass demonstrations. These older organizations had significant
achievements to their credit. The Supreme Court's 1954 *Brown* v. *Board of Educa-*

220

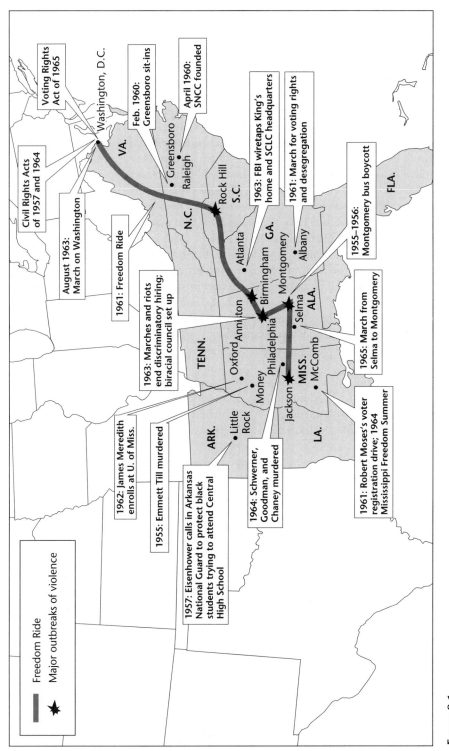

FIGURE 8.1
Key Events in the Civil-Rights Movement

Voting Rights Act of 1965

Feb. 1960: Greensboro sit-ins

April 1960: SNCC founded

1963: FBI wiretaps King's home and SCLC headquarters

1961: March for voting rights and desegregation

Civil Rights Acts of 1957 and 1964

August 1963: March on Washington

1961: Freedom Ride

1955–1956: Montgomery bus boycott

1963: Marches and riots end discriminatory hiring; biracial council set up

1965: March from Selma to Montgomery

1962: James Meredith enrolls at U. of Miss.

1955: Emmett Till murdered

1964: Schwerner, Goodman, and Chaney murdered

1961: Robert Moses's voter registration drive; 1964 Mississippi Freedom Summer

1957: Eisenhower calls in Arkansas National Guard to protect black students trying to attend Central High School

Washington, D.C.

VA.

Greensboro
Raleigh

Rock Hill

S.C.

FLA.

N.C.

Atlanta

Birmingham

GA.

Montgomery

Albany

TENN.

Oxford Anniston

Selma

ALA.

Philadelphia

Money

MISS.

McComb

Jackson

LA.

ARK.

Little Rock

Freedom Ride

Major outbreaks of violence

tion decision outlawing school segregation, for example, culminated years of legal effort by the NAACP.

After the *Brown* decision, fresh currents of activism had energized black America, especially in the South. The Montgomery bus boycott of 1955–56 coupled the familiar strategy of litigation with new tactics of nonviolent mass action. From the Montgomery campaign had emerged a new leader, Dr. Martin Luther King, Jr.; a new organization, the Southern Christian Leadership Conference (SCLC); and the Civil Rights Act of 1957, with its focus on voting rights.

The NAACP, Urban League, and SCLC remained active in the 1960s, but after the sit-ins, a vigorous new organization, the Student Nonviolent Coordinating Committee (SNCC), won support from both white backers of the black cause and young African Americans. This proliferation of organizations generated tensions and rivalries, but it also yielded a creative array of strategies that produced results no single organization could have achieved. The 1960s saw a broadening of direct-action approaches that sometimes sparked violent confrontation.

The civil-rights movement that arose in the later 1950s and crested in the 1960s profoundly threatened many white southerners, for whom a racially segregated society seemed the natural order. Rooted in slavery, the South's racial caste system was buttressed by custom, law, black disfranchisement, and, ultimately, the threat of violence. Through the first half of the twentieth century, two separate and unequal societies coexisted in the South. Strict segregation prevailed in schools, churches, courthouses, factories, residences, theaters, parks, even public restrooms. This caste system rested on ingrained white notions of racial superiority and a horror of the "mongrelization" that supposedly would result from a crumbling of the racial barrier. Any who challenged this wall of separation faced swift retribution. In one brutal example, Mississippi vigilantes lynched a fourteen-year-old black visitor from the North, Emmett Till, in 1955. The boy allegedly had whistled at a white woman.

Northern blacks also faced barriers and prejudice, and de facto segregation existed throughout the nation. But the white South, for reasons embedded in its history, had translated racist thinking into an elaborate, legally based caste system that relegated African Americans to second-class status. Accordingly, it was in the South that the civil-rights movement first took shape.

The "White South" was not a monolith. Differences in region, education, social class, and religious belief influenced white southerners' attitudes. The Deep South clung to segregation more rigidly than did the border states. Upper-class whites, better educated and more cosmopolitan, were more likely to recognize the inevitability of change. As we have seen, the region's business and professional elite often worked behind the scenes to ease racial tensions. Newspaper editors such as Ralph McGill of the *Atlanta Constitution* and Virginius Dabney of the *Richmond Times-Dispatch* spoke for this class by denouncing violence and by calling for enlightened responses to the civil-rights campaign. Southern academic centers such as the University of North Carolina at Chapel Hill harbored eloquent critics of segregation. Georgia novelist Lillian Smith had explored southern racial taboos and the horror of lynching in her 1944 novel, *Strange Fruit.* On the legal front, some southern judges backed segregation, but others, especially at the federal level, supported the black struggle. Federal district judge Frank M. Johnson, Jr., of Alabama, for example, despite vilification by white racists, consistently upheld

African Americans' constitutional rights. The revivalist Billy Graham, one of the nation's best-known white southerners, integrated his crusades and called racism "the most burning issue of modern times."

Nevertheless, the white South had an enormous investment in the prevailing caste system and in general saw any attacks on it, whether from local blacks or from northern liberals, as a dire threat. Preserving the status quo seemed especially urgent to poorer, uneducated southern whites. Such folk ranked low on the social hierarchy, but as long as the racial caste system survived, they knew that they stood at least above blacks in the pecking order. In the opposition stirred by the civil-rights campaign, poorer, socially marginal whites—and politicians and police officials who pandered to them—typically took the lead. Only a handful of white southerners resorted to actual physical violence to express their hatred of integration, but their actions reinforced the image of a white South united in murderous opposition to racial equality.

The intensity and scope of this new civil-rights activism caught Washington off guard. Official Washington was accustomed to working with leaders such as Roy Wilkins of the NAACP; the Urban League's Whitney Young; and, more recently, Martin Luther King, Jr. Administration and congressional leaders waffled uneasily as grassroots activism sprang up across the South. John F. Kennedy courted the black vote in 1960, although he responded only hesitantly to the rising demands for racial justice. But as the pace of demonstrations and the level of violence intensified, the federal courts, the White House, and Congress did extend decisive support at crucial junctures.

The civil-rights movement of the early 1960s did not unfold in an orderly fashion, one event at a time. Activists across the South simultaneously sought a variety of goals. And although Martin Luther King, Jr., and the SCLC played an important role, the maturing movement spawned new leaders. As young activists pushed beyond the tactics that had worked in Montgomery, King and the SCLC, not to mention the NAACP and the Urban League, struggled to redefine their goals and tactics. Whereas generational friction in white America arose over cultural issues, in black America it took the form of tense debates over how to conduct the freedom struggle.

Comprehending the civil-rights struggle requires a multifocal approach that keeps in view the strategies of sometimes fractious national organizations and leaders, the grassroots campaigns led by men and women seeking specific local objectives, the fears and anxieties of white southerners who saw their way of life under siege, and the national political stage where all these pressures and counterpressures coalesced into a reform movement of enormous magnitude. From the movement that historian C. Vann Woodward has dubbed the "second Reconstruction," nothing less than a new society was painfully emerging.

1960–1962: Tactical Innovation, Political Hesitation

The sit-ins that began at Greensboro captured the imagination of young blacks. At an April 1960 conference at Shaw University in Raleigh, North Carolina, some three hundred student leaders from more than fifty southern black schools and colleges, as well as delegates from northern schools, founded the Student Nonviolent Coordinating Committee (SNCC, pronounced "Snick"). White representatives from religious and student groups attended, but the movement was overwhelmingly black led. James M. Lawson, Jr., a divinity student at Vanderbilt University, drafted the new organization's statement of purpose. In a rousing address, Lawson criticized the NAACP and all "middle class conventional halfway efforts to deal with radical social evil." The key figure was not a student at all but fifty-seven-year-old Ella Baker, SCLC's executive director. Baker planned SNCC's founding conference and provided a modest grant from SCLC to cover expenses. After initial hesitation, both the NAACP and the SCLC threw their prestige and support behind the new student organization.

As the tempo of the sit-ins increased, white resistance kept pace. Governor Ernest Hollings of South Carolina, although not an extreme segregationist, warned that the prominence of protesting black ministers and religious leaders would not spare them from legal reprisals. "Our law enforcement officers have their Bibles, too," Hollings observed. Sit-in participants were assaulted, jailed, burned with lighted cigarettes, and scalded with hot coffee. Even some conservative black college administrators tried to stop the protests. But the demonstrators persisted, winning recruits and honing the strategy of nonresistance that so infuriated their opponents. From the sit-ins emerged the song that would become the civil-rights movement's anthem: "We Shall Overcome," an adaptation of an old slave melody.

The Congress of Racial Equality (CORE), meanwhile, resumed the Freedom Rides that it had initiated shortly after World War II. In 1946 the Supreme Court had barred racial segregation in public vehicles engaged in interstate commerce. The following year, CORE had tested this ruling with an integrated "Journey of Reconciliation" by bus through the South. In the 1960 case *Boynton* v. *Virginia,* the Supreme Court had extended its previous action by outlawing segregated bus and train stations, airport terminals, and other facilities related to interstate transit. But the South widely ignored these decisions, and early in 1961, CORE director James Farmer announced another Freedom Ride to integrate bus-station facilities.

On May 4, 1961, biracial teams of CORE volunteers headed south from Washington, D.C., on Trailways and Greyhound buses. They integrated station facilities in Virginia without incident, but as the vehicles lumbered into the Deep South, white racists mobilized. In Rock Hill, South Carolina, young toughs clubbed twenty-one-year-old John Lewis, a Nashville, Tennessee, divinity student, as he entered the white waiting room. In Anniston, Alabama, a mob armed with clubs and metal bars beat the Freedom Riders, inflicting permanent brain damage on one. When the bus's slashed tires deflated a few miles out of Anniston, whites following in cars smashed the windows, threw a smoke bomb inside, and assaulted the occupants as they escaped. A state trooper traveling on the bus in plain clothes at the order of the Alabama governor held the mob off with a pistol, preventing worse violence.

The mayhem intensified when the bus reached Birmingham, Alabama, a thriving industrial city and a hotbed of anti-integrationist sentiment. The town's most vocal politician, police commissioner T. Eugene "Bull" Connor, spewed bigotry. A high-school dropout and former radio sports announcer, Connor over the next few years would become the symbol of rabble-rousing racism at its rawest. In

Birmingham, the Freedom Riders endured attacks from about thirty men brandishing baseball bats and bicycle chains, with no police protection in sight.

Opposition to the Freedom Rides and sit-ins only accelerated the overall campaign's momentum. The movement was rapidly expanding beyond schools, bus stations, and lunch counters. As Ella Baker wrote in June 1960, "The current sit-ins are concerned with something much bigger than a hamburger or even a giant-sized Coke." James Lawson in a 1961 essay offered a radical analysis of American racism and of the movement's objectives:

> [I]f after over 300 years, segregation (slavery) is still a basic pattern rather than a peripheral custom, should we not question the American way of life which allows segregation so much structural support? . . .
> The sit-ins won concessions, not structural changes; the Freedom Rides won concessions, but not real changes.
> There will be no revolution until we see Negro faces in all positions that help to mold public opinion, help to shape policy for America.

As the movement unfolded, awareness of racism as a national issue spread. The recognition grew that deep-rooted patterns of racism contributed to the joblessness, poverty, and social disruption of the North's sprawling black ghettos. But before the nation could confront these larger realities, officially sanctioned segregation had to be extirpated from its southern bastion. This was the work of blacks of the 1950s and early 1960s who, with white supporters, marched; filed lawsuits; organized Freedom Rides, sit-ins, and boycotts; and in some cases suffered physical abuse, imprisonment, even death.

The civil-rights movement echoed loudly in Washington. As a candidate in 1960, John Kennedy had praised the sit-in movement and secured the release of Martin Luther King from jail. Once in office, Kennedy set up the Equal Employment Opportunity Committee, headed by Vice President Johnson, to combat discrimination in the federal government and in the hiring practices of firms with government contracts. At a time when blacks held only a miniscule share of federal positions, this effort paid off. In the administration's early days, joked Roy Wilkins of the NAACP, "everyone was scrambling around trying to find himself a Negro in order to keep the President off his neck."

Attorney General Robert Kennedy beefed up the Justice Department's anemic civil-rights division. Proceeding under the Civil Rights Act of 1957, the department sued thirty-two southern electoral boards for denying voting rights to blacks, in contrast to the Eisenhower administration's six such suits. When Mississippi blacks who registered to vote faced an economic boycott, the Department of Agriculture, on JFK's orders, distributed surplus food to them. In 1962, Congress passed an administration-backed constitutional amendment banning poll taxes, long used in some southern states to bar black voters. It was ratified in 1964.

Nevertheless, President Kennedy's overall civil-rights record proved decidedly mixed. Kennedy, who addressed the issue only episodically, was above all a practical politician interested in securing and holding power, not an idealist. He viewed the civil-rights movement not as an occasion for moral leadership but as a political problem to be managed. His narrow 1960 electoral victory made him extremely sensitive to the lily-white Southern Democratic party and its powerful sachems in

Congess. Despite urging by black leaders, Kennedy delayed introducing a civil-rights bill until mid-1963 and held back from outlawing racial discrimination in federally funded public housing until late 1962. As a candidate, he had pointed out that a president could effect the latter change "with the stroke of a pen." (Frustrated civil-rights advocates deluged the White House with pens.)

Under pressure from Mississippi's James Eastland, a notorious racist and chair of the Senate Judiciary Committee, Kennedy appointed to a Mississippi federal judgeship a segregationist, William Harold Cox, who used every possible stratagem to thwart the civil-rights cause. On one occasion, Cox referred to litigants seeking voting rights as "a bunch of niggers . . . acting like a bunch of chimpanzees." Bowing to the tradition of senatorial privilege, Kennedy named other segregationists to the federal bench as well. For the most part, the White House moved on civil rights only when forced by events.

The administration's response to the 1961 Freedom Rides illustrates this pattern. Preoccupied with the Berlin crisis, the president viewed the escalating drama in Alabama as a frustrating distraction. "Tell them to call it off. Stop them," he told an aide. Kennedy was also hampered by limited information. FBI director J. Edgar Hoover knew of Sheriff Bull Connor's willingness to allow attacks on the Freedom Riders in Birmingham but failed to pass along the information.

Kennedy did telephone Alabama's governor, who promised to protect the Freedom Riders, a pledge he promptly broke. The president also persuaded Greyhound officials to provide buses to transport the Freedom Riders out of Birmingham. But Kennedy neither sent federal marshals nor spoke out publicly except to issue a general call for law and order. Deprived of protection from the local police or from Washington, CORE volunteers flew from Birmingham to New Orleans on May 17, ending this phase of the Freedom Rides.

But John Lewis, working with SNCC leaders, organized a team of volunteers who rushed to Birmingham to continue the Freedom Ride. Police arrested them at the bus terminal, drove them to the Tennessee state line, and dropped them off beside the highway. Friends immediately drove them back to Birmingham, from which, on May 20, they set out on a Greyhound bus bound for Montgomery. Here, more violence broke out. With the local police nowhere in sight, a mob of more than a thousand whites screaming "Get those niggers!" attacked the Freedom Riders as they entered the bus station. John Lewis suffered a brain concussion; another Freedom Rider was brutally assaulted. John Siegenthaler, an observer from the Department of Justice, was beaten unconscious and kicked as he lay on the pavement. Prodded by the publicity, JFK finally took decisive action, ordering some four hundred U.S. marshals to the beleaguered city.

For decades, the terror that served as the ultimate enforcer of the South's caste system had drawn only casual attention from the white North. But the assaults on the Freedom Riders received major media coverage. *Life* and other magazines published vivid photographs and stories. Television news cameras caught rampaging whites brutalizing Freedom Riders. The media did not create the civil-rights movement, but in publicizing outrages, the press helped to push civil rights high on the national agenda.

On the evening of May 20, more than a thousand Montgomery blacks jammed into Reverend Ralph Abernathy's First Baptist Church. Martin Luther

King and others insisted that the Freedom Rides continue. Outside, a howling mob attacked blacks and hurled torches and stink bombs inside the sanctuary. At last the marshals moved in. For the first time since Little Rock in 1957, a president had drawn on federal power to protect black citizens exercising their civil rights.

The administration worked desperately behind the scenes to manage a social revolution whose intensity it barely grasped. James Farmer later recalled his fury when Attorney General Robert Kennedy advised a cooling-off period in the civil-rights struggle. "We had been cooling off for a hundred years," wrote Farmer. "If we got any cooler we'd be in a deep freeze." The movement's new slogan, "Freedom Now," evolved in reaction to the calls for restraint by white liberals and some conservative black leaders. When Robert Kennedy warned that civil-rights demonstrations would embarrass the president in his forthcoming meeting with Khrushchev, even Dr. King's enthusiasm for the administration turned into cold-eyed skepticism. "They don't understand the social revolution going on in the world," King concluded.

On May 24, Freedom Riders representing all the major civil-rights groups and all parts of the country set out from Montgomery bound for Jackson, Mississippi. The tension was high as they moved from city to city through a hostile region. "As we rolled toward Jackson," one Freedom Rider later recalled, "every blocked-off street, every back road taken, every change in speed caused our hearts to leap."

Robert Kennedy, still juggling divergent political interests, struck a deal with the governors of Mississippi and Alabama: The administration would not challenge the arrest and jailing of the Freedom Riders, provided that the governors held off the white mobs. The arrangement left Freedom Riders, male and female, to face harsh treatment far from the television cameras in obscure jails and penitentiaries. By the end of the summer, more than 1,000 volunteers had participated in Freedom Ride activities, and over 350 had gone to jail. James Farmer himself spent thirty-nine days behind bars. In late September, the attorney general finally secured an order from the Interstate Commerce Commission (ICC) barring racial segregation in all facilities serving interstate travelers and ordering that signs announcing this policy be prominently posted in all such facilities by November 1. During the next year, segregation in interstate travel gradually ended.

Events again spurred the administration to action in September 1962, when Mississippi governor Ross Barnett, a demagogic segregationist, personally blocked an attempt by James Meredith, a black air force veteran, to register at the University of Mississippi. Attorney General Robert Kennedy sent five hundred federal marshals to the university campus. "The eyes of the nation and all the world are upon you and upon all of us," President Kennedy reminded Mississippians. Nevertheless, on September 30, a mob incited by a Barnett radio address attacked the federal marshals, in a spasm of violence that left 2 dead and 375 injured. JFK, mobilizing a show of federal force, ordered some thirty thousand regular army troops and federalized national guardsmen to Oxford to restore order and ensure Meredith's safety. Barnett backed down, and Meredith enrolled.

FBI director J. Edgar Hoover, meanwhile, undertook a variety of clandestine activities to discredit the black freedom struggle. Pandering to Cold War fears, Hoover portrayed movement leaders as communist dupes or worse. In September 1963, Hoover's assistant for domestic intelligence drafted a memo describing

Martin Luther King as "the most dangerous and effective Negro leader in the country." Warning of the "social revolution" sweeping the nation, the memo called for "stepped-up [FBI] activities" to document the Communist party's supposed role in this upheaval. With Robert Kennedy's approval, the FBI wiretapped King's home and the SCLC headquarters in Atlanta. By this means, Hoover compiled a damaging file on King's private life, including evidence of extramarital affairs, that he used to besmirch the movement. A 1963 FBI document, "Communism and the Negro Movement," full of baseless innuendo, circulated through the government, provided ammunition for enemies of the civil-rights campaign.

But the movement involved more than high-level maneuverings and heavily publicized events. As Hoover pursued his vendetta and as the media highlighted the Freedom Rides, a grassroots effort had arisen in rural Mississippi. In the summer of 1961, Robert Moses, a New York high-school math teacher and SNCC volunteer, launched a voter registration drive in Mississippi, where only 5 percent of eligible blacks were registered to vote. In many rural areas, not a single black voted. The campaign centered on the town of McComb, a Ku Klux Klan stronghold. One of the volunteers, twenty-two-year-old Charles Sherrod, later described the SNCC workers' informal conversations with local blacks in lunch rooms and pool halls: "We would tell them of how it feels to be . . . in jail for the cause. . . . We referred to the system that imprisons men's minds and robs them of creativity. We mocked the system that teaches men to be good Negroes instead of good men."

As the SNCC volunteers tried to register black voters, hostile whites struck back. When Herbert Lee, a black farmer who had endorsed the voter-registration drive, was shot by a local white, a jury acquitted the killer, accepting his claim of "self defense." When a SNCC worker asked a local sheriff about jailed SNCC volunteers, the sheriff assaulted him brutally and then arrested him. One SNCC worker recalled, "[Fear] was always there, stretched like a tight steel wire between the pit of the stomach and the center of the brain."

Unlike the Freedom Rides, this lonely struggle drew little national attention. Some Justice Department observers briefly visited McComb, but the Kennedy administration declined to intervene despite blatant evidence of civil-rights violations. Many local blacks also fearfully stood aside, but others responded to SNCC's challenge. A sixteen-year-old high-school student spent September in jail after joining a sit-in at a local Woolworth's. Released in October, she led 115 of her classmates in a march on the McComb city hall.

As the McComb volunteers struggled on, setbacks elsewhere forced a reappraisal of civil-rights strategy. A campaign in Albany, Georgia, proved particularly trying. In the fall of 1961, SNCC, backed by King and SCLC, targeted Albany for a major desegregation campaign that organizers hoped would prod the administration to intervene. Month after month, Albany black residents marched for voting rights and to protest Albany's segregated schools, libraries, parks, and lunch counters. Hundreds were imprisoned, but the local white establishment handled the demonstrations shrewdly. The police treated the arrestees well, avoiding the brutality that could rivet television viewers and galvanize the White House. The police chief even prayed with the demonstrators prior to arresting them.

Divisions within the black community further weakened the Albany action. SNCC's youthful leaders ridiculed the NAACP as stodgy and timid, while the older organization resented SNCC's lack of appreciation for its efforts. NAACP head Roy Wilkins complained, "We paid some of the expenses of the Albany movement, only to be insulted for being on the wrong side of the generation gap." Privately, Wilkins also attacked Martin Luther King, Jr., whose growing prominence rankled him. Some local black leaders viewed *all* outside organizations as interlopers.

Late that year, when white leaders in Albany orally accepted the demonstrators' demands, King proclaimed victory and left town. The white establishment quickly reneged on its agreement, however, leaving Albany's walls of segregation firmly in place. This failure undermined the credibility of the civil-rights leadership and heightened blacks' frustration with the Kennedy administration, which had taken no steps to intervene.

Despite isolated successes, the movement seemed to flounder by the end of 1962. Eight years after the *Brown* decision, 92 percent of southern black children still attended segregated schools, most southern blacks could not vote, and segregation, although weakened, remained firmly in place across much of the South. In a strategy session that fall, SCLC leaders reached two sobering conclusions. First, the Albany disappointment made plain that moral suasion alone would not suffice; new federal laws were needed. Second, the Kennedy administration would not push such legislation except in the face of dramatic, media-grabbing confrontations. These conclusions led directly to a showdown in Birmingham, Alabama, that riveted the nation's attention in May 1963.

1963: Victory in Birmingham, Action in Washington

Birmingham, ranked by civil-rights leaders as America's most segregated big city, displayed the full spectrum of southern views on race. The city's white elite in their gracious homes deprecated poor whites' crude racism and violent assaults on civil-rights activists. Yet while some worked cautiously for racial change, others tacitly supported segregation. Birmingham also had the Ku Klux Klan and Bull Connor.

The SCLC targeted Birmingham at the urging of Reverend Fred Lee Shuttlesworth, pastor of the city's Sixteenth Street Baptist Church and an SCLC founder. To avoid the Albany mistakes, SCLC recruited 250 local black leaders to coordinate the drive. Intent on provoking encounters that would dramatize the city's institutionalized racism and prod Washington to action, SCLC set forth its strategy in a planning document tellingly labeled Project C—for confrontation. Along with marches, Project C included a boycott of Birmingham's department stores, which relied on African Americans' patronage while denying them equal employment opportunities.

On April 6, Reverend Shuttlesworth led a march on city hall and was arrested. Martin Luther King, with consciously planned symbolism, led a march on Good Friday and spent three days behind bars, where he composed the widely reprinted "Letter from Birmingham Jail," a central manifesto of the civil-rights movement. In the document, King explained the religious and philosophical underpinnings of the strategy of nonviolent civil disobedience. Disfranchised blacks jailed for disobeying local statutes, he pointed out, had had no voice in framing those statutes. To those who criticized the timing of the Birmingham protests, he commented wryly, "Frankly, I have never yet engaged in a direct action movement that was 'well timed.'" Articulating the anger spawned by segregation, he described his daughter's disappointment when he explained that she could not go to an amusement park advertised on television, and his sorrow on seeing "the depressing clouds of inferiority begin to form in her little mental sky, and [to] see her . . . unconsciously developing a bitterness toward white people."

Introducing an economic theme that would loom larger in the years ahead, King mentioned the "air-tight cage of poverty in the midst of an affluent society" that intensified black rage. If the moderate, religiously based movement that he represented failed, he warned, upheavals of incalculable ferocity could ensue: A bitter and alienated segment of the black community had already "lost faith in America," and was "perilously close" to violence.

Although "Letter from Birmingham Jail" won worldwide support, circumstances in Birmingham deteriorated. A series of marches, some comprising schoolchildren and students, drew the ire of Bull Connor's police, who attacked the singing, chanting demonstrators with clubs, cattle prods, police dogs, and high-pressure fire hoses. Many protesters suffered injuries or went to jail. Other signs confirmed King's warnings about simmering unrest in black America. When the

Birmingham, Alabama, 1963. *Fire hoses batter young black marchers as the city's white power structure fights in vain to preserve racial segregation.* (© Charles Moore/ Black Star)

KKK bombed SCLC's Birmingham headquarters in early May, some blacks struck back. In a frightening four-day outbreak, black gangs from the city's poorest neighborhoods roamed the streets, assaulting police, throwing rocks, bricks, and bottles, and burning white-owned businesses. Only urgent pleas by King and Shuttlesworth brought the rioting under control.

The climax came on Tuesday, May 7, as fire hoses ripped into four thousand black marchers assembled in a local park, tearing clothing from bruised bodies and knocking adults and children to the ground as though struck by bullets. Reverend Shuttlesworth was hospitalized. Bull Connor chortled when he heard the news, regretting only that the black leader had not been carried away in a hearse. Unlike McComb and Albany in 1962, the Birmingham violence attracted intense media coverage, and national outrage mounted. As the city's jails overflowed, marchers continued to pour from the Sixteenth Street Baptist Church, command center for the demonstrations.

At last the white elite had enough. Dismayed by the violence and by the economic boycott, and facing intense behind-the-scenes pressure from the Justice Department, a group of Birmingham political and business leaders on May 10, granted the SCLC's demands: an end to discriminatory hiring practices and the formation of a biracial council to supervise the dismantling of the city's structure of segregated facilities according to an agreed-upon timetable.

This triumph, hailed by Martin Luther King, Jr., as a "magnificent victory for justice," reverberated across the south. Some fifty southern cities desegregated in the summer of 1963. Nevertheless, change did not come painlessly. Bombings of homes and churches, police brutality, and even murders continued as white supremacists, sensing the dawn of a new order, struck out in impotent fury. Moreover, the locus of activism was shifting northward geographically and downward socially, into the ranks of the urban poor. As the uprising of Birmingham's black slum made clear, a struggle that had originated in the black middle class was now energizing a seething urban underclass trapped in poverty. Young ghetto blacks felt little patience with carefully planned campaigns or with King's doctrine of non-resistance.

As militancy rose, the mainstream civil-rights organization scrambled to keep up. "The [NAACP's] arena of combat," warned an NAACP official in May 1963, "has shifted from the courtroom to direct mass action." Martin Luther King, Jr., speaking in Chicago that June, told a cheering throng of five thousand, "We're through with tokenism and gradualism and see-how-far-you've-comeism. . . . We can't wait any longer. Now is the time." After mid-decade, King shifted his focus from integration—a goal of the black middle class—to the economic plight of the urban poor.

A leader no less charismatic than King most powerfully articulated the new militancy. Malcolm X, born Malcolm Little in 1925 in Omaha, was the son of a freelance Baptist preacher and a follower of black nationalist leader Marcus Garvey. In 1941 Little moved to Boston and drifted into the urban underworld of narcotics, prostitution, and burglary. Imprisoned in 1946, he converted to the Nation of Islam, or Black Muslims, an ascetic sect that brought discipline into the lives of its members, especially those in prison. Abandoning his "slave name," he became Malcolm X; the X stood for his lost African name.

❖❖ In Perspective: *Black Ministers and the Black Church*

The fact that Martin Luther King, Jr., and Malcolm X were religious leaders as well as prominent in the black freedom struggle underscores the importance of religion and of ministers in American black history. In slavery days, worship services provided spiritual comfort, strengthened slave communities, and offered a setting where the longing for freedom could be expressed. Free blacks in the antebellum North formed their own denominations, including the African Methodist Episcopal (AME) Church in 1816 and the AME Zion Church in 1821.

The black church remained strong after Emancipation, as many freedmen abandoned their ex-masters' churches and formed their own congregations. Commented one ex-slave (as recorded by a researcher): "Dat ole white preachin' wasn't nothin'. Old white preachers used to talk wid dey tongues widdout sayin' nothin', but Jesus told us slaves to talk wid our hearts." And ministers played a growing social role in African-American life. AME Bishop Daniel A. Payne was a prominent African-American leader in the mid- and later nineteenth century. Another AME bishop, Henry M. Turner (1834–1915), gave up on racist America and advocated the creation of a Christian nation in Africa to which U.S. blacks could return. Turner visited Africa four times in the 1890s in pursuit of his dream.

In the rural South, the preaching, singing, baptisms, revivals, picnics, weddings, and funerals of the black church knit together the community. As W. E. B. Du Bois wrote in *The Souls of Black Folk* in 1903: "The Negro church of today is the social centre of Negro life in the United States, and the most characteristic expression of African character." At the heart of this social institution were the ministers, whose emotional call-and-response preaching style—a style that Martin Luther King, Jr., used to great effect—engaged their congregations powerfully.

In the urban South, black ministers exerted leadership in their own communities and functioned as brokers in dealings with the white power structure. The Reverend Martin Luther King, Sr., father of the civil-rights leader and pastor of Atlanta's Ebenezer Baptist Church, was an influential figure in his own right long before his son achieved fame. Although much beloved figures, these charismatic black ministers could also be authoritarian, intensely moralistic, conservative in their social views, and jealous of their power. As Du Bois observed in 1903: "The Preacher is the most unique personality developed by the Negro on American soil. A leader, a politician, an orator, a 'boss,' an intriguer, an idealist—all these he is. . . . The combination of a certain adroitness

Released in 1952, Malcolm X traveled to Detroit to meet Black Muslim leader Elijah Muhammad, who assigned him to a Nation of Islam temple in Harlem. His charisma helped to boost the national membership to an estimated forty thousand by 1960. Sixty-nine Black Muslim temples, mostly in large northern cities, and several dozen radio stations carried the word to the black masses. The Nation of Islam preached strict moral purity and the superiority of the black race. Like Garvey's with deep-seated earnestness, of tact with consummate ability, give him his preeminence, and helps him maintain it."

As African Americans migrated North, they brought their faith with them. Every northern city had its black houses of worship, from large establishments like Harlem's Abyssinian Baptist Church to the storefront churches of the poor. The novelist James Baldwin, the son of a black preacher, himself preached as a teenager in a storefront church in Harlem. Baldwin's first book, *Go Tell It on the Mountain* (1953), drew upon his intimate knowledge of the black church.

And the black minister continued to function in the larger arena. When racial violence erupted, he was at the center of the crisis, sometimes advising Christian forbearance, sometimes calling for resistance. As race riots raged in 1919, one black bishop urged blacks to "protect their homes at any cost."

Music, whether mournful sorrow songs or toe-tapping, hand-clapping gospel songs, sustained black religious life from the beginning. The slave songs, blending African and Christian influences, expressed both spiritual longings and a people's desire for liberation. Songs such as "Go Down, Moses" recounted familiar Bible stories while also protesting slavery. In the twentieth century, countless African-American singers who became pop-music stars started out in black churches. Aretha Franklin, for example, the daughter of a famed black preacher, the Reverend C. L. Franklin, began her career as a singer in her father's New Bethel Baptist Church in Detroit.

When the freedom movement arose, black ministers (as well as many white religious leaders) inevitably became deeply involved. Some hesitated, perceiving a threat to their own role as power brokers. But others caught the vision and communicated it to their parishioners and to the larger community. None did so more effectively than Martin Luther King, Jr., whose strength lay in his roots in the black church. Another Baptist minister, the Reverend Jesse Jackson, a youthful King associate, would go on after King's assassination to build a career as a voice for the oppressed in America and abroad.

Perhaps no career better illustrates the prominent and complex social role of the minister in the African-American community than that of the Reverend Benjamin Hooks. Born in 1925, Hooks served as pastor of a leading Baptist church in Memphis (1956–64) and then of Detroit's Greater New Mt. Moriah Baptist Church in Detroit (1964–72). But he was also a lawyer, a criminal-court judge, the cofounder and director of a savings-and-loan association—and, from 1977 to 1993, executive director of the National Association for the Advancement of Colored People.

From the early nineteenth century to the end of the twentieth, the pulpit has been a highly effective launching pad for leadership in the black community. In the post–civil rights era with its complex challenges, black ministers continued to provide community leadership. Though still mostly male, their ranks now also included gifted and charismatic women, including the Rev. Bernice Albertine King, the daughter of Martin Luther King, Jr., and Coretta Scott King.

followers in the 1920s, Black Muslims denounced whites as "blue-eyed devils," rejected integration, and called for black pride, black institutions, and, ultimately, a separate black nation.

Whereas Martin Luther King, Jr., preached nonviolence, integration, and racial harmony, the fiery Malcolm X proclaimed a very different and—to whites—frightening message. Confronted by a violent oppressor, he insisted, the oppressed must use "any means necessary" to break their bonds. "[B]loodshed is a two-way street," he declared, "... dying is a two-way street, ... killing is a two-way street." By 1963 it was Malcolm, not Martin, who appeared most often on TV and in newspaper interviews and public forums. Flanked by stony-faced bodyguards, jabbing his finger to drive home his points, he made an unforgettable impression. Civil-rights leaders committed to racial integration deplored his separatist message. At a 1962 debate in Harlem, James Farmer challenged Malcolm X: "[D]on't tell us any more about the disease—that is clear in our minds. Now, tell us, physician, what is thy cure?" In answer, Malcolm X could only reiterate the utopian dream of a separate black homeland.

Malcolm X's success roused jealousies within the Nation of Islam, and Elijah Muhammad expelled him from the organization in 1963. After a 1964 African tour and pilgrimage to Mecca, he rejected racism of all kinds and spoke of the common bond linking humanity. Again he took a new name, one denoting his Mecca pilgrimage: El-Hajj Malik el-Shabazz. On February 21, 1965, as he spoke in a Harlem ballroom, three Black Muslim loyalists gunned him down.

Despite radical changes during his final months, many Americans still saw Malcolm X at the time of his death as a fomenter of violence. Editorial writers contrasted King, the apostle of peace, and Malcolm X, the preacher of hatred. In fact, as theologian James H. Cone argues in *Martin and Malcolm and America* (1991), the two leaders' views were converging in 1964–65, with King growing more radical and Malcolm tentatively exploring the possibilities of interracial cooperation.

By the 1990s, Malcolm X would become a folk hero in the inner cities. Rap singers chanted his words, and murals portraying his piercing gaze adorned building walls in black communities. Black filmmaker Spike Lee memorialized him in a 1992 movie. Malcolm X's enduring grip on the American imagination stemmed from the kaleidoscopic nature of his career: the early years as a street hustler; the uncompromising rhetoric of his Black Muslim days; the final, tentative message of racial understanding. His widow, Betty Shabazz, looking back in 1992, offered her own interpretation of her husband's message:

> He said freedom by whatever means necessary to bring about a situation where members of the African diaspora were respected and treated as human beings. . . . A lot of people . . . said "freedom by whatever means necessary" means violence. No, it's not violence. It's a comprehensive statement that says use more than one option. It could be political, social, education, or it could be self-defense.

The rise of Malcolm X and other black militants stimulated contributions to the NAACP, the SCLC, and other organizations now perceived as bastions of moderation. At a June 1963 meeting in New York, corporate leaders and foundation heads raised a fund of more than one million dollars for the major civil-rights groups. As the strategists of the Birmingham demonstrations had hoped, civil rights again dominated the national agenda. Not a sudden moral epiphany, but fear of social upheaval, rallied white public opinion in support of decisive action. The accelerating pace of black activism, the explosive buildup of racial tensions, and sober warnings of worse to come spurred the administration to move from behind-the-scenes manipulation to forthright leadership on civil rights. At Kennedy's direction, the White House prepared a tough new civil-rights bill to submit to Congress.

Another showdown in Alabama provided the occasion for Kennedy's long-delayed action. On June 11, 1963, fulfilling a campaign pledge to "stand in the schoolhouse door" to prevent integration, Governor George Wallace physically blocked access to two black students seeking to enroll at the University of Alabama. But the governor nimbly stepped aside when a Justice Department official read a federal court order mandating the students' admission. In contrast to the violence at the University of Mississippi the year before, integration at the University of Alabama proceeded peacefully.

On national television that night, JFK offered a plea for racial justice unprecedented from a U.S. president. Paraphrasing the Golden Rule, he declared, "Every American ought to have the right to be treated as he would wish to be treated, as one would wish his children to be treated." A century after the Emanicipation Proclamation, he went on, African Americans "are not yet freed from social and economic oppression. And this nation . . . will not be fully free until all its citizens are free." Kennedy offered a stark choice of supporting civil-rights reform or facing disaster: "The fires of frustration and discord are burning in every city, North and South," he warned. That very night, a hidden stalker shot and killed Medgar Evers, the president of the Mississippi NAACP.

On June 19, Kennedy sent his civil-rights bill to Congress. In sweeping language, it outlawed discrimination in all public places and empowered the Justice Department to sue school districts that delayed integration. To show their support for the bill, two hundred thousand black and white civil-rights advocates from an array of organizations gathered in Washington on August 28. The Kennedy administration initially opposed the march, fearing a backlash. But when the organizers held firm, the White House capitulated and worked closely with its planners.

Under a late-summer sun, a sea of marchers assembled at the Lincoln Memorial. Joan Baez sang "We Shall Overcome," Bob Dylan performed a tribute to Medgar Evers, and black singers Odetta and Mahalia Jackson added their voices. The labor leader and veteran civil-rights activist A. Philip Randolph eloquently urged passage of the civil-rights bill. But it was Martin Luther King's address that transformed a lobbying event into a memorably historic moment. A master orator at his peak, King used vivid, concrete images and familiar biblical language to make his point: "Now is the time to rise from the dark and desolate valley of segregation to the sunlit path of racial justice. . . . Now is the time to lift our nation from the quicksands of racial injustice to the solid rock of brotherhood. . . . We are not satisfied and we will not be satisfied until justice rolls down like the waters, and righteousness like a mighty stream."

In his now-famous extemporized conclusion, King in a few compelling phrases etched a vision of a society in which race did not matter:

> I have a dream that one day on the red hills of Georgia the sons of former slaves and the sons of former slaveowners will be able to sit down together at the table of brotherhood.
>
> I have a dream that one day even the State of Mississippi, a state sweltering with the heat of injustice, sweltering with the heat of oppression, will be transformed into an oasis of freedom and justice. I have a dream that my four little children will one day live in a nation where they will not be judged by the color of their skin but by the content of their character. I have a dream today.

Washington, D.C., August 1963. *Expressing idealism and unity of purpose, thousands of black and white civil-rights marchers rallied at the Lincoln Memorial. Soon the movement would splinter as the focus moved northward and the demands grew more radical.* (UPI/Corbis-Bettmann)

> I have a dream that one day down in Alabama with its vicious racists, with its Governor having his lips dripping with the words of interposition and nullification—one day right there in Alabama, little black boys and black girls will be able to join hands with little white boys and white girls as sisters and brothers. . . .
>
> When we let freedom ring, when we let it ring from every village and every hamlet, from every state and every city, we will be able to speed up that day when all God's children, black men and white men, Jews and Gentiles, Protestants and Catholics, will be able to join hands and sing in the words of that old Negro spiritual, "Free at last! Free at last! Thank God almighty, we are free at last."

But moments of moral exaltation are fleeting. Within two weeks, as if to mock King's eloquence, a bomb blast at Birmingham's Sixteenth Street Baptist Church killed four black girls. Furthermore, the movement's apparent unity in August 1963 masked widening rifts. Malcolm X, still in his separatist phase, ridiculed King's plea for unity. A. Philip Randolph originally had wanted to focus the march on the economic and social crisis of the urban black underclass, but this theme remained muted in favor of the more familiar message of racial integration and harmony. Even as King focused his peroration on the Deep South, attention was shifting northward, where the issues would prove more complex and the modes of protest more divisive. The most prophetic words were those that the marchers did not hear in Washington. In the original version of his speech, which more moderate leaders and administration officials pressured him to drop, John Lewis of SNCC had written:

> In good conscience we cannot support the administration's civil rights bill, for it is too little and too late. . . . The revolution is at hand, and we must free ourselves of

the chains of political and economic slavery. . . . Mr. Kennedy is trying to take the revolution out of the street and put it in the courts. . . . The black masses are on the march for jobs and freedom, and we must say to the politicians that there won't be a "cooling off" period.

Despite the Washington march, the administration's civil-rights bill languished in the Judiciary Committee owing to Senator Eastland's stalling tactics. Although Kennedy's June 1963 speech had conveyed a new level of moral commitment, the president failed to translate his late embrace of the cause into decisive legislative action. That task would fall to his successor.

1964: Breaking the Legislative Logjam

President Johnson took advantage of the nation's grief over Kennedy's assassination to give top priority to the stalled civil-rights bill. The mid-sixties brought a brief moment of near consensus in support of the black cause, and Johnson seized the opportunity.

As a Texas congressman, Johnson had opposed President Truman's civil-rights proposals, convinced that to do otherwise would end his political career. At the same time, he attacked racism and deplored political race baiting. In 1957, as a Senate majority leader harboring presidential ambitions, Johnson shepherded the Eisenhower administration's civil-rights bill through Congress, protecting his regional base by engineering some compromises favored by southern legislators.

As president, LBJ counted on his regional roots to overcome southern opposition to the Kennedy bill. To speechwriter Richard Goodwin, he confided, "Those Harvards [his term for the Kennedy team] think that a politician from Texas doesn't care about Negroes. . . . But I . . . always vowed that if I ever had the power I'd make sure every Negro had the same chance as every white man. Now I have it." Within days of Kennedy's assassination, LBJ met with the top civil-rights leaders and pledged quick action on this front.

A coalition of civil-rights organizations, liberal labor unions, women's groups, and religious bodies rallied support. Senator Hubert Humphrey praised church groups as "the most important force" in pushing for a civil-rights law. The National Council of Churches (NCC), an association of liberal Protestant denominations, lobbied, organized marches and letter-writing campaigns, and arranged speaking tours by civil-rights advocates. During the 1964 civil-rights debate, the NCC held daily services at a church near the Capitol. This religious involvement underscored the ethical dimension of the civil-rights cause. As James Reston of the *New York Times* wrote, "If there is no effective moral reaction out in the country, there will be no effective political reaction."

The civil-rights bill passed the House early in 1964. In the Senate, floor-leader Humphrey labored mightily to overcome stubborn opposition. President Johnson sat on the phone, cajoling waverers. For seventy-five days, opponents filibustered against the bill. At last on June 10, 1964, in a dramatic moment, the Senate voted to end the filibuster. Senator Clair Engle of California, unable to speak because of recent brain surgery, nodded his head "yes" from a wheelchair on the cloture vote. The next day, by a 73–27 tally, the Civil Rights Act of 1964 passed the Senate.

This omnibus measure targeted numerous expressions of racism in American life. The law made it easier for the attorney general to participate in private civil-rights cases and to prosecute segregated school districts and election officials who denied voting rights to blacks. Other sections forbade discrimination in hiring, in federally funded programs, and in public facilities such as restaurants, motels, theaters, and amusement parks. Finally, the law made permanent the Equal Employment Opportunity Commission, which would monitor compliance with laws against workplace discrimination. The far-reaching act represented a big step toward eradicating racism's institutional manifestations.*

Out of the limelight, grassroots civil-rights activists pursued the difficult task of local political organizing. After the March on Washington, Robert Moses and other SNCC leaders had resumed their voter-registration campaign in rural Mississippi. Through Moses's efforts, SNCC and CORE formed the Council of Federated Organizations (COFO) to coordinate the effort. Late in 1963, COFO organizers had laid plans for a major voter-registration drive in 1964, to be called Mississippi Freedom Summer. The question of whether to recruit northern white students proved divisive. Some argued that the presence of white volunteers would reduce the threat of violence and heighten media attention. Opponents warned that an influx of white volunteers would inhibit local blacks from developing their own leadership skills. Advocates of a biracial campaign won, and the call went out to northern colleges and universities. In June 1964, after a brief training period, nearly a thousand white northern student volunteers streamed into Mississippi.

The COFO campaign roused murderous opposition. In mid-June, three young men investigating an arson attack on a black church disappeared. They were Michael Schwerner, a white CORE staff member; Andrew Goodman, a white summer volunteer from the North; and James Chaney, a local black volunteer. The FBI soon arrested twenty-one Ku Klux Klan members, plus the local sheriff and his deputy, in the kidnapping plot. Six weeks later, the bodies were discovered in shallow graves at a dam construction site near Philadelphia, Mississippi. (*Mississippi Burning,* the 1988 Hollywood film about the case, not only presented a much more heroic picture of the FBI than the facts warrant but also insultingly suggested that all Mississippi blacks were cravenly terrified of Klan violence and utterly unable to stand up for their own rights.)

The summer also brought repeated bombings, arson, gunfire, and attacks on COFO volunteers. Despite a beefed-up FBI presence in Mississippi, J. Edgar Hoover, deploring the "overemphasis" on civil rights, declined to protect Freedom Summer volunteers. The violence further radicalized young black activists, hastening their turn from integration to economic and political demands and deepening their skepticism of King's message of nonresistance. For white volunteers, the experience stirred distrust of Johnson-era liberalism. Many would soon emerge as critics of the Vietnam War. The summer also drove a wedge between white and black civil-rights workers, as some southern blacks criticized the white volunteers

---

* In an action little noticed at the time, Title VII of the Civil Rights Act of 1964 barred discrimination on the basis of sex as well as of race. Although introduced by a southern legislator in an unsuccessful effort to discredit the bill, Title VII would play an important role in feminists' efforts against job discrimination.

as liberal do-gooders who after a few months in Mississippi would return to their safe, affluent world.

In the end, Mississippi Freedom Summer yielded mixed results. At COFO-run "Freedom Schools," black children and adults studied not only academic subjects but also African-American history and strategies for community organizing. Yet the goal of increasing blacks' political clout proved elusive: confronted by intransigent election officials, Freedom Summer volunteers registered only about twelve hundred new voters.

Despite the numerically scant results, the Mississippi Freedom Summer reverberated through the 1964 Democratic convention. As part of the project, COFO had formed the Mississippi Freedom Democratic party (MFDP) as an alternative to the all-white regular Democratic party. The MFDP named forty-two delegates and twenty-two alternates, including maids, carpenters, farmers, ministers, and teachers of both races, to the national Democratic party's August convention in Atlantic City. Initially the MFDP project was mainly symbolic, but when influential Democratic liberals endorsed it, COFO began to work to seat MFDP's delegation. Before the party's credentials committee, a parade of witnesses urged certification of the MFDP. The advocates included Martin Luther King, Jr.; Roy Wilkins; Michael Schwerner's widow; and Fannie Lou Hamer, a forceful forty-seven-year-old sharecropper and MFDP delegate who recounted the persecution she had suffered for trying to register to vote.

President Johnson opposed seating the MFDP, fearful of jeopardizing his election chances and angering the southern congressional leaders on whose support his Great Society reforms depended. Johnson worried, too, about Alabama governor George Wallace, whose appeal to white, working-class discontent had won him more than a third of the vote in Democratic primaries in Wisconsin, Indiana, and Maryland. Ever the compromiser, LBJ proposed that the MFDP delegates be designated "honored guests" of the convention—with no voting rights. The MFDP delegates refused to yield, but after heavy negotiations most civil-rights leaders accepted LBJ's compromise provided two MFDP delegates were seated as at-large delegates with voting rights. In addition, the regular Mississippi delegation would be required to pledge support for the party ticket, and in future conventions no delegations would be seated from states that disfranchised blacks.

The deal exacted a high price by deepening black activists' distrust of the possibilities of interracial cooperation. A disillusioned Fannie Lou Hamer later recalled, "We learned the hard way that even though we had all the law and all the righteousness on our side—that white man is not going to give up his power to us." What many SNCC and CORE volunteers viewed as the sellout of the MFDP, coming after the frustrations and violence of the Mississippi Freedom Summer, contributed to the radicalization of U.S. politics in the later 1960s. The events of 1964 eroded young black activists' faith in "working within the system." As one SNCC leader later recalled, "After Atlantic City, our struggle was not for civil rights, but for liberation."

SNCC's turn toward militancy and "black liberation" intensified when eleven of its leaders visited Africa in September 1964 as guests of the Marxist government of Guinea. John Lewis and another SNCC leader then traveled to Kenya, where they encountered Malcolm X on his own pilgrimage to the African homeland and for two days listened to him lecture on the need for black solidarity. Although SNCC did not embrace Malcolm X's ideology, his views influenced the movement in the later 1960s. Lewis, as president of SNCC from 1963 to 1966, steered the organization toward increasingly radical goals.*

1965: Selma and the Voting Rights Act

Having partially finessed the politics of race in the 1964 campaign, Johnson hoped to avoid another civil-rights battle and to give the South time to digest the Civil Rights Act of 1964. But as with President Kennedy, events forced his hand. Demanding action on a stronger voting-rights law, civil-rights leaders took steps to gain their objective.

Martin Luther King's Southern Christian Leadership Conference, relatively quiescent since the Birmingham campaign, again took the lead in 1965. Although still committed to nonviolence, King and other SCLC strategists increasingly saw peaceful resistance less in ethical than in tactical terms, as one means of bringing pressure to bear on Washington. Repeating the Birmingham strategy of deliberately courting confrontation, SCLC formulated new strategies for drawing national attention and forcing federal action on voting rights.

The target this time was Selma, Alabama, some fifty miles west of Montgomery, a bastion of white supremacy. The city had moved at a snail's pace to register the fifteen thousand eligible black voters. Selma also had its own version of Bull Connor—Sheriff Jim Clark—who announced his sentiments with a large button asserting: "NEVER!" Asked by a reporter whether a female demonstrator whom he had arrested was married, Clark sneered, "She's a nigger woman and she hasn't got a Miss or a Mrs. in front of her name."

Selma housed a small group of local activists led by Amelia and Samuel Boynton. When a SNCC voter-registration drive faltered, Amelia Boynton invited in SCLC. King's new militance emerged as he kicked off the Selma campaign in early January 1965: "We are not asking, we are demanding the ballot." Marchers besieged the courthouse, and soon more than two thousand sat in prison. But Sheriff Clark, taking a tip from the 1962 white strategy in Albany, at first avoided the kind of brutality that attracted media attention. On February 17, however, a state trooper shot civil-rights demonstrator Jimmy Lee Jackson. King announced a march from Selma to Montgomery to present a petition to Governor Wallace protesting Jackson's murder and demanding action on voting rights. Nonetheless, when LBJ privately pressured King to call off the march, King and his lieutenants shelved the idea and returned to Atlanta.

Other activists in Selma were not so easily diverted. On March 7, soon dubbed "Bloody Sunday," the Reverend Hosea Williams of the SCLC field staff, together with SNCC chairman John Lewis and local supporters, proceeded with the march. As the six hundred protesters approached the Edmund Pettus Bridge

---

* His faith in the system somewhat restored, Lewis would head the federal domestic-service program VISTA during the Carter administration, sit on the Atlanta city council from 1981 to 1986, and in the latter year win election to Congress.

Selma, Alabama, 1965. *This haunting photograph evokes the diversity of the civil-rights coalition that had coalesced by 1965, and emphasizes the way the movement employed patriotic and religious symbolism to further its goals.* (Bruce Davidson/Magnum Photos, Inc.)

over the Alabama River, they met Sheriff Clark with a hundred deputies and a similar number of state troopers. When the marchers refused an order to turn back, troopers and police, some on horseback, plowed into the throng, throwing tear gas, flailing nightsticks, and jabbing with electric cattle prods. Frightened and bloody, the marchers fell back. Fifty required hospital treatment.

Television once again carried the images to the nation and the world. Demands for federal intervention and for a federal voting-rights law rained down on Washington. Demonstrators attempted a sit-in at the White House as more paraded outside. Religious leaders poured into Selma in solidarity with the marchers.

As King and other top civil-rights leaders hastened to Selma, pressure mounted to complete the march. As one SNCC leader later recalled, "We were angry. And we wanted to show Governor Wallace, the Alabama State Highway Patrol, Sheriff Clark, Selma's whites, the federal government and poor Southern blacks in other Selmas that we didn't intend to take any more shit. We would ram the march down the throat of anyone who tried to stop us." Nevertheless, a federal judge banned the march, and President Johnson warned King that further violence would hurt the chances for a voting-rights bill, which he had now decided to introduce.

King had just won the Nobel Peace Prize and been named *Time*'s Man of the Year, but in the increasingly radical civil-rights movement, his leadership had come under challenge. Juggling conflicting pressures, he agreed to a symbolic gesture: The marchers would proceed to the Pettus Bridge, hold a prayer service, and return to Selma. But King failed to inform the marchers of the plan. With everyone primed for a trek to Montgomery, his instructions to return to Selma produced confusion and anger, deepening the rift in the movement. As in late 1962, the campaign again seemed to flounder.

Rabid segregationists, however, once more displayed their ability to reenergize the campaign whenever it flagged. Shortly after King's controversial "Tuesday turnaround," several whites attacked three Unitarian ministers on the streets of Selma. Chanting "Nigger lover," they assaulted James Reeb so badly that he died a few days later. Protesters continued to pour into Selma, now the focus of world attention, and outraged protests deluged the White House. On March 15, 1965, LBJ addressed a joint session of Congress to propose a voting-rights bill.

Moving beyond details, Johnson defined racism as "a challenge . . . to the values and purposes and the meaning" of America. "Should we defeat every enemy, and should we double our wealth and conquer the stars, and still be unequal to this issue, then we will have failed as a people and a nation." Praising the Selma demonstrators for touching the nation's conscience, Johnson defined the immediate challenge unambiguously: "Every American citizen must have an equal right to vote." He ended with the refrain of the civil-rights anthem: "We *shall* overcome." Black leaders across the ideological spectrum hailed the president's message. Martin Luther King, who watched the speech with the family of the murdered Jimmy Lee Jackson, telephoned the president to offer his praise.

The speech transformed the deadlock in Alabama. President Johnson pressured the local federal judge to issue a march permit and warned Governor Wallace that police brutality would not be tolerated. After a send-off sermon by King, eight thousand marchers set out from Selma. About three hundred continued all the way along Route 80, often in heavy rain but protected by a solicitous Alabama National Guard federalized by LBJ. Three thousand supporters joined them for a triumphant entry into Montgomery. Speaking to the throng near the statehouse where the Confederacy was born in 1861, King not only demanded passage of the voting-rights bill but also defined the movement's broadening agenda, calling for action on such issues as de facto housing segregation and joblessness in the urban black slums.

As so often in these years, a stab of violence followed the moment of triumph. That evening, night-riding Klansmen shot and killed Viola Liuzzo, a volunteer from Detroit, as she drove marchers back to Selma.

The Voting Rights Act of 1965, passed in August, authorized federal officials to register voters and to supervise elections in electoral districts with a clear record of racial bias. It outlawed the various devices long used in the South to exclude black voters. Together with the earlier voting-rights acts and the 1964 constitutional amendment outlawing the poll tax, this law at last opened the door of real political power to southern blacks. By mid-1966, half a million blacks had joined the South's voting rolls; by 1968, nearly four hundred blacks held elective office in the region. While southern whites defected to the Republican banner, African Americans transformed the South's once all-white Democratic party. Even in die-hard Mississippi, black registration rose from the single digits in 1960 to 59 percent by 1968. As blacks streamed to the polls, race-baiting politicians changed their tune. George Wallace, always a politician first and a racist second, successfully courted black voters in an Alabama gubernatorial campaign in 1982. President Johnson acknowledged the altered climate in 1965 by naming the first black cabi-

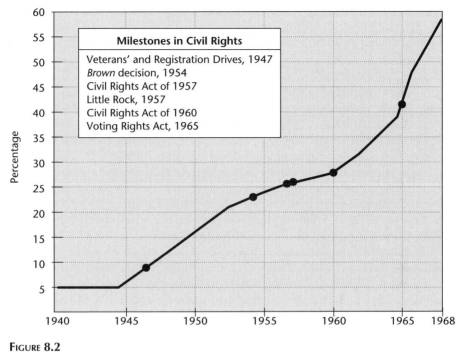

FIGURE 8.2
Percentage of Voting-Age Southern Blacks Registered, 1940–1968

net member, Robert C. Weaver, to head the new Department of Housing and Urban Development. In 1967 Johnson appointed NAACP lawyer Thurgood Marshall as the first black Supreme Court justice.

The year 1968 brought a final civil-rights measure: the Open Housing Act outlawing racial discrimination in the sale or rental of most housing units. By this time, however, one long cycle of civil-rights activism was over; new voices and new issues now held center stage.

The Civil-Rights Movement Reaches Hispanic Americans

The civil-rights movement had ramifying effects that extended far beyond black America. Mexican Americans, including roughly 4 million farm workers and barrio dwellers in the Southwest, were one of the groups most immediately influenced. The example of the black freedom struggle, particularly its more radical student-based wing, coupled with the stimulus of the War on Poverty, had an electrifying effect on young Mexican Americans of the second or third generation who were painfully conscious of the discrimination, educational liabilities, and lack of job opportunities their compatriots faced. In 1963 in New Mexico, Reies López Tijerina started a movement to reclaim ancestral lands appropriated from Mexican Americans by white settlers or by the federal government. Like southern civil-rights activists, Tijerina and some of his followers spent time in prison for their militant tactics. In Delano, California, in 1965, a Mexican-American labor leader, César Chávez, organized a strike of grape workers. This led to the formation of a union, the United Farm Workers of America, that attracted much media attention and organized an effective national boycott of nonunion grapes. Chávez's nonviolent strategies, influenced by his deep Catholic faith, were reminiscent of Martin Luther King's approach. In 1967, students at St. Mary's College in San Antonio, Texas, formed the Mexican American Youth Organization (MAYO), which soon led to a loose confederation of Mexican-American student groups nationwide.

A manifestation of the new consciousness in the younger generation was their preference for the term *Chicano* rather than "Mexican American," "Latin American," or the Census Bureau's clunky phrase "Spanish-surnamed Americans." Difficult to define precisely, the word suggested pride in Mexican cultural identity and in Mexico's revolutionary tradition, as well as skepticism about the assimilationist goal. One of MAYO's founders, José Angel Gutiérrez, even founded a Chicano political party, the Partido Raza (Party of United People). Like SNCC, these proliferating student-led organizations sponsored voter-registration drives, launched campaigns to address the social and economic problems of the barrios, and in general promoted group pride among Mexican Americans. As the sixties wore on, Mexican-American communities across the Southwest and the West Coast, both rural and urban, bubbled with protest politics and organizational ferment rooted in the example of the African-American freedom struggle.

Reflections on the Civil-Rights Struggle, 1960–1965

The African-American freedom struggle falls into two fairly distinct phases, with the demarcation line in 1965. The first stage, whose beginnings we examined in Chapter 5 and whose culmination we have just explored, focused on the southern caste system that denied most blacks the vote, excluded them from equal educational and job opportunities, and subjected them to a rigidly segregated and discriminatory social order.

This movement's immediate catalysts were the *Brown* decision of 1954, the Montgomery bus boycott, and the charismatic leadership of Martin Luther King, Jr. But with the sit-ins and Freedom Rides of 1960–61, the movement gained fresh energy and emerged from the shadow of any one individual, even one as gifted as Dr. King.

In this stage the leaders succeeded in building a broad consensus behind their goals because they spoke a vocabulary of individual rights and equality of opportunity enshrined in the American political tradition. With the end of legally enforced segregation across the South and the passage of the Civil Rights Act of 1964 and the Voting Rights Act of 1965, this phase of the struggle essentially closed. As historian J. Mills Thornton III has observed, the first stage of the civil-rights campaign ended "for the same reason that World War II ended: the enemies had been defeated."

Yet like a mountaineering expedition in which one successful ascent reveals even higher peaks in the distance, the successes of the early 1960s exposed the next challenge: the social problems, political impotence, and economic marginality of the black masses in the inner-city slums—the alienated outsiders to whom Malcolm X had appealed. After 1965, the focus shifted from voting rights and legally imposed segregation to the grievances of this black underclass. The rhetoric, often luridly embellished by fiery young radicals, centered not on constitutional rights and equal opportunity but on collective action on behalf of a specific portion of the African-American community. The ideological shift from equality of opportunity to equality of outcome would prove deeply divisive.

To concede that this first phase of the civil-rights movement did not address every dimension of racism in America is not to diminish what it did achieve. This stage of the struggle successfully challenged a caste system embedded in the culture, legal system, and social structure of the South. Demolishing a system of segregation and discrimination dating ultimately to the antebellum slave codes was an essential first step before more complex issues of racial inequity could be addressed.

This early phase of the civil-rights movement is also noteworthy for its decentralized, grassroots quality. If one looks only at the maneuverings of presidents, senators, governors, or national leaders such as Martin Luther King, Jr., one misses a key element of the story. Men and women like Robert Moses and Fannie Lou Hamer in Mississippi, Amelia Boynton in Selma, and Fred Shuttlesworth in Birmingham, no less than the better-known celebrities, are central to the story.

The civil-rights movement of the early sixties unfolded in places like Greensboro, Anniston, McComb, Albany, and Selma. Its true heroes were not Washington politicians or civil-rights bureaucrats but ordinary Americans who found within themselves extraordinary reserves of determination and courage. Local figures identified issues of immediate concern and devised creative strategies for addressing them. Sometimes they made use of national organizations like SCLC, yet they were more than bit players in a drama directed from afar that followed a single script. From this perspective, the movement dissolves into countless minidramas of personal empowerment and local community action.

Nor was the movement merely a melodrama pitting saints against villains. The civil-rights leaders were all too human, with their full share of flaws and foibles. The various organizations competed fiercely for contributions and media coverage, and some leaders made unseemly efforts to demean their rivals. Although this competition sometimes proved creative and offered activists a broad pallet of strategies, it also took its toll in effectiveness.

Within white America, too, the civil-rights struggle elicited a full spectrum of responses, from grim, murderous resistance to grudging acceptance of the inevitable to a deeply moral embrace of the cause of the oppressed. By a leap of imagination, one can even begin to understand the fears of social displacement and of a jeopardized way of life that motivated those who defied the drive for civil rights. Whites accustomed to a hierarchical social order suddenly confronted a mass uprising of the oppressed. In fear and fury, some lashed out in violence. The irony for them is that with every outbreak of violence, more supporters rallied to the civil-rights cause.

The mass media helped prepare the attitudinal change by which racial violence and the denial of full citizenship and even full humanity to African Americans came to seem offensive and intolerable. Not only did TV bring the reality of racial oppression into the nation's living rooms, but Hollywood, after years of portraying blacks in crude racist stereotypes, began to offer different images in the later 1950s and early 1960s. Black actors like Sidney Poitier and the singer Harry Belafonte portrayed characters who were sympathetic, if sometimes impossibly handsome, upright, and virtuous. In *The World, the Flesh, and the Devil* (1959), a movie that wove together several cultural preoccupations of the later 1950s, Belafonte, Mel Ferrer, and the beautiful Swedish actress Inger Stevens explored the possibilities of interracial cooperation as the only survivors of a worldwide nuclear holocaust. Poitier played the saintly Porgy in the film version of *Porgy and Bess* (1959), and in *The Lilies of the Field* (1963), he portrayed a kindly handyman who helps a group of nuns build the chapel of their dreams.

Perhaps the most revealing mass-culture product dealing with race in these years was Harper Lee's best-selling novel *To Kill a Mockingbird* (1960), made into an equally successful movie in 1962 starring Gregory Peck as a quietly courageous southern lawyer who defends a black man (played by Brock Peters) falsely accused of rape. Selected by several book clubs, Lee's prizewinning novel had sold over 11 million copies by 1975. Peck won an Oscar for his role in the film version. A fable of individual integrity and decency triumphing over racial hatred and the mob spirit, *To Kill a Mockingbird* captured an important part of the American mood in an early, idealistic stage of the civil-rights struggle, when the issues seemed clear and unambiguous to people of conscience and goodwill.

When all the complexity, ambiguity, and shades of gray are recognized, the profound historical and moral significance of the civil-rights movement shines through with startling clarity. No longer willing to tolerate a status quo rooted in racial exploitation and injustice, many thousands of black Americans, supported by large numbers of white Americans, took their fate into their own hands and transformed a society.

For the civil-rights establishment, the progression of events in the early sixties revealed the depth of African-American frustration and the explosive potential in the urban black slums. These years spurred the movement's leadership to devise new strategies and formulate more ambitious goals. They taught black-liberation activists another important lesson as well: Violent confrontation—even the threat of violence—was one sure way to gain attention in the media and in the centers of political power. This realization would give rise to more militant tactics consciously designed to elicit the kind of dramatic and visceral confrontations that brought results in 1960–65. Such a climate was hardly congenial to strategies that preached restraint, patient negotiation, and turning the other cheek.

As the career of César Chávez and the rise of the Chicano movement among young Mexican-American students make clear, the civil-rights movement also influenced political and social reforms not directly related to black America. Lyndon Johnson's War on Poverty, for example, gained urgency from the heightened awareness of the economic condition of inner-city blacks that emerged from the civil-rights movement. The antiwar movement of the later 1960s drew ideological and tactical inspiration from the civil-rights campaign.

Similarly, the women's movement of the 1970s owed an enormous debt to the civil-rights cause. The earlier campaign drew on the talents of countless women—not only the relatively well known, such as Rosa Parks, Ella Baker, Fannie Lou

Hamer, and Amelia Boynton, but thousands more, black and white, who marched, organized, joined sit-ins, and taught in Freedom Schools. The civil-rights campaign offered later feminists models of strong, committed women as well as a vocabulary for understanding oppression and strategies for confronting it. Still later, other activists, from Native Americans and people with disabilities to homosexuals and environmental crusaders, would draw on the ideology and strategy of the civil-rights pioneers. Few other social movements in American history have had such a protean and broad-ranging impact.

Conclusion

For all its transforming power, this phase of the civil-rights movement clearly was losing momentum even at its apparent zenith in 1965, as the consensus that had taken shape over the preceding decade splintered. As the focus shifted from South to North, from individual rights to the politics of class conflict, from moderate leaders to fiery young radicals, and from carefully planned demonstrations to seemingly nihilistic explosions of violence, Middle America moved from sympathetic support to fearful uneasiness.

Divisions over the Vietnam War further undermined the civil-rights cause. Martin Luther King's rapport with Lyndon Johnson turned to hostility as the black leader harshly criticized the president's war policies. Thousands of others who had cheered Johnson's stand on civil rights bitterly opposed his actions in Vietnam. White House speechwriter Richard Goodwin, looking back on LBJ's eloquent voting-rights speech of March 15, 1965, would reminisce years later, "God, how I loved Lyndon Johnson at that moment; how unimaginable it would have been to think that in two years' time I would—like many others who listened that night— go into the streets against him."

SELECTED READINGS

The Law and Politics of Civil Rights

David L. Armor, *Forced Justice: School Desegregation and the Law* (1995); Numan V. Bartley and Hugh D. Graham, *Southern Politics and the Second Reconstruction* (1975); Monroe Billington, "Lyndon B. Johnson and Blacks: The Early Years," *Journal of Negro History* (January 1977); Jack Bloom, *Class, Race, and the Civil Rights Movement* (1987); Carl M. Brauer, *John F. Kennedy and the Second Reconstruction* (1977); Dan T. Carter, *The Politics of Rage* [George Wallace] (1995); Chandler Davidson and Bernard Grofman, eds., *Quiet Revolution in the South: The Impact of the Voting Rights Act, 1965–1990* (1994); David Garrow, *Protest at Selma: Martin Luther King, Jr. and the Voting Rights Act of 1965* (1978) and *The FBI and Martin Luther King, Jr.* (1981); Richard Goodwin, *Remembering America: A Voice from the Sixties* (1988); Hugh Davis Graham, *The Civil Rights Era: Origins and Development of National Policy* (1990); Elizabeth Jacoway and David Colburn, eds., *Southern Businessmen and Desegregation* (1982); Steven F. Lawson, *Black Ballots: Voting Rights in the South, 1944–1969* (1976); Kenneth O'Reilly, *"Racial Matters": The FBI's Secret File on Black America, 1960–1972* (1989); Gary Orfield, *The Reconstruction of Southern Education:*

The Schools and the 1964 Civil Rights Act (1969); J. W. Peltason, *Fifty-eight Lonely Men: Southern Federal Judges and School Desegregation* (rev. ed., 1971); Mark Stern, *Calculating Visions: Kennedy, Johnson and Civil Rights* (1992); Charles Whalen and Barbara Whalen, *The Longest Debate: A Legislative History of the 1964 Civil Rights Act* (1985); Harris Wofford, *Of Kennedys and Kings: Making Sense of the Sixties* (1980).

Civil-Rights Leaders, Organizations, and Campaigns

Catherine Barnes, *Journey from Jim Crow: The Desegregation of Southern Transit* (1983); Taylor Branch, *Parting the Waters: America in the King Years, 1954–63* (1988); Eric R. Burner, *And Gently Shall He Lead Them: Robert Moses and Civil Rights in Mississippi* (1994); Seth Cagin and Philip Dray, *We Are Not Afraid: The Story of Goodman, Schwerner, and Chaney and the Civil Rights Campaign for Mississippi* (1988); Claybourne Carson, *In Struggle: SNCC and the Black Awakening of the 1960s* (1981); Clayborne Carson et al., *The Eyes on the Prize Civil Rights Reader* (1991); Sean Dennis Cashman, *African Americans and the Quest for Civil Rights, 1900–1990* (1991); William H. Chafe, *Civilities and Civil Rights: Greensboro, North Carolina, and the Black Struggle for Freedom* (1980); David Chalmers, *And the Crooked Places Made Straight: The Struggle for Social Changes in the 1960s* (1991); David L. Chappell, *Inside Agitators: White Southerners in the Civil Rights Movement* (1994); James H. Cone, *Martin and Malcolm and America: A Dream or a Nightmare* (1991); John Dittmer, *Local People: The Struggle for Civil Rights in Mississippi* (1994); Michael Eric Dyson, *Making Malcolm: The Myth and Meaning of Malcolm X* (1995); Charles W. Eagles, ed., *The Civil Rights Movement in America* (1986); Sara M. Evans, *Personal Politics: The Roots of Women's Liberation in the Civil Rights Movement and the New Left* (1980); Adam Fairclough, *To Redeem the Soul of America: The Southern Christian Leadership Conference and Martin Luther King, Jr.* (1987); James Farmer, *Lay Bare the Heart: An Autobiography of the Civil Rights Movement* (1985); James F. Findlay, *Church People in the Struggle: The National Council of Churches and the Black Freedom Movement, 1950–1970* (1993); David J. Garrow, *Bearing the Cross: Martin Luther King, Jr., and the Southern Christian Leadership Conference, 1955–1968* (1986); Herbert H. Haines, *Black Radicals and the Civil Rights Mainstream, 1954–1970* (1988); Richard H. King, *Civil Rights and the Idea of Freedom* (1992); David L. Lewis, *King: A Biography* (2d ed., 1978); Doug McAdam, *Political Process and the Development of Black Insurgency, 1930–1970* (1982) and *Freedom Summer* (1988); Neil R. McMillen, *The Citizens' Councils: Organized Resistance to the Second Reconstruction, 1954–64* (1971); Malcolm X, with Alex Haley, *The Autobiography of Malcolm X* (1965); Kay Mills, *This Little Light of Mine: The Life of Fannie Lou Hamer* (1993): Nicolaus Mills, *Like a Holy Crusade: Mississippi 1964 . . .* (1992); Aldon D. Morris, *The Origins of the Civil Rights Movement: Black Communities Organizing for Change* (1984); Charles M. Payne, *I've Got the Light: The Organizing Tradition and the Mississippi Freedom Struggle* (1995); Bruce Perry, *Malcolm: The Life of a Man Who Changed Black America* (1991); Fred Powledge, *Free at Last? The Civil Rights Movement and the People Who Made It* (1991); Mary Aickin Rothschild, *A Case of Black and White: Northern Volunteers and the Southern Freedom Summers, 1964–1965* (1982); Cleveland Sellers, *The River of No Return: The Autobiography of a Black Militant and the Life and Death of SNCC* (1973); Harvard Sitkoff, *The Struggle for Black Equality, 1954–1992* (1993); Robert Weisbrot, *Freedom Bound: A History of America's Civil Rights Movement* (1991); Stephen J. Whitfield, *A Death in the Delta: The Story of Emmett Till* (1989); Miles Wolff, *Lunch at the 5 & 10* (1990).

Hispanic Americans and the Chicano Movement

Albert Camarillo, *Chicanos in California* (1984) and "Latin Americans" in Mary K. Cayton, Elliott J. Gorn, and Peter W. Williams, eds., *Encyclopedia of American Social History*

(1993), Vol. II; John Chávez, *The Lost Land: The Chicano Image of the Southwest* (1984); Juan Gómez-Quinones, *Chicano Politics: Reality and Promise, 1940–1990* (1990); Richard A. Griswold del Castillo, *La Familia: Chicano Families in the Urban Southwest, 1848 to the Present* (1984); Richard Griswold del Castillo and Richard A. García, *César Chávez* (1995); Carlos Muñoz, *Youth, Identity, Power: The Chicano Generation* (1989); Armando Navarro, *Mexican American Youth Organization* (1995).

PART THREE

The Loss of Innocence

${B}$etween 1965 and 1974, American society reeled under a series of crises that pitted generation against generation, black against white, ethnic group against ethnic group, even women against men. The traumatic events of this period redirected and partially derailed the momentum for liberal reform that had taken shape in the late fifties and early sixties.

As this liberal momentum crested in 1964–65, Congress had enacted a remarkable body of legislation that attacked poverty and addressed such basic social issues as health care and environmental protection. Moreover, a broad national consensus had formed around the twin goals of ending racial segregation and transforming Lyndon Johnson's Great Society vision into reality. Johnson's sweeping electoral victory in November 1964 seemed a mandate to pursue this ambitious domestic agenda.

But the liberal consensus, always fragile, proved ephemeral. On the domestic front, growing cultural, social, and racial tensions foreshadowed conflict. Young black activists, rejecting the moderate leadership of Martin Luther King, Jr., espoused goals and strategies that alarmed white America. King himself adopted increasingly controversial positions, and northern cities erupted in racial violence. Simultaneously, as the affluent baby-boom generation reached college age, campus unrest and cultural rebellion intensified. Youthful radicals challenged their politically and now economically dominant parents, as well as the Old Left ideology of the 1930s and the Cold War liberalism personified by Kennedy and Johnson.

The liberal consensus might have survived had not President Johnson escalated the Vietnam War early in 1965. Just as the Berlin Wall once cut a city in half, the Vietnam experience bisects postwar American history. Johnson's decision to expand the conflict, rooted in twenty years of Cold War thinking and strategic calculations that seemed persuasive at the time, not only shattered a small Asian nation but exacerbated divisions at home. Although only a minority of Americans joined the antiwar movement, the drumfire of protest, heavily reported in the media, hastened the unraveling of the liberal dream. In 1968, with its street violence, political upheaval, and shocking assassinations, a torn nation reached its nadir of despair.

The chaos of 1965–68 pushed Americans powerfully to the right as citizens groped for stability and reassurance. The chief beneficiary of this shift was the durable Richard Nixon. Capitalizing on the conservative surge and building on the southern strategy that had become central to Republican planning, Nixon won the presidency in 1968 and laid the groundwork for a new political alignment that would wield influence for decades.

Nixon's most pressing task was to grapple with the war in Vietnam that had destroyed his Democratic predecessor. While maneuvering to avoid a humiliating defeat in Southeast Asia, Nixon and his national security adviser, Henry Kissinger, plotted to muffle antiwar protest at home. They succeeded; after a final outburst in the spring of 1970, the movement quietly expired. Nixon and Kissinger also initiated a reorientation of a U.S. foreign policy that seemed trapped in the straitjacket of Cold War platitudes. Adopting a strategy guided more by balance-of-power calculations than by anticommunist ideology, they pursued a policy of détente—lessening tensions—with the Soviet Union and a diplomatic opening to the People's Republic of China. Riding the crest of his diplomatic successes, Nixon handily won reelection in 1972.

Meanwhile, new social and cultural trends growing from the conflicts of the 1960s caught the nation's attention in the early 1970s. A heightened ethnic awareness clearly owed a debt to the black-pride movement. Movements as diverse as environmentalism, feminism, gay rights, and so-called New Age self-awareness fads all had their roots in the 1960s. Just as Nixon transformed the political landscape, so the social and cultural trends of the Nixon years would shape American life for years to come.

Yet despite Nixon's larger-than-life role on the global stage, his presidency ended in dismal failure. If the social crisis of the late 1960s played itself out on city streets and college campuses, the political crisis of 1973–74 began in secrecy and unfolded in the press, the courts, and the halls of Congress. Seeking to destroy his political enemies and to discredit critics of his Vietnam policies, Nixon and his top advisers conducted illegal activities that violated Americans' constitutional rights. He committed further crimes as he and his aides tried to cover up their wrongdoing. In August 1974, amid a grave constitutional crisis, Nixon resigned.

The interlinked traumas of urban upheaval, generational conflict, political violence, divisions over Vietnam, and two failed presidencies shattered the self-assurance engendered by the Eisenhower era and the confident liberalism of the early Kennedy-Johnson years. An oil crisis in the mid-seventies worsened matters by triggering inflation and stirring anxieties about what had once seemed a limitless supply of energy. At home and abroad, American prospects in 1975 seemed far more clouded than they had in 1955 or even in 1965. The malaise that would shadow American life had its foundation in the years to which we now turn.

CHAPTER 9

Radicalization: Black Power, the New Left, and the Counterculture

On August 11, 1965, as civil-rights activists applauded the new voting-rights act, Los Angeles policeman Lee Minikus made a routine speeding arrest of Marquette Frye, an intoxicated young motorist. But Minikus was white and Frye was black, and race soon injected itself into what became a confrontation. As a crowd of blacks gathered, the mood turned ugly, and more patrolmen materialized. As Frye and his brother resisted, they were felled by a policeman's billy club. A young black woman accused of spitting at the police was arrested and taken away in a squad car. One onlooker screamed: "We've got no rights at all! It's just like Selma!"

The police soon left, but the crowd remained angry, inflamed by false rumors that the arrested woman was pregnant and had been brutally beaten. Soon people began lobbing rocks at passing cars, attacking white drivers, and overturning and torching vehicles. As a heat wave blanketed the city, street violence, looting, and arson swept through Watts, a crowded section of Los Angeles housing 250,000 black residents. Thousands of blacks, many of them teenagers, roamed the streets. Despite the eventual presence of over fifteen thousand police and national guardsmen, the uprising raged for thirty-six hours, leaving thirty-four dead, nine hundred injured, and $30 million in property damage that turned the Watts business district into a charred ruin. Over the next three years, each summer brought new waves of riots in the black ghettos of urban America.

As the sixties waned, young black radicals, some inspired by Black Muslim leader Malcolm X, spoke a vocabulary of resistance and separatism strikingly different from the rhetoric of Martin Luther King, Jr. Activists shouted the slogans of Black Power, and city after city erupted in violence. A white backlash formed, splintering the already strained civil-rights coalition. The end of the 1960s found black America's anger—and white America's resentment—mounting. The unity and moral clarity of the early 1960s, and the era's achievements in combating segregation, seemed remote indeed.

As generational and ideological conflict divided the African-American community, young white radicals, mostly on the college campuses, challenged their parents' political and cultural values. New Leftists dissected Kennedy-Johnson liberalism, and a growing counterculture expressed its rebelliousness in dress, music, and even hairstyle. By the end of 1967, divisions over the Vietnam War exacerbated these conflicts, and American society floundered amid hostility and divisiveness. The upsurge of youthful radicalism that began in the mid-sixties would leave its stamp on the generation that experienced it. However, many Americans who lived through the sixties recoiled from the drama. Their revulsion triggered a conservative resurgence that would remain influential for decades.

Ghetto Upheavals and Black Power

A few days after the Watts riot, violence erupted in Chicago's black neighborhoods. The following summer, riots hit Chicago again, then Cleveland, Dayton, Milwaukee, and other midwestern cities. The cycle of inner-city turmoil climaxed in 1967, with outbreaks tearing apart more than twenty cities.

The most serious violence of 1967 struck Newark, New Jersey, and Detroit. Newark's black ghetto, beset by chronic poverty and unemployment, exploded on July 12. As in Watts, reports of police beating a black motorist triggered the outburst. By nightfall, an angry, cursing mob surrounded the police station. Over the next few days, the rioting spread. The city government clamped down on the mobs, and New Jersey's governor called in the National Guard. When the rioting and arson finally ebbed, twenty-five blacks had been killed.

Detroit's numerous antipoverty programs provided no shield against violence. On July 23, 1967, the mass arrest of patrons at an after-hours nightclub for liquor-law violations triggered six days of street fighting and burning that left the downtown in ashes. In one incident, an arsonist tossed a Molotov cocktail through the window of a small business. Fanned by hot summer winds, the flames soon

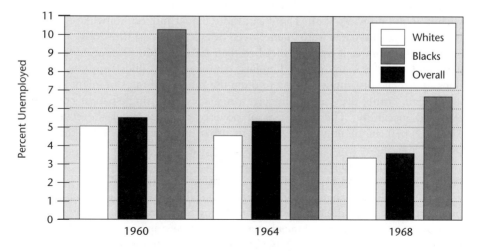

FIGURE 9.1

Unemployment Rates, 1960–1968

SOURCE: *Historical Statistics of the United States, Colonial Times to 1970* (1975).

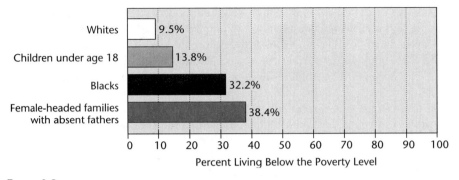

FIGURE 9.2

Poverty, 1969

SOURCE: U.S. Bureau of the Census, *Current Population Reports,* series P-60, No. 149, and unpublished data.

engulfed the entire block while residents tried in vain to quench the fire with garden hoses. Oddly, an almost festive mood prevailed. A contemporary account reported, "A spirit of carefree nihilism was taking hold. To riot and destroy appeared more and more to become ends in themselves." Other residents, by contrast, toured the riot-torn neighborhoods urging calm.

In retrospect, the 1965–68 riots should have come as no surprise. For decades northern cities had lured southern blacks seeking a better life. From 1940 to 1960, the net migration of blacks from South to North totaled more than 3 million, and the vast majority of these newcomers settled in metropolitan areas. Yet instead of finding improved lives, they more often were met with overcrowding and job discrimination. In 1966, when 32 percent of white workers held blue-collar or unskilled jobs, the comparable figure for blacks was 63 percent; many black men and women found no work at all. That year, more than 1 million nonwhite workers in the nation's central cities were unemployed or held only part-time jobs.

These urban black communities had their stable middle class and professional elite, and boasted many strong families, churches, and other supportive institutions. But social disruption was more often the rule. High rates of infant mortality, alcoholism, crime, drug abuse, teenage pregnancy, and single-parent households spawned instability. The grim fact of poverty dominated all the statistics. In 1966, 42 percent of nonwhites living in urban America fell below the federal poverty line.

The civil-rights movement had roused hopes in the ghettos that federal laws could not meet; analysts spoke of a "crisis of rising expectations." Some black leaders tried to direct the anger into organized political action, but the pressure-cooker mood in many cities discouraged reasoned long-term strategies. While the North did not have legally enforced racial segregation, the economic and social problems of the urban ghettos were inextricably entangled with the issue of skin color. Racism may have had a less blatant form in the North, but bigotry pervaded the region, affecting not just the labor market but every other facet of life. By a variety of informal techniques, and sometimes by restrictive clauses in property deeds, de facto residential segregation characterized all northern cities. Blacks who moved into white neighborhoods generally faced hostility and sometimes met with scrawled obscenities or a brick thrown through their window late at night. By the mid-sixties, with the burgeoning suburbs 95 percent white, poverty and discriminatory real-estate practices left blacks (and growing numbers of Hispanics) jammed in the inner city.

White political elites had paid scant attention as fast-growing black and Hispanic slums had sunk deeper into poverty and decay. With an eroding tax base owing to the flight of businesses and middle-class taxpayers to the suburbs, cities provided inadequate public services to those who remained, from schools to parks to garbage collection. Worse still, the highway and urban-renewal programs of the 1950s had left many city neighborhoods crisscrossed by freeways and access ramps, with the residents warehoused in ugly high-rise housing projects. These conditions provided ample fodder for the riots that erupted in the later 1960s.

Lower-class rioting as an expression of frustration and social tension was hardly new. In antebellum America, poor Irish immigrants had periodically exploded in protest against their economic plight and against the anti-Catholic prejudice of the Protestant majority. During and after World War I, race riots broke out in East St. Louis and Chicago, where a rapid influx of southern black workers had heightened social tensions and housing pressures. A 1943 outburst in Detroit took the lives of twenty-five blacks and nine whites and caused $2 million in property damage. That same year, Harlem exploded in several days of looting, burning, and property damage that left six dead and five hundred injured. Across the continent, in Los Angeles, Mexican Americans bore the brunt of another incident of wartime urban violence.

But despite the obvious catalysts and the historical precedents, the riots of 1965–68 stunned white America and official Washington. That they came after a decade of apparent progress in race relations made them all the more puzzling. Already grappling with his Vietnam War critics, President Johnson now also confronted threats to law and order in city after city. In July 1967, he created the National Advisory Commission on Civil Disorders, chaired by Governor Otto Kerner of Illinois. The 1968 Kerner Report rejected the charge that "outside agitators" or criminal elements had caused the upheavals. Moving beyond the immediate circumstances of specific riots, the study explored the larger pattern of white racism and rising black militance—combined with inner-city despair—that provided the breeding ground for violence. Noting that charges of police brutality had triggered many of the riots, the commission documented that most police forces remained overwhelmingly white, even in cities housing large black populations. The report also observed that although the riots had broken out spontaneously, participants often singled out white-owned businesses for arson and spared black-owned enterprises.

Concluding that "white racism is essentially responsible for the explosive mixture which has been accumulating in our cities since the end of World War II," the Kerner Commission warned, "Our nation is moving toward two societies, one black, one white—separate and unequal. . . . To pursue our present course will involve the continuing polarization of the American community and, ultimately, the destruction of basic democratic values."

While the urban black underclass seethed, some young blacks moved beyond Martin Luther King's integrationist agenda and nonviolent strategies to call for an ill-defined but militant Black Power. As the mainstream civil-rights movement lost steam, its original goals largely achieved, younger black radicals stepped in to fill the vacuum. SNCC led the way by electing as its head the firebrand Stokely Carmichael over the pacifist John Lewis. The militant Floyd McKissick replaced the more moderate James Farmer as director of CORE. Carmichael and McKissick turned up the rhetorical voltage sharply. On a march in Greenwood, Mississippi, in June 1966, Carmichael exhorted activists to "stop begging and take power—black power." When he hypnotically shouted "BLACK POWER! BLACK POWER! BLACK POWER!" and the crowd rhythmically responded, the media paid attention.

Black Power, Carmichael asserted, meant "smash[ing] everything Western civilization has created." At the 1966 CORE convention in Baltimore, he struck a separatist note: "We don't need white liberals. . . . We have to make integration irrelevant!" Early in 1967 he declared, "To hell with the laws of the United States. . . . If we don't get justice, we're going to tear this country apart."

Carmichael's successor as head of SNCC, young H. Rap Brown of Louisiana, outdid even Carmichael in rhetorical overkill. Violence, he announced in a much-quoted aphorism, "is as American as cherry pie." Speaking in Cambridge, Maryland, in July 1967 as flames engulfed Detroit, Brown harangued his volatile young audience with talk of guns and killing. The resulting wave of arson destroyed the heart of the city's black district. Soon after, Brown was arrested for inciting a riot. The moral idealism of the early civil-rights movement, and the apparent interracial unity displayed at the 1963 March on Washington, were little in evidence by 1967.

A West Coast manifestation of Black Power came in October 1966 when Huey Newton and Bobby Seale, young black college students in Oakland, California, founded the Black Panther party. Their manifesto demanded self-determination for the black community, full employment, decent housing, better education, and an end to police brutality. There were more radical goals too: exemption from military service for black males, all-black juries for blacks on trial, and "an end to the robbery by the capitalists of our Black Community." The new organization symbolized the angry mood among young urban blacks. In their paramilitary uniforms of black leather jackets and black berets, the Panthers won local celebrity and national media attention. Newton became "Minister of Defense" and Eldridge Cleaver, recently released from prison, "Minister of Information." In May 1967, as the California legislature debated a bill banning the carrying of loaded guns, Black Panther party members defiantly brought weapons into the capital building. When the Panthers became the targets of FBI surveillance and of raids by local police that sometimes resulted in fatalities, their fearsome aura increased.

Cleaver's autobiographical *Soul on Ice* (1968) expressed the rising self-awareness in urban black America. The nation's 20 million blacks, he declared, must awaken to the "vast power latent in their mass" and "hone [their numbers] into a sword with a sharp cutting edge." *Soul on Ice* was widely viewed as a no-holds-barred guide to the new spirit sweeping black America. A reviewer in the *New Republic* hailed it as "a book for which we have to make room—but not on the shelves we have already built."

Lacking a clear-cut program, Black Power primarily was a riveting slogan, expressing the mood of heightened militance among some younger blacks; impatience with the middle-class, church-based movement of Martin Luther King; contempt for patronizing white liberals; and, above all, pride in blackness. Beneath their incendiary rhetoric, Black Power advocates also offered a perceptive analysis of the racial power imbalance in America and its role in the exploitation of blacks. Martin Luther King had recognized this imbalance as well and had strived to strengthen black power by winning whites to the black cause through appeals to a shared moral tradition. The young radicals dismissed King's strategy and instead sought to weld black America into a powerful, disciplined cadre that would achieve its goals through group solidarity, collective effort, and intense racial consciousness.

The middle-class civil-rights organizations' strategy of building coalitions and working within the system held little appeal for Black Power devotees and their followers among the urban black poor. The oppressed should not collaborate with the oppressor, they insisted, or go hat in hand asking favors of the white enemy. Rather, some Black Power advocates espoused black political organizing, black business enterprises, black cultural institutions, and local control of schools and other institutions in black neighborhoods. This separatist vision had precedents in the mobilization of urban blacks by Marcus Garvey in the 1920s, and even earlier, but Black Power enthusiasts pushed the theme much further. These advocates laced their prescriptions with apocalyptic visions of revolution and retaliation against a demonized white oppressor. White and black critics alike dismissed this approach as a dangerous fantasy reflecting political naiveté and a failure of moral imagination.

But if the political aims of Black Power remained muddled, the movement's psychological meaning was clear. Indeed, it was in the realm of culture and consciousness, not politics, that the movement exerted its greatest long-range impact. Historian William L. Van Deburg, in his 1992 history of the movement, *New Day in Babylon,* sees Black Power as essentially a ritual of cultural empowerment and racial assertiveness. Van Deburg cites, for example, the playful fantasy of the black poet LeRoi Jones (who adopted the African name Amiri Baraka) of aliens arriving on a galactic quest for recordings by Art Blakey and other black jazz greats. In this sense, despite their repudiation of the civil-rights movement, Black Power champions displayed significant continuities with the earlier campaign. From the beginning, civil-rights leaders and local activists had focused on empowerment as well as on attacking Jim Crow and gaining voting rights. For them the word *freedom* encompassed racial pride, collective action, and breaking what historian David Chalmers has called "the white stranglehold on the black psyche." The call to Black Power intensified this concept of empowerment.

As Black Power enthusiasm swept the African-American community, especially the younger generation, in the late sixties, the black aesthetic summed up in the term *soul* became the test of racial authenticity. Artists and writers concentrated on creating work rooted in the black experience that spoke to a black audience. Young blacks abandoned elaborate hair-processing techniques and adopted the natural "Afro" look. Some donned colorful African dashikis. Well-educated blacks

Black Is Beautiful. *The "Black Power" movement that arose in the later 1960s took many forms, including an intensified pride by American blacks in their African heritage.* (© Mahon/Monkmeyer)

inspired by the new outlook consciously employed black dialect and nonstandard grammar. *Black* or *Afro-American* replaced *Negro* as the preferred racial designation. Black history courses sprang up on college campuses. In Detroit, the Reverend Albert Cleage opened his Shrine of the Black Madonna featuring a thirty-foot mural of a black Mary and baby Jesus.

Carrying the new racial consciousness to the world of sports, black sociologist Harry Edwards of California's San Jose State University urged black athletes to boycott the 1968 Summer Olympics in Mexico City as a protest against racism. Some black athletes joined the boycott; others participated in the games but protested in dramatic ways. When sprinters Tommie Smith and John Carlos mounted the victory stand to accept their gold and bronze medals, they lowered their heads and raised black-gloved fists as the "Star-Spangled Banner" was played. Like Rosa Parks's refusal to give up her bus seat in Montgomery in 1955 or the 1960 Greensboro sit-ins, their gesture was a defining moment in the rapidly evolving black-liberation movement.

Soul music captured the new mood. Aretha Franklin's "Natural Woman" (1967), Nina Simone's "Revolution" (1969), and the popular songs of James Brown, the Godfather of Soul, epitomized the awakening black consciousness. Tony Clarke's "Ghetto Man" (1969) conveyed the psychological toll of slum life:

Olympic Protest. *In a gesture that stirred both admiration and anger across America, track stars Tommie Smith and John Carlos raise black-gloved fists and bow their heads during the playing of the national anthem at the 1968 Summer Olympics in Mexico City.* (UPI/Corbis-Bettmann)

I never knew my papa's name
My ma scrubbed floors to keep me clad
And me and three brothers had to share one bed
When I was young I felt ashamed.

In one sense, the Black Power movement proved ephemeral. Even at its peak, canny entrepreneurs cashed in on the vogue with such products as "politically correct" Afro wigs and "Soul Brother" T-shirts. By the mid-1970s, the movement's erstwhile leaders had scattered, from expatriation in Africa (Stokely Carmichael) to evangelical Christianity and Republican politics (Eldridge Cleaver) to marketing barbecue sauce (Bobby Seale). Yet the cultural ferment summed up in the phrase "Black Power" exerted a profound long-range impact. For many thousands of African Americans, the movement both enhanced racial pride and heightened skepticism toward white America. Sinking deep roots into the black community, the assertive new outlook would be transmitted as a legacy to a younger generation of African Americans.

The Black Power movement, however, also contained an undercurrent of misogyny that dismayed many black women. When a young woman presented a paper on the position of women in SNCC in 1964, Stokely Carmichael sneered, "The only position for women in SNCC is prone." Such attitudes helped to raise the consciousness of a younger generation of African-American women and led to the formation of the National Black Feminist Organization in 1972. Black feminists noted the irony of Black Power advocates' ostentatiously rejecting everything white while retaining the most reactionary gender attitudes of 1950s America. Soon a talented group of black women writers, including Toni Morrison, Alice Walker, and Terry McMillan, would explore gender issues in the African-American community. The issue would remain touchy a generation later, as black women protested the coarse antiwoman messages in the lyrics of some black male rap groups in the early 1990s.

The Black Power movement also deepened the rift among the various civil-rights organizations. Martin Luther King, Jr., and the SCLC tried for a time to maintain links to the newly radicalized SNCC and CORE, but with little success. The young radicals ridiculed King as "Reverend Dr. Chickenwing." The more conservative NAACP and Urban League rejected the Black Power theme entirely. Black Power radicals, in turn, jeered the NAACP's Roy Wilkins as "a white man who somehow came out the wrong color."

Black Power pronouncements terrified white America. The language of racial assertiveness came from individuals who in fact wielded pathetically little power, but few noted this irony at the time as whites recoiled from the movement's new emphasis. After Martin Luther King's biblical cadences and uplifting vision of interracial cooperation, this rage-filled talk alarmed white America. The resulting white backlash would soon feed into a larger rightward turn in U.S. politics and culture.

Amid ghetto riots and young militants' calls for revolution, the efforts of mainstream civil-rights organizations to address the problems of the urban black poor faltered. In 1966 the SCLC tried in vain to mobilize Chicago's 800,000 blacks. Moving into a poor black district of the city, King announced a campaign for better housing and an end to discrimination in the real-estate market. King aides met with black gang leaders and advised planned action, not rioting. But Chicago mayor Richard J. Daley, while praising King's goals, shrewdly maneuvered to undercut King by mobilizing his powerful political machine, including local black politicians, and making such superficial but popular gestures as bringing portable swimming pools into the black slums that hot summer. As the SCLC campaign stumbled, Chicago blacks grew disillusioned. A black "Freedom Sunday" rally and march on city hall drew far fewer participants than expected, and some black youths even heckled King as he spoke. Laws against discrimination in the sale or rental of housing meant little to slum dwellers too poor to move to middle-class white suburbs, and the SCLC campaign struck many Chicago blacks as irrelevant. As one complained, "We're sick and tired of middle-class people telling us what we want."

A rally in a Chicago park in early August turned ugly as local whites, mostly second-generation European immigrants, threw bricks and shouted racial epithets. Late that month, Daley gave King a face-saving out: at a heavily publicized "summit conference," city officials and leading realtors made vague gestures toward open housing. Hailing the agreement as a significant victory against housing discrimination, King and his lieutenants left for Atlanta. In fact, little changed in Chicago. The intractable realities of urban black poverty and white resistance did not yield to the techniques that had worked in Birmingham and Montgomery. In contrast to the South of the 1950s and early 1960, writes historian Robert Weisbrot, "racism moved through Northern cities like Chicago in so many faceless, impersonal forms as to escape detection by a society inclined to ignore it."

In the volatile climate of the late 1960s, the consensus on civil-rights goals that had coalesced in 1964–65 evaporated. By the end of the decade, the movement lay in disarray. In retrospect, the cultural and psychological contributions of the Black Power campaign would become apparent, but many at the time deemed it nihilistic and divisive. In addition, the militance of alienated black radicals only further roused conservative anxiety levels when it found an echo among the younger generation of affluent white Americans.

The Personal Is Political:
The New Left and the Counterculture

As Black Power ideologues mocked the civil-rights establishment and proclaimed the virtues of soul, some white youths were making their own break with the politics and values of their elders. The unrest of the 1960s arose not only among blacks marginalized by racism and poverty, but also among privileged, middle-class white students at elite colleges and universities who repudiated Cold War liberalism and their parents' cultural style. Yet the two movements were linked. Many white students who emerged as radical activists in the mid-1960s had earlier rallied to the civil-rights cause, supporting the sit-ins or the 1964 Mississippi Freedom Summer. John Lewis, Robert Moses, Fannie Lou Hamer, and other black-movement leaders became role models and cultural heroes for young white activists.

President Kennedy's summons to public service had provided a spur to youthful idealism. The Peace Corps, the nuclear test ban, and rhetorical gestures to issues such as poverty and environmental protection had channeled the younger generation's reformist impulses into mainstream politics. But after Kennedy's assassination, many youthful activists renounced establishment politics. "The system" was now the enemy. Kennedy had been a hero; Johnson, the old-style politician, became the villain. The overbearing Texan lacked Kennedy's charisma, and although his domestic reform program won grudging praise on campuses, the Vietnam War rapidly eclipsed that support.

The rise of radical politics and campus unrest had demographic sources as well. The early postwar baby boom had by 1960 had created a teenaged "nation within a nation" totaling more than 20 million youngsters. With some 3 million baby boomers reaching college age each year and a higher percentage of high-school graduates going on to college,* higher-education enrollment soared from 3.6 million in 1960 to almost 8 million in 1970.

The institutions that greeted these eager young people—particularly the large public universities—were ill equipped to handle their vast numbers. Forced to fill

---

* The proportion of people 18 to 24 years old who were enrolled in colleges or universities surged, from 12.5 percent in 1946 to 32 percent by 1970.

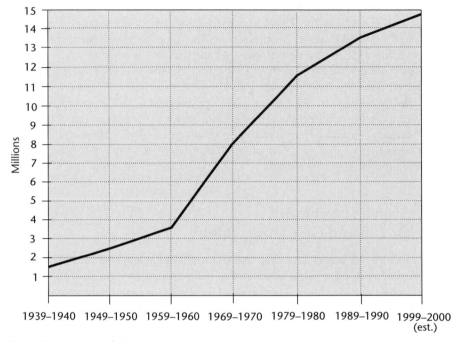

FIGURE 9.3

Total Enrollment in U.S.Colleges and Universities, 1939–2000
SOURCE: *World Almanac and Book of Facts, 1998* (1997).

out innumerable forms, wait in lines, sit in jammed lecture halls, and endure crowded dorms, students protested. In *The Uses of the University* (1963), University of California president Clark Kerr praised the modern "multiversity" for its intellectual diversity, but his characterization of universities as "service stations" and "knowledge factories" hinted at what students found alienating. Indeed, Kerr himself, celebrating the university as "a city of infinite variety," conceded that "some get lost in the city."

Unrest first erupted in the fall of 1964 at Kerr's flagship campus, the sprawling University of California–Berkeley. When administrators banned recruitment tables for civil-rights organizations from a campus area traditionally open to political activity, a coalition of groups organized the Free Speech Movement (FSM). Police arrested a young man who challenged the ban, and masses of students mobbed the police car. Later, FSM backers occupied Berkeley's administration building.

Mario Savio, a philosophy graduate student just back from the Mississippi Freedom Summer, emerged as the voice of the FSM—the first of a succession of 1960s leaders who articulated the escalating disgust with what became known as "the establishment." At one rally, Savio cried, "After a long period of apathy during the fifties, students have begun ... to act. ... There is a time when the operation of the machine becomes so odious ... that ... you've got to put your bodies upon the gears and upon the wheels, upon the levers, upon all the apparatus, and you've got to make it stop."

Through the fall and on into 1965, strikes, marches, and demonstrations paralyzed the Berkeley campus, until school officials eventually yielded on the specific point at issue. The FSM foreshadowed a nationwide wave of campus protest; soon, activists from coast to coast were portraying universities as cogs in a vast machine that was grinding up Vietnamese peasants as it dehumanized college students at home.

The most politically sophisticated expression of the new mood emerged in Students for a Democratic Society (SDS), an organization whose founders derived from an earlier radical tradition. In the 1960s, children of leftists who had supported radical causes in the 1930s—the so-called red-diaper babies—launched a fresh critical assault on capitalist America. Trying to revive a struggling New York socialist group, the League for Industrial Democracy, Michael Harrington and others had formed a youth branch, the Students' League for Industrial Democracy (SLID), in 1960. In 1961 a group of University of Michigan students took over SLID and renamed it Students for a Democratic Society. At a 1962 summer retreat at a United Auto Workers (UAW) center in Port Huron, Michigan, some sixty SDS students issued *The Port Huron Statement,* a founding text of the so-called New Left. The manifesto's principal author, Tom Hayden, of Detroit working-class origins, had just graduated from the University of Michigan, where he had edited the student newspaper. That summer, Hayden had been roughed up by local whites while visiting Robert Moses's voter-registration project in McComb, Mississippi.

Drawing on ideas already in the air in Left-liberal circles, *The Port Huron Statement* recounted the experiences that had shaped its authors' political outlook—nuclear fear, the civil-rights movement, and consciousness of the disparity between America's wealth and power and conditions in much of the rest of the world. "Although mankind desperately needs revolutionary leadership," the manifesto announced, "America rests in national stalemate, . . . its democratic system apathetic and manipulated." The document called for a campaign aimed at "breaking the crust of apathy and overcoming the inner alienation . . . of American college life." Anticipating the Berkeley Free Speech Movement, the statement challenged universities' "cumbersome academic bureaucracy" and faculty links to "the corporate economy" and defense contractors.

Despite its critical edge, *The Port Huron Statement* reflected Kennedy-era confidence and a belief in liberal ideals and the promise of democracy. Rejecting doctrinaire ideology—"We have no sure formulas, no closed theories"—it proposed a strategy of "participatory democracy." In practice, this slogan meant that cadres of activists would work for radical social and political change through grassroots political organizing. As ordinary citizens discovered their collective strength, manipulative, business-dominated politics would give way to more authentic democratic processes that promoted community rather than corporate interests.

SDS and *The Port Huron Statement* attracted notice among college students already politicized by the nuclear test-ban campaign and the civil-rights movement. By 1964 SDS boasted some fifteen hundred members on a score or more campuses. One early recruit, Harvard senior Todd Gitlin, later recalled:

[E]verything these people did was charged with intensity. They moved and attracted me as people in the same spirit that *The Port Huron Statement* first moved and attracted me as a manifesto. . . . They were . . . analytically keen and politically committed, but also, . . . these unabashed moralists cared about one another.

Full of hope, young SDSers, as Robert Moses and his SNCC co-workers had earlier done in Mississippi, set out to promote grassroots political action in the industrial cities. Funded by a small UAW grant, they moved into working-class communities. Their aim was to challenge society's power structure by helping residents to identify grievances and to devise collective strategies for forcing change.

But SDS evolved rapidly, and in 1963 came a more radical manifesto, *America and the New Era*. This tract denounced the "corporate liberalism" of the Kennedy administration and called for direct resistance to it, domestically and in the Third World. With the 1964 Gulf of Tonkin Resolution and Johnson's 1965 escalation of the Vietnam War (see pp. 280–282), SDS would shift from organizing the poor to organizing college students. If not the working class, then the learning class, would serve as the spark plug of radical change! In shifting its focus, SDS emerged as a leader of antiwar activism in the later 1960s.

The New Left was more than manifestos, however; as Gitlin's recollection suggests, it blended the personal and the political. In contrast to 1930s radicals, 1960s activists sought to change consciousness as well as the political system. As Tom Hayden has put it, "[M]ost of the sixties generation . . . were not interested in attaining office but in changing life-styles. They were not so interested in being opinion makers as in changing the climate of opinion." Depression-era radicals had identified with workers, as in Clifford Odets's 1935 play, *Waiting for Lefty*. To some extent, the New Left continued this identification with the labor movement in the early 1960s, as historian Peter B. Levy points out in *The New Left and Labor in the 1960s* (1994). In return, some union leaders, notably those of the United Auto Workers, initially supported SDS's community-organizing efforts in northern working-class neighborhoods (as well as SNCC's grassroots campaign in the rural South).

But the New Left did not identify solely with blue-collar workers as the vanguard of social change. They also allied themselves, at least ideologically, with marginalized groups and with social outcasts, even those stigmatized as insane. Some admired British psychiatrist R. D. Laing, who in *The Divided Self: An Existential Study in Sanity and Madness* (1965) romantically argued that psychosis could offer a liberating breakthrough to a deeper level of awareness and could be a rational response to an insane social order. Ken Kesey's novel *One Flew over the Cuckoo's Nest* (1962), was a favorite with campus radicals. Later made into a movie starring Jack Nicholson, it portrayed the "insane" as victims of a repressive society who possess more humanity than their keepers. New Left theorists did not literally view mental illness as simply a response to political repression, but on a metaphorical level the perspectives of Laing, Kesey, and others epitomized their understanding of the links between the personal and the political.

In their efforts to forge connections between the public and private realms, the New Left found certain social thinkers particularly relevant. Paul Goodman in *Growing Up Absurd* (1960) urged the young to move beyond conventional politics and to recover America's lost sense of community.

Norman O. Brown, professor of classics at Wesleyan University, urged rejection of external authority, including "the tyranny of books," in favor of inner sources of awareness. In *Life Against Death: The Psychoanalytic Meaning of History* (1959), Brown argued for intuition rather than rationality as the truest source of knowledge and celebrated the erotic potential of human bodies freed from socially imposed inhibitions. Hailing "polymorphous perversity," he argued that both academia and society at large needed "more Eros and less strife." Life's deepest mysteries "cannot be put into words," intoned Brown in a 1960 Phi Beta Kappa address at Columbia University, "at least not the kind of words which earn you your Phi Beta Kappa keys."

Herbert Marcuse (born 1898), a German philosopher who had come to America as a refugee from Nazism, also attracted New Left disciples. In *Eros and Civilization* (1954), Marcuse drew on both Marx and Freud to explore how elites manipulate sexual energy to maintain their power. Extending Freud's theory of repression, Marcuse argued that modern capitalist societies impose far more repression than is necessary to maintain order. This "surplus repression" is then manipulated by advertisers to promote consumption. Sexual repression, in short, fuels consumer capitalism. Marcuse, like Brown, offered a utopian vision of instinctual liberation.

In *One-Dimensional Man* (1965), Marcuse examined the mechanisms by which advanced capitalist states alienate men and women from their true selves and thwart their human potential. The manipulation of material wants is so skillfully managed, he argued, that most people have lost the capacity for political resistance, critical thought, or true sensual pleasure. Marcuse's apparent message—that breaking free of society's sexual taboos and "surplus repression" is not only an avenue to erotic fulfillment but a revolutionary political act as well—readily appealed to campus radicals. They encapsulated his thesis in an electric slogan: "Make love, not war."

The quest for the true self beneath the false, socially imposed self, a quest deeply rooted in the Romantic tradition, lent a distinctive flavor to 1960s radicalism. An intense subjectivity saturates *The Port Huron Statement,* as the authors probe their shifting psychic states—complacency, alienation, apathy, and so forth—and dream of a return to emotional wholeness through "self cultivation, self direction, self understanding, and creativity." All of this introspection reflected a central New Left tenet: the inner world of consciousness and the outer world of politics are inextricably connected.

Soon the media detected the emergence of a youthful "counterculture" that not only challenged liberal ideology intellectually but mocked conventional middle-class mores. Not all radical activists adopted alternative lifestyles, and not all members of the counterculture espoused radical politics. But the dual movements converged at many points. Both rejected what they considered the repressive authority of the established order, political and cultural. New Left leaders celebrated and often shared in the cultural rebellion of middle-class youth. As thousands of young men and women spurned the lifestyles and outlook of their parents' generation, SDS theorists predicted, a broader transformation in U.S. society would inevitably follow. And even the most politically naive counterculture youths sensed that their preferences in music, dress, and hairstyle were somehow linked to an unfolding process of political change. As historian David Burner writes in *Making Peace with the Sixties* (1996), a fundamental tenet of the dissenters of the early 1960s was that "the transformation of politics, culture, economics and society" must begin "with any number of personal decisions to live the transformed society."

Counterculture recruits found inspiration in dissident voices from the 1950s. They admired Salinger, Ginsberg, and Kerouac. They devoured the mordant humor of Lenny Bruce, Mort Sahl, Tom Lehrer, and other iconoclastic comics. They gyrated to rock-and-roll and identified with movie rebels like Brando and Dean. But 1960s cultural rebels politicized their rebellion in ways that gave the decade its unique flavor. Joseph Heller's *Catch-22* (1960) perhaps best anticipated the counterculture outlook. Set in World War II, Heller's novel captured the casual inhumanity, bizarre irrationality, and hilarious bumbling of officialdom engaged in vast enterprises such as the conduct of war. At the end, the antihero Yossarian paddles off on a raft bound for neutral Sweden, a forerunner of thousands of young draft resisters who soon headed for Canada, Scandinavia, and elsewhere.

The young men and women of the counterculture displayed lively imagination in rejecting bourgeois convention. They let their hair grow and eschewed makeup; they burned candles and incense and decorated their rooms with Eastern symbols; they bought clothes from the Salvation Army or military-surplus stores. Tie-dyed T-shirts, army fatigues, and long cotton dresses, sandals, beads, and peace symbols became their uniform. They engaged in premarital sex more openly than their elders had. The introduction of the oral contraceptive ("the Pill") in 1960 and the intrauterine device (IUD) later in the decade facilitated this sexual revolution. So did sex studies, such as William Masters's and Virginia Johnson's *Human Sexual Response* (1966) and even Helen Gurley Brown's slickly popularized *Sex and the Single Girl* (1962). In 1968 *Life* magazine offered Middle America a prurient look at unmarried undergraduate couples living together in off-campus apartments. Counterculture youth were hardly the first to discover sex, but they invested their erotic adventures with ideological meaning. To flout the dominant culture's sexual repressiveness was also to reject its political ideology, its fetishistic consumerism, and, eventually, its war in Southeast Asia.

As the sixties wore on, drugs—mostly marijuana but also stronger substances such as lysergic acid diethylamide (LSD)—pervaded the youth culture as well as parts of the "straight" world. Marijuana and cocaine had been familiar in jazz circles for years, and peyote, a cactus-bud hallucinogen used in Native American religious rites, had appeared on the Beat scene in the late 1950s. LSD, first synthesized in England, reached Greenwich Village in the early sixties and hit the West Coast soon after.

Looking back from a time when heroin and crack addiction in inner-city slums and even "recreational" cocaine use among white-collar professionals exact a tragic toll, it takes an imaginative leap to recapture the benign view of drugs held by many young people in the early days of the counterculture. For a time, marijuana and even LSD appeared as relatively harmless avenues to deeper levels of consciousness. Together with rock, long hair, and psychedelic posters, drugs became part of a counterculture scene that promoted a sense of community and demonstrated youthful alienation from the oppressive, uptight adult world.

"Tune In, Turn On, Drop Out." Timothy Leary, erstwhile Harvard psychologist shown here in 1968, became the Pied Piper of LSD and other consciousness-altering substances for the 1960s counter-culture. (Black Star)

The high priest of LSD was Timothy Leary, a Harvard psychologist who discovered hallucinogenic mushrooms in Mexico. Fired from Harvard in 1963, Leary became a full-time missionary for LSD through his *Psychedelic Review* and League for Spiritual Discovery. "Tune in, turn on, drop out," he counseled the young. Leary cheerfully combined the sexual and the pharmacological revolutions, describing LSD in a 1966 *Playboy* magazine interview as "the most powerful aphrodisiac known to man."

Another drug-culture guru, novelist Ken Kesey, founded a commune near San Francisco in 1964 with a group of hangers-on called the Merry Pranksters. That spring Kesey and the Pranksters drove east in a psychedelically painted 1939 school bus, wired for sound. The group visited Leary at a Hudson Valley estate provided by a well-heeled patron. They also conducted "acid [LSD] tests": at multimedia concerts and light shows, they dropped acid into foods or drinks, sometimes without recipients' knowledge.

Above all, the counterculture defined itself through music—first folk, then rock. Joan Baez, a classically trained Boston folksinger active in the civil-rights movement, became the balladeer of social engagement. Bob Dylan, born Robert Zimmerman in Hibbing, Minnesota, joined the Greenwich Village folk scene in 1961. His hugely successful second album, *The Freewheelin' Bob Dylan* (1963), included political songs such as "A Hard Rain's Gonna Fall" and "Blowin' in the Wind." The last, with its call to political commitment—"How many times can a man turn his head/Pretending he just doesn't see?"—sold more than a million copies in a version recorded by another popular group, Peter, Paul & Mary. "The Times They Are A-Changin'," by Bob Dylan, was prophetic.

In Perspective: *The Politics of Music*

T he political and cultural upheavals of the 1960s found expression through music. Arlo Guthrie's sardonic antiwar song "Alice's Restaurant" and the harsh dissonance of Jimi Hendrix's version of "The Star-Spangled Banner" at the 1969 Woodstock festival captured the spirit of the counterculture better than any speech.

In articulating their protest musically, sixties activists were continuing a long tradition of expressing dissident political views and advocating change through the medium of song. In colonial America, following ancient customs brought over from England, street hawkers in Boston, New York, and Philadelphia sold penny broadsides featuring song lyrics, set to well-known popular tunes, that commented on the political events of the day. As the Revolution approached, these broadsides took on a sharper edge and a distinctly anti-British tone.

In antebellum United States, touring singing groups were enormously popular, and their performances often had a political and reformist aspect. Most famous of all were the Hutchinson Family Singers, Abby Hutchinson and her four brothers, who toured the North in the 1840s. Abby ("the sweet canary of New Hampshire") was the Joan Baez of her day. She joined her brothers to perform not only such sentimental favorites as "The Snow Storm" and "My Mother's Bible," but also songs promoting an array of reform causes. "Cold Water" advocated temperance, "The Slave's Lament" championed abolitionism, and the ballad "There's a Good Time Coming" became the anthem of antebellum reformers. Even after the family group broke up following Abby's marriage in 1849, she continued to sing before women's rights conventions in the 1850s and 1860s.

During the era of industrialization in the late nineteenth century, radicals and labor activists used music to protest the exploitation of workers. A song that circulated among the immigrant coal miners of northeastern Pennsylvania began:

Come, listen, fellow-workingmen, my story,
      I'll relate,
How workers in the coal-mines fare in
      Pennsylvania State;
Come, hear a sad survivor, from beside his
      children's graves,
And learn how free Americans are treated
      now as slaves.

Communists and socialists joined voices in the "Internationale." The Swedish immigrant Joseph Hillstrom (Joe Hill), an itinerant laborer, songwriter, and activist, contributed many satirical songs, often set to popular hymn tunes, to the Industrial Workers of the World's *Little Red Songbook*. After Hill was convicted of murder in Salt Lake City and executed by a firing squad in 1915, in what many considered a gross miscarriage of justice, he himself was memorialized in the most famous song to emerge from the American labor movement, "The Ballad of Joe Hill."

Amid the Great Depression of the 1930s, songs again expressed the endurance and discontents of suffering Americans. Oklahoma's Woody Guthrie (1912–67), singer, songwriter, and radical, wrote what would become an anthem of the American Left, "This Land Is Your Land" (1940). America belongs to all its citizens, Guthrie's rousing ballad proclaimed, not just to the rich and powerful. Pete Seeger carried on the tradition of musical leftist politics in the Cold War era.

In the 1950s and early '60s, Tom Lehrer's songs helped rouse opposition to the nuclear arms race. Stanley Kubrick sharpened the satirical edge of his antinuclear film *Dr. Strangelove* (1964) by staging his nuclear Armageddon to the accompaniment of such jaunty war songs as "When Johnny Comes Marching Home." The Australian folk song "Waltzing Matilda" echoes through another movie of nuclear annihilation, *On the Beach* (1959). Not only the speeches of antinuclear activists, but music, helped mobilize public opinion against the bomb.

The civil-rights movement is inextricably identified with "We Shall Overcome," sung at countless rallies and protests as well as in jail cells. An African-American gospel song, "We Shall Overcome" took on new meaning in the context of the black freedom struggle. Billie Holiday's rendition of "Strange Fruit" and Nina Simone's searing version of Kurt Weill's "Pirate Jenny" from *The Threepenny Opera* offered chilling commentary on lynching, racial injustice, and a coming day of reckoning.

Of course, music can be used not just to stir protest, but also to mobilize public opinion in support of government policies, or to promote patriotism. During the Civil War, Julia Ward Howe's "Battle Hymn of the Republic," with its powerful biblical imagery, helped convince northerners of the righteousness of their cause. Confederate troops, meanwhile, marched off to war to the jaunty strains of "Dixie," *their* national anthem. In World War I, songs like "Over There" stirred Americans to support the war effort; in World War II an outpouring of patriotic songs such as "God Bless America" served the same purpose. Even during the 1960s, not all songs celebrated the counterculture or the antiwar cause. Merle Haggard's patriotic "Okie From Muskogee," for example, sharply attacked the pot-smoking, long-haired opponents of the war.

Although the tradition of political music diminished somewhat after the 1960s, it remained alive. The environmental movement spawned many songs lamenting the destruction of endangered species and rain forests. In the 1980s and 1990s, rap music, rooted in a long tradition of African-American protest music and satirical verse recited orally, featured young ghetto blacks lashing out against a hostile social order. Some criticized rappers for misogyny, for antiwhite racism, or for advocating violence, but, like it or not, rap's raw power and unvarnished lyrics did carry on the centuries-old tradition of dissidents and outsiders using music to express their grievances, their seething anger, and sometimes their idealistic vision of a better world to come.

There's a battle
Outside and it's ragin'.
It'll soon shake your windows
And rattle your walls
For the times they are a-changin'.

With President Kennedy's violent death, the urban riots, the Black Power phenomenon, and the Vietnam escalation as a backdrop, Dylan's songs caught the
edgy new mood on campus. In the early sixties, his politics had reflected the civil-
rights movement and Kennedy liberalism, and his music remained in the folk vein.
By 1965, as his lyrics grew more radical, his style evolved as well. At the Newport
Folk Festival that summer, he dismayed purists by playing "folk rock" on an electric guitar. Songs like "Maggie's Farm" and "Desolation Row" sneered at the establishment and limned an apocalyptic vision of looming cataclysm.

Early in 1964, the Beatles jetted in from Liverpool sporting long hair and boyish
smiles. After their TV debut on the Ed Sullivan show, Beatlemania swept teenage
America. Thanks largely to John Lennon, the Beatles soon outgrew their insipid early
repertoire ("I Want to Hold Your Hand") and became more original musically and
more radical politically. They found a new audience on college campuses. Originally
inspired by U.S. rock-and-roll performers and by African-American rhythm-and-
blues artists, the Beatles in turn shaped American popular music of the 1960s
and beyond. As an English import, the group exemplified the cultural cross-
fertilization made possible by the new technologies of LP records and global air
travel.

As drug use swept the counterculture, groups such as San Francisco's Jefferson
Airplane and The Grateful Dead incorporated LSD-inspired lyrics and encouraged
the use of marijuana and other controlled substances at their concerts. Dylan's
"Mr. Tambourine Man" and the Beatles's "Lucy in the Sky with Diamonds" (a
thinly disguised hymn to LSD) testified to the role of drugs in the music scene. The
"Human Be-In" held at San Francisco's Golden Gate Park on January 14, 1967, became a day-long counterculture love feast featuring Day-Glo banners, psychedelic
costumes, nonstop music making by bands and blissed-out participants—and the
ubiquitous ingestion of mind-altering substances. A flower-bedecked Timothy
Leary wandered about in white, proselytizing for LSD.

New Left celebrity Jerry Rubin tried to promote radical politics at the Be-In,
but by this time the New Left and the counterculture were on diverging trajecto-
ries. As the leftists pursued theoretical disputations and protested U.S. imperialism,
a large portion of the counterculture, propelled by the logic of consumerism, succumbed to the lure of drugs, new varieties of rock, and the elaborate accou-
trements of their alternative lifestyle. Leary spoke of his LSD crusade as the "Politics of the Nervous System," but his own career was orbiting into outer space. As
historian William O'Neill has observed, "To 'turn on and drop out' did not weaken
the state. Quite the contrary, it drained off potentially subversive energies. . . .
[M]any adult Americans [were already] dependent on drugs like alcohol and tran-
quilizers. Now the young were doing the same thing."

For all its criticism of consumer capitalism, the counterculture flourished among college-age children of the well-to-do and in fact depended on affluence. And for all the talk of linking the personal and the political, many young people, especially those seduced by mind-altering substances, turned from action to sensation. "We've become obsessed with experience," mourned critic Benjamin Mott in 1969. A narcissistic preoccupation with the self and its potential for gratification would prove to be one of the sixties' more enduring—and questionable—legacies.

The media loved the counterculture. San Francisco's "Human Be-In," gushed *Newsweek,* was "a psychedelic picnic, a hippie happening." *Time* pronounced San Francisco's Haight-Ashbury district the counterculture's "vibrant epicenter" as "flower children" converged there in 1967 for the "Summer of Love." By the early 1970s, however, the drug culture's darker side—its passivity, the "bad trips" (drug overdoses), the exploiters and psychotics lurking on the fringes—had given the entire counterculture the aura of a pleasant idyll turned sinister.

But just as one should avoid facile caricatures of the Black Power movement, one should be wary of reducing the counterculture to its drug-induced excesses. The counterculture challenged the tepid and conformist features of 1950s and early 1960s culture. In this respect its influence proved long-lasting. Long after the "Summer of Love" and the "Human Be-In" had become quaint exhibits in the museum of 1960s nostalgia, the underlying impulses of the counterculture, and of its more politicized twin, the New Left, would continue to shape American life as the youth of the 1960s moved into adulthood.

This point is illustrated in the area of gender relations. The women's movement that would soon transform America (see Chapter 12) drew influence not only from the civil-rights campaign but also from the rise of the New Left and the counterculture. Indeed, SDS's community-organizing efforts, like the antisegregation campaigns in the South, gave many young women invaluable political experience. The bible of modern feminism, Betty Friedan's best-selling *The Feminine Mystique,* appeared in 1963, the same year as SDS's *America and the New Era.* In 1966 the National Organization for Women (NOW) was founded. At its national conference in 1967, NOW demanded an end to legal restraints on abortion and addressed other issues that would dominate the feminist agenda in the years ahead. Neither Friedan nor most of the early NOW activists were themselves New Leftists or counterculture devotees, but those movements created a climate that encouraged women to question gender stereotypes along with other cultural and ideological baggage.

The New Left, like the Black Power movement, also stimulated the rise of feminism in a negative sense. SDS and other radical movements remained male dominated, as young men provided the leadership, established the agenda, and set the tone of "movement" culture. As angry female activists denounced gender discrimination and *sexism* (a word coined as a direct analogue to *racism*), they initially met a dismissive response. When female SDS members raised gender issues at SDS's 1965 conference, male leaders barely past adolescence shouted them down. But women persisted, laying the groundwork for a reform movement in the 1970s. At an antiwar rally in Washington, D.C., in January 1968, five thousand women marched separately as the Jeanette Rankin Brigade, honoring a congresswoman who in 1917 had voted against America's entry into World War I.

Conclusion

The early and mid-1960s stand as a crucial transitional era in postwar U.S. social history, as currents of protest and discontent gathered across the nation. Far from the power centers of Washington or Wall Street, ferment stirred among young urban blacks, radical students, educated middle-class women, and growing numbers of the younger generation. Although they pursued different goals, these groups collectively challenged the social, political, and cultural status quo. Building on the civil-rights movement and the promise of change in the Kennedy and early Johnson years, these movements unleashed yeasty activist energies that would remain potent long after the sixties had ended.

Behind all the converging social trends—the ghetto riots, Black Power, the rise of the New Left and the counterculture, the reawakening of feminist consciousness—lay the inescapable reality of Vietnam. This scourge blotted out LBJ's domestic achievements and exacerbated the hydra of other conflicts—political, social, and cultural—confronting the nation in the 1960s. As the turbulent decade wore on, the war that began as a troubling distraction burgeoned into an all-consuming obsession.

SELECTED READINGS

Inner-City Riots and the Black Power Movement

Alan I. Altschuler, *Community Control: The Black Demand for Participation in Large American Cities* (1970); Michal R. Belknap, ed., *Urban Race Riots* (1991); James Burton, *Black Violence: Political Impact of the 1960s Riots* (1978); Clayborne Carson, *In Struggle: SNCC and the Black Awakening of the 1960s* (1981); Robert Conont, *Rivers of Blood, Years of Darkness* [Watts riot] (1968); Theodore Draper, *The Rediscovery of Black Nationalism* (1970); James Forman, *The Making of Black Revolutionaries* (1985); Sylvia R. Frey, *Water from the Rock: Black Resistance in a Revolutionary Age* (1991); Herbert H. Haines, *Black Radicals and the Civil Rights Mainstream, 1954–1970* (1988); John T. McCartney, *Black Power Ideologies* (1992); Allen J. Matusow, "From Civil Rights to Black Power," in Barton J. Bernstein and Allen J. Matusow, eds., *Twentieth-Century America: Recent Interpretations* (1967); Manning Marable, *Race, Reform and Rebellion: The Second Reconstruction in Black America from 1945 to 1982* (1984); James R. Ralph, Jr., *Northern Protest: Martin Luther King, Jr., Chicago, and the Civil Rights Movement* (1993); *Report of the National Advisory Commission on Civil Unrest* (1968); Cleveland Sellers with Robert Terrell, *The River of No Return: The Autobiography of a Black Militant and the Life and Death of SNCC* (1973); Harvard Sitkoff, *The Struggle for Black Equality, 1954–1992* (1992); William L. Van Deburg, *New Day in Babylon: The Black Power Movement and American Culture, 1965–1975* (1992); Milton Viorst, *Fire in the Streets: America in the 1960s* (1979).

The Rise of the New Left and the Counterculture

Terry H. Anderson, *The Movement and the Sixties* (1995); John Borkima and Timothy L. Lukes, eds., *Marcuse: From the New Left to the Next Left* (1994); Wini Breines, *Community and Organization in the New Left* (1983); David Burner, *Making Peace with the Sixties* (1996); Morris Dickstein, *Gates of Eden: American Culture in the 1960s* (1977); Sara Evans, *Personal Politics: The Roots of Women's Liberation in the Civil Rights Movement and the New Left* (1979); David Farber, ed., *The Sixties: From Memory to History* (1994); Todd Gitlin, *The Sixties: Years of Hope, Days of Rage* (1987); Clinton Heylin, *Bob Dylan* (1991); Maurice Isserman, *If I Had a Hammer: The Death of the Old Left–and the Birth of the New Left* (1989); Cyril Levitt, *Children of Privilege: Student Revolt in the Sixties* (1984); Peter B. Levy, *The New Left and Labor in the 1960s* (1994); James Miller, *"Democracy Is in the Streets": From Port Huron to the Siege of Chicago* (1987); Edward P. Morgan, *The 60s Experience: Hard Lessons About Modern America* (1991); R. David Myers, ed., *Toward a History of the New Left: Essays from Within the Movement* (1989); Philip Norman, *Shout! The Beatles in Their Generation* (1981); William Novak, *High Culture: Marijuana in the Lives of Americans* (1980); Tim Riley, *Tell Me Why: A Beatles Commentary* (1988); Stanley Rothman and S. Robert Lichter, *Roots of Radicalism* (1982); Kirkpatrick Sale, *SDS* (1973); Anthony Scaduto, *Bob Dylan* (1971); William C. Seitz, *Art in the Age of Aquarius, 1955–1970* (1992); Bob Spitz, *Dylan: A Biography* (1986); George R. Vickers, *The Formation of the New Left: The Early Years* (1975); Jon Wiener, *Come Together: John Lennon in His Time* (1984).

CHAPTER 10

Out of Control: War in Vietnam, Protest at Home

T hey come by the hundreds, walking slowly down the sloping path and gazing silently at the black marble wall on which are inscribed the names of more than 57,000 young Americans. Some visitors weep quietly; others leave a flower or a message; still others seek out the name of a son, a brother, or a friend.

This is the Vietnam Veterans Memorial in Washington, D.C., designed by Yale art student Maya Ying Lin, an intensely moving monument in a city filled with statuary. Other Washington monuments honor revered leaders or recall proud events; this one commemorates the nation's longest and most controversial war—a conflict that devastated the people it sought to save and that catalyzed wrenching divisions at home. Lacking victory or celebration, the war's conclusion left only relief that a long ordeal had ended. The Vietnam Veterans Memorial stands as a reminder not only of dead young soldiers but of strategies gone grievously awry, the collapse of two presidential administrations, vast human suffering, and an America torn by internal strife. In 1580 the words of English playwright John Lyly foreshadowed the Vietnam War's ultimate meaning for the United States: "The wound that bleedeth inward is most dangerous."

As we saw in Chapter 9, the wound of Vietnam festered in a body politic already feverish. The upheavals that tore U.S. society in the late 1960s had roots in earlier ideological and cultural conflicts. As the Vietnam struggle escalated, the mood turned angrier in the African-American community, and the New Left and the counterculture, already well entrenched, spearheaded a sharp challenge to the administration's war policies. The domestic turmoil that had first erupted in the mean streets of the nation's black ghettos now spread to the campuses of the nation's most prestigious universities.

Although the Vietnam conflict came to be called "Johnson's War," it was not entirely of his making. Its roots stretched back to decisions and actions taken by Dwight Eisenhower and John Kennedy, and indeed to a whole nexus of entrenched Cold War assumptions. But Johnson's 1965 decision to commit U.S. power and prestige fully in an internecine war raging halfway around the world had reverberations that neither he nor anyone else anticipated. By 1968 not only the civil-rights cause and the liberal consensus, but the American social fabric itself, seemed about to unravel.

Vietnam 1963–1967: The Years of Escalation

When Lyndon Johnson took office in November 1963, some sixteen thousand U.S. military personnel were in Vietnam as advisers to the South Vietnamese army. The White House was committed to maintaining a noncommunist government in Saigon, where a coup had recently overthrown and assassinated Ngo Dinh Diem. Over the next four years, Johnson vastly expanded this investment; by the end of 1967, 485,000 U.S. troops were fighting in South Vietnam and U.S. bombers were raining death across much of North and South Vietnam. But despite billions of dollars and a mighty military effort, the U.S. goal of a stable, popularly supported anticommunist government in South Vietnam stayed maddeningly out of reach.

The American commitment to a full-scale war in Vietnam had evolved gradually, through a series of decisions reflecting strategic calculations in Washington and Hanoi, the North Vietnamese capital. In March 1964, after much debate, North Vietnam had decided to escalate its military role in South Vietnam to unify the country under the rule of Hanoi and the Vietnamese Communist party. Ho Chi Minh, General Vo Nguyen Giap, and other top leaders, having defeated the French in 1954, bitterly resented the United States' snatching national unification from their grasp. To carry out the plan, North Vietnamese soldiers quietly slipped south to join the 23,000 Vietcong (VC), the military arm of South Vietnam's communist-led National Liberation Front, already on the scene. In addition to the VC, fifty thousand local self-defense militia stood ready. Regular North Vietnamese army units moved south as well. Hanoi improved and extended the Ho Chi Minh trail, a vast network of roads and paths linking North and South Vietnam.

President Johnson, alerted to these moves by the U.S. ambassador in Saigon, Henry Cabot Lodge, fretted about becoming bogged down in the conflict. As he put it, he felt like a catfish that had swallowed "a big juicy worm with a right sharp hook in the middle of it." Another coup in Saigon in January 1964 brought to power yet another general and underscored South Vietnam's political instability.

Despite Johnson's doubts, many factors drove him to up the ante in Vietnam. Secretary of State Dean Rusk, Defense Secretary Robert McNamara, National Security Adviser McGeorge Bundy, Walt Rostow of the State Department policy planning staff, and the Joint Chiefs of Staff all warned that without a strong U.S. military response to Hanoi's moves, South Vietnam would surely fall to the communists. This collapse, they cautioned, could expand China's power in Asia, particularly because Hanoi was siding with Beijing in the worsening Sino-Soviet dispute. Moreover, it could jeopardize Japan's security. Invoking President Eisenhower's domino theory, they predicted that if South Vietnam fell, Laos, Cambodia, Malaysia, Burma, and perhaps other nations of the region would topple into the communist camp as well. Because each of these nations had a common colonial past and ample reason to welcome indigenous radicals who championed the cause of independence, the theory seemed plausible. Moreover, Indonesia's unstable ruler, Sukarno, was granting increasing influence to the Indonesian Communist party. Beijing's nuclear-weapons program, culminating in an atomic-bomb test in October 1964, deepened fears of China's future role.

Johnson's advisers further believed that abandoning South Vietnam would stir doubts among America's allies about Washington's reliability. If America allowed a communist takeover in South Vietnam, Dean Rusk asked rhetorically, how could the NATO allies trust Washington's pledge to defend West Berlin? More broadly, the situation in Vietnam appeared to fit the new Cold War paradigm that had evolved in the early 1960s. As we have seen, this new conceptual framework focused less on preparation for direct military confrontation with the Soviet Union and more on strategic calculations involving the developing nations of Asia, Latin America, and Africa. Washington planners concluded that here, under the guise of anticolonial "wars of national liberation," the Cold War would be decided—not in a single Armageddon moment but in a series of local insurgencies. These uprisings, the administration surmised, would involve guerrilla bands inspired by Marxist ideology and equipped by Moscow or Beijing. The Sino-Soviet rivalry for the allegiance of the developing world; the strategic pronouncements of Mao Zedong and other Chinese leaders, with their emphasis on encouraging local insurgencies; and the success of Fidel Castro's revolution in Cuba lent credence to this analysis. Vietnam seemed the ideal opportunity to test America's ability to compete in the new arena.

This view of the Cold War derived ultimately from George Kennan's containment doctrine, with its picture of the Soviets' endlessly probing for weak spots in which to inject their power and influence. Yet Kennan had focused on Europe and other key geopolitical regions. By the early 1960s, "containment" implied a commitment to intervene anywhere in the world that emerged as a cockpit of Cold War confrontation. In addition, Walt Rostow and others continued to portray the Cold War struggle as more than military. These strategists envisioned the use of economic aid and development programs to help Third World nations to evolve into modern, prosperous democracies that would be immune to the lure of communism. But economic development required political stability, so the suppression of guerrilla uprisings and leftist insurgencies—General Maxwell Taylor's "flexible response" capability—became the essential first step to achieving America's larger foreign-policy goals. Thus, economic development and democratic nation-building, on the one hand, and counterinsurgency efforts on the other, were complementary features of the same strategic blueprint. As General Taylor put it, "We should have learned from our frontier forebears that there is little use planting corn outside the stockade if there are still Indians around in the woods outside." Once again, Vietnam seemed the perfect laboratory to test the new strategy.

For President Johnson, the Vietnam effort and the Great Society program were two sides of the same coin. As historian Lloyd Gardner argues in *Pay Any Price: Lyndon Johnson and the Wars for Vietnam* (1995), LBJ believed that once the communist insurgency had been quelled, a New Deal style reform could be exported to Vietnam. Through a massive development program, a liberal U.S. government would transform the lives of Vietnamese peasants just as it was uplifting the poor in America's inner cities. Ultimately, Johnson paid a heavy price for this linkage: as support for the Vietnam War eroded, so did support for the Great Society.

As Johnson weighed his options in Vietnam, a dilemma arose in the Caribbean that underscored the Cold War issues at stake. In 1962, leftist Juan Bosch had won the presidency of the Dominican Republic in that island-nation's first free election since 1924, but a right-wing military coup soon overthrew him. When pro-Bosch forces rebelled against this military dictatorship in April 1965, President Johnson, fearing "another Cuba," sent in thirty-three thousand marines and army troops to squelch the uprising.* Nine thousand U.S. troops stayed as late as 1966, when a presidential candidate acceptable to the Dominican army, and to Washington, defeated Bosch in a second election. LBJ avowed, "We don't intend to sit here in our rocking chair with our hands folded and let communists set up any governments in the Western Hemisphere." The Dominican intervention suggested that similar boldness in Vietnam could produce an equally satisfactory outcome.

To compound Cold War ideology, America had long viewed Asia as its special province. After the Spanish-American War of 1898, the United States had occupied the Philippines and had ruled the islands until 1946. During World War II, thousands of GIs had given their lives battling Japanese aggression. In the early 1950s, U.S. forces had prevented a takeover of South Korea by communist-led North Korea. This long history doubtless stirred in Johnson's mind as he pondered his course in Vietnam.

Domestic political calculations also dictated a strong stand in Southeast Asia. For years the Democrats had borne the onus of having "lost China," and Johnson, like Kennedy, vowed not to become the president who "lost Vietnam." With an election looming, Johnson was determined not to appear weaker than Kennedy, who had stood tall during the Berlin and Cuban crises. In addition, memories of the 1938 Munich Conference haunted the debate; the British and French had caved in to Hitler's territorial demands in Czechoslovakia and spurred the German dictator to further expansion. Would a failure to resist "communist aggression" in Vietnam similarly whet the appetite of Moscow and Beijing?

In hindsight, the flaws in the case for escalation seem all too evident. The peasant society of Vietnam had little strategic or economic significance for the United States. The domino theory ignored the complexity of the various societies supposedly lined up ready to fall. And as Kennan himself often complained, advocates of the containment doctrine who portrayed an aggressive Soviet Union or China muscling into every nook and cranny of the globe ignored the caution that usually guided both nations' foreign policy and blurred crucial distinctions between vital and peripheral regions. Nor did the Korean or Dominican precedents suggest much about the likely outcome of intervention in Vietnam; each situation was unique. As for China, the Vietnamese historically viewed their giant neighbor with intense suspicion, making it unlikely that Beijing would turn Vietnam into a puppet state. In general, broad-brush analyses by Washington's Cold War strategists missed the nuances of specific situations. They tended to ignore, for example, the importance of nationalism for Hanoi's leaders, viewing it as a rhetorical fig leaf masking more sinister objectives orchestrated from abroad.

---

* Other member nations of the Organization of American States, pressured by Washington, supplied an additional two thousand men.

Still, the case against intervention was far less clear-cut in 1964 than it would appear a generation later. Johnson's decisions about Vietnam, in short, were not bizarre aberrations; they arose from what appeared to be legitimate strategic calculations based on a virtual consensus among foreign-policy experts, the media, and the American public in the early and mid-1960s. The wonder is not that Johnson chose escalation but that he proceeded so cautiously. Affirming America's commitment to a noncommunist South Vietnam, he initially rejected calls for a major buildup. At the end of 1964, U.S. troop strength in Vietnam stood at 23,300. Early that year, however, Johnson had approved covert military action, including air raids against North Vietnamese and Pathet Lao (Laotian communist) bases in Laos and shelling of North Vietnamese installations by South Vietnamese gunboats. Even more ominously, Johnson laid the groundwork for a full-scale war with the Gulf of Tonkin Resolution of August 1964.

On the night of August 1–2, 1964, North Vietnamese torpedo boats attacked the U.S. destroyer *Maddox* as it conducted espionage in the Gulf of Tonkin off North Vietnam. Earlier, South Vietnamese gunboats had shelled a North Vietnamese island, and Hanoi no doubt held the *Maddox* responsible for that attack as well. The *Maddox* drove off the torpedo boats and, on Johnson's orders, continued its spying mission, joined by another destroyer, the *Turner Joy.* Two nights later, tossing on stormy seas and relying on radar and sonar rather than visual sightings, the two vessels reported another torpedo attack. Follow-up messages cast doubt on the first report, and no firm evidence of an attack ever surfaced. Johnson privately conceded the ambiguity of the situation ("For all I know the Navy was shooting at whales"), but he used the incident to request from Congress blanket authorization to respond as he chose to any future aggression. As National Security Adviser Mc-George Bundy later commented, such incidents were like streetcars: if you missed one in the search for a pretext for a policy change, another would soon come along.

The Gulf of Tonkin Resolution, which passed the House unanimously after a half-hour's discussion, stated:

> Congress . . . supports the determination of the President . . . to take all necessary measures to repel any armed attack against the armed forces of the United States and to prevent further aggression. . . . The United States is, therefore, prepared, as the President determines, to take all necessary steps, including the use of armed force, to assist any member or protocol state of the Southeast Asia Collective Defense treaty requesting assistance in defense of its freedom.

The Senate passed the measure 88–2, with only Wayne Morse of Oregon and Alaska's Ernest Gruening in dissent. Later opponents of the war, George McGovern of South Dakota and Gaylord Nelson of Wisconsin, harbored doubts but voted for the resolution nevertheless. The more typical response was that of Senator Richard Russell of Georgia, who proclaimed, "Our national honor is at stake. We cannot and will not shrink from defending it." In public-opinion polls, Johnson's approval ratings jumped 30 points, to 72 percent.

Johnson opted for a resolution of this sort rather than a formal declaration of hostilities, which he feared might draw the Soviet Union or China directly into the conflict. Furthermore, as McGeorge Bundy advised him, a declaration of war would have "heavy domestic overtones." Adopting the useful fiction that South Vietnam was an independent nation, Bundy portrayed the planned action as simply an effort to help an ally defend itself against a domestic insurgency.

The Gulf of Tonkin Resolution, together with later appropriations to pay for the conflict, provided the legislative foundation for the Vietnam War. The resolution, as Lyndon Johnson observed, was "like Grandma's nightshirt, it covers everything." When he requested this authorization, Johnson concealed the operations already under way and the detailed war plans waiting in the Pentagon. In the 1964 election campaign, Johnson had reassured voters made uneasy by Barry Goldwater's bellicose rhetoric. "We seek no wider war," LBJ promised. "We don't want our American boys to do the fighting for Asian boys."

In 1965, however, the political instability in Saigon, combined with North Vietnam's military campaign in the south, precipitated a series of decisions that moved the United States from a limited commitment to all-out war. In August 1964, Nguyen Khanh, South Vietnam's military ruler, had assumed near-dictatorial powers, sparking protests among Buddhists and other dissident groups. In February 1965, as protests flared in the streets of Saigon, Khanh fled the country. "I'm sick and tired of this coup shit," exploded Johnson.

Johnson's advisers had been advocating an air war against North Vietnam; with the Saigon government unraveling, their exhortations grew more urgent. General Maxwell Taylor, the new ambassador to South Vietnam, cautioned, "To take no positive action now is to accept defeat in the fairly near future." On February 24, LBJ approved Operation Rolling Thunder, a large-scale bombing campaign drafted by the Joint Chiefs of Staff. Soon U.S. bombers were conducting more than three thousand raids monthly north of the 17th parallel, the dividing line between the two Vietnams. To justify this move, Johnson cited recent Vietcong attacks on U.S. military installations, including one at Pleiku in Vietnam's central highlands that had killed nine Americans. Johnson again concealed from Congress and the public the larger plan underlying his action. Instead, he presented his decision as merely a specific response to a particular incident. Thus, by "indirection and dissimulation," with no opportunity for full-scale debate, as historian George Herring has written, the nation edged closer to open war.

What was Johnson's objective as he took these fateful steps? What would have constituted "victory" in Vietnam? The goal was not North Vietnam's surrender or even the overthrow of the Hanoi government. Instead, the United States strove to inflict enough damage through bombing (and later to kill enough Vietcong and North Vietnamese troops) to prevent Hanoi from unifying all Vietnam under the communist banner. Sufficiently heavy attrition, U.S. war planners believed, would compel Hanoi to accept America's war aim: an independent, noncommunist government in the south. This agenda rested on three assumptions: first, that a large show of force would persuade Hanoi to give up the struggle; second, that a government could be established in Saigon capable of leading a viable noncommunist state; and third, that the American people would support the war long enough for the first two goals to be achieved. None of these premises proved sound.

One step up the escalation ladder led to the next. With the launching of the bombing campaign, General William C. Westmoreland, the U.S. military commander in Vietnam, requested U.S. combat forces to defend the airbase at Danang from VC attack. In early March 1965, in a replay of legendary World War II Pacific island invasions, thirty-five hundred U.S. marines sloshed ashore near the base. Greeting them were bouquet-bearing young Vietnamese women and a banner proclaiming, "Welcome to the Gallant Marines." By moving from an advisory to a ground-combat role, the United States had crossed another critical threshold.

The numbers (and the casualties) rose steadily over the next three years. Upping the ante at a strategy session in Honolulu in April, General Taylor and the Joint Chiefs asked that about forty thousand U.S. soldiers be assigned to Vietnam. The initial plan, to concentrate the troops around key U.S. installations, soon gave way to a more aggressive mission. In May, Congress approved Johnson's request for $700 million to pay for the expanded war.

As the commitment of troops and dollars grew, the revolving door in Saigon whirled on. In June, a cabal of junior officers staged yet another coup. Air Vice Marshal Nguyen Cao Ky became premier. A French-trained pilot with a rakish mustache and a glamorous wife, Ky sported gold-rimmed sunglasses, black jumpsuits, and modish silk scarves. Once more, further escalation seemed the answer to political chaos. Westmoreland and the Joint Chiefs requested another 150,000 troops. Only a major enlargement of the war, McNamara claimed, could achieve America's goals in Vietnam. Walt Rostow, now very influential in Johnson's inner circle, enthusiastically supported the buildup. The president received the same advice from the "Wise Men," an informal group of senior counselors led by Dean Acheson.

Bucked up by this near unanimity, Johnson in mid-July 1965 ordered a vast expansion in both the air and ground war. In the initial phase of Operation Rolling Thunder, Johnson had sharply limited the choice of targets. "They can't even bomb an outhouse without my approval," he had boasted. Now he authorized expanded bombing in North Vietnam and the bombing of suspected enemy concentrations in South Vietnam as well. Monthly B-52 sorties soon increased to nearly five thousand. Johnson also approved sending fifty thousand more GIs to South Vietnam immediately, with an additional fifty thousand to follow. Equally important, the president authorized a basic change in strategy. The combat troops sent earlier had served defensive duty, protecting the Danang airbase and other U.S. installations. This was a variant of the enclave strategy advocated by James Gavin, a retired U.S. army general who urged that the United States defend only Saigon and other major South Vietnam cities, not the whole country. Americans, he reasoned, would support a defensive mission with minimal casualties almost indefinitely—certainly long enough to force North Vietnam to the negotiating table.

But Westmoreland and the Joint Chiefs resisted Gavin's strategy. "No one ever won a battle sitting on his ass," jeered General Earle Wheeler, chairman of the Joint Chiefs. Under intense pressure, Johnson agreed to a more aggressive plan. After July 1965, the U.S. combat role in Vietnam shifted from defense to a search-and-destroy mission aimed at seeking out and killing the maximum number of Vietcong and North Vietnamese forces. Alone in the administration, Undersecretary of State George Ball continued to object. Ball warned Johnson, as he had Kennedy, of "an open-ended commitment of U.S. forces, mounting U.S. casualties, [and] no assurance of a satisfactory solution." "Once on the tiger's back," he added, "we cannot be sure of picking the place to dismount."

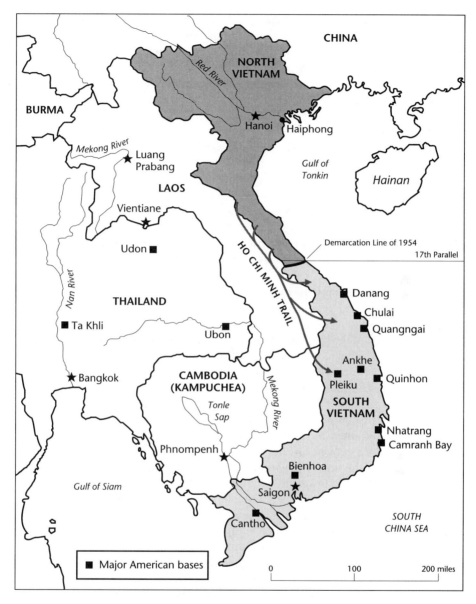

FIGURE 10.1
The Vietnam War to 1968

In his July 1965 decisions, Johnson chose options somewhat short of what his generals recommended. He confined the bombing to the southern part of North Vietnam, and he granted Westmoreland 100,000 more troops rather than the requested 150,000. Nevertheless, even this represented a massive escalation. By the end of 1965, 184,000 U.S. troops had amassed in South Vietnam. U.S. combat deaths had edged above six hundred, and the shift to a search-and-destroy strategy made heavier future losses inevitable. July 1965 was thus the pivotal point toward full-scale war. Yet Johnson, desperate to avoid controversy that would jeopardize his Great Society programs, once more hid the full magnitude of the escalation.

In 1966 and 1967, the air and ground war grew exponentially. Washington planners especially favored air strikes, for here the Americans dominated overwhelmingly and suffered relatively light losses. Sorties against North Vietnam increased to more than a hundred thousand in 1967,* and the target range moved steadily north to include factories and oil tanks on the very outskirts of Hanoi and the port city of Haiphong. The civilian toll was heavy. All told, U.S. bombs killed an estimated one hundred thousand North Vietnamese civilians.

Nevertheless, General Westmoreland in an August 1966 report to President Johnson, saw "no indication that the resolve of the leadership in Hanoi has been reduced." A 1966 study ordered by Defense Secretary McNamara confirmed that the air war was having scant impact on either Hanoi or the guerrilla insurgency in the south. As a prominent Hanoi physician told journalist Stanley Karnow after the war, "There was an extraordinary fervor then. . . . [T]he bombs heightened rather than dampened our spirits."

The North Vietnamese moved factories underground, built a network of tunnels and shelters, and rebuilt roads and bridges with lightning speed. By 1967 some six thousand tons of supplies arriving daily from China and the Soviet Union diluted the effects of the bombing. Soviet aid increased sharply when Khrushchev's successor, Leonid Brezhnev, launched a drive to win Hanoi's allegiance.

The bombing campaign exacted a high price. From 1965 to 1968, North Vietnam's air defenses shot down nearly a thousand U.S. aircraft, valued at some $6 billion. Nearly six hundred captured pilots would serve the North Vietnamese as bargaining chips when peace talks began. The ground war in South Vietnam, too, grew in scope and intensity. A major battle in Ia Drang Valley in Pleiku Province in November 1965 proved a watershed. The battle pitted a battalion of the U.S. Seventh Cavalry (the unit commanded by General Custer at the disastrous Battle of Little Big Horn in 1876) against a much larger North Vietnamese force. The battle left 230 American soldiers dead and 240 wounded. But the North Vietnamese toll of three thousand dead implied a favorable "kill ratio," confirming Westmoreland's judgment that a war of attrition eventually would break Hanoi's will.†

Westmoreland requested ever more troops, and through 1966 Johnson complied. In June of that year, the president authorized 431,000 U.S. troops in Vietnam by the following summer. Nevertheless, the ground war continued to fare badly. Most search-and-destroy patrols proved futile. Operation Cedar Falls, a major search-and-destroy mission early in 1967 that sent thirty-five thousand troops to the so-called Iron Triangle region north of Saigon, illustrates the pattern. The soldiers destroyed entire villages identified as VC hideouts. In Ben Suc, U.S. military forcibly

---

* The bombing was not constant throughout the year. It declined during Vietnam's rainy season (September to May) when visibility was poor, and it increased in other months.

† The story of the battle of Ia Drang, *We Were Soldiers Once . . . and Young* (1992), by Harold G. Moore, a battalion commander, and Joseph L. Galloway, a journalist who was present, powerfully conveys the reality of the Vietnam combat experience.

Quang Ngai Province, 1967. *Having evacuated the inhabitants, a U.S. Army team nicknamed the "Zippo squad" (after a brand of cigarette lighter) burned down this village to deny its use by the Vietcong. Here a GI rests following the operation.* (© Philip J. Griffith/ Magnum Photos, Inc.*)*

removed people to a refugee camp and flattened their village with earth-moving equipment. (During a similar operation in 1968 involving the Mekong Delta community of Ben Tre, a U.S. officer memorably commented, "It became necessary to destroy the town in order to save it.") But most enemy troops in the area simply withdrew into nearby Cambodia and returned when the operation was over.

The ground war in South Vietnam was augmented from the air, with bombers pouring explosives on suspected enemy centers. In free-fire zones covering most of South Vietnam, B-52s could bomb at will. Ironically, South Vietnam, America's ally, absorbed more than double the bomb tonnage dropped on North Vietnam, at a fearful cost in civilian lives. Gunships, including converted C-47 transport planes, rained deadly fire on VC forces. Helicopters of the First Air Cavalry Division deployed troops and evacuated the wounded. The use of napalm added to the toll. This gluelike flaming explosive, made of jellied petroleum and phosphorus, adheres to whatever it touches, including human skin. Over the course of the war, U.S. bombers dropped an estimated 400 million pounds of napalm.

An array of technological aids backed the ground war. IBM computers in Saigon identified likely points of VC attack. Infrared viewing devices pinpointed enemy hideouts. On Secretary of Defense McNamara's orders, the marines bulldozed and wired a twenty-five-mile-wide strip between North and South Vietnam to create an electronic barrier against infiltration. In Operation Ranchhand, the United States sprayed millions of gallons of herbicides and chemical defoliants such as Agent Orange over South Vietnam to deny the enemy concealment in the jungle. "Only you can prevent forests," sardonically joked the men who handled the stuff. Johnson's policies brought environmental disaster to Vietnam while his wife preached beautification at home. The North Vietnamese commander General Giap ridiculed the U.S. reliance on technology and statistical measures of success. The Americans "question the computers . . . and then go into action," he jeered. "But arithmetical strategy doesn't work . . . [w]hen a whole people rises up."

While strategists pored over their computer printouts in Washington and Saigon, the ground war itself unfolded in the jungles, river deltas, and highlands of South Vietnam, with Vietnamese and American forces both paying a tremendous price. For American soldiers in the field, nicknamed "grunts," a year-long tour of duty brought fatigue, psychological trauma, and the ever-present danger of death or severe injury from a sniper or land mine. The contrast between conditions in the field and the amenities of major bases like Danang added a surreal dimension to the war. These centers boasted bowling alleys, movie theaters, and PXs loaded with reminders of home: the latest magazines, soft drinks, hamburgers, beer, and ice cream. Yet familiar treats offered only fleeting escape from the war's realities. Plucked from city streets, farms, and small towns, often possessing only a high-school education and little experience of the world, these young men found themselves trapped in an utterly alien environment. They confronted a foe familiar with the land and its people and trained in guerrilla combat. Set-piece battles were few. Days of boredom might explode in murderous fire from an unseen sniper during a reconnaissance mission or in a stealthy VC attack on a base camp.

For the thousands of women who served in Vietnam, the war brought its own special traumas. As many as forty thousand worked for private organizations such as the Red Cross. Some eleven thousand came to Vietnam as army nurses or in other noncombatant positions with the U.S. military. One army nurse recalled, "Our job was to look [wounded soldiers] in the eye and convince them that everything was all right. . . . [Y]ou finally built up a facade and could literally look at somebody dying and smile like Miss America or whatever we personified to them." Historian Marilyn Young has perceptively observed, "The war gave many women responsibilities and a sense of power usually denied them in civilian life. But this new status too was confusing and even distressing in that there was no way to extricate it from the death and dehumanization that were its occasion."*

Ultimately, remembered moments rather than mind-numbing statistics best convey the reality of Vietnam for those caught in its coils. Recounting the confusion of battle at Ia Drang in November 1965, one journalist recalled a seventeen-year-old's brush with death: "In the middle of all that, a kid wearing a white T-shirt stumbled out of the trees. . . . We all started yelling and waving to him to go back. . . . When he turned around we could see his back was shredded, the red blood startling against the white shirt." This youth survived, at least on that day; thousands perished. Another veteran remembered a single death among many. On a search-and-destroy patrol, a shot rang out of the jungle, hitting one of the men:

> The man . . . was writhing on the ground, his back arching up. He was gasping, hoarse, dragging air into his lungs. There was a perfect round hole about the size of a pencil, right in the middle of his sternum.
>
> Then he stopped moving. . . . I looked at him—blond, All-American, crewcut with these pale ice-blue eyes. I stood up and looked back into those eyes. Those eyes looked right through me, right through my skull and out the back of my head. I turned around and looked at the sky in the direction that his eyes were looking to see what he was staring at. I thought I was going to see something.
>
> It ran through my mind for a moment, "Did his mother feel something, did his father feel something, did anybody? Was she reaching for a can of peas in the supermarket and feel a tug or a jolt and not know what it was? Does anybody close to him know that he just died?"

---

* In 1993 a statue honoring the army nurses of Vietnam was erected near the Vietnam Veterans Memorial in Washington, D.C.

Many soldiers bitterly resented risking their lives in a conflict whose purpose seemed obscure and that was stirring fierce dissent at home. One veteran angrily rejected the claim that the war could have been won if only Washington and the American people had supported it long enough. "The bureaucrats didn't push us into a winnable war and then tie our hands," he charged. "What they did was actually far worse. They put us into a war that was as unwinnable as it was immoral. They put us into a war that even they could not explain, and so, young men died for old men's pride."

Although marked by moments of courage and heroism, the war also exacted a high price morally. In a struggle that blurred distinctions between friend and foe, some GIs came to despise all Vietnamese as "gooks." Napalmed bodies became "crispy critters." Ally and enemy looked identical, and soldiers struggled to distinguish them. Some broke under the pressure. One recalled an incident in which a few GIs, after twenty days in a free-fire zone, stopped a Vietnamese man and his daughter riding a motorbike. After ripping up the man's identification papers so that he could be classified as Vietcong, they killed him and raped his daughter "like an animal pack," then shot and mutilated her. Recounting this incident in graphic detail, the veteran continued:

> I got back to the World [the United States], but it wasn't the World that I had left. . . . I did not fit into the real world any more. . . . When my mom came to see me, she was a different person. . . . I couldn't communicate with her. I just looked at her. . . . I would just sit in the room in the hospital and my mind would flash back. I would have dreams about the Nam and action. I could see myself fighting, when I'm actually sitting in a VA hospital on the bed. I could see myself back in the Nam.

Of course, atrocities occurred on both sides. The VC and NLF forces killed wounded enemy troops, assassinated civilians who worked for the Saigon government, devised ambushes that killed and maimed patrolling GIs, and held prisoners under terrible conditions. (After the war, American suspicions that the North Vietnamese had taken far more GI prisoners than they officially acknowledged would roil American politics for decades and disrupt efforts to normalize relations with Vietnam.) Furthermore, North Vietnam's communist rulers proved ready to sacrifice hundreds of thousands of lives to achieve their goals. Nevertheless, the atrocities by U.S. forces, some of which gradually filtered out, received the heaviest attention from the American media, shaping home-front perceptions of the war.

The bombing raids and search-and-destroy missions only forestalled the collapse of the Saigon regime, at enormous cost. The U.S. death toll reached 16,500 by the end of 1967—with almost 10,000 killed in that year alone. The monetary cost hit $21 billion in 1967. The Vietnamese paid the highest price in death, suffering, and disruption. From 1961 on, 451,000 South Vietnamese civilians died as a result of the war, with more than twice that number wounded. Some 6.5 million were uprooted from their homes and turned into refugees. U.S. officials sometimes portrayed the massive disruption of the civilian population as a strategic plus. As General Westmoreland responded when a reporter asked him about the refugee problem, "It does deprive the enemy of the population, doesn't it."

Despite the U.S. effort, the war failed in its central purpose: to force Hanoi to accept an independent, noncommunist South Vietnam. Ho Chi Minh matched the

U.S. escalation step by step. Regardless of ghastly attrition rates, fresh waves of North Vietnamese troops arrived in the field as a younger generation came of age. By mid-1966, Hanoi could count on a force of more than 430,000 in South Vietnam, including North Vietnam regulars, VC, and local militia. When casualties reached prohibitive levels, the troops lay low awaiting reinforcements or regrouped in the North. Some withdrew to jungle bases in nearby Laos and Cambodia. Hanoi counted on outlasting the invaders, confident that America's tolerance for the bloodletting would eventually wear thin. As U.S. casualties mounted, predicted the astute General Giap, "their mothers will want to know why. The war will not long survive their questions."

The United States also launched a pacification and nation-building program in South Vietnam designed to insulate the population from Vietcong influence and to build loyalty to the Saigon regime. Toward this end, Americans built schools and clinics in "pacified" areas. Saigon's New Life Hamlet Program, which replaced the Strategic Hamlet program described earlier, moved villagers to new settlements in regions supposedly under Saigon's control. (When this program grew unpopular, a variant was introduced called *Ap Doi Moi,* or *"Really* New Life Hamlet Program.") A related effort, the Revolutionary Development Program, sent teams of South Vietnamese experts into villages for community building. But peasants conditioned to distrust officials remained leery of these emissaries from Saigon, and the

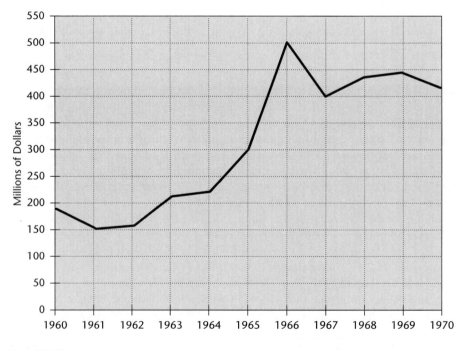

FIGURE 10.2

U.S. Government Grants and Credits to South Vietnam, 1960–1970

SOURCE: *Historical Statistics of the United States, Colonial Times to 1970* (1975).

VC or the North Vietnamese often assassinated the village leaders of the most successful efforts.

Westmoreland's office gave priority to its military operations over the political goals of pacification and nation building, and the two programs bore little relation to each other. In May 1967, to resolve tensions between the military command and the pacification effort, Johnson placed the latter under Westmoreland's direct authority and chose an eager young National Security Council staffer to head it. Devising a computerized Hamlet Evaluation Survey, this official soon reported proudly that 67 percent of South Vietnam's peasants supported the Saigon government. This statistical precision roused suspicions, particularly because Westmoreland's predecessor, a commander notorious for his unflagging optimism, had reported precisely the same percentage in 1963. In fact, the military effort directly undermined the political goals. The continual bombing and search-and-destroy missions that shredded the fabric of life in this peasant society eroded any hope of creating a viable nation on the U.S. model. Every bombing raid over South Vietnam was a propaganda gift to the Vietcong, allowing them to portray America as the outside aggressor that was devastating Vietnam. One American official later bleakly observed, "It was as if we were trying to build a house with a bulldozer and wrecking crane."

Some historians argue that by the early 1970s the pacification program was slowly achieving its goals. But by that time home-front support for the war was rapidly evaporating, and in any event the successes rested upon a local infrastructure wholly dependent on the U.S. military presence and on U.S. aid.

As Americans commandeered the war, they pushed the South Vietnamese aside and lost any prospect of a Vietnamese solution of the dispute. South Vietnam's forces stood at 800,000 by 1967 but high desertion rates eroded the units' combat effectiveness. The American presence also unleashed runaway inflation in South Vietnam, and the devastation in rural areas drove throngs of refugees into crowded urban shantytowns. Once-lovely Saigon became a teeming warren of bars, brothels, and black markets crowded with GIs. Even in remote villages, shacks made entirely of flattened beer cans cropped up—symbols of the American impact on Vietnamese society.

Saigon politics remained as muddled as ever. Prime Minister Ky was lavishly feted by President Johnson at a meeting in Honolulu early in 1966, but his graft-ridden regime exercised little real power and never won the trust of most South Vietnamese. In March 1966, Buddhists in Hué and Danang demonstrated against the Ky regime, prompting U.S. officials to pressure Ky to modify his authoritarian rule. With much fanfare, the government adopted a constitution, complete with bill of rights. Distrusting the impulsive Ky, U.S. officials shifted their support to his more stable sidekick, General Nguyen Van Thieu. In a September 1967 election marked by irregularities worthy of LBJ's 1948 Senate campaign, Thieu won a weak plurality of the votes (35 percent) and became president. Ky settled for the vice-presidency, but intrigue and turmoil persisted.

The U.S. military command, meanwhile, remained firmly upbeat. Inflated enemy body counts ("If it's dead and Vietnamese, it's VC," was the rule in the field) ballooned still further as they rose through the chain of command. The flow of heartening but fanciful statistics not only lulled the U.S. public and official

Washington but locked the military commanders themselves onto a doomed course. Military historians harshly criticize Westmoreland's obsession with quantitative yardsticks of kill ratios achieved, sorties run, tonnage dropped, acres defoliated, and villages pacified. As they see it, the preoccupation with statistics masked a failure of strategic vision and an appalling blindness to the war's social and political context. In Washington, the Joint Chiefs mostly parroted Westmoreland's version of the war and rubber-stamped his calls for more troops. Up and down the chain of command, the military had a huge psychological and institutional investment in presenting the war in a favorable light.

But all the while, journalists were filing stories and capturing scenes on film that belied the optimistic official briefings. As early as 1965, a reporter coined the term *credibility gap* to describe the growing distrust of the government's version of the war. As relations between the military and the press soured, some officers accused reporters of disloyalty. Acid rivulets of doubt began to corrode the bright facade of official optimism.

Gnawing Doubts at High Levels

The war persisted and so did Johnson's fundamental problems. The Saigon regime showed little long-term viability; nation building in South Vietnam had made meager progress. Hanoi, despite punishing losses, pursued its efforts to drive out the Americans and unite Vietnam. No one knew how long the American people would stand behind the war effort. To shore up support, LBJ initiated several "peace offensives." As early as April 1965, he offered Hanoi a regional development program for the Mekong River delta bigger than Franklin Roosevelt's TVA. A brief bombing halt accompanied this carrot, but to no avail. On Christmas Eve 1965, Johnson once more stopped bombing, largely for public-relations purposes. As Dean Rusk cabled Ambassador Lodge in Saigon, in order to build support for the major escalation of the war planned for 1966, it was necessary to convince the public that "we have explored fully every alternative but that the aggressor has left us no choice." On January 31, 1966, Johnson resumed the air strikes.

Outsiders periodically attempted to mediate. In June 1966, professing to have positive signals from Hanoi, a Polish diplomat launched a peace initiative. This effort collapsed, however, in part because Johnson refused even a temporary bombing halt. Indeed, in December, as low-level talks were about to begin in Warsaw, U.S. B-52s raided rail facilities on the edge of downtown Hanoi. Early in 1967, British prime minister Harold Wilson and Soviet leader Alexei Kosygin floated a British-Soviet initiative to bring the two sides to the negotiating table. This attempt failed as well, much to Wilson's annoyance.

As 1967 opened, General Westmoreland, as usual, reported progress on all fronts. Yet in March, he and the Joint Chiefs called for another big escalation: 200,000 more troops, mobilization of the reserves, expansion of the war to VC staging areas in Cambodia and Laos, heavier bombing in the North, and mining of the ports through which supplies reached North Vietnam. Hard-liners in Congress ("hawks" in the lingo of the day) such as senators John Stennis of Mississippi and Henry Jackson of Washington supported the call for escalation. A top aide to

Westmoreland, General William Depuy, summed up the hard-line view: "The solution in Vietnam is more bombs, more shells, more napalm . . . till the other side cracks and gives up."

The appearance of military unanimity is misleading, however. As Robert Buzzanco shows in *Masters of War: Military Dissent and Politics in the Vietnam Era* (1996), Pentagon analysts had long expressed doubts about U.S. military involvement in Southeast Asia. Air force strategists could show convincingly the futility of a ground war in Vietnam; army analysts could demonstrate clearly that air power could not prevail against a guerrilla foe. But President Johnson did not encourage a diversity of opinion, and the hierarchical nature of military decisionmaking tended to keep such differences out of public view.

The steady escalation of the military's demands finally set off warning bells in the White House. "When we add divisions, can't the enemy add divisions?" Johnson queried Westmoreland. "And, if so, where does it all end?" Key Johnson advisers harbored suspicions that the military had lost sight of political reality in Vietnam and at home. George Ball, who had left the government, stepped up his criticism. President Johnson's press secretary, Bill Moyers, voiced skepticism and departed. Even Secretary of Defense Robert McNamara, so closely identified with the Vietnam escalation that antiwar activists derided "McNamara's War" and jeered his rare public appearances, was growing disillusioned. His analytic and quantitative techniques, including the 1966 study showing the air war's negligible effects, offered little evidence that the U.S. strategy was paying off. In October 1966, on a fact-finding trip to Vietnam, McNamara told Johnson that he saw "no reasonable way to bring the war to an end soon." Furthermore, he had moral qualms about the devastation that mighty America was wreaking on a small Asian country. In a May 1967 memo to Johnson, McNamara reflected, "The picture of the world's greatest superpower killing or seriously injuring 1,000 non-combatants a week, while trying to pound a tiny, backward nation into submission on an issue whose merits are hotly disputed, is not a pretty one."

McNamara's doubts came amid growing opposition to the war on college campuses and among a vocal minority of legislators, religious leaders, and editors. Picketers targeted campus Reserve Officer Training Corps (ROTC) programs and recruiters for the Dow Chemical Company, the maker of napalm. The Spring Mobilization Committee, a coalition of peace and civil-rights groups, announced a New York City march for April 15, 1967. The event attracted from 125,000 to 400,000 demonstrators. (Crowd estimates for 1960s antiwar rallies vary wildly, depending on who was doing the estimating.) A San Francisco rally on the same day drew thousands more. Fighting back, the administration launched an illegal CIA domestic surveillance operation, code-named CHAOS, that compiled dossiers on antiwar organizations and leaders.

As 1967 dragged on, McNamara pressed for a scaling back of the war. To this end, he argued for a bombing halt or cutback, a cap on force levels in Vietnam, and a shift from search-and-destroy missions to protection of South Vietnam's major cities—General Gavin's enclave plan. McNamara also hinted that the United States might modify its rigid opposition to any National Liberation Front role in governing South Vietnam. In August, the defense secretary told the Senate Armed Services Committee, "Enemy operations in the south cannot, on the basis of any report I have seen, be stopped by air bombardment—short, that is, of the virtual annihilation of North Vietnam and its people." In November, McNamara resigned. LBJ, personalizing the issue, convinced himself that McNamara's increasingly public doubts represented a political double-cross engineered by Robert Kennedy.

Full of self-pity, an exhausted Johnson pored over the dispatches and casualty reports. Endless White House meetings probed for a course that might hold promise. A bleary-eyed LBJ haunted the White House Situation Room at night, selecting targets for the next day's bombing raids. George Ball's 1964 warnings about the difficulties of dismounting the tiger now seemed prophetic. With McNamara's departure, the wagons circled tighter. Dean Rusk and Walt Rostow, who had become national security adviser in 1966, still supported the war. So did McGeorge Bundy, now in private life, although he harbored reservations.

While Johnson rejected McNamara's plan to scale back, he also found the military's call for further escalation dismaying. "Bomb, bomb, bomb, that's all they know," he complained of his generals. Another major buildup, the president feared, would require a tax increase that could tilt wavering U.S. public opinion decisively against the conflict. On the other hand, withdrawal might outrage the hawks and trigger the dreaded accusation that he had "lost" Vietnam.

On November 1, Johnson reconvened the "Wise Men." Far gloomier than in 1965, they saw no alternative but to stay the course, yet they warned LBJ of the political costs of escalation: The prolonged stalemate was eroding domestic support for the war, a fact obvious to anyone who watched television or read newspapers. Appalled by this formula for more war and killing, George Ball exploded at the panel of aging statesmen and bankers, "You're like a flock of buzzards sitting on a fence, sending the young men off to be killed. You ought to be ashamed of yourselves."

Congressional opposition mounted as well. Senator J. William Fulbright of Arkansas, chair of the Senate Foreign Relations Committee, emerged as a powerful critic. As early as February 1966, Fulbright's committee held special hearings on the war. Dean Rusk and other administration leaders were grilled sharply, and James Gavin, George Kennan, and others criticized the war's underlying strategic assumptions. The hearings helped crystallize antiwar sentiment.

Although Johnson turned down the military's call for 200,000 more troops and an expanded air and sea war, he approved 55,000 additional men and allowed the high rate of bombing to continue. As in 1965, Johnson again presented his decision as a middle way between two extremes. In fact, it translated into further substantial escalation. The United States had undertaken the 1965 escalation in the confident hope of forcing Hanoi to yield. The 1967 escalation was the desperate action of a drained president and a defensive administration aware of their failure to achieve the war's goals but fearful of the backlash that open admission of failure would trigger. The very fact of the war itself had become the major rationale for slogging on.

Johnson mounted a propaganda offensive to flog waning home-front support. Under a White House mandate to report good news, the flow of impressive body counts continued. In April 1967 Johnson brought General Westmoreland home to address a joint session of Congress. Standing stiffly at attention, the six-foot South

Carolinian looked every inch the general as he smartly saluted the cheering legislators. But since the administration defined Vietnam as a limited intervention to help a friendly government put down a guerilla insurgency, LBJ was never able to mobilize the nation for full-scale war, as President Roosevelt had during World War II.

Further, behind the facade of unanimity, the tense debate in the White House persisted. Even McGeorge Bundy, now one of the "Wise Men," advised LBJ that his generals' grasp on reality had slipped and that Johnson must find a way to quell rising domestic opposition. Geopolitical shifts in Asia underscored the need for a policy reassessment. In 1966 President Sukarno and the Indonesia Communist party had fallen from power in an army coup, rendering the more extreme forms of the domino theory less plausible. That same year, China turned inward in a drive for Marxist ideological purification known as the Great Cultural Revolution, and its already peripheral involvement with the Vietnam conflict dwindled.

"The Wound That Bleedeth Inward . . ."

Growing home-front opposition, fed by journalistic coverage from Vietnam that was becoming more skeptical, vastly complicated the president's efforts to sustain a consensus behind the war. The Vietnam struggle did not create the New Left or the counterculture—both had got well under way earlier—but after 1965, the conflict functioned as the white-hot focus of campus unrest and radical organizing. The discontents that had been building in American society now centered on a single issue, the Vietnam War.

SDS and the Black Power ideologues already had challenged the established order in the early 1960s. As the administration plunged the nation into full-scale war in Vietnam, the crisis of legitimacy deepened. To the war's opponents, the government became at first the object of suspicion, then of ridicule, and finally of scorn and hatred. For some on the radical fringe, America's political enemies became heroes, as the idealism and reformist mood of these years turned to bitter alienation.

The antiwar movement—or simply "the movement"—began in March 1965 with a "teach-in" at the University of Michigan after Johnson announced the bombing war against North Vietnam. Adapting the term from the civil-rights sit-ins, the organizers conducted an all-night round of lectures and discussions about the war. Within days, teach-ins cropped up at the University of Wisconsin, Harvard, and other schools. In April, SDS organized the first large demonstration against the war: a march on Washington that drew twenty thousand protesters. That spring and fall, local committees and groups from Berkeley to New York City initiated antiwar actions and marches. In January 1966, Johnson ended automatic draft deferments for college students, intensifying campus antiwar activity. From a small cadre of radical activists, SDS grew to a loosely knit national organization. Local chapters initiated protest actions, with the national office exerting minimal supervision. Indeed, the movement soon expanded beyond the control of any single organization.

For all its intensity, the movement initially had a comparatively narrow base. Its early leaders were often alumni of the test-ban and civil-rights movements, and

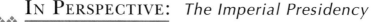

❖❖   IN PERSPECTIVE: *The Imperial Presidency*

The reaction against LBJ for waging war in Vietnam without explicit congressional approval—a reaction that culminated in the punitive War Powers Act of 1973—represented a particularly bitter phase in a debate that dates back to the founding of the nation. The framers of the Constitution, having repudiated the imperial claims of George III, feared that the presidency would evolve into a quasimonarchical institution. They surrounded the office with many constraints, balancing the president's prerogatives by giving at least equal authority to the legislative branch, especially the power of the purse. In principle, no president can spend a penny that has not been appropriated by the people's representatives in Congress.

Although the Whigs of the 1830s professed to find monarchical tendencies in "King Andrew" Jackson, the presidency remained weak through most of the nineteenth century. (The major exception was Abraham Lincoln's exercise of sweeping powers during the Civil War.) Theodore Roosevelt (1901–9) and Woodrow Wilson (1913–21) significantly enlarged the office. Roosevelt pursued an activist approach in conservation, business regulation, and foreign affairs ("I took Panama," he later boasted after wresting from Colombia the land on which the Panama Canal was built.) The Wilson administration assumed broad economic and censorship powers during the war years of 1917–18. Warren G. Harding and Calvin Coolidge in the 1920s, guided by their probusiness laissez-faire ideology, reverted to an earlier, narrower presidential role. Ironically, however, it was Coolidge who produced one of the more flowery characterizations of the presidency. The office, he mused, "does not yield to definition. Like the glory of the morning sunrise, it can only be experienced, it cannot be told."

With Franklin D. Roosevelt, the modern presidency took shape. Battling the Depression, FDR proliferated agencies, built a deeply loyal personal following, and expanded the presidential office. Since his administration, presidents have been expected to set the national agenda and to introduce congressional programs that shape public discourse. Yet Roosevelt also stirred the old fears of a presidency slipping into dictatorship. When he tried to enlarge the Supreme Court in 1937 to give it a more liberal coloration, albeit by constitutional means, Congress slapped him down. Roosevelt broke tradition by seeking, and winning, a third term in 1940 and a fourth in 1944, but Congress retaliated posthumously with the Twenty-second Amendment (ratified in 1951), which limits presidents to two terms.

most came from liberal, politically attuned families. In some cases, as we have seen, their parents had been socialists or communists in the 1930s. Antiwar leaders at the elite private or public institutions tended to be the liberal arts majors. Generally from affluent backgrounds, they saw the college years as a time to explore ideas rather than to train for a vocation; protest proved a natural extension of this focus. Fewer activists came from the sciences, engineering, or the professional

The postwar presidency continued to grow in size and influence. In 1973 historian Arthur Schlesinger, Jr., published a cautionary study, *The Imperial Presidency.* (Schlesinger had earlier written admiring studies of two presidents—Andrew Jackson and Franklin Roosevelt—who had contributed to the expansionary process, and he had served as a speechwriter for a third, John F. Kennedy.) Richard Nixon's gross abuses of the office, culminating in his forced resignation, produced a temporary reaction against strong chief executives. Yet despite periodic shifts in the balance of power, the general trend toward a stronger presidency continued under Republicans and Democrats alike. Ronald Reagan repeatedly insisted on the need to trim the federal government, and the presidency in particular, yet during his two terms, total civilian employment in the executive branch increased from 2.8 million to 3 million. Moreover, for all Reagan's railings against government power, the Iran-contra affair, one of the more flagrant abuses of executive power in American history, unfolded during his watch.

Students of the presidency such as historian Henry F. Graff attribute its growth in the modern era not to individual ambition but rather to trends largely beyond control. The end of World War II left the United States as the world's collossus, and the advent of the Cold War gave the president the grandiose title "leader of the Free World." The president literally took on the power to launch a world-destroying holocaust. Simultaneously, as social problems grew more complex and more national in scope, the programs, administrative tasks, and regulatory functions assigned to the executive branch expanded exponentially. Television contributed to the "imperial presidency" as well, turning the occupant of the White House into a media celebrity and granting him instant access to millions worldwide.

As the Cold War waned, some analysts foresaw a diminished presidency. Columnist Leslie H. Gelb of the *New York Times* wrote in 1993:

> Success feeds power. And President Clinton has little prospect of a power-building success in foreign policy, one that would catapult him to new stature at home and abroad. . . . For 50 years, Presidents have defined themselves decisively and dramatically by their actions on the world stage. . . . Mr. Clinton is not likely to have such opportunities. . . . [He] faces mostly quicksand and mudholes.

Other observers, however, wonder whether decisive achievements on major domestic issues such as economic revitalization and health-care reform will serve as the functional equivalent of the bold foreign-policy initiatives by which earlier presidents enhanced their stature. If the long-term trends of nearly a century persist, the growth in presidential power seems likely to continue. Nevertheless, the checks and balances devised by the founders in 1787 remain effective. Confounding the dark warnings of Lyndon Johnson's antiwar critics in the sixties, the nightmare of a president so powerful and so megalomaniacal as to make a mockery of constitutional government has never materialized.

schools. Fraternity and sorority members, conservative students, and the politically passive generally remained aloof. As the war continued, however, more campuses and a broader spectrum of students were drawn in.

Politically engaged writers joined the cause. The poet Robert Lowell, invited to a White House cultural festival in 1965, wrote a public letter to President Johnson refusing to attend because of the war. At the event itself, John Hersey read from his book *Hiroshima,* and critic Dwight Macdonald circulated an anti-war petition. (Actor Charlton Heston huffed, "Are you really accustomed to signing petitions against your host in his own home?") When the "festival" finally ended, President Johnson sighed, "At least nobody pissed in the punchbowl."

Dramatist Barbara Garson, a veteran of the Berkeley Free Speech Movement, dashed off *MacBird!* a parody of Shakespeare's *Macbeth* featuring a thinly disguised Lyndon and Lady Bird Johnson as the murderous Scottish monarchs. Published in 1966, *MacBird!* sold more than a hundred thousand copies. Critic Mary McCarthy visited Vietnam in 1967 and in a series of essays on the air war in the *New York Review of Books* described B-52 Superfortresses flying over an already shattered land, seeking new targets: "The Air Force seems inescapable, like the eye of God, and soon, you imagine . . . , all will be razed, charred, defoliated by that terrible searching gaze."

With Bob Dylan's performance at the 1965 Newport folk festival and Barry Maguire's popular hit that year, "Eve of Destruction," the music of the counterculture also took on a sharp antiwar edge. Folksinger Pete Seeger, a link to an older generation of radical activism, evoked the Vietnam quagmire in "Waist Deep in the Big Muddy" (1967), which he performed on "The Smothers Brothers Comedy Hour," a popular television show.

The media played a crucial role in shaping perceptions of the war and of the home-front protests. Although President Johnson blamed an unpatriotic press for undercutting support for the war and glorifying the protesters, the reality was more complex. As historians Daniel Hallin and Clarence R. Wyatt have documented, the media initially portrayed the war favorably and generally endorsed the administration's justifications for it. But as time passed, doubts about the official version of the war increased. By late 1966, the *New York Times* was reporting wild exaggeration in official reports of the success and accuracy of the bombing campaign. By 1968, media mistrust of the government's rationale for the war and claims for its success was at a high level. And shocking TV images of flaming villages, dying GIs, or children and aged peasants fleeing U.S. bombs proved more potent than "talking heads" explaining why America was in Vietnam.

The media's role in influencing attitudes toward the home-front protests, too, was complicated. Certainly TV images and print accounts of the protests rocking Washington and some of the nation's campuses publicized, and at times magnified, the opposition. Learning from the civil-rights movement, protesters skillfully exploited television and displayed a vivid sense of theater: flaming draft cards, coffins, and skull masks made for compelling television. But how individ-uals interpreted the images depended on their political orientation. Scenes of mass protest that the war's opponents applauded roused dismay among conservatives. Already upset by inner-city riots, conservatives saw a society trembling on the brink of anarchy. Further, as historian Melvin Small demonstrates in *Covering Dissent: The Media and the Anti-Vietnam War Movement* (1994), media coverage of the protests was notably hostile and superficial. The media, including the major newsmagazines and the TV networks, focused on scenes of violence and confrontation more than on peaceful demonstrations, and typically ignored the content of protest speeches or the substance of opponents' arguments against the war.

Responses to Vietnam: The Faces of Opposition and Support

Not only campus protesters, but many other Americans of liberal leanings also argued against involvement in Vietnam. Church groups, too, already mobilized by the civil-rights campaign, passed antiwar resolutions and joined marches. As early as 1965, twenty-seven hundred ministers and rabbis, in a full-page *New York Times* ad, demanded, "Mr. President, In the name of God, stop it!" The differences among Hollywood celebrities epitomized the larger divisions within society. Whereas many stars such as Gregory Peck, Dustin Hoffman, and Jane Fonda vehemently opposed the war, others, including John Wayne, Bob Hope, Clint Eastwood, and Frank Sinatra, just as vigorously supported it.

Was social class an important determinant of attitudes toward the war? The evidence is mixed. George Meany, head of the AFL-CIO, backed Johnson's war policies. An AFL-CIO poll of some thirty-five hundred labor leaders in 1967 found some 40 percent in support of the administration's prosecution of the war, nearly an equal number advocating further escalation, and only about 20 percent favoring deescalation or withdrawal from Vietnam. A few highly publicized incidents during which cursing construction workers assaulted peace marchers (see Chapter 11) buttressed the image of massive blue-collar support for the war. But polls in 1964

Miami, 1972. Vietnam veterans protest the war at the Democratic National Convention. President Nixon, elected in November 1972, would defuse protests with his policy of "Vietnamization" of the war, which gradually reduced the number of U.S. ground troops in Vietnam. (George W. Gardner/The Image Works)

and again in 1968 revealed nearly identical patterns of support for and opposition to the war among the working class, the lower-middle class, and the upper-middle class.

The evidence for the role of religious belief in shaping attitudes toward the war is similarly mixed. Eminent Protestant figures, such as William Sloane Coffin, the chaplain of Yale University, and Reinhold Niebuhr of Union Theological Seminary, opposed the war, as did leaders of the major liberal Protestant denominations. Naturally, pacifists like A. J. Muste and the historic peace churches—the Quakers, Mennonites, and Brethren—shared these views. Nevertheless, other Protestant spokespersons supported the war. Paul Ramsey, a professor of religion at Princeton, argued in a series of books and articles that America's role in Vietnam met Christianity's classic just-war criteria. Prowar sentiment flourished among fundamentalist and evangelical Protestants. *Christianity Today,* a leading evangelical journal, strongly supported the war. The evangelist Billy Graham proclaimed in 1965: "Communism has to be stopped somewhere, whether it is in Hawaii or on the West Coast. The President believes it should be stopped in Vietnam." Even in the liberal, social-activist denominations, the leadership often opposed the conflict more strongly than did the laity. Despite the antiwar activism of a few high-visibility Catholic pacifists such as the Berrigan brothers, Philip and Daniel, support for the war ran high among American Roman Catholics. Vigorously anticommunist and sympathetic with the plight of South Vietnam's many Catholics, U.S. Catholics backed the war at a ratio from 6 to 10 percentage points higher than did Protestants. Jews were the first religious group to turn decisively against the war. As early as 1966, fully 63 percent of American Jews favored immediate withdrawal or a negotiated settlement in Vietnam, whereas only a minority of Protestants and Catholics embraced these dovish positions. Leading rabbis strongly condemned Johnson's escalation on moral grounds.

Gender was another significant variable. Opposition to the war among women at all educational and socioeconomic levels, and of all races and religions, ran about 10 percentage points higher than opposition among the comparable male cohort.

Although the conventional wisdom at the time held otherwise, young people as a whole supported the conflict more strongly than any other age cohort. In April 1965, as Johnson's escalation unfolded, 76 percent of Americans under age thirty approved of the war, while only 51 percent of those aged forty-nine or older backed it. A mere 10 percent of eighteen to twenty-two year olds, one study found, ever participated in any antiwar activity. Through 1967, a majority of this age cohort supported or acquiesced in Johnson's policy.

Further, despite the heavy media attention accorded to campus antiwar protests, many college students supported the war. The nation's twenty-five hundred institutions of higher learning in the 1960s constituted a spectrum of schools, from large state universities to conservative church colleges. Students and faculty on many of these campuses generally backed the war, and fewer than half of the schools ever witnessed any organized antiwar activism. The stereotype of college students standing united in opposition to the war while superpatriotic blue-collar workers cheered Johnson's escalation remains little more than a caricature, based on selective memories and distorted media images.

The widely held belief that nearly all campuses were wracked by demonstrations and that college students uniformly opposed the war had several sources. First, opposition to the war did emerge quickly and strongly at some of the nation's best-known institutions of higher learning, including elite private universities such as Harvard and major public universities such as Michigan and Berkeley. Second, for brief intervals, notably in the spring of 1970, campus protest spread very widely indeed, reinforcing the illusion that this phenomenon continued during the entire period of the war. Third, as campus activists conducted marches and rallies and occupied buildings, they created images of campus protest that pervaded the media from 1965 on. Finally, campus opponents of the war, even when in the minority, brought to their cause a passion and urgency generally lacking among those who supported Vietnam or felt ambivalent about it.

Of all sectors of U.S. society, none opposed the war more strongly than the African-American community. A few conservative black leaders—Roy Wilkins of the NAACP, Republican senator Edward Brooke of Massachusetts, U.N. diplomat Ralph Bunche—supported the war, or at least did not openly oppose it, but they were a tiny minority. The inner-city riots and the rising militance of young black activists unfolded against the background of a war that took a disproportionate toll among African Americans* and that cut deeply into domestic social programs. In these circumstances, the black community, despite its support for LBJ's domestic programs, turned quickly against his Vietnam policies. As early as March 1966, when most white Americans supported the war, a majority of blacks already opposed the conflict. Of all groups surveyed, African-American women invariably showed the lowest levels of support for the war.

Opposition to the war linked prominent blacks who otherwise differed radically. The prizefighter Muhammed Ali, a Black Muslim, lost his heavyweight crown for refusing to register for the draft. The fiery orators of SNCC and CORE included the Vietnam War in their denunciations of white America, and Martin Luther King, Jr., attacked the war as early as 1965, breaking with Johnson and angering many Americans who still backed the president. Repeatedly in 1966–67, King highlighted the war's negative impact on African Americans. He pointed out the high proportion of young blacks in combat in Vietnam and deplored the war's devastating effect on social programs that benefited African-Americans. As long as Vietnam drained the nation's human and economic resources, he asserted in April 1967, the crisis in the inner cities would only worsen. Having lauded Johnson for his civil-rights stand two years earlier, King now denounced the administration as "the greatest purveyor of violence in the world today."

Despite the vocal opposition, however, the American public as a whole turned only slowly against the war, and never with anything approaching unanimity. A hefty 61 percent of Americans supported Johnson's escalation in 1965, with only 24 percent opposed. As late as the summer of 1967, a majority of citizens still backed Johnson's war policies, with antiwar activists in a distinct minority. As peace advocates marched, hawks implored true patriots to rally 'round the flag.

---

* In the early stages of the war, blacks accounted for 23 percent of the U.S. fatalities. By 1969 the figure had dropped to 14 percent–still higher than blacks' 11 percent share of the population.

Senator Russell Long of Louisiana, launching a McCarthyite-like attack on activists "who encourage the Communists to prolong the war," orated, "I swell with pride when I see Old Glory flying from the Capitol. . . . My prayer is that there may never be a white flag of surrender up there."

Many Americans of all ages, education, and social class endorsed such sentiments. With LBJ defining support for the war as a test of patriotism and true citizenship, most Americans in this first stage of escalation gave the president and his policies the benefit of the doubt. Certainly the families and friends of the young men in Vietnam did not look sympathetically on critics who attacked the war as immoral or unwinnable.

Hostility toward campus demonstrators further influenced many citizens' position on the war. Many working-class and middle-class Americans viewed the youthful protesters as pampered offspring of a privileged elite. They had been reared too permissively, the litany typically went, and now they petulantly demanded their way in shaping national policy. The media's tendency to focus on moments of confrontation between demonstrators and the police or other authority figures heightened these stereotyped perceptions. This gut-level aversion to campus demonstrators and street marchers would crest in 1968–70, but it was present from the beginning. For many conservatives, distaste for the war's opponents proved stronger than their distaste for the war itself.

As Vietnam and its domestic fallout dominated the news, numerous Americans tried to carry on as usual. The bestsellers in these years of escalating war and

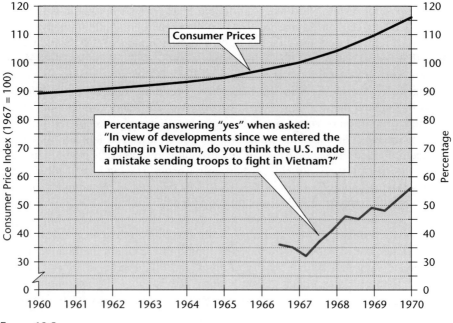

FIGURE 10.3

Inflation and Public Opinion on the Vietnam War, 1960–1970

SOURCE: *Historical Statistics of the United States, Colonial Times to 1970* (1975) and Gallup poll data.

protest tellingly included such titles as *Happiness Is a Warm Puppy* (1963) and Jacqueline Susann's steamy sex novel *Valley of the Dolls* (1966). Movies receiving Academy Awards for best picture included three escapist musicals: *My Fair Lady* (1964), *The Sound of Music* (1965), and *Oliver!* (1968).

Yet even Americans who detested the protests could not see the light at the end of the tunnel in Vietnam that the administration professed to discern. As casualties mounted, victory seemed ever more remote. Citizens' growing doubts about the war were worsened by its dismaying economic costs, which soared to $20.6 billion in fiscal 1967, a year that saw the sharpest rise in the defense budget since 1943. As early as December 1965, the Council of Economic Advisers cautioned Johnson that a significant tax increase would be needed, but for two years, the president avoided such a step. Johnson wanted desperately to provide both "guns and butter"—that is, to finance the war in Vietnam *and* his Great Society programs—without a tax hike.

Johnson's unwillingness to raise taxes led to overly optimistic projections of the war's cost and probable duration. In 1965 Defense Secretary McNamara predicted that hostilities would cease by June 30, 1967—not for any clear military reason but because that was the end of the fiscal year. In 1967 a congressional committee estimated that the war's costs in that year alone would exceed the administration's projections by $5 billion to $6 billion. This juggling with figures and dates further undermined the administration's credibility.

Granted, the war fed the 1960s economic boom and stimulated employment. The jobless rate fell steadily in 1963–69, to an eventual low of 3.5 percent. But the conflict also increased federal deficits and fueled inflationary pressures, deepening Americans' uneasiness about the economic implications of the war.

At last in August 1967, Johnson proposed a 10 percent surcharge on individual and corporate taxes, which Congress passed the following June. Immediately after the president's tax-increase proposal, with no dramatic worsening in the news from Vietnam, a plurality of Americans for the first time turned against the war. In August 1967, 46 percent of those polled now viewed the war as a "mistake," with 44 percent still in support. This had ominous implications for Lyndon Johnson. Rising inflation and the threat of higher taxes stirred grave questions about the war even among Americans who did not oppose it on ideological or moral grounds.

Conclusion

Faced with stalemate in Vietnam and an eroding base at home, Johnson hesitantly agreed to a major review of the quagmire. In a September 1967 speech he modified the U.S. terms for peace talks and, like McNamara earlier, even hinted at a role for the National Liberation Front in ruling South Vietnam. Cautiously, the administration moved toward turning over more of the fighting to South Vietnam, a strategy of "Vietnamization" that President Richard Nixon would implement more fully.

Capitalizing on the shifting mood, a coalition of antiwar groups called a march on Washington for October 16, 1967. Some hundred thousand participants rallied on the Mall. Thirty-five thousand of them, chanting "End the War" and "Hell No,

We Won't Go," proceeded to the Pentagon, where they sat down at the entrance facing a line of armed guards. Soon the light from burning draft cards flickered in the darkness. Eventually military police cleared the demonstrators. Arresting 660 and clubbing many, they stirred memories of police violence against civil-rights activists. One young college student later recalled:

> We were out on the grass, chanting, "Peace now. Peace now." This went on for quite a long time, and then all of a sudden there was sort of a signal, and people were being hit by soldiers or MPs [military police]. . . . I remember people falling on me, and I remember seeing blood. It was all kind of chaos. One minute was peaceful and fun, and then all of a sudden they're hitting.

Those arrested included the Jesuit peace activist Daniel Berrigan; pediatrician Benjamin Spock, a veteran of the nuclear-test-ban campaign; and novelist Norman Mailer, who described the march in *The Armies of the Night* (1968).

Johnson dragged Westmoreland home again in November for another round of optimistic speeches. "[Victory] lies within our grasp—the enemy's hopes are bankrupt," the general optimistically told the National Press Club. But LBJ's edginess was apparent. "This is not Johnson's war," the president shouted angrily to reporters that fall. "This is America's war."

At the same time, a major battle appeared about to erupt around Khe Sanh, in northwest South Vietnam, where the North Vietnamese reportedly had massed forty thousand troops. As Westmoreland urgently reinforced Khe Sanh's marine battalion, Johnson watched anxiously. Was this Dien Bien Phu all over again? Or would Khe Sanh at last provide the decisive victory that could turn the war around? In fact, Khe Sanh was a diversion. As 1968 opened, the enemy would strike a very different and unexpected blow, not at a remote outpost but at centers of American strength throughout South Vietnam. The Tet Offensive of January 1968 not only proved a pivotal point in the war but also became the overture to the bleakest, most divisive year in postwar American history.

SELECTED READINGS

The War in Vietnam

Christian G. Appy, *Working-Class War: American Combat Soldiers and Vietnam* (1983); C. D. B. Bryan, *Friendly Fire* (1976); William A. Buckingham, Jr., *Operation Ranch Hand: The United States Air Force and Herbicides in South East Asia, 1961–1971* (1982); Larry E. Cable, *Conflict of Myths: The Development of American Counterinsurgency Doctrine and the Vietnam War* (1986); Phillip Davidson, *Vietnam at War* (1991); George C. Herring, *America's Longest War: The United States and Vietnam* (rev. ed., 1985) and "Vietnam Remembered," *Journal of American History,* (June 1986) [essay review of seven books by Vietnam veterans]; Tom Holm, *Wounded Souls: Native American Veterans of the Vietnam War* (1996); Stanley Karnow, *Vietnam: A History* (1983); Richard Moser, *The New Winter Soldiers: GI and Veteran Dissent During the Vietnam Era* (1996); J. B. Neilands et al., *Harvest of Death: Chemical Warfare in Vietnam and Cambodia* (1972); James S. Olson and Randy Roberts, *Where the Domino Fell: America and Vietnam, 1945–1990* (1991); Bruce Palmer, Jr., *The 25-Year War: America's Military Role in Vietnam* (1984); Andrew J. Rotter, ed.,

Light at the End of the Tunnel: A Vietnam War Anthology (1991); Jonathan Schell, *The Village of Ben Suc* (1967) and *The Real War* (1987); Neil Sheehan, *The Bright and Shining Lie: John Paul Vann and America in Vietnam* (1988); Jack Shulimson and Maj. Charles M. Johnson, *The U.S. Marines in Vietnam: The Landing and the Buildup, 1965* (1978); Wallace Terry, ed., *Bloods: An Oral History of the Vietnam War by Black Veterans* (1984); James Clay Thompson, *Rolling Thunder: Understanding Policy and Program Failure* (1980); Marilyn B. Young, *The Vietnam Wars: 1945–1990* (1991).

Vietnam: The Strategic Planning Process

Loren Baritz, *Backfire: A History of How American Culture Led Us into Vietnam and Made Us Fight the Way We Did* (1985); Larry Berman, *Planning a Tragedy: The Americanization of the War in Vietnam* (1982) and *Lyndon Johnson's War: The Road to Stalemate in Vietnam* (1989); Anne E. Blair, *Lodge in Vietnam: A Patriot Abroad* (1995); H. W. Brands, *The Wages of Globalism: Lyndon Johnson and the Limits of American Power* (1995); Robert Buzzanco, *Masters of War: Military Dissent and Politics in the Vietnam Era* (1996); Warren I. Cohen and Nancy Bernkopf Tucker, eds., *Lyndon Johnson Confronts the World: American Foreign Policy, 1963–1968* (1994); Ilya V. Gaiduk, *The Soviet Union and the Vietnam War* (1996); Lloyd C. Gardner, *Pay Any Price: Lyndon Johnson and the Wars for Vietnam* (1995); Leslie H. Gelb with Richard K. Betts, *The Irony of Vietnam: The System Worked* (1979); James William Gibson, *The Perfect War: The War We Couldn't Lose and How We Did* (1986); John Girling, *America and the Third World* (1980); David Halberstam, *The Best and the Brightest* (1972); George C. Herring, "American Strategy in Vietnam: The Postwar Debate," *Military Affairs* (April 1982), and *LBJ and Vietnam: A Different Kind of War* (1994); Michael H. Hunt, *Lyndon Johnson's War: America's Cold War Crusade in Vietnam* (1996); Richard A. Hunt, *Pacification: The American Struggle for Vietnam's Hearts and Minds* (1995); Edward P. Metzner, *More Than a Soldier's War: Pacification in Vietnam* (1995); Edwin Moïse, *Tonkin Gulf and the Escalation of the Vietnam War* (1997); Harry G. Summers, *On Strategy: The Vietnam War in Context* (1981); Kathleen J. Turner, *Lyndon Johnson's Dual War: Vietnam and the Press* (1981).

The Domestic Response to the War

Some of the titles already listed cover home-front responses to the war as well. See also Michael A. Anderegg, *Inventing Vietnam: The War in Film and Television* (1991); John Bokima and Timothy J. Lukes, *Marcuse: From New Left to the Next Left* (1994); David Burner, *Making Peace with the Sixties* (1996); David Farber, ed., *The Sixties: From Memory to History* (1994); Owen W. Gilman, *Vietnam and the Southern Imagination* (1992); Daniel C. Hallin, *The "Uncensored War": The Media and Vietnam* (1986); David W. Levy, *The Debate over Vietnam* (1990); Anne C. Loveland, *American Evangelicals and the U.S. Military, 1942–1993* (1996); Myra McPherson, *Long Time Passing: Vietnam and the Haunted Generation* (1984); Thomas Powers, *Vietnam, the War at Home: the Antiwar Movement, 1964–1968* (1984); Jo Ann Robinson, *Abraham Went Out: A Biography of A. J. Muste* (1981); Timothy E. Scheurer, "Myth to Madness: America, Vietnam, and Popular Culture," *Journal of American Culture* (Summer 1981); Melvin Small, *Covering Dissent: The Media and the Anti-Vietnam War Movement* (1994); Robert M. Stevens, *Vain Hopes, Grim Realities: The Economic Consequences of the Vietnam War* (1976); Clyde Taylor, ed., *Vietnam and Black America: An Anthology of Protest and Resistance* (1973); Clarence R. Wyatt, *Paper Soldiers: The American Press and the Vietnam War* (1993); Nancy Zaroulis and Gerald Sullivan, *Who Spoke Up? American Protest Against the War in Vietnam, 1963–1975* (1984).

CHAPTER 11

1968 and the Nixon Years

On May 17, 1968, a band of nine antiwar activists entered a draft-board office in the Baltimore suburb of Catonsville, led by the brothers Philip and Daniel Berrigan, Catholic priests and radical opponents of the Vietnam War. As a secretary screamed, "Don't you take my files!" the nine loaded some three hundred file folders into baskets, carried them to the parking lot, and set fire to them using homemade napalm. While the bonfire blazed, they encircled it, held hands, and recited the Lord's Prayer. Alerted beforehand, television crews crowded around. Philip Berrigan received six years in federal prison for the Catonsville burning. Looking back in the mid-1980s, he reflected, "My instinct is, if a person hotly objects to what his or her government is doing, then it's necessary to take a position against it—to resist it."

The Berrigans were part of a rising swell of discontent with the Vietnam War. The Tet Offensive in January 1968 crystallized this deepening mood. After three years of mounting casualties and soaring costs, a majority of Americans finally turned against "Johnson's War." But frustration with the war did not translate into support for the New Left or the counterculture. On the contrary, continued campus unrest, two shocking assassinations early in 1968, and violence at the Democratic convention that summer sparked revulsion against radicalism. Richard Nixon's victory that November, reflecting this conservative shift, began an era of Republican dominance of the White House that, except for one four-year interlude, would continue until 1993.

Reversing course in Vietnam, Nixon and his national security adviser, Henry Kissinger, pursued negotiations and gradually cut U.S. troop levels; the last American combat units left South Vietnam in 1973. Within two years, the Saigon government collapsed, erasing Washington's twenty-year effort to maintain a noncommunist South Vietnam. Yet even amid peace talks, the war had persisted, and when Nixon expanded the ground war to Cambodia early in 1970, new protests erupted. By that time, however, the New Left and the counterculture were on the wane, victims of internal divisions and the nation's rightward shift.

While withdrawing from Vietnam, Nixon and Kissinger reoriented U.S. foreign policy, crafting a strategy of détente—an easing of tensions—with China and the Soviet Union. Domestically, the new president displayed the same innovativeness and opportunism that characterized his foreign policy. In dealing with welfare policy and economic issues, as with the communist powers, he willingly abandoned long-held Republican positions if it seemed politically expedient to do so. Shrewdly exploiting discontents and fears in grassroots America, he focused on building a new Republican majority among alienated voters.

1968: "The Center Cannot Hold"

Throughout the Vietnam War, the two sides had observed an informal cease-fire during Tet, the festive Vietnamese New Year—until 1968, when the National Liberation Front and the North Vietnamese chose Tet—January 31—to launch a coordinated assault on cities, bases, and provincial capitals across South Vietnam. While the siege at Khe Sanh preoccupied the U.S. military command, 84,000 NLF and North Vietnamese troops stealthily maneuvered into position. NLF sympathizers in the cities joined in the attack. In a move that devastated American morale, nineteen NLF guerrillas penetrated the U.S. embassy compound in Saigon and held out for six hours before American soldiers finally gunned them down.

In Vietnam's ancient capital of Hué, the NLF held power for nearly four weeks, executing as many as three thousand officials and others identified with the Saigon regime. U.S. officials pointed to this massacre as proof of their contention that a communist victory in South Vietnam would mean a bloodbath. After U.S. bombing and shelling pounded Hué to ruins, marines retook the city on February 25.

The Tet Offensive introduced a new stage of savagery in the war. Under the CIA's Phoenix Program, the Thieu government murdered some twenty thousand suspected opponents of the regime who had revealed themselves as NLF supporters during Tet. Thousands more were jailed. The post-Tet phase also produced the most notorious American atrocity of the war: the My Lai massacre. On March 16, 1968, a U.S. platoon commanded by Second Lieutenant William L. Calley, Jr., entered the village of My Lai in Quang Ngai province on a search-and-destroy mission. Finding no Vietcong, Calley's men, under pressure to maintain the weekly "body count," systematically shot more than three hundred peasants—women, children, and old men. In the spasm of violence, they raped women, mutilated

Vietnam 1968. *A wounded GI evacuated from Hué, a scene of fierce fighting during the Tet Offensive. The military brass tried to put a positive spin on the outcome of Tet, but in the United States it sharply intensified opposition to the war. (John Olson/*Life Magazine,* © Time-Warner)*

bodies, slaughtered domestic animals, and burned the village to the ground. The story of My Lai broke in 1969 despite official efforts to suppress it. As other veterans and journalists spoke up, an even more chilling realization emerged: My Lai was unique only in its scale; the killing, rape, and torture of civilians occurred far more often than anyone had believed.*

Having beaten back the Tet invaders and regained precarious control of South Vietnam's cities, U.S. authorities portrayed the Tet Offensive as a major U.S. victory. The communists had gambled everything and failed. "The enemy is on the ropes," General Westmoreland crowed. The North Vietnamese, despite the disappointing military outcome of the Tet operation, steeled themselves for more fighting. Whatever its military significance, Tet proved a propaganda disaster for the Johnson administration. Respected newsman Walter Cronkite asked, "What's going on here? I thought we were winning." If Tet was an NLF defeat, mused Senator George Aiken of Vermont, what would an NLF victory look like? Support for the war dropped to 41 percent, and Johnson's approval rating sank to a pathetic 26 percent. Key periodicals, including *Time, Newsweek,* the *New York Times,* and the *Washington Post,* broke with the administration over Vietnam.

Another round of campus antiwar protests in the spring of 1968 compounded Johnson's woes. Demonstrations erupted on more than a hundred U.S. campuses, involving upwards of four hundred thousand young men and women and many faculty members. The movement spread even into high schools, and to Paris and Berlin. Many schools canceled classes as students flocked instead to hastily organized teach-ins and gathered in dorm lounges for discussions of the war. At one such meeting at the University of Massachusetts, a young woman arose to speak. Was her brother's death in Vietnam meaningless? she tearfully asked. The question hung in the air, unanswerable.

At Columbia University in New York City, black militants and the local SDS joined forces to protest Columbia's ROTC program, campus recruitment by the military and Dow Chemical, and Columbia's plan to build a gymnasium in nearby Harlem, a plan that would eliminate some black housing. The confrontation lasted for two months. Two mass sit-ins produced eight hundred arrests. For nearly a week, protesters occupied five campus buildings, including the president's office.

As the war dragged on, the protests grew more confrontational. The speeches at rallies became more militant, the attacks on the Establishment more sweeping. Some activists moved from marches and speechmaking to acts of civil disobedience. More than sixty performers recorded Dylan's antiwar "Blowin' in the Wind." Folksinger Phil Ochs declared in one song:

> Call it "peace" or call it "treason,"
> Call it "love" or call it "reason,"
> But I ain't marchin' anymore.

---

* In the legal aftermath of the My Lai affair, a military court in 1971 convicted Lieutenant William Calley of premeditated murder of South Vietnamese civilians and sentenced him to life imprisonment. In fact, he went free in 1974 after serving thirty-five months, mostly under house arrest at Fort Benning, Georgia. Many felt that in singling out Calley, despite his proved complicity in the massacre, the army had failed to confront the larger pattern of atrocities against civilians in Vietnam.

FIGURE 11.1
The Tet Offensive

The two sides eyed each other across a widening chasm of mistrust that poisoned the political climate. Hounded by protesters, Johnson limited his domestic travel to military bases. The only difference between himself and John Kennedy, he complained, was that his assassination was more drawn out. Federal intelligence agencies stepped up their surveillance of antiwar organizations. Hundreds of paid informants supplied information on antiwar leaders and organizations and even on elected officials who spoke out against the war.

Amid rising domestic discord, the high-level reassessment of the war triggered by Westmoreland's 1967 request for 206,000 more troops proceeded urgently. Westmoreland himself was removed from active command and became army chief of staff. The new secretary of defense, Clark Clifford, the Democratic stalwart who had helped to craft Harry Truman's 1948 election strategy, urged Johnson to scale back the war. Even Dean Acheson, at a gloomy meeting of the "Wise Men" in March 1968, counseled ending the conflict.

On the political front, Johnson faced rebellion in his own party. In January, Senator Eugene McCarthy of Minnesota launched a campaign for the Democratic presidential nomination on an antiwar platform. A devout Catholic and a poet, McCarthy initially portrayed his candidacy as a moral gesture, but thousands of enthusiastic volunteers responded. The "Dump Johnson" movement even lured student activists back to party politics. In preparation for door-to-door canvassing, young men shaved beards and cut their hair; young women made similar bows to conventionality, to be "neat and clean for Gene."

In the New Hampshire primary on March 12, McCarthy won a stunning 42 percent of the Democratic vote against the incumbent. As disillusioned hawks joined the parade against Johnson, hope buoyed the antiwar camp. The New Hampshire primary also set the stage for an even more formidable challenge to Johnson by Robert Kennedy, who had resigned as U.S. attorney general in 1964 and had won election to the U.S. Senate from New York. Four days after the New Hampshire vote, he threw his hat into the ring. Remnants of John Kennedy's old team, along with a wave of voters, rallied to the new Kennedy banner.

The third of four sons in a fiercely competitive family, nicknamed "the runt" for his small size, Robert Kennedy had built a reputation for ruthlessness dating back to his days as an aide of Senator Joseph McCarthy. As attorney general, he had pursued Jimmy Hoffa of the corrupt Teamsters' Union and authorized wiretaps on Martin Luther King, Jr. By 1967–68, however, he showed growing sensitivity to the alienated young and the poor.

For a few weeks, the presidency seemed within his grasp. Lambasting LBJ for unleashing "the darker impulses of the American spirit" and linking the war to America's home-front crises, Kennedy pledged "to end the bloodshed in Vietnam and in our cities, . . . to close the gap . . . between black and white, between rich and poor, between young and old, in this country and around the world."

As Johnson watched his political base crumbling, he came to a decision. In a television address on March 31, 1968, LBJ announced a partial bombing halt, called for negotiations, and concluded with the terse announcement: "I shall not seek, and I will not accept, the nomination of my party for another term as your President." He wanted to devote his remaining months in office to the search for peace, he said. Johnson's withdrawal threw the campaign wide open. While McCarthy and Kennedy split the antiwar vote, Vice President Hubert Humphrey joined the race as well, hoping to rebuild the traditional Democratic coalition of farmers, blacks, Hispanics, union members, and big-city ethnic voters. Despite private doubts, Humphrey had publicly defended the war.

Governor George Wallace of Alabama also announced his candidacy for president on a third-party ticket, the American Independent party. Having "stood in the schoolhouse door" in 1963 to flaunt his opposition to integration, Wallace appealed to southern and working-class whites resentful of blacks, campus agitators, and hippies. In rabble-rousing speeches, he denounced antiwar protesters and "pointy-headed intellectuals." Choosing as his running mate General Curtis LeMay, a superhawkish former head of the Strategic Air Command, Wallace rose in the polls to 21 percent by September.

The ugly national mood reflected by the Wallace surge exploded in violence on April 4, 1968, as an assassin gunned down Martin Luther King, Jr., on the balcony of a Memphis motel room. White ex-convict James Earl Ray was arrested and found guilty of the murder. Rumors circulated that Ray had hoped to collect a bounty for King's death posted by white supremacist groups.*

In a sermon the night before his death, the thirty-nine-year-old King had described the threats on his life and had prophetically concluded:

> Like anybody, I would like to live a long life. . . . But I'm not concerned about that now. I just want to do God's will. And He's allowed me to go up to the mountain. . . . And I've seen the promised land. I may not get there with you. But I want you to know tonight, that we, as a people, will get to the promised land. And I'm happy tonight. . . . Mine eyes have seen the glory of the coming of the Lord.

James Earl Ray's gun silenced not only a civil-rights leader but one who since 1965 had opposed the Vietnam War and championed the urban black poor. Despite the failure of his 1966 Chicago campaign, King had continued to stress economic issues. Indeed, he had come to Memphis to support a strike by the city's mostly African-American garbage collectors.

King's murder unleashed a new round of inner-city violence. An outburst of rioting and arson hit Chicago, Washington, D.C., and many other cities, leaving forty-three dead. In Washington, arsonists and looters devastated parts of the area between the White House and the Capitol. In Chicago, Mayor Daley issued shoot-to-kill orders against arsonists.

Two months after the King murder, another assassination shocked the nation. Robert Kennedy had swept the Indiana and Nebraska primaries, but McCarthy had triumphed in Oregon. The California primary on June 5 loomed as the crucial test. Kennedy won; then that night he, too, fell to an assassin's bullet in a Los Angeles hotel. The killer, Sirhan Sirhan, was a Palestinian who resented Kennedy's pro-Israel stand.

The King and Kennedy murders, against a backdrop of political turmoil and burning cities, sharpened the sense of a society unraveling and hastened the rightward shift of American politics. The era of resurgent liberalism that had begun with John Kennedy's election in 1960 was over.

At the Democrats' Chicago convention in August, Vice President Humphrey won a first-ballot nomination. In a wildly inappropriate speech, he buoyantly trumpeted his campaign theme: "the politics of joy." Humphrey boasted a strong liberal record, but he bore the stigma of "Johnson's War." He first drafted a platform

---

* Ray confessed to the murder, but later recanted. In 1997, members of King's family, alleging that the assassination was the product of a larger conspiracy that included high government officials, called for a new trial of Ray. Ray died in 1998.

Columbia University, 1968. *As the Vietnam War escalated, so did protests on the na-tion's campuses, such as this one in front of Columbia's Low Library. But many Ameri-cans were dismayed by the turbulence, giving rise to a powerful conservative back-lash.* (Barton Silverman/New York Times Company/Archive Photos)

plank pledging greater efforts for peace, but when Johnson angrily protested, Humphrey embraced the administration's position, further alienating antiwar De-mocrats. The New York delegation, filled with die-hard Kennedy loyalists, defi-antly sang "We Shall Overcome" repeatedly on the convention floor.

The convention's most unforgettable moments occurred in Chicago's streets, thronged with five thousand antiwar activists. Principled protesters mingled with publicity seekers from the counterculture's fringe. Abbie Hoffman and Jerry Rubin, cofounders of a parody political movement, the Youth International (Yip-pie) party, presented a pig as their presidential nominee and issued fanciful threats to pour LSD into the city water supply. An unamused "Boss" Daley vowed to re-store order. On the night of Humphrey's nomination, protesters jammed North Michigan Boulevard. Helmeted Chicago police waded into the throng, clubbing wildly. Many activists, as well as television crews and journalists, suffered beatings, some severe. Tear gas drifted into the lobbies of nearby hotels. TV images of rampaging police and bloody protesters reinforced the fearful impression of a society gone mad. An investigative panel later concluded that although the police were provoked, they had ignored citizens' rights and unleashed a "police riot."

The beneficiary of this chaos was Richard Nixon. Since his defeat in the 1962 California gubernatorial race, Nixon had patiently rebuilt his Republican party credentials at gatherings of the party faithful across the nation. In 1968 Nixon out-maneuvered his rivals—governors Ronald Reagan of California, George Romney of Michigan, and Nelson Rockefeller of New York—to win the nomination. The

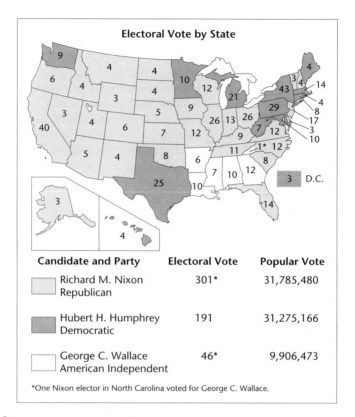

Electoral Vote by State

Candidate and Party	Electoral Vote	Popular Vote
Richard M. Nixon Republican	301*	31,785,480
Hubert H. Humphrey Democratic	191	31,275,166
George C. Wallace American Independent	46*	9,906,473

*One Nixon elector in North Carolina voted for George C. Wallace.

FIGURE 11.2
Presidential Election of 1968

carefully staged GOP convention in Miami seemed a model of tranquility in contrast to Chicago. Nixon's acceptance speech introduced his campaign theme: "new
leadership in America."

Capitalizing on the public's revulsion against the war, Nixon assured voters
that he had a secret peace plan for Vietnam. And amid rising dismay over domestic turmoil, he assured the "forgotten Americans"—the uneasy middle class—that
he would toughen law enforcement. "Law and order" became the code for crack-
ing down on protesters, militants, and anyone else who challenged the status quo.
Nixon's vice-presidential choice, jut-jawed Spiro Agnew, the governor of Maryland, echoed this theme. The Republican team battled George Wallace for support
in the South, where the lily-white Democratic party had fallen into disarray as the
black electorate had grown. Shrewdly crafted GOP TV commercials juxtaposed
images of war and disorder with Nixon's soothing voice pledging peace and tranquil times and linked Hubert Humphrey with violence and upheaval.*

---

* Journalist Joe McGinniss, having won the confidence of top Republican campaign strategists,
later produced a devastating account of this media campaign, *The Selling of the President* (1969).

Considering their initial liabilities, Humphrey and his running mate, Senator Edmund Muskie of Maine, ran a strong race. Starting sixteen points behind Nixon in the polls, Humphrey by the end had pulled even. Had the campaign gone on a week longer, some analysts believe, he would have won. In late September Humphrey finally broke with the administration, calling for a total bombing halt and a shift of the fighting from U.S. to South Vietnamese forces.

The breakthrough toward peace that could have put Humphrey over the top never came. After Johnson's March 31 address, the North Vietnamese had agreed to talks in Paris. W. Averell Harriman represented the United States, and Hanoi sent a former foreign minister. The talks started in mid-May but quickly deadlocked. North Vietnam demanded a full bombing halt; the United States insisted on concessions in return. By October, Hanoi had agreed to stop sending North Vietnamese units south and shelling South Vietnamese cities, and Johnson announced the bombing halt. But President Thieu of South Vietnam boycotted the talks, and they remained mired in details. In the campaign's final weeks, to undermine Humphrey's chances, Nixon's manager, John Mitchell, discouraged Thieu from accepting a peace agreement until after the election.*

Nixon won six Deep South states and every state west of the Mississippi except Texas and Washington. He lost only eight states of the Upper South, Midwest, and Northeast to Humphrey. Wallace carried five Deep South states. Nixon got 43.4 percent to Humphrey's 42.7 percent and Wallace's 13.5 percent. In the closest electoral-college tally since 1916, Nixon received 301 votes, Humphrey 191, and Wallace 46. Had Humphrey carried California instead of narrowly losing it, Nixon would have fallen short of an electoral-college majority, and the election would have gone to the House of Representatives.

Social unrest, the Vietnam stalemate, and middle-class resentment of Johnson's antipoverty program all fed into Nixon's win. The New Right movement also played a role, nurtured by conservative ideologues like William F. Buckley and by the 1964 Goldwater campaign. Although won by a slim margin, the 1968 election signaled a profound rightward shift in American politics.

George Wallace demonstrated surprising strength in the North. Indeed, Wallace in retrospect can be seen as a pivotal figure who mobilized resentments that would soon drive mainstream politics. Populist politicians had once energized angry voters by directing their resentment against the rich and corporate elites. As Thomas B. Edsall and Mary D. Edsall have noted, Wallace by contrast offered a new set of villains as a focus of working-class hostility: college students, intellectuals, the media, and Washington bureaucrats.[†] The Alabama governor also exploited a growing white backlash against a decade of civil-rights activism and federal programs aimed at the inner-city poor.

As Mary C. Brennan argues in *Turning Right in the Sixties: The Conservative Capture of the GOP* (1995), this rightward thrust was long in preparation. Even in the

---

* The full story is recounted in Jules Witcover, *The Year the Dream Died: Revisiting 1968 in America* (1997).

† Thomas B. Edsall with Mary D. Edsall, *Chain Reaction: The Impact of Race, Rights, and Taxes on American Politics* (1991).

1950s, some conservatives found the Eisenhower administration too easygoing toward communism and the welfare state. Former president Herbert Hoover warned that the "Karl Marx virus" had infected the Republican party. The conservative shift picked up steam in the 1960s, though often obscured by activism on the Left. With George Wallace yapping at his heels, Richard Nixon successfully mobilized this emerging conservative movement.

The most decisive loser in 1968 was Lyndon Johnson. Johnson's consensus style initially had served him well in the domestic realm, as he sought to grant everyone a slice of what one historian described as "the giant pizza in the sky he called the Great Society." But LBJ's preference for consensus over hard choices ultimately failed him even in the domestic sphere, and in Vietnam his efforts proved disastrous. His escalation of the war never achieved its objectives, and in 1968 he paid the price.

Back on his Texas ranch, LBJ let his graying hair grow long, conveying the odd impression of an aging hippie, and spoke wistfully of his Great Society. He died of a heart attack in January 1973, at the age of sixty-four.

Nixon's War: Vietnam, 1969–1975

Vietnam had ended Johnson's career and broken him psychologically; now Richard Nixon, fascinated by foreign policy, welcomed the challenge. The cabinet could handle domestic affairs, he believed; the chief executive should concentrate on global issues. Nixon's national security adviser, Henry Kissinger, emphatically agreed. The deep-voiced, owl-eyed Kissinger had lived in the United States since 1938 when his family had fled Nazi Germany. After serving in World War II and working with U.S. occupation forces in Germany, he graduated from Harvard and stayed on to earn a Ph.D. and to teach government. In *Nuclear Weapons and Foreign Policy* (1957), Kissinger advocated the deployment of tactical nuclear weapons, in addition to intercontinental ballistic missiles, to advance U.S. strategic interests. A foreign-policy adviser in the 1950s to Nelson Rockefeller, Kissinger filled a series of various government positions in the 1960s. He thus was already a fixture in Washington when Nixon brought him to the White House in 1969.

The two men, although very different, shared a love of power and a taste for strategic thinking. Both were secretive, and distrustful of the bureaucracy and even their own staff. Someone compared Kissinger's aides to mushrooms: "They're kept in the dark, get a lot of manure piled on them, and then get canned." Nixon functioned as his own secretary of state, with Kissinger at his side. The man who actually held that title, William Rogers, was a Wall Street lawyer largely ignorant of foreign affairs. "No secretary of state is really important," Nixon believed. "The President makes foreign policy."

The new team's priority was obviously Vietnam. When Nixon took office, the United States had 545,000 troops in Vietnam, and nearly 31,000 Americans had already died there. Nixon's cryptically stated goal—"peace with honor"—was to withdraw U.S. ground forces so as to reduce the casualties that fueled home-front protest, and turn the ground fighting over to U.S.-trained ARVN (Army of the Republic of Vietnam) forces. Through "Vietnamization" of the war, Nixon still hoped to secure a settlement favorable to U.S. interests. After assuring President Thieu of America's continued support, Nixon in June 1969 announced the withdrawal of 25,000 U.S. troops. By the end of 1970, American troop strength in Vietnam stood at 280,000; by December 1971, 140,000, only about half of them combat troops.

The ARVN forces still relied on U.S. training, weapons, vehicles, communications, and air support. Moreover, Nixon stepped up both the pacification program and the Phoenix Program, aimed at eradicating the VC infrastructure, and escalated the bombing of communist bases in Laos. In March 1969, amid a major North Vietnamese offensive, Nixon ordered the secret bombing of North Vietnamese bases and supply trails in neighboring Cambodia. By April 1970, B-52s had dumped 110,000 tons of bombs on the tiny country.

When the *New York Times* reported the Cambodian bombing, Kissinger ordered the FBI to wiretap the telephones of a National Security Council aide and other suspected leakers. Soon the illegal wiretaps expanded to journalists and White House aides. The tangle of illegal activities that would drive Nixon from office in 1974 originated in this 1969 effort to conceal the Cambodian air war.

Nixon's goal was to pressure Hanoi to accept U.S. terms even as American troop strength declined. As Kissinger commented, "I refuse to believe that a little fourth-rate power like North Vietnam does not have a breaking point." Nixon put the matter in Orwellian terms: "The true objective of this war is peace. It is a war for peace." The bombing also served to convince Hanoi that Nixon was capable of any level of escalation. As he later explained to his aide Robert Haldeman:

> I call it the madman theory, Bob. . . . I want the North Vietnamese to believe I've reached the point where I might do anything to stop the war. We'll just slip the word to them that, "For God sakes, you know Nixon is obsessed about Communists. We can't restrain him when he's angry—and he has his hand on the nuclear button"—and Ho Chi Minh himself will be in Paris in two days begging for peace.

In fact, the cease-fire talks remained stalemated as Nixon continued to back the Thieu regime and insist that Hanoi withdraw its troops from South Vietnam. Hanoi, in turn, demanded full U.S. withdrawal and a government in Saigon that excluded Thieu. Kissinger met secretly with the North Vietnamese negotiators in Paris in 1969 and 1970, but to little effect. When Ho Chi Minh died in September 1969, Hanoi's new leaders vowed to carry on the struggle.

As Vietnamization failed to end the war, youthful alienation deepened. The counterculture crested in August 1969 when four hundred thousand young people gathered on a farm near Woodstock, New York, for a rain-drenched three-day festival featuring rock music, marijuana and other substances, and communal good feeling. The event proved remarkably trouble-free, and the counterculture acquired a new name: the Woodstock Nation. For decades after, participants would recall the festival as a defining moment of their youth. Although more a cultural phenomenon than a political event, Woodstock in part became a vast antiwar rally. Antiwar themes and political alienation pervaded the music, most memorably in Jimi Hendrix's sardonic version of "The Star Spangled Banner."

The more explicit antiwar movement, dormant since August 1968, also revived. Movement leaders designated October 15, 1969, as Vietnam Moratorium Day. Thousands of protesters left jobs and classes to rally in Boston, New York, and other cities and college towns. Coretta Scott King, carrying on her slain husband's cause, led a candlelight parade of 30,000 in Washington, D.C. The weekend of November 13–15 saw another mass rally in Washington organized by an antiwar coalition called the New Mobilization. As a cold rain whipped the capital, 45,000 participants walked from Arlington National Cemetery to the Capitol, each carrying a candle and a placard bearing the name of a soldier killed in Vietnam. They called out the names as they passed the White House and at the Capitol deposited the placards in twelve wooden coffins. (While most of the participants joined in the peaceful "March Against Death," several thousand descended on the Department of Justice shouting "Smash the state!" After ripping down and burning the U.S. flag, they raised an NLF flag in its place.) On Saturday, a throng variously estimated from 250,000 to 800,000 gathered on the Mall to decry the war. President Nixon let it be known that he had spent the day watching football on television. At about the same time, the *New York Times*'s revelation of the My Lai massacre intensified revulsion against the war.

Vietnamization eroded the morale of both U.S. and South Vietnamese troops who remained in the field. Units openly evaded combat; two infantry units flatly refused orders. Among GIs, drug use and racial tension soared. The army reported more than two thousand cases of "fragging"—attacks on officers by their own men—in 1970. A Marine colonel warned in the *Armed Forces Journal* in June 1971, "Our army that now remains in Vietnam is in a state approaching collapse, . . . drug-ridden and dispirited where not mutinous."

Still Nixon pressed on. On April 30, 1970, the president announced a joint U.S.–South Vietnamese ground attack on North Vietnamese bases in Cambodia. The goal, he asserted, was to eradicate the semimythic nerve center of Hanoi's war effort. Nixon and Kissinger had a larger, twofold aim, however. First, they sought to escalate pressure on North Vietnam to settle the war on America's terms. Second, they wished to support Cambodia's new pro-Western ruler, the right-wing military officer Lon Nol, who had overthrown the neutralist Prince Norodom Sihanouk a few weeks earlier. For years, Sihanouk had managed to keep the worst of the war's ravages from Cambodia. After 1970, as a result of U.S. involvement, Cambodia was sucked into the maelstrom, with horrendous consequences for its people.

In announcing the Cambodian invasion, Nixon insisted that if America allowed communism to overrun Southeast Asia, the United States would become a "pitiful, helpless giant" respected by no one. Failure in Vietnam, he cautioned, would signal "that despite its overwhelming power the United States, when a real crisis comes, will be found wanting." Linking his foreign and domestic policies, the president warned that radicals were undermining American institutions at home just as "small nations all over the world find themselves under attack from within and from without."

The Cambodian invasion revived the flagging antiwar cause. In a largely symbolic action, congressional opponents of the war terminated the 1964 Gulf of Tonkin Resolution under which Johnson had escalated the war. The angry aftermath of Nixon's speech saw classes canceled at over a third of the nation's colleges and universities, including Kent State University in Ohio, where radicals had recently burned the ROTC building. Ohio's Republican governor, seeking his party's Senate nomination, took a hard line and ordered the Ohio National Guard to Kent State. On

May 4, nervous guardsmen in gas masks—pharmacists, accountants, and salesmen activated on a few days' notice—raked a crowd of students with M-1 rifle fire, killing two young men and two young women and injuring nine others. Apologists later claimed that the students had mortally threatened the troops, but insults and a few rocks thrown hardly justified the murderous fusillade. One guardsman later confessed that he had taken off his glasses to don his gas mask and could see only a blur as he fired into the crowd. Ten days later, amid campus protests over Vietnam and other issues at Jackson State College in Mississippi, state troopers sprayed a dormitory with gunfire, killing two women and wounding nine.

The protests and campus killings of May 1970 marked the end of the major cycle of antiwar activism. Why did a force that had roused such passion fade so quickly? Nixon's Vietnamization strategy and the decline in U.S. casualties clearly played a central role. The weekly toll of U.S. combat deaths fell from nearly two hundred in 1969 to thirty-five by early 1971. Further, Congress in March 1969 limited the draft to nineteen-year-olds, to be chosen by lottery on the basis of birth date. Males twenty and older no longer faced military duty. In January 1972, Congress ended the draft entirely.

A government propaganda campaign also helped to weaken the movement. Nixon sneered at antiwar activists as "bums." Vice President Agnew, exploiting working-class resentment of college protesters, called the demonstrators an "effete corps of impudent snobs." The FBI spied on SDS and other antiwar (and civil-rights) groups by bugging their telephones, stealing their mail, paying informants, and planting rumors designed to discredit the leaders. In October 1968, the FBI warned its field offices that "the New Left with its anti-war and anti-draft entourage" would likely continue to disrupt campuses, and urged a maximum effort "to destroy this insidious movement."

Nixon, his paranoid streak fed by class resentments rooted in childhood, the hostility of the liberal media, and the skullduggery that he believed had cost him the presidency in 1960, became obsessed with eradicating his enemies. To this end, he approved an elaborate—and patently illegal—plan by a White House aide for discrediting antiwar groups and leaders. Although not implemented because it overlapped with the FBI's ongoing program, the plan reflected the White House's siege mentality.

Federal efforts to stifle the movement found parallels in state and local action against radicals, including the 1970 Kent State killings. In May 1969, police fired on six thousand protesters in Berkeley, California, killing one and blinding another. The National Guard, ordered in by Governor Ronald Reagan, occupied Berkeley for over two weeks. As tensions flared again in April 1970, Reagan snapped, "If it takes a bloodbath, let's get it over with. No more appeasement."

Through informants, agents provocateurs, forged letters, and other means, the FBI also targeted the militant Black Panthers, described in 1968 by J. Edgar Hoover as "the greatest threat to . . . internal security" facing America. In the predawn hours of December 4, 1969, Chicago police raided the headquarters of the Illinois Black Panthers. A hail of police gunfire cut down the party's charismatic state leader, Fred Hampton, and another local leader, Mark Clark, and wounded four others. A federal court later awarded the survivors, and the families of Hampton and Clark, $1.85 million in damages.

Incited by the government's inflammatory pronouncements and episodes of official repression, the public mood turned ugly. In opinion polls, most Americans rated campus unrest as a greater danger than the Vietnam War itself. A citizenry increasingly fearful of domestic turmoil generally sided with the authorities against "student rioters." Even as the war in Southeast Asia wound down, hostility toward "hippies," youthful radicals, and campus protesters remained intense, especially among older Americans. Yet this anger had a class as well as a generational dimension. Working-class Americans resented affluent college students who protested at home while poorer youth bore the brunt of combat in Vietnam.

On May 8, 1970, four days after the Kent State shootings, construction workers at the New York World Trade Center, shouting "Kill the commie bastards," attacked a group of antiwar marchers, injuring seventy. A similar demonstration by "hard hats" erupted in St. Louis. Soon after, President Nixon proudly accepted a hard hat at a White House ceremony. On May 20, a hundred thousand New Yorkers, mostly construction workers and longshoremen, staged a prowar march, waving flags and singing "God Bless America." Nixon's "silent majority" had found its voice, and it was a howl of rage against college youth and others of the privileged classes. To these angry Americans, those opposing the war were heaping contempt on military service, patriotism, loyalty, and duty.

But the movement also fell victim to internal erosion and conflicts. As frustration with the war mounted, many activists followed Timothy Leary's advice to drop out. SDS collapsed in 1969 in bitter factional feuding between doctrinaire Maoists organized as the Progressive Labor party (PLP) and radical activists who called themselves the Weathermen.* By the end, lamented Todd Gitlin, a leader in its heady early days, SDS "had degenerated into a caricature of everything idealists find alienating about politics-as-usual: cynicism, sloganeering, manipulation." Far from articulating a bold vision of political renewal, the organization had become a swamp of soggy ideological disputes "that only the most dedicated—or masochistic—would bother to try slogging through."

Cut off from former friends and allies, a few hundred Weathermen went underground to "bring the war home" to America and to foment the revolution that their ideology assured them was imminent. The Weathermen and their sympathizers sought not U.S. withdrawal from Vietnam but U.S. *defeat* there. An NLF victory, they hoped, would hasten revolution at home and end American imperialism worldwide. The organization thus embraced the view of the war held by its most hawkish backers: A loss in Vietnam would destroy America's credibility worldwide.

In October 1969, several hundred Weathermen organized the "Days of Rage" in Chicago, smashing store windows and trashing parked cars. From September 1969 to May 1970, a handful of militants carried out some 250 bombings nationwide, including ROTC headquarters, draft boards, and other symbols of militarism or capitalism. One underground activist, arrested for bombing a Bank of America branch near Santa Barbara, explained, "It was the biggest capitalist thing around." On March 6, 1970, three Weathermen died when a blast rocked the Manhattan

---

* The name came from a Bob Dylan line "You don't need a weatherman to know which way the wind blows." Shedding gender specificity, this faction later became known as the Weatherpeople or the Weather Underground.

townhouse where they were making bombs. In August 1970, four radicals at the University of Wisconsin in Madison parked a truck loaded with explosives by a campus building housing the Army Mathematics Research Center. The explosives detonated in the middle of the night, shattering the building and killing a late-working student, himself an opponent of the war.

This extremist wing grew more visible as the antiwar movement weakened. On May 1, 1971, thirty thousand hard-core activists arrived in Washington intent on "shutting the government down." As several of them blocked traffic, others broke windows and rampaged in the streets. A few days earlier, members of the recently formed Vietnam Veterans Against the War had publicly thrown away their medals and campaign ribbons in an angry ceremony at the Capitol. Yet neither street theater nor ventures in "smashing the state" had much apparent effect on the Nixon White House.

Unable to stop the war, some activists focused on exposing the process by which America had entered the conflict. Secretary of Defense McNamara, before leaving office, had asked his aides to compile from Pentagon files a history of the process by which the Kennedy and Johnson administrations had planned and prosecuted the war. In March 1971, one of these aides, Daniel Ellsberg, now an antiwar activist, gave the explosive documents to the *New York Times.* Nixon tried to halt publication, but the Supreme Court upheld the *Times*'s claim to First Amendment protection. The so-called *Pentagon Papers* revealed a pattern of official secrecy and deception of both Congress and the public and fed a suspicion of government that would deepen in the years ahead.

The publication of the *Pentagon Papers* intensified Nixon's and Kissinger's obsession with press leaks. On Nixon's orders, aides Robert Haldeman and John Ehrlichman assembled a secret team of former FBI and CIA operatives to trace leaks by using wiretaps and other means. Appropriately nicknamed the Plumbers, the group carried out a series of illegal operations. In their first project, the Plumbers broke into the office of Daniel Ellsberg's psychiatrist, seeking evidence that would discredit Ellsberg and, indirectly, the entire antiwar movement.

Meanwhile, the Paris talks dragged on. In May 1971, Kissinger offered to pull out within seven months of a cease-fire in exchange for the return of prisoners of war and Hanoi's pledge to stop sending troops to South Vietnam. When Hanoi and the NLF (now renamed the Provisional Revolutionary Government, or PRG) made a promising counteroffer, the peace talks took on new life. With South Vietnamese elections due in the fall of 1971, Hanoi's chief negotiator Le Duc Tho made the radical proposal that the process be honest, confident that Thieu would lose a fair election. Instead, Thieu rigged the outcome to give himself 94.3 percent of the vote. The Paris talks sputtered.

Nixon and Kissinger were simultaneously pursuing improved relations with China and the Soviet Union (see p. 321), and they informed both superpowers that peace in Vietnam would further that goal. Both Moscow and Beijing discreetly advised Hanoi to reach a settlement, but to no effect. On March 30, 1972, hoping to overwhelm the Saigon government as U.S. troop strength dwindled, Hanoi resumed full military operations in South Vietnam. As two hundred thousand North Vietnamese and PRG forces attacked, the ARVN forces fell back in panicked disarray.

⁓ Fearful of a humiliating rout, Nixon ordered new bombing around Hanoi and Haiphong. "The bastards have never been bombed like they're going to be bombed this time," he vowed grimly. As the North Vietnamese advanced, taking Quang Tri City on May 1, Nixon stepped up the bombing of the north and of North Vietnamese strongholds in Quang Tri province and along the Cambodian border. Land already pockmarked by years of bombing again endured incessant B-52 raids. In the heaviest air strikes of the war, the United States dropped 112,000 tons of explosives on North Vietnam in June alone. Nixon also announced the mining of Haiphong harbor to disrupt the flow of supplies to North Vietnam, a step that the military had long urged. ⁓

Americans lulled by three years of Vietnamization suddenly confronted a newly raging war. This time, however, U.S. casualties were low. Of GIs remaining in Vietnam, only six thousand were assigned to combat duty. Although U.S. bombers and weapons remained crucial to the conflict, the large-scale protests of the Johnson era had faded. As Senator George McGovern of South Dakota observed, when the corpses changed color, American interest diminished.

⁓ In October, Hanoi made key concessions, agreeing to a cease-fire before a political settlement and accepting Thieu's regime as one of two "administrative entities" in South Vietnam, the other being the PRG. A commission made up of the PRG, the Thieu government, and neutralist elements, the negotiators agreed, would determine South Vietnam's political future. Kissinger, eager for a deal as the U.S. election neared, initialed a draft agreement on October 22. "Peace is at hand," he promised. ⁓

President Thieu denounced the draft, rightly fearing for his future once the Americans withdrew. Nixon himself was incensed by an accord that all but abandoned the Saigon regime. Talks resumed, but Le Duc Tho rejected the changes that Thieu demanded in the agreement. Nixon, safely reelected, used the delay to transfer over $1 billion in military hardware to the Saigon government and promised Thieu "swift and severe" retaliation if Hanoi violated the agreement.

On December 18, with the Paris talks stalled, Nixon ordered renewed bombing around Hanoi and Haiphong and further mining of Haiphong harbor. In twelve days of these around-the-clock "Christmas bombings," thirty-six thousand tons of bombs fell, more than in the entire 1969–71 period. Amid worldwide denunciations of Nixon's action, it seemed for a time that the antiwar movement might reignite. However, the Paris talks resumed, and on January 27, 1973, Kissinger and Le Duc Tho initialed a cease-fire accord, essentially the same one agreed to the previous October. Two months later, the last U.S. troops left South Vietnam. Nineteen years after the 1954 Geneva Accords and eight years after the 1965 escalation, America's longest and most inconclusive war ended, at least in terms of U.S. casualties. During "Nixon's War," 20,553 Americans had died, together with an estimated 107,000 ARVN forces and more than 500,000 North Vietnamese and PRG troops. The civilian toll ran into the hundreds of thousands.

Rooted in a Cold War mindset that had evolved since World War II, the Vietnam War had exacted a high price in life and resources, battered America's reputation abroad, and raised questions about the nation's world role. For years, Vietnam memories would fuel an aversion to any U.S. military involvement abroad. When President George Bush took the nation into war in 1991 in the Persian Gulf, he did so in part, he asserted, to help Americans "kick the Vietnam syndrome once and for all."

The war also increased the power of the presidency. In pursuing the conflict, Nixon and Kissinger, accelerating a trend already evident in the Kennedy and Johnson years, had vastly enlarged the role of the White House and the National Security Council in implementing foreign policy. In November 1973, over Nixon's veto, Congress passed the War Powers Act. This law requires the president to notify Congress "in every possible instance" before sending troops into combat or into situations where hostilities appear imminent. Furthermore, troops must be withdrawn within six months unless Congress approves their further deployment. Had the law been in place in 1965, Lyndon Johnson would have found it difficult to take the nation into war without congressional and public debate. But the War Powers Act left unresolved the basic tension between the executive and the legislative branches over committing U.S. forces, and the issue remained under debate.

Vietnam stands as a watershed in postwar American history. It represented the culmination of twenty years of Cold War thinking. But in its aftermath, the nation turned to new concerns and set new priorities. Above all, the war raised questions about the meaning of our national experience. After Vietnam, Americans could no longer unquestioningly accept certitudes about the nation's benign world role. Stanley Hoffmann, professor of government at Harvard, looked back on the ordeal in 1979. Focusing on the role of Nixon and Kissinger, he wrote, "At the root of this tree of evils one finds an extraordinary arrogance ... , a self-intoxicating confidence in our capacity to manipulate other societies." Through the Vietnam experience, as a theologian might put it, America lost its innocence and learned the meaning of sin.

Realpolitik and Détente

For Nixon and Kissinger, extricating the United States from Vietnam constituted only one move in the larger chess game of global politics. Their overall goal was détente with the Soviet Union and China. Détente served many functions. Nixon and Kissinger used the lure of improved relations to persuade Beijing and Moscow to pressure Hanoi to reach a settlement in Vietnam. And Nixon the politician realized that easing Cold War hostilities could raise his stock with moderates and liberals in the 1972 election.

At first glance, Nixon seems miscast in the role of either strategist or advocate of détente. His early worldview had reflected the simplistic polarities of the Cold War, and he had made his reputation by denouncing communism. But Nixon's thought had evolved. Shrewd, opportunistic, and highly intelligent, he adapted quickly to changed political realities. His 1967 article in *Foreign Affairs,* "Asia After Viet Nam," had won notice for its strategic analysis and its early recognition that the Vietnam trauma would reduce Americans' tolerance for "the role of the United States as world policeman." With the Soviets achieving nuclear parity with the United States and the Chinese gaining nuclear strength, he had further noted, the world power balance was fundamentally shifting. Revealing his thinking on both global diplomacy and domestic politics, Nixon mused to journalist Garry Wills in 1968 that in coming years, "a man who knows the world will be able to forge a whole new set of alliances."

Nixon remained suspicious of both the Soviets and the Chinese, but he had concluded that normalizing relations with these Cold War adversaries would serve U.S. interests. His approach was more pragmatic and less ideologically driven than anyone familiar with his early career might have predicted.

Even more explicitly than Nixon, Henry Kissinger—national security adviser and, after 1973, secretary of state—held a realpolitik view in which power calculations, not moral judgments, shaped foreign policy. On occasion Kissinger quoted Goethe: "If I had to choose between justice and disorder, on the one hand, and injustice and order on the other, I would always choose the latter." His first book had analyzed the conservative statesmen who had reconfigured Europe after the Napoleonic wars. Kissinger shared Nixon's view that America must outgrow Cold War slogans and reconceptualize international relations. Above all, the two men saw a historic opportunity to advance American interests by exploiting the split between the communist superpowers, China and the Soviet Union.

Both Nixon and Kissinger realized that the United States no longer dominated the world as it had after World War II. The Soviet Union and China were nuclear powers, and Western Europe, too, had emerged as a key player. On the economic front, the inflation that began in the mid-1960s had weakened the dollar, and Germany and Japan were ascending as major trading competitors. In 1971, for the first time since 1894, the United States ran a trade deficit, as imports surpassed exports. For Nixon and Kissinger, strengthening America's world economic standing was crucial. In a 1971 speech in Kansas City, facing a projected trade deficit of $48 billion, Nixon presciently declared, "Economic power will be the key to other kinds of power . . . in the last third of this century."

In their quest for détente, Nixon and Kissinger focused first on China. Ever since the Chinese communists' victory in 1949, the United States had treated this vast nation as a pariah. Clinging to the fiction that Jiang Jieshi's Taiwan regime was China's true government, Washington had refused any dealings with Beijing, and had thwarted its efforts to join the UN. Now Nixon and Kissinger saw advantages in better relations with China. They believed that "playing the China card," for example, could help to extract concessions from the Soviet Union on arms control and other issues. The Chinese, worried about the 1 million Soviet troops along their border, discreetly welcomed closer ties with the United States, despite the two nations' contrasting ideologies.

Nixon first signaled the shift in 1970 by speaking of "the People's Republic of China" rather than the usual "Red China" and by expressing curiosity about the distant land that no American president had ever visited while in office.* Beijing responded by inviting a touring U.S. table tennis team to visit China. Practicing "Ping-Pong diplomacy," the Chinese players—the world's best—politely lost to the visitors or took care not to beat them too badly. In June 1971, Henry Kissinger secretly flew to Beijing for meetings with Chinese leaders.

Kissinger's visit laid the groundwork for Nixon's historic February 1972 trip to China. At the airport, the president shook hands with Premier Zhou Enlai, erasing John Foster Dulles's insulting refusal to greet Zhou at the 1954 Geneva Confer-

---

* President Ulysses S. Grant had stopped in China on a world tour after leaving the White House.

❖❖ IN PERSPECTIVE: *The Nuclear Threat*

The 1972 SALT I and ABM treaties brought a ray of hope to the long effort to restrain the nuclear arms race. At every stage from 1945 through the 1980s, powerful forces either propelled this effort forward or, more often dragged it down. These forces included Cold War suspicions, periodic upsurges of popular nuclear fear, and advances in the technology of destruction.

Nothing thwarted nuclear arms control more than the harsh realities of the Cold War. U.S.-Soviet hostility repeatedly sabotaged efforts to regulate missile competition. The Limited Nuclear Test Ban Treaty of 1963 did not include underground tests because the mutually suspicious superpowers could not agree on verification procedures.

Grassroots fear of atomic war also influenced arms-control efforts, often in unexpected ways. As one example, after Hiroshima and Nagasaki, frightened U.S. scientists used terrifying descriptions of the bomb's effects to urge public demand for international control of atomic energy. In the long run, however, their campaign roused support not for disarmament but for keeping ahead of the Russians in nuclear competition. In the late fifties and early sixties, fear of radioactive fallout from nuclear tests led to strong popular support for a test-ban treaty. This grassroots movement helped to produce the 1963 ban on atmospheric tests. Nevertheless, with protests focused on fallout rather than on the larger nuclear threat, the activist momentum faded after 1963, even though the nuclear arms race continued unabated.

The ambiguous effects of nuclear fear and of antinuclear protest again became evident in 1981–83, when a campaign to freeze the nuclear arms race won broad backing. As in 1946, activists won recruits with graphic descriptions of thermonuclear annihilation. President Reagan, however, exploited the campaign for his own purposes. In a March 1983 TV address, Reagan professed his horror of nuclear war, but rather than suggest a freeze, he proposed a missile-defense system. As Americans debated Reagan's Strategic Defense Initiative (SDI), the freeze movement expired.

Technological advances complicated arms control as well. Moscow's testing of an atomic bomb in 1949, for example, led President Truman to launch a race for the hy-

---

ence. Later, Nixon drank toasts with Zhou and Mao Zedong as an orchestra played "America the Beautiful." At the Great Wall of China, the president enthusiastically observed, "This truly is a great wall." He attended a ballet choreographed by Mao's actress wife, who confided to Nixon that her favorite movie was *Gone With the Wind*. The visit ended with a joint communiqué calling for increased contacts between the two nations. Full diplomatic recognition would not come until 1979, but Nixon had mended relations with a major Cold War adversary.

Next came détente with the Soviet Union. Nixon and Kissinger still embraced containment doctrine, and they maneuvered in many parts of the world to check Moscow's influence. But they viewed the Soviet Union as simply another player in drogen bomb—a race that physicist Edward Teller assured him the United States could win. The Soviets quickly developed their own H-bomb, upping the nuclear ante still higher. Another breakthrough that frustrated arms-control efforts came in the 1970s, when U.S. technicians developed missiles that could carry multiple, independently targeted nuclear warheads or "reentry vehicles" (MIRVs). Although SALT I limited the number of *missiles,* it did not restrict the number of *warheads* that each missile could carry. Thus, thanks to MIRVing, the nuclear arms race roared on despite the 1972 accord.

With the Cold War's end, the superpowers' nuclear competition faded at last. In 1992 Washington and Moscow agreed upon a treaty imposing deep cuts on strategic missiles. In 1993, after soaking up $30 billion, the SDI program was put on the back burner. But a witches' brew of nuclear danger still simmered. The issue of safely storing tons of radioactive waste from missiles and nuclear-power plants posed problems of enormous complexity, both technologically and politically. Moreover, dismantling the former Soviet Union's nuclear arsenal proved a tricky business. Newly independent Ukraine, for example, resisted giving up the missiles on its soil, not out of any intention to use them but because of their value as economic bargaining chips.

Despite the easing of superpower tension, the threat of proliferation persisted, a part of the nuclear dilemma from the beginning. The 1968 Nuclear Nonproliferation Treaty (NPT), signed by 153 states, had failed to halt the spread of nuclear weapons. As Iraq, North Korea, and other nations ruled by authoritarian regimes pursued weapons research, the specter of nuclear terrorism stalked humanity. In 1993 North Korea withdrew from the NPT. India conducted five nuclear weapons tests in 1998.

One group still haunted by the nuclear threat were the Americans exposed to radiation from weapons testing. In 1988 Congress permitted veterans who had served as human guinea pigs in nuclear tests to file service-related disability claims if they developed one of thirteen types of cancer. In 1989, former civilian employees at the Nevada test site sued the U.S. government for failing to adopt adequate safety procedures. Many citizens exposed to windborne fallout in eastern Nevada and southern Utah lived in fear of developing cancer. In *American Ground Zero: The Secret Nuclear War* (1993), photojournalist Carole Gallagher offered a gripping memoir of this bitter legacy. Ironically, the most devastating effects of a program designed to protect American had been wrought on the American people themselves. Post-Cold War revelations made clear that Soviet testing, too, had exposed thousands of troops and civilians to highly dangerous radiation levels.

Nearly thirty years after SALT I, in short, the nuclear menace lives on. Americans who had hailed the atomic bomb in 1945 could scarcely have guessed what lay ahead.

---

the global power game, not as an outlaw state. The Soviets—facing China to their east and NATO and a restive group of satellites to their west, spending vast sums on armaments, and grappling with weak agricultural output and other economic problems—welcomed Washington's overtures. In 1971, at Nixon's initiative, the United States and the Soviet Union, with the other wartime allies, signed an agreement ensuring western access to Berlin in return for West Germany's pledge not to absorb the city into the Federal Republic. The issue that had sparked so many Cold War crises was thus neutralized.

Hard bargaining with the Kremlin paved the way for another of Nixon's historic visits. In May 1972, fresh from Beijing, Nixon's entourage arrived in Moscow.

The stepped-up fighting in Vietnam raised problems, but Nixon told the Soviet leaders, "There must be room in this world for two great nations with different systems to live together and work together."

Improved trade relations remained a prime goal of détente, and in Moscow Nixon completed a deal whereby the Soviets agreed to buy $750 million in American wheat. This arrangement eased the trade deficit and earned Nixon points in the farm belt. Yet missiles, not wheat, dominated Nixon's Moscow agenda. The years since the 1963 test-ban treaty had seen little arms-control progress, as the two nations' nuclear arsenals had vastly increased. In 1969, however, the two sides began talks in Geneva on a strategic arms limitation treaty, known by the acronym SALT I. Nixon and Kissinger secretly completed the SALT negotiations with Soviet ambassador Anatoly Dobrynin in Washington. (Typically, they concealed the meetings from both the Geneva negotiators and the State Department.) The treaty, signed by Nixon and Brezhnev in Moscow, froze each side's arsenals of land-based and submarine-launched missiles for five years. However, SALT I did little to slow the nuclear arms race, because it failed to address the latest technological advance: MIRV, or multiple independently targetable reentry vehicles. Through MIRVing, up to fourteen separately targeted warheads could be attached to a single missile. MIRVed missiles were highly destabilizing, for they increased the odds of destroying most of the enemy's retaliatory missiles and thus encouraged a first strike.

More important was the Anti-Ballistic Missile (ABM) Treaty, signed as part of the SALT accord. Over the years, nuclear strategists had insisted that deterrence theory—the premise that a nation vulnerable to a decisive counterattack would never initiate a nuclear assault—offered the best safeguard against nuclear war. But deterrence could work only if neither side possessed a defense against nuclear weapons. If one nation successfully deployed a full missile-defense system, that nation theoretically would be free to launch a nuclear attack, or to try nuclear blackmail, without fear of reprisal. Such calculations underlay the ABM Treaty, by which both sides pledged not to develop nationwide missile-defense systems. On a 1973 visit to the United States by Soviet leader Leonid Brezhnev, the two sides agreed to pursue a more comprehensive arms-control treaty.

As Nixon and Kissinger addressed superpower relations, they also maneuvered in the Middle East, where the United States found itself walking a tightrope. As Israel's patron, Washington supplied the military and economic aid that ensured the Jewish state's survival. Yet Americans depended on oil from the Arab states. Complicating the picture, the Mideast had become a Cold War arena, where the United States and the Soviet Union vied for allies. In the Six Day War of 1967, Israel had defeated its Arab foes and occupied the Golan Heights on its northern border with Syria, the Egyptian-held Sinai peninsula and Gaza Strip, and the West Bank of the Jordan River and the Old City of Jerusalem, hitherto controlled by Jordan. In October 1973, backed by Soviet arms, Egypt and Syria launched a war against Israel to redress their grievances. The attack came on Yom Kippur, the holiest day of the Jewish year. Israel, aided by an airlift of U.S. arms, fought off the attackers and pursued Egyptian troops across the Sinai. The war strained détente, as Brezhnev threatened to send troops to Egypt and the Pentagon went to a high level of nuclear alert. To halt Israel's counterattack, the United

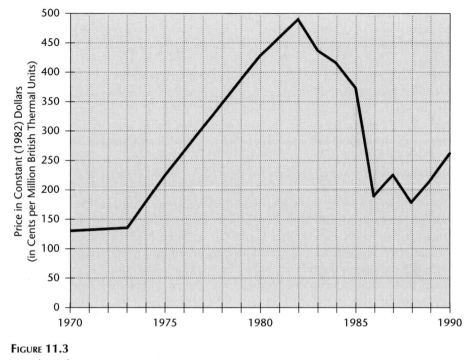

FIGURE 11.3

Crude Oil Prices, 1970–1990

SOURCE: U.S. Energy Information Administration, *Annual Energy Review.*

States withheld military supplies. Clearly, in areas of regional conflict the Cold War remained very much alive.

The Yom Kippur War illustrated the links between foreign policy and the domestic economy. Angered by U.S. support for Israel, the oil-producing Arab states halted oil shipments to the United States from October 1973 to March 1974. Although the United States imported only 12 percent of its oil from the region, the American public felt the pinch. Fuel and gasoline shortages plagued the nation and gasoline prices soared from forty cents to fifty-five cents a gallon, spurring inflation and alarming motorists accustomed to cheap fuel. Stock prices plummeted as the boycott's effects bit in. Hitting all sectors of the economy, the oil crisis contributed in 1974–75 to the nation's worst recession since the 1930s.

The embargo focused attention on longer-term problems, too, including rising energy costs. Since OPEC's founding in 1960, oil prices had quadrupled. This increase was justified, according to the oil-producing nations, because their oil reserves were finite, and inflation forced them to pay higher prices for imported manufactured goods. The crisis also underscored America's disproportionate consumption of the world's natural resources. Home to only 6 percent of the population, the United States gobbled 40 percent of the earth's resources.

For both strategic and economic reasons, then, Nixon and Kissinger concluded that the United States must mend fences with the Arabs. During two years of "shuttle diplomacy" on a plane dubbed the "yo-yo express" because it took off and landed so often, Kissinger jetted to Middle East capitals negotiating disputes, currying favor with the Arab states, and countering Soviet influence. Although he failed to resolve the region's underlying animosities, he did make progress. As early as November 1973, he negotiated a cease-fire between Israel and Egypt and persuaded Israel to withdraw from Egyptian and Syrian land seized in the 1973 war. In return, the Arabs' oil boycott ended. Escaping the Watergate crisis at home, President Nixon toured the region in June 1974. Egypt's new president, Anwar el-Sadat, having broken with the Soviets, now warmed to the United States.

Oriented toward power, the Nixon-Kissinger team readily supported authoritarian and even dictatorial regimes that served American strategic or economic interests. The administration granted millions of dollars in military assistance and foreign aid to the autocratic shah of Iran, the corrupt Ferdinand Marcos of the Philippines, South Africa's white-supremacist government, repressive regimes and military dictatorships in Argentina, South Korea, Brazil, Nigeria, and other nations. This realpolitik approach ignored nations that did not at the moment fit into Washington's grand design but that might become crucial in the future. It also allied the United States with rulers hated by their own people. When these despots fell, as they invariably did, the United States was reviled as well, making it difficult for Washington to build good relations with the new governments.

The administration's realpolitik manifested itself most brutally in Chile. In a three-way 1970 presidential election, the Chileans gave Marxist Salvador Allende a plurality. The administration feared that Allende would jeopardize the large Chilean investments of major U.S. corporations such as International Telephone and Telegraph (ITT). Kissinger and Nixon also saw Allende as a potential Castro who would transform Chile into a client state of Moscow. As Kissinger mused, "I don't see why we need to stand by and watch a country go communist due to the irresponsibility of its own people." Working through the CIA, Nixon plotted a military coup to prevent Allende from taking office. When this effort failed, Nixon secretly channeled $10 million to the CIA to disrupt Allende's government and to "make the [Chilean] economy scream." The president also cut off aid to the country and persuaded international monetary agencies to deny it development loans.

When Allende tried to break up Chile's large landholdings and nationalized nearly $1 billion in U.S. corporate investments, the campaign against him grew more urgent. In September 1973, a military junta overthrew the government and murdered Allende. Nixon quickly recognized the new regime, and U.S. economic relations with Chile resumed. The CIA's role in the coup remains murky, but the administration clearly helped to create the conditions that led to it. When Chile's new rulers resorted to such brutalities that even the U.S. ambassador protested, Kissinger snapped icily, "Cut out the political science lecture."

Richard Nixon and Henry Kissinger reshaped the conceptual foundations of postwar U.S. foreign policy.* In the 1950s and 1960s, the architects of U.S. diplomacy tended to assume a bipolar world and to substitute crisis management and ideological formulas for long-range strategic analysis. Nixon and Kissinger, by con-

---

* Although Nixon's role ended with his resignation in August 1974, Kissinger remained secretary of state until January 1977.

trast, envisioned a multipolar world in which power arose not only from military might but from economic and geopolitical realities. The emphasis on economic factors in diplomacy would prove especially important in laying the intellectual groundwork for the post–Cold War world of the 1990s.

Downplaying ideology, both men saw self-interest and long-term strategic calculations as the key to nations' behavior, and they molded U.S. policy accordingly. As historian John Lewis Gaddis writes, "It was the overall calculus of power that was important, not the defeats or victories that might take place in isolated theaters of competition." Concentrating on areas that they believed truly involved U.S. interests, they moved away from a foreign policy driven by brushfire crises. Specifically, they disengaged from Vietnam, which Kissinger dismissed as "a small peninsula on a major continent." (Their determination to withdraw from that small peninsula on their own terms proved very costly, however.) Instead, they opened the door to China, negotiated seriously with the Soviets, and pursued U.S. interests in the Middle East. Their strategy echoed the realist approach to foreign policy enunciated by George Kennan in the late 1940s. Downgrading ideology, Kennan, too, had stressed national interest. After Kissinger became secretary of state, Kennan observed, "Henry understands my views better than anyone at State ever has."

The diplomacy of the Nixon-Kissinger years also responded to specific long-term trends, notably the Sino-Soviet split, Moscow's rise to nuclear parity, and problems that plagued both the Soviet and the American economies. Tension and jealousy plagued the partnership of this odd couple once described by Nixon as "the grocer's son from Whittier and the refugee from Hitler's Germany, the politician and the academic." Yet with a remarkable concordance of worldviews, objectives, and styles of operation, they left their stamp on American diplomacy.

The duo had detractors. Conservative Republicans such as Ronald Reagan and various "neoconservative" Democrats criticized them for supposedly weakening America's defenses through the SALT treaty and cuts in military spending.* Some Democrats deplored the amorality and unconcern for human rights of their single-minded concentration on national interest and balance-of-power diplomacy. Unquestionably, their foreign policy had its brutal side, as their handling of Allende revealed.

Détente with Beijing and Moscow represents Nixon's greatest achievement. It did not end the Cold War, but it moved the conflict to a less dangerous plane. And the nation's premier Cold Warrior accomplished this turnaround. As historian Stephen Ambrose observes, Nixon's key asset was that he did not have to contend with Nixon: "Had anyone but Nixon tried to promote détente, Nixon . . . would have rallied the right wing to kill it." The president had this fact in mind when he told the Chinese, "In America, . . . those on the right can do what those on the left can only talk about."

In pursuing their grand strategy, Nixon and Kissinger centralized policymaking and resorted to secrecy and deception. Both looked askance at popular movements,

---

* Although advocates of U.S. strategic superiority wanted the savings gained through withdrawal from Vietnam to be plowed into other areas of military spending, U.S. outlays for defense declined at a steady rate of 4.5 percent from 1970 to 1975. Defense Secretary Melvin Laird, who presided over this scaleback, became a central target of conservative attack.

such as the antiwar protests, that aimed at influencing foreign policy. Diplomacy, they believed, should be left to the experts (another link with the elitist Kennan). Both bypassed the foreign-policy bureaucracy and used back channels to deal with foreign leaders. "Without secrecy," Nixon insisted, "there would have been no opening to China, no SALT agreement with the Soviet Union, and no peace treaty ending the Vietnam War." But the deviousness took its toll by creating a climate of suspicion and fostering intrigues that ultimately would drag Nixon down.

Kissinger's reputation, too, fell after he left office. He had no role in the new Republican ascendancy that began in 1981, and his reputation for toadying to the powerful, his arrogance toward subordinates, and his contempt for the foreign-policy bureaucracy all hurt his standing in the long run. His self-serving memoirs did little to salvage his image, and a massive biography published in 1992 denigrated him with grim single-mindedness.* But the reaction was as extreme as the earlier adulation, when cartoonists had portrayed him as a cape-wielding "Super-K." For all his flaws and the drawbacks of his worldview, Kissinger remains a towering figure. Emulating his heroes, the conservative statesmen of an earlier day, he set out to impose intellectual coherence on a foreign policy that had too often substituted rhetoric and bluster for broad-gauge thinking. To a great extent he succeeded—although in history's ever-shifting terrain, success is often written in the sand.

Domestic Policy: New Departures, Conservative Affirmations

Nixon would have preferred to concentrate on foreign affairs and turn over domestic issues to his cabinet, but in the modern world, the two were interwoven. As Lyndon Johnson had learned and as the 1973–74 Arab oil embargo underscored, events abroad had political and economic ramifications at home. Furthermore, Nixon's approach to foreign affairs and domestic issues was remarkably consistent. At home, too, he proved unexpectedly open to innovation. The same opportunism and even cynicism that led him to Beijing and Moscow after winning fame as an anticommunist zealot also gave him a nondogmatic adaptability in approaching domestic issues. The fact that he had won only 43 percent of the vote in 1968 and faced opposition-party majorities in both the House and Senate no doubt encouraged this flexibility.

In his early years in office, Nixon adopted moderately progressive positions, adhering to the Eisenhower strategy of accepting reforms—the New Deal, the Fair Deal, and now the Great Society—while curbing their "excesses" and administering them more economically. He signed Democratic bills raising social security benefits, increased federal funds for low-income public housing, and even expanded the Job Corps. His first term saw increases in spending on mandated social-welfare programs, especially social security, Medicare, and Medicaid. Far from bucking this trend, Nixon in a January 1971 TV interview sketched a vision of post-Vietnam America reminiscent of Lyndon Johnson at his most expansive:

---

* Walter Isaacson, *Kissinger: A Biography* (1992).

If we can get this country thinking not of how to fight a war, but . . . of clean air, clean water, open spaces, of a welfare reform program that will provide a floor under the income of every family with children in America, . . . a new approach to government, reform of education, reform of health . . . then we will have the lift of a driving dream.

Nixon's most surprising departure from laissez-faire orthodoxy came with his 1969 proposal to provide a guaranteed minimum income to every U.S. family. The initial annual minimum, $1,600 for a family of four, plus food stamps, represented nearly $9,000 in early-1990s buying power. This so-called Family Assistance Plan (FAP) was the brainchild of Nixon's urban-affairs adviser, Daniel Patrick Moynihan. Although a Democrat and a former Kennedy administration official, Moynihan had ideas that appealed to Nixon, who appointed him head of the newly created Urban Affairs Council. Moynihan proposed to replace the nation's cumbersome social-welfare system, widely criticized for perpetuating a culture of dependence, with straight cash payments to bring society's poorest members up to an agreed-upon minimum. All this would be done, Moynihan hoped, without reducing the incentive of the needy to better themselves by working. In a television interview, Moynihan defended his plan: "The problem of the poor people is they don't have enough money. . . . Cold cash! It's a surprisingly good cure for a lot of social ills." Whereas Johnson's Great Society envisioned an array of federal programs to battle poverty, the FAP approach bypassed the welfare bureaucracy in favor of funneling money directly to the poor.

Winning approval in the House, the FAP failed in the Senate. Conservatives denounced it as socialistic, and liberals balked at the low level of payments. Although unsuccessful, the scheme reveals Nixon's capacity for domestic innovation and anticipated an issue—welfare reform—that would rise to prominence in the 1990s. Many leftists not normally among Nixon's admirers cheered the FAP. Michael Harrington, the socialist whose *The Other America* had highlighted the problem of poverty a decade earlier, called it "the most radical idea since the New Deal."

Nixon's flexibility also emerged in his response to the nation's economic problems, although not at first. Johnson's "guns-and-butter" effort to finance both the Vietnam War and domestic social programs without raising taxes had ignited inflation and increased the federal deficit. These problems worsened in Nixon's early years. In 1970, as the inflationary spiral continued, Congress authorized the president to freeze wages and prices. But Nixon demurred; not only did most economists oppose such controls, but Nixon as a young lawyer in the wartime Office of Price Administration had developed a strong aversion to elaborate federal regulation and bureaucratic red tape.

Instead, Nixon tried to curb inflation by cooling the economy. To this end, he trimmed government spending and prodded the Federal Reserve Board to tighten credit. The policy not only failed to halt inflation but contributed to a business downturn. With production falling, the stock market weakening, and the jobless rate rising, the nation edged into recession. The economic fallout of Vietnamization—returning job-seeking veterans and canceled defense contracts—worsened the problem. Boeing, the Seattle aircraft giant, slashed its work force from 101,000 to 44,000. A strike at GM exacerbated economic woes. As the economy sputtered, the Democrats gleefully attacked "Nixonomics" and gained twelve House seats in the 1970 midterm election, widening their already formidable majority.

In January 1971, unemployment rose to nearly 6 percent. Spending on the federal food-stamp program mushroomed from $250 million in 1969 to $2.2 billion in 1971. The 1971 federal deficit spurted to more than $23 billion, nearly matching Johnson's record 1968 deficit. To make matters worse, as we have seen, 1971 brought the first U.S. trade deficit since the 1890s. On the world's money markets, the dollar fell to its lowest point since 1949. In 1969 Americans had named Vietnam as the nation's most pressing problem; in 1971, inflation topped the list.

Demonstrating the same pragmatism that characterized his quest for détente, Nixon abruptly reversed course. In August 1971, he announced a program of federal economic intervention such as he had rejected only months earlier. In the first phase of his anti-inflation program, the president slapped a ninety-day freeze on prices, wages, and rents.* In the second phase, launched in November, he capped annual wage increases at 5.5 percent and price and rent increases at 2.5 percent. Stressing voluntary compliance, Nixon nevertheless set up the Cost of Living Council with authority to enforce these restraints. To stimulate the economy, he announced a 10 percent tax credit for corporate investment and other pump-priming steps.

To address the weak dollar and the growing trade deficit, Nixon imposed a 10 percent surcharge on imports. He also suspended the convertibility of the dollar into gold at the official price of $35 per ounce—an artificially high valuation that was hurting America's export business. Henceforth, the dollar would "float," finding its own value in the international currency market. As the dollar became cheaper in relation to other currencies, Nixon hoped, U.S. products would attract more foreign buyers.

Proclaiming his conversion to Keynesian economics, with its advocacy of deficit spending as an economic stimulus, Nixon offered a "full employment" budget for 1972 that projected an $11.6 billion deficit. Fiscal conservatives protested, but the president defended his plan. As long as U.S. workers lacked jobs, he proclaimed in Rooseveltian phrases, deficits were justified. Like all other presidents, Nixon had shaped his economic program with one eye on the forthcoming electoral campaign.

For a time the medicine seemed to help. Inflation slowed, and the trade gap narrowed. The stock exchange broke 1000 for the first time late in 1971, a big psychological lift. But welfare and health-care payments; rising imports, especially of fuel-efficient Japanese cars; and soaring energy costs stemming from the Arab oil boycott all worked against recovery. The roller-coaster stock market dipped below 800 by the end of 1973, and the trade deficit widened. Inflation spiraled upward, hitting 11 percent in 1974, with energy and food leading the way. Unemployment reached 8.5 percent by 1975.

---

* Nixon took this action under powers granted the president by the Economic Stabilization Act, passed by the Democratic-led Congress in August 1970. At the time, Nixon had insisted he would never use these powers.

The picture looked bleak on all fronts. In constant dollars, median family income, having risen steadily since World War II, stagnated between 1970 and 1975. Similarly, U.S. productivity, which rose by more than 3 percent annually from 1947 to 1965, dropped to an anemic 1.4 percent in 1971–75. The long cycle of economic expansion that had started after World War II began grinding to a halt, and the productivity that had kept the economy humming for more than two decades sputtered ominously. Americans sensed that the downturn involved more than just the usual pattern of a brief recession followed by a strong rebound. Severe structural problems had emerged.

Circumstances had led Nixon to impose the most drastic economic controls since World War II and to adopt stimulus strategies that were anathema to earlier Republicans. The federal government's sense of obligation to foster prosperity—a legacy of the New Deal and the Employment Act of 1946—had become entrenched in the nation's polity, no matter which party held power. Ironically, Nixon's conversion to Keynesian theory came as economists were growing skeptical of government's ability to fight recessions. Battling complex long-term problems, neither Nixon nor his successors found the magic formula for assuring economic health.

In his role as party leader, Nixon continued to woo the middle-class and blue-collar white vote so crucial to his 1968 victory. Kevin Phillips explained the strategy in *The Emerging Republican Majority* (1969). To gain dominance, Phillips argued, Republicans must enlarge their traditional conservative base to include "middle Americans." These voters had once rallied to Franklin Roosevelt, but their Democratic loyalties had withered under antiwar demonstrations, black militancy, and soaring welfare costs. Political parties succeed, Phillips claimed, by understanding "who hates whom" and then exploiting those hatreds.

Nixon brought to politics the same pragmatism that defined his approach to foreign affairs. Indeed, his political style mirrored his diplomatic style. As the Sino-Soviet bloc had broken up, he and Kissinger had maneuvered to realign global power relationships to America's advantage. Similarly, as the New Deal coalition splintered, Nixon looked for opportunities to woo disaffected voting blocs.

To this end, the president balanced heretical economic proposals such as FAP and deficit spending with a more predictably conservative stance on other issues. He vetoed more than twenty spending bills passed by the Democratic Congress. In the fall of 1971, he refused to sign a bill providing day-care centers for working mothers. Such "communal approaches" to child rearing, he charged, would "sovietize" America's children. "Good public policy," he avowed, "requires that we enhance rather than diminish . . . parental involvement with children."

The president also articulated middle-class frustration with the federal bureaucracy by calling for a reduction in Washington's role in American life. To this end, he proposed in his 1972 budget message an annual rebate of $5 billion to the states, with the money to come from cuts in federal aid programs for minorities and the poor. In an obvious play for suburban votes, he predicted that his program would generate a 30 percent cut in local property taxes.

In October 1972, two weeks before the election, Congress passed Nixon's revenue-sharing bill, distributing more than $30 billion in federal revenues over a five-year period to state, county, and local governments. At the same time, Congress placed a $2.5 billion annual cap on federal welfare spending. As Washington cut funding for social programs, the theory went, local governments would pick up the slack. But big cities, awash in poverty and social problems, complained that state legislatures used the federal-rebate windfall to cover their own chronic budget shortages and neglected urban needs.

Nixon's courting of the "hard hats" who demonstrated against antiwar marchers reflected a calculated campaign to attract voters disturbed by campus unrest and left-wing protests. The Justice Department's prosecution of eight antiwar activists on conspiracy charges arising from the demonstrations at the 1968 Democratic convention also served Nixon's purposes, confirming conservatives' worst nightmares about radicals. The trial, held in Chicago from October 1969 to March 1970 before short-tempered Judge Julius Hoffman, turned into a media circus, and the defendants, including Yippie showmen Abbie Hoffman and Jerry Rubin, took over an already politicized event. They openly ridiculed an increasingly apopleptic Judge Hoffman and otherwise disrupted the proceedings. Beneath the farcical surface, a serious political psychodrama unfolded as the Nixon administration demonstrated that the forces of law and order, represented by the strong leader in the White House, could stand firm against anarchy.

Kevin Phillips's "emerging Republican majority" included blue-collar workers, as well as Catholic ethnics, anti-Castro Cuban exiles, and upwardly mobile suburbanites. GOP strategists played on such groups' fears of social disorder and charged that the Democrats were more interested in minorities and welfare clients than in the concerns of hard-working, patriotic citizens. The party of FDR, they told wavering Democrats, had been hijacked by antiwar protesters, New Left radicals, and entrenched bureaucrats out of touch with grassroots America. With George Wallace planning another presidential run in 1972, Nixon also stepped up his effort to attract southern white voters.

Nixon's confidant John Mitchell, whom he appointed attorney general, helped to implement the president's southern strategy. The mournful-looking, pipe-puffing former partner in Nixon's New York law firm had managed Nixon's 1968 campaign. As attorney general, he opposed extension of the 1965 Voting Rights Act and thwarted enforcement of the 1968 Fair Housing Act. When he sued to delay school desegregation in Mississippi, even attorneys in his own Justice Department protested. The Supreme Court slapped down this effort in *Alexander* v. *Holmes County* (1969), ordering that school desegregation proceed "at once."

When the Court in *Swann* v. *Charlotte-Mecklenburg Board of Education* (1971) approved school busing to achieve racial balance, Nixon found the kind of gut issue on which he thrived. He denounced the decision and demanded that Congress outlaw the policy. When HEW officials and Justice Department civil-rights lawyers drew up integration plans involving busing for several cities, the president fired off an angry memo to Ehrlichman: "*Knock off this Crap.* I hold [HEW and Justice Department officials] personally accountable to keep their left wingers in step with my express policy—Do what the law requires and not *one bit more.*"

Nixon's southern strategy emerged most blatantly in his Supreme Court nominations. When Chief Justice Earl Warren retired in 1969, Nixon nominated Warren Burger of Minnesota, a moderately conservative federal judge of the U.S. Court of Appeals of Washington, D.C. The Senate easily confirmed the choice. When another vacancy opened in 1969, Nixon offered a nomination clearly intended to please southern whites: federal appeals-court judge Clement F. Haynsworth of South Carolina, the home state of Senator Strom Thurmond, who had played a key role in helping Nixon carry the South in 1968. (The 1948 Dixiecrat candidate for president, Thurmond had later become a Republican.) A bitter opponent of the 1954 *Brown* decision and other examples of judicial activism, Thurmond favored jurists who believed in "strict construction" of the Constitution and avoided social issues such as racial integration.* Haynsworth filled the bill in this respect, but he also had a record of opposing labor unions and civil rights. Moreover, conflict-of-interest problems had arisen in cases that he had handled. The Senate rejected him, 55–45, with seventeen Republicans joining in a stinging rebuke of Nixon.

Nixon followed the Haynsworth nomination with a totally unqualified candidate, G. Harrold Carswell, a Florida appeals-court judge. The American Bar Association and legal scholars deplored Carswell's nomination. As a candidate for the Georgia legislature in 1948, the judge had declared, "Segregation of the races is proper and the only practical and correct way of life. . . . I have always so believed and I shall always so act." Carswell had renounced this statement, but he could not shake the charge of incompetence. Nixon's key liaison man with Congress advised the president: "[Most senators] think Carswell's a boob, a dummy. And what counter is there to that? He is." One Carswell supporter, Republican senator Roman Hruska of Nebraska, even tried to turn Carswell's mediocrity into an asset. Many Americans were mediocre, Hruska pointed out; didn't they deserve Supreme Court representation as much as any other group? Despite Hruska's argument, the Senate in April 1970 turned back the Carswell nomination, 51–45. Extracting maximum political mileage from the episode, Nixon denounced the vote as an insult to the South. Among white southerners, accustomed to lost causes, Nixon's popularity soared.

Having made his gesture to the South, Nixon next nominated a moderate jurist, Harry Blackmun of Minnesota, who won easy confirmation in May 1970. To fill the next two Supreme Court vacancies, which came in 1971, Nixon nominated Lewis Powell and William Rehnquist. Powell, a Virginian, boasted a distinguished record, including presidency of the American Bar Association. Rehnquist, a classmate of John Ehrlichman at Stanford Law School, had been a Goldwater Republican in 1964. As an assistant attorney general under John Mitchell, he had shown himself to be a hard-nosed "law-and-order" advocate, supporting secret wiretaps, for example, when he was convinced that "national security" necessitated them. Both nominees won confirmation.

Once elevated to the Supreme Court, Burger, Blackmun, and Rehnquist all steered a moderate-to-liberal course. The new court took a tough stand on issues of obscenity and law enforcement but avoided reversing the liberal rulings of the Warren era. On some issues, such as affirmative action, school busing, and abortion, it moved in directions deplored by many conservatives. Blackmun, for example, wrote the majority decision in *Roe* v. *Wade,* the landmark 1973 decision upholding a woman's constitutional right to an abortion.

---

* Strict constructionists hold that in interpreting the Constitution, the courts should follow the precise meaning intended by the framers; the other view, broad construction, sees the Constitution as a flexible, growing document, adaptable to changed circumstances and conditions. The confrontation of the two approaches dates back to the time of Jefferson and Hamilton.

Conclusion

Richard Nixon's first term and the first year of his second brought striking initiatives and landmark achievements: disengagement from Vietnam, détente with the Soviet Union, the opening to China, and resourceful diplomacy in the Middle East. Domestically, he moved beyond traditional Republican positions in several key areas. A consummate politician, Nixon capitalized on the country's rightward turn and rallied his "silent majority" of suburbanites, blue-collar voters, white southerners, and others unsettled by recent events. More than anyone else, he set the terms of American political discourse for the coming decades.

But history's verdict on Nixon would prove far harsher than seemed possible in 1973. Behind the scenes, the president had engaged in and encouraged illegalities that would produce the gravest crisis in the history of the presidency. As the nation grappled with broad-ranging social and cultural changes in the early 1970s, it also endured an ordeal that historians would sum up with a single word: Watergate.

SELECTED READINGS

1968 and the Vietnam War, from Tet to Cease-fire

Many of the works listed in the Selected Readings of Chapters 9 and 10 are relevant to the first two sections of Chapter 11 as well. In addition, see Jerry L. Avorn, *University in Revolt: A History of the Columbia Crisis* (1968); William C. Berman, *America's Right Turn: From Nixon to Bush* (1994); Michael Bilton and Kevin Sim, *Four Hours in My Lai* (1992); Mary C. Brennan, *Turning Right in the Sixties: The Conservative Capture of the GOP* (1995); Bernard Brodie, "The Tet Offensive," in Noble Frankland and Christopher Dowling, eds., *Decisive Battles of the Twentieth Century* (1976); Dan T. Carter, *The Politics of Rage: George Wallace, the Origins of the New Conservatism, and the Transformation of American Politics* (1995); David Caute, *The Year of the Barricades: A Journey Through 1968* (1988); Todd Gitlin, *The Whole World Is Watching: Mass Media in the Making and Unmaking of the New Left* (1980) and *The Sixties: Years of Hope, Days of Rage* (1987); Lewis L. Gould, *1968: The Election That Changed America* (1993); Andrew Kopkind and James Ridgeway, eds., *Decade of Crisis: America in the 60s* (1972); Stephen Lesher, *George Wallace: American Populist* (1994); Michael Mandelbaum, "Vietnam: The Television War," *Daedalus* (Fall 1982); Joan Morrison and Robert K. Morrison, *From Camelot to Kent State: The Sixties Experience in the Words of Those Who Lived It* (1987); Jack Newfield, *Robert Kennedy: A Memoir* (1970); Richard M. Nixon, *RN: The Memoirs of Richard M. Nixon* (1978); Keith W. Nolan, *Battle for Hué: Tet, 1968* (1983); W. J. Rorabaugh, *Berkeley at War: The 1960s* (1989); David Rudenstine, *The Day the Presses Stopped: A History of the Pentagon Papers Case* (1996); Herbert Y. Schandler, *The Unmaking of a President: Lyndon Johnson and Vietnam* (1977); William Shawcross, *Sideshow: Kissinger, Nixon and the Destruction of Cambodia* (1979); Melvin Small, *Johnson, Nixon, and the Doves* (1988); Carl Solberg, *Hubert Humphrey* (1984); Ronald H. Spector, *After Tet: The Bloodiest Year in Vietnam* (1993); Irwin Unger and Debi Unger, *Turning Point, 1968* (1988); Jules Witcover, *The Year the Dream Died: Revisiting 1968* (1977).

Nixon-Kissinger Foreign Policy

The general histories of the Cold War cited in the Chapter 2 Selected Readings are relevant to the Nixon-Kissinger years as well. See also Stephen E. Ambrose, *Nixon: Tri-*

umph of a Politician (1987); Coit D. Blacker, *Reluctant Warriors: The United States, the Soviet Union, and Arms Control* (1987); McGeorge Bundy, *Danger and Survival: Choices About the Bomb in the First Fifty Years* (1988); Alan Dowty, *Middle East Crisis* (1984); Lawrence Freedman, *The Evolution of Nuclear Strategy* (1981); Raymond L. Garthoff, *Détente and Confrontation: American-Soviet Relations from Nixon to Reagan* (1985); John Girling, *America and the Third World* (1980); Seymour M. Hersh, *The Price of Power: Kissinger in the Nixon White House* (1983); Walter Isaacson, *Kissinger: A Biography* (1992); Henry Kissinger, *White House Years* (1979) and *Years of Upheaval* (1983); Walter LaFeber, *Inevitable Revolutions: The United States in Central America* (1985); Robert S. Litwack, *Détente and the Nixon Doctrine: American Foreign Policy and the Pursuit of Stability* (1984); Keith L. Nelson, *The Making of Détente: Soviet-American Relations in the Shadow of Vietnam* (1995); Herbert Parmet, *The World and Richard Nixon* (1990); Gareth Porter, *A Peace Denied: The United States, Vietnam, and the Paris Agreement* (1975); Steven J. Spiegel, *The Other Arab-Israeli Conflict: Making America's Middle East Policy from Truman to Reagan* (1985); C. L. Sulzberger, *The World and Richard Nixon* (1987); Tom Wicker, *One of Us: Richard Nixon and the American Dream* (1991); Daniel Yergin, *The Prize: The Epic Quest for Oil, Money, and Power* (1991).

Domestic Politics in the Early Nixon Years

Vincent Burke and Vee Burke, *Nixon's Good Deed: Welfare Reform* (1974); David Calleo, *The Imperious Economy* (1982); Thomas Byrne Edsall with Mary D. Edsall, *Chain Reaction: The Impact of Race, Rights, and Taxes on American Politics* (1991); Joan Hoff, *Nixon Reconsidered* (1994); Roger L. Miller, *The New Economics of Richard Nixon* (1972); Daniel Patrick Moynihan, *The Politics of a Guaranteed Income: The Nixon Administration and the Family Assistance Plan* (1973); Leon E. Panetta and Peter Gall, *Bring Us Together—the Nixon Team and the Civil Rights Retreat* (1971); Herbert Parmet, *Richard Nixon and His America* (1990); A. James Reichley, *Conservatives in an Age of Change: The Nixon and Ford Administrations* (1981); Garry Wills, *Nixon Agonistes: The Crisis of a Self-Made Man* (1970)

❖ ❖ ❖

CHAPTER 12

Reform in the Nation, Crisis in Washington

On the afternoon of August 7, 1974, facing the supreme crisis of his life, President Richard Nixon gathered his family in the White House solarium: wife Pat, daughters Tricia and Julie with their husbands Edward Cox and David Eisenhower, grandson of the revered Dwight Eisenhower. In a quintessentially Nixonian touch, the president summoned the White House photographer to record the moment "for history." In the photograph, Nixon's tightly clenched fists belie his smiling face. A moment after the staged shot, the photographer captured a sobbing Julie embracing her father as Tricia turns away weeping and Edward gamely smiles on. When the photographer at last departed, the family shared a grim, silent dinner. Nixon announced his resignation the following evening and left the White House by helicopter the next day. For the first and so far the only time, a U.S. president had involuntarily left office before the expiration of his term.

Nixon's efforts to conceal his role in a break-in at the Democratic party headquarters during the 1972 campaign had spawned further crimes, and by the summer of 1974 he faced two choices: resign or be impeached. But the president's personal crisis paled in contrast to the nation's. Watergate stretched the fabric of constitutional government to the limit. Following the distrust that had dogged LBJ's final White House years, the scandal further weakened the presidency, and Americans' trust in government sank to all-time lows.

Watergate dominates the seventies, making it difficult for historians to delineate the decade's larger contours. In contrast to both the sixties and the eighties, the seventies remain curiously ill focused. In part, the period was marked by reaction and passivity after the traumas of the sixties. While Nixon rallied his "silent majority," some erstwhile activists and counterculture members bade farewell to radicalism and cultural protest and shifted their focus inward. But the sixties cast a long shadow, and the decade's political and cultural trends did not vanish as the new decade began. Despite the collapse of the New Left and the counterculture, the reformist energies and drive for cultural innovation that had infused these movements persisted. The context changed, but many activists turned to new causes, including environmental protection and feminism.

336

As in the sixties, this new wave of social activism stirred opposition, and movements that threatened the status quo or challenged strongly held values triggered a powerful conservative response. The political counterrevolution embodied in the Wallace movement and in Richard Nixon's election in 1968 continued through the 1970s, laying the groundwork for the election of Ronald Reagan in 1980.

The nation may have longed for a break as the sixties ended, but history offers no time-outs. The seventies brought fresh political crises, new movements and causes, and deepening social and cultural divisions. Janus-like, the decade faces both backward and forward; in some respects a continuation of the sixties, it also prefigured trends that would occupy the nation in the years that followed.

Escapism and the Collapse of the Counterculture

The culture and politics of the seventies unfolded amid the wreckage of the antiwar movement and the apparent collapse of the counterculture. The New Left faded as Nixon's policy of Vietnamization neutralized its most potent issue and as the political climate turned hostile. Bitter ideological disputes finished off an already weakening movement. The counterculture also suffered from commercial exploitation, drug abuse, and the actions of a few disturbed individuals attracted by its aura of nonjudgmental tolerance. A more insidious force silently eroded these movements as well: time. With each passing year, more erstwhile activists and counterculture devotees started families, began professional training, entered the job market, or otherwise reached a truce with the society they had earlier reviled or ridiculed.

As resourceful promoters coopted the counterculture's music and fashions,* the movement itself took a lurid turn and then collapsed. In December 1969, Charles Manson, a psychotic drug cultist, and his "family" of young followers recruited in San Francisco's Haight-Ashbury district ritually murdered actress Sharon Tate and four others in Tate's Beverly Hills home. A few publications on the counterculture's far outer fringe hailed Manson as a hero; to conservatives, the horror embodied everything they feared in the movement. In 1970, the year the Beatles broke up, a rival British rock group, the Rolling Stones, set out to make a documentary movie like the highly profitable film version of the Woodstock festival. The Stones staged a free concert at Altamont Raceway near San Francisco and, cultivating their outlaw image, hired the Hell's Angels motorcycle gang to provide security in return for $500 worth of beer. The event proved a disaster: Concertgoers harrassed physicians trying to treat drug-overdose victims; the Hell's Angels assaulted several people and fatally knifed a young man as he approached the stage; three people died in drug-related accidents. The Manson murders, Altamont, and other evidences of antisocial, exploitive impulses mocked the counterculture's avowals of peace and love.

In a post-Altamont article, "The End of the Age of Aquarius," Todd Gitlin criticized the movement's failure to confront the havoc of drugs. "Why doesn't this contaminated culture, many of whose claims are based on the virtues of drugs,

---

* *Hair,* a musical celebrating the "Age of Aquarius" (also the title of a popular counterculture song) and featuring eye-popping nudity, opened on Broadway in 1968.

help its own brothers and sisters?" he lamented. Would the youth culture "leave anything behind but a market?" Years later, Gitlin—by then a Berkeley sociologist—reflected on the movement's sad end: "The revolutionary mood had been fueled by the blindingly bright illusion that human history was beginning afresh because a graced generation had willed it so. Now there wasn't enough life left to mobilize against all the death raining down." As the counterculture grew older, a few remained outside the mainstream and preserved the styles of the sixties in a kind of cultural time capsule. The Grateful Dead, a musical group popular with the counterculture, retained a loyal following into the 1990s. For most, however, their season of youthful rebellion survived only in memory.

As the counterculture and the antiwar movement faded, the cultural climate shifted markedly. Except for Watergate, the 1970s struck many people at the time and since as rather featureless and devoid of memorable highlights. One history of the decade bears the tongue-in-cheek title *It Seemed Like Nothing Happened.* Indeed, the decade was generally free of the riots, assassinations, campus turmoil, bitter confrontations, and superheated rhetoric that for many Americans defined the sixties. Brandeis University's Center for the Study of Violence, having opened in 1966, closed in 1973.

A shell-shocked nation turned to reassuring icons of mass culture. The antiwar, anti-Establishment, and drug-induced music of the late 1960s gave way to songs such as Don McLean's bittersweet and enigmatic 1971 hit "American Pie." John Denver's crooning "Rocky Mountain High" (1972) recommended unspoiled nature rather than LSD for spiritual transcendence. Groups like Led Zeppelin and The Who carried on the hard-rock tradition but without the overt political content of late-sixties rock.

Television fed the escapist mood. The three major networks—CBS, ABC, and NBC—pushed their revenues from $1 billion to $3 billion in the 1970s. Their offerings typically featured situation comedies, 1950s nostalgia (*Happy Days, Laverne and Shirley*), sexual titillation, and police dramas such as *Kojak* and *Hawaii Five-O.* There were exceptions, of course. The long-running comedy-drama *M*A*S*H* premiered in 1972, marked by witty dialogue and the exploration of humane values in a Korean War medical unit. The show's implicit pacifist message captured the nation's post-Vietnam mood. For the most part, however, 1970s TV, driven by ratings and marketing demographics, lived down to the "vast wasteland" label that an FCC chairman had applied to it in 1961. A *New York Times* TV critic complained late in the decade that the medium was "dropping rapidly to kiddie levels."

Television in the seventies only fitfully reflected America's diversity. The hugely successful ABC miniseries *Roots* (1976) offered a panorama of the African-American experience, but other series featuring blacks were less impressive. George Jefferson on *The Jeffersons* was a weak buffoon, and the prancing teenager J. J. on *Good Times* perpetuated the grinning, blackface minstrel stereotype. Asians, Hispanics, and Native Americans appeared but rarely.

Hollywood shared in the infantilization of mass culture in the 1970s, despite a few gripping movies such as *The Deerhunter* (1978), a portrayal of the psychological effects of Vietnam service. Typical escapist fare included Sylvester Stallone's *Rocky* (1976), *Superman* (1978), and Steven Spielberg's and George Lucas's *Star Wars*

(1977) with its comic-book storyline and computer-generated intergalactic warfare. These films transferred the sixties' sense of powerful and insidious forces seeking global control from the arena of political activism to the realm of fantasy.

The so-called new ethnicity of the seventies similarly continued in depoliticized form a cultural trend rooted in the sixties. Calls for black pride had originally arisen as part of the larger freedom struggle. In the seventies, the affirmation of African-American identity not only inspired the "Roots" phenomenon but stimulated the self-awareness among white ethnic groups applauded in Michael Novak's *The Rise of the Unmeltable Ethnics* (1973). For many blue-collar and middle-class ethnics, allegiance to the Democratic party had been a tradition since the 1930s. Now, as old party loyalties crumbled, a generalized affirmation of ethnic identity, freed from political connotations, offered an alternative form of group identification.

The new ethnicity also evoked a simpler age in an era of unsettling social change, often through hazy memories of a semimythic past. Many first- or second-generation immigrants had submerged their ethnicity in order to seize the opportunities that came with "Americanization." Now, with the transition successfully accomplished, the newly self-conscious ethnics of the 1970s could indulge in a sentimental journey into their past from the security of their mainstream lives. But like most generalizations about the 1970s, this one must be qualified. Despite its ambiguous meanings and its silly side (like buttons reading "Kiss Me, I'm Italian"), the new ethnicity also represented a healthy defiance of the white-bread blandness of the fifties and the corporate world's tendency to reduce Americans to blocs of consumers living in "media markets."

The heightened awareness of race, class, and ethnicity in American life underlay the most popular TV show of the seventies, *All in the Family.* The series starred Carroll O'Connor as Archie Bunker, a bigoted longshoreman and part-time taxi driver who spouted venom against blacks, radicals, feminists, Jews, and other groups that he deemed threatening. Archie's wife Edith, brilliantly played by Jean Stapleton, offered occasional insights into the experiences that had shaped his worldview. "He'll never be more than what he is now," she says sadly in one show, "even though he had dreams once." The show's producer, liberal Democrat Norman Lear, intended to satirize bigotry, but audience surveys revealed that many viewers applauded Archie's diatribes and his scornful attacks on "Meathead," his liberal son-in-law.

Another portrayal of working-class frustration emerged in the 1979 film *Breaking Away,* which explored the lives of blue-collar youth in the university town of Bloomington, Indiana. With nuance and regional authenticity, *Breaking Away* conveyed the disorientation of post-Vietnam America as well as the class tensions and economic changes of the 1970s. Walking on the university campus, a displaced stonecutter reduced to selling used cars tells his son, "I cut the stone for this building. I was one fine stonecutter. I loved it. I was damned proud of my work." The hero, a recent high-school graduate who imagines himself an Italian bicycle racer, is devastated when a real-life, corporate-sponsored Italian racing team uses unfair tactics to prevent him from winning a race. "Everybody cheats," he surmises bitterly. "I just didn't know."

Novelists, too, examined ethnic sensibilities and tensions. Saul Bellow's *Mr. Sammler's Planet* (1970) and Bernard Malamud's *The Tenants* (1971) probed the uneasy relations between blacks and Jews. Toni Morrison's debut novel *The Bluest Eye* (1970) told of poverty-bound Pecola Breedlove, who dreams of having blue eyes like Dick and Jane in her school reader. Torn by conflicting aspirations, Pecola descends into madness: "Elbows bent, hands on shoulders, she flailed her arms like a bird in an eternal, grotesquely futile effort to fly. Beating the air, a winged but grounded bird, intent on the blue void it could not reach—could not even see—but which filled the valleys of the wind."

A few 1960s activists, meanwhile, went underground or joined rural communes. Others, still suspicious of the Establishment's technocratic expertise, embraced mysticism and the occult. Zen Buddhism and teenage Indian gurus won followers; interest in astrology, Native-American religion, and techniques for heightening psychic awareness and "self-actualization" soared. One former SDS leader, writing in 1971, offered a snapshot of a radical in transit from public to private concerns:

> I am less involved in changing America. . . . This does not mean that I am less angry or upset or horrified by this country than before. If anything, I am more profoundly and intuitively aware, day to day, of what an ugly society this is and how desperately it needs change. But my information comes less and less from the papers—more and more from my own experience with it.

As ex-radicals embraced a "New Age" sensibility, cultural critic Edwin Schur captured the trend in the title of a 1976 book: *The Awareness Trap: Self-Absorption Instead of Social Change.*

Other erstwhile activists, less mystically inclined, turned to physical fitness and material acquisitions. Many young, urban professionals (later dubbed Yuppies) whose acquisitive tastes would shape American life in the 1980s were veterans of the counterculture. In *The Greening of America* (1970), Charles Reich of Yale Law School, himself a late-blooming flower child, argued that a more peaceful and harmonious society would arise effortlessly and spontaneously as the counterculture's values spread by a kind of osmosis. Some movement dropouts welcomed Reich's message. Indeed, in 1976 journalist Tom Wolfe labeled the baby boomers the "Me Generation." The 1983 movie *The Big Chill* would offer a sad image of cynical ex-sixties radicals in avid pursuit of money, sex, and power.

Historian Christopher Lasch in *The Culture of Narcissism* (1979) argued that the counterculture's dissident lifestyles and the New Left's politics of confrontation, initially undertaken to challenge suburban conformity and power-elite manipulation, had degenerated into "a politics . . . of style without substance." In approaching politics as "a mode of self-dramatization," charged Lasch, movement activists had contributed to the obsessive "navel gazing" of the 1970s. Citing psychiatrists' reports of patients needing immediate gratification and incapable of long-term planning, Lasch linked the turn toward narcissism to the nation's worsening economic problems:

> Having no hope of improving their lives in any of the ways that matter, people have convinced themselves that what matters is psychic self-improvement: getting in touch with their feelings, eating health food, taking lessons in ballet or belly dancing, immersing themselves in the wisdom of the East, jogging, learning how to "relate," overcoming the "fear of pleasure."

New Activist Energies

Not all former radicals sold out; not all of the political activism and counterculture energies of the sixties metamorphosed into careerism or narcissism in the 1970s. Although the specific forms of protest and cultural alienation faded, a host of 1960s activists carried into the 1970s and beyond the commitment to social justice and the skeptical view of mainstream culture that they had acquired through civil-rights advocacy, antiwar protests, and the counterculture. As historians Maurice Isserman and Michael Kazin have written:

> The movements and events of the 1960s generated an attitudinal penumbra that glimmered long after SDS and SNCC had been eclipsed. Chastened by the collapse of "the movement," many pragmatic radicals entered the left wing of the Democratic party, helping transform its stance on foreign policy and producing at least a strong rhetorical commitment to equal rights for all disadvantaged groups. . . . [T]housands of others took up jobs and professions that did not represent a break with their earlier political aspirations. They became social workers, union and community organizers, public school teachers, Legal Services lawyers, or doctors involved in occupational or neighborhood health programs.

Thus, although political reaction, cultural exhaustion, and mass-culture escapism compose part of the seventies picture, the decade also gave rise to a series of significant cultural and social movements rooted in the sixties. As cultural critic

Challenging the "Insolent Chariots." *The antiwar protest energies of the 1960s found new outlets in the 1970s, including environmentalism. America's love affair with Detroit cooled as gas prices soared and environmental activists publicized the pollution caused by exhaust emissions. Tougher regulation resulted.* (AP/Wide World Photos)

Morris Dickstein observed in 1977, "The sixties are over, but they remain the watershed of our recent cultural history; they continue to affect the ambiance of our lives in innumerable ways."

The environmental movement, for example, which arose in the early seventies, drew strength from the distrust of the technocratic order that had pervaded the New Left and the counterculture. As one counterculture theorist wrote grandly in 1969, "[Our] primary project . . . is to proclaim a new heaven and a new earth so vast, so marvelous that the inordinate claims of technical expertise must of necessity withdraw to a subordinate and marginal status."

The responses to the moon landing of July 21, 1969, similarly anticipated some of the environmental movement's central themes. On one level, this culmination of a project launched by John Kennedy seemed a triumph of technocratic know-how. Television viewers thrilled as astronaut Neil Armstrong stepped on the lunar surface and delivered his prepared epigram: "That's one small step for [a] man, a giant leap for mankind." Yet many observers also expressed fears that the achievement would add fuel to America's long infatuation with technology. Others warned that space missions would push the arms race into the heavens. Still others argued that such costly ventures ate up resources better directed to pressing social needs on earth.

Environmentalism and the related theme of energy conservation were not, however, simply extensions of the ideological preoccupations of the 1960s. A series of unsettling trends and events hastened their emergence. Through World War II, America had produced more oil than it consumed. Yet as the long postwar boom got under way, oil use outran domestic supply, and Americans began to rely heavily on imports and offshore drilling in the Gulf of Mexico and along the Pacific Coast. A stark reminder of the hazards of these operations came in 1969 as leaking rigs in California's Santa Barbara channel turned seawater to oily scum, blackened beaches, and killed fish and shorebirds. TV images of napalmed children in Vietnam gave way to oil-soaked cormorants flapping helplessly on the beach.

A Santa Barbara citizens' group drafted the "Declaration of Environmental Rights" (1970). Echoing Rachel Carson's *Silent Spring,* the document insisted that Americans accustomed to unlimited natural resources must pay more attention to the environmental cost of their profligate lifestyle:

> We need an ecological consciousness that recognizes man as member, not master, of the community of living things sharing his environment. . . . We must find the courage to take upon ourselves as individuals responsibility for the welfare of the whole environment. . . . We must redefine "progress" toward an emphasis on long-term quality rather than immediate quantity.

On April 22, 1970, millions of Americans adopted an idea of Senator Gaylord Nelson of Wisconsin and observed the first Earth Day by cleaning up beaches and vacant lots and attending environmental teach-ins. The high-spirited mood reflected the early naiveté and deceptive harmony of a cause that would prove both divisive and complex, but Earth Day symbolically placed the environment high on the public agenda for the seventies and beyond.

Two measures of 1970 expanded the growing body of environmental law. The Water Quality Improvement Act and the Clean Air Act aimed at purifying the nation's air and waterways. The latter measure set emissions standards for auto exhausts. That year, President Nixon, attuned as always to voters worries, signed bills creating the Environmental Protection Agency and the Occupational Safety and Health Administration with broad powers to enforce federal environmental and worker-safety regulations.

Nonetheless, the Nixon team viewed environmentalism with suspicion. Nixon's interior secretary chose Earth Day to approve an Alaska oil pipeline opposed by environmentalists. John Ehrlichman avowed, "Conservation is not the Republican ethic," no doubt making Theodore Roosevelt spin in his grave. On a 1971 Ehrlichman memo lamenting the economic toll of pollution controls, Nixon scribbled, "I completely agree—We have gone overboard on the environment." The head of the Atomic Energy Commission ridiculed those who questioned nuclear-reactor safety: "We can't live in a Garden of Eden and still have a technological society."

The environmental movement continued to grow, however, influenced not only by oil spills but also by the more chronic problems of air and water pollution, shrinking wilderness areas, and declining natural resources. The media, having celebrated consumption and endless growth in the 1950s, began to strike a different note. Calls for achieving a "sustainable economy," rather than heedlessly exploiting the world's resources, found a receptive audience. Ecology, once a specialized academic field, became a fad. A cynical California politician called it "the political substitute for the word 'mother.'"

Shaped by a culture that had long worshipped technology and boundlessness, Americans began to envision limits and a less exploitive coexistence with the natural order. Dozens of books—including Barry Commoner's *The Closing Circle* (1971), Frances Lappe's *Diet for a Small Planet* (1971), and E. F. Schumacher's *Small Is Beautiful: Economics as If People Mattered* (1973)—signaled the shift. The new consciousness also propelled the career of Ralph Nader, the young lawyer who in *Unsafe at Any Speed* (1965) had attacked the U.S. auto industry for putting flashy design above safety. Nader's muckraking gave rise to the National Traffic and Motor Vehicle Safety Act of 1966. In the later 1960s and the 1970s, advocacy groups nicknamed "Nader's Raiders" lobbied against dangerous products, ranging from gas pipelines to insecticides. Nader funded his operation in part with money that he won from General Motors in a legal battle.* Emulating Nader, many young law-school graduates turned to the field of public advocacy in the 1970s.

While environmental advocates pitched their appeal to all Americans, other groups drew inspiration from the civil-rights and Black Power movements in their more narrowly targeted struggles against oppression. Thus, the early seventies also saw a sharp rise in activism by specific groups pursuing their own agendas. If the "new ethnicity" phenomenon was largely apolitical, the rising self-consciousness of Hispanics, Native Americans, gays, and feminists found intensely political outlets.

---

* GM had hired detectives to spy on him, and Nader had sued for invasion of privacy. GM settled out of court for $425,000.

Native American Militancy, June 1971. *Young AIM (American Indian Movement) activists remained defiant after federal marshals ended their occupation of Alcatraz Island in San Francisco Bay. (© Ilka Hartmann/Jeroboam, Inc.)*

Among Mexican Americans, the new militance that had arisen in the 1960s (see p. 243) continued. Activist energies found outlets not only in national advocacy groups such as the Mexican American Legal Defense and Education Fund but also in numerous grassroots organizations addressing local issues. Cesar Chavez maintained a high level of national visibility as leader of the United Farm Workers of America (UFWA), which he defined as a "cross between . . . a movement and . . . a union." It included Filipino and other farm workers as well as Mexican Americans. Although the UFWA settled its strike against thirty-three grape-growing agribusinesses in 1970 and declared an end to the five-year national grape boycott, the struggle for better conditions continued. As the militant UFWA leader Dolores Huerta declared in 1973: "[T]his is a real war—all of the growers and right-wing elements . . . are trying to crush the farm workers. . . . [W]e have to act like it's a real war."

Political awareness among the Hispanic population was intensified by its rapid rate of growth. As a result of both immigration and natural increase, the Mexican-American population grew from 4.5 million to 8.7 million in the 1970s. The 1980 federal census also recorded more than 330,000 residents from other Central American countries, especially El Salvador, Guatemala, and Nicaragua, of whom 61 percent had arrived within the past ten years.

In the late 1960s and early 1970s, a pantribal Native-American organization, the American Indian Movement (AIM), took direct action. In 1969 eighty of its members claimed Alcatraz island in San Francisco Bay. Demanding that Alcatraz become an Indian cultural center, they occupied the island until 1971. In 1972 AIM occupied the Bureau of Indian Affairs in Washington, D.C., charging governmental violations of treaty obligations. A year later, AIM seized a trading post at

Wounded Knee, South Dakota, where, in 1890, the U.S. Army had massacred three hundred Teton Sioux. After a seventy-one-day siege, the occupation ended. Federal charges against the occupiers of Wounded Knee were dropped in 1974 after it was found that the government had withheld evidence and used illegal wiretaps in building its case.

Native American protests spurred action. In 1970 the federal government restored forty-eight thousand acres to the Taos Pueblo of New Mexico, including the sacred Blue Lake region taken over by the U.S. Forest Service in 1906. The Alaska Native Land Claims Act (1971) restored 40 million acres to the native peoples of Alaska and granted over $960 million to tribal villages and associations in compensation for lands taken when Alaska became a state. In 1972 the federal government transferred to the Yakima Indians of Washington State some twenty-one thousand acres of the Mount Rainier Forest Reserve. Eight years later, the Supreme Court upheld a lower-court award of $107 million in damages to the Sioux of South Dakota and endorsed the Sioux claim that the Black Hills had been illegally seized from them during the 1870s gold rush. That same year, Congress granted $81.5 million to various tribes of northern Maine in settlement of claims based on Maine's violation of a 1790 statute prohibiting the sale or disposal of Indian lands without congressional approval.

The Nixon administration also initiated an important change in the law governing relations between the federal government and Native Americans. In 1953, Congress had ended all federal benefits for Indians as a distinct category of citizens and had abolished the tribes' legal standing under federal law. In the 1960s, responding to protests, Washington modified the termination policy and made tribal governments eligible to participate in antipoverty and Great Society programs. President Nixon in 1970 urged Congress to abandon the termination policy altogether. Criticizing government paternalism as well, Nixon supported the Indian Self-Determination Act (1974). This law restored the legal status of Indian tribes and granted them authority over federal programs on their reservations and more control of tribal schools and colleges.

Homosexuals, another group historically subject to discrimination, had also grown more assertive amid the cultural ferment of the late 1960s. A symbolic turning point came on June 29, 1969, when police raided the Stonewall Inn, a gay bar in Manhattan's Greenwich Village. Homosexuals had tolerated such harassment in the past, but now the patrons resisted, pelting the police with bottles and stones. Having formerly found precarious security in a shadowy subculture, growing numbers of homosexual men and lesbians "came out of the closet" in the 1970s. Embracing the "Gay Rights" banner, they proclaimed their sexual preference, formed organizations, founded newspapers, and protested discrimination. The National Gay Task Force,* founded in 1973, launched campaigns to include homosexuals as a protected class in civil-rights laws barring job or housing discrimination. Dade County (Miami), Florida, was among the jurisdictions to pass such legislation. Responding to pressure, the American Psychiatric Association in 1973 removed homosexuality from the list of mental disorders in its diagnostic manual.

---

* In 1986 the name was changed to the National Gay and Lesbian Task Force.

A Revived Women's Movement

Of all the movements to arise in the wake of the upheavals of the sixties, the most sweeping was the new feminism. After winning the vote in 1920, the women's movement had faded. Nineteen-fifties mass culture had reinforced strict gender distinctions: women in the home, men in the workplace; women as emotional, men as rational; women as sexual prey, men as predators. Yet even in the fifties, these polarities bore little resemblance to reality. For example, as we have seen, the percentage of women in the workplace actually rose in the decade. Instead, the stereotypes expressed the anxieties of a postwar decade seeking stability and traditional values in early marriage, close families, and suburban domesticity.

Betty Friedan's *The Feminine Mystique* (1963), which had sold 1.3 million copies by 1967, challenged these images. Friedan herself was hardly the typical 1950s housewife. A Smith College graduate with a background in radical politics, she had hired a nearly full-time maid while launching a career as a writer. Nevertheless, in *The Feminine Mystique* she voiced the frustrations of many women of her generation as they confronted what she called "the problem that has no name." She wrote, "Each suburban wife struggled with it alone. As she made the beds, shopped for groceries, matched slipcover material, ate peanut butter sandwiches with her children, chauffeured Cub Scouts and Brownies, lay beside her husband at night—she was afraid to ask of herself the silent question: 'Is this all?'" Friedan hit a nerve. Letters poured in revealing a reservoir of repressed anger. "I've seen too many women say they would 'do something' when the last children went to school,'" wrote one woman. "The something has usually been bridge, bowling or drinking." *The Feminine Mystique* welded diffuse discontent into a movement. Such was the "subterranean explosive urgency" of this discontent, Friedan later wrote, that once ignited, "it spread like a nuclear chain reaction."

Pre–World War I feminists had focused on gaining the vote. Those of the 1920s had concentrated less on women's issues than on social-justice and peace concerns. The new feminism of the 1960s and 1970s, by contrast, more closely resembled the original women's-rights movement of the antebellum era.* Its leaders launched a broad-gauge campaign for full gender equality in American life. In time, the movement would divide into radical and moderate wings, but this initial phase was characterized by cohesiveness and confidence. In founding the National Organization for Women in 1966 (see p. 273), Friedan and others dedicated it to "equality of opportunity and freedom of choice" for all women and their "full participation in the mainstream of American society." The new feminist agenda, NOW made clear, embraced not only politics but culture, including changes in the mass media's "false images of women" and, in the domestic realm, "a different concept of marriage, an equitable sharing of the responsibilities of home and children and of the economic burdens of their support." By 1977 NOW had sixty-five thousand members. The Women's Political Caucus, founded in 1971, lobbied both parties on

---

* The goals of pre–Civil War women's rights advocates such as Elizabeth Cady Stanton included not only the vote but freer access to higher education and the professions, married women's property rights, more equitable divorce laws, and other reforms.

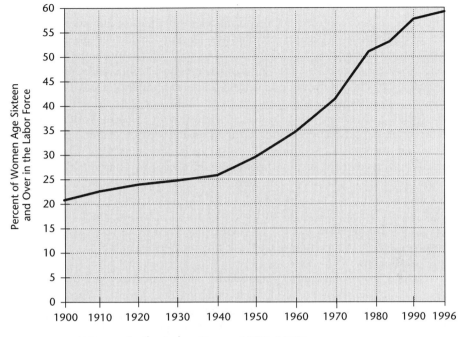

FIGURE 12.1   *Women in the Labor Force, 1900–1996*

SOURCE: *Historical Statistics of the United States, Colonial Times to 1970,* Part I (1975); *Statistical Abstract of the United States, 1997* (1997), p. 403.

behalf of women's issues. Despite changes since the 1950s, women still faced wage discrimination in the workplace and remained underrepresented in politics, the media, higher education, most professions, and the managerial ranks of business.

The movement gained a sharper, more radical edge as it attracted recruits with experience from the civil-rights and antiwar campaigns of the 1960s. As young women protesting the exploitation of southern blacks or Vietnamese peasants had found themselves exploited by male leaders, their resentment had built. Challenging the older liberals of NOW (as Black Power advocates were challenging the mainstream civil-rights groups), these younger feminists attacked the sexual status quo in new and radical ways. The broader sixties climate of protest and of skepticism toward the Establishment encouraged the questioning of gender roles as well.

The civil-rights and antiwar campaigns provided tactics, a vocabulary, and a taste of activism for thousands of protofeminists. Movement experience also taught feminists how to attract media attention. They picketed the *Ladies Home Journal* offices just as antiwar protesters had picketed ROTC buildings. At Atlantic City in 1968, they paraded a sheep as Miss America, as the Yippies had nominated a pig for president. Emulating the draft-card burners, they immolated curlers, bras, and high-heeled shoes in "freedom trash cans." Students at an Iowa college echoed the southern sit-ins and staged a "nude-in" when a *Playboy* representative visited campus.

Robin Morgan's *Sisterhood Is Powerful* (1970) and Gloria Steinem's *Ms.* magazine (1972) captured the exuberance of a burgeoning movement. Feminist writers explored issues ranging from wage inequities to media stereotypes to the merits of the clitoral orgasm. Journals such as *Signs* offered feminist explorations of literature, history, and social theory. Feminist theologians challenged patriarchal religion. *Our Bodies, Ourselves,* a women's health manual written by eleven women, became a bestseller in 1973, appealing to women who felt infantilized by the male medical establishment. Rape-crisis centers, battered-women shelters, and feminist "consciousness-raising" groups proliferated.

Reviving a sexual revolution whose origins lay in the pre–World War I bohemian culture of Greenwich Village, many young women claimed as their due the sexual freedom long considered an option only for men. Aided by a readily available array of contraceptive methods and access to abortion, they experimented widely and postponed long-term commitments. As married women abandoned unsatisfying or abusive relationships, the divorce rate rose from 2.2 per 1,000 population in 1960 to 5.2 in 1980. The nation's lesbian community, emerging from furtive obscurity like its gay counterpart, grew more vocal. Even the conservative *Reader's Digest* acknowledged the sweeping effects of the "Women's Liberation" movement.

Changes in women's employment status, under way since the fifties, provided the economic context of the new feminist consciousness. Women, married and single, poured into the workplace in the seventies; the percentage of gainfully employed women rose from 44 percent in 1970 to 51 percent by 1980. The reasons were often less ideological than economic. As inflation eroded families' income, women went to work to make up the gap. The changing patterns of women's work, in turn, affected marriage and birth rates. Many young working women chose to

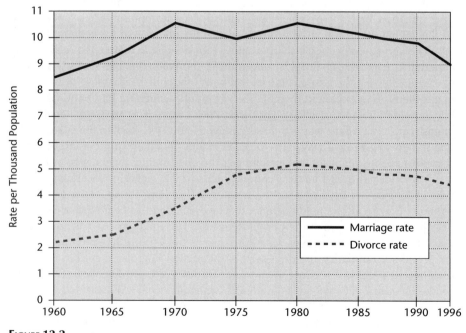

Figure 12.2
Marriage and Divorce Rates, 1960–1996

remain single, opting instead for relationships outside marriage. Many who were married delayed starting a family or chose to have only one or two children. The birthrate dropped from a postwar peak of 25.3 per 1,000 population in 1957 to 18.4 in 1970 and 14.8 by 1975. Again economic calculations played a role; as inflation took its toll, couples eager to sustain the standard of living they had become accustomed to limited the number of their offspring.

For many women, these changes opened new possibilities for careers, higher education, and professional training. But the new openness could also stir confusion and uncertainty as marriage and domesticity became only one of many options. And millions of working-class women and those living in inner-city slums remained little affected by the demographic shifts and feminist ferment of these years.

On the political and judicial front, a series of victories for women, following on the Civil Rights Act of 1964, which had banned gender as well as racial discrimination in employment, came with deceptive ease. In 1972 Congress barred gender discrimination in higher education and sent to the states for ratification the equal rights amendment (ERA) to the Constitution outlawing discrimination on the basis of sex. Within three years, thirty-two states had ratified the amendment, and final approval seemed certain. In 1973 the Equal Employment Opportunity Commission ordered the American Telephone and Telegraph Company to pay millions in back wages to women as well as minority employees to rectify past discrimination. That same year came *Roe* v. *Wade,* the Supreme Court's landmark decision upholding women's constitutional right to abortion.*

Gender discrimination and stereotyping continued to pervade the nation's institutions and culture, however. Men tended to be promoted more rapidly than women, and paid more for comparable jobs. One female insurance broker wrote, "I just had this notion that I could pull myself up by my bootstraps. And my bootstraps kept breaking." In the 1970s, the proportion of women attorneys rose from 3 percent to 13 percent and of women physicians from 7 to 10 percent, evidence of progress but also of the long road to full equality. Gloria Steinem lamented at mid-decade, "We are triumphantly galloping toward tokenism."

TV did portray a bright professional woman on *The Mary Tyler Moore Show,* but even she reported to a male boss (played by Ed Asner) whom she invariably addressed as "Mr. Grant." But, this rare exception was more than matched by programs such as *Three's Company* and *Charlie's Angels* featuring sexual innuendo and young women in provocative costumes and situations. The head of ABC instructed the producers of *Three's Company* to make the show "the same kind of breakthrough in sexiness that 'All in the Family' was in bigotry." Originally planned to celebrate women professionals, *Charlie's Angels* with its three female detectives quickly degenerated into an exploitation show featuring skimpy outfits and wet T-shirts.

Recruits to the women's movement remained overwhelmingly white, middle class, and college educated. While some black and Hispanic women responded, in-

---

* "Jane Roe" (so-called to protect her privacy) was a Dallas woman who in 1970 brought suit against the district attorney of Dallas County, Texas, an official named Wade, challenging the constitutionality of a Texas statute making it a crime to perform an abortion except to save the life of the mother. (Ironically, she emerged in the 1990s as an anti-abortion activist.)

cluding writers like Alice Walker and Toni Morrison, many remained skeptical and accused white feminists of diverting attention from the more pressing issue of racism. In 1971 the editor of *Essence,* a magazine for black women, called the new feminism "basically a family quarrel between white women and white men." Even this assessment overstated the case. Working-class white women tended to be unsympathetic to the effort. Catholic and evangelical Protestant women bristled when the women's movement welcomed lesbians and abortion-rights advocates.

By mid-decade, as we shall see, a backlash against the new feminism would set in. Phyllis Schlafly, a conservative activist, formed a "Stop ERA" organization in 1972. Within the women's movement, conflict between moderate and radical wings and between lesbians and heterosexual women only worsened tensions. Male uneasiness about the new feminine assertiveness, expressed ironically in Woody Allen's nostalgic *Play It Again Sam* (1972), added fuel to the controversy. In Allen's movie, the Humphrey Bogart character rasps through gritted teeth, "Dames are simple. I never met one who didn't understand a slap in the mouth or a slug from a forty-five." As with the civil-rights movement, the initial gains of the women's movement opened a hornet's nest of debate, with legislative and judicial successes often undermined by rising opposition and resistance in the larger society.

In sum, the seventies, in some respects a decade of reaction and quiescence, also sustained the cultural revolution of the sixties and propelled it in new directions. The new feminism, the gay-rights movement, Native-American activism, and the environmental cause all had roots in the political and cultural ferment of the sixties. And as in the sixties, this reformist activism aroused hostility in parts of blue-collar and middle-class America. Just as many Americans of the late sixties who had no enthusiasm for the Vietnam War still decried the antiwar movement, so citizens who favored environmental protection often disliked the more outspoken environmental activists. Similarly, Americans who endorsed the principle of gender equality reacted with dismay to radical feminism, legalized abortion, and even the rising numbers of women in the workplace. The gay-rights movement stirred especially intense reactions among millions of Americans who found homosexuality personally threatening or offensive to their beliefs. Cumulatively, these movements challenged a familiar social order and raised troubling issues. The resulting anxieties often translated into Republican votes and contributed to the growing climate of reaction. For poorer, less educated Americans, the tension triggered the same kind of class resentments that in the late sixties had been directed against university-based antiwar activists.

The politics of race remained central in the 1970s. In contrast to the early civil-rights movement, when the struggle to stop legalized segregation appealed to all people of goodwill, racial issues in the seventies tended to be divisive. The nation remained split between affluent, overwhelmingly white suburbs and poor, largely black and Hispanic inner-city slums, but no Martin Luther King, Jr., or Lyndon Johnson arose to prod the nation to a renewed crusade against the inequities of American life.

Instead, many citizens viewed many of the social issues most worrisome to middle-class and blue-collar Americans—crime, drug abuse, decaying cities, rising rates of teenage pregnancy, soaring welfare costs—as racial in origin rather than as byproducts of endemic poverty. Just as native-born Americans of the late nineteenth century had blamed the problems of an industrializing age on immigrants, so racial and ethnic minorities tended in the 1970s to be held responsible for conditions that were largely beyond their control. As we shall see, a racist backlash focused on such volatile issues as school busing gathered steam in parts of white America as the decade wore on. While environmentalists campaigned and educated white women organized, the problem of race festered, provoking uneasiness but little positive action.

A profound failure of leadership in these years exacerbated the loss of political purpose and nurtured the gathering reactionary backlash. Early in Nixon's second term, when the nation and its elected representatives might have begun to address a broad range of domestic issues, America was instead distracted by a grave political crisis.

Watergate: The Nation in Crisis

The term "Watergate," like "Teapot Dome" from the 1920s, encompasses a complex tangle of events. Although the scandal stemmed mainly from criminal activities carried out by the Nixon administration during the 1972 presidential campaign and the subsequent attempts to cover up those crimes, it had larger sources and im-

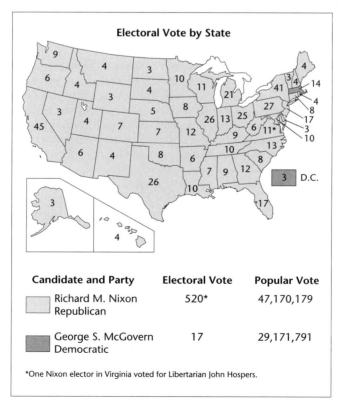

FIGURE 12.3

Presidential Election of 1972

In Perspective: *Presidential Scandals and Trust in Government*

Though the Watergate scandal was unique in the scale of criminality involved and in its outcome—the resignation of a president—it was, in fact, simply one in a long series of scandals that have periodically swirled around the White House. Some involved sex, some money, and some the constitutional abuse of power, but all riveted the nation's attention as they unfolded.

One of the earliest presidential scandals involved Andrew Jackson. In the 1828 electoral campaign, opposition newspapers accused Jackson of adultery, because he had married Rachel Robards in 1791 before her divorce had become final, even though both she and Jackson thought it had. (Jackson supporters responded by accusing his opponent, John Quincy Adams, of being an aristocrat who wore silk underwear.) Scandal tore at the Jackson administration itself in 1829 when the secretary of war, John H. Eaton, married Peggy O'Neale Timberlake, the daughter of a Washington tavernkeeper. Vice President John C. Calhoun and his wife snubbed the Eatons, deeming Peggy to be socially inferior and of shady reputation. This infuriated Jackson, split the cabinet, and in 1830 contributed to Calhoun's resignation. As often happens, the scandal had a political dimension, since Jackson already suspected (correctly) that Calhoun had presidential ambitions himself.

The most scandal-ridden administration of the nineteenth century was Ulysses S. Grant's (1869–77). Though a brilliant Civil War general, Grant was a weak president, and his two terms produced an orgy of high-level corruption. His vice president profited from his connections with a fraudulent railroad-construction company, his private secretary took money from a ring of distillers who were cheating the government of whiskey taxes, and his secretary of war accepted bribes from persons seeking appointments to operate profitable Indian trading posts in Oklahoma. The degeneration of the presidency from Washington to Grant, wrote the historian Henry Adams, was alone enough to disprove all theories of inevitable progress.

Politics and sex again became entangled in 1884 when Republicans accused the Democratic presidential candidate Grover Cleveland of having fathered an illegitimate child years before. "Ma, Ma, Where's my Pa?" they chanted at Cleveland rallies. When Cleveland admitted the charge and made clear that he had supported the child, the voters overlooked his youthful indiscretion, electing him president not only in 1884 but again in 1892.

---

plications. The specific actions that brought Nixon to the verge of impeachment in 1974 revealed the no-holds-barred style of politics that he had practiced for years and exposed fundamental flaws in his character. The crisis, in turn, raised questions about the power and accountability of the executive branch that went to the heart of the U.S. system of governance.

The scandal began, appropriately, under cover of darkness. In the early morning hours of June 17, 1972, a night watchman at the Watergate apartment complex

The worst pre-Watergate presidential scandal came during the administration of Warren G. Harding (1921–23). Like Grant's tarnished presidency, Harding's brief White House tenure (he died in office of a heart attack) was riddled with financial wrongdoing. His attorney general took bribes to fix cases, his director of veterans affairs stole vast sums, and his interior secretary accepted payoffs from oil companies seeking access to oilfields that were part of the government's strategic oil reserve. One of these reserves was in Teapot Dome, Wyoming (so named because of the distinctive shape of a local geological formation), and the term "Teapot Dome" came to describe all the Harding financial scandals. Harding also had a mistress, Nan Britton, whom he occasionally invited for secret trysts in a White House cloakroom. But the full dimensions of the Harding scandals became known only later. In fact he was a popular president, and his death on August 2, 1923, was widely mourned.

Watergate was hardly the end of presidential scandals, as we shall see in later chapters. A major crisis gripped the Reagan White House when the press revealed that top Reagan advisers, if not Reagan himself, had approved the secret transfer of funds to the contras, insurgents fighting the leftist government of Nicaragua, despite Congress's explicit prohibition of such aid. The money came from another secret operation, the clandestine sale of U.S. arms to Iran, a nation widely and correctly viewed as deeply hostile to America. The popular Reagan rode out the storm, but for a time the "Iran-contra affair" held the public's fascinated attention nearly as fully as Watergate had earlier.

The administration of President Bill Clinton had its share of scandals, both financial and sexual. The financial scandals involved charges of campaign finance irregularities, and also the role of the Clintons in a failed real-estate venture, Whitewater, and a collapsed savings-and-loan association during his year as governor of Arkansas. The sexual scandals (which stirred considerably more public interest) involved a series of alleged extramarital relationships or improper sexual advances by Clinton, the most spectacular one involving a young White House intern, Monica Lewinsky.

The presidency as an institution survived all these scandals, but they eroded public trust in government, particularly in recent decades. The Watergate crisis, coming after evidence of deceptions by the Johnson and Nixon administrations in their pursuit of the Vietnam War, severely jolted Americans' confidence in government and in elected officials. Indeed, "Watergate" sank so deeply into the public consciousness that subsequent scandals were often given nicknames that involved the suffix "-gate," such as "Irangate." (Some humorists even alluded to the Clinton-era sex scandals as "Fornigate"!) Much of the antigovernment mood that prevailed in the United States from the 1970s through the end of the century can be traced directly to Watergate and subsequent presidential scandals and attempted cover-ups. Presidents come and go; the impact of the scandals in which they become involved, like the policies they initiate, lives on after them.

---

in Washington, D.C., noticed a door lock taped open. He called the police, who arrested five burglars in the offices of the Democratic National Committee (DNC). One intruder was James W. McCord, Jr., a former CIA agent and chief of security for Nixon's campaign organization, the Committee to Reelect the President, headed by Attorney General John Mitchell. (The committee's preferred acronym was CRP, but the press and public favored CREEP.) The others, Cuban exiles from Miami, had participated in the Bay of Pigs invasion.

The White House and other high administration officials denied any knowledge of what Nixon's press secretary pooh-poohed as "a third-rate burglary attempt." The incident did indeed seem trivial compared to Nixon's trips to China and the Soviet Union earlier that year. As the summer wore on, the White House continued to portray Watergate as a bungled "caper" by overzealous underlings. A few weeks after the incident, John Mitchell, citing family problems, resigned as campaign manager. Mitchell's successor as attorney general, Richard Kleindienst, promised a full Justice Department investigation. Watergate sank to the back pages, and the campaign moved forward.

After the disastrous 1968 convention, the Democratic party had adopted sweeping reforms. As one result, the 1972 convention at Miami Beach included delegates from many groups hitherto underrepresented in party affairs: women, young people, blacks, Hispanics, radical activists. The party's traditional power brokers such as Chicago's Mayor Daley and union officials exerted less influence than in earlier conventions. As one delegate quipped, convention visitors saw more hair and fewer cigars.

One potential candidate, Senator Edward M. Kennedy of Massachusetts, the surviving brother of the famous clan, had been tarred by a nasty scandal in July 1969 when a car he was driving had plunged into Nantucket Sound off Chappaquiddick Island late one night, and Kennedy's young female passenger had drowned. Questions swirled around the tragedy and its aftermath, scuttling the senator's White House hopes. With Kennedy out of the running, Senator George McGovern of South Dakota, front-runner in the primaries, won a first-ballot nomination. A historian and former Methodist minister, McGovern favored immediate U.S. withdrawal from Vietnam, amnesty for Vietnam draft resisters, and broad domestic reforms. The first of McGovern's many problems arose with the revelation that his running mate, Senator Thomas Eagleton of Missouri, had on three occasions received electroshock therapy for depression. Eagleton withdrew, and McGovern, after several top Democrats turned him down, tapped Kennedy brother-in-law R. Sargent Shriver to complete the ticket.

The Republican convention, also in Miami Beach, renominated Nixon and Agnew by acclamation. The party platform opposed school busing and amnesty for draft evaders. Already the strong favorite, Nixon gained additional ground in May when Governor George Wallace, again running as a third-party candidate, was shot by a deranged man at a rally in Maryland and left paralyzed.

Nixon made few appearances and refused to debate McGovern, relying on TV ads and on surrogate speechmakers instead. Nevertheless, he won a landslide victory: 49 states and 520 electoral votes. McGovern, his support confined mainly to hard-core antiwar and liberal constituencies, carried only Massachusetts and Washington, D.C. Nixon garnered 49 million popular votes to McGovern's 29 million. Although the Republicans gained thirteen House seats, they remained in the minority, and the Democrats actually picked up two Senate seats. In any showdown, Nixon would face a strongly Democratic Congress. The clash came soon.

Despite the administration's efforts, the Watergate break-in refused to vanish. An address book carried by one of the burglars had linked the operation to E. Howard Hunt, who worked for Nixon aide Charles Colson. Also implicated was G. Gordon Liddy, counsel of CREEP's finance committee. Both Hunt and Liddy had taken part in earlier clandestine operations as members of the White House Plumbers (see p. 318). The FBI quickly traced money in the burglars' possession to CREEP, and bit by bit the story emerged. Hunt and Liddy had planned the burglary, probably on the instructions of John Mitchell and deputy campaign director Jeb Stuart Magruder. In February 1972, Liddy had detailed the plan in a meeting with Mitchell, Magruder, and White House counsel John W. Dean III, who in turn had briefed the White House chief of staff, Bob Haldeman. Nixon himself probably approved the plan in advance. As one investigator surmised, "If Haldeman knew, the President knew."

In an earlier break-in at the DNC late in May, the burglars had photographed documents and tapped the telephones of Lawrence O'Brien, chairman of the DNC, and another Democratic official. The second tap had worked well, and reports on the illegally recorded conversations went to Haldeman. But the O'Brien tap proved faulty, and the June 17 break-in was planned to correct the problem.

Why did the Nixon campaign attempt such a high-risk crime? FBI director J. Edgar Hoover had died in early May 1972, disrupting Nixon's normal channels of political intelligence. Perhaps, some scholars theorize, he was forced to improvise. The immediate impetus for the break-in was Nixon's urgent desire to learn how much O'Brien knew about contributions to the Republican campaign by large corporations in exchange for preferential treatment, and about his shady financial dealings with billionaire Howard Hughes. More broadly, the operation continued a pattern of wiretaps and break-ins initiated by Nixon and Kissinger. Watergate, in short, was only part of a web of criminal activity spun in the Oval Office.

In mid-September 1972, a grand jury indicted the five burglars, together with Hunt and Liddy. In late September, Bob Woodward and Carl Bernstein of the *Washington Post* revealed that Mitchell, as attorney general, had managed a secret fund intended to gather damaging information on Nixon's political enemies and potential challengers. They also uncovered another fund targeted at sabotaging Democratic presidential hopefuls in the primaries by forging letters, planting spies, stealing campaign plans, and feeding false information to the media.

The White House indignantly denied all the charges and accused the *Post* of irresponsible journalism. Outside Washington, however, the Watergate break-in and the follow-up stories roused little interest. McGovern called the Nixon White House "the most corrupt administration in history," but most voters dismissed the charge as campaign hyperbole.

Despite Nixon's outward calm, the Watergate arrests had set off panic bells in the White House and triggered a massive effort by the president and his aides to conceal their complicity in the Hunt-Liddy operation and other crimes. John Dean, hinting vaguely that CIA security matters were involved, pressured acting FBI director L. Patrick Gray III to curb the FBI's Watergate investigation and to transfer FBI records in the case to Dean. Haldeman, drawing on a secret fund that he kept in his White House safe, gave $400,000 in cash to an intermediary for transfer to the seven Watergate defendants to ensure their silence. Jeb Stuart Magruder and other White House staffers lied to the FBI, the grand jury, and the press about the role of CREEP and the White House in the break-in.

In January 1973, the trial of the Watergate Seven began before U.S. district court judge John Sirica, who grilled witnesses sharply. All seven defendants were convicted. Living up to his nickname "Maximum John," Sirica threatened them with long prison terms unless they told what they knew. In late March, Sirica read an explosive letter from James McCord revealing that the White House had paid him off and had promised him a pardon if he kept quiet. An outraged Sirica called for further investigation.

On another front, Patrick Gray, testifying in February before the Senate Judiciary Committee on his nomination as permanent FBI director, had revealed John Dean's close involvement in the FBI's investigation of Watergate. That month, the Senate also created the Special Committee on Presidential Campaign Activities to investigate the spreading scandal. Seventy-seven-year-old Sam Ervin, Democrat from North Carolina, chaired the committee. On March 21, John Dean warned Nixon, "We have a cancer—within, close to the Presidency, that's growing. It's growing daily."

Nixon counterattacked on April 30. Claiming that he had only just learned the full story of the burglary and the cover-up, he blamed everything on John Dean, whom he fired. With lavish praise, he also announced the departure of chief of staff Haldeman and adviser John Ehrlichman. All earlier White House statements about Watergate, instructed Nixon's press secretary, were now "inoperative." Nixon then replaced Attorney General Richard Kleindienst with Elliot Richardson, a Boston Brahmin of sterling reputation. On May 18, Richardson chose Archibald Cox, a law professor at Harvard, as a special prosecutor with broad powers to investigate the Watergate matter. Two investigations were thus under way: the special prosecutor's, which could involve criminal prosecution, and the Ervin Committee's, which could lead to impeachment.

On May 11, in still another twist, a California federal judge exonerated Daniel Ellsberg in the Pentagon Papers case. In the course of this trial, the break-in at the office of Ellsberg's psychiatrist had come to the light. The press also reported that John Ehrlichman had dangled the prospect of the FBI directorship before the judge, in what seemed like a bribe for an Ellsberg conviction.

The Ervin Committee began televised hearings on May 17. For six months, Americans watched fascinated as witnesses uncovered the crimes and plots hatched in the Nixon White House. The beetle-browed Senator Ervin, who referred to himself as a "simple country lawyer," possessed impressive constitutional expertise and a razor-sharp mind. Inexorably, the investigation circled closer to the Oval Office. Jeb Magruder now conceded that he and John Mitchell had helped to plan the break-in. Nixon's lawyer admitted that he had raised $220,000 for the Watergate defendants and had managed a half-million-dollar fund earmarked for sabotage and espionage against Democrats. Mitchell, now in serious jeopardy himself, gave a fuller view of what he called the "White House horrors." Furious over Nixon's making him the fall guy, John Dean testified against his former boss and White House colleagues. Nixon himself, Dean testified, had directed the cover-up from the start. Dean's assertions fleshed out a developing picture of Watergate as only part of a pattern of illegal and unethical activities carried out at the president's initiative against politicians, journalists, and others on the president's "Enemies List." In an August 1971 memo to Ehrlichman, Dean himself had outlined a campaign of wiretaps, tax audits, and other forms of harassment "to screw our political enemies."

Charles Colson, another master of political chicanery, orchestrated such activities as the forging of State Department cables to make it appear that President John Kennedy had ordered the murder of Ngo Dien Diem in 1963. The aim was to damage Senator Edward Kennedy, whom Nixon feared as a potential rival. Senator Ervin found especially heinous this assault on the memory of a man "sleeping in the tongueless silence of the dreamless dust for nine years."

The criminal goings-on, including the Watergate payoffs, together with legitimate campaign expenses, had been financed by a vast pool of cash raised from corporate contributors in return for special treatment. The International Telephone and Telegraph Corporation, for example, paid much of the cost of the 1972 Republican convention after Nixon apparently intervened to help ITT in a 1971 antitrust case. The dairy industry contributed hugely after Nixon backed higher price supports for milk. The seamy record extended to Nixon's personal finances as well. Prodded by reports in the press, a congressional tax committee found that Nixon owed some $475,000 in back taxes and interest for 1969–72. The president's tax returns revealed a pattern of questionable deductions, including inflated valuations placed on presidential papers contributed to the National Archives.

The Watergate scandal had broadened incredibly, but only Dean's testimony linked Nixon to criminal activity. Republican Senator Howard Baker of Tennessee asked the key question of the Ervin hearings: "What did the President know, and when did he know it?" On July 16, 1973, Nixon aide Alexander Butterfield unexpectedly opened a way to answer Baker's query. Nixon, testified Butterfield, had secretly tape-recorded all conversations held in the Oval Office. The Ervin Committee and special prosecutor Cox, seeking direct evidence that might tie Nixon to the cover-up, demanded that Nixon release the relevant tapes. But the president refused, invoking national security and "executive privilege." Instead, he offered to provide summaries of the requested tapes, their accuracy to be verified by Senator John Stennis (D., Mississippi), seventy-two years old, deeply conservative, and partially deaf. Cox rejected this offer.

On Saturday, October 20, after Cox had secured a court order for the release of the tapes, Nixon instructed Attorney General Richardson to fire the prosecutor. Richardson refused, and resigned. The deputy attorney general also refused. He too was fired. Finally, the third-ranking Justice Department official, Solicitor General Robert Bork, signed the order dismissing Cox. With this action, Richardson later wrote, Nixon abused his power "more blatantly than at any other stage in the whole sordid history of Watergate. A government of laws was on the verge of becoming a government of one man."

The Final Stage of the Crisis

Public reaction to Watergate had built slowly. Nixon's politics had broad appeal, he had compiled an impressive diplomatic record, and he had just won an overwhelming mandate for a second term. But the erosion of his popular support was ominously steady. In this context, the "Saturday Night Massacre" precipitated an uproar. Impeachment demands mounted. Automobile horns blared around the White House, where picketers' signs urged, "Honk for Impeachment." On NBC-TV, a commenta-

Democracy in the Streets. *Clad in prison garb and sporting a Nixon mask, a demon-strator in Washington, D.C., made his views clear as the Watergate cover-up unrav-eled.* (AP/Wide World Photos)

tor declared, "The country tonight is in the midst of what may be the most serious constitutional crisis in its history." Under heavy pressure, the president appointed a new special prosecutor, Leon Jaworski. A Houston lawyer and former president of the American Bar Association, Jaworski was a friend of Lyndon Johnson and other prominent Texas Democrats, but he had supported Nixon in 1972.

Watergate now dominated the media. Woodward and Bernstein of the *Post* re-lied heavily on an unnamed informant whom they nicknamed "Deep Throat." One plausible theory holds that "Deep Throat" was an FBI official upset by Nixon's compromising of the Bureau's integrity.*

Compounding Nixon's troubles, Vice President Spiro Agnew resigned in Oc-tober 1973 after a grand jury found that he had accepted bribes while governor of Maryland and as vice president. In a negotiated settlement, Agnew pleaded *nolo contendere*—in effect a guilty plea—to a single tax-evasion charge. In exchange for the government's agreement not to prosecute, Agnew paid a $10,000 fine and re-ceived a three-year suspended sentence. As provided by the recently enacted Twenty-fifth Amendment, Nixon nominated as Agnew's successor House Minority Leader Gerald R. Ford, who won quick confirmation by the Senate and House.

Stories circulated of Nixon's heavy drinking. During the October 1973 Yom Kippur War, Henry Kissinger took control. Even the decision to declare a high state of nuclear alert was made by Kissinger, Secretary of Defense James Schlesinger, and a few other officials at a midnight White House meeting as Nixon slept.

---

* The FBI's L. Patrick Gray and Alexander Haig, Nixon's chief of staff, have also been suggested.

On November 12, 1973, a year after Nixon's electoral victory, *Time* magazine called on him to resign. Pressed at a gathering of newspaper editors to discuss his tax problems and other matters, the president finally exploded, "I am not a crook!" As Nixon's approval rating sank to 27 percent, the sharpest one-year drop since polling began in the 1930s, columnist Elizabeth Drew described him as "running and maneuvering like a hunted man." In a defiant State of the Union address on January 30, he declared, "One year of Watergate is enough. . . . I have no intention . . . of ever walking away from the job that the people elected me to do."

Even as Nixon battled on, however, the House Judiciary Committee was gathering evidence of presidential wrongdoing—a first step toward impeachment. For the first time since 1868, the removal of a president by Congress seemed a real possibility.* In February 1974, by an ominous 410–4 vote, the House granted the Judiciary Committee full subpoena powers to pursue its investigations.

On March 1, a grand jury in Judge Sirica's court indicted Haldeman, Ehrlichman, Mitchell, four other former White House and CREEP staff members, and "other persons known and unknown" for conspiracy to obstruct justice. The charges included wiretapping, destroying documents, promising executive clemency, paying hush money, and lying to investigators. The indictments relied heavily on the testimony of John Dean, who had pleaded guilty to a single conspiracy charge and was cooperating with the grand jury. A few days later, Sirica turned over to the Judiciary Committee the grand jury's sealed report naming Nixon as an "unindicted coconspirator" in the cover-up.

On a swing through the Midwest and South to shore up support, Nixon met mostly hostile crowds. Republican candidates in the upcoming midterm election distanced themselves from the president. Even Vice President Ford told an audience of Republican faithful, "The political lesson of Watergate is this. Never again must America allow an arrogant, elite guard of political adolescents like CREEP to bypass the regular party organization and dictate the terms of a national election."

On May 9, 1974, the Judiciary Committee began formal impeachment hearings. In June, to divert attention from Watergate, Nixon toured the Middle East, where a million people cheered him in a Cairo motorcade, and made another trip to Moscow. But what should have been diplomatic triumphs, now seemed mere diversions from the domestic crisis. The release of the Ervin Committee's devastating final report in early July, a veritable catalog of presidential wrongdoing, brought impeachment another step closer.

Meanwhile, the tussle over the tapes had continued. In November 1973, Nixon had turned over to special prosecutor Jaworski some recordings that convinced Jaworski of Nixon's complicity in criminal activities. The tape for June 20, 1972, three days after the break-in, contained a gap of some eighteen minutes. Nixon's secretary loyally claimed to have erased this section inadvertently while answering the telephone. Alexander Haig, Haldeman's successor as White House

---

* The impeachment powers of Congress, involving an initial finding by the House of Representatives and trial in the Senate, with removal from office by a two-thirds vote of the Senate, are grounded in Articles I and II of the Constitution, which set out the procedures for removing a president, vice president, or other civil officers for "Treason, Bribery, or other high Crimes and Misdemeanors."

chief of staff, blamed some "sinister force of energy." Most Watergate scholars hold Nixon himself responsible.

In April, Sirica ordered Nixon to give tapes of sixty-four post-Watergate conversations to Jaworski. Instead, Nixon released his own edited version of forty-two taped conversations, with many cuts and alterations. In one conversation, for example, he proposes "to get off the cover-up line." In the Judiciary Committee's later version of the same tape, the words are, "to get on with the cover-up plan." Nixon entirely edited out his order to John Mitchell on March 22, 1973: "I want you to stonewall it, let them plead the Fifth Amendment, cover-up or anything else."

Even these doctored transcripts revealed the sleazy tone of the Nixon White House, as the president and his aides hatched plots against Nixon's many "enemies." The words "expletive deleted" recur repeatedly, adding another phrase to the lexicon of Watergate. The revelations of the tapes wrought deep dismay. In a typical editorial, the Republican *Omaha World-Herald* deplored "the appallingly low level of political morality in the White House." Watergate, coupled with a 15 percent inflation rate, was devastating public morale.

On May 20, Judge Sirica again ordered Nixon to release the subpoenaed tapes. This time, Nixon's lawyers appealed Sirica's order to the Supreme Court. Still stonewalling, Nixon in June wrote to House Judiciary chairman Peter Rodino and U.S. district judge Gerhard Gesell that he alone would decide what evidence he would release, even under judicial or congressional subpoena.* The *New Yorker* wrote, "The President's two letters . . . are not just one more set of legal arguments. They are briefs against Constitutional government. They are a proposal for a new form of government, in which a President, once elected, is beyond restraint." On July 24, in *United States* v. *Nixon,* Chief Justice Warren Burger read the Supreme Court's unanimous ruling: Nixon must obey Sirica's subpoena and turn over the tapes in the interests of "criminal justice." That same day, the House Judiciary Committee began six days of debate on the impeachment resolutions. Upwards of 35 million Americans followed the mesmerizing drama on TV or radio. Committee member Barbara Jordan from Texas declared, "My faith in the Constitution is whole, it is complete, it is total, and I am not going to sit here and be an idle spectator to the diminution, the subversion, the destruction of the Constitution."

On July 27, the Judiciary Committee approved, 27–11, the first article of impeachment, charging Nixon with obstruction of justice in his attempt to impede the Watergate investigation and to "cover up, conceal, and protect those responsible." In committing these deeds, the article concluded, Nixon had "acted in a manner contrary to his trust as President and subversive of constitutional government." All twenty-one Democrats and six of the seventeen Republicans voted for this article. Two further articles, approved a few days later, cited Nixon's use of the FBI, Internal Revenue Service, and CIA to abuse "the constitutional rights of citizens" and his defiance of a congressional subpoena to release the tapes.†

---

* Gesell had ordered release of the tapes as evidence in a separate case involving the prosecution of John Ehrlichman and Charles Colson for their role in planning the break-in at the office of Daniel Ellsberg's psychiatrist.

†The committee voted down two additional articles of impeachment. One accused Nixon of violating Congress's war-making powers with his secret bombing of Cambodia; the other accused him of demeaning the presidency by his handling of his personal finances, a reference to his massive underpayment of his federal income taxes.

On August 6, after again justifying his withholding the tapes, Nixon released them. Here at last was the "smoking gun": conclusive proof of Nixon's direct role in the criminal obstruction of justice. On June 23, 1972, Haldeman had explained Dean's scheme to Nixon: the White House, citing "national security," will instruct the CIA to tell the FBI to halt its Watergate investigation. Nixon replied:

> All right. Fine. . . . You open that scab there's a hell of a lot of things and . . . we just feel that it would be very detrimental to have this thing go any further. . . . Play it tough. That's the way they [our enemies] play it and that's the way we are going to play it. . . . Don't lie to them to the extent to say there is no involvement, but just say this is sort of a comedy of errors, bizarre, without getting into it. . . . [The CIA] should call the FBI in and say that we wish for the country, don't go any further into this case, period!

The March 21, 1973, tape, in which Nixon approved paying more hush money to E. Howard Hunt in response to Hunt's blackmail threat, proved damaging as well. In other tapes, Nixon urged his aides to lie to the grand jury—for example, "You can say I don't remember. You can say I can't recall."

In early August, even before Nixon released the tapes, 66 percent of the American people had favored impeachment. With the tapes' release, the figure rose higher. Even Nixon's last-ditch supporters now jumped ship. At a meeting of Republican senators on August 6, Senator Barry Goldwater growled, "There are only so many lies you can take and now there has been one too many. Nixon should get his ass out of the White House—today!" On August 7, GOP congressional leaders confirmed to Nixon that impeachment and removal from office appeared certain.

On August 8, Nixon announced his resignation in a television address. Obliquely apologizing for "any injuries that may have been done in the course of the events that led to this decision," he referred to Watergate only briefly and instead recited his foreign-policy triumphs. The next day, after Nixon's emotional, and somewhat incoherent, farewell to his staff, he and Pat boarded a helicopter for the first leg of their flight to California. In his inaugural address, Gerald Ford declared, "Our long national nightmare is over."

Conclusion

Nixon's reputation fell into deep eclipse following his resignation, worsened rather than salvaged by President Ford's unconditional pardon of him a month later. But his amazing ability to bounce back remained intact. Slowly easing into the role of elder statesman, he revisited the scenes of his foreign triumphs and wrote extensively on global politics. By 1992, the twentieth anniversary of Watergate, Nixon had regained a degree of grudging public respect. His favorite bird, someone quipped, must be the phoenix.

Historians remain wary. Earlier presidential scandals, such as the Whiskey Ring of the 1870s and Teapot Dome of the 1920s, had involved the all-too-human motive of greed. Watergate entailed abuses that revealed contempt for the U.S. Constitution and for citizens' most basic rights.

The constitutional crisis of 1972–74—the gravest that the nation had faced since the Civil War—arose from the intersection of long-term trends and Nixon's own character. Since Franklin Roosevelt's day, the executive branch had steadily expanded in power. The FBI wiretap on Martin Luther King, Jr., authorized by Robert Kennedy, the escalation of the Vietnam War secretly planned by Johnson and his advisers, the clandestine bombing of Cambodia by Nixon and Kissinger, and other abuses of presidential power all paved the way for Watergate. As Nixon pointed out, every president since Franklin Roosevelt had authorized wiretaps. Lyndon Johnson, in fact, had approved a wiretap on Nixon's campaign plane in 1968.

But in the Nixon White House, isolated improprieties became commonplace. On the world stage, Nixon and Kissinger had operated at a rarefied level as they reshaped global alignments. Such power can breed a kind of megalomania, in which one feels exempt from the rules that govern others. In Nixon's case, the headiness of power combined with the paranoid streak in his character. Even as president he remained the suspicious outsider, seeing enemies everywhere. This outlook elicited precisely the hostility that Nixon imagined. "Opponents are savage destroyers, haters," he reminded himself early in 1974. "[Their] whole purpose . . . is to discredit, destroy, harass everybody around the President." He reacted instinctively: "Time to use full power of the President to fight overwhelming forces arrayed against us."

From his early days in politics, Nixon had conducted underhanded campaigns. Moreover, he had attracted aides who shared his suspicious nature and his compulsion to annihilate the opposition. This pattern led inexorably to the illegalities and abuses of power that climaxed in Watergate. The post-Watergate conspiracy, which Nixon orchestrated "from day one," as Bob Haldeman later conceded, reflected Nixon's lifetime record. To him, Watergate was simply another vendetta of the kind that punctuated his entire political career. In superpower diplomacy, his ruthlessness and penchant for intrigue at times served him well; in the domestic arena, these traits proved fatal.

After Nixon resigned, editorial writers sighed in relief that "the system worked"—the rule of law had prevailed. But the outcome was by no means certain. Only amid bouts of indecision and temporizing did Congress move ponderously toward impeachment. In the last analysis, it was Nixon's own ingrained habits of distrust and deceit, symbolized by his secret taping of even his closest advisers, that undid him. As the conspirators turned on each other, the whole skein of illegality unraveled. Historian Stanley Kutler writes, "Lies became the quicksand that engulfed Nixon, estranged him from his natural political allies, and eventually snapped the fragile bond of trust . . . that binds government and the people."

"The system worked," but Watergate revealed its vulnerability to those who will stop at nothing in their pursuit of power. Many observers at the time believed that Watergate had permanently crippled the presidency. And, indeed, Nixon's immediate successors did inherit a much diminished office.

"The system worked," but Nixon's resignation offered no guarantee that it would survive another challenge by an even more ruthless successor. The Iran-contra scandal of the Reagan years (see Chapter 14) offered a reminder that no single crisis, even one as searing as Watergate, could grant permanent immunity against constitutional abuses.

"The system worked," but at a high price. For over a year, Watergate obscured other urgent issues. In the long run, Watergate weakened the public's confidence in government. Like Hiroshima and the Vietnam War, Watergate haunts the nation with its legacy of unanswered questions—not only concerning its details but, more profoundly, about the vulnerability of a constitutional system too often taken for granted.

Watergate tainted scores of lives and derailed numerous careers. More than seventy persons were eventually convicted or pleaded guilty for their role in the scandal. Bob Haldeman, John Ehrlichman, and John Mitchell each served a year and a half in jail. Eight other White House aides or campaign officials also went to prison. G. Gordon Liddy served the longest term, from January 1973 to September 1977.

Henry Kissinger's judgment on his former boss was harsh: "In destroying himself, Nixon had wrecked the lives of almost all who had come into contact with him." Nixon's darker side brought out the worst in others. John Ehrlichman confessed to Judge Sirica, "I abdicated my moral judgments and turned them over to someone else." More serious than the personal toll was Nixon's assault on the fabric of American government. That the fabric endured—however precariously one can never be sure—testifies to the farsighted wisdom of earlier, and finer, American statesmen.

SELECTED READINGS

Social Groups and Movements in 1970s America

Rodolfo F. Acuña, *Occupied America: A History of Chicanos* (3d ed., 1988); Lois Banner, *Women in Modern America* (1984); Mary Francis Berry, *Why the ERA Failed* (1986); Albert Camarillo, *Chicanos in California: A History of Mexican Americans in California* (1984); Stephen Cornell, *The Return of the Native: American Indian Political Resurgence* (1988); Barbara Deckard, *The Women's Movement: Political, Socioeconomic, and Psychological Issues* (1983); Martin Duberman, *Stonewall* (1993); Alice Echols, *Daring to Be Bad: Radical Feminism in America, 1967–1975* (1989); John D'Emilio, *Sexual Politics, Sexual Communities: The Making of a Homosexual Minority in the United States, 1940–1970* (1983); Sara Evans, *Personal Politics: The Roots of Women's Liberation in the Civil Rights Movement and the New Left* (1978); David J. Garrow, *Liberty and Sexuality: The Right to Privacy and the Making of* Roe v. Wade (1994); Susan M. Hartmann, *From Margin to Mainstream: American Women and Politics Since 1960* (1989); Bell Hooks, *Ain't I a Woman? Black Women and Feminism* (1981); Carolyn Johnson, *Sexual Power: Feminism and the Family in America* (1992); Jonathan Katz, *Gay American History: Lesbians and Gay Men in the U.S.A.: A Documentary History* (1992); Eric Marcus, *Making History: The Struggle for Gay and Lesbian Equal Rights, 1945–1990* (1992); Donald G. Mathews and Jane S. De Hart, *Sex, Gender, and the Politics of ERA* (1990); Michael Novak, *The Rise of the Unmeltable Ethnics* (1972); Kenneth R. Philip, ed., *Indian Self-Rule: First-Hand Accounts of Indian-White Relations from Roosevelt to Reagan* (1986); Margaret Rose, "From the Fields to the Picket Line: Huelga Women and the Boycott, 1965–1975," *Labor History* (Summer 1990); Leigh W. Rutledge, *The Gay Decades: From Stonewall to the Present* (1992); Randy Shilts, *Conduct Unbecoming: Gays and Lesbians in the U.S. Military* (1993); Melissa Walker, *Down from the Mountaintop: Black*

Women's Novels in the Wake of the Civil Rights Movement, 1966–1989 (1991); Winifred D. Wandersee, *On the Move: American Women in the 1970s* (1988).

Watergate

Stephen E. Ambrose, *Nixon* (1987); Charles Colson, *Born Again* (1976); Congressional Quarterly, *Watergate: Chronology of a Crisis* (2 vols., 1973–1974); John W. Dean III, *Blind Ambition: The White House Years* (1976); James Doyle, *Not Above the Law: The Battles of Watergate Prosecutors Cox and Jaworski* (1977); John Ehrlichman, *Witness to Power* (1982); H. R. Haldeman, *The Ends of Power* (1978); Jim Houghan, *Secret Agenda: Watergate, Deep Throat, and the CIA* (1984); Leon Jaworski, *The Right and the Power: The Prosecution of Watergate* (1976); Stanley I. Kutler, *The Wars of Watergate: The Last Crisis of Richard Nixon* (1990); J. Anthony Lucas, *Nightmare: The Underside of the Nixon Years* (1976); Jeb Stuart Magruder, *An American Life: One Man's Road to Watergate* (1974); New York Times, *White House Transcripts* (1974); Richard Oudes, ed., *From the President: Richard Nixon's Secret Files* (1989); Jonathan Schell, *The Time of Illusion* (1975) and *Observing the Nixon Years* (1989); Arthur M. Schlesinger, Jr., *The Imperial Presidency* (1973); Peter Schrag, *Test of Loyalty: Daniel Ellsberg and the Rituals of Secret Government* (1974); John J. Sirica, *To Set the Record Straight* (1979); Fred D. Thompson, *At That Point in Time: The Inside Story of the Senate Watergate Committee* (1975); Bob Woodward and Carl Bernstein, *All the President's Men* (1974) and *The Final Days* (1976).

1970s Politics, Environmental Issues, and Cultural Trends

James L. Baughman, *The Republic of Mass Culture* (1992); Peter N. Carroll, *It Seemed Like Nothing Happened: America in the 1970s* (1982); Thomas Byrne Edsall with Mary D. Edsall, *Chain Reaction: The Impact of Race, Rights, and Taxes on American Politics* (1991); Robert Booth Fowler, *The Greening of Protestant Thought* (1995); Todd Gitlin, *Inside Prime Time* (1985); Samuel Hays, *Beauty, Health, and Permanence: Environmental Politics in the United States, 1955–1985* (1987); Maurice Isserman and Michael Kazin, "The Failure and Success of the New Radicalism," in Steve Fraser and Gary Gerstle, eds., *The Rise and Fall of the New Deal Order, 1930–1980* (1989); Sam Kushner, *Long Road to Delano: A Century of Farmworkers' Struggle* (1975); Christopher Lasch, *The Culture of Narcissism* (1979); Charles McCarry, *Citizen Nader* (1972); Martin V. Melosi, *Coping with Abundance: Energy and Environment in Industrial America* (1985); Carolyn Merchant, *Major Problems in American Environmental History: Documents and Essays* (1993); Allan Schnaiberg, *The Environment: From Surplus to Scarcity* (1980); Edwin Schur, *The Awareness Trap: Self-Absorption Instead of Social Change* (1976); Robert Sklar, *Prime-Time America: Life on and Behind the Television Screen* (1980); Donald Worster, *The Wealth of Nature: Environmental History and the Ecological Imagination* (1993).

PART FOUR

Uncertain Triumph

The contemporary era, from Watergate to the present, has seen profound changes at home and a radically altered international picture. These years have also witnessed a swing in the political pendulum, from conservatism to a cautious liberalism tempered by public suspicion of government. Richard Nixon's disgrace intensified this revulsion against Washington, but the roots of the antigovernment mood lay deeper, in Middle America's resentment of the Vietnam debacle, a costly welfare system, school busing, federal affirmative action pro grams, and conflict over abortion and other issues. In the later 1970s, inflation and other economic problems exacerbated middle-class anxieties and the reactionary spirit. The immediate beneficiary of these discontents, Jimmy Carter, rode the antiestablishment wave to the White House in 1976. But Carter's generally unsuccessful one-term presidency suffered both from his personal flaws and from factors largely beyond his control, including runaway inflation, soaring energy costs, and a humiliating hostage crisis in Iran.

Carter's ineffectual term accelerated the electorate's rightward shift, and Ronald Reagan, a well-known champion of conservative causes, capitalized on the insurgent mood. Reagan's program, featuring laissez-faire economics, Cold War militance, and a rollback of big government, won support from an electorate in full flight from New Deal/Fair Deal/Great Society–style liberalism. The "Reagan revolution" brought big tax cuts, deregulation of key sectors of the economy, slashes in social programs, and massive increases in military spending. With inflation under control and the affluent profiting from favorable tax and regulatory policies, the decade saw a glow of prosperity. Giddy real-estate speculation, a wave of high-stakes corporate takeovers, and a general aura of conspicuous consumption marked the Reagan years.

The Reagan political coalition survived long enough to send heir-apparent George Bush to the White House in 1988. But Bush had neither Reagan's charisma nor his clear-cut domestic agenda, and his administration drifted despite military exploits in the Persian Gulf that earned him a brief spurt of popularity.

With the election of 1992, the baby boomers, now well into midlife, elevated one of their own—Bill Clinton—to the White House. Clinton shared the ideological allegiances of many members of this generation, including feminism and environmentalism. Indeed, at the outset he appointed women to key posts and assigned his wife a central role in shaping health-care policy. His vice president, Al Gore, had written a book much admired by environmentalists.

Although heir to an activist liberal tradition extending from Franklin Roosevelt to Lyndon Johnson, Clinton himself reflected the more conservative political climate of the post-Reagan era. After a disastrous initial effort to promote a massive and unwieldy health-reform program, Clinton shifted course. Intent on shedding the Democrats' reputation as a big-government "tax-and-spend" party, he called for spending cuts, a smaller government, and welfare reform. Sweeping Republican gains in the 1994 midterm election pulled Clinton further to the right and away from classic liberal positions. He collaborated with Republicans on a budget-balancing plan and signed a historic welfare-reform bill designed to limit benefits for the poor through a tough-minded, decentralized, work-oriented approach. Aided by a booming economy, Clinton won a second term in 1996, but as the decade ended, and Clinton wrestled with a series of scandals involving his personal behavior, neither he nor the Republican Congress seemed inclined to bold new initiatives.

Despite the glow of prosperity, economic problems remained, especially the enormous task of uplifting an urban underclass trapped in welfare dependence. Millions in the inner cities, along with blue-collar workers displaced by the industrial decline of these years, found themselves marginalized in an emerging high-tech economy that required fewer and more highly trained workers.

As the political merry-go-round whirled on, the United States experienced social and economic shifts that would shape U.S. history in the twenty-first century. American society grew increasingly multiracial and multiethnic, and gender roles, family structure, and even sexual identity seemed fluid and variable. The political system, the cultural arena, and social institutions all bent before the winds of change. On the economic front, an agrarian society that had evolved into the world's industrial leader experienced an equally profound transformation. As the old industrial base eroded, a new economic order based on global markets, electronic data processing, the delivery of services, and the transmittal of knowledge and information began to emerge. Simultaneously, a new world of mass entertainment based on futuristic electronic technologies and vast corporate conglomerates loomed. While visionaries hailed these developments, others nervously pointed to the social and cultural tensions and economic hardship that seemed destined to mark the transition to the brave new world.

The closing decades of the twentieth century brought world changes that were no less dramatic. The Cold War, which had shadowed so much of American history since 1945, ended abruptly in the late 1980s as the Soviet empire collapsed, a victim of unremitting competition with the West and its own debilitating weaknesses. The United States now confronted a freshly complex globe in which the forces of consolidation and of disintegration warred for ascendancy. Islamic fundamentalism in the Middle East; ethnic conflicts in Eastern Europe; famine and feuding clans and ethnic groups in Africa; and the longer-term scourges of poverty, illiteracy, over-population, and environmental deterioration all clamored for attention. As the year 2000 approached, a long cycle of American history that had begun with the victory celebrations of 1945 drew to a close, and the contours of a new era, one marked by urgent challenges both at home and abroad, slowly came into focus.

CHAPTER 13

Picking Up the Pieces: Post-Watergate America

In 1976 the United States threw a year-long party to celebrate the two hundredth anniversary of the American Revolution. The American Revolution Bicentennial Commission sponsored a cornucopia of activities. Citizens in Albany, Georgia, performed a musical honoring the Constitution. The "American Freedom Train," laden with five hundred historic documents and funded by GM and other corporations, toured the nation. A VFW post in Ohio reenacted Washington's crossing of the Delaware. The Smithsonian Institution, with backing from General Foods, sponsored the "Festival of American Folklife." "The Bicentennial Wagon Train Pilgrimage," funded by Gulf Oil Company, lumbered across the nation from west to east and encamped at Valley Forge on July 4, 1976. That day, as President Ford delivered inspirational speeches, fireworks burst across the nation and a breathtaking flotilla of sailing vessels entranced New Yorkers.

Despite the hoopla, the United States was still unsettled by the aftershocks of an era marked by assassinations, riots, and demonstrations. Watergate, history's worst presidential scandal, had left raw scars. Economic problems exacerbated the edgy mood. As energy prices soared, a combination of inflation and recession that journalists dubbed "stagflation" struck, and U.S. industry eroded. Gerald Ford, a Republican, and then Jimmy Carter, a Democrat, left the White House after brief presidencies that brought more frustration than achievement. Moreover, as the country moved to the right both culturally and politically, a reactionary groundswell gained momentum. By 1980 it would startlingly alter the political landscape.

More than 150 years earlier, the German philosopher Georg Friedrich Hegel had described America as "the land of the future . . . , a land of desire for all those who are weary . . . of old Europe." As recently as 1941, the press tycoon Henry Luce had hailed "the American Century." By 1976 such soaring rhetoric was rare. Anxiety, not euphoria, marked the bicentennial year. Sociologist Daniel Bell discerned a "loss of faith in the nation's future." The nation's third century, Bell speculated, could well provide "yet another illustration of the trajectory of human illusions." To many Americans, such apprehensions seemed fully warranted.

A Ford, Not a Lincoln

Watergate left a diminished presidency. Gerald Ford, after completing Nixon's second term, failed to win election in his own right. Ford's Democratic vanquisher, Jimmy Carter, served only one term. With mixed results, both leaders fought a hydra-headed array of economic problems that dominated the late seventies.

Gerald Ford's roots lay in the Middle America that Nixon had so avidly courted. His parents divorced when he was an infant, and he was adopted by his mother's second husband, a Grand Rapids businessman whose name he took. The tall, athletic Ford played football at the University of Michigan, earned a law degree from Yale, and practiced in Grand Rapids. In 1948 he won election to Congress, and in 1965 he became minority leader. With his friendly smile and reputation for honesty, Ford enjoyed wide respect. His integrity and modesty ("I'm a Ford, not a Lincoln") provided refreshing contrast to the scheming Nixon of the Watergate tapes.

But Ford's pardon of Richard Nixon in September 1974 "for all offenses against the United States which he . . . has committed or may have committed or taken part in" knocked his approval ratings from 72 to 49 percent. Ford denied that he had struck a bargain with Nixon and argued that an indictment and possible imprisonment of the ex-president would have prolonged the agony of Watergate. But suspicions of an unsavory deal—the executive office for Ford, pardon for Nixon—however unjustified, shadowed his presidency to the end. Ford's most recent biographer concludes that there was no deal: Ford's reasons for the pardon were those he stated publicly. He goes on to argue, however, that Ford seriously mishandled the pardon by failing to insist that Nixon apologize to the American people for his actions and give up his claim to his presidential papers and to the notorious Oval Office tapes (John Robert Greene, *The Presidency of Gerald R. Ford* [1995]).

Ford showed little of Nixon's openness to innovation. As a congressman he had opposed most of Johnson's Great Society program, and in his first year in office, he vetoed thirty-nine bills passed by the Democratic Congress, including one mandating increased regulation of strip mining. Espousing a 1920s-style laissez-faire ideology, he called for "maximum freedom for private enterprise." In 1974, Ford vetoed the Freedom of Information Act, which, reflecting the post-Watergate mood, granted citizens access to their government files. Congress promptly overrode his veto. Despite delays and restrictions, the law ultimately opened the FBI and other agencies to public scrutiny and checked abuses of individual rights.

Ford encountered economic problems that had been temporarily eclipsed during Watergate. Inflation ranked first in urgency. Oil prices had risen 350 percent after the 1973 Yom Kippur War, and the 1973–74 Arab oil boycott had pushed the inflation rate to a horrendous 11 percent in 1974. Taking office amid this price surge, Ford rejected Nixon's ineffective wage-and-price controls and chose a more ideologically congenial voluntarist approach. In the fall of 1974, Ford grandly announced his "Whip Inflation Now" (WIN) program to persuade businesses to restrain prices voluntarily. When the effort fell flat, Ford conceded that it was "probably too gimmicky." With the oil boycott's end, inflation dropped to about 8 percent in 1975 and 5 percent in 1976 (it would spurt upward again in the late 1970s).

Compounding Ford's problems, the worst recession since the Great Depression struck in 1974–75. As business stagnated, the unemployment rate hit 8.3 percent in 1975. To stimulate recovery, Congress cut taxes by some $23 billion in 1975. The economy rallied, but the tax cut worsened the budget deficit, which in turn, increased inflationary pressures. The recession battered the nation's cities, already floundering as businesses and middle-class taxpayers fled to the suburbs. By late 1975, New York City edged toward bankruptcy, barely able to meet its payroll or pay the interest on its bonds. When New Yorkers in Congress proposed a federal bailout, President Ford refused. "Ford to City: Drop Dead" headlined a Manhattan tabloid. Congress approved emergency loan guarantees, averting the immediate crisis, but urban America's long-term problems continued.

Exploiting the economic mess, the Democrats devised the "Discomfort Index" by combining the inflation and unemployment rates. From 1972 to 1975, this measure nearly doubled. In the 1974 midterm election, frustrated voters increased the Democratic majorities in both the House and Senate. While some of the administration's inflation-fighting measures—spending cuts, the Federal Reserve Board's tightening of credit—had contributed to the problem, the downturn also had roots in economic changes (see pp. 379–383) beyond either party's control. Inflation, for example, stemmed mainly from the oil boycott and the resulting price hikes. The initial panic that produced long lines at service stations soon abated, but Americans used to paying thirty-five cents for a gallon of gas stared in disbelief as prices edged toward seventy cents a gallon. Although gas cost far less in the United States than in Western Europe, the increases shocked a public accustomed to cheap fuel. As an added irritant, U.S. oil-company profits more than doubled from 1972 to 1974 as domestic oil prices rose along with the cost of imported oil. Reacting to soaring gasoline prices, Congress in the Energy Policy and Conservation Act of 1975 for the first time set fuel-efficiency standards for U.S. automobiles. In a further fuel-saving measure, Congress set a national speed limit of 55 miles an hour, triggering more grumbling from drivers.

In international relations, Ford had a hard act to follow, even though Henry Kissinger, appointed secretary of state in 1973, remained in that post. Ford's brief tenure offered few opportunities for foreign-policy initiatives, and in general he pursued Nixon's policies and handled the consequences of Nixon's actions.

Under Ford, the final scenes of the Vietnam debacle unfolded. "Vietnamization" had not stopped the fighting in the region. Indeed, the 1973 Paris agreement proved less a peace treaty than a license for the war to proceed without U.S. ground troops. America remained very much a player, however. U.S. naval and air power hovered nearby in the Gulf of Tonkin, in Thailand, and on Guam. Thieu's regime hired six thousand hastily discharged U.S. army officers as "civilian" advisers. After the cease-fire ended U.S. bombing in Vietnam and Laos, Nixon had ordered a hundred additional B-52s to join the bombing raids on Cambodia, in a show of continued support for Thieu. "This was appalling," the secretary of the air force later wrote. "You couldn't even figure out where you were going to put them all. . . . How were you going to base them?" U.S. bombing of Cambodia continued until August 15, 1973, when a congressional ban took effect.

As B-52s rained 250,000 tons of bombs on Cambodia's villages, fields, and jungles, ostensibly to destroy Khmer Rouge (Cambodian communist) strongholds, the consequent devastation created two million refugees in a population of seven

Old Beyond Their Years. *Cambodian refugee children eye the camera. President Nixon's massive bombing of neutral Cambodia caused many civilian casualties, filled refugee camps, and worsened the nation's political instability. (© Steve Weinrebe)*

million and, ironically, hastened the collapse of Lon Nol's U.S.-backed regime. The B-52s and the 1970 invasion had driven the North Vietnamese deeper into Cambodia and exacerbated the country's social and political chaos. In April 1975 the Hanoi-backed Khmer Rouge unseated Lon Nol and launched a reign of genocidal savagery. Before the Vietnamese overthrew the Khmer Rouge dictator Pol Pot in January 1979, his regime had slaughtered as many as two million people— 25 percent of the population. Recounting these events in his 1979 book *Sideshow,* British journalist William Shawcross reached a harsh conclusion about Washington's role: "Cambodia was not a mistake; it was a crime."

In South Vietnam, President Thieu, relying on Nixon's pledge of U.S. support, had refused to cooperate with the Provisional Revolutionary Government, and in 1974 he resumed the war. Without direct U.S. military power to back him, his cause was precarious. Soon after Nixon's resignation in August 1974, Congress rejected Kissinger's urgent request for $1.5 billion in military aid to South Vietnam. This denial crippled the South Vietnamese military and ended whatever slim chance Thieu might have had to cling to power a bit longer.

North Vietnamese forces, advancing down the peninsula, captured Phuoc Long province, north of Saigon, in January 1975. The end now came with shocking suddenness, Pleiku and Danang fell, and Hué yielded without a fight despite Thieu's order to hold it at all costs. The retreat turned into a rout, at a heavy cost in dead and wounded. In late April, after a three-hour speech denouncing the United States for reneging on its pledges, Thieu fled to Taiwan with fifteen tons of luggage.* Saigon fell on May 1 and was promptly renamed Ho Chi Minh City. In a

---

* Thieu eventually settled in Great Britain. His vice president, the flamboyant Nguyen Cao Ky, became a prosperous liquor-store operator in California.

final humiliating scene, South Vietnamese who had worked for American officials frantically scrambled aboard helicopters atop the U.S. embassy roof as North Vietnamese forces closed in.

Vietnam memories would long haunt the American psyche and influence the nation's approach to global politics. On one hand, Americans were determined to avoid another Vietnam. On the other, they feared lest the world discount U.S. resolve. In this context, relatively minor incidents took on special significance. For example, in May 1975, when Cambodia's communist regime seized a U.S. merchant vessel, the *Mayaguez,* Ford spurned negotiations and ordered a military rescue by two thousand U.S. Marines. The thirty-nine *Mayaguez* crew members were "rescued"—at a cost of forty-one marines' lives. (In fact, the Cambodians had released the crewmen before the operation began.) The symbolic value of Ford's macho display just weeks after the hasty evacuation from Saigon was clear. *Newsweek* hailed Ford's "daring show of nerve and steel." The families of the dead marines were left to count the cost of this fleeting boost to American self-esteem.

Yet post-Vietnam reluctance to engage U.S. power underlay Congress's refusal to sanction U.S. intervention in the African nation of Angola, which became a cockpit of Cold War conflict after gaining its independence from Portugal in 1974. As civil war erupted, the United States and China backed one faction, Moscow another. When the Soviets flew in Cuban troops in 1975, Kissinger proposed massive aid to the U.S.-backed faction. Gripped by the "no more Vietnams" spirit, Congress refused. Kissinger disgustedly concluded that a traumatized nation was embracing isolationism. Other powers, he feared, would assume that Washington had "lost the will to counter adventurism or even to help others to do so." But Kissinger's own prescriptions struck many citizens as the very adventurism that had dragged the nation into the Vietnam quicksand.

Détente, another Nixon legacy, advanced haltingly. At a 1974 meeting in Vladivostok, Ford and Soviet leader Leonid Brezhnev made some progress on SALT II, an arms-control treaty. But final agreement eluded them; despite the rhetoric of détente, Cold War suspicions lingered. Nevertheless, a summit conference at Helsinki in August 1975 constituted the foreign-policy highlight of the Ford years. At this meeting, the nations of Europe, including the Soviet Union and its satellites, agreed to stabilize their national boundaries and the East-West power balance. Equally important in the long run, they also adopted a set of accords on human rights and freedom of travel. These agreements strengthened the forces of political change behind the Iron Curtain. At the time, however, U.S. Cold Warriors and many Americans of Eastern European origin denounced the Helsinki Accords for conceding Soviet hegemony in Eastern Europe.

A Sea of Troubles: The Carter Years

Domestic issues dominated the Ford years, and as the recession dragged on, the 1976 Democratic presidential nomination looked tempting to potential candidates. Aspirants included Senator Lloyd Bentsen of Texas; Senator Henry Jackson of Washington State (dubbed "the senator from Boeing" for his close links to the Seattle aerospace giant); California's maverick governor Jerry Brown, with a penchant

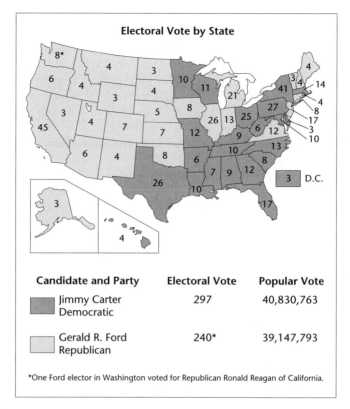

Electoral Vote by State

Candidate and Party	Electoral Vote	Popular Vote
Jimmy Carter Democratic	297	40,830,763
Gerald R. Ford Republican	240*	39,147,793

*One Ford elector in Washington voted for Republican Ronald Reagan of California.

FIGURE 13.1
Presidential Election of 1976

for New Age mysticism; and James Earl (Jimmy) Carter, Jr., of Georgia, who had served a term as governor and then returned to the family's peanut business.

Like George McGovern in 1972, Carter benefited from the Democratic party reforms instituted after 1968, which increased the role of primaries and grassroots activists in the choice of candidates. He also was helped by television, which allowed obscure candidates to win national visibility almost overnight. Supporters of Carter's better-known opponents jeered "Jimmy who?" but he won the Iowa and New Hampshire primaries and soon had the nomination sewn up. As his running mate, he chose Senator Walter Mondale of Minnesota, a leading northern liberal.

Carter offered a pledge of simple honesty ("I will never lie to you") that before Nixon would have sounded ridiculous. He struck a populist note as he accepted the nomination in New York's Madison Square Garden, proclaiming, "It's time for the people to run the government." A devout Baptist whose sister Ruth Carter Stapleton was an evangelist and faith healer, Carter proclaimed himself a "born-again" Christian who strove to apply his faith in daily life. This open avowal of faith epitomized a larger religious trend that molded American life and politics in the 1970s (see pp. 389–392). In *Electing Jimmy Carter: The Campaign of 1976* (1994), Carter's 1976 speechwriter Patrick Anderson describes Carter's evangelical religion as "basic to the idealism and decency that made him attractive to millions who didn't otherwise share his . . . beliefs." Anderson further argues, however, that this same devout evangelical piety contributed to Carter's aura of sanctimony and self-righteousness, which increasingly grated on voters as his term progressed.

On the Republican side, President Ford withstood a challenge by former governor Ronald Reagan of California to win the nomination in his own right. On taking office, Ford had chosen as his vice president former governor Nelson Rockefeller of New York, a leader of the party's liberal eastern wing. For the 1976 campaign, however, seeking to consolidate his conservative flank, he named Senator Robert Dole of Kansas as his running mate.

Carter proved an inept campaigner, and he won a scant 50.1 percent of the popular vote. The stricken economy and Watergate memories, exacerbated by the Nixon pardon, had cost Ford the victory. As a pro-civil-rights southerner, Carter earned 94 percent of the black vote, providing his victory margin in thirteen states. The new president retrieved some—although by no means all—of the white working-class voters who had defected to Nixon or Wallace in 1968 and 1972.

Revealing the depth of post-Watergate voter alienation, fewer than 55 percent of those eligible had bothered to cast a ballot. Voter turnout had long been falling, but 1976 marked a low point. Apathy, it seemed, was the true winner in 1976, summed up in a cynical bumper sticker: DON'T VOTE, IT ONLY ENCOURAGES THEM.

On Inauguration Day, highlighting the contrast with Nixon's imperial presidency, a waving Carter walked from the Capitol to the White House with his wife, Rosalynn, and daughter, Amy. Throughout his term, Carter would project a casual image, favoring blue denims and sports shirts and carrying his own garment bag aboard Air Force One. Fulfilling a campaign pledge, he immediately pardoned some ten thousand Vietnam War draft resisters. Veterans' organizations protested, but most Americans welcomed this gesture toward healing still-raw wounds.

On domestic issues, Carter built a far from negligible record. Honoring a platform promise to the teachers' union, a power in Democratic politics, he created the Department of Education in 1979. (The former Department of Health, Education and Welfare became the Department of Health and Human Services.) His civil-service reform bill, passed in 1978, introduced a merit-pay system and made it easier to fire incompetents. At Carter's behest, Congress created a $1.6 billion environmental "Superfund" to clean up the nation's worst pollution sites. The new president set aside over 100 million acres in Alaska, eyed by developers, as parkland, forest reserves, and wildlife areas. Carter appointed a record number of women and minorities to federal office, including three women cabinet members. Civil-rights veteran Andrew Young became UN ambassador.

Carter's political skills proved lame, however, and he failed to achieve such major domestic goals as welfare reform and strengthening of the underfunded social security system. The creation of a national health-insurance system—a liberal objective since Truman's day—also went unrealized. Despite Democratic majorities in both houses, his relations with Congress remained prickly. As early as 1977, TV journalist Eric Sevareid commented, "[Carter] has the mind of an engineer. . . . He's got a lot of little filing cabinets in his mind that he seems able to use as needed. But he doesn't seem to have much stylistic change of pace, and I fear he will become less and less stimulating." Happiest when analyzing issues and devising paper solutions, the president lacked Lyndon Johnson's talent for political deal-making. The outsider's role that had helped him win the election also stymied his efforts to work with Congress. His personality caused problems as well; beneath the surface affability, he proved aloof and self-righteous. As his popularity fell, he withdrew still more, relying on a tight circle of advisers he had brought from Georgia.

On the economic front, the same problems that had bedeviled Ford—inflation, recession, rising energy costs—haunted Carter as well. In October 1978, with inflation at 9 percent, Carter announced a program of voluntary wage-and-price restraints. But inflation kept spiraling, reaching 13.4 percent in 1979. By 1980 the dollar was worth only forty cents compared to 1967. Unemployment, having declined after 1975, crept up again, reaching 7 percent in 1980, and nearly double that number among black and Hispanic workers. The recession erased the gains of the War on Poverty. By 1978, 29 percent of black families and 23 percent of Hispanic families fell below the poverty line, more than three times the rate for whites.

In a maddening paradox, remedies for one part of the economic crisis worsened another. For example, to fight the recession, Congress, at Carter's request, cut taxes by $34 billion in 1977 and appropriated $4 billion for public-works spending. But the stimulus came too late and only intensified inflationary pressure. Conversely, as the Federal Reserve Board tightened credit—the classic remedy to cool an overheated economy—interest rates soared as high as 20 percent, pushing home mortgages and business loans out of reach and deepening the recession. Carter never unraveled these dilemmas to devise a coherent economic plan.

The president's attempt to resolve energy issues, his top domestic priority, proved equally frustrating. A graduate of the U.S. Naval Academy, he applied his considerable analytic skills to the problem. In April 1977 a sweater-clad Carter sat by an open fire in the White House library and addressed the nation on energy. In a phrase coined by William James, he called the issue the "moral equivalent of war." Soon Congress created the new Department of Energy with a mandate to enforce energy legislation and to formulate national energy policy.

Carter sought to force Americans to conserve by raising the cost of energy. Moreover, he aimed to reduce America's foreign oil imports, which grew from 35 percent of total consumption in 1973 to nearly 50 percent in 1977. In an energy bill presented before a joint session of Congress two days after his address to the nation, Carter proposed phasing out the price controls that kept the cost of domestic oil and natural gas artificially low, while taxing domestic oil production to prevent windfall profits by oil and gas companies. He also called for stiffer federal taxes on gasoline, tax penalties on cars that violated federal fuel-efficiency standards, tax credits for conservation measures, and increased use of coal, although under strict antipollution requirements.

The bill met strong opposition from oil and gas companies, which favored the end of price controls but opposed heavier taxes and federal regulation. Political ideology shaped the debate as well. Believers in the free market favored policies, such as easing environmental rules and lifting price controls on oil and natural gas, designed to encourage drilling for new reserves. Liberals emphasized measures to encourage conservation. The energy law that finally passed in October 1978 after long bargaining contained elements of both positions. It lifted price controls on natural gas in phased steps and penalized gas-guzzling cars. It also provided incentives for coal use by industry and energy-saving measures by consumers, including solar heating units. The law fell short of Carter's dream of a "national energy policy," but it was a step in this direction. The public remained skeptical, however, fearful of higher energy costs and unconvinced that the situation was as dire as Carter claimed.

The energy crisis took on new urgency in 1979–80 when OPEC instituted a second round of price increases. A revolution had unseated Iran's pro-U.S. government, and Iran's new regime, together with the other radical OPEC states of Iraq, Libya, and Algeria, pushed the cartel to raise prices sharply. Soon Saudi Arabian light crude, the industry benchmark, was selling for over thirty dollars a barrel, ten times the pre-1973 price. Long queues again formed at service stations, and gasoline prices broke the dollar-a-gallon barrier. The days of cheap and unlimited energy had ended. Rising energy costs rippled through the economy, from producing and transporting consumer goods to college tuition and hospital fees. Americans paid over $16 billion in higher prices in these years, directly related to OPEC's price hikes. U.S. oil companies, by contrast, boomed as energy prices rose. Exxon's first-quarter profits in 1980, $1.9 billion, ranked the highest of any corporation in history.

Capitalizing on the drive to conserve energy, the nuclear-power industry promoted this panacea as the obvious way to conserve fossil fuels, cut pollution, and reduce U.S. reliance on imported oil. The industry had a case: utilizing water power, nuclear energy was renewable. Under normal operations, nuclear plants, unlike coal-burning generators, did not pollute. President Carter, who had served aboard nuclear submarines in the navy and often consulted Admiral Hyman Rickover ("the father of the nuclear submarine"), supported this option.

But environmentalists, already dubious about nuclear power because of its military connotations, warned of accidents and the hazards of radioactive-waste disposal. In February 1974, an antinuclear activist in Massachusetts loosened the bolts on a 500-foot tower marking the site of a planned nuclear-power plant. The tower crashed to the ground. Turning himself in, the activist explained his gesture as an act of conscience against a project that he considered dangerous. As the antinuclear movement gathered momentum, led by such groups as New Hampshire's Clamshell Alliance and California's Abalone Alliance, the activist spirit of the 1960s and even the test-ban fervor of the 1950s revived. The 1970s campaign bridged the earlier protests and the nuclear-weapons freeze campaign of the early 1980s (see p. 408).

An accident at the Three Mile Island nuclear power plant near Harrisburg, Pennsylvania, in March 1979 bore out the critics' warnings. Some 800,000 gallons of radioactive water burst from a cooling unit, threatening the Susquehanna valley and its people with grave hazards. Tension mounted as the crisis unfolded. Jimmy Carter toured the plant to reassure the public, but his toothy grin seemed forced. In a convergence of mass culture and reality, the 1979 movie *China Syndrome,* starring the 1960s antiwar activist Jane Fonda, dramatized the kind of accident that had actually occurred a few weeks earlier. Three Mile Island, its impact amplified by the coincidental release of *China Syndrome,* dealt the nuclear-energy industry a heavy blow. More than thirty planned plants were canceled, and new orders fell to zero.

President Carter doggedly pursued his battle for a comprehensive energy policy, targeting the federal price controls that kept domestic oil prices artificially low. Price controls were already scheduled to end in 1981, but in April 1979 Carter announced an immediate, phased decontrol of domestic oil prices. Again he called for a windfall-profits on the oil companies, with the revenue to go for public transportation, alternative-energy development, and heating-bill assistance for the poor. Simultaneously he proposed a freeze on imported oil and a government program to produce synthetic fuels from coal and shale. Congress took no action on these ideas, and the president geared up for yet another energy speech, his fifth.

The public's weariness with Carter's lectures on these complex issues deepened. As he wrote in his memoirs, "My repeated calls for action on energy had become aggravating, and were . . . falling on deaf ears." Furthermore, his pollster convinced him that the basic problem was not public resistance to energy conservation but a crisis of morale and loss of confidence in Carter himself. This led to one of the more unusual episodes in the history of the presidency. Canceling his scheduled speech, Carter retreated to Camp David with Rosalynn and a few close advisers for ten days of brainstorming about his and the nation's problems. Scores of men and women from various walks of life shuttled in and out to conduct a kind of rolling seminar for one student: the president of the United States. As Carter and his wife scribbled notes, economists, preachers, journalists, and academics offered their opinions.

After the retreat, Carter gave his postponed speech, which he now used to explain his diagnosis of a national "malaise." America's inability to solve its energy problems, he insisted, reflected "a moral and spiritual crisis, . . . a loss of a unity of purpose." In phrases redolent of the pulpit, the president upbraided Americans for abandoning the old values:

> In a nation that was proud of hard work, strong families, close-knit communities, and our faith in God, too many of us now tend to worship self-indulgence and consumption. . . . But we've discovered that owning things and consuming things does not satisfy our longing for meaning. . . . [P]iling up material goods cannot fill the emptiness of lives which have no confidence or purpose.

Citing Vietnam, Watergate, inflation, and other reasons for the decline of civic spirit, Carter conceded, "The gap between our citizens and our Government has never been so wide." But he ended on a cautiously hopeful note:

> There are two paths to choose. One is . . . the path that leads to fragmentation and self-interest. Down that road lies a mistaken idea of freedom, the right to grasp for ourselves some advantage over others. . . . All the traditions of our past, all the lessons of our heritage, all the promises of our future point to another path, the path of common purpose and the restoration of American values.

Many agreed that the nation suffered from a failure of nerve, often blamed on the psychic aftershock of Vietnam, which some compared to Great Britain's loss of empire. Opinion polls showed increases in feelings of alienation and powerlessness. Although Carter was hardly the first chief executive to urge a renewal of national purpose, people had wearied of White House sermonizing. In fact, Americans castigated Carter himself for a failure of leadership and a tendency to blame others for his own deficiencies. The president's firing of three cabinet members after his "malaise" speech and the resignation of two others highlighted this pattern of blame shifting. The fact that the secretaries of energy and HEW were among those dismissed underscored Carter's failure to resolve the problems to which he himself had given top priority.

Defining energy policy as the test of whether "we can seize control again of our national destiny," Carter sent to Congress a ten-year, $140-billion energy plan that encompassed research on synthetic fuels, higher oil and natural-gas taxes, and tougher automobile fuel-efficiency standards. Except for funding synthetic-fuel research and imposing a windfall-profits tax on oil companies, Congress once more took little action. Carter's four-year battle for a national energy policy had produced a few victories, much acrimony, and many frustrating setbacks.

By 1979 nearly 75 percent of the American people disapproved of Carter's performance—worse than Nixon's lowest ratings. At the *Boston Globe,* a joke title for an editorial on a Carter speech accidentally was printed: "More Mush from the Wimp." In August 1980, as mounting problems battered the White House, a *Time* magazine columnist, offered a harsh judgment of Carter's performance:

> Carter is today a political cripple . . . because the larger issues have swamped him. . . . In his own inexperience and uncertainty, the President could not define a mission for his Government, a purpose for the country, [or] a means of getting there. . . . Carter's mind fixed on the small parts of the effort and not the whole.

No one doubted Carter's honesty, brilliance, or sense of duty, but he lacked key traits that make a successful president. Not blessed with the oratorical power of a Franklin Roosevelt, the charisma of a Jack Kennedy, the manipulative genius of a Johnson, or even the cynical opportunism of a Nixon, Carter gamely soldiered on in the face of deepening disapproval. After Johnson's and Nixon's involuntary departures and Ford's caretaker term, yet another failed presidency loomed.

But the economic problems confronting the nation in the late seventies could well have overwhelmed even the ablest leader. No American president had the power, short of war, to stop OPEC's oil-price increases, the driving force behind the inflationary spiral. Adding to the economic conundrum, the baby-boom generation continued to flood the job market. In fact, the U.S. economy generated more than 26 million new jobs in the seventies, but the rising tide of job seekers only pushed unemployment rates upward. The combination of recession and inflation also made devising a coherent economic policy virtually impossible. The classic Keynesian solution to recession, adopted by both Democrats and Republicans in the postwar years, featured increased federal spending, tax cuts, and eased credit to stimulate recovery. But these measures made money and credit more plentiful and hence worsened inflation. Thus, the Carter administration vacillated between mutually contradictory strategies.

Lobbying by different interest groups further complicated decisionmaking. These pressures increased, ironically, after passage of the campaign finance law of 1974. This post-Watergate reform measure provided for public financing of presidential campaigns through a check-off system on federal income-tax forms but permitted political-action committees (PACs) to contribute up to five thousand dollars to any one candidate. By contributing to an array of PACs, a corporation or lobbying group could multiply its influence with a candidate. By 1980, the number of PACs approached three thousand, each a bulging political cash-cow promoting its particular legislative agenda. Union PACs, for example, blamed unemployment on imports and called for higher tariffs and trade restrictions. Business PACs took advantage of the recession to launch a general assault on federal regulation of business. Carter reacted by deregulating the airline, trucking, and railroad industries and persuading Congress to ease banking controls, thereby launching a wave of deregulation that President Reagan would pursue enthusiastically in the 1980s.

Conservative critics also blamed the nation's economic woes on the social-welfare system. Massive welfare spending, they charged, fed the federal deficits, which in turn worsened the recession. The critics had a point. Social-welfare spending, although proportionately modest when compared to that of Sweden and other Western democracies, did climb sharply in the 1970s. Adjusted for inflation, public assistance, including welfare, jumped by 47 percent, the food-stamp program by 546 percent, Medicaid and other medical services by 186 percent, and on down the list. Overall, this sector of the federal budget, adjusted for inflation, more than doubled from 1970 to 1979, when it accounted for a whopping 61.7 percent of the total budget.

This trend placed enormous strains on the economy. As entitlement programs like social security expanded and as welfare costs mounted with the deepening recession, the federal deficit ballooned. The government borrowed money to cover the shortfall and to service the public debt—the legacy of past deficits—and commercial interest rates rose under the resultant credit squeeze. Rising interest rates in turn inhibited home buying, consumer credit buying, and business borrowing for expansion. Few professed to have answers to the worsening dilemmas.

A Sputtering Economy

Beneath the inflation and unemployment that helped to torpedo Carter's presidency lay deeper, more ominous trends. The nation's industrial infrastructure, based in gritty midwestern cities such as Pittsburgh, Buffalo, Cleveland, and Detroit, was crumbling. Cleveland made unwelcome history in 1978 by becoming the first U.S. city since the 1930s to default on its bonds. One by one, plagued by foreign competition, aging equipment, rising labor costs, and shifting consumer tastes, the factories that had made America the world's industrial leader from the 1880s through World War II closed their gates. Journalists labeled the region the "Rust Belt." With the decline of basic industries, union membership fell. In 1970 about 28 percent of the nonagricultural labor force was unionized; by 1980 the figure had dropped to 23 percent. The erosion of organized labor in turn weakened a central prop of the Democratic party and contributed to the conservative drift of American politics.

Two core industries, automobiles and steel, typified the trend. In the 1950s and 1960s, U.S. automakers had ruled the domestic market. True, the Volkswagen "Beetle," an ungainly German import, had sold 4 million units by 1970, and other imports were edging into the market as well, but as late as 1970, the Big Three—General Motors, Ford, and Chrysler—still accounted for 89 percent of U.S. auto

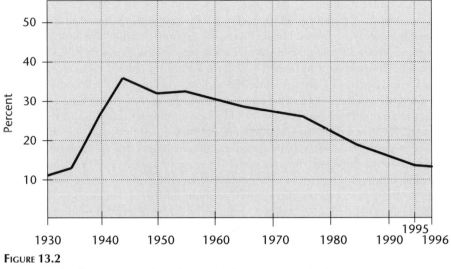

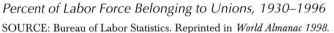

FIGURE **13.2**

Percent of Labor Force Belonging to Unions, 1930–1996

SOURCE: Bureau of Labor Statistics. Reprinted in *World Almanac 1998.*

sales. All this changed in the seventies. With gasoline prices soaring and buying power eroded by inflation, car buyers welcomed affordable, more fuel-efficient imports like Japan's Toyota and Datsun. Ad campaigns stressing economy—summed up in the slogan "Datsun Saves"—challenged Detroit's traditional emphasis on glamour and style. Detroit, geared toward producing bulky six-passenger sedans, failed to convert in time, and its market drifted away. By 1980 imports had grabbed 34 percent of the U.S. auto market. The United States now imported 3.2 million foreign cars annually, about 60 percent of them from Japan. U.S. auto exports rose as well in the decade, but not enough to counterbalance the deluge of imports. Detroit's automotive giants, once America's pride, seemed to have become lumbering dinosaurs.

As the decade ended, conditions worsened. GM sank into the red in 1980 for the first time since 1921. Ford lost $1.2 billion that year. The weakest of the Big Three, Chrysler, slid toward bankruptcy. Only $1.5 billion in federal loan guarantees in 1980 saved Chrysler from immediate disaster.* The Chrysler bailout was orchestrated by the company's chairman, Lee Iacocca, whose campaign for federal aid illustrated how quickly laissez-faire ideology can fade when corporate survival is at stake. He later wrote, "[T]he last thing in the world I wanted to do was turn to the government. . . . I've always been a free enterpriser, a believer in survival of the fittest. Once the decision was made, however, I went at it with all flags flying."

Troubles in the auto industry aggravated the recession. GM, Ford, and Chrysler, employing 98 percent of U.S. autoworkers, laid off more than 225,000 workers in 1974 alone. Additional thousands faced lengthy "temporary leaves."

---

* The controversial bailout worked. Chrysler returned to profitability in 1982 and the following year repaid the loans in full, including $23.4 million in interest to the federal government.

Skilled workers anticipating a comfortable retirement found themselves haunting employment offices instead. With 17 percent of the U.S. labor force directly linked to the auto industry, Detroit's problems rippled across the entire economy.

The steel industry, bedrock of America's industrial might, presented a similarly bleak picture. In earlier times, the great steel mills of Pittsburgh, Youngstown, Wheeling, and other steel towns had provided jobs for millions of hard-working immigrants. As late as 1950, the annual output of U.S. steel mills stood at 97 million tons—nearly half the world's total. But change loomed. In 1959, with the steel industry plagued by a long strike, steel imports exceeded exports for the first time in the century. By 1980 U.S. steel output accounted for only 14 percent of total world production. In that year the Soviet Union, Japan, and the European Community (the twelve-nation consortium of European nations), all exceeded the United States in steel production, with Canada and Brazil offering strong challenges as well. An industry dominated by the United States since the 1880s was faltering badly.

Although steel's decline had connections to the auto industry's troubles, the crisis went deeper, reflecting management's failure to adapt to new technologies, including the basic oxygen furnace, which replaced the old open-hearth system, and the production of steel in continuous sheets rather than in separate ingots. Foreign steelmakers such as Japan's giant Nippon Steel embraced these innovations, abandoning old mills and building new ones. The U.S. steel industry, by contrast, heavily invested in older mills, resisted the new technology. As late as 1963, not one of the six top U.S. steel companies possessed the more modern furnace. By 1980 Japan could make a ton of steel for one-third less than it cost U.S. producers. Even more telling, Japanese steel companies plowed twice as much of their profits back into research and development as did U.S. companies.

The U.S. companies' behavior represented a departure from the boldness that had once characterized American steelmakers. "Well, what shall we throw away this year?" Andrew Carnegie once demanded of his directors. Instead of emulating Carnegie and investing in technologies that might pay off years in the future, post–World War II steelmakers, answerable to dividend-hungry stockholders, maximized short-run profits. Buoyed by Cold War military spending, they counted on a ceaseless flow of Pentagon contracts. Furthermore, despite the myth of open competition, the U.S. steel industry was in fact a largely noncompetitive oligopoly of big companies, each with its established market share, charging uniform prices. This arrangement also discouraged innovation.

Statistics on overall U.S. productivity (that is, output per man- or woman-hour of work) proved revealing as well. During the long postwar boom from 1947 to the mid-1960s, the United States enjoyed average annual productivity increases of 3.2 percent. From 1965 to 1973, however, productivity growth averaged only 2.4 percent annually, a one-third drop from the earlier period. In the problem-plagued 1970s, the rate of increase slowed still more, and by 1978–80, productivity was declining in absolute terms. At the same time, wage raises for unionized workers, often tied to inflation-driven cost-of-living increases, far outstripped productivity.

In explaining declining productivity, analysts reflected their ideological bias. Conservatives wrung their hands over government regulations, soaring worker-benefit packages, and an indolent, overpaid unionized labor force. Liberals stressed short-term profit-taking, inadequate schools and job-training programs, and the lack of a governmental strategy for nurturing new technologies. But whatever their ideology, most analysts pinpointed weak investment in research and development as a key problem. Not only the steel industry but many other corporations shied away from the costly long-term research investment essential to better productivity.

As U.S. productivity declined, that of the nation's trade competitors surged. This was especially the case in Japan and West Germany, the World War II foes whose economies, ironically, had rebounded with American aid. In 1980 Toyota produced five times as many cars per worker as did Detroit automakers. As foreign-made products flooded in, U.S. imports far outran exports. The 1971 trade deficit, the first since 1888, amounted to $2.3 billion. By 1981 the figure had climbed to $28 billion; soon it would rise far higher. Not only cars but television sets, appliances, shoes, clothing, and countless other products now increasingly came from abroad, a shift that severely undercut U.S. manufacturers.

Inflation and budget deficits plagued Western Europe as well, and despite America's economic difficulties during the seventies, the U.S. economy remained the world's largest. And although unemployment persisted, the labor force grew by millions of workers in the 1970s. While the trade gap widened with the surge of imports, U.S. exports more than doubled in the decade. For all its problems, America still enjoyed a standard of living unmatched in the rest of the world.

Some analysts saw an economy not in decline but in transition. In any dynamic economy, they pointed out, some sectors erode as others expand. They noted U.S. dominance in aerospace, electronics, information processing, and other high-tech fields, and the success of companies such as Rochester's Xerox Corporation, a leader in the burgeoning photocopying industry. The computer field struck many as a beacon of promise for the future. The earliest computers, called mainframes, were bulky and expensive, affordable only by the government and large corporations. IBM's 360 series, introduced in 1965, set the new standard for mainframes. Miniaturization came in the 1970s, transforming the industry. First, transistors replaced bulky vacuum tubes. Then sophisticated integrated circuitry made possible desktop computers as powerful as the behemoths of a decade earlier. By the mid-1970s, as computer sales edged upward, more and more people found employment in the growing industry, especially near Boston and San Francisco.

Personal-computer (PC) sales took off as the decade ended. In 1976 two college dropouts in Cupertino, California—Steven Jobs and Stephen Wozniak—built a prototype in the Jobs's family garage. (Like Henry Ford tinkering in his garage in the 1890s, the story would become the stuff of legend.) After selling early models to local hobbyists, Jobs and Wozniak founded Apple Computers in 1977. The company caught on at once; sales soared to $117.9 million by 1980. The "Cupertino comet" made *Fortune* magazine's list of the nation's top 500 corporations faster than any other company in history. IBM introduced its first PC in 1981, and other companies rushed into the market. The computer revolution was under way.

Thus, signs of renewal as well as warning signals marked the economy. As the industrial work force fell, jobs in the service sector increased. To a degree, of course, this shift simply continued a well-established trend. Each decade since 1900 had seen increases in the service-sector work force and corresponding declines in the percentage of farmers, manual laborers, factory operatives, and other

blue-collar workers. But this long-term trend accelerated in the 1970s as basic industries declined. The United States of 1980 more closely resembled the middle-
class consumer-and-service society portrayed in Edward Bellamy's 1888 utopian
novel *Looking Backward* than it did Karl Marx's vision of a vast industrial proletariat
mired in misery.

The service sector was broad, however, and those entering it did not necessar-
ily rise in status. Along with doctors, lawyers, executives, and other white-collar
workers, this category also included the low-status, semiskilled jobs: domestic service, car washing, supermarket checkout, restaurant and fast-food work, and so on.
Such positions paid far less than unionized jobs in industry. Laid-off factory workers sometimes found new jobs only by taking a sharp income cut in the lower
ranks of the service sector. Some economists spoke of the "de-skilling" of the work
force. Other analysts warned of a bimodal labor force with highly paid white-collar
professionals at one end, unskilled service workers (often minorities and recent immigrants) at the other, and little in between. For better or worse, they argued, the
economic trends of the 1970s offered a preview of the future.

The economy thus presented a mixed picture, of bright spots amid disturbing
trends, in the 1970s. While the southwestern oil belt, the necklace of high-tech industries encircling Boston, and California's "Silicon Valley"* south of San Francisco boomed, the industrial heartland stagnated. In the inner cities, minority
youths seemed permanently frozen out of an economy that increasingly demanded
specialized skills and advanced education.

With billions going for defense and for mandated entitlement programs at a
time when revenues were depressed by recession, the deficit soared from $8.7 bil-
lion in 1970 to a whopping $72.7 billion in 1980. By the decade's end, the total
federal debt approached $1 trillion. Carter's 1976 pledge to balance the federal
budget by 1980 had become a bitter joke as his term ended. Worse lay ahead, but
in the seventies the flood tide of federal red ink was already rising ominously.

To many, the nation's best years lay in the past. Eighty years after historian
Frederick Jackson Turner had explored the meaning of the closing of the geo-
graphic frontier, the end of the industrial frontier and the can-do spirit associated
with it seemed at hand. Worry and resentments rooted in economic problems increasingly infiltrated the cultural and political climate as the seventies wore on.

Backlash: Culture and Politics in the Later Seventies

The 1970s defies easy categorization, for divergent trends unfolded simultaneously.
Self-absorbed narcissism, for example, coexisted alongside activist energies. Environmentalism, feminism, gay-rights protests, and other movements remained
strong, even winning legislative and legal victories, yet the public sphere as a
whole seemed diminished. Amid the crosscurrents, one trend emerged with clarity: The liberalism that had peaked in 1964–65 inexorably lost support, a development that laid the groundwork for a conservative triumph in the late seventies.

---

* The nickname came from the silicon chip, a key component in the new integrated circuitry that
made possible the miniaturized personal computer.

Tom Wolfe's "Me Generation" continued to display narcissistic self-absorption, which Christopher Lasch, writing in 1979, saw as the decade's key trend. "Americans have retreated to purely personal preoccupations," Lasch announced. Faced with Nixon's disgrace, economic problems, and weak performances by Ford and Carter, many Americans gave up on politics and civic engagement. Like Voltaire's Candide, they cultivated their own gardens instead. The years following the Civil War and both world wars had all witnessed a turn from public to private concerns, and the aftermath of Vietnam brought a similar reaction.

The evidence for this shift was everywhere. Escapist novels like Erich Segal's *Love Story* (1970) and Peter Benchley's *Jaws* (1974) spawned hit movies. Baby boomers "gentrified" decaying urban neighborhoods, creating islands of trendy sophistication amid inner-city blight. A jogging fad swept the middle class, inspiring a 1978 *Newsweek* story that began with the Whitmanesque line, "I hear America puffing." James Fixx's *The Complete Book of Running* sold 800,000 copies. (Sales fell after Fixx died of a heart attack while jogging.) The fitness vogue also heightened interest in natural foods and healthy diets. Beef sales fell; fish and chicken consumption rose. Low-calorie "lite" foods and beverages crowded the supermarket shelves. The loosening of sexual taboos that in the 1960s had been linked to radical protest now proceeded on its own, unencumbered by ideology. The lavishly illustrated *Joy of Sex* by the aptly named Alex Comfort became a 1970s bestseller.

As two-career households proliferated, often because of economic necessity, couples postponed having children or placed their offspring in daycare facilities. In 1977, 35 percent of all children under age five spent their days with a nonrelative or in a child-care center. Semimythic stories circulated of middle-class parents' scrambling to place their darlings in prestigious nursery schools that would enhance the little ones' chances of gaining admission to an Ivy League college.

The activist energies of the 1970s often found conservative, even reactionary, outlets, as the national mood tacked sharply to the right. This conservative impulse took many forms and found numerous targets. Some former leftists and liberals, repelled by the excesses of the 1960s, moved rightward. Warning against the lure of left-wing utopian ideologies and invoking traditional moral and spiritual values, the neoconservatives praised the free-enterprise system and preached a vehement anticommunism.

The rightward shift manifested itself outside the political arena as well. Indeed, one reason for the fragmented nature of conservative protest in the 1970s is that Nixon's forced resignation stymied the movement's political expression. As Thomas and Mary Edsall wrote, "Watergate . . . effectively choked off the growth of conservatism from 1973 through 1976. . . . [I]nstead of finding an outlet within the political system, rightward pressure built throughout the decade to explosive levels. . . . Watergate resulted in a political system out of sync with larger trends." The resentments first exploited by George Wallace and Richard Nixon in the 1960s intensified in the mid-seventies, but lacking an effective political outlet, they flowed into other channels.

This disjunction between the political process and the national mood produced striking anomalies. For example, while the Supreme Court issued rulings protecting the rights of arrested persons and convicts, and even for a time abolished the death penalty, many Americans, alarmed by rising crime rates, demanded a crackdown on criminals.* Similarly, as the Equal Employment Opportunity Commission and other federal agencies promoted minority rights and developed affirmative-action programs, many whites turned against what they labeled "reverse discrimination."

The growing conservatism of the 1970s also had economic sources. Oil shocks, recessions, inflation, and industrial decline directly affected millions of families. In 1973, for the first time since World War II, the median income of the average U.S. family, adjusted for inflation, actually fell. The decline continued in 1974 and 1975. Various factors worsened the economic pinch. Congress regularly increased social security taxes in these years, thereby reducing workers' take-home pay. Millions of Americans also experienced "bracket creep." As cost-of-living clauses in union contracts pushed their wages up (with no increase in buying power because of inflation), they found themselves in a higher tax bracket, forking over a larger share of their earnings to Uncle Sam.

The most direct expression of nagging economic worries was a grassroots tax revolt. In 1978 California voters by a two-to-one margin passed Proposition 13. The law slashed real-estate taxes, creating havoc for the state's education and welfare systems. Similar referenda soon appeared on ballots across the nation. President Carter's pollster declared in awe, "This isn't just a tax revolt. It's a revolution against government." Conservative congressman Jack Kemp of New York exulted, "We've changed the focus of politics in America from their ground to our ground. . . . They're now arguing on our turf."

Economic anxieties also fueled a broader reaction against Johnson-style liberalism with its emphasis on expanding the rights and improving the status of disadvantaged social groups. In a time of prosperity, the majority had supported such programs. But as Middle America saw its own status eroding, sympathy for such reforms vanished. In its place, hostility against welfare recipients and a broad spectrum of groups demanding special attention and more equitable treatment intensified.

The women's movement became a prime target of this backlash. As the economy weakened, the flow of women into the workplace stirred resentment among men fearful of losing their own jobs. Conservatives attacked "radical feminism" as proabortion, antifamily, tainted by lesbianism, and a general threat to traditional values. Working-class women sensed that the feminist movement mainly addressed the concerns of college-educated and professional women, and turned against it, illustrating the power of class over gender. Marabel Morgan's *The Total Woman* (1975) appealed to such resentments, urging women to eschew agitation and discover new meaning in traditional roles. "A total woman caters to her man's special needs," she wrote, "whether it be in salads, sex or sports." Formulaic romance novels set in distant times and exotic locales featured dreamy women ravished by domineering males. These "bodice rippers" sold 20 million copies in the 1970s. As 1950s-style gender roles blurred, the romance novels conjured up a fantasy world in which "men were men and women were women."

---

* According to FBI statistics, the number of reported violent crimes (murder, robbery, assault, and rape) rose from 738,000 in 1970 to 1,345,000 in 1980.

In 1978 twenty thousand feminists gathered in Houston for the National Women's Conference. The rhetoric sizzled as delegates enjoyed what journalist Gail Sheehy called "a giant self-esteem bath." But in a counterrally, eight thousand conservative women cheered Phyllis Schlafly, who proclaimed, "The American people do not want the ERA, and they do not want government-funded abortion, lesbian privileges, or [federally funded] . . . universal child care." Schlafly's fifty-thousand-strong Eagle Forum fought the equal rights amendment as the entering wedge of a radical assault on morality and tradition.

In the end, the ERA fell victim to the antifeminist backlash. Although the amendment needed only three more states for ratification as the 1979 deadline neared, the process bogged down despite Congress's granting a three-year extension for ratification. ERA would force women into combat, opponents charged, and even require unisex toilets. One anti-ERA Missouri housewife baked and sold 450 coconut cakes and sent the proceeds to Schlafly.

The battle over abortion proved even more emotion laden. *Roe* v. *Wade,* the 1973 Supreme Court decision establishing women's right to terminate pregnancy, called forth the highly vocal right-to-life movement. As the number of legal abortions rose from 18,000 in 1968 to 1.3 million in 1977—more than three for every ten live births—opinion polls showed deep divisions over the issue. An uncertain middle group, although hesitant to criminalize the procedure, harbored doubts about its ethics. This opened the way for a well-organized assault on *Roe* v. *Wade* led by the Roman Catholic church, Protestant evangelical groups, and Orthodox Jews.

In 1976, Congress barred the use of Medicare funds to finance abortions. To the dismay of pro-choice forces, the Supreme Court upheld this ban in 1977. In 1978 Congress extended the ban on federally funded abortions to military personnel and their families and to Peace Corps volunteers. By 1980, abortion had become a defining issue in American political culture.

As the homosexual-rights movement expanded, it, too, drew hostile attention. Thousands of gays and lesbians "came out," marching in "Gay Pride" parades and protesting discrimination. Beginning around 1973, under pressure from the Gay and Lesbian Alliance, states and municipalities adopted gay-rights ordinances barring discrimination on the basis of sexual orientation. But reaction soon set in. Conservative religious leaders denounced homosexuality as a sign of national degeneracy. Right-wing politicians deplored the movement as an example of 1960s-style liberalism run amok. When Miami adopted a gay-rights statute in 1977, pop singer Anita Bryant mounted a protest campaign. "If homosexuality were the normal way, God would have created Adam and Bruce," she pointed out. In a referendum, Miamians repealed the statute by a two-to-one margin. Voters rejected similar measures in other cities as well.

Above all, the conservative backlash focused on issues of race. In the 1950s and early 1960s, a consensus had supported civil rights and antipoverty programs aimed at uplifting inner-city minorities. In the altered climate of the 1970s, that consensus collapsed. Goodwill gave way to resentment, and cities torn by racial violence elected get-tough "law-and-order" candidates. As the struggle against racial discrimination shifted northward, it sparked complex reactions involving not only race but social class. Two issues catalyzed the tensions: school busing to achieve racial balance and affirmative-action plans to compensate for past discrimination.

Gay Pride, San Francisco, 1978. *Buoyed by the black freedom struggle and the women's movement, homosexuals, too, began to protest discrimination. But such demonstrations also helped fuel a strong conservative reaction. (© Rose Skytta/Jeroboam, Inc.)*

Busing plans ignited angry white protest in many cities, as busing opponents championed the "neighborhood school." Critics denounced busing as federal meddling with a local issue in the interests of an abstract social ideal. The fact that the officials who mandated the school busing schemes often lived in affluent suburbs unaffected by the plans added a class dimension to the resentment. The most heated dispute erupted in Boston. There, local black leaders had pressed for a school-integration plan, but the city's school committee had refused. In 1974 federal judge W. Arthur Garrity, finding "systematic . . . segregation" in Boston's schools, ordered the school committee to develop a desegregation plan that included busing. Irish-American and other ethnic neighborhoods of South Boston and Charlestown—insular, conservative, and economically hard-pressed—exploded at the meddling of affluent "limousine liberals" like Garrity. That fall, white students boycotted South Boston High School, and their supporters stoned black students arriving by bus from nearby Roxbury. When a white youth was stabbed, a mob trapped 135 black students in the school for four hours. Eerily echoing Little Rock in 1957, white parents marched under banners such as ROAR (Restore Our Alienated Rights). Young white thugs, one of them wielding a flagpole bearing the stars and stripes as a weapon, beat a young black lawyer outside Boston City Hall. President Ford, following Nixon's script, fueled the protests by denouncing forced busing.

The seventies also saw bitter fighting over plans—especially quota systems—to increase blacks' access to skilled jobs, education, and the professions. The issue reached the courts when Allan Bakke, a white, sued the medical school of the University of California at Davis, charging that his rejected application was stronger than that of others who had been admitted under a racial quota system. In 1978 the Supreme Court, by a 5–4 vote upheld Bakke's claim and ordered the school to enroll him. Ruling that admissions offices might consider race as one factor in their decisions, the court forbade the setting of specific quotas for minorities. Justice Thurgood Marshall, veteran black civil-rights activist who as an NAACP attorney had argued the *Brown* v. *Board of Education* case in 1954, angrily dissented, citing the nation's history of discrimination. Affirmative-action programs, even quotas, he declared, were an appropriate minimal response by white America to centuries of racial injustice.

Memories of the 1963 March on Washington, when all Americans of goodwill had seemed to agree on a civil-rights agenda, faded as race-related issues spawned acrimony. Jimmy Carter, who owed his election to African-American voters, appointed a number of blacks to office but did not place race high on his agenda. Issues that had seemed clear-cut in the sixties now appeared riddled with ambiguity. Even some black leaders criticized busing to achieve integration, for example, urging more attention to upgrading black schools. In *The Declining Significance of Race* (1978), William Julius Wilson, a black sociologist, argued that the central division in modern America was no longer between the races but between middle-class, upwardly mobile Americans—white and black—and the inner-city underclass cut off from jobs, education, and hope.

The backlash hit other minorities as well, including the more than 12 million Hispanics, 60 percent of them Chicanos of Mexican origin. Not only did the Hispanic jobless rate exceed the national average, but the wages of male Hispanic workers averaged only 70 percent of white male earnings. One and a half million job-seeking Hispanics entered the United States legally in the 1970s, including 637,000 from Mexico, 760,000 from the Caribbean, and 132,000 from Central America. Many more came clandestinely, mostly from Mexico. Yet in this anxious decade, the Hispanic poor were less an object of solicitude than a target of resentment, viewed as competitors in a constricting labor market.

The nation's Asian population also rose sharply in the 1970s as 1.8 million immigrants arrived from the Philippines, Korea, China, Vietnam, India, and other Pacific Rim nations. Fueled by immigration, the ranks of Asian Americans grew to 3.7 million by 1980, contributing to the rich diversity of the American demographic palette. Again, however, economic stress produced an edge of hostility toward these newcomers, who were viewed as rivals for scarce jobs. This response, too, contributed to the decade's broader conservative tendency.

Some social observers expressed fears of society's splintering into self-seeking groups. Channeled positively, such heightened group consciousness can lead to a quest for new sources of community, as in the rise in ethnic awareness and interest in family roots. But fear of social fragmentation also expressed itself as hostility to all those—blacks, gays, feminists, abortion-rights advocates, job-hungry immigrants, welfare recipients, even prisoners—who seemed to demand special attention and privileges in difficult times. Other groups demonized under various labels—"liberals," "the mass media," "secular humanists"—were seen as threats to "traditional values," a catch-all term for the supposed moral and cultural unity of earlier, simpler days.

Both the search for community and the new conservatism found an outlet in religion. A fifteen-year trend of declining church attendance reversed in the mid-1970s, owing in large part to an upsurge in evangelicalism. In the 1950s, despite the popularity of revivalist Billy Graham, the mainstream liberal denominations had set the tone of American Protestantism. Many observers of religious trends, particularly liberals, had long believed that Protestantism's theologically conservative wing, known as evangelicalism, and its even stricter variant, fundamentalism, had been fatally discredited by the 1925 Scopes case, in which a Tennessee high-school teacher was tried for violating a state law barring the teaching of evolution in the public schools.

Yet evangelicalism not only survived but flourished, sustained by a grassroots network of local congregations, church colleges, publishing houses, and influential regional leaders. In the 1970s, the liberal denominations lost membership, but groups like the evangelical Assemblies of God church burgeoned. A powerful faction within the giant Southern Baptist Convention adhered to biblical literalism. As the larger culture became more conservative, evangelical churches, with their biblical emphasis and clear-cut moral codes, were well situated to benefit. The decade also saw a surge in private Christian academies founded by evangelicals dismayed by the public schools' "secularism" and by such social realities as teenage sex, alcohol abuse, and increasing drug use. "Born-again" celebrities included Bob Dylan, Watergate conspirator Charles Colson, and former Black Panther Eldridge Cleaver. Jimmy Carter saturated his speeches with the language of evangelicalism, promising a government as "good and honest and compassionate and as filled with love" as the American people themselves.

Many Americans troubled by the social fragmentation and impersonality of modern life welcomed the close sense of community offered by the typical evangelical congregation. In *Why Conservative Churches Are Growing* (1972), Dean M. Kelley accused the liberal denominations of neglecting their own members in their fervor for social action, while evangelical churches more fully met parishioners' spiritual and psychological needs.

In a 1978 survey, 22 percent of Americans identified themselves as evangelicals; other polls put the total as high as one-third. Although strongest in the South, with its high concentration of Protestants, and among the less well educated, evangelicalism flourished in all regions and at all socioeconomic levels. Reinforced by conservative Catholics, Mormons, and Jews, Protestant evangelicals wielded potent influence in 1970s America.

Evangelicals exploited the paperback revolution to spread the gospel. Thousands of Christian bookstores marketed evangelical paperbacks that racked up massive sales. One popular genre used Bible prophecy to explain world events. The nonfiction bestseller of the 1970s, Hal Lindsey's *The Late Great Planet Earth* (1970), found the Cold War, the nuclear arms race, Russia's destruction, and the emerging global economy all foretold in the Bible. In the last days, he predicted, the Antichrist, a demonic figure portended in the Bible, will win a universal following and control all commerce by means of giant computers and orbiting TV satellites.

But if television posed dangers, it also served evangelicals well. Indeed, TV preachers led the evangelical resurgence. From his headquarters in Tulsa, Oral

IN PERSPECTIVE: *That Old-Time Religion*

❖❖

The election of a born-again Christian, Jimmy Carter, as president in 1976 focused attention on the continued vitality of evangelical Protestantism, a surprise to many who long ago had written its obituary.

In nineteenth-century America, evangelicalism was a powerful force. From the revivals on the Kentucky frontier in 1801 to a long series of urban revivals led by Charles Finney, Dwight L. Moody, and others, evangelical piety pervaded American life. While missions, Sunday schools, and tract societies spread the faith in the cities, Methodist circuit riders and missionaries carried the Word to isolated interior settlements. Evangelicals led many nineteenth-century reforms; Harriet Beecher Stowe, author of the antislavery bestseller *Uncle Tom's Cabin* (1852), was the daughter of a prominent evangelical minister, Lyman Beecher.

By the end of the century, however, evangelicalism seemed on the wane. From the 1890s through the 1920s, the liberal Social Gospel dominated mainstream Protestantism. Evangelicals fought back, battling "modernism" and codifying the fundamentals of their faith, including the verbatim inspiration of the Bible and the resurrection and Second Coming of Jesus Christ. In the interwar years, regional leaders such as Aimee Semple McPherson of Los Angeles attracted large congregations and employed the new medium of radio to spread the message.

The faith continued to make steady gains after World War II, thanks to evangelists like Billy Graham and organizations such as Youth for Christ. The Assemblies of God church and other charismatic or "pentecostal" groups that featured divine healing and emotional worship grew rapidly. In the 1970s and 1980s, with mainstream Protestantism in decline, evangelicalism attracted waves of new adherents. Evangelical paperbacks sold by the millions; "Bible-believing" independent churches proliferated across the land; TV preachers entered countless homes via cable and satellite; and evangelical missionaries made dramatic inroads among the Catholic populations of Latin America.

Long ignored, evangelicalism drew increasing scholarly notice. In *American Evangelicalism: Conservative Religion and the Quandary of Modernity* (1983), sociologist James Davison Hunter examined how evangelicals both resist and accommodate contemporary trends in a process that he called "cognitive bargaining." For example, evangelical authors published many self-help books offering techniques for achieving

Roberts built a vast TV ministry based on evangelical preaching and divine healing. Jimmy Swaggart of Louisiana, Jack Van Impe of Michigan, Jim and Tammy Bakker of South Carolina, and many others reached worldwide audiences via satellite. Pat Robertson's Christian Broadcasting Network (CBN) aired many of these programs. Robertson's own "700 Club" featured talk-show-style interviews with evangelical leaders. The "pope" of the electronic church, Jerry Falwell of Lynchburg, Virginia, broadcast his weekly "Old Time Gospel Hour" on 325 TV stations personal happiness and emotional well-being—popular themes in the general culture—but written from a specifically evangelical theological perspective. Returning to the theme in *Culture Wars: The Struggle to Define America* (1991), Hunter portrayed religious conservatives as key players in a battle for the nation's soul. "America," he wrote, "is in the midst of a culture war that [reverberates] . . . not only within public policy but within the lives of ordinary Americans everywhere."

What were the political implications of this struggle? Some believers repudiated the wicked world and withdrew into their own spiritual realm. At its most extreme, this separatist impulse produced phenomena such as David Koresh's Branch Davidian sect, whose members barricaded themselves in a heavily armed compound near Waco, Texas, to await the end. In April 1993, after a long standoff with the FBI, Koresh and most of his followers perished in a fiery holocaust that tragically fulfilled their prophecies of a final Armageddon-like confrontation.

More typically, however, religious conservatives turned to politics to realize their moral vision. In the 1980s, the Moral Majority led by televangelist Jerry Falwell enthusiastically supported the Reagan movement. In the 1990s, Pat Robertson's Christian Coalition mobilized conservative activists who ran for school board, city council, and other local offices, building a righteous nation at the grassroots level. Founded in 1989, the Christian Coalition boasted 350,000 members in 750 chapters by 1993. In many states and communities, well-organized religious conservatives maneuvered for control of the Republican party.

Scholars observing this trend saw a decline in traditional denominational loyalties and a rise in special-agenda groups—the Christian Action Council, the Christian Heritage Center, the National Pro-Family Coalition, and scores of others—that pursued specific agendas while sharing a common goal. Nineteenth-century evangelicals had formed single-issue organizations such as the Anti-Saloon League (1895) but had lacked the computer-based direct-mail techniques available to their modern-day successors. Mobilizing around what they saw as defining moral issues, politically active religious conservatives embraced symbolic causes such as creationism, school prayer, and "family values," and battled abortion, pornography, homosexuality, radical feminism, sexual permissiveness in the media, sex education in the schools, government support for "obscene" art, and the worldview that they denounced as "secular humanism." One skeptic defined the latter term as "a label used by the Far Right to attack virtually everything that they disagree with about the schools and society at large."

Mark Twain once dismissed reports of his death as "greatly exaggerated," and the same might be said of evangelical religion in modern America. Amid turbulent world events and unsettling social changes at home, millions of Americans still find meaning and reassurance in religious beliefs and folkways. As they enter the public arena to apply their religious vision to public policy, they demonstrate once again evangelicalism's central role in U.S. history and life.

and 300 radio stations. Televangelists reached millions each week and raked in massive contributions from what they fondly called their "television family." By the decade's end, they had become a major force not only in religion but also in politics.

Energized by the TV preachers, evangelicals engaged political and cultural issues. Via TV, magazines, paperbacks, and local pulpits, they deplored the nation's moral breakdown. The Reverend Tim LaHaye, writing in 1980, cited an array of trends, including divorce, pornography, abortion, gay rights, and "militant femi-nism," that made America a modern Sodom and Gomorrah.

The political mobilization of the Christian Right, initially directed against fed-eral efforts to deny tax-exempt status to Christian schools, quickly gained momen-tum and broadened in focus. The Moral Majority, for example, an organization founded by Falwell in 1979 to spearhead America's spiritual regeneration at the ballot box, attracted numerous adherents and intense media attention. On the mass-media front, politicized evangelicals decried sex magazines like *Playboy,* of-fensive movies, TV shows, and rock music. The Reverend Don Wildmon's Na-tional Federation for Decency organized boycotts of advertisers that sponsored sexually suggestive TV shows. Turning to education, evangelicals prescribed prayer in the schools and eradication of "secular humanism" from textbooks. Strongly patriotic, they urged morality in government, denounced the Soviet Union, and called for increased military spending to fight "godless communism."

The popularity of the TV evangelists underscored the urgent longing for con-nectedness and moral clarity spawned by the later 1970s cultural disarray, eco-nomic troubles, and political failures. In Robert Altman's 1975 movie *Nashville,* lonely, unfulfilled people hover like moths around Nashville's glamorous country-music stars while a sound truck for a mysterious, unseen presidential candidate blares endlessly in the city's streets. Nostalgia for a sense of community lost some-where in the past surfaced in cultural products as diverse as the bicentennial proj-ects of 1976, the 1977 *Roots* miniseries, and Woody Allen's poignant chronicling of a failed relationship in *Annie Hall* (1977). It emerged, too, in the pop-culture mythologizing of America's past offered in John Jakes's *Kent Family Chronicles,* which sold 30 million copies between 1974 and 1980.

Right-wing political movements exploited this volatile stew of economic wor-ries and white backlash, evangelical moralism and traditionalist longings. Conserv-ative think tanks such as Washington's Heritage Foundation (1973), financed by Colorado beer baron Joseph Coors, funded New Right intellectuals. William F. Buckley's venerable *National Review* flourished. Mass-mail specialist Richard Viguerie, a Louisiana-born Roman Catholic, marshaled computerized lists of names to raise funds for conservative causes and candidates. Viguerie's single-issue appeals focused on emotion-laden themes: gun control, abortion, gay rights, the death penalty, and school prayer. John Dolan's National Conservative Political Ac-tion Committee assembled a war chest of more than $4 million to defeat liberal candidates. The American Conservative Union in 1978 boasted 300,000 members and contributions of $3 million. Jerry Falwell summed up the ultimate political ob-jective of all this organizational effort: "We have enough votes to run the country. And when the people say, 'We've had enough,' we are going to take over."

As the Watergate trauma faded, the New Right found its political legs. In 1976 candidate Jimmy Carter moved to the right, downplaying his party's traditional championing of the underdog and emphasizing instead such themes as fiscal re-straint, governmental efficiency, and tax-code revision. Even so, working-class whites abandoned the Democratic ticket in ominous numbers that year. In 1960, 61 percent of working-class whites had voted for John F. Kennedy; in 1976, only 53 percent of the voters in this category cast their ballots for Carter.

By the 1978 midterm election, the political realignment was fully under way. Much of the $17.3 million spent by PACS that year came from conservative sources. Right-wing PACs targeted key liberal legislators for defeat and key conservatives for support, using computerized mailing lists to reach receptive voters in the targeted states and districts. With an overall voter turnout of under 38 percent, such motivational tactics proved effective: targeted liberal legislators fell, while New Right favorites such as Jesse Helms, seeking a second term in North Carolina, sailed to victory. Antiabortion candidates backed by the National Right-to-Life Committee won elections across the nation, Proposition 13 passed in California, and Republicans enjoyed a net gain of nearly three hundred seats in state legislatures across the nation.

The rightward drift affected both parties—conservative Democratic mayors in Los Angeles and Philadelphia capitalized on the white backlash—but the main beneficiary was the GOP. Arising from the ashes of Watergate, the Republicans gradually remade themselves. Historically the party of privilege, the GOP now redefined itself as the vehicle of grassroots resentments and fears. The successes of 1978 portended a far more dramatic triumph two years later. With inflation raging, unemployment rising, and family income continuing to sag in 1978–80, the anger surging throughout Middle America intensified.

In the 1960s, liberalism had come under attack from the Left; now it faced a far stronger assault from the Right. Political conservatism had once been the domain of corporate America and the monied class, who had denounced high taxes, big government, and federal regulation. These issues remained alive, but the New Right democratized conservatism, reaching out to the grassroots not only with political and economic appeals but with cultural and moral themes lamenting the alleged breakdown of values and tradition in American life.

The New Right showed a genius for mobilizing free-floating grievances; whether it had the capacity to govern remained to be seen. One last crisis, centered in distant Iran, drove the final nail into Jimmy Carter's political coffin and buoyed conservative Republican hopes as the 1980 election neared.

Carter Diplomacy and the Middle East Hostage Crisis

As in the Ford years, Richard Nixon's agenda continued to shape U.S. foreign policy during Carter's term. In 1979, Carter formalized full diplomatic relations with the People's Republic of China, completing the process that Nixon and Kissinger had initiated a decade earlier. Carter also set out to apply his problem-solving skills to international issues, but forces beyond his control ultimately thwarted his ambitions abroad, just as they did at home.

In assembling his foreign-policy team, Carter drew on his contacts as a member of the Trilateral Commission, a private organization started in 1972 by David Rockefeller, head of Chase Manhattan Bank, and Zbigniew Brzezinski, professor of international relations at Columbia University. The commission brought together political, economic, and strategic leaders of the United States, Western Europe, and Japan to address issues of global concern. As secretary of state, Carter named Cyrus Vance, a New York lawyer and pillar of the foreign-policy establishment. As national security adviser, he chose Brzezinski. The son of a pre–World War II Polish diplomat, Brzezinski, like Kissinger, had emigrated to America as a youth. A confirmed Cold Warrior, he deeply distrusted Moscow. U.S. foreign policy in the late 1970s reflected the personalities and ideology of these three men.

Like Woodrow Wilson, Jimmy Carter believed that morality had an important role in foreign policy. Avowing his commitment to human rights around the world, he implicitly rejected Kissinger's realpolitik approach, which largely ignored the internal policies of nations friendly to U.S. interests. Cyrus Vance found Carter's goals congenial. Using U.S. influence, along with threats to cut off foreign aid, he prodded Chile, Argentina, Ethiopia, South Africa, and other nations to improve their human-rights record. Carter and Vance focused more on Africa and Latin America than had Nixon and Kissinger, who had viewed these regions simply as arenas for pursuing the superpower game.

Carter particularly hoped to make Latin America a showcase of his human-rights policy, yet when leftists rebelled against Nicaragua's right-wing dictator, Anastasio Somoza, in 1977, Carter showed more concern about the spread of communism than about Somoza's brutal suppression of the insurgency. When the rebel Sandinistas (named for an earlier revolutionary hero, Augusto Sandino) overthrew Somoza in 1979, Carter recognized the new regime but gave it little attention. In El Salvador, terrorist "death squads" supported by the ruling junta assassinated many thousands, including the archbishop of El Salvador and four American Roman Catholic missionaries in 1980. Washington's protests proved ineffectual. When Carter's term ended, he left festering problems in both countries to his successor.

In Panama, by contrast, Carter's moralism and U.S. strategic interests converged. In the 1960s, alarmed by anti-American demonstrations in Panama, President Johnson had begun talks to renegotiate the one-sided 1903 treaty by which the United States owned and operated the Panama Canal. Under Carter, the two nations agreed on a pair of treaties. The first restored Panamanian sovereignty to the Canal Zone; the second pledged the United States to transfer operations of the canal to Panama by 1999. The Senate approved the treaties 68–32—the bare two-thirds necessary. Although the agreements safeguarded U.S. security interests, the New Right seized upon them as another symbol of the failure of American will.

Extending another Nixon initiative, Carter at first pursued détente with Moscow. Meeting in Vienna in June 1979, Carter and Leonid Brezhnev initialed the SALT II Treaty limiting each nation to 2,250 missile launchers. When Carter submitted the treaty to the Senate for ratification, it met a storm of protest. Conservatives denounced it for accepting the principle of nuclear parity instead of U.S. superiority. Hawkish neoconservative Democrats formed a lobbying group, the Committee on the Present Danger, to fight the treaty. To reassure his hard-line critics and in response to pressure from Brzezinski to hang tough against the Soviets, Carter approved a new nuclear missile system, the MX, to replace the older Minuteman ICBMs. He also sanctioned a giant new missile-launching submarine, the Trident, ratcheting up the nuclear arms race even as he tried to push SALT II through the Senate.

Prospects for the ratification of SALT II collapsed in December 1979 when the Soviets invaded Afghanistan, on their southern border, to squelch a militant Islamic fundamentalist movement that jeopardized the pro-Soviet regime in Kabul and threatened to spread to Islamic regions of the Soviet Union itself. Many Americans, convinced of Moscow's desire to rule the world, saw the action as proof of their worst fears. National security adviser Brzezinski, already suspicious of détente, pushed Carter toward a tough anti-Soviet stance. Under his influence, Carter's human-rights policy became mainly a club for bludgeoning Moscow. Amid rising anti-Soviet sentiment, Carter withdrew SALT II from the Senate. Pronouncing the Afghan invasion "the most serious threat to world peace since World War II," he canceled various trade agreements with the Soviets and even pulled the United States out of the 1980 Moscow Olympics.

On January 23, 1980, addressing a joint session of Congress, the president proclaimed the Carter Doctrine. The Soviet invasion of Afghanistan, he warned, had brought them within three hundred miles of the Persian Gulf and menaced the flow of oil to the West. Echoing the 1947 Truman Doctrine, Carter proclaimed that any "attempt by an outside force to gain control of the Persian Gulf" would be deemed a grave threat to the United States. Détente lay in shambles. The harshly anti-Soviet tone of the early Reagan years was set by Jimmy Carter in 1980.

Carter's greatest foreign-policy achievement and his costliest failure both came in the Middle East. In the Nixon-Ford years, Henry Kissinger had worked in vain for a comprehensive peace settlement in this conflict-ridden region. President Carter avidly pursued this goal, impelled in part by his evangelical beliefs, which gave special meaning to Israel, God's chosen nation, and its history. Carter's peacemaking impulse gained a boost in November 1977 when Egyptian leader Anwar el-Sadat initiated peace talks with the Israelis.

In September 1978 Carter invited Sadat and Israeli prime minister Menachem Begin to Camp David for further negotiations. For thirteen days, with Carter as mediator, the bargaining progressed. On September 18, Carter announced that a "framework" of peace had been agreed on. On March 26, 1979, Sadat and Begin signed a peace treaty at the White House. Egypt recognized Israel, and Israel agreed to return the Sinai peninsula to Egypt by 1982. True peace in the Middle East remained a distant vision, but Carter served as midwife to an important first step. Amid mounting frustrations on the domestic front, the Egyptian-Israeli accord scored a rare success for an embattled president.

But events in the Middle East also brought Carter's administration to its nadir. Since 1953, Iran had been ruled by Shah Reza Pahlavi, whose army defended U.S. interests in the Persian Gulf. Having crushed his domestic opponents with CIA help in 1953 (see p. 112), the shah had backed U.S. policy and brutally repressed his internal foes. Yet he proved no match for the fundamentalist energies roiling the Islamic world. In January 1979, the shah fled Iran in the face of a revolutionary uprising led by the Ayatollah Ruhollah Khomeini, a leader of Islam's intensely orthodox Shiite sect that hated the shah's secular, Westernizing regime.

When Carter admitted the shah to the United States for cancer treatment, Iran's Shiites exploded. With the blessings of Khomeini, who regularly denounced the United States as "the Great Satan," Shiite militants occupied the U.S. embassy

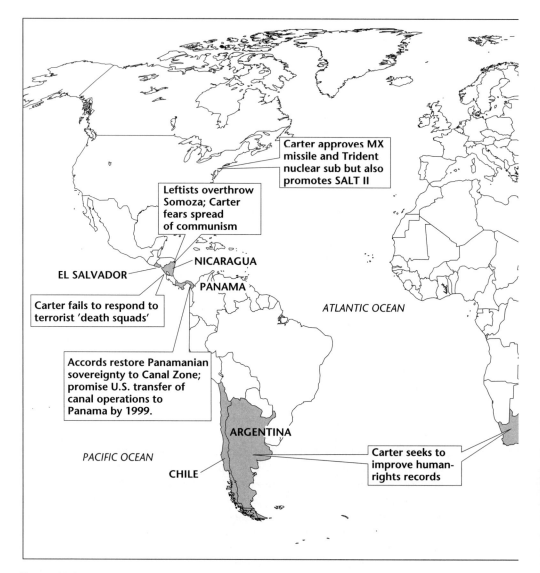

Carter approves MX missile and Trident nuclear sub but also promotes SALT II

Leftists overthrow Somoza; Carter fears spread of communism

NICARAGUA

EL SALVADOR

PANAMA

ATLANTIC OCEAN

Carter fails to respond to terrorist 'death squads'

Accords restore Panamanian sovereignty to Canal Zone; promise U.S. transfer of canal operations to Panama by 1999.

ARGENTINA

PACIFIC OCEAN

CHILE

Carter seeks to improve human-rights records

FIGURE 13.3
Carter Diplomacy

in Tehran and seized seventy-six American hostages. Six escaped unseen, and the kidnappers soon released thirteen embassy employees, all of them blacks or women. Washington expelled Iranian students and froze Iranian assets in the United States but seemed powerless to break the impasse.

The "hostage crisis," reported daily in the media, dominated the rest of Carter's term. The Khomeini regime took full advantage of America's obsession with the prisoners. The nightly news brought images of blindfolded hostages paraded by their captors and of kidnappers using American flags to carry out

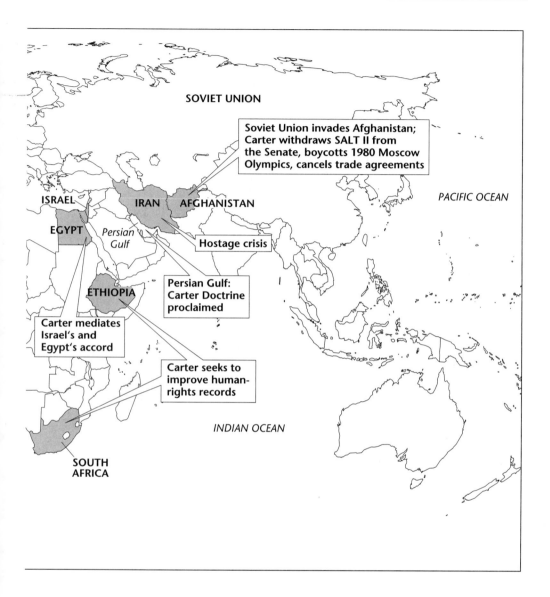

SOVIET UNION

Soviet Union invades Afghanistan;
Carter withdraws SALT II from
the Senate, boycotts 1980 Moscow
Olympics, cancels trade agreements

ISRAEL

IRAN   AFGHANISTAN

PACIFIC OCEAN

EGYPT

Persian Gulf

Hostage crisis

Persian Gulf:
Carter Doctrine
proclaimed

ETHIOPIA

Carter mediates
Israel's and
Egypt's accord

Carter seeks to
improve human-
rights records

INDIAN OCEAN

SOUTH
AFRICA

garbage. The more the U.S. media focused on the hostages, the greater their propaganda value became for Iran.

In April 1980, an attempted U.S. rescue operation failed as three helicopters broke down in dust storms in the Iranian desert. During the evacuation, a helicopter and a C-130 transport collided, killing eight Americans. The catastrophe heaped additional humiliation on the United States. Secretary of State Vance, who had opposed the operation, resigned. Carter's approval ratings, already feeble, sank even further. The ordeal consumed him. Recalling the protracted crisis in his memoirs, Carter admitted, "The release of the American hostages had become al-most an obsession with me."

Conclusion

As the inflation-recession cycle continued, a weakened Jimmy Carter faced the 1980 electoral campaign. Responding to critics on the Right, Carter called for cuts in federal welfare spending, an approach that upset liberal Democrats without win-ning back the alienated white working class.

Late in 1979, Senator Edward Kennedy, the last surviving Kennedy brother, challenged Carter for the Democratic nomination. The president fended off the threat, in part because Chappaquiddick still clouded Kennedy's reputation, but Carter lost the general election. Returning to private life, he founded the Carter Presidential Center at Atlanta's Emory University, where he organized seminars and conferences aimed at the peaceful resolution of regional conflicts. He also worked with a volunteer group that rehabilitated slum housing. Although his repu-tation, like Nixon's, would later revive, few Americans in 1981 regretted seeing him leave the White House that he had entered so exuberantly four years earlier.

The decade that had begun with the invasion of Cambodia and the killings at Kent State at last dragged to a close. Few argued with the judgment passed by *Time* magazine: "Nobody is apt to look back on the 1970s as the good old days." After the turmoil of the 1960s, it is small wonder that Americans in the 1970s seemed drained by psychic fatigue. Giving up on the public sphere and the quest for a common vision, they fragmented into diverse interest groups, pursued private goals, or embraced causes that often seemed based more on suspicion and fear than on positive values. Jimmy Carter correctly identified a national "malaise" in his much-maligned speech of 1979, but proved unable to lead the United States out of its collective funk. By 1980 the nation clearly craved ideological direction and new sources of political energy. Eager to provide that direction and energy, the New Right delivered its messiah: Ronald Reagan.

SELECTED READINGS

Politics and the Economy in the Ford and Carter Years

Carl Abbott, *The New Urban America: Growth and Politics in the Sunbelt Cities* (1981); Patrick Anderson, *Electing Jimmy Carter: The Campaign of 1976* (1994); Ken Auletta, *The Underclass* (1981); Michael A. Bernstein and David E. Adler, eds., *Understanding Ameri-can Economic Decline* (1994); Barry Bluestone and Bennett Harrison, *The Deindustrializa-tion of America* (1982); James Cannon, *Time and Chance: Gerald Ford's Appointment with History: 1913–1974* (1993); Jimmy Carter, *Keeping Faith* (1982); Thomas Byrne Edsall with Mary D. Edsall, *Chain Reaction: The Impact of Race, Rights, and Taxes on American Pol-itics* (1991); Gerald R. Ford, *A Time to Heal* (1979); Betty Glad, *Jimmy Carter* (1980); John Robert Greene, *The Presidency of Gerald R. Ford* (1995); David Halberstam, *The Reckoning* (1986) [decline of the U.S. auto industry]; John P. Hoerr, *And the Wolf Finally Came: The Decline of the American Steel Industry* (1988); Burton I. Kaufman, *The Presidency of James*

Earl Carter, Jr. (1993); David P. McCaffrey, *The Politics of Nuclear Power* (1991); A. James Riechley, *Conservatives in an Age of Change* (1980); J. Harvey Wilkerson, *From Brown to Bakke* (1979); William Julius Wilson, *The Truly Disadvantaged: The Inner City, the Underclass, and Public Policy* (1987); Jules Witcover, *Marathon* (1977) [1976 election]; Daniel Yergin, *The Prize* (1991) [U.S. and world petroleum industry].

Social and Cultural Trends in the Seventies

Peter Carroll, *It Seemed Like Nothing Happened* (1983); Alan Crawford, *Thunder on the Right* (1980); John Crewden, *The Tarnished Door: The New Immigrants and the Transformation of America* (1983); Donald W. Dayton and Robert K. Johnston, eds., *The Variety of American Evangelicalism* (1991); Ethics and Public Policy Center, *No Longer Exiles: The Religious New Right in American Politics* (1993); Jo Freeman, *The Politics of Women's Liberation* (1979); James William Gibson, *Warrior Dreams: Paramilitary Culture in Post-Vietnam America* (1994); Douglas Glasgow, *The Black Underclass* (1980); Christopher Lasch, *The Culture of Narcissism* (1978); Michael Lienesch, *Redeeming America: Piety and Politics in the New Christian Right* (1993); Kristen Luker, *Abortion and the Politics of Motherhood* (1984); George M. Marsden, *Understanding Fundamentalism and Evangelicalism* (1991); Michael Moritz, *The Little Kingdom: The Private Story of Apple Computer* (1984); Maureen Muldoon, *The Abortion Debate in the United States and Canada: A Source Book* (1991); George H. Nash, *The Conservative Intellectual Movement in America Since 1945* (1976); Timothy J. O'Neill, *Bakke and the Politics of Equality* (1985); Jerome Price, *The Antinuclear Movement* (1982); Quentin J. Schultze, *Televangelism and American Culture* (1991); Edwin Schur, *The Awareness Trap: Self-Absorption Instead of Social Change* (1976); Suzanne Staggenborg, *The Pro-Choice Movement* (1991); Melvin Urofsky, *The Continuity of Change: The Supreme Court and Individual Liberties, 1953–1986* (1991); Winnifrid D. Wandersee, *On the Move: American Women in the 1970s* (1988); William J. Wilson, *The Declining Significance of Race* (1978); Mark Royden Winchell, *Neoconservative Criticism* (1991); Robert Wuthnow, *The Restructuring of American Religion: Society and Faith Since World War II* (1988).

America and the World in the Seventies

James Bill, *The Eagle and the Lion: The Tragedy of American-Iranian Relations* (1987); Zbigniew Brzezinski, *Power and Principle* (1983); Alan Dawson, *55 Days: The Fall of South Vietnam* (1977); Raymond L. Garthoff, *Détente and Confrontation: American-Soviet Relations from Nixon to Reagan* (1987); John F. Guilmartin, Jr., *A Very Short War: The Mayaguez and the Battle of Koh Tang* (1995); Arnold R. Isaacs, *Without Honor: Defeat in Vietnam and Cambodia* (1983); William E. LeGro, *Vietnam from Ceasefire to Capitulation* (1981); George D. Moffett, III, *The Limits of Victory: The Ratification of the Panama Canal Treaties* (1983); William B. Quandt, *Camp David* (1987); Barry Rubin, *Paved with Good Intentions* (1983) [U.S.-Iranian relations]; David Schoenbaum, *The United States and the State of Israel* (1993); Lars Schoultz, *Human Rights and U.S. Policy Toward Latin America* (1981); William Shawcross, *Sideshow: Kissinger, Nixon, and the Destruction of Cambodia* (1979); Gary Sick, *All Fall Down: America's Tragic Encounter with Iran* (1986); Gaddis Smith, *Morality, Reason and Power: American Diplomacy in the Carter Years* (1986); Strobe Talbott, *Endgame* (1979) [SALT II]; Cyrus Vance, *Hard Choices* (1983).

CHAPTER 14

Prime-Time Politics:
The Reagan-Bush Years

Jimmy Carter paced the White House halls all night on January 19, 1981, hoping to announce, as his final presidential act, that Iran had released the U.S. hostages. Even as he rode to the inaugural ceremony on January 20, his eyes puffy from lack of sleep, Carter was on the phone, seeking word of the hostages' release. But this final balm eluded him. Not until a few minutes after Ronald Reagan took the oath of office did Iran, after 444 days, at last free the Americans.

Taking office under these auspicious circumstances, Reagan set about achieving the political agenda of the New Right, whose advocates had gained ground steadily in the 1970s. At the time, his policies won broad support. In retrospect, Reagan's two terms saw grave economic problems ignored or worsened. The federal deficit and trade gap widened, and the industrial infrastructure crumbled even further. As corporate profits soared, the nation's inner cities decayed.

Avidly pursuing the Cold War, Reagan accelerated the military-spending increases and rhetorical assaults on Moscow that had begun during Carter's administration. He particularly focused on battling communism in Africa and Latin America. Indeed, the latter campaign spawned the worst scandal of his presidency, the Iran-contra affair. Yet by the end of his watch, sweeping changes within the Soviet Union heralded the Cold War's end and the final, incongruous act of Reagan's long career: a warm embrace of the world's top communist in Moscow's Red Square.

The Reagan revolution mobilized the mood of reaction that had gripped Middle America in the troubled 1970s. The individualistic, acquisitive, and conservative outlook that Reagan personified had cultural as well as political manifestations, and the 1980s remains indelibly the Reagan era. After his departure various negative consequences of his policies emerged, but the public never seemed to hold Reagan responsible. Envious Democrats would dub him the "Teflon president."

In 1988, Vice President George Bush defeated Michael Dukakis to win the presidency. As when William Howard Taft succeeded the larger-than-life Theodore Roosevelt early in the twentieth century, Bush's single term seemed pale and anticlimactic after eight years of Reagan. In characterizing the Bush years, historians would speak of a "caretaker" presidency or a "status quo" presidency. For many Americans, the high point of the Bush years was the drama of the Persian Gulf War. Bush's approval ratings soared in the war's aftermath, but in retrospect even that conflict seemed a less clear-cut triumph than it did at the time.

The New Right Takes Charge: 1980–1984

In electing Richard Nixon in 1968, frustrated voters had rejected radicalism, redistributive liberalism, and affirmative action in favor of conservatism and the status quo. The process had continued in the 1970s, fed by economic worries and white blacklash. New Right activism crested in 1980, a watershed year in American political history.

On the Democratic side, Senator Edward Kennedy's convention speech evoking the party's reformist tradition won a nostalgic ovation, but in the end the divided and dispirited Democrats renominated Carter.

The confident Republicans turned to Ronald Reagan, who had easily bested five challengers in the Republican primaries. The most liberal of the five, Congressman John Anderson of Illinois, later ran in the general election as an independent. Reagan chose as his running mate one of his erstwhile rivals, George Bush, a party stalwart who had held a variety of government posts, most recently as director of the CIA.

The GOP platform attacked abortion and the equal rights amendment. Exuding Cold War militance, it criticized SALT II and demanded increased military spending. On the economy, the platform embraced two seemingly contradictory goals: major tax cuts and a balanced budget. Reagan's acceptance speech, a preview of his campaign, stressed lower taxes, less government regulation, and a beefed-up national defense. Praising "family values" and the free-enterprise system, he ended with a paean to "this . . . beloved and blessed land."

Reagan's acting skills shone in a televised debate with Carter. His rhetorical query, "Are you better off today than you were four years ago?" resonated with voters battered by inflation. When Carter warned of the dire consequences of Reagan's policies, Reagan smiled benevolently and sighed, "There you go again." On voting day, Reagan won a narrow 51 percent of the popular vote. Carter trailed with 41 percent, and Anderson picked up 7 percent. Reagan carried 44 states; only Georgia and Minnesota (the home states of Carter and Mondale), Hawaii, Maryland, Rhode Island, West Virginia, and Washington, D.C., withstood his appeal. The Republicans won control of the Senate for the first time since losing it in 1954 and cut the Democrats' majority in the House from 119 to 50. The vote revealed an anti-Carter, anti-inflation protest as well as an affirmation of the New Right agenda, but Reagan confidently claimed a clear mandate for his program, and the new Congress largely went along.

The oldest president ever elected, Reagan was sixty-nine when he took office. Yet aided by his Hollywood training and his skillfully dyed hair, he projected a sprightly image. Of Irish immigrant stock (the name was originally O'Regan), he grew up in Dixon, Illinois, where his alcoholic father supported the family during the Depression as a local New Deal relief administrator.

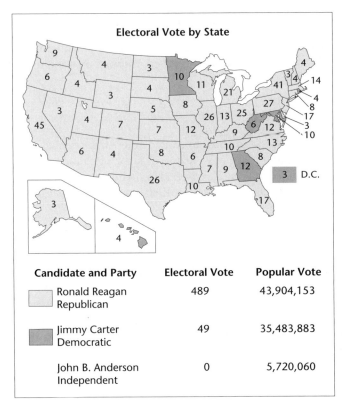

FIGURE 14.1
Presidential Election of 1980

Reagan graduated from Eureka College in Illinois and worked as a radio sports announcer in Des Moines. In 1937, after taking a screen test arranged by a friend, he signed a contract with Warner Brothers. He appeared in supporting roles in a series of movies that ended with *The Killers* (1964)—his only part as a villain. His best-known role, as the dying football player George Gipp in *Knute Rockne–All American* (1940), gave rise to his nickname, the Gipper.

Reagan voted for Roosevelt in 1932, but as a postwar president of the Screen Actors Guild amid investigation of communist influence in Hollywood, he had turned to the right. In 1954 he began hosting TV's "General Electric Theatre" and became GE's corporate voice. A ceaseless round of speechmaking in these years fixed his palette of political ideas. Reagan's second marriage in 1952, to actress Nancy Davis, a staunch conservative, deepened his right-wing political bent. A Reagan TV speech for Barry Goldwater in 1964 won national attention.

As governor of California (1966–75), Reagan denounced campus antiwar protests and in 1970 stood firm against student demonstrators protesting the Cambodian invasion. He resumed his speechmaking to conservative audiences after leaving the governorship and soon gained a national following.

A seasoned politician and well-known conservative, Reagan was also a creature of the media. Reagan watchers marveled at the chasm between the media image molded by scripted TV speeches and staged appearances and the person behind the image. The former was charismatic, eloquent, and deeply thoughtful about politics and the human condition. The latter, while capable of charm, was detached and rather vague, bored by details, and fairly inarticulate except when recounting an anecdote that supported his conservative ideology. A surge of nostalgic affection for Harry Truman in the 1980s perhaps reflected Americans' awareness of the contrast between the down-to-earth, plainspoken Truman and the media-savvy Reagan.

Exuding optimism in his inaugural address, Reagan lauded private initiative as the key to renewal. "Government is not the solution to our problem," he announced in a well-worn line. "Government *is* the problem." The inaugural became a festival of privilege, as private jets shuttled in Hollywood stars and the Reagans' rich friends. At Washington's elegant Union Station, scene of one inaugural party, street people mingled with invited guests to filch hors d'oeuvres from the groaning tables.

The new administration nearly ended tragically ten weeks after it began when, on March 30, 1981, a deranged young man fired six bullets at Reagan as he emerged from a Washington hotel. One bullet hit presidential press secretary James Brady, inflicting brain damage. Brady and his wife would later champion the cause of gun control.* Another bullet punctured Reagan's lung. He survived after surgery, although in graver condition than the public realized. Borrowing a movie line, he quipped, "I forgot to duck." His already high approval ratings soared.

Another defining moment early in Reagan's term came in August 1981 when the 11,600-member Professional Air Traffic Controllers Organization (PATCO) called an illegal strike. The president fired the strikers when they defied a back-to-work order. Some found his action callous, but many Americans, judging PATCO workers arrogant and overpaid, applauded his tough stance. The failed PATCO strike symbolized the weakened clout of organized labor. Indeed, by 1987 only 17 percent of American workers belonged to unions, down from 23 percent in 1980.

Reagan's domestic program, a pastiche of New Right themes, featured four key elements: tax cuts, reduced federal regulation, increased military spending, and—somewhat improbably—a balanced budget in three years. As a further, unstated goal, the administration hoped to reduce the government's commitment to affirmative action for minorities and zealous enforcement of the civil-rights laws.

Reduced taxes, Reagan claimed, citing the ideas of California economist Arthur Laffer, would jump-start the economy as consumers spent their windfall and as businesses invested in new plants and technology. The resulting boom would increase tax revenues even at lower rates. Laffer summed up this theory, known as supply-side economics, in the "Laffer curve," a chart showing economic

---

* The Bradys' long campaign gained a partial victory on November 30, 1993, when Congress passed the so-called Brady Bill requiring a five-day waiting period for the purchase of a handgun, to allow for a background check of the prospective purchaser.

activity rising as tax rates fell. Most economists viewed Laffer's simplistic theory as wishful thinking. George Bush, during his own try for the Republican nomination in 1980, had called it "voodoo economics." Once on the ticket, Bush reversed himself, an early example of the kind of behavior that would gain him a reputation for opportunism. Yet the *Wall Street Journal* and other influential voices endorsed Laffer's ideas, and Ronald Reagan, long convinced that high taxes served as socialism's entering wedge, had proved an easy convert.

Reagan's tax-cutting, probusiness ideology won a boost also from George Gilder, who argued in *Wealth and Poverty* (1981) that of all economic systems, capitalism most fully expressed humankind's highest spiritual aspirations. The capitalist, he declaimed, must have "faith in man, faith in the future, . . . faith in the mutual benefits of trade, [and] faith in the providence of God." In these years of rising evangelical fervor, the line between social policy and religious dogma thus often blurred.

Reagan's youthful budget director, David Stockman, shared his boss's tax-cutting fervor. Stockman had joined SDS in the sixties, but in 1976 he went to Congress as a Republican. For him, as he revealed in a candid *Atlantic Monthly* interview in December 1981, tax cuts were part of a larger project: to move toward a "minimalist" government and to dismantle the welfare state. Supply-side economics, he conceded, was simply the old "trickle-down" theory: if the rich get richer, the benefits will seep down to the rest of society. As budget director, he proposed a 30 percent tax cut. Only slightly modifying this request, Congress in May 1981 approved a 25 percent cut: 5 percent in 1981 and 10 percent in each of the next two years.

Conservative southern Democrats called "boll weevils" joined congressional Republicans in supporting the call for spending cuts. The long list of slashed social programs included food stamps, child nutrition, job training, and Aid to Families with Dependent Children. Ironically, despite cuts of $45 billion in specific programs, total federal spending on social welfare, including entitlement programs, such as social security and Medicare, rose from $313 billion in 1980 to $533 billion by 1988. Even Reaganites could do no more than chip away at the welfare state. Yet the slashes in social spending were significant, reflecting both a budget-balancing impulse and fears of growing welfare dependency. Charles Murray, a former social worker, expressed this frustration in *Losing Ground: American Social Policy, 1950–1980* (1984). Social programs intended "to provide more for the poor," Murray charged, had merely "produced more poor instead."

In simplest terms, the tax cuts and reduced social spending of the early 1980s redistributed income from the poor to the wealthy. In 1980 the poorest 20 percent of U.S. households received 4.9 percent of total after-tax income. By 1985 this figure had fallen to 4.6 percent. In the same period, the after-tax income share of the top 20 percent of households rose from 40.6 percent to 42.6 percent, the highest since World War II. In actual dollar terms, the inflation-adjusted annual income of the poorest 10 percent of American families fell by 10.5 percent over 1980–85. By contrast, the very richest Americans, the top 1 percent, saw their taxable income from salaries and investments spurt upward between 1980 and 1990.

The income decline among the poor cannot be blamed entirely on Reagan's economic policies. The loss of factory jobs also depressed income statistics, as did

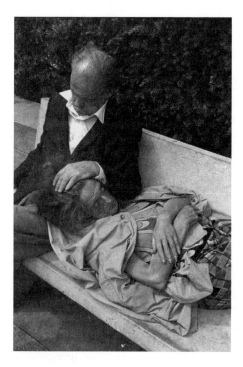

The Weary Blues. *Beneath the booming prosperity of the Reagan years, severe social problems festered. A homeless man and woman, wearily resting on a park bench in Philadelphia, were witnessed by a photographer in 1986.* (© James Conroy)

rising immigration. The Hispanic population, fed by a steady flow of newcomers from Mexico and the Caribbean nations, grew by 53 percent in the 1980s. As immigrants continued to flood in from the Philippines, China, Korea, and Vietnam, the Asian-American population doubled. Although some of the new arrivals, particularly those from Asia, were well educated and moved quickly into good jobs, most began their life in America at the lowest rungs of the economic ladder.

Although the administration insisted that a "safety net" protected the truly needy, cuts in social spending made life harder for the poor. The number of homeless grew markedly. A policy of deinstitutionalizing the chronically mentally ill, implemented in these years, added to the ranks of street people. In 1987 one of five American children lived in poverty, up by 24 percent from 1979. A few activists still championed the cause of the poor, but to unreceptive ears. Marian Wright Edelman of the Children's Defense Fund calculated that the money spent annually on operating a private dining room for the secretary of defense would restore morning snacks for 1 million low-income schoolchildren, one of many Reagan-era budget cuts. In *Rachel and Her Children: Homeless Families in America* (1988), Jonathan Kozol described life in a New York City welfare hotel:

> There are families in this building [who] . . . , like refugees . . . in the midst of war, cling to each other and establish a small zone of safety. [But] most people here do not have resources to create a zone of safety. Terrorized already on arrival, they are quickly caught up in a vortex of accelerating threats and are tossed about like bits of wood and broken furniture and shattered houses in an Arkansas tornado. Chaos and disorder alternate with lethargy and nearly absolute bewilderment in face of regulations they cannot observe or do not understand.

Reaganomics struck even at Americans who had jobs. In 1988, *U.S. News and World Report* found that some 9 million working adults earned incomes below the poverty level, including "people like Glen Witbeck, a short-order cook whose $8,000 annual salary doesn't stretch to cover his two little girls' medical bills. . . . Or Pamela Kelley, a onetime airline-passenger screener who shifted to canned food at home because pot roast was too expensive for her and her two-year-old daughter." An advanced degree offered no guarantee of upward mobility in the spotty Reagan economy. In 1988 the Ambassador Cab Company of Cambridge, Massachusetts, reported six Ph.D.s among its drivers.

Not even the middle class particularly benefited from the tax cuts. State taxes rose to cover new costs caused by drops in federal spending, and other charges and fees went up as well. In 1983 Congress raised social security taxes, further diluting the effects of the income-tax cut. Overall, the average family's total tax burden remained about the same or rose slightly in these years. And although Reagan justifiably boasted of 20 million new jobs created in the 1980s, these were often service-sector positions with low pay, few benefits, and little prospect of advancement. As in the 1970s, many skilled workers in declining industries found their wages cut as they left the factory for unskilled work in the lower ranks of the service sector.

Reagan's first term did bring the end of the raging inflation of the 1970s. Owing to the Federal Reserve's continued tight-money policy and a drop in world oil prices, the inflation rate fell from 13.5 percent in 1980 to 1.9 percent by 1986. But the other component of the 1970s economic crisis, the recession, worsened as the Fed's credit policies, designed to starve inflation, impeded business recovery. The "Reagan recession" of 1981–82 produced painfully high jobless rates. With some 10 million Americans out of work in 1982–83, the unemployment rate for both years remained stuck at 9.5 percent, the highest since 1941. Bank failures and business bankruptcies soared. The recession gradually bottomed out, however, and in November 1982 the stock market began a five-year rise. The later Reagan years would bring better times.

Just as the Fed's credit policies had mixed effects, so, too, did other measures of the early 1980s. For example, the 1983 hike in social security taxes that diluted the economic stimulus intended by the income-tax cut was part of a much-needed overhaul of the entire social security system. The reforms shored up a program hard hit by expanding benefits, ballooning Medicare costs, and a tide of retirees. Among other changes, the 1983 reform taxed the benefits of well-to-do retirees and restricted automatic cost-of-living benefit increases.

Implementing a New Right goal backed by many economists and by Jimmy Carter, the administration also set out to deregulate the economy. Indeed, many Reagan appointees scorned the entire concept of federal regulation. Secretary of the Interior James Watt of Colorado, a leader of the "Sagebrush Rebellion" promoting private development of public lands, did his best to reduce federal control and to open these lands to exploitation. Watt's religious beliefs reinforced his laissez-faire ideology. Asked at his confirmation hearing whether he wished to protect the environment for future generations, he responded that he did not know how many generations remained before the Second Coming. Watt's bigotry (he characterized one advisory panel as "a black, a woman, two Jews, and a cripple") soon made him a liability, and Reagan dumped him in 1983. Nevertheless, the antiregulatory ideology that he personified lived on. The budget of the Environmental Protection Agency was slashed. The head of EPA, in charge of the $1.4 billion Superfund to clean up hazardous sites, showed favoritism toward polluters, with whom she had close links. An EPA official indicted for lying to Congress served three months in jail. The head of the Securities and Exchange Commission (SEC), a Wall Street insider and true believer in deregulation, radically reduced the SEC's oversight of the stock market.

The deregulation spirit pervaded the Federal Home Loan Bank Board, too, an oversight agency for the savings and loan (S&L) industry. The subsequent wave of risky speculation and outright fraud left many S&Ls in ruins by the end of the 1980s (see p. 440). A multibillion-dollar federal program to salvage failed S&Ls and to reimburse depositors became part of the price of the deregulation mania.

Reagan's choice to head the Federal Communications Commission, another disciple of deregulation, ridiculed the notion that TV had a public-service role. "Television is just another appliance," he insisted. "It's just a toaster with pictures. . . . [It is] time to move away from thinking about broadcasters as trustees, [and to] treat them the way almost everyone else in society does—that is, as business." Under his chairmanship, the FCC increased the amount of time that television stations could air commercials and dropped the rule that some programming time must be devoted to public-service broadcasts.

During Reagan's tenure, the Federal Trade Commission, the Occupational Safety and Health Administration, the Department of Transportation, the Justice Department's antitrust division, and other agencies sabotaged the regulatory laws that they existed to uphold. In his inaugural address, Reagan had joked, "It's not my intention to do away with government," yet zealots in his administration often seemed determined to do just that.

Along with tax cuts and deregulation, a beefed-up military topped Reagan's agenda. The 1980 GOP platform had warned of a post-Vietnam decline in U.S. armed might; and once in office, Reagan launched the largest military expansion in peacetime history. Excluding veterans' affairs, the defense budget surged from $157 billion in 1981 to $273 billion in 1986. The administration's enthusiasm for reactivating battleships illustrated the symbolic component of the military buildup. These dinosaurs had little utility in an era of missiles, nuclear submarines, and communications satellites that could easily track them; nevertheless, Reaganites' nostalgia for the glory days of World War II, when battleships had symbolized U.S. power, ignored such arguments.

Secretary of Defense Caspar Weinberger presided over this buildup. As President Nixon's budget director, Weinberger had fought wasteful spending. Now at the Pentagon, he opened the tap wide. In his annual reports to Congress, Weinberger warned apocalyptically about America's "dangerous slide" in military preparedness and defended his huge budget requests as essential to U.S. security.

Reagan's admirers would later argue that the frantic military spending forced Moscow into a foolhardy effort to keep pace and thereby drove the Soviet system into crisis. The U.S. buildup may have been a factor, but political and economic conditions within the Soviet sphere itself probably explain the U.S.S.R.'s collapse more accurately. Whatever its global impact, Reagan's military expansion had profound effects at home. It benefited defense contractors and buttressed their political clout, and it generated thousands of jobs, especially in the Sun Belt. Glamorous high-tech weapons systems proliferated on the drawing boards. But ballooning defense budgets also enlarged the federal deficit, worrying even conservatives. *Business Week* warned against the Pentagon's runaway budget in a 1987 article entitled "Defense Spending: The Wild Blue Yonder."

Many Americans, including the conservative, patriotic, blue-collar and middle-class citizens who made up Richard Nixon's "silent majority," cheered Reagan's martial emphasis. Smarting over the Vietnam defeat, taught to expect the worst of the Soviet Union, and angered by OPEC rulers and Middle Eastern sheiks who seemed to tweak Uncle Sam's nose with impunity, they welcomed the morale boost that came from pouring billions into military hardware. In liberal churches, on college and university campuses, and among peace advocates and antinuclear activists, however, the arms expansion met opposition. The Federal Emergency Management Agency (FEMA), with its plans to disperse city dwellers to rural areas if nuclear war threatened, helped to revive nuclear anxiety. President Reagan contributed to the growing uneasiness by taking no arms-control initiatives in his first two years.

Events in Europe fed nuclear worries. Seeking parity with Soviet missiles in Eastern Europe, NATO and the Carter administration had agreed to deploy 572 U.S. missiles in Great Britain and West Germany in 1979. NATO also affirmed its "first-use" policy on nuclear weapons: a Soviet thrust into Western Europe could trigger a nuclear response. Reagan's first secretary of state, Alexander Haig, described the utility of "nuclear warning shots" in conventional war situations.

As the missile deployment proceeded, protests spread across Europe. With TV newscasts showing antinuclear marchers in Great Britain, Germany, and elsewhere, U.S. activists also mobilized. The antinuclear power movement of the 1970s now targeted nuclear weapons. Protests reached levels not seen in America since the test-ban campaign of a quarter century before.

The movement coalesced around the "nuclear freeze" idea: while pursuing arms-reduction talks, the nuclear powers should declare a mutual freeze on building, testing, and deploying nuclear weapons. In the winter of 1981–82, town meetings in New England passed freeze resolutions. In June 1982, 800,000 nuclear protesters—the largest political rally in U.S. history—gathered in New York's Central Park. That fall, voters in nine states, including California and Wisconsin, approved nuclear-freeze referenda.

Religious bodies endorsed the movement. *The Challenge of Peace,* a 1983 statement by the nation's Catholic bishops, raised grave doubts about U.S. nuclear policies. College students, writers, artists, and filmmakers joined the campaign. In the 1983 movie *WarGames,* an out-of-control Defense Department computer nearly obliterates the world. Jonathan Schell's *The Fate of the Earth* (1984) pondered the meaning of a nuclear holocaust that could leave a planet devoid of all memory that human beings had ever existed. *The Day After,* a 1984 ABC-TV special, portrayed the effects of nuclear war on Kansas. Scientists warned that the atmospheric effects of thermonuclear war could lower average temperatures over vast regions and bring on a permanent "nuclear winter."

Meanwhile, however, Reagan had struck back in a TV speech on March 23, 1983. Conceding the horror of nuclear war, the president offered his remedy: not a nuclear freeze but the Strategic Defense Initiative (SDI), a space-based defensive shield with computerized laser beams and other high-tech weaponry to destroy incoming missiles. Reagan's proposal, a surprise to the Pentagon, was the brainchild of physicist Edward Teller, "the father of the H-bomb," whom Reagan much admired.

Nicknamed "Star Wars" by the media, SDI drew criticism from scientists who derided its futuristic technology, including complex computer systems that could never be fully tested except under actual attack conditions. Arms-control specialists warned that SDI would violate the 1972 Anti-Ballistic Missile Treaty, which had outlawed missile-defense systems that might tempt a nation to deliver a first strike. Nonetheless, legislators unwilling to invite accusations of neglecting the nation's defense voted funds for SDI research that eventually totaled $30 billion. The program stumbled on until 1992, when the Bush administration quietly shelved it. In 1993 the *New York Times* revealed that key SDI tests had been rigged, not only to deceive the Soviets but also to ensure continued funding. However impractical, SDI had served Reagan's immediate political purpose: by 1984 the nuclear-freeze movement was fading fast.

Increased defense spending coupled with tax cuts drove the annual federal deficit from $74 billion in 1981 to $185 billion in 1984. During Reagan's first term, the total federal debt surged from $994 billion to $1.8 trillion. This result did not surprise the administration. Budget director David Stockman in his 1981 *Atlantic Monthly* interview admitted that slashing taxes while massively increasing military appropriations would yield huge budget deficits. In fact, he had gambled that Congress, faced with soaring deficits, would make radical cuts in domestic spending, and thereby severing what he called "the umbilical cords of dependency" running from Washington to every corner of the nation. In short, the administration deliberately induced budget deficits to starve domestic social spending.

Attuned to the nation's conservative mood, Reagan also sympathized with the white backlash that had fueled the New Right. He had opposed the civil-rights acts of 1964 and 1965 and in private told stories of a mythic "welfare queen" who had amassed a fortune by defrauding the welfare system. Emulating the Nixon-Ford foot-dragging approach to civil rights, the Reagan White House encouraged local school boards to resist mandatory busing orders and slashed the budgets of the Equal Employment Opportunity Commission and the Office of Federal Contract Compliance. As head of the Justice Department's civil-rights division, Reagan named a corporate lawyer who had no background in civil rights. In a telling illustration of the decade's mood, this official openly proclaimed his goal of reversing the division's vigorous support for affirmative-action programs.

New Militance: Reagan and Foreign Policy

If Reagan's domestic policy reversed the activism of discredited liberals, his foreign policy was highly activist, reflecting the New Right's intense anti-communism. The administration mobilized to fight communism and leftism in the Third World, especially in Latin America, and adopted a highly belligerent stance toward the Soviet Union. Reagan continued and amplified the anti-Soviet tone of Jimmy Carter's final year in office. But the White House also faced foreign challenges that did not

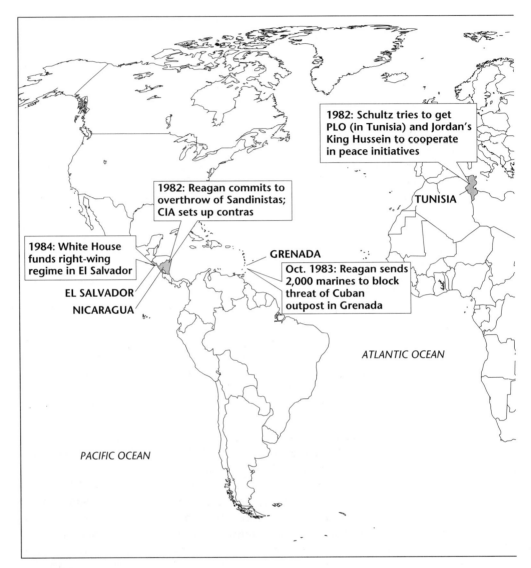

1982: Schultz tries to get
PLO (in Tunisia) and Jordan's
King Hussein to cooperate
in peace initiatives

TUNISIA

1982: Reagan commits to
overthrow of Sandinistas;
CIA sets up contras

1984: White House
funds right-wing
regime in El Salvador

EL SALVADOR
NICARAGUA

GRENADA

Oct. 1983: Reagan sends
2,000 marines to block
threat of Cuban
outpost in Grenada

ATLANTIC OCEAN

PACIFIC OCEAN

FIGURE 14.2
Reagan and the World, 1980–1984

lend themselves to the stark polarities of Cold War ideology, especially in the Middle East. Despite the Israeli-Egyptian treaty, peace proved elusive. White House attention initially centered on Lebanon, an unstable nation prey to its powerful neighbors Syria and Israel. The Palestine Liberation Organization (PLO) had its headquarters in the Lebanon capital of Beirut, and in southern Lebanon thousands of displaced Palestinians lived in squalid refugee camps.

In June 1982, countering a terrorist faction within the PLO, Israel attacked PLO strongholds and established an Israeli-controlled "security zone" in southern Lebanon. The invasion led to a massacre of Palestinian refugees by Lebanese

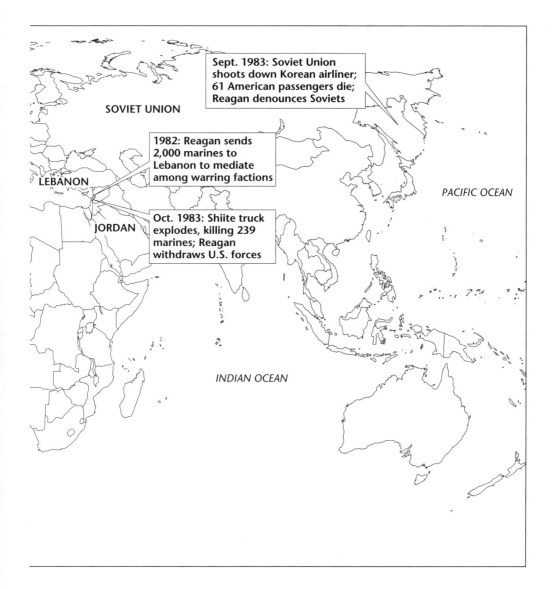

Christian militia linked to Israel. The PLO high command, expelled from Lebanon, shifted to Tunisia. President Reagan, as part of an international force overseeing the PLO withdrawal and trying to mediate among warring factions, ordered two thousand U.S. Marines to Lebanon. Because of America's close ties to Israel, radical Shiite Muslim groups reviled the marines. In October 1983 a Shiite terrorist drove a truck loaded with explosives into the lightly guarded U.S. barracks near the Beirut airport. The shattering blast killed 239 marines. Fifty French troops died in a related attack. Reagan withdrew the remaining U.S. forces.

At the same time, Secretary of State George Shultz, who replaced Alexander Haig in 1982, tried in vain to revive the stalled Middle East peace process. Deeming the PLO a key to long-term stability in the region, Shultz sought to bring PLO leader Yasir Arafat and Jordan's King Hussein into the negotiations. Yet Israeli security fears, Syria's intransigence, and PLO suspicions of Hussein all conspired to scuttle Shultz's efforts. So, too, did growing Jewish settlements in the West Bank territories seized by Israel from Jordan in the 1967 war.

Closer to home, the Reagan administration fought radical insurgencies in Latin America. Plagued by explosive population growth and vast disparities of wealth and poverty, this region had long suffered military coups and guerrilla violence. Reagan, ever the Cold Warrior, saw in all these complexities the hand of Moscow. Here was an opportunity to resume the anticommunist struggle abandoned in Vietnam, but this time with success. In El Salvador, the White House helped to fund a right-wing military regime fighting a guerrilla insurgency backed by Nicaragua and Castro's Cuba. But aware that a less repressive regime was more likely to win popular support, the State Department backed the moderate José Napoleon Duarte in a 1984 presidential election. Duarte's victory did not end the brutality of El Salvador's ruling elite, however. Death squads linked to the army continued to murder civilians, from poor farmers to teachers and physicians suspected of opposing the regime.

In Nicaragua, President Reagan, accusing the Marxist-led Sandinistas of aiding the rebels in El Salvador, not only reversed Carter's policy of recognition but committed the United States to the Sandinistas' overthrow. The Soviet Union, he charged, wanted to turn Nicaragua into another communist enclave like Cuba. Under director William Casey, the CIA in 1982 organized, trained, and financed the contras, an anti-Sandinista guerrilla army based in Honduras and Costa Rica. Some top contra leaders had close links to the discredited Somoza dictatorship, overthrown in 1979. Infiltrating Nicaragua, the contras conducted raids, carried out sabotage, and used a CIA manual that explained how to "neutralize" local Sandinista officials. Civilians suffered heavily in the shadowy war, but the contras won Reagan's praise as "the moral equivalent of our Founding Fathers."

Home-front critics of the CIA-run contra war accused the administration of perpetuating the old practice of backing Latin American elites against the masses and of deceiving the American people in the process. Others feared a repeat of the Vietnam disaster. In December 1982, Congress halted military aid to the contras for one year. In April 1984, the *Wall Street Journal* reported that CIA agents, with the written approval of President Reagan, had mined Nicaragua's harbors, running the risk of sinking Soviet or other foreign vessels. Members of the Senate Intelligence Committee, charged with overseeing the CIA, exploded in anger, for CIA head Casey had concealed the operation from them. In October 1984 the House passed an amendment introduced by Representative Edward Boland of Massachusetts imposing a two-year ban on contra aid.

Amid the controversy, the contra insurgency itself faltered. In 1988 the Sandinistas and the contras would reach a truce arranged by President Oscar Arias Sánchez of Costa Rica and by other Central American leaders. To the end of his term, however, Reagan continued to hope for a contra victory.

On another Latin American front, U.S. Marines in October 1983 invaded the tiny West Indian island nation of Grenada, where Cuban-backed radicals had seized power. The United States ostensibly aimed to rescue U.S. students attending a Grenada medical college, yet the White House proclaimed a larger purpose: to prevent the emergence of another outpost of Cuban-Soviet power and to show America's post-Vietnam willingness to protect its interests. Expelling Cuban workers building an airfield, the Marines installed a pro-U.S. government in Grenada.

With Soviet troops still in Afghanistan and Reagan accusing Moscow of mischief in Latin America, relations with Moscow worsened. In a March 1983 address to evangelical leaders, Reagan lambasted the Soviet Union as an "evil empire" and "the focus of evil in the modern world." Relations further deteriorated that September when a Soviet fighter shot down a Korean airliner that had flown far into Soviet air space. All 269 passengers, including 61 Americans, died, and the circumstances remained unclear. Rejecting Moscow's charge that the plane had been conducting espionage, the White House and right-wing political groups used the disaster to step up their denunciations of Soviet perfidy.* Détente, floundering at the end of Carter's term, now seemed moribund.

U.S. foreign policy during Reagan's first term saw a sharpening of Cold War hostility, evidenced by increased military spending and the neglect of arms control. Belligerent pronouncements and vigorous resistance to Soviet expansion, real or imagined, in Latin America completed the picture. These measures won applause from the New Right, as proof that America's post-Vietnam funk had lifted. Although a tonic at home, Reagan's ideologically driven diplomacy failed to sustain Nixon's détente initiative, or to take into account the indigenous sources of the conflicts raging in the poverty-wracked nations south of the U.S. border.

Buoyed by the new militance in foreign affairs, Reaganism crested in the 1984 election year. Belying the carping of liberal critics, most Americans rated Reagan's first term a success. He had chalked up some achievements, and even the setbacks did not hurt his standing. Reagan's unabashed patriotism stirred a powerful response, and sports fans waving the stars and stripes and chanting "We're Number One" at the 1984 Summer Olympics in Los Angeles summed up the expansive mood. Although the Democrats had gained twenty-six House seats in the 1982 midterm election, Reagan's popularity posed a serious hurdle for Democratic presidential hopefuls. Walter Mondale of Minnesota, Carter's vice president and a prominent liberal, won the party nomination, but not without a fight. Senator Gary Hart of Colorado beat him in the New Hampshire primary. Chicago's Jesse Jackson, a former aide of Martin Luther King, Jr., was supported by many African Americans. In the end, though, Mondale, backed by the party leadership, lined up the labor and teacher unions, women's organizations, and other interest groups, and earned the nomination. Criticizing Reagan's military buildup and belligerent rhetoric, Mondale pleased union backers by calling for import quotas on manufactured products from abroad.

---

* In 1992, with the Cold War over, Moscow admitted that the intrusion had come about because of navigational error.

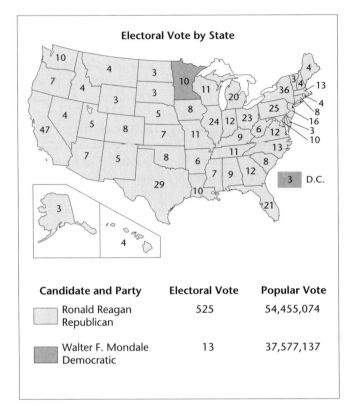

FIGURE 14.3
Presidential Election of 1984

Mondale named as his running mate Congresswoman Geraldine Ferraro of New York, the first woman to appear on a major party presidential ticket. But his prospects faded when he announced in his acceptance speech that as president he would raise taxes. Mondale hoped that this admission would win him points for candor, but to many voters it simply confirmed GOP charges that Democrats were the "tax-and-spend" party.

Despite soaring deficits, Reagan again promised a balanced budget and blamed free-spending Democrats in Congress for sabotaging this goal. In a TV debate, the seventy-four-year-old president jokingly pledged not to make a campaign issue of his fifty-six-year-old opponent's "youth and inexperience." The Reagan-Bush ticket triumphed in a landslide. Without a third-party challenge as in 1980 to siphon off support, Reagan garnered 59 percent of the popular vote. Mondale carried only his home state of Minnesota and the District of Columbia. Even with Ferraro on the ticket, he failed to carry New York or to win a majority of women voters. Blacks and Hispanics (except for pro-Reagan Cuban exiles in Florida) voted heavily Democratic but could not stem the Reagan tide. Portraying Mondale as a captive of "special interests," Reagan ran well in white working-class neighborhoods, where the Democratic vote dropped by 15 percent from the 1980 totals.

The 1984 election revealed the scope of the post-1960 shift in U.S. politics. In place of the liberal consensus stood a new coalition of disaffected Middle Americans forged in the conservative social climate and economic stresses of the 1970s. The New Right comprised an unstable but potent alliance of wealthy Americans, corporate leaders, evangelicals, Catholic ethnics, and white blue-collar workers. Although highly diverse, these groups shared an antipathy to intrusive federal regulations and cultural trends that threatened "traditional values." With one voice, they decried public policies that favored minorities, welfare recipients, feminists, homosexuals, and others who seemed to seek preferential treatment.

The election outcome also reflected the population shifts of these years. Whereas the Northeast and Midwest grew only slightly in 1970–90, the South's population exploded from 63 million to 87 million; the Pacific states, from 27 million to 39 million. California, having already passed New York as the most populous state in the 1960s, grew still more in the 1980s, from 24 million to 30 million. These changes contributed to the 1984 Reagan landslide as the South and West, enjoying the lion's share of Reagan-era military spending, voted solidly Republican. In the onetime Democratic bastion of Texas, for example, 64 percent of the voters chose Reagan. Across the Sun Belt, a similar story unfolded.

Iran-Contra Scandal and a Waning Cold War: Reagan's Second Term

Reagan's second inaugural address again struck a note of soaring optimism and love of country. But Reagan's mellow rhetoric obscured the sink-or-swim ideology and cuts in social programs that underlay his message. For all its inspiration, Reagan's themes—individualism, acquisitiveness, and competition—offered no unifying vision other than a rather jingoistic patriotism. Moreover, a rising cycle of Middle East terrorism and the Iran-contra affair marred Reagan's foreign policy of 1984–88. The latter scandal for a time threatened to cripple another presidency. In retrospect, however, the most momentous developments of Reagan's second term unfolded not in Washington but in Moscow, where dramatic events portended nothing less than the collapse of the Soviet Union and the end of the Cold War.

Three Supreme Court retirements, two during his second term, enabled Reagan to place his stamp on the judicial branch. In 1981 he had appointed Sandra Day O'Connor of Arizona, the first woman to serve on the high court. When Chief Justice Warren Burger retired in 1986, Reagan elevated William Rehnquist, a Nixon appointee, to the chief justiceship and named to the vacancy the conservative Antonin Scalia, a federal judge who had taught at the University of Chicago Law School. Scalia soon emerged as a rigid advocate of presidential power. The third opening, in 1987, sparked a fight. The Senate rejected Reagan's first nominee, Robert Bork. Opinionated, sarcastic, and harshly critical of judicial activism, Bork struck many as unsuited by both temperament and judicial philosophy for the Supreme Court. Reagan's next choice withdrew after revelations that he had smoked marijuana while a Harvard Law School professor. Reagan finally turned to Anthony M. Kennedy of San Francisco, who gained easy confirmation. Although chosen for their conservative credentials, O'Connor and Kennedy would emerge in the 1990s as centrists in contrast to the Court's more doctrinaire right wingers.

On the economic front, Reagan in his second term achieved one goal that had eluded Jimmy Carter. The tax-reform law of 1986 plugged some loopholes and exempted millions of poor Americans from paying taxes. But it also extended the regressive feature of Reaganomics, cutting tax rates for the wealthiest Americans to a maximum of 28 percent. On the other hand, inflation remained low, and unemployment declined in the later 1980s. Yet in Washington the red ink gushed on. After soaring to $238 billion in 1986, the federal deficit still stood at $206 billion in 1989, the year Reagan left office. Washington borrowed billions each year merely to pay interest on the ever-rising $3 trillion national debt, straining the credit market and threatening to push up interest rates and bring back recession. Only heavy purchases of U.S. government securities by investors in Japan and Western Europe staved off this disaster.

As the deficit grew, Congress at last trimmed the Pentagon's budget. The rate of increase in defense spending, in constant dollars, fell from 8.8 percent in 1985 to under 1 percent in 1988. Budget worries also led to the Gramm-Rudman-Hollings Act of 1985, which aimed to achieve a balanced budget by the early 1990s by mandating specific deficit-reduction targets. In 1986, however, the Supreme Court ruled that one of its key enforcement provisions violated the constitutional principle of separation of powers.

The United States' international economic position weakened in Reagan's second term as the trade gap widened. In 1987 Americans imported $160 billion more than they exported, with imports from Japan and other Asian nations accounting for nearly 80 percent of the total. Alarmed, the administration pressured Japan to open its domestic market to more U.S. imports and to stop "dumping," or selling exports below cost to maintain market dominance. In 1987, Reagan retaliated for Japan's dumping of microchips and imposed duties on Japanese electronics. The White House rejected calls for more protectionism from sectors of the economy hurt by imports, however, and in 1988 signed a free-trade pact with Canada to eliminate most trade barriers between the two nations by 1999.

While the defense industry, the service sector, and certain high-tech businesses prospered in the eighties, other elements of the economy continued to languish. Joblessness among inner-city minorities remained a chronic problem. As Americans caught the acquisitive spirit, total consumer debt exploded from $302 billion in 1980 to $671 billion by 1988. All of these problems—the deficit, the trade gap, the uneven economy, the upsurge in credit buying—fostered uneasiness. On October 19, 1987, the five-year stock-market boom crash-landed with a 500-point plunge. In the worst one-day drop ever, the value of the nation's stocks shrank by 20 percent. The market slowly recovered, but the 1987 collapse exposed the nagging doubts induced by six years of Reaganomics.

Despite such economic woes, world events and their domestic fallout dominated Reagan's second term. In 1988, George Shultz launched a final Middle East peace effort. He based his approach on a "land for peace" formula: Israel would give up the occupied territories in Gaza and the West Bank in return for security guarantees by the PLO and the Arab nations. Under U.S. pressure, PLO head Yasir Arafat renounced terrorism and conceded Israel's right to exist. But Israel's government, now headed by the right-wing Likud party, which favored continued Jewish settlements on the West Bank, rejected Shultz's efforts.

Terrorism, not peace hopes, more typically preoccupied the White House in these years. The 1983 bombing of the U.S. Marine barracks in Beirut heralded a larger campaign of fear launched by shadowy groups linked to the PLO, to Iran's Hezbollah (Party of God), and to Libya's ruler, Muammar el-Qaddafi. Terrorists demanding the release of Israeli-held Palestinians hijacked airplanes and attacked airports across Europe. In June 1985, 135 passengers aboard a TWA flight hijacked over Greece endured seventeen nightmarish days of captivity. That October, PLO agents seized an Italian cruise ship and murdered a wheelchair-bound Jewish-American passenger. In April 1986, terrorists linked to Libya bombed a Berlin discotheque popular with GIs. An irate Reagan ordered a bombing raid on military sites around Tripoli. The cycle of terrorism escalated. In December 1988, a Pan Am jet en route from London to New York crashed over Scotland, killing all 259 aboard, including numerous Americans. Investigators found evidence of a bomb hidden in the baggage section. In 1991 the U.S. and British governments officially accused Libya of masterminding the bombing.

A wave of political kidnappings also hit Beirut, a hotbed of Palestinian and Shiite ferment. From 1982 to 1985, terrorists seized nine Americans. One, the head of the CIA bureau in Beirut, died in captivity, probably under torture. Hostages from various European nations were taken as well. Although Reagan agonized less publicly over the hostages than had Carter, he was equally preoccupied with winning their freedom.

Two administration goals—release of the Beirut hostages and support for the contras—led to the web of misdeeds known as the Iran-contra affair. In August 1985, unbeknown to Congress or the public, President Reagan had approved the sale of 504-TOW antitank missiles to Iran, then at war with Iraq. National security adviser Robert McFarlane had directed the deal. In return, officials hoped that Tehran would use its influence to secure the release of the U.S. hostages in Beirut. Israel shipped the arms, with a former member of the shah's secret police acting as middleman. In all, the United States sold 2,004 TOWs and 18 HAWK antiaircraft missiles to Iran. The effort bore little fruit; three hostages were freed, but three more were seized, and Iran remained stridently anti-American. The deal contradicted Reagan's pledge never to negotiate with terrorists and mocked his pressure on other nations to boycott Iran. It also violated the Arms Control Export Act and an arms embargo against Iran imposed by Congress in 1979.

On November 3, 1986, a Beirut newspaper broke the story of these arms shipments and added startling details. In May 1986, the paper said, Robert McFarlane (having resigned as national security adviser the previous December) had flown with a shipment of HAWK parts to Tehran, bearing a Bible autographed by President Reagan for presentation to the Ayatollah Khomeini. McFarlane and Reagan both issued denials, but evidence soon confirmed that Washington had indeed sold arms and curried favor with the same U.S.-hating regime that had perpetrated the hostage ordeal of 1979–81.

Later in November came still more explosive news: Funds from the Iranian arms sales had been secretly diverted to the contras, at a time when Congress had explicitly forbidden such aid. Lieutenant Colonel Oliver North of the U.S. Marine

Corps, a National Security Council aide, had directed the operation from his White House office. Using various middlemen, North had funneled millions of dollars to the contras. Further circumventing the Boland amendment, he had also raised some $37 million for the contras from Saudi Arabia and other governments, as well as from wealthy U.S. conservatives. North's operation had its own airplanes, pilots, ship, and communications system. The deal unfolded in deep secrecy, with no accountability to Congress or the public.

When this story broke, North and his secretary shredded key documents and erased computer files just before FBI investigators arrived. Some files remained on backup disks, however, and provided crucial evidence of North's activities. On November 25, President Reagan praised North as "a national hero"—but dismissed him nevertheless. John Poindexter, McFarlane's successor as national security adviser, resigned.

In December, Reagan named an investigative panel headed by ex-senator John Tower of Texas. Its March 1987 report criticized Reagan's lax management style but blamed the Iran-contra debacle mainly on White House aides, especially Chief of Staff Donald Regan, who also resigned. On TV, President Reagan denied knowing of any illegalities but admitted "mistakes."

In May–July 1987, a joint House-Senate committee conducted hearings on the scandal. Under two Democratic cochairmen, the committee heard 250 hours of testimony, much of it televised to a fascinated nation. Oliver North sat ramrod straight in full-dress uniform during his six days of testimony. He admitted lying under oath, destroying documents, and falsifying records to conceal the White House role in the arms-for-hostages and contra-diversion schemes, but he insisted that love of country had motivated his every action. He claimed that he had kept his superiors informed and that he had worked closely with CIA director William Casey (who died in May 1987) to develop a covert-operations network beyond the reach of Congress. Many people thought North mawkish and self-serving, but others found his patriotism inspiring. North remained a hero to the political Right for years after.

Pipe-smoking John Poindexter admitted that he had approved North's plan to divert funds to the contras but loyally insisted that he had not told Reagan, in order to give the president "plausible deniability." Poindexter also revealed that he had destroyed Reagan's written approval of the initial arms sale to Iran, to spare him future political embarrassment.

In its report, the joint committee cited a litany of illegal acts, including failure to notify Congress of the arms sales, destroying and altering official documents, and diverting funds to the contras despite Congress's ban. The committee also noted a pervasive contempt for the law and for Congress by North and others. The committee found no evidence of Reagan's direct knowledge of criminal activity but echoed the Tower Commission's criticism of lax White House procedures. The scandal, the report concluded, had not only strained relations between the White House and Congress but also diminished the credibility of the presidency—and, indeed, of the United States.

Attorney General Edwin Meese in the meantime, after a casual initial investigation, had appointed special prosecutor Lawrence Walsh to handle the criminal aspects of the case. In March 1988, a federal grand jury indicted North, Poindexter, and two of North's intermediaries on various charges. Robert McFarlane pleaded guilty to misleading Congress (a misdemeanor) and cooperated with the prosecution. In May 1989, North was convicted of destroying evidence and other offenses. A federal judge fined him $150,000 and ordered him to perform twelve hundred hours of community service. (By this time North was earning up to $200,000 a month on the lecture circuit.) In June 1990, a jury found John Poindexter guilty on five felony charges; he received a six-month jail term. A federal appeals court reversed both convictions on a legal technicality in 1991.*

In contrast to Richard Nixon's fate, the Iran-contra scandal left Reagan relatively unscathed. Not only did the president enjoy a deeper reserve of goodwill, but no "smoking gun" comparable to the Nixon tapes linked him directly to illegal activities. Many Americans, too, agreed that the operation, however misguided, arose from motives of patriotism. Yet the affair again underscored the vulnerability of constitutional government to executive abuse. When North's secretary justified her shredding of documents (and smuggling of others out of the White House) by asserting that "sometimes you have to go above the written law," the arrogance of power became apparent.

As the Iran-contra affair receded, events on the main Cold War stage seized the limelight. Under President Mikhail Gorbachev, who came to power in 1985, the Soviet Union changed profoundly. Decades of Communist party control had stifled the Soviet economy and led to massive shortages in food and consumer goods. In addition, unrest simmered in Eastern Europe and in the Soviet republics, including Latvia, Estonia, and Lithuania, swallowed up by Moscow in 1940. To foster his twin goals of *glasnost* (openness) and *perestroika* (restructuring), Gorbachev urgently sought improved relations with the West.

A hint of the new order came during arms-control talks between Reagan and Gorbachev at Geneva in 1985 and Reykjavik, Iceland, in 1986. Although differences over inspection procedures and SDI derailed the Reykjavik summit, the two nations in 1987 agreed on the INF (Intermediate Nuclear Forces) Treaty, providing for the withdrawal of some twenty-five hundred missiles from Europe. Whereas the 1972 SALT I Treaty had simply capped future missile levels, the INF Treaty for the first time eliminated an entire category of weapons. In December Gorbachev traveled to Washington to sign the treaty. The Soviet leader also announced a reduction in Soviet military forces and troop withdrawals from Eastern Europe and Afghanistan.

As the pace of change quickened, Americans contemplated the unthinkable: the end of the Cold War. Ronald Reagan, despite his years of anti-Soviet rhetoric, responded imaginatively to the new realities. In May 1988, the Senate having consented to the INF Treaty, the president flew to Moscow for the final signing. Talks also continued on a strategic-arms reduction (START) treaty. For several days the two leaders socialized and posed for the media.

Reagan's cordiality with Gorbachev dismayed the Far Right, but most Americans sighed in relief as the Cold War crumbled. Diplomatic historian John Lewis

---

* The judge ruled that the convictions had rested in part on congressional testimony given under grants of immunity against self-incrimination.

Home on the Range. *As the Cold War thawed, President Reagan met Soviet leader Mikhail Gorbachev at Reagan's Rancho Mirage in Santa Barbara, California. Gorbachev himself would soon be swept aside by the forces of reform he had unleashed.* (AP/Wide World Photos)

Gaddis wrote early in 1989, "[D]uring his eight years as president, Ronald Reagan has presided over the most dramatic improvement in U.S. Soviet relations—and the most solid progress in arms control—since the Cold War began. History has often produced unexpected results, but this one surely sets some kind of record."

A Decade of Greed

Reagan's contempt for government, coupled with his glorification of self-interest, helped spawn a series of Washington scandals in which officials placed personal gain above the public interest. The so-called Wedtech affair is typical. For years, the Welbilt Corporation in the Bronx, a machine shop founded by the son of Puerto Rican immigrants, had tried to win government contracts set aside for minority-owned companies. Its fortunes rose dramatically when it hired lawyer E. Bob Wallach, a close friend of Attorney General Edwin Meese, and retained the Washington public-relations firm headed by Lynn Nofziger, Reagan's former political director. With these patrons, the renamed Wedtech Corporation won $250 million in no-bid minority Pentagon contracts. In 1986, shortly before the Small Business Administration cut Wedtech from its minority-business program, Nofziger and other insiders who had aided the corporation's rise sold their stock for $10 million. Clouded in scandal, Wedtech soon went bankrupt. Wallach and others were indicted on fraud, conspiracy, bribery, and other criminal charges.

Deceptive pricing, inflated labor costs, and other Pentagon-procurement abuses proliferated as runaway military spending and slack regulation invited fraud. Defense contractors freely indulged in what Haynes Johnson of the *Washington Post* called "plunder in the name of patriotism." Arkansas senator David Pryor spoke of "an eight-year feeding frenzy at the Department of Defense." By 1985 nearly fifty Pentagon contractors had come under investigation.

The most unsavory of all federal agencies in the Reagan years was the Department of Housing and Urban Development (HUD), where top officials funneled millions in federal contracts to contractors and consultants with political connections. James Watt, for example, back in the private sector after his brief tenure as secretary of the interior, earned $420,000 by making a few telephone calls to HUD for friends. Other insiders profited handsomely for their role in securing HUD contracts. As the HUD scandals unfolded, even Reaganites held their noses. Conservative columnist James J. Kilpatrick wrote, "The more one hears of this rotten affair, the worse it gets."

Dedicated public servants still worked in Washington, but a climate of opportunism and greed hung over the capital. By 1989, 138 administration officials had run afoul of the law. Among Reagan's inner circle, deputy chief of staff Michael Deaver received a three-year suspended sentence for perjury related to influence-peddling charges. Lynn Nofziger's conviction under the 1978 Ethics in Government Act was later overturned on appeal. Edwin Meese underwent a fourteen-month criminal investigation by a special prosecutor on charges including bribe taking, filing a false income-tax return, and conflict of interest in his actions as attorney general. In 1988 Meese's two top aides resigned, disgusted by his official conduct. In the end, Meese escaped indictment.

The laissez-faire individualism and shriveled social vision of the Reagan presidency helped shape the larger culture of the 1980s. As in the Gilded Age and the 1920s, amassing wealth became a national obsession. President Reagan declared in 1983, "What I want to see above all is that this remains a country where someone can get rich." The 1960s had honored John Kennedy and Martin Luther King, Jr., as heroes; the eighties idolized entrepreneurs who flaunted their wealth and power. Donald Trump, a pudgy New York real-estate tycoon, became a celebrity for his flamboyant lifestyle and a 1987 book on dealmaking. Chrysler head Lee Iacocca revealed his success formulas in *Iacocca* (1985). Some pushed him for president. Leona Helmsley, wife of another New York real-estate baron, posed as the regal "Queen" in ads for one of her husband's hotels, the Helmsley Palace.

In the decade's go-go economic climate, high-flying dealmakers ruled Wall Street. The years 1985–87 saw twenty-one corporate mergers involving stock transfers of over $1 billion each. The torrent of mergers eventually totaled more than twenty-five thousand, many of them hostile takeovers by raiders seeking a quick killing. T. Boone Pickens, Ivan Boesky, Carl Icahn, and other raiders became household names. Having acquired a company, they wrote off weaker divisions as tax losses and sold the remaining units at huge profits. They ignored the impact of their maneuverings on workers or local communities.

Junk bonds, high-risk stocks offered to speculators attracted by possible vast profits, financed this wave of corporate takeovers, and young Michael Milken reigned as the junk-bond king. Displaying a genius for complex takeover deals, Milken directed the junk-bond division of the Drexel Burnham Lambert firm from his office in Beverly Hills. Using the telephone like a bodily appendage, he worked around the clock to set up intricate deals. His 1987 income, including profits on his own stock holdings, exceeded $1 billion. Milken's annual High Yield Bond Conference in Los Angeles earned a revealing nickname: the Predators' Ball.

The turbulent history of the savings-and-loan (S&L) industry exemplified the economic climate of the eighties. S&Ls had traditionally given small investors a modest but secure return on home-mortgage loans. The high interest rates of the late 1970s, however, had impelled S&Ls to raise *their* rates to attract deposits, even though much of their capital was tied up in low-interest mortgages. In the deregulated climate of the 1980s, many S&Ls resorted to risky investments and high-pressure marketing tactics to lure new depositors, some of whom invested their life savings. Congress increased federal insurance on S&L deposits from $20,000 to $100,000, attracting still more funds. Many S&Ls, especially in the Southwest, made large loans on high-risk commercial ventures: malls, apartment complexes, office towers, and so on. As S&L interest rates soared, full-page newspaper ads promised fantastic returns and generated an infusion of deposits that the S&Ls sank into ever more shaky real-estate projects.

As we shall see in Chapter 15, the giddy economic carnival of the Reagan years soon shuddered to a halt. As the economy turned sour, hundreds of S&Ls went bankrupt, and some S&L officials faced criminal indictments. The era of endless corporate takeovers, highly leveraged buyouts, and junk-bond millionaires faded. Ivan Boesky, Michael Milken, Leona Helmsley, and others went to jail for various white-collar crimes. Jerry Sterner's 1989 play, *Other People's Money,* dissected the get-rich-quick mania of the Reagan years and chronicled the destruction of a venerable New England firm by corporate raiders. Commented Sterner:

> There hasn't been a more selfish generation in the United States since this country was founded. . . . We suffer from a disease. . . . It's called instant gratification. We expect it from our politicians, our investments, . . . even our wars. We've come from an era of "What can I do for my country?" to "What's in it for me?" to "What's in it for me TODAY?"

Other writers, too, captured the decade's mood. In *Rabbit Is Rich* (1981), John Updike chronicled the success of his fictional hero Rabbit Angstrom as a prosperous Toyota dealer. Mystery writer Sara Paretsky examined the sleazy world of Yuppie lawyers and white-collar lawbreakers in 1980s Chicago in *Guardian Angel* (1992). And Tom Wolfe's *Bonfire of the Vanities* (1987) did for the eighties what F. Scott Fitzgerald had done for the twenties in *The Great Gatsby.* The novel offered a panorama of New York City life, from stockbrokers' Park Avenue penthouses to the harsh streets of Brooklyn and the South Bronx.

Reflecting the economic climate, the mass media became more consolidated as conglomerates swallowed up one company after another. By 1990 one such conglomerate, controlled by S. I. Newhouse, owned twenty-seven newspapers; the upscale magazines *Vanity Fair, Vogue, House and Garden,* and the *New Yorker;* and the publishing behemoth Random House. An infusion of foreign capital transformed the once-staid world of book publishing. The German corporation Bertelsmann, the Australian-born tycoon Rupert Murdoch, and the British press lord Robert Maxwell all acquired major U.S. publishing firms in the 1980s.

The consolidating process extended to the newspaper world as well. By 1986 twelve newspaper chains accounted for nearly half of total U.S. daily circulation. The ultimate generic newspaper, *USA Today,* had appeared in 1978. With its color graphics and human-interest stories, *USA Today* lacked regional flavor or editorial distinctiveness. This concentration of media ownership muffled the intellectual diversity and clash of opinion on which a healthy democracy and vibrant culture depend.

The movie industry, too, reeled under a wave of corporate takeovers. Gulf + Western Corporation acquired Paramount Studios. Time Inc. bought Warner Communications, already an entertainment octopus, for $13 billion in 1989. At the same time, the movie studios entered TV production and sold their film libraries to TV networks or to independents like Ted Turner, whose Atlanta superstation broadcast nationwide via satellite. The Disney Corporation not only made movies but produced TV series, owned a record company, and ran theme parks in Florida and California. By the late eighties, the mass-culture industry had become so interconnected that the tangled relationships nearly defied sorting out.

As with the print media, foreign capital poured into the entertainment industry in the 1980s. Japan's SONY Corporation acquired Columbia Pictures for $3.4 billion in 1989. The Matsushita Corporation, a leader in consumer electronics, snapped up MCA-Universal, another U.S. media conglomerate, for $7 billion. Bertelsmann bought RCA Records, and Rupert Murdoch gained control of 20th-Century Fox. By 1990 four of the five top U.S. record companies were foreign owned. Sustained by multinational corporate investment and multibillion-dollar deals, U.S. mass culture in the 1980s extended its reach to every realm of national life. The nation's inner cities might be decaying, the schools in crisis, and class divisions widening, but the vast machinery of commercial amusement hummed on.

Early in the twentieth century, John Dewey and other intellectuals had noted the paradox of economic consolidation at a time when society seemed to be fragmenting in other ways. A similar phenomenon happened in the 1970s and 1980s. As individualist ideologies reigned supreme, corporate consolidation proceeded rapidly. The United States seemed able to achieve in the economic arena the cohesion that eluded it in the civic realm. Underscoring the paradox, an increasingly consolidated mass media targeted a more and more segmented market. As a result, the common culture eroded further, and the outlets for civic discourse diminished. While thoughtful periodicals such as *Harper's* and the *Atlantic Monthly* limped along, special-interest periodicals focused on narrow market niches. Magazine publishers targeted readers interested in photography, golf, the Civil War, antiques, travel, computers, fitness, specific cities and regions, and countless other topics.

Radio grew more segmented as well, as stations targeted particular audiences. Some featured news; others offered nonstop call-in programs; still others catered to musical tastes ranging from "Top 40" and "Easy Listening" to country, religious, and rock. Stations for black and Hispanic listeners proliferated. National Public Radio (NPR) had begun in 1971 with funding from the federal government and listener contributions. By the eighties, some three hundred noncommercial public-radio stations appealed to affluent, well-educated listeners with classical music, jazz, and in-depth news analysis.

Technology promoted both the segmentation and the privatization of popular culture. For example, the rise of cable TV splintered the viewing audience among

IN PERSPECTIVE: *Politicians, the Media, and Campaign-Finance Reform*

❖❖

No matter how people differed about Ronald Reagan's political ideology, on one point everyone agreed: He was a master of television. And small wonder—Reagan was, after all, a trained actor. As one staff member later recalled, whenever the cameras focused on Reagan and he began to speak, they could relax: The master was in control.

In one sense, this was nothing new. American politicians have loved (or loved to hate) the media for two centuries. In the earliest days of the Republic, long before CNN or Larry King, newspapers left no doubt about their political allegiance. As early as the 1790s, some newspapers tirelessly promoted the Federalist party of John Adams and Alexander Hamilton; other papers just as vigorously championed the emerging Republican party of Thomas Jefferson.

By the campaign of 1840, when the Whig William Henry Harrison ran against the Democrat Martin Van Buren, the politics of media imagemaking were in full swing. Serious issues faced the nation, but the campaign mainly involved mudslinging newspaper editorials and raucous torch-light parades at which Harrison supporters carried miniature log cabins and swigged hard cider, symbolizing their candidate's allegedly humble Western origins. In fact, Harrison was of aristocratic Virginia stock, and the Whigs were the party of the well-to-do, but in the arena of media manipulation, facts have never been a serious impediment. No president was above the allure of the media. When John Wilkes Booth shot Abraham Lincoln at Ford's Theater in April 1865, Lincoln was carrying in his pocket a well-thumbed packet of press clippings.

By the early twentieth century the media had expanded beyond newspapers to include radio and film, and politicians quickly adapted. Just as contemporary presidents invite sports heroes and celebrities to the White House to bask in their reflected glory, so did earlier chief executives. When Charles A. Lindbergh became an instant celebrity in 1927 for his solo flight across the Atlantic, President Calvin Coolidge quickly invited him to Washington for a joint press appearance.

President Franklin D. Roosevelt was a legendary master of radio, and the media fully cooperated in concealing Roosevelt's inability to walk: Movie newsreels and newspaper photos invariably showed a jaunty, vigorous Roosevelt seated at his desk, relaxing in a comfortable chair, riding in a car, or occasionally standing at a podium, but never in a wheelchair or painfully walking with crutches, dragging the heavy steel of his leg braces.

---

an array of channels. By 1989 the three major networks' audience share had shrunk to 61 percent. Many viewers now watched channels specializing in religion, business, black interests, sports, and so on. Direct-marketing channels hawked jewelry, cosmetics, fashions, and kitchenware. Viewers could catch first-run movies on Home Box Office, continual news on CNN, erotica on the Playboy Channel, and

Both John F. Kennedy and Richard Nixon played the media like a violin. At the height of Kennedymania in the early 1960s, the media vied to publish photographs or transmit TV images of the handsome young president with his beautiful, adoring, whispery-voiced wife and their two sweet children. Nary a hint of Kennedy's incessant philandering—including romps with young women in the White House swimming pool when Jackie went traveling—reached the public until long after his death. As for Nixon, aficionados of media manipulation still speak in awed tones of the 1952 "Checkers" speech, in which he tearfully dragged in the family dog as he wheedled his way back into public favor after revelations of a secret campaign fund contributed by wealthy backers.

But while the symbiotic relationship between politics and the media has been a part of American public life from the beginning, there is also no question that the advent of television raised the stakes immeasurably. The dominance of the catchy sound bite, the attack ad, and the soft-focus image of family togetherness—with its inevitable corollary, the decline of serious discussion of complex issues—increased enormously in the decades after 1950.

So, too, did the price tag of running for office in an era when the key to victory was no longer the public forum where serious matters were discussed, but the professionally crafted media campaign. At all levels, from the presidency down to judgeships and mayoral races, television added enormously to the cost of campaigning, turning politicians into nonstop fundraisers and leading to endless discussions of—but little action on—campaign-finance reform. Some proposed much shorter campaigns, in the British manner; others suggested that TV stations be required to provide free time to all candidates to debate the issues on a regular basis, as an alternative to paid commercials and evening-news sound bites.

But campaign-finance reform, too, has been around for a long time. In 1883, after President James A. Garfield was shot by a disappointed (and insane) officeseeker, Congress passed the Pendleton Act, which, among other provisions, forbade political candidates from soliciting contributions from federal workers. In 1939, disgruntled congressional Republicans, suspecting that WPA relief funds and New Deal arts and theater programs had been manipulated to influence the 1938 congressional elections, passed the Hatch Act forbidding federal employees from participating in electoral campaigns.

Whether the latest drive for campaign-finance reform will succeed remains to be seen. So, too, does the question of whether American politicians can ever wean themselves from the fifteen-second sound bite and the manipulative TV commercial to once again address the electorate in a thoughtful way, as Abraham Lincoln and Stephen A. Douglas did in 1858, when they conducted a senatorial campaign by debating the vital issues of the day in long, grueling face-to-face debates up and down the state of Illinois. What a concept!

even gavel-to-gavel coverage of Congress on C-Span. Another new technology promoting privatized leisure, the videocassette recorder (VCR), enabled people to record TV shows for later viewing and to watch rented movies at home. Introduced in the 1960s, VCRs enjoyed explosive growth in the 1980s. By mid-decade, 70 percent of American homes had VCRs.

Ironically, the mass-culture industry itself offered sharp-edged critiques of its own manipulative techniques. In *Network* (1976), a movie satirizing television news, a network desperate for higher ratings promotes a mentally disturbed newscaster (played by Peter Finch) as "the mad prophet of the airwaves," with Faye Dunaway as an ambitious programmer willing to do anything to increase the network's audience share. In the 1987 film *Broadcast News*, actor William Hurt played a cynical TV news anchor who resorts to fakery and deception to further his career. Despite such exposés of the media's strategies to expand their audience (thereby allowing them to charge higher advertising rates), the public seemed passively to accept more of the same.

In his 1953 novel *Fahrenheit 451,* Ray Bradbury had imagined a citizenry for whom the world of the media was the only reality; by the 1980s, some found Bradbury's nightmare disturbingly at hand. The Walkman—a radio and tape cassette unit worn on the head, muting the sounds of the outside world—symbolized a larger trend toward privatized pleasure and away from social engagement. Nineteen-fifties social critics had feared a blandly homogeneous, standardized culture. By the 1980s, the question had sharpened: Could a highly segmented populace caught up in socially isolating patterns of consumption and mass-media diversion sustain a common public discourse or even a sense of community?

One mass-culture trend remained glaringly obvious: television's dominance. Average daily viewing time crept to nearly seven hours by 1990, up from about six hours in 1970. In a 1976 survey, 51 percent of Americans rated television their "most believable" news source; only 22 percent described newspapers in this way. Ironically, the big magazine success of the postwar era was *TV Guide,* founded in 1952. With rare exceptions, the masters of this ubiquitous medium continued to aim abysmally low in the 1980s. Escapism, violence, and sexual innuendo filled the screen. The popular *A-Team* featured cartoon cut-out crime fighters. The successful *Miami Vice* offered music videos and fashion statements in the guise of limp police drama.

The FCC's lax regulation under Reagan made television more than ever a vehicle for commerce. By 1990 annual TV ad revenues surpassed $26 billion. Enormous talent and technical expertise went into producing commercials for cars, breakfast cereals, pet food, breath fresheners, and hemorrhoid remedies. A parade of Saturday morning children's cartoons with formulaic plots and simulated violence peddled plastic toys and sugared breakfast cereals. Even public TV's award-winning educational program *Sesame Street* sparked criticism for mimicking commercial TV. "Commercials" for "the letter R" or "the number 7," for example, further acculturated children to actual TV ads and the consumerist ethos that lay behind them.

The link between television and professional sports tightened in the 1980s. A thirty-second commercial during the Super Bowl could cost as much as $675,000. By 1990 the Super Bowl accounted for eight of the ten largest audiences in TV history. Contract negotiations between the professional sports leagues and the networks became major corporate events. Details of superstars' multimillion-dollar contracts and product endorsements filled the sports pages. Because the big-money professional sports were mostly male dominated, television sharpened the disparity in the attention given to men's and women's sports at the high school and college levels.

Critics deplored television's effects on politics. In *Amusing Ourselves to Death* (1985), Neil Postman contrasted the infantile level of TV campaigning to the more elevated public discourse of the nineteenth century, as exemplified by the Lincoln-Douglas debates. Indeed, from 1968 to 1988, the average TV "sound bite" in reporting presidential campaigns shrank from 42 to 10 seconds.* TV's role in the electoral process, already great by the 1960s, increased in the 1980s. Haynes Johnson of the *Washington Post* perceptively wrote, "Ronald Reagan and television fitted into American society like a plug into a socket. . . . He was the Sun King, presiding over the new national celebration from the White House. Under his reign, all lines blurred; news and entertainment, politics and advertising." In one example of the power of visual images, Leslie Stahl of ABC News showed scenes of Reagan's visit to the Special Olympics (an event for physically impaired competitors) during the 1984 campaign. As the segment played, Stahl read a report documenting the administration's spending cuts on programs for the handicapped. To Stahl's surprise, a Reagan media adviser called to thank her for the wonderful story. When she reminded him of her negative commentary, he taunted her, "Nobody heard what you said. They just saw the five minutes of beautiful pictures of Ronald Reagan. They saw the balloons, they saw the flags, they saw the red, white, and blue. Haven't you people figured out yet that the picture always overrides what you say?"

The Reagan-era ethos found its TV apotheosis in the prime-time soap opera *Dallas,* which chronicled the business deals and torrid sex life of oilman J. R. Ewing. Another popular show explored "Lifestyles of the Rich and Famous." Fantasy and reality blurred when Reagan's first wife, Jane Wyman, starred in *Falcon Crest,* another TV drama of intrigues among the wealthy. By contrast, America's minorities, migrant workers, rural poor, and others left behind in the glitzy 1980s rarely appeared on TV. The popular *Cosby Show,* a throwback to 1950s domestic sitcoms, portrayed the family of an affluent black professional couple but ignored the far larger portion of the black population: the inner-city poor.

The differences over Vietnam that in the 1960s had raged in the streets erupted again in the 1980s, this time on the cultural front. While films such as *The Deer Hunter* (1978), *Platoon* (1986), and *Born on the Fourth of July* (1989) explored the experience of combat and the war's psychological toll, Sylvester Stallone's *Rambo* (1985) offered a comic-strip version of the war in which America triumphs, as the national mythology held that it should. Even Maya Ying Lin's design for the Vietnam Veterans Memorial raised angry disputes. Some found the listing of the dead on a black marble wall somber and defeatist and demanded a monument emphasizing military valor instead. Texas billionaire Ross Perot campaigned for a more conventionally patriotic memorial. In the end, a group statue was erected near the memorial wall, but its three young soldiers look more fatigued and uncomprehending than heroic.

Among Hollywood mixed fare in the 1980s, the most successful movies provided fantasy and diversion. Stephen Spielberg's fairy tale *E.T.* (1982), for example, recounted the friendship between a small boy and a lost wanderer from outer space. *E.T.* fans praised it as a parable of cross-cultural understanding, but a wave

---

* A sound bite is a catchy phrase uttered by a politician in hopes that it will be shown on TV.

of escapist movies with little apparent social significance soon followed. *Porky's* (1982) offered a steamy adolescent fantasy of life and sex among 1950s teenagers. In the series of cartoonlike *Rocky* movies, Sylvester Stallone played a prizefighter who prevails over various fearsome opponents. Apart from the better Vietnam films, the real world rarely impinged, even in fictional form, on such fare. In one notable exception, the 1987 hit *Wall Street,* Michael Douglas played a corporate buccaneer who gets his comeuppance. Douglas also costarred in *Fatal Attraction* (1987), in which a psychotic career woman (Glenn Close) nearly destroys his marriage after a weekend sexual fling. To some critics, the movie tapped into a rising level of hostility toward professional women.

Pop music increasingly involved the high-tech marketing of images. On MTV, a pop-music channel, rock groups and singers lip-synched their hits in minidramas called music videos. Michael Jackson, a global superstar, became a reclusive eccentric whose androgynous and racially ambiguous image heightened his mystique. Madonna blatantly flaunted her sexuality as she branched out from popular music to movies, TV videos, and concert tours.

Music-reproduction technology continued its long evolution with the advent of the compact disc (CD) in 1982. The CD, in which laser beams "read" dots molded into concentric circles on a metallic disk, provided remarkably high fidelity, although some found the sound, like the decade, a bit sterile. On Broadway, the 1980s saw the rise of extravagant sound-and-light shows whose flashy production outshone the music or the story. The most successful of these high-tech musicals, *Les Misérables,* derived, ironically, from Victor Hugo's tale of the poor of Paris.

Personal computers, the hot new data-processing technology of the 1970s, proliferated in the 1980s. By 1988 some 45 million Americans owned PCs. Students now took PCs rather than typewriters to college. Even small businesses did their recordkeeping by computer. Library research speeded up enormously as continually updated electronic databases replaced card catalogs and bulky multivolume indexes. The number of public schools using PCs in instruction rose from 1,035 in 1985 to 2,355 four years later. Some visionaries foresaw a day when computer instruction would render human teachers largely superfluous.

Critics worried that the new technologies of entertainment and communication would produce a generation that experienced life vicariously as computer bytes, TV images, or aural messages emanating from a CD player. In a media-dominated world, they feared, both the capacity to respond to direct experience and the sense of social connectedness would atrophy.

As in earlier decades, TV roused criticism for allegedly producing a nation of "couch potatoes" who passively absorbed an endless stream of programming in the isolation of their living rooms. A car-bomb explosion in Beirut, starving children in Ethiopia, upheavals in Eastern Europe, a drive-by shooting, a fashion show at a suburban mall, reports of the dreadful new disease AIDS, commercials for perfumes and weight-loss products—all flickered by on the tube, creating a mishmash of unconnected sensory impressions. One critic described Americans as "metaphorically chained to their TV screen and, like Plato's cave dwellers, blind to the real world behind them, unable to differentiate between shadow and substance." Such judgments overstated the passivity of mass-culture consumers and understated the degree to which Americans remained linked to actual social networks and the real world through family, church, neighborhood, and work. Nevertheless, the media's dominance raised legitimate concerns.

Mass culture remained America's hottest export and helped to reduce the trade deficit. The *Economist* of London summed matters up in 1989: "America is to entertainment what South Africa is to gold and Saudi Arabia is to oil." By the late 1980s, the U.S. entertainment industry earned $5.5 billion annually in foreign exchange. The U.S. music industry, mainly rock and other pop genres, garnered 70 percent of its revenues from overseas sales. One show-business executive commented, "Hollywood, unlike Detroit, has found a product that the Japanese can't improve on."

The world's image of America increasingly derived from mass-culture exports. A Jamaican journalist bitterly noted, "Because of what they see on television, everyone in Jamaica thinks . . . that everything in America is wonderful. . . . It makes people think that money and material wealth are the only ways to be rich in this world." Certainly American democracy continued to inspire other peoples in the 1980s, particularly in regions breaking free of communism. But the mass media exported another image of the United States as well: a society of self-seeking individuals absorbed in the pursuit of money, amusement, and material possessions.

Amid rampant individualism, the sense of community waned. In *Habits of the Heart: Individualism and Commitment in American Life* (1985), the University of California sociologist Robert Bellah and four colleagues examined contemporary U.S. society and found it wanting. The title echoed Alexis de Tocqueville's warning in *Democracy in America* (1835) of an individualism so powerful that each citizen would be "shut up in the solitude of his own heart." Probing the historic roots of the American obsession with the self, the authors speculated that in modern America this extreme individualism had been severed from a balancing social vision. Their interviews with middle-class men and women revealed a pervasive longing for stronger communal bonds. The search for an alternative to radical individualism, they suggested, could lead back to religion and to republican political thought, with its stress on the common good and its sense of shared obligations. "Our problems today," they concluded, "are not just political. They . . . have to do with the meaning of life. . . . We are beginning to understand that our common life requires more than an exclusive concern for material accumulation."

Critics of *Habits of the Heart* questioned its sermonlike tone and its assumption that a recovered religious or even "republican" tradition could give rise to a new sense of community. Yet Bellah's picture of middle-class America at the high noon of Reaganism was disturbing.

And what of democratic self-government and the general welfare in a society caught up in individualistic pursuits? The decade's media-dominated politics and socially barren ideology added immediacy to these perennial questions. Benjamin Barber, commenting in *Harper's* magazine on the individualistic theme of Reagan's second inaugural address, offered a sharply critical assessment:

> [T]he great American dream has always been a *public* dream. . . . Entrepreneurs may make money, but only citizens can make justice. The struggle for common goods–clean air, justice, peace–is a common struggle in which democratic govern-

ment is our only ally. President Reagan asks much of individuals but nothing of citizens; he burdens the market with demands for progress and prosperity, but of the community and the government that is the community's instrument he asks nothing.

Ronald Reagan's farewell address, delivered on January 11, 1989, proved a vintage performance. After highlighting his achievements and gliding over failures, he concluded with a lump-in-the-throat call for a rebirth of patriotism.

Reagan's popularity had remained high throughout his two terms, enhanced by prosperity and the sudden outbreak of peace. Insiders, however, depicted a remote, uninvolved figure. In part, these traits reflected the infirmities of age, but more than any other president in memory, Reagan was a performer—the "Great Communicator"—smiling on cue and reading speeches with consummate acting skill. As one astute biographer observed, "Acting took early hold of him, and never let him go." Unconcerned with details and most at ease in front of the camera, Reagan seemed more a master of ceremonies than a president. Tom Shales of the *Washington Post* commented, "Historians can decide if Ronald Reagan was a great president, but any TV viewer can see he has been a great leading man." During White House briefings, Reagan displayed shocking ignorance of basic issues and relied instead on shopworn anecdotes. Supporters contended that he preferred to sketch broad goals while leaving details to others. Yet his tendency to reduce complex issues to formulaic bromides represented a triumph of ideology over pragmatism rare in U.S. politics.

The most damaging picture of the Reagan presidency came from insiders. David Stockman revealed not only the cynicism of the Reagan economic plan but also the intellectual vacuity of the White House inner circle. Donald Reagan, forced out during the Iran-contra scandal, got his revenge in a book that portrayed his boss as a puppet controlled by his handlers: "He listened, acquiesced, played his role, and waited for the next act to be written." A daily schedule leaked to the press showed that Reagan's every public word was scripted, down to the most trivial small talk. Insiders also described the behind-the-scenes power of Nancy Reagan, who sometimes planned her husband's trips on the basis of astrological advice. Mrs. Reagan epitomized the materialism of the era as well, wearing high-fashion gowns on loan from New York couturiers delighted by the free advertising.

To his admirers, Reagan had restored patriotism, rebuilt an eroded military, ended inflation, stimulated the economy, and reaffirmed the old verities of individualism and self-reliance. One of his fans, Great Britain's conservative prime minister Margaret Thatcher, affirmed, "He has left America stronger, prouder, greater than ever before." But skeptics saw him as substituting right-wing rhetoric for serious policy analysis and, with his ridicule of "the government," contributing to a corrosive cynicism about politics. Certainly Reagan was likeable, with impulsive warmth when confronted with individual need. But the ideology that he so artfully championed revealed an impoverished social vision.

Reagan's critics are left to account for his phenomenal popularity, certified by two sweeping electoral victories to which millions of "Reagan Democrats" contributed. Of the old New Deal coalition, only black Americans resisted the lure of Reaganism; the white working class defected in droves. Journalist Garry Wills in

Reagan's America (1987) saw Reagan's serene confidence as one key to his appeal: "Self-assurance reassures others, and that has not been the least of Reagan's gifts to us, at a time when the nation needed some reassuring." The *Albuquerque Journal,* in assessing Reagan's farewell address, acknowledged the thinness of his "Don't worry, be happy" message but concluded that what had been true in 1981 remained true in 1989: "America really likes Ronald Reagan."

Ultimately, the issue is not Reagan as a person but his policies. The "Reagan revolution" cut social services and ratcheted up the arms race while emasculating federal regulatory agencies and shifting resources away from the neediest Americans. Celebrators of the top-down prosperity of the mid- and later 1980s typically ignored problems such as the trade gap and the growing federal deficit. They also overlooked the plight of lower-income Americans and urban minorities, as well as displaced industrial workers and even struggling members of the middle class.

In retrospect, the eighties seem years of drift, with rhetoric supplanting substance and short-term private gain substituting for long-term public advance. Reagan did not single-handedly cause the materialism, selfishness, and vulgarity of the 1980s, but his endless praise of unrestrained individualism encouraged some of the era's less appealing features. Urgent national issues—from inner-city joblessness, troubled schools, and drug abuse to environmental threats, the AIDS epidemic, and health care—suffered neglect as persons intent on quick gain set the political and cultural tone. Despite Reagan's personal decency and kindly manner, the decade to which he gave his name offered little by way of inspiration or guidance to the future. Instead, Reagan primarily bequeathed to his successors an array of festering problems.

Campaign '88

In 1988, Vice President George Bush claimed his chance at the top spot. As Bush won a string of primaries, challengers including televangelist Pat Robertson and Kansas senator Bob Dole fell by the wayside, and the nomination was his. Bush's acceptance speech evoked a psychological mood rather than proposing a program as he called for "a kinder, and gentler nation." He also pledged, "Read my lips: No new taxes." Bush tapped Indiana senator Dan Quayle, son of a conservative newspaper publisher, as his running mate. Few discerned presidential qualities in Quayle, and doubts about him deepened with revelations that during the Vietnam War, which his family's newspapers had supported, he had pulled strings to avoid the draft.

Among the Democratic aspirants, Jesse Jackson, again the favorite among African Americans, bettered his 1984 showing with white voters in several state primaries. But the field quickly thinned. Senator Gary Hart of Colorado withdrew after the *Miami Herald* revealed his affair with a Florida model. The ultimate victor was Governor Michael Dukakis of Massachusetts, a Greek American whose state had prospered in the 1980s, in part because the military buildup had showered contracts on the electronics and computer industries around Boston. As his running mate, he chose Senator Lloyd Bentsen of Texas. Dukakis initially surged to a wide lead in the polls. Democrats saw Bush, with his penchant for malapropisms,

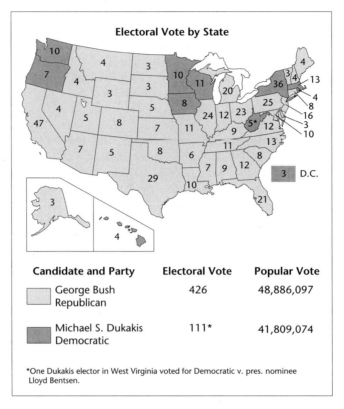

FIGURE 14.4
Presidential Election of 1988

as an easy target. "Poor George," gibed one Democratic leader, "he was born with a silver foot in his mouth."

But Dukakis's lead soon evaporated. An inept campaigner, he bored even fellow Democrats. He refused to challenge the Reagan-Bush ideology and instead stressed his alleged administrative competence. By contrast, Bush pointed to the new jobs, reduced world tensions, and low inflation of the 1980s. Naturally, he ignored the budget deficit and Iran-contra scandal, as well as other embarrassments. The Bush forces further damaged Dukakis with insidious TV commercials. The most notorious of these featured Willie Horton, a black convict who had committed rape and murder while on a weekend pass under a Massachusetts prisoner-furlough program. Implying that Dukakis was soft on crime, the commercial also subtly exploited racial stereotypes. Both sides pandered to the ubiquitous television cameras: Bush visited flag factories; Dukakis posed in an army tank. With the candidates marketed as if they were deodorants, serious debate rarely interrupted the sound bites and photo opportunities.

Aided by prosperity and Dukakis's ineffective campaign, Bush grabbed 54 percent of the popular vote. Carrying forty states, including vital California and Texas, he dominated the electoral tally 426–112. Dukakis claimed only ten states plus the

District of Columbia. Except for West Virginia, he lost every southern and border state. Yet despite Bush's triumph, voters returned Democratic majorities to Congress. This outcome reflected the advantage of incumbency in good times, reinforced by heavy PAC contributions. The White House thus was controlled by one party and Congress by the other, with neither inclined to cooperate. The resulting impasse contributed to four years of what by 1992 would come to be called "gridlock."

Marking Time: The Bush Interlude

George Herbert Walker Bush, the son of a Connecticut senator, epitomized New England's WASP elite. An Episcopalian and avid sportsman, he attended a private academy and then Yale College, where he led the baseball team and gained admission to the venerable secret society Skull and Bones. In World War II, Bush flew fifty-nine bombing missions, was shot down, and won the Distinguished Flying Cross. After the war he married Barbara Pierce, daughter of a prominent magazine publisher, and moved to Texas, where he entered the oil business. He turned to politics, winning election to Congress in 1966, but lost to Lloyd Bentsen in a 1970 Senate race. Out of his Texas years came a close friendship (tempered by a well-concealed rivalry) with James Baker III, an astute alter ego whom Bush would appoint as secretary of state.

In the 1970s Bush held various appointive posts, including CIA director. As vice president, he avoided entanglement in the Iran-contra affair but also gained a reputation for opportunism. On the abortion issue, for example, he abandoned a long-held pro-choice position and courted the antiabortion vote. "I will do anything to win," Bush once candidly told an interviewer. His gauzy inaugural address called on Americans to ignite "a thousand points of light" and to view the future as "a door you can walk right through into a room called tomorrow."

As Bush uttered these banalities, a series of stunning events were unfolding abroad—events that cumulatively spelled nothing less than the end of the Cold War. The upheavals in the Soviet Union and Eastern Europe accelerated early in Bush's term. In 1989, as communist regimes long propped up by Soviet power collapsed, Lech Walesa of Poland's independent labor movement Solidarity and Václav Havel, a Czech playwright and former political prisoner, were elected presidents of their nations. In Rumania, the dictatorship of Nicolae Ceausescu and his wife ended as the pair was hunted down and shot.

Most amazing of all was the lightening pace of events in Germany. Unrest rumbled across East Germany in the summer of 1989, as demonstrators boldly protested the oppressive regime headed by the aging hard-line communist Erich Honecker. With Honecker's forced resignation in October, his successor, Egon Krenz, nervously promised reforms. But few anticipated what would come next. On the evening of November 9, in a move that would have been unthinkable only a short time before, Krenz opened the Berlin Wall. As the news spread, jubilant Berliners flocked to the squat gray barrier that had long bisected their city. Their celebration continued far into the night. At the historic Brandenburg Gate, near what had once been Hitler's Reichstag, young people danced atop the wall. Others used hammers and chisels to chip off souvenir bits of cement.

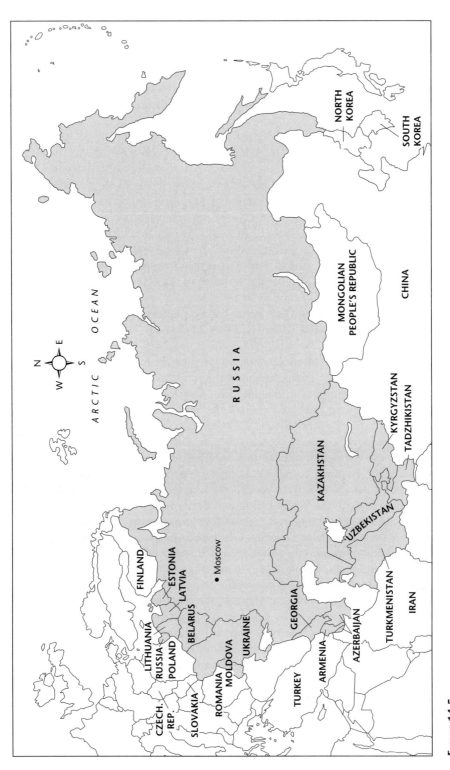

FIGURE 14.5
The Former Soviet Union

The next day, East Berliners by the tens of thousands poured through once heavily guarded checkpoints for their first view of life beyond the wall. One woman, overwhelmed by the shops along West Berlin's glittering and elegant Kurfürstendamm, murmured, "There is so much color, so much light. It's incredible." A blind man came with his seeing-eye dog. "I just wanted to smell the air of a free Berlin," he explained. Another East Berliner returned several books to a West Berlin library that he had borrowed twenty-eight years earlier, the day before the wall went up in 1961. "Berlin Is Berlin Again!" shouted the city's newspapers. Soon after, Leonard Bernstein conducted a gala performance of Beethoven's stirring Ninth Symphony in the reunited metropolis, restoring *Freiheit* ("Freedom") for *Freude* ("Joy") in the choral movement. The opening of the Wall proved the prelude to the collapse of East Germany's communist regime. The division of Germany, a legacy of World War II, ended in October 1990 as the Bonn government assumed power over all Germany.

Soon the Soviet Union itself fragmented. Mikhail Gorbachev had hoped to introduce democratic socialism while preserving the Soviet Union and heading a reformed Communist party. But in 1991 the forces that he had unleashed overwhelmed him. As the party's grip weakened, the Soviet economy faltered and nationalism reawakened in the Soviet republics. The three Baltic republics of Estonia, Latvia, and Lithuania gained their independence. In August, Soviet military officers alarmed by the pace of change staged a coup and briefly held Gorbachev captive. President Boris Yeltsin of the Russian Republic, backed by a mass outpouring of Muscovites, defied the coup leaders' tanks and restored Gorbachev to freedom. But Yeltsin himself, riding a tide of Russian nationalism and revulsion against communist rule, soon muscled Gorbachev aside. Later in 1991, the Soviet Union formally split up, its fifteen republics forming an amorphous Commonwealth of Independent States. The Communist party collapsed, and Gorbachev suddenly found himself a private citizen. Europe's last great empire had dissolved into a jumble of new nations torn by ethnic turmoil, border disputes, and economic problems, united only in their repudiation of bolshevism. Statues of communist leaders toppled; Leningrad resumed its ancient name of St. Petersburg. In May 1992, speaking at Westminister College in Missouri, the scene of Churchill's "Iron Curtain" address of 1946, Gorbachev declared the Cold War over.

For Americans reared on "the Soviet threat," the change proved difficult to absorb. Relief, disorientation, and residual mistrust vied for dominance. As John Updike's Harry Angstrom reflected in *Rabbit at Rest* (1990), "It's like nobody's in charge of the other side any more. I miss it, the cold war. It gave you a reason to get up in the morning." For Russia and the other former Soviet republics, the transition from a state-run economy to a free-market system on the Western model—but without commercial banks, investment capital, or a free-enterprise tradition—proved monumentally difficult. As Russia's economy foundered, Yeltsin urgently sought Western help. Washington dragged its feet, but in 1992, prodded by Richard Nixon, Bush proposed a $35 billion aid package. Russian leaders, as well as some Western economists, urged a far more ambitious program lest Russia revert to despotic rule.

The Cold War's end accelerated the arms-control process. In August 1991 President Bush flew to Moscow to sign the START treaty cutting the two nations' nuclear arsenals by one-quarter. In June 1992, Boris Yeltsin, in Washington seeking aid, accepted still deeper cuts in ICBMs. Tacitly conceding the altered balance of power, Yeltsin agreed to give up all of Russia's land-based MIRV missiles, whereas the United States would cut its submarine missile force only by half. The Russian president also pledged to deactivate all missiles targeted on the United States.

NATO and the Soviet-sponsored Warsaw Pact signed a nonaggression agreement in 1990. With the Warsaw Pact's collapse soon after, NATO announced a 50 percent troop reduction. For decades, the existence of a common foe had cemented the Western alliance. With the Soviet threat gone and with Western Europeans forging a single economic bloc, the question of America's future relationship with Western Europe gained urgency. Indeed, the end of the Cold War disoriented U.S. foreign policy, long grounded in the single theme of anticommunism. From Truman to Reagan, containment of the U.S.S.R. had given coherence to American diplomacy. Suddenly the old formulas seemed irrelevant. Unlike the Nixon-Kissinger team, Bush had no grand strategy; he simply reacted to events as they occurred. Like Nixon, Bush savored the role of world leader, but although he served in stirring times, he did little to put his personal imprint on U.S. foreign policy.

The new era rattled the Pentagon too. Bush's secretary of defense, Dick Cheney, proposed a 4 percent annual reduction in military spending and a 25 percent cut in the military over five years. Democrat Les Aspin, chair of the House Armed Services Committee, advocated doubling Cheney's proposed cuts. Whatever the levels, job losses were inevitable. At the peak of the Reagan buildup, annual military spending had neared $375 billion, and 1.4 million Americans had worked in military-related jobs. By 1992 military spending had fallen below $300 billion, and defense jobs declined by some 200,000.

Bush won plaudits for his performance during the Persian Gulf War of 1990–91, but the long-term results proved ambiguous. On August 2, 1990, Iraq invaded its neighbor, the tiny but oil-rich Kuwait, with which it had a long-running dispute over control of the vast Rumaila oil field. Iraqi dictator Saddam Hussein, eager to gain access to the Persian Gulf, claimed that historically Iraq had ruled Kuwait. Even before the attack, Saddam had roused fears with his anti-Israel threats, his hostility to other Arab states, and his nuclear- and chemical-weapons research. Nevertheless, during Iraq's war with Iran (1980–88), Washington had given Saddam weapons and satellite intelligence to aid his battle against Tehran's anti-American Shiites. Using an Italian bank as a front, the Reagan White House and the CIA had secretly funneled weapons, electronics, and computers to Saddam. The flow of aid and military hardware had increased under George Bush, even though the Iran-Iraq war had ended and Iran had softened its anti-American tone after Ayatollah Khomeini's death of 1989.

With Saddam's invasion of Kuwait, President Bush suddenly shifted gears. Comparing the Iraqi strongman to Hitler, Bush denounced the attack on Kuwait as a threat to regional stability and a violation of international law. Perhaps most important, Saddam's action jeopardized two major oil producers with close ties to the West, not only Kuwait but also neighboring Saudi Arabia.

The Reality of War: Kuwait, 1991. *In a scene from the Persian Gulf War that did not appear on prime-time television, three GIs impassively consider the body of an Iraqi soldier incinerated by American firepower. (© 1991 Peter Turnley/Black Star)*

A unanimous UN Security Council slapped trade sanctions on Iraq, ordered its withdrawal from Kuwait by January 15, 1991, and authorized member states to use "all means necessary" to achieve this end. The Pentagon rushed U.S. air and sea power to the Persian Gulf and deployed 400,000 ground forces in Saudi Arabia. Bush assembled a coalition of nations led by the Saudis, Great Britain, Egypt, and France. Avoiding LBJ's mistake in Vietnam, he cultivated home-front backing by defining the issues starkly: resisting aggression and protecting U.S. strategic interests. He then spelled out his goal: Iraq's withdrawal from Kuwait.

On January 12, 1991, over the opposition of Democrats who argued for more time to allow the sanctions to take effect, both houses of Congress authorized military action. Four days later, the Allies launched Operation Desert Storm under U.S. commander General H. Norman Schwarzkopf. For a week, 2,000 Allied warplanes rained bombs on Iraqi forces in Kuwait, military targets in Iraq, and strategic sites in Baghdad itself. On February 23, after U.S. Marines feinted an amphibious assault, 200,000 ground forces moved across the desert into Kuwait. What Saddam called "the mother of all battles" proved pitiably one-sided. U.S. forces destroyed 3,700 Iraqi tanks, while losing only 3. The United States counted 467 wounded and 148 dead, 35 of whom were killed accidentally by U.S. fire. An estimated 100,000 Iraqis died, both soldiers and civilians. The war's most dramatic moments came when Iraq, trying to provoke another Arab-Israeli war, fired Soviet-made Scud missiles against Tel Aviv and other targets in Israel as well as at

U.S. staging areas in Saudi Arabia. U.S. Patriot missiles destroyed most incoming Scuds or threw them off course by exploding in their general vicinity. Americans watched fascinated as CNN broadcast scenes of the aerial fireworks live.

Indeed, the whole war played well on TV. Unlike the harrowing scenes from Vietnam, death or human suffering rarely intruded on the images of surrendering Iraqis and abandoned Iraqi equipment. This was no accident; having learned the lesson of Vietnam, the Pentagon restricted press access to the war. The skillfully edited shots of bombs exploding on distant targets, some filmed through the bomb-sights of U.S. aircraft, resembled the simulated combat of video games.

As Americans savored the media-enhanced victory, Bush gloated, "By God, we've licked the Vietnam syndrome once and for all." Before a wildly cheering Congress, Bush proclaimed: "We hear so often about our young people in turmoil; how our children fall short; how our schools fail us; how American products and American workers are second-class. Well, don't you believe it. The America we saw in Desert Storm was first-class talent." Bush's approval rating spurted to 89 percent; Schwarzkopf enjoyed a hero's welcome. In contrast to the Vietnam era, citizens hailed the returning troops. The untelevised war, including the heavy loss of Iraqi lives, hardly impinged on the American consciousness.

The euphoria soon faded, however. Iraq had left Kuwait, but Saddam remained in power. The cease-fire provided for the UN-supervised ending of Baghdad's nuclear- and chemical-weapons programs, but Saddam raised many roadblocks. Revelations about Washington's earlier aid to Saddam further diluted the sweet tang of victory. The political bonus to Bush of the Desert Storm triumph soon dissipated.

President Bush also confronted disturbing events in China, where an aging communist oligarchy clung to power while edging toward a freer economy and pursuing détente and trade with the West. In 1989, when Chinese students calling for democracy occupied Beijing's Tiananmen Square, the government eventually ordered a tank assault that left hundreds dead. A systematic crackdown on dissidents followed, including arrests and public executions. Bush condemned the brutality and proposed economic sanctions, but he resisted congressional demands that he sever trade and diplomatic relations with Beijing.

Bush's essentially reactive foreign policy manifested itself as well in South Africa. In 1986, overriding a Reagan veto, Congress had barred all U.S. trade or corporate investment in South Africa with its all-white government and its system of apartheid. These sanctions and other countries' efforts induced South Africa to moderate its racial stance. A breakthrough came in 1990 when President F. W. de Klerk released Nelson Mandela, leader of the African National Congress (ANC), the major political organization of black South Africans, after years of detention. In 1991, as de Klerk dismantled apartheid, President Bush lifted U.S. sanctions. In a dramatic moment in September 1993, Mandela appeared before the UN to call for an end to all economic sanctions against his nation. In South Africa's first universal election, in April 1994, the ANC won 63 percent of the vote, and ex-political prisoner Mandela became president of his country.

Elsewhere in Africa, a severe drought in 1992 threatened 40 million people with famine, especially in war-torn Somalia with its 6.7 million people. Relief agencies stepped in, and the United States, under UN auspices, supplied emergency food shipments. When warring factions diverted relief shipments to the black market, President Bush ordered in thirty thousand U.S. troops to protect food deliveries. His action reflected less a strategic decision than a response to TV images of famished Somalis. The U.S. role in Somalia would soon generate controversy, but at the time the nation supported Bush's action. As one citizen told a reporter, "You see these starving kids on T.V., and you think how could we not do this?"

In Latin America, the Soviet collapse reoriented U.S. policy. Bush and Baker reversed Reagan's failed contra policy in Nicaragua, and backed efforts to reintegrate the contras into the country's politics. A 1990 election brought an anti-Sandinista coalition to power. In neighboring EL Salvador, U.S.-promoted peace talks finally bore fruit in 1992. The guerrillas and the government signed an agreement inaugurating various reforms, and the costly twelve-year civil war ended. Foreign policy and domestic concerns intersected in December 1989 when U.S. forces invaded Panama to capture strongman Manuel Noriega, accused of aiding the flow of cocaine from Colombia and Peru to U.S. cities. The action cost five hundred Panamanian and twenty-three U.S. lives, but it won applause in America and from many Panamanians relieved to be rid of Noriega. In 1992, convicted of drug trafficking by a federal court in Miami, Noriega went to prison. As with U.S.-Iraqi relations, however, the story proved complex. Noriega had long been on the CIA payroll, and only after his drug trafficking became too blatant to ignore did Washington move against him.

If the Cold War's end eased some regional conflicts, it worsened others. In the former Soviet Union and Eastern Europe, long-suppressed ethnic and religious hatreds erupted, perplexing U.S. diplomats accustomed to dealing with a unified Soviet bloc. Territorial disputes between Armenians and Azerbaijanis cost hundreds of lives. In 1992 Czechoslovakia split into the Czech Republic and Slovakia. Old animosities turned murderous in the Balkans when Yugoslavia's communist state splintered in 1991. The region was historically unstable as a result of tensions and territorial disputes between Catholic Croatians, Orthodox Serbs, and a small minority of Muslims. As Yugoslavia's western provinces of Slovenia, Croatia, and Bosnia-Herzegovina proclaimed their independence, the Serb-dominated federal government in Belgrade launched military operations first in Croatia and then in Bosnia aimed at Croats and Muslims living in areas dominated by ethnic Serbs. Serbian guerrillas besieged Sarajevo and other Bosnian cities, killing residents, cutting off food and medicine, and leaving hundreds of thousands homeless. Troops loyal to Serbian president Slobodan Miloslovic murdered, raped, imprisoned, and deported Muslims and other non-Serbs in a campaign of "ethnic cleansing" reminiscent of the Nazis. (In World War II, the tables had been turned. Then, Croatian fascists allied with Hitler had brutalized the Serbs.) UN-imposed sanctions against Serbia had little effect, and proposals for military intervention initially won scant support. President Bush, wary of engaging American forces in such a complex situation, confined the U.S. role to assistance in safeguarding UN food and relief convoys sent to Sarajevo and other besieged centers in Bosnia.

The administration's most substantial diplomatic achievement, significantly, came on the economic front and underscored Washington's shifting post–Cold War priorities. In August 1992, U.S., Canadian, and Mexican trade representatives completed the North American Free Trade Agreement (NAFTA). Under the treaty, the three nations created a single trading bloc containing more people and more production than the European Community. Bush would pass to his successor the task of persuading Congress to ratify NAFTA, but he defined its larger meaning: "The Cold War is over. The principal challenge now facing the United States is to compete in a rapidly changing, expanding global marketplace."

In sum, the Bush administration compiled a mixed diplomatic record, highlighted by the NAFTA accord and coordination of the international response to Iraqi aggression. Beyond these partial successes, the shapers of U.S. foreign policy groped uncertainly toward what Bush hopefully called a "new world order." As historian Stephen Graubard observed, "Like many Americans of his generation, Bush had become so habituated to living with the Cold War, was so much formed by its values, that he lacked any moral or political compass to guide him when he wished to turn away from its simple and brutal verities." As Graubard noted, Bush was hardly alone in this uncertainty and loss of direction.

Bush's domestic record proved even more lackluster, as the nation grappled with a tangle of economic problems. The annual trade deficit hovered at around $40 billion in the early nineties. In 1992 Bush converted a planned visit to Asia into a trade mission. The heads of GM, Ford, and Chrysler, invited along by the president, ham-handedly pressured the Japanese to buy more U.S. cars. When a flu attack caused Bush to collapse and vomit on Japan's prime minister at a state dinner, the mishap seemed symbolic of America's foreign-trade woes.

The federal budget deficit continued to rise as the impact of the tax cuts and increased military spending of the 1980s, together with the cost of ever-growing entitlement programs, became painfully evident. In 1990 Congress and the president agreed on a five-year deficit-reduction package. The plan cut spending and, breaking Bush's "read my lips" pledge, increased a variety of taxes. Yet the deficit still soared, reaching $290 billion in 1992. The costs of entitlement programs, the S&L bailout,* and coming baby-boom retirements threatened a continued flow of red ink in future years. So did interest payments on the $4 trillion national debt, which by 1992 was eating up $200 billion annually, 15 percent of all federal spending.

If the trade and budget deficits remained abstract to many citizens, the recession that hit in 1990 proved all too real. Unemployment rose; sales, housing starts, and business investment plummeted. By mid-1992, despite some hopeful trends, consumer confidence remained depressed, and the jobless rate stood at 7.8 percent. The GNP, which had grown 14 percent during Reagan's two terms, increased but an anemic 2.2 percent in the recession-battered Bush years. The problem had several sources, including reduced defense spending and a collapse of the commercial real-estate market after overexpansion in the 1980s. A further cause lay in the boom of the eighties, when Americans had plunged heavily into debt, not to finance long-term investment but to sustain high levels of consumption. The bill came due in the early 1990s, and the economy reacted by contracting sharply.

---

* In 1989, Washington set up procedures for bailing out the nation's insolvent S&Ls, whose depositors were federally insured up to $100,000. Budget experts estimated the cost at $195 billion through 1998. In the most notorious case, Charles Keating, chairman of California's Lincoln Savings & Loan, was convicted in December 1991 of securities fraud for inducing seventeen thousand investors to buy $250 million worth of uninsured bonds.

As usual, the recession hit the poor most severely, but it also brought bad news for the middle class and exacerbated a long-term economic erosion. From 1989 to 1991, median household income (adjusted for inflation) fell from $31,750 to $31,125. High-school and college graduates faced the worst job market in memory in 1992. Of recent college graduates who were employed, 20 percent held jobs not requiring a degree. In *Boiling Point: Republicans, Democrats and the Decline of Middle Class Prosperity* (1993), Kevin Phillips documented that the real income of the middle class had been falling since 1973, worsened by the tax cuts of the 1980s that had redistributed income from the lower and middle ranks to the wealthy. The baby-boom generation born between 1946 and 1964, observed anthropologist Katherine Newman in *Declining Fortunes: The Withering of the American Dream* (1993), was "the first . . . since the Great Depression that can expect to have a *lower* standard of living than its parents." The anxieties gnawing at the middle class would profoundly influence the politics of 1992.

Although Bush at various times proclaimed himself both "the environmental president" and "the education president," he won scant praise on either front. He signed the Clean Air Act of 1990, a bipartisan measure intended to reduce smog, acid rain, and industrial pollution, but he also appointed officials who undercut the rules that they were pledged to enforce. These appointees advocated expanded logging on public lands, more oil exploration in Alaska, and the commercial development of protected wetlands. The Competitiveness Council, an agency headed by Vice President Quayle, attacked environmental regulations for supposedly stifling business growth. Bush's petulant, defensive speech at the Earth Summit, a 1992 environmental conference in Rio de Janeiro, boasting of his environmental record and attacking his critics, further alienated environmental activists.

Not until 1991 did Bush unveil an education agenda. The plan included national student testing, competency exams for teachers, and a system by which students could attend private or church-run schools at public expense. While private-school administrators praised the "school choice" idea, the Carnegie Foundation for the Advancement of Teaching and others criticized it as doing little to help a public-school system battered by recession and neglect.

Two Supreme Court justices retired during Bush's term. Bush's first nomination, in 1990, went to Judge David Souter of New Hampshire. Despite his scant record on major issues, Souter proved thoughtful and open in his confirmation hearings, and he won easy confirmation. Together with Sandra Day O'Connor and Anthony Kennedy, Souter emerged as a centrist on abortion and other highly charged legal matters.

Bush's 1991 choice of Clarence Thomas to replace Thurgood Marshall proved more divisive. Both black, the two men were otherwise very different. Marshall, an NAACP attorney before joining the high court, had long upheld liberal and civil-rights causes. Thomas, an ideological conservative, had risen from a poor Georgia boyhood to attend Holy Cross College and Yale Law School. Head of the Equal Employment Opportunity Commission (EEOC) under President Reagan, he had been appointed a federal judge only in 1990.

Mindful of the fate of the loquacious Robert Bork, Thomas mostly refused to discuss his legal views in his confirmation hearings, including his position on abortion. But the hearings took a startling turn when a former associate at EEOC, Anita

Hill, accused Thomas of sexual harassment. Thomas angrily denied the charges, and Republican committee members harshly grilled Professor Hill. In the end, Thomas narrowly won Senate confirmation, 52–48. Once on the bench, he consistently took the most conservative position. Judges must try to discern the "original intent" of every law, he held, including the Constitution and the Bill of Rights, and not twist them to "address all [the] ills of our society."

The crisis in the inner cities, rooted in joblessness and lack of economic opportunity, got only sporadic federal attention in the Bush years. Jack Kemp, the former professional football player who headed the Department of Housing and Urban Development, urged tax incentives to encourage inner-city job creation by private capital, but the White House showed scant interest. After the Rodney King riots, Bush and Congress agreed on a $5 billion urban aid package, but Washington's attention soon waned. Addressing the nation's $50 billion illegal drug traffic, Bush urged a doubling of the federal antidrug budget and named William Bennett, a former secretary of education, as "drug czar." Bennett adopted a get-tough policy that included jailing drug dealers, but although drug-related arrests rose to a million each year, he had little to show for his efforts and soon departed in frustration.

Conclusion

As the Bush administration wore on, presided over by a benign but often vague chief executive, it increasingly seemed a kind of postscript tacked onto the Reagan era. Marked by short-term bursts of energy, the Bush years lacked sustained momentum, clear objectives, or focused energy. A twelve-year presidential cycle that had begun with the excitement and ideological fervor of Reagan's first term was ending in a period of rather aimless drift.

SELECTED READINGS

Ronald Reagan and Reagan-Era Politics

Frank Ackerman, *Reaganomics* (1982); Sidney Blumenthal, *The Rise of the Counter-Establishment: From Conservative Ideology to Political Power* (1988); Sidney Blumenthal and Thomas Byrne Edsall, eds., *The Reagan Legacy* (1988); Paul Boyer, ed., *Reagan as President: Contemporary Views of the Man, His Politics, and His Policies* (1990); William J. Broad, *The Star Warriors* (1985) and *Teller's War: The Top-Secret Story Behind the Star Wars Deception* (1992); Lou Cannon, *President Reagan* (1991); John F. Cogan, *Federal Budget Deficits: What's Wrong with the Congressional Budget Process* (1992); Robert Dallek, *Ronald Reagan: The Politics of Symbolism* (1984); Thomas Byrne Edsall with Mary D. Edsall, *Chain Reaction: The Impact of Race, Rights, and Taxes on American Politics* (1991); Rowland Evans and Robert Novak, *The Reagan Revolution* (1981); Jack W. Germond and Jules Witcover, *Blue Smoke and Mirrors* (1981) [1980 election]; Haynes Johnson, *Sleepwalking Through History: America in the Reagan Years* (1991); Jonathan Lash, *A Season of Spoils: The Story of the Reagan Administration's Attack on the Environment* (1984); Sar A. Levitan and Clifford M. Johnson, *Beyond the Safety Net* (1984); Charles Murray, *Losing Ground: American Social Policy, 1950–1980* (1984); Peggy Noonan, *What I Saw at the Revolution: A Political Life in the Reagan Era* (1990); Kevin Phillips, *The Politics of Rich and Poor* (1990); Kirkpatrick Sale, *Power Shift: The Rise of the Southern Rim and Its Challenge to the Eastern Establishment* (1975); Bob Schieffer and Gary Paul Gates, *The Acting President* (1989); Herman Schwartz, *Packing the Courts* (1988); C. Brant Short, *Ronald Reagan and the Public Lands: America's Conservation Debate, 1979–1984* (1989); David A. Stockman, *The Triumph of Politics: How the Reagan Revolution Failed* (1986); Garry Wills, *Reagan's America* (1987).

U.S. Foreign Policy, 1981–1988

Michael R. Beschloss and Strobe Talbot, *At the Highest Levels: The Inside Story of the End of the Cold War* (1994); Seweryn Bialer and Michael Mandelbaum, eds., *Gorbachev's Russia and American Foreign Policy* (1988); Raymond Bonner, *Weakness and Deceit: U.S. Policy and El Salvador* (1984); Thomas Crothers, *In the Name of Democracy; U.S. Foreign Policy Toward Latin America in the Reagan Years* (1991); Theodore Draper, *A Very Thin Line: The Iran-Contra Affairs* (1991); John Lewis Gaddis, *The United States and the End of the Cold War* (1992); Raymond L. Garthoff, *The Great Transition: American-Soviet Relations and the End of the Cold War* (1994); Patrick Glynn, *Closing Pandora's Box: Arms Races, Arms Control, and the History of the Cold War* (1992); Roy Gutman, *Banana Diplomacy* (1988); David E. Kyvig, ed., *Reagan and the World* (1990); Michael Mandelbaum and Strobe Talbott, *Reagan and Gorbachev* (1987); Constantine Menges, *Inside the National Security Council* (1988); Morris H. Morley, *Washington, Somoza, and the Sandinistas* (1994); Kenneth Oye et al., *Eagle Defiant: U.S. Foreign Policy in the 1980s* (1983) and *Eagle Resurgent? The Reagan Era in American Foreign Policy* (1987); David Schoenbaum, *The United States and the State of Israel* (1993); Charles D. Smith, *Palestine and the Arab-Israeli Conflict* (2d ed., 1992); Strobe Talbott, *Deadly Gambits: The Reagan Administration and the Stalemate in Nuclear Arms Control* (1984).

Economic Trends, Protest, and Social Thought in the Eighties

Carl Abbott, *The New Urban America: Growth and Politics in the Sunbelt Cities* (1981); Robert Bellah et al., *Habits of the Heart* (1985) and *The Good Society* (1991); Connie Bruck, *The Predators' Ball: The Inside Story of Drexel Burnham and the Rise of the Junk Bond Raiders* (1989); Paul S. Dempsey, *The Social and Economic Consequences of Deregulation* (1988); Barbara Ehrenreich, *Fear of Falling: The Inner Life of the Middle Class* (1989) and *The Worst Years of Our Lives* (1990); Benjamin Friedman, *Day of Reckoning: The Consequences of American Economic Policy Under Reagan and After* (1988); Larry N. Gerston et al., *The Deregulated Society* (1988); J. David Hoeveler, *Watch on the Right: Conservative Intellectuals in the Reagan Era* (1991); Harry Hurt, *The Lost Tycoon: The Many Lives of Donald J. Trump* (1993); J. Anthony Lukas, *Common Ground: A Turbulent Decade in the Lives of Three American Families* (1986); Frances Fox Piven and Richard A. Cloward, *The New Class War: Reagan's Attack on the Welfare State and Its Consequences* (1982); Clyde V. Prestowitz, Jr., *Trading Places: How We Allowed Japan to Take the Lead* (1988); Jerome Price, *The Antinuclear Movement* (1982); Patricia Cayo Sexton, *The War on Labor and the Left: Understanding America's Unique Conservatism* (1991); James B. Stewart, *Den of Thieves* (1991) [Wall Street trading scandals]; Sidney Weintraub and Marvin Goodstein, eds., *Reaganomics in the Stagflation Economy* (1983); William J. Wilson, *The Truly Disadvantaged: The Inner City, the Underclass and Public Policy* (1987).

Popular Culture in the Eighties

"America's Hottest Export: Pop Culture," *Fortune,* December 31, 1990; Michael A. Anderegg, *Inventing Vietnam: The War in Film and Television* (1991); Bob Carroll et al., *The*

Hidden Game of Football (1988); Richard M. Clurman, *To the End of Time: The Seduction and Conquest of a Media Empire* (1992) [merger of Time, Inc. and Warner Communications]; Stuart Ewen and Elizabeth Ewen, *Channels of Desire: Mass Images and the Shaping of American Consciousness* (2d ed., 1992); "Fancy Free: A Survey of the [U.S.] Entertainment Industry," *Economist* London, December 23, 1989; Jane Feuer, *Seeing Through the Eighties: Television and Reaganism* (1995); Todd Gitlin, *Inside Prime Time* (1985) and *Watching Television* (1986); Ron Grover, *The Disney Touch* (1991); Daniel Ichbiah, *The Making of Microsoft* (1991); Donald Lazere, ed., *American Media and Mass Culture: Left Perspectives* (1987); Steven Levy, *Insanely Great: The Life and Times of Macintosh, the Computer That Changed Everything* (1993); Nicholas Mills, ed., *Culture in an Age of Money* (1991); Edward Palmer, *Television and America's Children: A Crisis of Neglect* (1988); Neil Postman, *Amusing Ourselves to Death* (1985); Randy Roberts and James S. Olson, *Winning Is the Only Thing: Sports in America Since 1945* (1989); Michael Sorkin, ed., *Variations on a Theme Park: The New American City and the End of Public Space* (1993); Michael Winship, *Television* (1988).

George Bush and the Bush Presidency

Philip John Davies, ed., *An American Quarter Century: U.S. Politics from Vietnam to Clinton* (1995); Michael Duffy, *Marching in Place: The Status Quo Presidency of George Bush* (1992); Jack W. Germond and Jules Witcover, *Whose Broad Stripes and Bright Stars: The Trivial Pursuit of the Presidency, 1988* (1989); Nicholas King, *George Bush: A Biography* (1980); David Mervin, *George Bush and the Guardianship Presidency* (1996); Kevin P. Phillips, *The Politics of Rich and Poor: Wealth and the American Electorate in the Reagan Aftermath* (1990); John Podhoretz, *Hell of a Ride: Backstage at the White House Follies, 1989–1993* (1993); Richard Rose, *The Post-Modern President: George Bush Meets the World* (1991).

Bush and the World: Foreign Affairs and the Persian Gulf War

Rick Atkinson, *Crusade: The Untold Story of the Persian Gulf War* (1993); Zbigniew Brzezinski, "The Cold War and Its Aftermath," *Foreign Affairs* (Fall 1992); Alan Friedman, *Spider's Web: The Secret History of How the White House Illegally Armed Iraq* (1993); Stephen R. Graubard, *Mr. Bush's War: Adventures in the Politics of Illusion* (1992); Richard Hallion, *Storm over Iraq: Air Power and the Gulf War* (1992); Roger Hilsman, *George Bush vs. Saddam Hussein* (1992); Kim R. Holmes and Burton Yale Pines, *George Bush's New World Order* (1991); Robert D. Kaplan, *Balkan Ghosts: A Journey Through History* (1993); John D. Martz, *United States Policy in Latin America: A Decade of Crisis and Challenge* (1995); Gale Stokes, *The Walls Came Tumbling Down: The Collapse of Communism in Eastern Europe* (1993); Bernard Trainor, *The Generals' War* (1995); U.S. News and World Report, *Triumph Without Victory: The Unreported History of the Persian Gulf War* (1992).

CHAPTER 15

The Clinton Years: The Search for New Directions at Century's End

By 1992, with the economy stagnant, a frustrated electorate vented its discontent at the polls. After twelve years of Republican rule, voters ushered Democrat Bill Clinton into the White House. Domestically, Clinton launched his term by proposing a sweeping national health-care plan reminiscent of the New Deal or the Great Society at their most expansive. When it failed in Congress, the pliant Clinton moved toward the center and scaled back his ambitious domestic program. The 1994 midterm election, which produced Republican majorities in both houses of Congress, pushed Clinton further to the right, and he joined Congress in crafting a welfare-reform program that partially dismantled a federal welfare system whose origins dated to the 1930s. Though Clinton won reelection in 1996, the opening stage of his second term produced little of note. Amid a prevailing antigovernment mood, both the Democratic White House and the Republican Congress proceeded cautiously, avoiding high-visibility initiatives.

World trends continued to flow America's way in the nineties, but the task of devising a comprehensive post–Cold War foreign policy proved no easier for Clinton than it had for Bush. The Soviet Union's collapse eased global tensions and blessedly reduced fears of nuclear war, but the new world reality posed novel challenges for the United States internationally, from Bosnia to China. As the global economy became more and more integrated, economic concerns increasingly dominated the diplomatic process.

Beyond Washington, U.S. society presented a complex mosaic of trends in the later 1990s. A booming economy and a soaring stock market muted the economic anxieties that had gripped the nation earlier, but despite the rosy statistics nagging problems remained, many of them focused on the chronic poverty and joblessness of the inner cities. As Americans struggled to define a common national purpose amid rampant consumerism, individual ambition, and interest-group politics, debate swirled around such diverse issues as taxes, abortion, affirmative action, education, the mass media, and the health-care needs of an aging population.

The emerging global economy, the rise of entertainment conglomerates, and new communications technologies—especially personal computers and the

Internet—made clear that twenty-first-century America would be very different from the America of 1950 or even of 1980. As so often in the past, the pace of social and technological change proved both exhilarating and unsettling. Nostalgia, religious piety, and a conservative concern for tradition and "family values" loomed large as Americans uneasily contemplated their future on the eve not just of a new decade or a new century, but a new millennium.

Campaign '92

George Bush had made extravagant promises in 1988. In addition to the "Read My Lips: No New Taxes" pledge, broken in 1990, he had spoken glibly of 30 million new jobs. His call for a "kinder, gentler America" had suggested concern for those left behind in the 1980s. In fact, Bush disdained what he called "the vision thing" and largely ignored domestic issues. Apart from a law barring discrimination against persons with disabilities, even Bush's admirers had trouble identifying domestic achievements. Bush boasted of ending the Cold War and standing up to Iraq, but his flip-flop on taxes and his neglect of economic issues amid a recession severely weakened him. By the summer of 1992, Bush's approval rating had sagged to 34 percent, and fewer than 20 percent of Americans approved his handling of the economy.

Bush's earlier, post–Persian Gulf popularity had led top Democrats like New York governor Mario Cuomo to opt out of the 1992 presidential race. Into the vacuum stepped various candidates with only regional reputations, including Governor Bill Clinton of Arkansas. The personable and telegenic Clinton battled rumors of extramarital affairs, charges that he had avoided the Vietnam War draft, and insinuations of "character flaws" summed up in the epithet "Slick Willy."

Public cynicism about politics-as-usual emerged on many fronts in 1992. *JFK,* a movie postulating a bizarre conspiracy theory to explain Kennedy's assassination, scored big at the box office. The PAC (political-action committee) money that showered down on Washington intensified the anti-incumbency mood. In 1992 Speaker of the House Tom Foley received $401,000 in PAC contributions, and majority leader Richard Gephardt raked in a whopping $1.2 million.

The insurgent mood inspired the third-party candidacy of Ross Perot, a Texan whose EDS Corporation, a data-processing firm, had made him a billionaire. Perot's politics remained obscure apart from a deficit-cutting obsession, but he enjoyed a reputation for can-do activism. Above all, he was an outsider, untainted by old-style politics. Bypassing the primaries, he revealed his White House aspirations on a TV call-in show and then confined himself mainly to such forums, which he enlivened with salty one-liners. Millions flocked to Perot's banner, stirring fears that the election, for the first time since 1824, might be thrown into the House of Representatives.* But the mercurial Perot, angered by media scrutiny and tripped

---

* If no presidential candidate receives an electoral-college majority, Article II, section 3 of the Constitution places the decision in the hands of the House of Representatives, each state delegation casting a single ballot.

up by his own off-the-cuff style, withdrew from the race in July. He reentered to participate in the televised presidential debates but never regained his momentum.

Bill Clinton, despite his liabilities, easily won the Democratic nomination. Born in 1946, he grew up in a household dominated by an abusive stepfather. Young Clinton adored Elvis Presley and briefly contemplated a career as a saxophonist, but instead he attended Georgetown University, Oxford University as a Rhodes scholar, and Yale Law School. In 1978, at age thirty-two, he won election in Arkansas as the nation's youngest governor.

Clinton's acceptance speech focused on health care, education, jobs, and economic growth and earned him a spurt in the polls. So did his choice of Senator Al Gore of Tennessee as running mate. To attract younger voters, Clinton appeared on MTV and a popular TV talk show, sporting sunglasses and saxophone. Hillary Clinton, also a Yale Law graduate and a high-powered lawyer, had initially put off many voters who considered her too aggressive, but she softened her public image—challenging Barbara Bush to a cookie recipe contest, for example—and emerged as an asset to her husband's cause.

Both Clinton and Gore belonged to the Democratic Leadership Council (DLC), a moderate group intent on wooing back Reagan Democrats. To this end, the DLC combated the Democrats' reputation as a "tax-and-spend" party beholden to minorities and special interests. Clinton thus distanced himself from Jesse Jackson and from union leaders. His acceptance speech praised "the hardworking Americans who make up our middle class" and included tough talk on welfare. The party platform echoed the theme, describing welfare as "a second chance, not a way of life." Clinton called for a two-year limit on welfare payments, coupled with education, job training, and child-care programs to help recipients to find work. He demanded tough laws to compel delinquent fathers, or "deadbeat dads," to support their offspring. A sign at Clinton headquarters summed up the campaign's key theme: "It's the Economy, Stupid." Clinton pledged to make the sluggish economy his top priority. Advised by fellow Rhodes scholar Robert Reich, who would be appointed secretary of labor, Clinton called for government programs to promote economic growth through education and job training.

A faltering Bush never offered a coherent second-term agenda, and Vice President Quayle, already a butt of humor, drew more ridicule when he misspelled *potato* while presiding over a school spelling bee. Yet the Republicans faced deeper problems than Quayle's spelling. The coalition that had twice elected Richard Nixon and Ronald Reagan was inherently unstable. It comprised an uneasy alliance of laissez-faire ideologues who hated "big government," and corporate executives and wealthy citizens who favored lower taxes but often took a liberal stand on social issues. The coalition also accommodated millions of white working-class and middle-class Americans, frequently Protestant evangelicals or Catholic ethnics, concerned with such issues as abortion, pornography, homosexuality, school prayer, "family values," and alleged favoritism to minorities. Through the 1980s, the Soviet threat and the prevailing aura of prosperity, together with Reagan's charisma, had held the coalition together. But by 1992 the Cold War had ended, the economy was in recession, and Reagan had been replaced by the lackluster Bush.

As the GOP splintered, the party's well-organized right wing flexed its muscle. Bush's post–Persian Gulf complacency further emboldened critics within his own

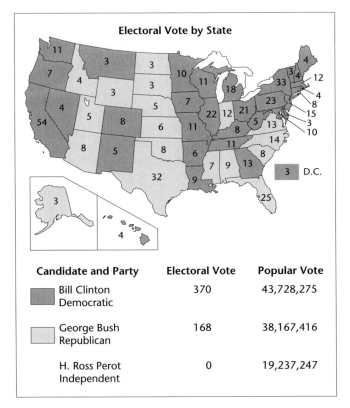

FIGURE 15.1
Presidential Election of 1992

party. In several early primaries, Bush faced a strong challenge by conservative columnist Pat Buchanan. The party platform embodied the New Right's cultural agenda. The convention celebrated Barbara Bush and Marilyn Quayle for devoting themselves to their husbands' careers and attacked Hillary Clinton as a "radical feminist." Delegates representing Pat Robertson's Christian Coalition cheered a slashing speech by Pat Buchanan vowing all-out ideological war on a variety of cultural and moral issues.

Bush's campaign strategist James Baker sketched a high-minded theme: President Bush, having devoted his first term to global issues, would focus on domestic problems in his second term. Yet the campaign quickly sank to the low level that seemed the new political norm. Issues were reduced to sound bites, and innuendo and stereotypes substituted for thoughtful discussion. Clinton blamed Bush for chronic economic problems that had complex causes. When Bush, on the other hand, denounced the Democratic platform for omitting "three simple letters, G-O-D," even jaded political observers groaned.

Election day 1992 thrilled victory-starved Democrats. Clinton won 43 percent of the vote to Bush's 38 percent and an electoral margin of 370–168. Exploiting economic discontent, Clinton won back Reagan Democrats and cut deeply into

Republican strongholds in the southern and mountain states. More than 75 percent of African-American voters voted Democratic. Both houses of Congress went Democratic, placing the legislative and executive branches under the control of the same party for the first time in twelve years. Still, the outcomes also sent a cautionary signal to Bill Clinton: 19 percent of voters had opted for Ross Perot, the best third-party showing since Theodore Roosevelt's in 1912. As for George Bush, the *New York Times* summed up a prevailing view in a postelection editorial entitled "The Half-Way Man." The *Times* conceded Bush's foreign-policy achievements but observed that on domestic policy he "created the disquieting and ultimately fatal impression that he didn't know what to do, and worse, didn't much care."

A Chastened Liberalism: Clinton at the Helm

As in 1960, the 1992 election brought both a change of party and a generational shift. George Bush would be the last president to have fought in World War II and to have lived through the entire Cold War as an adult. With Clinton and Gore, and 110 new members of Congress, the baby boomers emerged as the nation's leaders. This generation's formative memories were not of Munich, Pearl Harbor, Stalin, and Bing Crosby, but of the Peace Corps, civil-rights marches, antiwar protests, John Kennedy, Woodstock, and the Beatles. The Clintons' daughter, Chelsea, was even named for a popular sixties ballad, Joni Mitchell's "Chelsea Morning."

The election dramatized the emergence of women in American public life. Voters sent six women to the Senate and forty-eight to the House of Representatives. California became the first state to elect two women senators—Barbara Boxer and Dianne Feinstein. Women still remained a small minority in Congress, but the men's club atmosphere was fading.

Clinton's appointments further highlighted the new gender dynamics of U.S. politics. He chose women to head the Environmental Protection Agency, the Council of Economic Advisers, and the U.S. delegation to the United Nations. Breaking precedent further, he appointed the first woman attorney general, Janet Reno, a Florida prosecutor. Donna Shalala, chancellor of the University of Wisconsin, Madison, became secretary of health and human services; Hazel O'Leary, vice president of Northern States Power Company of Minneapolis, was appointed secretary of energy. When a Supreme Court vacancy occurred in 1993, Clinton chose Ruth Bader Ginsburg, a federal appeals court judge. The president also made clear that Hillary Rodham Clinton would be more than a ceremonial First Lady. He gave her an office in the White House West Wing—the official side— and named her to head the Task Force on National Health-Care Reform.

Fulfilling a campaign call for "a government that looks like America," Clinton chose Ron Brown, African-American chairperson of the Democratic National Committee, as secretary of commerce, and two Hispanics, Henry Cisneros, the mayor of San Antonio, and Federico Peña, to head HUD and the Department of Transportation, respectively. The new Congress reflected greater variety as well, with not only more women but also thirty-eight African Americans (up from twenty-five), seventeen Hispanics (up from ten), the first Korean-American congressman, and the first American Indian senator, Ben Nighthorse Campbell of Colorado.

January 1993: New Democrats in Power. *All smiles, President Bill Clinton and Vice President Al Gore exchange greetings after taking their oaths of office.* (AP/Wide World Photos)

Clinton's early weeks as president brought some hard lessons in Washington politics. Fulfilling a campaign pledge, he called for an end to the exclusion of homosexuals from military service. The move roused fierce controversy, and in the end the president submitted the issue to a study commission, which came up with a compromise "don't ask, don't tell" policy. Clinton's first two choices as attorney general both withdrew after allegations that they had hired illegal aliens for child-care services or had failed to pay social security taxes for domestic employees. The media feasted on "Nanny-gate."

Shaping his administration's domestic themes, Clinton initially addressed three key issues: economic renewal, deficit reduction, and health care. Clinton came to office pledged to focus "like a laser beam" on the economy, but in pursuing the dual goals of economic revitalization and deficit reduction, Clinton got conflicting advice. Moderate Democrats of the DLC variety and budget hawks like Leon Panetta and Alice Rivlin (director and deputy director of the Bureau of the Budget) wanted to prove that Democrats could be fiscally responsible. They thus gave highest priority to deficit reduction. Social-activist Democrats such as Marian Wright Edelman of the Children's Defense Fund, in which Hillary Clinton and Donna Shalala were active, wanted substantial spending on a wide range of social programs.

In late February 1993, Clinton offered his economic plan. An amalgam of the different viewpoints, the strategy combined an array of spending cuts and tax increases aimed at a net deficit reduction of $325 billion over four years. Cuts included a further tightening of military outlays, a one-year freeze on federal salaries, and elimination of a hundred thousand federal jobs through attrition. The plan capped Medicare and Medicaid payments to doctors and hospitals and reduced funding for such big-ticket projects as the space station and the superconducting supercollider. Clinton's proposed tax hikes hit the richest Americans with the stiffest increases, went much easier on the middle class, and spared families earning under $30,000 a year.

Clinton's new spending proposals, totaling $169 billion in economic "stimulus and investment" over four years, aimed at job creation and economic growth. Along with increases in Head Start and worker-training programs, the president called for tax credits for small-business investment and creation of a national fiber-optic data network. Finally, he recommended a national service corps by which college students could pay off federal education loans through community work. To avoid the familiar Republican charge that the Democrats favored "big government," Clinton insisted that the chief impetus for economic growth must come from the private sector. Echoing Ross Perot and Ronald Reagan, he declared, "The time has come to show the American people that we can limit [government programs], that we can not only start things but we can actually stop things."

Mixed economic signals complicated the debate over the need for a stimulus. The GNP, adjusted for inflation, rose by 2.1 percent in 1992, after a decline in 1991. But unemployment still stood at around 7 percent through 1993, with the number of long-term jobless stuck at about 2 million. In parts of the country, notably California, the jobless rate remained as high as 10 percent. Thirty-six million Americans struggled below the poverty line, and the number of Americans receiving food stamps reached the highest point since the program began in 1964. Large-scale layoffs by GM, IBM, Sears, aerospace companies, and other top corporations further weakened the job market. Many displaced skilled workers took positions in the service sector at steep cuts in wages. A 1993 study of two thousand workers fired by RJR-Nabisco Corporation, for example, revealed that those who found employment elsewhere on average earned less than half their former pay.

Military spending cuts and consequent layoffs in defense industries also clouded the economic picture. Boeing prepared to trim its work force by fifty thousand; McDonnell-Douglas, by ten thousand. By 1995, the Pentagon estimated, nine hundred thousand defense workers would lose their jobs. In March 1993, the Defense Department announced the closing of thirty-one military bases and cutbacks at others. To ease the pain, President Clinton proposed a program to retrain displaced workers, to aid communities hit by base closings, and to help defense industries convert to civilian production.

In early August, after long debate, Congress by razor-thin margins enacted a five-year economic plan quite different from Clinton's original proposal. The president's requested tax increase survived more or less intact. The bill raised the top tax rate from 31 to 36 percent while further easing the tax burden of the poor. To this extent, the measure partially reversed the retrogressive features of the Reagan-era tax cuts. But the measure appropriated only a fraction of what Clinton had sought for education, retraining, and apprenticeship programs. Furthermore, the bill's deficit-cutting potential was limited, both because the tax increase remained modest and because the spending cuts spared the mushrooming entitlement programs such as Medicare and social security.

Ominously, the bill passed without a single Republican vote, and with many Democratic defections. Nevertheless, the passage of even a modified economic plan spared Clinton a major embarrassment early in his term.

Clinton's economic plan included the North American Free Trade Agreement (NAFTA). Negotiated by the Bush administration, the plan incorporated Mexico into the free-trade zone already created by the United States and Canada. NAFTA roused both strong support and harsh criticism. Union leaders and their political friends, including House majority leader Richard Gephardt, warned of job losses to Mexico. Supporters of NAFTA, including most economists, conceded that low-wage jobs in labor-intensive industries might be lost. However, they insisted that NAFTA would create more high-wage jobs by opening the Mexican market to U.S. machinery and other products.

The treaty posed tricky political challenges for Clinton, since it threatened to alienate the blue-collar workers whom the Democrats hoped to win back. Ross Perot mounted a demagogic attack on the agreement, but the public was wearying of Perot's negativism and his slippery use of facts. The House of Representatives in November passed NAFTA by a comfortable 234–200 margin, handing Clinton another political victory. The administration followed up the NAFTA success with a campaign for expanded U.S. trade opportunities in Asia. In addition, it completed an agreement to lower trade barriers among the members of the General Agreement on Tariffs and Trade (GATT), the umbrella organization of the world's trading nations established in 1948.

As for NAFTA, by 1997 it was clear that the treaty had only a slight effect on the U.S. economy; some 117,000 U.S. citizens had applied for the benefits offered to workers displaced by the treaty, but in a booming economy this was negligible. The treaty's principal effects were felt in Mexico, as it promoted not only trade but also economic reform, U.S. investment, and joint Mexican-U.S. business ventures. Politically, the treaty strengthened ties between the two nations; as one Clinton administration official candidly put it: "We bought ourselves an ally with NAFTA." An improving Mexican economy promised other benefits as well. As the *Economist* of London observed in July 1997: "[A] prosperous Mexico is more likely to . . . see fewer of [its young people] become illegal immigrants or drug smugglers."

Next on Clinton's agenda came health-care reform, a goal of liberals since the 1930s. The problem had two elements: coverage and cost. Some 37 million Americans, most of them poor, lacked medical insurance. Millions more, including many middle-class citizens, feared losing coverage in an uncertain economy. And costs continued to soar as patients demanded access to the latest treatments and technologies and as physicians prescribed batteries of expensive tests and procedures to forestall possible malpractice suits. From 1980 to 1992, Medicare and Medicaid payments ballooned from $48 billion to $196 billion and expanded from 8 percent to 14 percent of the federal budget.

Hillary Clinton's health-care task force set out to devise a program to control runaway costs and to extend coverage to those who lacked it. In October 1993, the administration unveiled a plan that called for a system by which all Americans would be guaranteed medical and dental coverage and an array of preventive services. The plan proposed to contain costs by limiting Medicare and Medicare reimbursements, capping health-insurance premiums, and fostering competition among providers. By means of financial incentives, the new system would enroll all Americans into large regional purchasing groups, called health alliances, to monitor costs and negotiate with health-care providers. Individuals could join either a fee-for-service plan, enabling them to choose their own physicians, or a less expensive health maintenance organization (HMO). A seven-member national health board chosen by the president would oversee the nation's overall health budget. Under Clinton's plan, Medicaid would continue to protect the poor. To cover the plan's estimated $100 billion in added initial costs, Clinton proposed stiff new taxes on tobacco. With tobacco-related illnesses killing 418,000 Americans annually, adding massively to health-care costs, this proposal won general support.

The president took the plan to the people, stressing the security of guaranteed health coverage. Consciously emulating Franklin Roosevelt's 1935 campaign for social security, Clinton proposed a "health security card" modeled on the social security card that had reassured Depression-era Americans. Hillary Clinton, meanwhile, defended the plan in congressional testimony. Critics warned of government meddling, bloated bureaucracies, and a decline in health-care quality and ease of access. Several experts questioned whether the plan would produce the savings that Clinton envisioned. The 290,000-member American Medical Association, long a foe of "socialized medicine" and armed with a $7 million lobbying budget, attacked key parts of the plan. Former drug czar William Bennett blasted it as "a monumental assault . . . on individual liberty."

Other critics focused on the secretive process by which the plan had been formulated, and the central role of Hillary Clinton, who held no elective office. The lobbying attacks and the drumfire of criticism took their toll, and in September 1994 the administration dropped its efforts to bring its comprehensive health-care reform measure to a vote in the Senate. In the aftermath of this defeat, Hillary Clinton played a much less public role. The entire health-care debacle represented a major setback for the administration, and decisively shaped President Clinton's future course.

Even before the health-care defeat, it was clear that although Clinton drew on New Deal symbolism, the liberalism that he espoused differed markedly from the past. He recognized the nation's rightward shift and the collapse of the liberal consensus. Whereas at times he echoed FDR's confidence in governmental answers to society's ills and LBJ's calls for compassion to the poor, Clinton more typically stressed such classic conservative themes as individual responsibility, free enterprise, and the dangers of big government. His health plan, for example, rejected Canada's centralized, government-run system in favor of a decentralized plan of "managed competition" that mixed private enterprise and public oversight. Clinton's liberalism still embodied notions of entitlement—such as the right of all Americans to health care—but he also stressed fiscal restraint, managerial efficiency, and the importance of the private sector. Although not ignoring the poor, Clintonian liberalism focused on the economic anxieties of the vast American middle class.

The new president's approach reflected the electorate's rejection of 1960s-style liberalism, as well as the pervasive voter cynicism about government that Perot had exploited. In contrast to Lyndon Johnson's soaring rhetoric and ambitious reform agenda, Clinton's tone was restrained and his initiatives cautious. Tellingly, while Clinton pushed health-care reform, Vice President Gore led a task force that developed proposals for "reinventing government" by cutting paperwork, trimming bureaucratic fat, and tightening management controls. The Clinton administration, in short, offered a bargain-basement vision of government's role in social change that was tempered by harsh economic and political realities.

As Clinton's first term unfolded, the public verdict on his chastened liberalism remained tentative. The conservative coalition that had arisen in the 1970s and captured the White House in 1980 remained a force. Pat Robertson's Christian Coalition, having shown its muscle at the 1992 GOP convention, patiently elected candidates to local school boards and town councils. Robertson's organization rallied the Christian Right not only on such social themes as school prayer and pornography but also on political issues such as the budget deficit and health care. Neoconservative intellectual William Kristol, Dan Quayle's former chief of staff, derided Clinton's program as the product of a decayed liberalism that had "lost its force, its real conviction, and its real confidence in itself."

The failure of the administration's health-care plan showed Clinton's vulnerability, and Republicans scented victory as the 1994 midterm election approached. Clinton was further weakened by allegations of wrongdoing when he was governor of Arkansas, including the Whitewater matter, a complex real-estate deal involving alleged illegalities, and a sexual harassment suit filed by a female state employee. The 1993 suicide of Vincent Foster, a Clinton confidant and deputy White House counsel, churned more rumors. Seizing the moment, Georgia congressman Newt Gingrich drafted a conservative manifesto he called the Republicans' "Contract with America." Amid much hoopla, several hundred GOP candidates signed it, turning the midterm election, normally dominated by local issues, into an ideological referendum. On election day, Republicans won control of both houses of Congress.

When the newly elected Congress convened early in 1995, the House of Representatives hummed with activity. Jubilant Republicans elected Newt Gingrich as speaker; conferred honorary membership on Rush Limbaugh, a conservative radio commentator; and set about enacting the "Contract with America" agenda. One early measure prohibited "unfunded mandates," that is, federal requirements imposed on the states without money to carry them out. The House also passed a constitutional amendment requiring a balanced federal budget. Criticized by most economists as a simplistic panacea, this measure died in the Senate. Tackling an issue high on the list of voter worries, the new Congress passed, and Clinton signed, a crime bill that included tougher sentencing provisions and other measures aimed at "getting tough on criminals."

Attention soon focused on another issue that aroused passionate feelings: welfare reform. Americans across the political spectrum agreed that the federal welfare system, which encouraged long-term dependency rather than preparation for gainful employment, needed overhauling. The number of women and children receiving benefits under the largest federal welfare program, Aid to Families with Dependent Children (AFDC), grew from 8 million in 1970 to 12.6 million in 1996. And since welfare benefits increased with the number of children, the system appeared to reward out-of-wedlock pregnancies. With the out-of-wedlock birthrate running at 33 percent, and one in seven American children on welfare, this issue hit home.

Candidate Clinton in 1992 had pledged to "end welfare as we know it," but it was the congressional Republicans, as well as Republican governors such as Wisconsin's Tommy Thompson, who pushed the issue most actively. In August 1996, after vetoing two earlier bills, Clinton signed a historic welfare-reform bill passed by the Republican Congress. Sharply curtailing Washington's sixty-year role in welfare, the new law ended AFDC, and instead turned over to the states responsibility for devising their own welfare program, partially funded by federal block grants, under tough federal guidelines. With some exceptions for hardship cases, the law limited able-bodied welfare recipients to two years of continuous benefits, with a five-year lifetime maximum. It also cut the food-stamp program, slashed benefits to legal immigrants, and authorized states to deny Medicaid to persons dropped from the welfare rolls.

Supporters of the hard-edged new law praised it as an essential first step in correcting the abuses of a bloated program that had outlived its original purpose. By ending long-term dependency, they claimed, it would encourage self-respect and self-reliance. "[P]eople who are able-bodied are actually going to have to get trained to go to work," declared John Kasich, chairman of the House Budget Committee, "because they can't be on welfare all of their lives." Critics, however, charged that it would push vast numbers of women and children into poverty, and that it reflected an attack by well-to-do Americans on the poor. Since blacks and Hispanics were heavily represented on the welfare rolls, critics argued that in some cases the enthusiasm for "welfare reform" simply reflected ill-disguised racism.

As the sweeping new law went into effect, its long-term impact remained unknown. Would fifty state welfare systems succeed any better than the discarded federal system? Would the states be willing to fund the job training, counseling, child care, and public-sector employment essential to any meaningful welfare-reform program? And how would the tough new system fare in times of recession? Such questions went unanswered amid broad public approval of "welfare reform."

Clinton's signature on the Republican welfare-reform bill, marking his decisive break with the liberal tradition, split the Democratic party. Half of the Democrats in the House and twenty-one of the forty-six Democrats in the Senate, including such liberal stalwarts as Edward M. Kennedy of Massachusetts, voted against the bill. Labor unions; advocacy groups for immigrants and the poor; and organizations representing African Americans, Latinos, and women—traditional Democratic strongholds—uniformly opposed the bill. Clinton, with his eye on the polls and on the America's middle class with its rich harvest of votes, ignored the protests. He did, however, promise to work for changes in the law's harsher features and for more funding of training programs to help welfare recipients find jobs.

Clinton's first Supreme Court appointee, Ruth Bader Ginsburg, joined Sandra Day O'Connor to become the second woman justice. To fill another vacancy in 1994, Clinton appointed Stephen Breyer of Harvard Law School. Far more skeptical of social activism than the Warren Court of the 1950s, the Clinton-era Supreme Court was more libertarian, often championing individual rights against government infringement. In one 1997 ruling, for example, the Supreme Court extended First Amendment protection to the Internet, the computer-based communications system, overturning a portion of the Communications Decency Act of 1996 that had sought to protect the nation's mouse-wielding juveniles from pornography. In another 1997 ruling, the Court overturned part of a 1993 federal gun-control law as an infringement of states' rights. The death in 1997, at ninety-one, of former Justice William J. Brennan, Jr., a stalwart on the Court during its heyday of liberal activism, served as a reminder of how radically the Court—and the nation—had changed course. "The life of the man is over," observed Brennan's close friend Justice David Souter in a eulogy. "So is the liberal era when Justice Brennan's voice was the voice of the Supreme Court."

1996: Clinton Reelected

The GOP sweep in 1994 did not, as Republicans had hoped, translate into a presidential victory two years later. The Republicans suffered from ideological divisions, heightened by feuding among the party's congressional leaders. House Speaker Gingrich attracted a firestorm of criticism in 1995 when he permitted two partial shutdowns of the government as a tactical maneuver in congressional budget wrangling with the White House. President Clinton, meanwhile, bouncing back

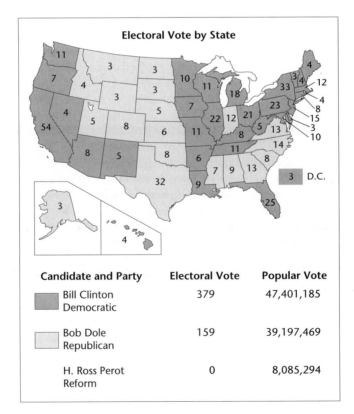

Electoral Vote by State

Candidate and Party	Electoral Vote	Popular Vote
Bill Clinton Democratic	379	47,401,185
Bob Dole Republican	159	39,197,469
H. Ross Perot Reform	0	8,085,294

FIGURE 15.2
Presidential Election of 1996

from the health-care defeat, benefited from a booming economy as the 1996 election neared.

While the Democrats renominated Clinton and Gore, Republicans initially placed their hopes in General Colin Powell, an African American and a much-admired former chairman of the Joint Chiefs of Staff. But Powell declined to run, and Senator Bob Dole bested a weak field of contenders to win the GOP nomination, with Jack Kemp as his running mate. A plainspoken Kansan who had been severely wounded in World War II, Dole was a long-time power in the Senate, most recently as majority leader. The seventy-three-year-old Dole compaigned gamely but ineptly, showing only flashes of his razor-sharp humor. On election day, Clinton handily gained a second term, carrying thirty-one states plus the District of Columbia. Clinton won 49 percent of the popular vote to Dole's 41 percent, while a die-hard 8 percent went for Ross Perot. Although the Republicans retained control of Congress, the much-predicted conservative revolution did not materialize. The message of the 1996 election, which the *New York Times* called a "mid-course correction," was one of moderation, not extremism. The shock of the 1996 Oklahoma City bombing (see p. 494) may have helped diminish the appeal of extremist ideology, as Americans saw where it could ultimately lead.

Hugging the Middle of the Road: Domestic Issues in Clinton's Second Term

Bill Clinton hewed so closely to a centrist or slightly right-of-center position in his second term that he seemed more a moderate Republican than a classic "tax-and-spend" New Deal–style Democrat. The preferred stance of Clintonian Democrats, observed historian Allan Brinkley, was to be "moderate, responsible, and non-frightening, but marginally more progressive than the Republicans." The Democratic party of Franklin Roosevelt in 1936, or George McGovern in 1972, were but fading memories in the later 1990s.

Embracing a cherished Republican goal—a balanced-budget—Clinton in July 1997, after two years of negotiation, signed an omnibus bill that mandated a balanced budget by 2002 while providing $94 billion in net tax cuts. The measure slashed the capital gains tax (another long-time GOP objective), raised to $1.2 million the portion of estates exempted from death taxes, and created numerous tax loopholes for the very wealthy. Fulfilling a pledge in Gingrich's 1994 Contract with America, it included a $500 tax credit for each child. The spending cuts included reduced payments to health-care providers under Medicare and Medicaid. While Republicans and Clinton-Gore "New Democrats" praised the bill, a dwindling band of Democratic liberals charged that it favored the rich. Some parts of the final bill did reflect Clinton's social concerns, including tax relief for college-tuition costs; $24 billion over five years for health care for children without health insurance; and the restoration of Medicaid and disability benefits to legal immigrants, cut off in the 1996 welfare-reform act.

A few cautionary notes were heard. What would happen to the budget after 2002, some asked, when the baby-boom generation retired, left the tax rolls, and began to receive Medicare, social security, and other benefits? Skeptics noted that

most of the spending cuts were delayed to the end of the five-year period, after
Clinton had left office. They also pointed out that prosperity and post–Cold War
cuts in defense spending had already largely achieved the law's budget-balancing
goal. After peaking in 1992 at $290 billion, the federal deficit fell in 1997 to under
$23 billion, the lowest since 1974. Indeed, as the boom continued, Clinton early in
1998 promised a balanced budget four years ahead of the 2002 deadline.

On another front, the hazards of tobacco suddenly came to the foreground in
1997. Since 1965, cigarettes had carried a mandated health warning, but more and
more victims of lung cancer and other tobacco-related diseases sued the tobacco
companies for misleading advertising and for concealing their product's hazards.
Some states sued as well, seeking to recover the costs of providing health care to
smokers. In June 1997, the tobacco industry reached a landmark $368 billion set-
tlement with the attorneys general of some forty states. The companies agreed to
pay $50 billion in punitive damages and $318 billion to settle liability claims and
to reimburse states for tobacco-related medical costs. The agreement further restricted tobacco advertising, set heavy fines if teenage smoking did not decline by
60 percent in ten years, and gave the Food and Drug Administration authority to
regulate tobacco as a lethal and addictive substance. In return, the tobacco industry
received protection from lawsuits and immunity from further penalties for past
actions.

While some praised the agreement, anti-tobacco crusaders and many public-
health officials criticized it for not going far enough. President Clinton expressed
the fear that tobacco companies would deduct the costs of the settlement as a business expense, thus reducing their tax payments and jeopardizing his budget-
balancing hopes. Clinton also called for tougher antismoking measures and stiffer
penalties on tobacco companies if teenage smoking did not decline.

The plan required congressional approval, and as of early 1998 the outcome
remained uncertain. Warned C. Everett Koop, a former surgeon general:
'[R]emember, the tobacco companies are a sleazy bunch of people who misled us,
deceived us, and lied to us for three decades. Under this settlement . . . , the tobacco lobby will still be there, and they will never stop." With the industry allocating $30 million to influence Congress, bankrolling pro-tobacco politicans such as
Senator Jesse Helms of North Carolina, and recruiting prominent former senators
and governors as lobbyists, Koop's warning seemed well taken. While the debate
raged on, Mississippi, Florida, and Texas reached separate settlements with the tobacco companies. In the Florida agreement, the industry, in return for legal immunity, pledged to pay the state $11.3 billion for health-care costs related to smoking
and accepted various specific strategies for cutting teenage smoking.

The role of money in politics, so vividly demonstrated in the tobacco wars,
was further highlighted by a 1997 Senate inquiry into charges of illegal Democratic
fundraising in 1996, including hundreds of thousands of dollars in laundered
money allegedly solicited by fundraisers John Huang and the Little Rock restaura-
teur Charlie Trie from corporate sources in China, Korea, Thailand, Hong Kong,
Indonesia, and elsewhere. Chaired by Republican senator Fred Thompson, the
hearings publicized such episodes as Vice President Gore's appearance at a
fundraiser at a Buddhist temple in California where monks vowed to poverty had
miraculously raised $140,000 for the Democratic cause. Two Chinese immigrant

housewives of modest means explained to the committee how they happened to contribute $25,000 to the Democratic National Committee. Big contributors were rewarded with rounds of golf with President Clinton, nights in the Lincoln bedroom at the White House—and possibly special treatment on sensitive trade and export issues. Republicans called on Attorney General Janet Reno to appoint a special counsel to investigate the charges, but she refused.

The administration dismissed the charges as politically motivated. Pointing out that both parties had scrambled for contributions in the 1996 campaign, which had cost a staggering $2.2 billion in all, Democrats argued that campaign-finance reform, like the balanced-budget issue, should be approached in a nonpartisan way. The hearings ended inconclusively, tangled in such details as precisely which bank accounts contributions had been deposited in and which telephones Gore had used in raising a total of $40 million. Whether actual illegalities had occurred remained unclear, but the hearings underscored the obscene cost of running for office in the era of television, and encouraged public cynicism about the political clout that money could buy. When the Senate in October 1997 buried a campaign-finance bill proposed by Republican John McClain of Arizona and Democrat Russell Feingold of Wisconsin, the cynicism only deepened. But California voters in November 1996 did adopt Proposition 208, creating the strictest campaign-finance rules in the nation, holding out hope that Congress and the White House might yet summon the will to address the issue at the national level.

In general, the administration seemed somewhat adrift, at least on the domestic-policy front, as Clinton's second term wore on, while among Republicans, the cocky confidence of 1994 had long since faded. Ineligible for reelection, Clinton was already viewed as something of a lame duck as early as 1997. He seemed preoccupied with his place in history, and he announced one lofty goal after another. He called for a national dialogue on race relations, and appointed a commission to lead it. He urged measures to protect the environment, combat global warming, fight crime, promote literacy, encourage volunteerism by young people, improve children's health, spur technological innovation, increase computer access in the schools, and set national standards for education. For a while he focused on uniforms for schoolchildren; late in 1997 he embraced Republican calls to reform the Internal Revenue Service. Clinton's enthusiasms often proved short-lived, however, as his notoriously short attention span propelled him on to other issues, always in quest of the political center of gravity at any given moment.

Despite his favorable approval ratings, Clinton's support seemed tepid rather than deep and passionate. While the investigations and legal proceedings involving his alleged financial and sexual improprieties stirred no public indignation comparable to Watergate or the Iran-contra affair, they cumulatively took their toll. (In 1996 the media reported that Clinton's third-grade teacher had given him a C for conduct.) In 1997, as a measure of his political vulnerability, Congress denied Clinton the so-called fast track authority he requested to conduct trade negotiations on an accelerated basis. Soon after, a Labrador retriever, Buddy, joined the Clintons' pet cat, Socks, in the White House, but despite many winsome photographs, the political payoff among a jaded electorate proved disappointing.

Essayist Josef Joffe, writing in *Time* magazine in October 1996, offered an intriguing assessment: "Clinton is both right and left. He is the first postmodern President, the first to turn 'anything goes' into a political creed. Call him the son of the White Queen who, as she told Alice, sometimes 'believed six impossible things before breakfast.'" How could such a superficial and mercurial leader enjoy such electoral success? Joffe asked, and offered his own answer: "[Voters] who have traditionally heeded the call of class, religion, or ethnicity have become nimble-footed shoppers in the market of political goodies." The leader and the era, it appeared, were perfectly synchronized.

America and a Changing World

The end of the Cold War left America as the world's only superpower, yet U.S. foreign policy in the 1990s seemed curiously unfocused. Reversing President Bush's priorities, Clinton initially devoted little attention to foreign affairs, leaving matters to his dour and taciturn secretary of state, Warren Christopher. In 1996, Christopher was succeeded by the more feisty and outspoken Madeleine Albright, the U.S. ambassador to the United Nations. Born in 1937 into a Czech Jewish family that soon fled Prague to escape the Nazis, Albright was reared as a Catholic. As secretary of state, she became the highest-ranking woman ever to serve in the U.S. government.

Clinton's vacillations regarding Somalia and Bosnia illustrated the diplomatic pattern of his early presidency. He endorsed Bush's decision to send U.S. troops to Somalia to protect food intended for famine victims. But this humanitarian mission soon gave way to an effort to restore order in Somalia's anarchic capital, Mogadishu, and specifically to capture elusive warlord Mohammed Farah Aidid. The U.S. force was part of a larger UN peacekeeping army, and UN secretary general Boutros Boutros-Ghali had played a central role in redirecting the Americans' mission. As U.S. casualties mounted, so did home-front calls for U.S. withdrawal. Cartoonists drew Somalia in the shape of Vietnam. TV scenes of starving Somali children gave way to images of dead GIs. In October 1993 Clinton announced full withdrawal in six months and emphasized that in the interim he, not Boutros-Ghali, would decide the U.S. role. But he also increased the U.S. force in Somalia to ten thousand, and suspicions that Washington had lost its way continued. In December 1993, Secretary of Defense Les Aspin became the first member of Clinton's cabinet to be forced out, in part because he was perceived as indecisive on a variety of military issues, including the Somalia operation. In March 1995 the last UN peacekeeping forces, including the U.S. contingent, withdrew from Somalia.

Somalia illustrated a larger problem in redefining America's global role. During the Cold War, U.S. policy in the Third World, for better or worse, had been shaped by strategic calculations. Somalia's ports, for example, had been prized as a key to control of the Indian Ocean. The Cold War's end reduced the Third World's strategic importance at the same time that it unleashed a Pandora's box of ethnic and religious hatreds. This confluence of forces left American foreign policy rudderless, prey to passing gusts of media-influenced public opinion. The administration seemed unable to clarify the extent to which it wished to commit U.S.

The Endless Quest for Mideast Peace. *Secretary of State Madeleine Albright meets with Palestinian leader Yasir Arafat in 1997. Despite persistent U.S. prodding, the Mideast peace process seemed stalled as the 1990s ended.* (Gamma)

power and prestige in situations that did not involve vital American national interests.

The same dilemma hamstrung U.S. policy toward the ongoing conflict in Bosnia and Herzegovina, where fighting among ethnic Serbs, Bosnian Muslims, and Croatians had left 100,000 dead by early 1993, created 3.6 million refugees, and wrought untold suffering. Clinton ordered the U.S. Air Force to drop food and relief supplies to besieged Bosnian Muslims, but like Bush he initially refrained from a deeper military engagement. Clinton did endorse a plan negotiated by European Community representatives that divided Bosnia and Herzegovina into a patchwork of ethnic regions. But the warring factions at first showed little interest, and the murderous fighting raged on.

Late in 1995, responding to a U.S. initiative, leaders of the warring factions in Bosnia came to a conference in Dayton, Ohio, where they signed a treaty ending the war and providing for separate Serbian and Muslim-Croatian jurisdictions in Bosnia, under the umbrella of a vaguely described coalition government. President Clinton committed 20,000 U.S. troops to Bosnia to monitor the cease-fire and facilitate implementation of the Dayton accords. This task proved remarkably difficult, as ethnic hatreds and territorial expansionism raged on. In 1998 more than 8,500 U.S. troops remained in Bosnia as part of a NATO stabilization force. But the fragile cease-fire generally held, and Clinton touted Bosnia as at least a qualified success for post–Cold War American diplomacy.

Meanwhile, conditions in Russia and elsewhere in the former Soviet sphere remained volatile. In 1993, as falling productivity and hyperinflation battered the

Russian economy, right-wing nationalists and former Communist *apparatchiks* in the parliament tried to unseat President Boris Yeltsin. Visions of a Russia awash in anarchy and civil war, or even of a return to dictatorship and renewed Cold War tensions, haunted Washington. The crisis peaked in October, as Yeltsin's hard-line opponents, nostalgic for the days of empire and one-party rule, made a last stand in the parliament building. After several tense days, Yeltsin crushed the resistance. Clinton and other Western leaders endorsed Yeltsin but mainly watched from the sidelines. In Russian parliamentary elections later that year, disgruntled voters backed a constitution proposed by Yeltsin but gave surprising support to the party of Vladimir Zhirinovsky, a rabid Russian nationalist, anti-semite, and neofascist who openly admired Adolf Hitler. Washington responded with renewed expression of support for Yeltsin. Battling economic problems, political instability, and organized crime, Yeltsin clung to power into 1998 and Russia continued its rocky transition to democracy and capitalism. To facilitate the process, President Clinton, meeting with Yeltsin in Helsinki in March 1997, supported Russia's membership in the World Trade Organization. In the same spirit, the world's major industrialized nations (the so-called Group of Seven, or G7) invited Russia to participate in their 1997 annual conference in Denver, renamed the Summit of Eight.

Europe's new power realities were starkly underscored in 1997 when NATO invited Hungary, Poland, and the Czech Republic, all former Soviet satellite states, to join. To ease Moscow's objections, NATO gave Russia a voice in shaping NATO policy and agreed not to introduce nuclear weapons into the new members' territory. The precise function of the expanded post–Cold War NATO remained unclear. While some NATO officials spoke of an enlarged security system extending "from Vancouver to Vladivostok," President Clinton and the U.S. State Department played down the military theme and spoke of NATO's political role in promoting democracy and amicable relations among the new Eastern European members.

On another front, the hijackings and other terrorist acts that had tormented Carter and Reagan abated in the early 1990s. But in February 1993, horror struck in the United States itself when terrorists planted a massive bomb in a parking garage under the twin towers of New York's World Trade Center, a vast 110-story complex housing 50,000 workers and 350 companies. The blast killed six people and left scores of victims of smoke inhalation and other injuries. Thousands of office workers and tourists had to grope their way down smoke-filled stairs. In 1994, four Shiite fundamentalists, followers of a militant sheik earlier implicated in the assassination of Egypt's Anwar el-Sadat, were convicted of the bombing. In 1997 the man considered the mastermind of the plot, Ramzi Ahmed Yousef, was convicted and faced life imprisonment. The tragedy offered a sobering reminder of the dangers that still stalked the world despite the easing of superpower tensions.

While the end of the Cold War unleashed conflicts in the former Soviet realm, in the Middle East it initially appeared to reduce tensions. Cut adrift by their former patron Moscow, hard-line Arab leaders like Syria's Hafez-al Assad grew more flexible. Secretary of State James Baker had nudged the Arabs toward talks with Israel while simultaneously pressuring Israel to stop building Jewish settlements on the occupied West Bank. President Bush had added to the pressure by withholding loan guarantees urgently sought by Israel to settle 360,000 Jewish immigrants who had poured in from the former Soviet Union. Premier Yitzhak Shamir of Israel's right-wing Likud party showed little interest in peace talks, but Shamir's successor, Yitzhak Rabin of the Labour party, who came to power in 1992, proved more receptive. When Rabin curbed Jewish settlements in the West Bank and proposed limited Palestinian self-government in the territories, Bush approved the loan guarantees. While Secretary of State Christopher pursued the Baker initiative, Rabin initiated secret talks with Yasir Arafat's Palestine Liberation Organization. September 1993 brought a startling breakthrough. Israel and the PLO announced an accord granting the Palestinians limited autonomy in the Gaza Strip and in the West Bank city of Jerico. In return, Arafat renounced terrorism and recognized Israel as a nation. On September 13, 1993, flanking a smiling Bill Clinton, the two leaders signed the accord at the White House. Encouraged by Washington, Israeli peace talks with Jordan and Syria moved forward.

As always, however, Middle East peace proved maddeningly elusive. Israeli-Palestinian hostilities remained high, particularly after an Israeli gunman shot and killed twenty-nine worshippers at an Arab mosque in the predominantly Palestinian city of Hebron in 1994. Then in November 1995, an Israeli youth fanatically opposed to the peace process assassinated Prime Minister Yitzak Rabin at a Tel Aviv peace rally. In 1996, Benjamin Netanyahu of the conservative Likud party was elected prime minister. Tensions flared as the Israelis opened a tunnel entrance near a Muslim religious site on Jerusalem's Temple Mount. In 1997 they began construction of a Jewish settlement in a region of East Jerusalem claimed by the Palestinians. By a 130–2 vote, the UN General Assembly condemned this action as illegal, but a series of deadly terrorist bombings of Israeli civilians by Palestinians linked to the radical Hamas organization deepened the intransigence of Israeli hard-liners. "The struggle for Jerusalem has begun," declared Israel's police minister grimly.

President Clinton, while condemning the terrorism, pressed Netanyahu to avoid provocations and to speed the agreed-upon withdrawals. In January 1997 Netanyahu announced a partial withdrawal from Hebron, but the process stalled as hard-liners in Netanyahu's own Likud party objected, giving rise to more Palestinian protests and more Hamas-inspired suicide bombings. On a brief and abortive Middle East visit in September 1997, Secretary of State Albright called on Yasir Arafat to crack down on Hamas terrorism, sharply criticized Netanyahu's policies, and pushed for renewed momentum on the peace process. "I am not going to come back here just to tread water," she announced brusquely upon her departure. As so often in the past, the high hopes of 1993 had faded. The *New York Times* noted with disappointment: "The Israeli-Palestinian peace effort has fallen into a coma, and the prospects for recovery anytime soon are bleak."

On another Middle East front, Iraqi president Saddam Hussein, despite his defeat in the Persian Gulf War, remained a threat as he chafed under UN economic sanctions, including an embargo on Iraqi oil exports. A ruthless dictator with a shaky grip on power, Saddam was for that reason all the more dangerous. In 1997, Saddam sought to bar Americans from the UN inspection team sent to Iraq after the Gulf War to dismantle his admitted stockpile of chemical-biological weapons (sometimes called "the poor man's atomic bomb") and to prevent further development of these nightmarish weapons of mass destruction. With France and Russia

Frustration with Iraq. *Despite his defeat in the 1990–91 Persian Gulf War, tough UN sanctions, and U.S. threats of renewed military attack, Iraqi strongman Saddam Hussein clung to power, stirring fears that he was building an arsenal of chemical and biological weapons.* (© 1996 Dana Summers/The Orlando Sentinel)

eager to resume trade with Iraq, Saddam hoped to exploit divisions in the alliance against him. In the short run the alliance held, Saddam backed down, and the inspectors returned. But Iraq under his rule remained worrisome.

In neighboring Iran, too, bitterly anti-American Muslim fundamentalists still held sway. But the landslide election of Mohammed Khatami, a somewhat more moderate Shiite leader, as Iran's president in 1997 suggested that Iran's hard-line position might be softening. While still denouncing the U.S. government, Khatami expressed goodwill toward "the American people."

Although problems in Eastern Europe and the Middle East remained, Asia—and especially trade with Asia—also loomed large on Washington's foreign-policy agenda as the 1990s wore on. And small wonder: In 1996, the United States ran up trade deficits of $47 billion with Japan and $37 billion with China. The trade deficit with all the Pacific Rim nations together soared to $102 billion. Given such numbers, the administration tirelessly pressured Japan, China, and other Asian nations to open their doors to more U.S. products. Pursuing this goal, the administration gave high priority to an eighteen-nation Asia-Pacific Economic Cooperation Forum that met in Manila in November 1996. The conference agreed on a phased elimination of all tariffs on computers and electronic equipment by 2000.

The danger that trade calculations would override other important diplomatic goals became starkly evident in American relations with China, which remained firmly in the control of a Communist party that encouraged free-market experimentation while stifling democracy and denying basic human rights to its citizens. Walking a tightrope in formulating its China policy, the Clinton administration agreed to diplomatic visits and in November 1996 granted "most favored nation" trading status to China (that is, China received the same trading privileges America accorded to other nations). Secretary of State Albright visited China in 1997, followed by a delegation that included Vice President Gore and House Speaker Gingrich. On the latter visit, China signed major trade agreements with the U.S. corporations Boeing and General Motors. Amid the mutual congratulations, Gingrich firmly insisted that any Chinese-U.S. relationship must address China's human-rights abuses. Chinese exiles in America and private human-rights organizations—and, much more cautiously, the Clinton administration—pressed China to democratize its political system and grant its people political and religious freedom.

Later in 1997, Chinese president Jiang Zemin paid a state visit to the United States. (Among his stops were Colonial Williamsburg and Drexel University in Philadelphia, where his son had earned a Ph.D. in engineering.) Jiang's visit, undertaken in part to enhance his prestige at home, became a magnet for protests. Except for a few symbolic gestures, however, including the release from prison of one prominent activist, the Chinese ignored the protests. In an era when global trade loomed ever larger, economic considerations were clearly driving America's China policy.

After the abortive Somalia intervention, Washington had generally neglected Africa with its many problems. President Clinton sought to rectify this neglect in 1998 (and shore up support with African-American voters) with a swing through sub-Saharan Africa, a region of poverty, indebtedness, and authoritarian rule, but with signs of political and economic progress as well. In prosperous South Africa he honored President Nelson Mandela; in Uganda, Botswana, Rwanda, and Senegal he praised movements toward democracy, wildlife protection, and economic development. As elsewhere in the world, Clinton emphasized U.S. commercial interests, preaching the message of "trade not aid."

At times, the administration seemed out of step with the rest of the world, as in its resistance to a humanitarian campaign to ban land mines. Nearly 100 million land mines deployed worldwide, many of them having long outlasted the conflicts that gave rise to them, annually killed or wounded some twenty-five thousand innocent people, often children. In September 1997, citing military considerations in Korea, the United States refused to join nearly one hundred nations in signing a treaty outlawing land mines. When the American Jody Williams won the 1997 Nobel Peace prize for her role in organizing the global campaign against land mines, she strongly condemned the Clinton administration's refusal to sign the treaty.

While the administration pushed for continued global involvement, particularly on trade and economic issues, many Americans, including some powerful politicians, held back in suspicion. This neo-isolationist "go it alone" attitude often focused on the United Nations. In 1996, the United States refused to support a second term for UN Secretary General Boutros Boutros-Ghali, a target of right-wing attack in America. In his place, the UN chose a candidate acceptable to America, the U.S.-educated Kofi Annan of Ghana. Despite this concession, conservatives in

Congress continued to withhold over $1 billion in back dues owed by the United States to the UN, charging that the world organization was overstaffed and poorly administered. The UN, in turn, rejected U.S. efforts to reduce its annual assessment, which was based on America's share of the global economy. Senator Jesse Helms, chair of the Senate Foreign Relations Committee, when not defending the tobacco industry, battled the United Nations and other international organizations he deeply distrusted. Some religious fundamentalists denounced the United Nations as part of a demonic conspiracy to take over the world and destroy America.

As the Cold War receded, the United States moved cautiously and sometimes uncertainly in exercising its power and defining its global interests. For the first time in half a century, no single, overarching goal could provide clarity and coherence to American foreign policy. Instead, many different and often maddeningly complex problems had to be addressed as they arose, often simultaneously, in different parts of the world. A tendency in the media to present complex issues in luridly melodramatic terms and to demonize individuals like Saddam Hussein, a legacy of the era of World War II and the Cold War, further complicated the effort to develop a coherent long-term foreign policy.

In general, the Clinton administration sought to preserve U.S. national security, advance U.S. economic interests, build up a framework of international order, and to some extent promote America's tradition of upholding democracy and human rights. When these goals conflicted, as in American relations with China, or when they stirred domestic opposition, as in policy toward the United Nations, problems arose.

From the days of Woodrow Wilson through the Carter and Reagan administrations, a concern for democracy, freedom, and human rights had suffused American foreign policy. "Realists" like Henry Kissinger had objected that national interest, not an effort to reform other nations' internal practices, should guide U.S. diplomacy, but human-rights concerns remained important. Indeed, this was inevitable in an open society in which foreign policy to some extent arose from popular beliefs and attitudes. Initially, President Clinton appeared to share this outlook, as he came to office pledging to oppose dictatorships "from Baghdad to Beijing." But as economic and trade considerations increasingly dominated the administration's approach to the world, human rights received little but lip service.

While aspects of America's world role in the 1990s merited criticism, it was also important not to lose sight of the broader picture of a world breathtakingly transformed in a few years' time. An American of 1980 suddenly propelled forward to the end of the nineties would scarcely have believed his or her eyes. The Cold War was over; America's long-time antagonist the Soviet Union was no more. With capitalism triumphant globally, nearly 90 percent of the world's population was linked by common trading agreements, in contrast to some 25 percent in 1980.

Our hypothetical time traveler would have been equally amazed to learn that the nuclear threat that had menaced the world for a half a century, while not totally gone, had radically diminished. Meeting in Helsinki in March 1997, President Clinton and Boris Yeltsin signed the START III Treaty (subject to ratification by their respective legislatures) cutting each nation's stock of long-range nuclear warheads to 2,500 or fewer. By the standards of 1945 this was still an awesome arsenal, but in contrast to the bristling nuclear armadas at the height of the Cold War, it represented a dramatic reduction.

Total U.S. military spending fell by some 38 percent between 1985 and 1997. As late as 1988, some 6 percent of America's gross domestic product went for military purposes; a decade later, the figure had fallen to just over 3 percent. In the Pentagon's quadrennial review submitted to Congress in 1997, Defense Secretary William Cohen projected even deeper cuts. In Cohen's scenario, the number of attack submarines would drop from 73 to 50, bombers from 202 to 187, active military personnel from 1.45 million to 1.36 million, and so forth. As always in a democracy, this process stirred controversy. Some argued that the cuts in military spending should go much further, while others hawkishly insisted that the reductions were dangerously weakening the nation. The underlying reality stood out boldly, however: While the world remained a dangerous place as the 1990s ended, and while the United States had no doubt fumbled some of the challenges of the post–Cold War era, the globe was in many ways a far less terrifying place, and America a far less militarized society, than had been true a scant fifteen years before.

A Booming Economy—But Not for All

Central to much of U.S. history in the mid- and later 1990s—from Clinton approval ratings and welfare reform to the budget-balancing bill and the stress on trade agreements in the nation's foreign policy—is the fact that these were years of strong and sustained prosperity. The benefits of this prosperity were not evenly distributed, and the good times were accompanied by warning signals. But the prosperity was real, and it decisively influenced the course of events. The economic upturn looked particularly impressive since it came at a time when the economies of Germany and Japan, as well as "Asian tigers" such as Thailand, Indonesia, and South Korea, the smoking pacesetters of the seventies and eighties, fell into recession or even, in the case of South Korea and Indonesia, catastrophically collapsed.

The beginning of the decade gave little hint of what lay ahead. As we have seen, a sluggish economy helped defeat George Bush in 1992. For a time, it seemed that the chronic structural ills that had stalled economic growth after the bleak watershed year of 1973 would persist indefinitely. In December 1991, after a dismal sales year, GM announced plans to close twenty-one plants and to slash its labor force by seventy thousand. The revelation that top management at the Big Three automakers had received fat raises and stock benefits as their firms lost billions and laid off workers stirred bitter resentment. IBM lost $4.97 billion in 1992 and, in a difficult step for a company proud of never having laid off employees, revealed plans to shed twenty-five thousand workers. IBM stock plunged to half its value.

But some economic indicators began to turn upward in 1991, and by 1993 the turnaround was clear. The resulting boom roared on into 1998, with many economists predicting continued expansion. The gross domestic product, which measures aggregate economic growth, rose from $5.5 trillion in 1990 to nearly $8 trillion in 1997. Corporate profits surged from $313 billion in 1990 to $735 billion in

1996, and still higher in 1997. In the expansive climate, corporate mergers and acquisitions hit record levels in 1997. The year's largest merger united two telecommunications giants, as Worldcom acquired MCI for $36.5 billion. By 1997, thirty of the world's one hundred biggest multinational corporations, dealing in everything from pharmaceuticals to computer software, were headquartered in the United States.

The South enjoyed the most rapid growth, but nearly all regions basked in the glow of prosperity. The Midwest, the gritty industrial powerhouse dismissed in the 1980s as "the Rust Belt," bounced back as industries downsized and retooled, and as exports surged. Thanks to microprocessing and other new technologies, marvelled the *Economist,* American industry had "reinvented manufacturing." California, battered by defense-industry cuts, enjoyed an economic renaissance, creating four hundred thousand new jobs from June 1996 to June 1997. The laggard Los Angeles economy, once heavily dependent on aerospace industries, became far more diversified in the 1990s.

As investors rushed to share in the boom, the stock market soared. With occasional dips and blips, stock prices streaked upward after 1992 in one of the longest sustained bull markets in U.S. history. The Dow Jones Industrial Average, a key indicator, which stood at 2679 in 1990, soared to over 9000 by the spring of 1998. Mutual funds flourished as millions of Americans poured more and more money into the market. Computer and communications stocks did especially well. In 1997, the stock price of an Internet company called Yahoo that had yet to show a profit increased by 500 percent. "Is this a wonder economy or what?" crowed *Business Week* in mid-1997; "On Top of the World," gushed *Newsweek.* The market's recent performance, agreed the *New York Times* early in 1998, was "nothing short of amazing."

How did the boom affect ordinary Americans? Corporate executives, white-collar professionals, highly skilled workers, and citizens fortunate enough to have inherited wealth or accumulated savings to invest in the stock market obviously did very well. For others, the picture was mixed. On the plus side for consumers, the inflation rate, in contrast to some other periods of prosperity, remained low in the 1990s, dropping to 1.7 percent in 1997. Indeed, for five months early in 1997, overall prices actually fell—the longest sustained period of price decline since the 1950s.

Jobs became plentiful as businesses hired more workers to meet production demands. The economy added 13.5 million jobs in 1993–97—nearly 3 million of them in 1997 alone. The welfare rolls shrank by almost 10 percent in 1996, even before the welfare-reform law took effect, as more marginal workers found jobs. By November 1997 the jobless rate stood at 4.6 percent, the lowest since 1973. Economists and journalists became almost euphoric in the face of such statistics. Commenting on 1997's "stunning job growth," President Clinton's chief economic advisor, Janet L. Yellen, exulted: "We're in the best of all possible worlds." The 1990s, said the *New Republic* in 1997, "will be seen in future decades as a golden age in American history."

Not all was peaches and cream, however. Some economists worried about the low rate of savings. Others warned that as the baby boomers retired, placing heavy demands on Medicare and an underfunded social security system, the federal deficit would once again mushroom, depressing the economy. Still others noted that while the total volume of goods and services grew in the 1990s, the annual increase in the productivity *rate* (that is, output per worker) remained stuck at around 1 percent, in contrast to the 1945–73 era of economic growth, when the productivity rate had risen dramatically. (Some analysts argued, however, that older methods of calculating productivity underestimated the new forms of economic growth, in which intangibles such as electronic communications and information processing loomed large.)

Further, the benefits of prosperity were unevenly distributed. For example, while the jobless rate among white workers dropped to a minuscule 3.8 percent by 1997, for Hispanic workers it stood at around 7 percent, and for African Americans, nearly 10 percent. Employment rates for all groups improved in the 1990s thanks to the economic upturn, but the disparities remained. Among black teenagers, the unemployment figure approached 30 percent. The fact that the 1997 jobless rates for minorities were the *lowest* in decades merely underscored the serious and chronic nature of this problem. A lack of education and of the skills demanded by an increasingly high-tech economy, analysts found, were key factors in these differential employment rates. The importance of skills and education in the new economic environment was brutally evident in the statistics. From 1974 to 1996, the family income of Americans with college degrees rose by 28 percent; for those with only a high-school education, the figure was an anemic 3 percent. As for those at the very bottom, the poverty rate fell in the 1990s, but in 1996 it was still 13.7 percent—higher than in 1989. In the inner cities it rose to 21 percent, and in some deeply depressed neighborhoods it reached 40 percent.

Even for the vast majority of workers who did hold jobs, wages did not begin to keep pace with corporate profits or stock prices. Corrected for inflation, wages remained flat for most of the 1990s (although by 1997, as the labor market tightened and businesses competed for a dwindling number of available workers, wages did rise somewhat). Indeed, from 1991 through 1997, as corporate profits, the stock market, and U.S. exports all went through the roof, the average income of the lower 60 percent of American families, adjusted for inflation, actually declined slightly. The lack of pressure for higher wages resulted from various factors, including the flood of imports from Asian nations with lower wage scales, workers' job anxieties about "downsizing" and high-tech automation, and the continued decline of labor unions. By the end of the nineties, only 10 percent of workers in the private sector were unionized. Lacking the clout of collective action, workers generally had to be content with the wages they were offered.

Not only did wages fail to keep pace with overall rates of economic growth, but almost 20 percent of the U.S. labor force held part-time or temporary positions at lower wages and often without health coverage or other benefits. While the percentage of part-time workers remained fairly constant from the 1970s through the 1990s, and while most part-timers claimed that they preferred this option, the pattern was nevertheless troubling. The nation's largest "employer" in the 1990s was Manpower, Inc., a clearinghouse for temporary workers. Many big companies had a two-tier labor force, with an elite of highly trained, well-paid workers, and a second tier of less skilled, lower-paid part-timers. The 1990s also saw a surge in the number of part-time college teachers. Though often holding a Ph.D., these marginal instructors earned less, enjoyed fewer benefits, and lacked long-term job security.

An extreme example of the part-time phenomenon in industry was the sprawling United Parcel Service with its familiar brown trucks and brown-uniformed delivery persons. Of UPS's 185,000 employees in 1997, 60 percent were part-timers earning less than half the hourly rate of the company's full-time employees. (A decade earlier, part-timers had constituted only 42 percent of the UPS work force.) The issue of part-time work, in fact, was a key factor in a 1997 strike of UPS workers. One of the few successful labor actions of the 1990s, the strike produced an agreement by UPS management to shift more part-timers to full-time status.

The boom times of the 1990s did not diminish the enormous disparities of wealth and poverty in America; indeed, the gap widened. At the top of the scale, upper-class and upper-middle-class Americans prospered thanks to their social connections, their stock holdings, or the education and skills they brought to the job market. At the other end were not only those in poverty, but millions of workers, many lacking advanced job skills and holding only a high-school diploma at best, earning low wages in marginal, part-time, or temporary jobs. The chasm between the two was vast. In 1997, after six years of sustained growth, the top 20 percent of U.S. families enjoyed an average income of $117,489—almost thirteen times the average income of the bottom 20 percent ($9,254). In New York State, the income of the top group was nearly *twenty times* that of the lowest group. As with the employment data, these numbers in part reflected racial and ethnic differentials: the average income of Hispanic and African-American families in 1997

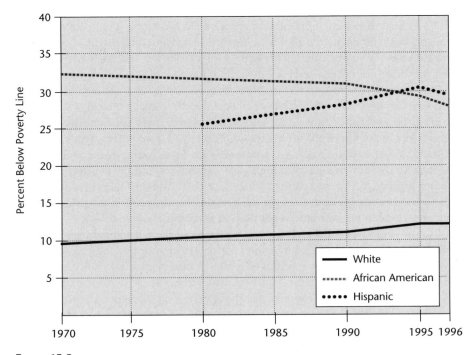

FIGURE 15.3

Poverty, Race, and Ethnicity in America, 1970–1996

SOURCE: Bureau of the Census, in *World Almanac, 1998.*

was only 58 percent that of white, non-Hispanic families. Observed economist Elizabeth McNichol of Washington's Center on Budget and Policy Priorities: "It used to be that when the economy grew, everybody gained, but in the last generation that hasn't been true."

These disparities roused remarkably little protest. As is the way of politicians, both the Clinton administration and the Republican leaders of Congress took credit for the positive economic news and played down the less rosy parts of the picture. For some leaders, the nation's burgeoning exports seemed the only economic indicator that counted. "Corporate success in global competition has become an overriding goal," noted business reporter Louis Uchitelle in the *New York Times* in 1997, "even at the price of greater wage inequality." Among those stuck at the lower end of the economic ladder, a mood of resignation rather than anger or protest seemed to prevail. A 1997 study found a striking correlation between wealth and voting: the well-to-do protected their status and interests at the polls; the disadvantaged, apparently having lost faith in the political process, took little interest in elections. Representative John Conyers of Michigan said in 1996: "I have never heard ... more complaints about the government's insensitivity to what people need in this country ... , [but] instead of ... angry protests at the polls, it turns into a whimper."

The sometimes mind-numbing statistics documenting these economic disparities translated into tangible realities. While an auto dealer in Wichita, Kansas, reported selling twenty-two $35,000 BMW luxury cars in one six-week period in 1997, millions of Americans struggled at the economic margins. Robert Reich, former secretary of labor in the Clinton administration, summed up the situation vividly in 1997: "For all its riches, the United States now has a greater percentage of its citizens in prisons or on the streets, and more neglected children, than any other advanced nation."

In short, while the prosperity of the 1990s was real and important, it came hedged with reservations. This helps explain why the national mood remained cautious, even pessimistic, not confident and expansive as it had been in the 1950s, for example. With the recessions, unemployment, inflation, downsizing, and other economic problems of the 1973–91 years fresh in memory, and with the income of most workers flat or rising only slightly, Americans welcomed the prosperity, but did not assume—as many had in the more innocent fifties—that it would last forever. The average workweek lengthened, as employees worked longer, and took overtime, to salt away as much as they could against a possible downturn. As Don Simon, an employee at the Cessna aircraft plant in Wichita, observed of his $17.50-an-hour job in 1997: "We've had 60- or 70-hour weeks. I'm just stashing it away in the pillow so I can retire early." While the economy boomed, the national mood remained edgy and uncertain.

A Diverse People: Contemporary Social Trends

As they tentatively assessed an economic boom whose blessings seemed to be rather capriciously distributed, Americans also struggled to absorb demographic and social trends that would mold U.S. life for the foreseeable future. The nation's

❖❖ In Perspective: *The Multiculturalism Debate*

"E pluribus unum," the nation's motto proclaims: "Out of many, one." Yet in the post-1960 decades, the ideal of a common national culture proved elusive. As U.S. society grew more fragmented, with an array of groups clamoring for cultural as well as political equality, debate raged over how literature and history should be taught.

The so-called multiculturalism controversy took many forms. Advocates for women, African Americans, Native Americans, Hispanics, Asian Americans, gays and lesbians, and other groups protested the way in which traditional pedagogy had ignored or marginalized them. Even evangelical Christians, once the dominant cultural group, complained that the academic world ignored and devalued their beliefs. In English departments, academics argued over whether to reconstruct a canon dominated by works of "dead white European males." Instructors devised new courses that privileged works by women, persons of color, and Third World writers. History textbook writers and publishers scrambled to give more space to non-elites.

Some observers, however, saw in these efforts an erosion of any sense of common American identity: the *pluribus* seemed triumphant, the *unum* in retreat. In *Cultural Literacy: What Every American Needs to Know* (1987), E. D. Hirsch, Jr., cautioned that American culture was becoming a "tower of Babel." Yet many judged Hirsch's own effort to define a common culture traditionalistic and exclusionary. The University of Chicago classicist Alan Bloom, an unabashed elitist, defined culture more narrowly still. In his best-selling polemic, *The Closing of the American Mind* (1987), Bloom lamented the erosion of standards and called for an intellectual elite that would disdain the ephemera of politics, social conflict, and mass culture to ponder the great themes of Western civilization. Historian Arthur Schlesinger, Jr., in *The Disuniting of America* (1991) urged a renewed effort to define a common core of American citizenship and culture. Finally, historians warned lest the impulse to enhance the self-esteem of minority groups encourage shoddy history.

The dispute spilled over into politics. Cities such as Miami with large Hispanic populations debated resolutions making English the official language. President Reagan's choice to head the National Endowment for the Humanities, Lynn Cheney (spouse of Defense Secretary Dick Cheney), battled multiculturalism and lauded the classical tradition. Pat Buchanan, the conservative columnist who briefly ran for president in 1992, rallied the forces of the Right at the Republican convention, stridently summoning cheering supporters to take back "our cities, our culture, and our country." These critics often idealized the past's cultural unity and intellectual harmony in contrast to today's fragmentation and raucous conflicts. In fact, a close look at history from ancient Greece onward shows not harmony but conflict and disputatiousness remarkably similar to our own era.

It is not surprising that the "multicultural" demand eventually became so vehement. Up to the very recent era, courses in history and literature did focus on the exploits and writings of white male elites of European origin. In U.S. history courses, Indians appeared solely as a quickly vanquished foe, blacks mainly as victims of slavery, and Hispanics and Asian Americans hardly at all. Absent, too, was working-class culture, of whatever ethnic character. A few women merited notice, but the historical experience of women as a whole—half the population—was ignored. As these groups asserted themselves politically, the corresponding demand to rectify decades of cultural distortion soon followed.

Some proponents of "multiculturalism" and "politically correct" speech dismissed their critics as expressing the bigotry and xenophobia that have always existed in America. Indeed, as early as the 1740s, Benjamin Franklin warned of the German immigrants who were "polluting" Pennsylvania's Anglo society with their alien ways and language. Throughout American history, prejudice against newcomers and minorities has led to periodic demands for exclusion and control.

Yet the contemporary debate involves more than just covert prejudice and has unfolded in a unique cultural setting. In the past, minorities were either powerless or had far less power than the dominant elite. In modern America, advocates for the underdog occupy powerful positions in government, the media, and academia. When demands for the redress of minority grievances in the cultural realm come from such quarters, they can be accompanied by credible threats to impose sanctions that will enforce acceptable standards of conduct and expression. This potential for abuse raises legitimate concerns about "Big Brother" and the repression of individual freedom. It also can encourage a culture of victimization, in which individuals and groups demand legal redress for insensitive behavior or speech that, however deplorable, may be the price of a free society. Conflicts once fought out in private now land in the courts. Furthermore, the obsession with "political correctness" can stifle discussion in the classroom and elsewhere, as people become so fearful of giving offense that they choose to remain silent rather than express potentially unpopular views. Thus, the debate over multiculturalism and "political correctness" can inhibit the vigorous give-and-take on which democracy thrives.

Some observers have tried to move the controversy off dead center. In *Beyond the Culture Wars* (1992), Gerald Graff of the University of Chicago viewed the debate as evidence not of disintegration but of cultural renewal. Passivity over issues of cultural meaning is far more to be feared than discord, Graff contended. He urged teachers to incorporate the cultural debate into the curriculum as a way of bringing texts alive for students. Despite occasional excesses, the multiculturalism debate has in fact pumped new energy into education. Textbooks and course syllabi now more closely reflect the ethnic and gender realities of the larger society. Students vigorously debate issues of gender, race, and social class in canonical works that they once accepted without question.

One champion of multiculturalism, the Japanese-American historian Ronald Takaki, insists that only by recognizing the reality of cultural diversity can the "E pluribus unum" dream ever be realized. Hopes for a genuinely inclusive culture, Takaki wrote in *A Different Mirror* (1993), lie in "'unlearning' much of what we have been told about America's past and substituting a more inclusive and accurate history of all the peoples of America." Takaki's point is well taken, but the risks remain: Intolerance in pursuit of multiculturalist or "politically correct" goals can lead to new forms of prejudice, pressures toward a sterile conformity, and the prospect of a backlash damaging to all concerned. Clearly this complex debate is far from resolved as the end of the century approaches.

population of some 267 million in 1997 comprised a mosaic of immigrants and native-born, Native Americans, blacks, Asians, whites, and Hispanics of diverse racial and ethnic origins. The population also included growing numbers of persons of mixed race who resisted checking one box or another on the census forms. Each of these vast groups, in turn, included an array of subgroups differentiated by geography, religion, cultural roots, and economic status.

Immigration in the 1980s and 1990s rose to the highest levels since the early twentieth century. Five million immigrants arrived in 1985–90, and the flow continued thereafter at a pace that approached or exceeded a million a year. In 1996, for example, 900,000 legal immigrants arrive, joined by an estimated 300,000 illegal immigrants, for a total of 1.2 million. This influx produced a population that by 1998 was nearly 10 percent foreign born, up from 4.7 percent in 1970; in California, the foreign-born figure exceeded 20 percent. In the 1950s, the media had portrayed America as blandly homogenous. Unrealistic even then, the stereotype collapsed a generation later as diversity, not uniformity, characterized U.S. society. By 2050, the Census Bureau predicted, non-Hispanic whites would comprise a scant 53 percent of the population.

For Native Americans, these years brought a quickening of ethnic pride. More than 1.7 million persons identified themselves as American Indians in the 1990 census, over twice the 1970 total. These figures reflected not only natural increase but also the growing numbers of Indians eager to affirm their ethnic roots. A network of some thirty tribal colleges provided educational opportunities and cultural sustenance. Under a 1961 law permitting tribes to buy or develop land for commercial purposes, Indians pursued business ventures ranging from vacation resorts to gambling casinos. The latter generated revenue but also led to intratribal disputes and conflicts with opponents of commercialized gambling. Yet Indians remained among the nation's poorest citizens. Both on the reservations and in the cities, joblessness, alcoholism, and inadequate health care inexorably took their toll.

But Native-American communities fought back. A number of tribes, including the Oneida of Wisconsin, used casino earnings to fund alcohol-treatment centers. Staff members of the treatment center at the Pine Ridge Indian Reservation in South Dakota used traditional methods such as the sweat lodge, and reminders of the warnings of Native-American leaders like Crazy Horse, to help young people overcome alcoholism. Said Tim Giago, the editor of the newspaper *Indian Country Today,* in 1997: "Our people are becoming more aware of our traditional ways and culture. And they're realizing that drunkenness was not part of it."

The Asian-American population continued to expand as well, fed by immigration from the Philippines, Korea, and Vietnam and by well-established Chinese-American and Japanese-American communities. In 1990 Los Angeles was more than 9 percent Asian, up from 5 percent a decade earlier. With their strong family culture and emphasis on academics, Asian-Americans showed high rates of college attendance and upward mobility. As in most other immigrant groups, however, generational tensions plagued these communities as young people wavered between traditional ways and the lure of the mass culture.

The African-American population remained divided along economic lines. At one end of the spectrum, the black professional and upper-middle class enjoyed good incomes, stable families, and college degrees. In 1990, 12 percent of college students were black, more than double the 1965 rate and close to the ratio of the general population. From 1967 to 1990, the proportion of black workers earning more than $50,000 (in constant 1990 dollars) rose from 7 percent to 15 percent. In 1990 some 46 percent of African Americans in the labor force held white-collar jobs. In 1995, the average income of black married couples was 87 percent of that of white married couples, up from 79 percent in 1989, while the annual earnings of blacks with college degrees averaged about $30,000. Communities like Cranwood in Cleveland, Chicago's Auburn Park, and Baldwin Hills in Los Angeles featured the attractive homes and well-tended lawns of this black professional and middle class. The more than six hundred thousand black-owned businesses in the 1990s included giant TLC Beatrice International, a food processing and distribution company with 1996 sales of $2.2 billion. Prominent black scholars like Henry Louis Gates, Cornel West, and William Julius Wilson of Harvard and writers like Toni Morrison and Alice Walker played key roles in the nation's cultural life. Thousands of African Americans were prominent in the music, sports, and entertainment fields. Increasing numbers of blacks held elective and appointive office at all levels of government.

At the other end of the scale were the impoverished inner-city blacks, perhaps a third of all African Americans in 1990. From this battered group, whose education often ended well before high-school graduation, came the blacks who accounted for 55 percent of all murder arrests and 69 percent of all arrests for robbery. Although strong families, thriving churches, and vigorous social institutions existed in the inner city, the social pathologies were powerful. Among black youngsters aged fifteen to nineteen, the death rate by homicide stood at nearly ten times the rate for white youths in the early 1990s. In a trend for which analysts offered various explanations, pregnancy rates among black teenagers spiked upward in the 1970s and 1980s. In 1989, 66 percent of all black births were to single women, in contrast to 18 percent in 1950. Often scarcely beyond childhood themselves, these new mothers frequently had no means of support. As a result, more than two-thirds of all black children had been on welfare by their eighteenth birthday.

Lacking the training for skilled jobs that in any event were often located in distant suburbs, youths faced life on the streets or marginal service-sector jobs in car washes or fast-food establishments. Inner-city crime, welfare dependency, and teenage pregnancy were inseparable from the problem of joblessness. For the unskilled, one economist observed, the America of the early 1990s had become "a harder, rougher place."

Illegal drug use, although found at all income levels and among all races, reached epidemic proportions in inner-city minority neighborhoods plagued by poverty. In some two hundred urban areas, drug gangs waged lethal struggles over the lucrative cocaine and heroin trade. In many communities, children as young as eight or nine, lured by drug dealers' gold jewelry and flashy cars, acted as lookouts or made deliveries. The drug of choice in the inner cities was crack, an extrapotent form of cocaine. Public-health officials estimated that from thirty thousand to fifty thousand "crack babies" came into the world annually, addicted at birth. Of the eight hundred thousand African Americans in prison in 1998 (comprising nearly half the 1.7 million prison population), many were young males convicted of drug-related crimes.

Caught in the coils of joblessness, welfare dependence, and destructive behavior, millions in the inner cities seemed in the 1990s at risk of becoming a permanent undercaste. Books such as Alex Kotlowitz's *There Are No Children Here* (1991) and movies like John Singleton's *Boyz 'N the Hood* (1991), with its portrayal of young Los Angeles blacks devastated by drugs and gang warfare, evoked the individual human tragedies behind the aggregate statistics.

Inner-city tensions exploded into violence in Los Angeles in 1992 amid black outrage over the Rodney King case. On March 3, 1991, L.A. police had arrested King, a twenty-five-year-old black man, after a high-speed chase on the freeway. Though unarmed, the intoxicated King showed signs of resisting arrest. After zapping him with a 50,000-volt stun gun, the police forced King to the ground, and four officers took turns kicking and clubbing him with heavy truncheons, causing serious injury. Eleven other policemen stood by and watched. Unknown to the police, a nearby resident had captured the mayhem on videotape. Four policemen faced trial, but despite the videotape, a jury acquitted them in April 1992. As word of the verdict spread, violence erupted in South Central Los Angeles, a black and Hispanic district. For thirty-six hours, gangs roamed the streets, burning and looting. Black youths viciously beat a white truck driver. Rioters especially targeted the shops of Korean merchants. In scenes unhappily reminiscent of the 1960s, entire blocks went up in flames. "Can't we all get along," pleaded Rodney King in a televised call for calm. When an uneasy quiet returned, Los Angeles counted 44 dead, nearly 1,800 injured, 6,345 arrests, and $500 million in property damage. The "Rodney King riots" starkly underscored the pressure-cooker environment of inner cities mired in poverty and joblessness.

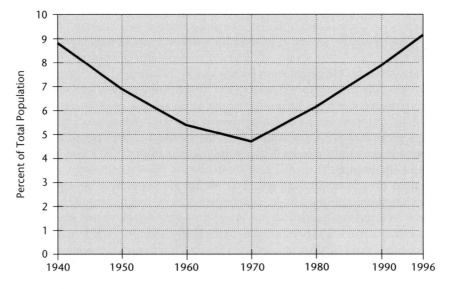

FIGURE 15.4

*Foreign-Born Residents in the United States, 1940–1996,
as Percentage of Total Population*

SOURCE: Bureau of the Census, in *World Almanac 1998.*

Even for this portion of the black community, however, the later 1990s brought evidence of improved conditions. The African-American poverty rate fell to all-time lows in 1995 and after. In contrast to the general population, median black family income rose significantly in the later 1990s, with the strongest gains among the poor. The black teenage birthrate fell by 17 percent in 1991–96, and the rate of out-of-wedlock births dropped slightly as well. The inner-city murder rate—often linked to drugs and gang warfare—also declined, contributing to a sharp drop in the overall violent-crime rate in America. By the late 1990s the high-school graduation rate for young African Americans was about the same as for whites. The statistics remained sketchy, but the trend seemed encouraging. As a spokesperson for a Washington think tank that studies trends in the black community observed in 1996: "[T]his is a short period of really very substantial and significant gains. . . . [B]y virtually every measure of well-being, African Americans have been on a significant uptrend during the '90s." In the "Million Man March" of October 1995, hundreds of thousands of black males gathered in Washington, D.C., to affirm their family responsibilities. Though sponsored by the Reverend Louis Farrakhan of the small Nation of Islam sect, the event's larger symbolism resonated in the black community and beyond.

The 1996 welfare-reform law and tough new state rules had a significant impact on the African-American community, since some 40 percent of the women and children receiving AFDC benefits were black. From a peak of 14 million in 1994, the welfare rolls plummeted thereafter: by 7 percent in 1995, 11 percent in 1996, and an estimated 18 percent or more in 1997. While some ex-welfare recipients sank deeper into poverty, early data suggested that at least half went to work, many with the help of state-funded job-training, placement, transportation, and childcare programs. In New Jersey, out-of-wedlock births fell sharply after a 1992 law barred increased welfare payments to women who had more children. Welfare-reform advocates hoped to see a similar pattern develop nationwide as the ideology of "work not welfare" took hold.

In 1998 the nation's 28 million Hispanics—nearly triple the 1970 total—composed America's fastest-growing minority. Indeed, demographers predict that by 2010, Hispanics will supplant blacks as the nation's largest minority, and by 2050 comprise one-quarter of the U.S. population. The nation's Hispanic population included more than 18 million Mexican Americans centered in the Southwest; Cuban Americans living in Florida; and immigrants from the Caribbean and Central America residing along the East Coast. Puerto Ricans, who are U.S. citizens, arrived in great numbers as well. Like earlier immigrants, Hispanics came to America seeking a better life, especially as falling oil prices rocked the Mexican economy. Between 1980 and 1985, the Hispanic population of California and Florida grew by some 30 percent; Texas's, by 23 percent. By 1990 both Miami and Los Angeles were one-third Hispanic.

Despite the 1986 immigration law that tightened border controls and imposed tougher restrictions on hiring undocumented aliens, as many as 12 million Hispanics lived in the United States illegally in the early 1990s. With few health benefits or other protections, they worked long hours for low wages as domestics, garment workers, and migrant farm laborers. Hispanic family, church, and cultural institutions provided support, but life in America was harsh, scourged by drugs, crime, school dropout, and teenage pregnancy. While Hispanics benefited from the economic boom of the 1990s, the overall growth in the Hispanic population, from immigration and natural increase, meant that the poverty rate hovered at around 30 percent through much of the decade, making Hispanics the nation's poorest minority group.

Ironically, shared poverty often pitted minority groups against each other. Inner-city blacks resented Korean-American shopkeepers. And tensions erupted as poor blacks and Hispanics competed for the same low-wage jobs. When Hispanics seeking better conditions moved from inner cities to outlying suburbs, they often faced discrimination. In the working-class Chicago suburb of Addison, for example, the white ethnics from earlier waves of immigration who ran the town reacted with hostility when Hispanics arrived in the 1980s, bulldozing housing in the Hispanic district for alleged building-code violations.

But the Hispanic-American story was not only one of poverty and problems. The Hispanic middle class grew by 25 percent in the 1990s. A 1992 Census Bureau study found 862,000 Hispanic-owned businesses, and the number burgeoned thereafter. And Hispanic Americans, like other minority groups, organized to defend their interests. The largest advocacy group, La Raza, vigorously articulated Hispanic concerns. The displaced Hispanics of Addison fought back, filing a class-action lawsuit supported by the U.S. Justice Department. Addison's town fathers settled the suits in 1997, pledging to construct affordable housing to replace the demolished residences, pay moving costs and compensation to the displaced families, and construct parks and a community center in Hispanic neighborhoods. Other cities reached similar settlements in response to charges of anti-Hispanic discrimination.

America's rich diversity in the 1990s found religious expression as well, with some 800,000 Buddhists, 900,000 Hindus, more than 5 million Muslims, and thousands of adherents of other non-Western religions contributing to the tapestry of faith. The Muslim community included not only immigrants from Muslim countries, but some 2 million African Americans. Only about 80,000 of these adhered to the racist Nation of Islam (NOI) headed by Louis Farrakhan; the vast majority followed the son of NOI founder Elijah Muhammed, who after his father's death in 1975 converted to the mainstream Sunni Islamic faith. For some, this was a return to an ancestral faith, since at least 20 percent of the Africans transported to America as slaves were Muslims. By 2020, it is predicted, Islam will replace Judaism as the nation's largest religion after Christianity. The U.S. military added its first Muslim chaplain in the 1990s, and in 1996 the Clintons celebrated the end of Ramadan (the Islamic holy month) with a group of Muslim children at the White House. U.S. Muslims vigorously challenged stereotypes about their faith, especially many Americans' tendency to link Islam with the use of terrorism in pursuit of political goals—a practice that violates Islamic belief and is repudiated by all but a tiny fringe of fanatics.

In any survey of American society at century's end, the changing status of women must inevitably loom large. The statistics were impressive. Women writers, artists, and scholars, moving rapidly toward full equality with their male colleagues, energized the cultural and intellectual scene, and women's history emerged as a lively field. In the realm of black literature, once largely a male do-

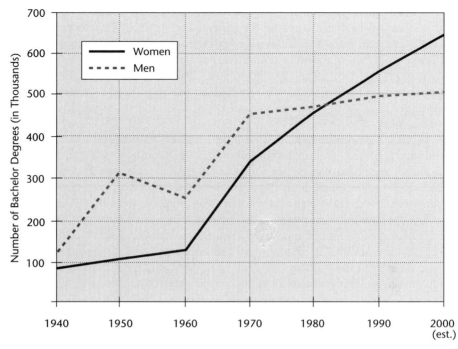

FIGURE 15.5
Number of Bachelor (B.A.) Degrees Awarded, 1940–2000,
Actual and Estimated, by Gender
SOURCE: *World Almanac, 1998.*

main, women such as Alice Walker, Maya Angelou, and Toni Morrison now held sway. Morrison won the Nobel Prize for literature in 1993. Moreover, the proportion of women in the work force rose from 42 percent in 1970 to 57 percent by 1991 and remained at that level through the 1990s. Even Rabbit Angstrom's long-suffering wife, Janice, became a realtor. Women found employment at all levels, from domestic service and the building trades to white-collar jobs. By 1998 some 30 percent of working women held executive and managerial positions. By 1997, 63 percent of female high-school graduates were going on to college, in contrast to 61 percent of male graduates. In the fall of 1997 at the University of Wisconsin, Madison, 42 percent of the entering medical students and 44 percent of the entering law students were women. Nevertheless, the top ranks of business and the professions remained male bastions as employed women clustered in the lower ranks of the labor force, held down by subtle but entrenched patterns of gender discrimination that became known as the "glass ceiling." In a 1997 poll by CBS News, 72 percent of women under thirty said that women are discriminated against in obtaining executive jobs.

Shifting marital and family patterns shaped women's lives as well. With births to unmarried women still at high levels and nearly half of all marriages ending in divorce, single-parent families, usually headed by a female, grew steadily. The proportion of children living in traditional, two-parent families fell from 85 percent in

1970 to around 70 percent in 1991. (For non-Hispanic white children, the figure was 76 percent; for black children, 33 percent, and for Hispanic children, 63 percent.) The birthrate remained low, with couples opting for one or two children or none at all. All these trends directly influenced women's life choices. As the journal *Public Interest* noted in 1993, "In a long-life-expectancy, low-birth-rate society, there really is no serious alternative to major lifelong working careers for most women. The career of full-time wife, mother and homemaker has simply ceased to be an adequate life project."

Amid these profound changes, feminism came under assault from conservatives who deplored its emphasis on autonomy and careers as antifamily and a threat to "traditional values." In *Backlash: The Undeclared War Against American Women* (1991), Susan Faludi saw a systematic drive in politics, fashion, and advertising to reassert old stereotypes of women as subordinate, deferential sex objects.

With greater autonomy came a heightened awareness of all forms of exploitation, including rape and sexual harassment. Susan Brownmiller's *Against Our Will: Men, Women, and Rape* (1975) had placed this issue on the feminist agenda, and it remained there in the eighties and nineties. Businesses and educational institutions adopted tough sexual-harassment codes. But this issue, too, stirred controversy. In *The Morning After: Sex, Fear, and Feminism on Campus* (1993), Katie Roiphe argued that the broadening of "rape" to include a wide range of ambiguous sexual encounters represented a resurgence of Victorian prudery in a more politically correct guise. Conservative writer Charles Sykes in *A Nation of Victims* (1993) attacked what he called the "sexual nightmare" of some feminists who were peddling "the politics of victimization."

Abortion, too, continued to rouse strong emotions a quarter century after the 1973 *Roe* v. *Wade* decision. Books such as *Life Itself: Abortion in the American Mind* (1992) by journalist Roger Rosenblatt and *Life's Dominion* (1993) by law professor Ronald Dworkin sought grounds for compromise, but such efforts failed to sway the committed partisans of either camp. While the pro-choice advocates defended unrestricted access to abortion as a right, the antiabortion group, mostly Catholics and evangelical Protestants, denounced the procedure as immoral. Abortion foes portrayed their cause as part of a larger crusade to affirm the sanctity of all life. Pro-choice advocates linked their battle to the wider campaign for gender equality; the war against abortion rights, they insisted, was part of a broader drive to subordinate women. Interestingly, some prominent feminists expressed reservations about abortion, and opinion polls generally showed greater opposition to abortion among women than among men.

Civil disobedience, once the province of antiwar and civil-rights activists, now became a technique of antiabortion groups like Operation Rescue, whose members courted arrest in their demonstrations against clinics and even against individual physicians. A handful of anti-abortion activists crossed the line into violence. From 1978 to 1993, extremists bombed or set fire to more than a hundred clinics. In March 1993, an antiabortion activist in Pensacola, Florida, shot and killed a physician whose photograph had earlier appeared on a "Wanted" poster circulated by Operation Rescue. In 1994, a mentally disturbed young man on the fringe of the antiabortion movement shot and killed the receptionists at two abortion clinics in the Boston suburb of Brookline. In 1997, bombs damaged abortion clinics in Tulsa and Atlanta. Nearly all "pro-life" leaders condemned violence, but these acts revealed the passions that the issue had catalyzed.

From time to time, the abortion issue reached the courts and Congress. In 1992 the Supreme Court upheld parts of a Pennsylvania law limiting abortion rights by a 5–4 vote. Justice Thomas took the occasion to call for a reversal of *Roe,* but Justice Souter outraged abortion foes by joining the majority in coupling a partial endorsement of the Pennsylvania law with a strong defense of *Roe* itself. The majority ruled that "an entire generation has come of age free to assume *Roe*'s concept of liberty in defining the capacity of women . . . to make reproductive decisions. . . . To overrule *Roe* . . . [would cause] profound and unnecessary damage to the Court's legitimacy, and to the Nation's commitment to the rule of law." Indeed, the bitterness of the controversy obscured the fact that a broad national consensus supported the Supreme Court's position. This consensus approved the availability of abortion in the first trimester of pregnancy but also endorsed the right of states to impose restrictions such as waiting periods and parental notification (or even parental consent) for minors. The Clinton administration firmly upheld the prochoice position. In 1996, President Clinton vetoed a Republican bill to ban late-term or "partial birth" abortions, arguing that this should be a medical decision, not a political one. On the GOP side, the Republican National Committee early in 1988, by a 114–43 vote, rejected a proposal to make opposition to late-term abortions a "litmus test" for all Republican candidates seeking party support.

While debate swirled around the abortion issue, the actual number of abortions, after rising steadily from 1974 to a 1990 peak of 1.4 million, slowly declined thereafter, to an estimated 1.2 million in 1997. Public attitudes toward abortion appeared to be shifting as well. A *New York Times*/CBS poll in 1998, the twenty-fifth anniversary of *Roe* v. *Wade,* found only qualified support for legal abortion. The respondents overwhelmingly backed the right to an abortion in cases of rape, risks to the mother's health, or the possibility of serious defects in the baby, but strong opposition under other circumstances. For example, only 25 percent supported the right to an abortion when giving birth would interrupt a woman's career—a drop from 37 percent in 1989. in the ever-shifting realm of public opinion, a consensus appeared to be developing around the position that while legal abortion should be preserved, it should be socially discouraged, hedged in with restrictions, and available only under specific circumstances. How this would translate into future legislation and legal rulings, if at all, remained unclear.

As the abortion controversy raged on, the women's movement itself, after the excitement and solidarity of the 1970s, entered a period of self-examination, as feminists questioned their assumptions and strategies. As early as 1981, in *The Second Stage,* Betty Friedan criticized feminists who focused on career issues and women's rights and left concerns about the family to conservatives. As the national mood became more conservative, feminists found themselves on the defensive. While 74 percent of women told pollsters in 1997 that women's status had improved since 1970, fewer than 20 percent described themselves as "feminists," down from around 35 percent in 1989. Even more revealingly, the women who said they would prefer an outside job to full-time homemaking fell from about 70 percent in 1974 to about 40 percent in 1997. "People are saying that all feminism ever got us is more work," reported Heidi Hartman, the director of a research organization on women's issues, in 1997.

Environmentalism, another legacy of the 1970s, remained strong through the 1990s, though, like the woman's movement, it, too, experienced a backlash amid controversies over complex issues. Environmental concerns sharpened in March 1989 when the giant oil tanker *Exxon Valdez* ran aground in Prince William Sound, Alaska. The ship dumped 10.8 million gallons of crude oil that blackened miles of coastline; killed hundreds of sea otters, bald eagles, and shorebirds; and endangered Alaska's fisheries. George Bush deplored the disaster but insisted that America's energy needs required continued oil drilling in Alaska. Similar clashes between conflicting interests proliferated. In the Pacific Northwest, for example, the campaign to preserve the last old-growth forests and their delicate ecosystem, including the northern spotted owl, angered loggers and timber companies worried about jobs and profits.

The environmental movement took on fresh urgency as new health threats emerged. Scientists warned of acid rain, a product of atmospheric pollution that kills plant and animal life in lakes and forests. They also pointed to the thinning of the Earth's ozone layer caused by chlorofluorocarbon gases from spray cans and other sources. Ozone filters out carcinogenic ultraviolet radiation. In addition, scientists grew alarmed by the threat of global warming as atmospheric pollution prevented the Earth's heat from escaping. Such reports built support for the Clean Air Act of 1990 (see Chapter 14). At the local level, cities urgently established recycling programs to avoid choking on their own refuse, estimated to reach 216 million tons per year by 2000.

In *Earth in the Balance* (1992), then-senator Al Gore of Tennessee spotlighted the environmental crisis. The industrialized world continued to deplete dwindling natural resources and energy supplies, while in poor nations such as Egypt and India, the drive for economic development often overrode environmental concerns. In South America and parts of Asia, rain forests rich in biological diversity and ecologically vital to the entire world faced destruction. Recognizing the global dimensions of the issue, the UN in 1992 convened Earth Summit, in Rio de Janeiro, an event that drew thirty-five thousand participants. The delegates signed treaties related to biodiversity and global warming and endorsed "Agenda 21," a sweeping, although nonbinding, manifesto.

The success of the Clinton-Gore ticket in 1992 brought joy to environmentalists, but in his first three years Clinton focused on other matters and neglected environmental issues. However, when the Republican-dominated Congress elected in 1994 tried to roll back two decades of environmental regulation, the administration was prodded into action, and in 1996–98 it played a more active environmental role. The administrator of the Environmental Protection Agency (EPA), Carol Browner, successfully protected her agency from GOP attacks. In 1996, Clinton secured passage of a bill strengthening the regulation of pesticides. In 1997, despite fierce industrial lobbying, Clinton approved tough new EPA regulations on the emissions of pollutants that produced smog and soot, caused respiratory problems (particularly for children, the elderly, and asthmatics), and contributed to global warming.

Clinton's belated environmental activism played well politically. In a 1996 poll, 57 percent of Americans said that the environment must be protected even if job losses resulted. The GOP's opposition to environmental-protection laws proved deeply unpopular. The administration also had the weight of scientific evidence on its side, especially on the issue of global warming. In 1998 the National Oceanographic and Atmospheric Administration reported that average temperatures worldwide had risen by a degree since 1900, and that 1997 was the warmest year on record. The report further concluded that pollutant emissions likely played a role in this disturbing trend. Scientific data also pinpointed a major source of the problem: the United States, with per capita emission of pollutants of some 20 metric tons per year, in contrast to Europe's total of around 8 metric tons per capita.

In December 1997, delegates from 150 nations gathered in Kyoto, Japan, to negotiate a global treaty to control the emissions of the heat-trapping gases that contribute to the "greenhouse effect" implicated in global warming. When the conference threatened to bog down in disputes between poor nations and rich, industrialized nations over the rates of emission reduction, Vice President Gore flew to Kyoto to push the negotiations forward. The delegates were bombarded by lobbyists representing not only environmental groups but also automobile, steel, petroleum, and other industries; the latter warned of economic disaster if a strict treaty were adopted. The intense business lobbying further illustrated the role of economic calculations in shaping post–Cold War U.S. foreign policy. The delegates eventually agreed on a treaty, but the prospects for ratification by the U.S. Senate remained unclear, particularly when the chief business lobby allocated $13 million to defeat it.

Encouraging news from the private sector came in 1998 when the U.S. auto industry (in part to fend off their Japanese competitors) announced a major commitment to developing lower-emission vehicles, and to improving the record of the high-polluting light trucks and sport-utility vehicles beloved of U.S. consumers in the 1990s. "No car company will be able to thrive in the 21st century," declared the head of General Motors, "if it relies solely on internal combustion engines."

Another troubling environmental problem was the disposal of deadly radioactive waste from decades of nuclear-power and nuclear-weapons production. In 1997, scientists reported a higher-than-expected rate of water seepage in the manmade cavern deep under Nevada's Yucca Mountain, the government's designated waste-disposal site. Experts foresaw years of study before any nuclear waste was actually stored at Yucca Mountain, if ever. Despite the lobbying, political maneuvering, and honest scientific disagreements, environmental issues were clearly destined to remain high on the national—and global—agenda as a new century dawned.

Health Issues, Scientific Innovations, Mass Culture Trends

Just as nagging problems and periodic crises marked U.S. foreign relations in the 1990s despite the Cold War's demise, so an array of domestic concerns preoccupied Americans in these years, despite the booming economy. Complex medical developments, rapid changes in the mass-culture realm, and the continuing computer revolution all made the end of the twentieth century a time of edgy adjustment and earnest debate, as Americans grappled with large-scale social and technological transformations and the difficult policy issues and ethical dilemmas they sometimes posed.

On the biomedical front, as the U.S. population aged, the nation confronted an array of ethical issues including assisted suicide for the terminally ill, the soaring cost of nursing-home care, and the challenge of maintaining the quality of life for the old. Feminist pioneer Betty Friedan, now in her seventies, addressed this issue in *The Fountain of Age* (1993). Grey power received a major boost when NASA announced that Senator John Glenn, who in 1962 had become the first American to orbit the earth, had been cleared for a ten-day space mission in October 1998, when he would be 77. If Glenn's feat succeeded, predicted a NASA official, "children will look at their grandparents differently."

The beginnings of life raised thorny issues as well, not all of them related to abortion. As childless couples sought help from science, problems of medical ethics arose, ranging from fertility drugs that sometimes produced multiple births ranging from twins to sextuplets, to the science-fiction prospect of human cloning—an issue that moved a step closer to reality in 1997 when scientists in Edinburgh, Scotland, cloned a sheep. A stark reminder of the health toll of tobacco addiction came early in 1998 when a congressman released tobacco-industry documents revealing a clear strategy of attracting children and young people. President Clinton stressed the "imperative" necessity of tougher controls on cigarette advertising and sales to minors.

The nation in the 1990s continued to grapple with the scourge of AIDS (acquired immunodeficiency syndrome), the fatal disease first identified in 1981. By

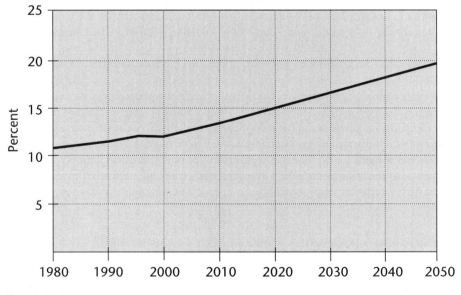

FIGURE 15.6

Percentage of U.S. Population Aged 65 or Older, 1980–2050 (Actual and Projected)

SOURCE: Bureau of the Census, in *Statistical Abstract of the U.S., 1997.*

The AIDS Quilt. *"America does not have a person to waste,"* President Bill Clinton vowed to AIDS marchers in Washington, D.C., in 1993 as he proposed strengthening funding for AIDS research. (Gregory Zabilski)

the end of 1997, more than 380,000 Americans had died of AIDS. An estimated 650,000–850,000 were infected with the human immunodeficiency virus (HIV), a precursor of AIDS, of whom some 233,000 had the disease in full-blown form. The epidemic took a global toll. The UN in 1996 estimated some 22 million HIV/AIDS cases worldwide, with sub-Saharan Africa, South and Southeast Asia, and Latin America hardest hit. The U.S. AIDS picture brightened somewhat at the end of the 1990s. Thanks to improved therapies and growing knowledge about prevention, AIDS-related deaths in America fell by 26 percent in 1997. In California, a hard-hit state, the number of deaths dropped by 60 percent in the first half of 1997. A leader of the San Francisco AIDS Foundation hailed this "astonishingly good news," but warned that the crisis was far from over.

AIDS spreads by the direct transmission of bodily fluids. The most vulnerable populations are homosexuals or bisexuals, persons having unprotected sex with infected individuals, drug users sharing needles, and babies born to infected mothers. Early in the epidemic, blood transfusions also spread the virus. With no cure in sight, public-health agencies urgently advised protective measures, including the use of condoms. The AIDS epidemic had cultural ramifications as well. Actor Rock Hudson, who had hidden his homosexuality during his movie career, died of AIDS in 1985. Basketball superstar Earvin "Magic" Johnson and tennis pro Arthur Ashe announced in 1991–1992 that they were HIV positive. Ashe, who had become infected from a blood transfusion, died in 1993.

While some viewed the disease as God's "punishment" of homosexuals, gay-rights and AIDS activists protested the ostracizing of sufferers and called for expanded research budgets and quicker testing of promising drugs. The radical group ACT UP used direct-action techniques to publicize their cause. Hospice organizations and support networks helped people with the disease, and a giant AIDS quilt made of panels crafted by victims' friends and relatives toured the nation. In novels, in plays such as Larry Kramer's *The Normal Heart* (1985) and Tony Kushner's epic *Angels in America* (1993), and in movies such as *Philadelphia* (1993), starring Tom Hanks, writers and filmmakers explored the devastation of AIDS and the courage that it could call forth. The AIDS crisis added urgency to the larger debate over the allocation of medical-research funds, the availability of promising but untested drugs, and other complex issues.

The defeat of the Clinton health-care plan in 1993 did not end governmental involvement in health issues. The soaring cost of Medicare, the 1960s program to cover health services to the elderly and severely disabled, caused deepening worry as the decade wore on. With 38 million beneficiaries, Medicare cost $196 billion in 1996, 12 percent of the federal budget—surpassed only by social security and defense spending. Total U.S. health-care spending represented 14 percent of the gross domestic product (up from 7 percent in 1970), in contrast to 7–10 percent in European countries. And worse lay ahead. As the nation's 75 million baby boomers retired after 2010, annual Medicare costs could soar to $312 billion, creating horrendous budget deficits. Adding to the concerns about Medicare, a 1996 federal audit concluded that in 1995 the government had overpaid hospitals, physicians, and other health-care providers by $23 billion—14 percent of Medicare's total cost!

Medicare was clearly spiraling out of control, and despite such powerful lobbies as the American Association of Retired Persons, Congress moved to rein in costs. In the 1997 budget negotiations, the Senate approved raising the age of Medicare eligibility from 65 to 67, and increasing premiums for the well-to-do. The House demurred, but the trend was clear as Congress set up a bipartisan federal advisory panel to address the problem; Congress also capped Medicare payments to Health Maintenance Organizations (HMOs), causing many of them to raise monthly premiums and copayment fees for prescription drugs. One of the largest providers, Humana, in 1998 tripled its fee for drugs prescribed for Medicare patients.

Meanwhile the inflationary increases in health-care costs slowed, as millions of Americans joined HMOs—private, for-profit, managed-care providers. By 1996, 58 million Americans were enrolled in HMOs or similar plans, and 75 percent of doctors worked at least part-time for an HMO. The HMOs did cut costs, but sometimes at patients' expense. As stories mounted of patients denied needed treatment by their HMO or of new mothers sent home from the hospital after one day, public anger grew and the government stepped in. Regulatory measures were proposed at both the state and federal levels, including a Clinton administration plan for a "bill of rights for health-care consumers" setting mandatory HMO guidelines and requiring HMOs to inform consumers about their policies. It took no crystal ball to see that health-care issues would only grow more urgent in the twenty-first century, and that government would be a key player as the revolution in health care continued.

Worries about health care and other pressing issues did not impede Americans' quest for entertainment, as the mass-culture trends of the 1980s (see Chapter

14) continued in the prosperous 1990s. Movies, television, resorts, theme parks, professional sports, gambling casinos, travel agencies, and the pop-music industry all flourished as Americans sought leisure-time diversion. In 1996, 700,000 visitors toured Graceland, Elvis Presley's garish mansion in Memphis. As in the past, escapist fare dominated the mass media. The two top-grossing movies of 1996, *Independence Day* and *Twister,* both loaded with special effects, dealt, respectively, with invading aliens and killer tornadoes. Together they took in more than half a billion dollars. *Titanic,* a 1997 Hollywood spectacular, retold the story of that ill-fated vessel's 1912 sinking. As computer-animation technology grew more sophisticated, movies blended real action and animation in ways that were hardly distinguishable. In 1996, *Life* magazine named moviemaker Steven Spielberg the most influential American of his generation, celebrating him as "our Homer and our Hans Christian Andersen, an epic fairy-tale maker with a Midas touch."

Seinfeld, the top TV comedy of the 1990s, involved a cast of likeable but self-absorbed and mildly neurotic New Yorkers as they confronted in wildly bizarre ways the petty irritations of everyday life and tried, with little success, to hold jobs and build long-term relationships. In 1994, network TV news programs devoted 491 stories to the case of O.J. Simpson (a football star and media celebrity suspected of murdering his ex-wife and a friend), in contrast to the 409 stories about that year's midterm elections, a notable turning point in contemporary politics. Indeed, television's cultural power and ubiquity influenced the political process profoundly. Political campaigns became hardly distinguishable from toothpaste promotions, as advertising agencies "packaged" candidates and TV commercials featured manipulative visual images, memorable (if meaningless) sound bites, and "attack ads" discrediting the opponent. The popularity of confessional TV talk shows influenced politicians' self-presentation, as they told heart-tugging stories of parental abuse, injured children, and other traumas that had shaped their outlook. Ronald Reagan's patented catch-in-the-throat was legendary, and although Bill Clinton's mastery of the politics of emotion ("I feel your pain") provoked ridicule, it was effective.

Meeting Americans' voracious appetite for entertainment involved mind-boggling sums of money. CD sales surged to around $10 billion in 1996, nearly three times the 1990 total. *Seinfeld* generated $200 million a year for NBC. In high-level negotiations early in 1998, ABC paid $4.4 billion to televise *Monday Night Football* for eight years and ESPN acquired the cable rights to National Football League (NFL) games for $4.8 billion. The total contract negotiations produced $18 billion for the NFL over an eight-year period, and made the NFL the major supplier of programming to the TV industry.

Corporate conglomerates with vast and complex holdings increasingly dominated the mass culture. The Disney Corporation, with 1996 revenues of $19 billion, counted ABC, ESPN, a movie studio, and the Disneyland and Disney World theme parks among its crown jewels. Another media giant, Viacom ($12 billion in 1996 revenues) controlled Paramount Pictures and MTV, the popular music-video channel, along with many other holdings. King of the media moguls was the Australian Rupert Murdoch, who became a U.S. citizen in 1985. In 1997, after decades of acquisitions, Murdoch's parent corporation owned 789 businesses in fifty-two countries. His U.S. holdings included Fox movie studios (producers of *Independence Day*), the Fox TV net-

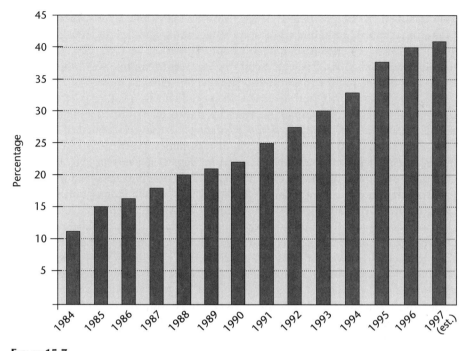

FIGURE 15.7

Percentage of U.S. Households Owning Computers, 1984–1997

SOURCE: Electronic Industries Association, in *World Almanac 1998*.

work, 22 television stations, the *New York Post, TV Guide,* the Los Angeles Dodgers baseball team, and HarperCollins publishing company. What the *Washington Post* called Murdoch's "planet-girdling ring of satellite TV systems" could theoretically broadcast simultaneously to 75 percent of Earth's population.

The personal-computer revolution gained momentum as the century ended. PC sales jumped from 4 million in 1990 to nearly 11 million in 1997. By 1997, 41 percent of U.S. households had computers, nearly double the 1990 total, and 65 percent of senior high schools had computers equipped with CD-ROM players.

Like the entertainment industry, the computer-software business was dominated by giant corporations, many centered in Silicon Valley, but with outposts in Texas, Washington State, and the Northeast. Biggest of all was the Seattle giant Microsoft, founded by Harvard dropout Bill Gates III, son of a prominent Seattle lawyer. By the late 1990s, Gates was the richest person in America. Trumpeting its cheerful slogan "Where do you want to go today?," Microsoft dominated the software industry with an array of computer operating systems and applications. With $9 billion in cash and a stock-market valuation of $160 billion (three times that of General Motors), Microsoft in 1997 absorbed its onetime rival, Apple Computer, founded by former wunderkind Steve Jobs and Steve Wozniak in the 1970s. After years of operating in an almost totally unregulated environment, Microsoft in 1997 confronted a Justice Department antitrust suit charging it with unfair competitive practices such as installing its own Internet browser, Explorer, in its Windows 95 operating system. Like Standard Oil or Carnegie Steel in an earlier era, the Microsoft juggernaut crushed or bought out weaker competitors through its sheer size, wealth, and ruthlessness. In 1995–97, Microsoft acquired forty-seven computer software, Internet, or entertainment companies. How successful Washington would be in trimming Microsoft's sails remained to be seen.

The computer made possible the multibillion-dollar video-game industry; revolutionized personal communications through the electronic system known as e-mail; and opened to users a vast world of global information exchange and discussion through the Internet, a supernetwork of many smaller computer networks. Developed in rudimentary form by the Department of Defense in 1969, the Internet soon took on a life of its own. With some 30 million Internet users in the United States in 1997, observers predicted that half of U.S. households would be part of the system by 2000. The World Wide Web, developed in Geneva in the early 1990s, represented a further elaboration of the Internet's potential. With images, movement, and sound, the World Wide Web represented an even richer, more varied Internet environment.

In contrast to the corporate consolidation represented by Microsoft, the Internet was decentralized to the point of anarchy, infusing it with a heady excitement but also giving rise to periodic calls for censorship, as in the Communications Decency Act of 1996. The Supreme Court, as we have seen, ruled this law unconstitutional in 1997, shifting from government censors to parents the responsibility for shielding minors from the Internet's proliferating pornographic Websites. Civil libertarians cheered, but antipornography groups such as Enough is Enough bemoaned this further blow to morality and decency.

Inevitably, the democratization of the computer inspired both utopian visions and hand-wringing warnings. Critics claimed that it encouraged rote memorization and stifled creativity, but politicians from Al Gore to Newt Gingrich hailed the spread of computer-based teaching, as did some academic defenders. Seymour Papert, a learning researcher at MIT, argued in *The Children's Machine: Rethinking School in the Age of the Computer* (1993) that imaginative, interactive computer programs could challenge and stretch pupils' imaginations.

Other critics warned of numbed moral sensibilities in a generation reared on computer-based video games, which often featured extreme violence without consequences. In *War of the Worlds: Cyberspace and the High-Tech Assault on Reality* (1995), Mark Sloutka offered a broader critique, contending that the virtual reality of the computer screen can become more "real" for users than the actual world around them. Underscoring such fears, teachers reported that schoolchildren were bonding emotionally with their digital "pets" (a fad of the late 1990s) and grieving when they "died" from lack of "feeding." In the same vein, sociologist Sherry Turkle, in *Life on the Screen: Identity in the Age of the Internet* (1995), saw a weakening of fixed identity as people assumed different roles in the anonymity of chat groups and interactive Websites. The Internet, she suggested, was the ultimate "postmodern" phenomenon, foreshadowing a destabilized, decentered self, and a dissolving of reality. Despite such apprehensions, however, America's love affair with the computer showed no signs of tapering off.

The giant, dinosaur-like computers of the late 1940s, a byproduct of World War II, with which this history began, had by the 1990s spawned a vast progeny of personal computers that were revolutionizing American life. Yet, to historians looking back from 2050, the communications revolution of the late twentieth century may well seem only the sketchiest prelude to what the twenty-first century held in store. Beyond the technological wizardry, what would be the social and political effects of this revolution? Would powerful computers lead to ever-greater concentrations of governmental and corporate power? Or would the private, free-for-all world of the personal computer and the Internet make the twenty-first century more like the nineteenth, when individualism flourished and the government and other large-scale institutions played comparatively little role in ordinary citizens' lives?

Anticipation and Apprehension as a New Millennium Dawns

As Americans confronted a momentous turn of the calendar—the arrival not only of a new century but of a new millennium—the national mood, while in some ways quite upbeat, seemed curiously uneasy and ambivalent, with notes of anxiety mingling with the more positive chords. Certainly Americans welcomed the end of the Cold War, the lowered threat of nuclear war, and the prosperity of the 1990s. They applauded in 1997 when NASA's Pathfinder space probe landed a small exploratory vehicle on Mars that sent back stunning photos of the Martian surface, and when the orbiting Hubbell telescope returned breathtaking images of vast star systems in the process of emerging and disintegrating. Who could not feel pride as U.S. scientists expanded the frontiers of human knowledge?

But for many Americans, the lightening pace of social, cultural, technological, and even scientific change in these years also proved disorienting and unsettling, stirring a mood of conservatism and nostalgia that sometime edged over into reactionary hostility and suspicion. Too much was changing, too fast! Many responded by clinging to the familiar, or by lashing out at those who seemed responsible.

Some observers saw this anxious mood as a lingering aftereffect of decades when fear and apprehension had been fully justified. As New York senator Daniel Moynihan observed in 1997: "Perceptions lag. It takes time for a culture that was deeply pessimistic about the future and deeply anxious about the present during the Cold War to come out of that." Others found the cause in postwar domestic history. The almost three decades of economic growth that had followed World War II, concluded economist Robert J. Samuelson in *The Good Life and Its Discontents* (1995), had created unrealistic expectations of endless expansion and personal entitlement, leaving Americans in an "almost permanent state of public grumpiness."

Whatever the reasons, the unease and anger coursing through the nation's political and cultural life surfaced in unexpected ways. When the National Endowment for the Arts gave modest grants to artists and photographers whose work some found offensive, the public outcry seemed out of all proportion to the money involved. When the Smithsonian's National Museum of American History announced an exhibit in 1995 marking the fiftieth anniversary of the atomic bombing of Japan that included a range of historical judgments regarding Truman's decision, as well as information on the bombs' human toll, veterans' groups, patriotic organizations, and sympathetic politicians protested loudly, and the exhibit was canceled. Historian John Dower noted the irony of "demanding a pristine, heroic, official version of a war that presumably was fought to protect principled contention and the free play of ideas."

Some Americans—mostly native-born whites—found the nation's increasingly multiethnic, multicultural profile deeply upsetting, and came to see themselves as embattled and under siege. One result was another of the periodic upsurges of hostility to immigrants that have marked U.S. history. As legal and illegal newcomers, often poor and ill educated, and typically from Latin America or Asia, arrived in great numbers in these years, they encountered growing hostility. Stricter rules imposed in 1997 raised the economic barrier for immigration and made it harder for recent immigrants to bring in relatives. The notoriously porous U.S.-Mexican border was more heavily fortified and patrolled. In 1997, U.S. Marines patrolling for drug smugglers shot and killed a Mexican youth herding sheep along the border.

But the anti-immigrant sentiment was muted, since the newcomers supplied crucial agricultural labor in the West, and took low-paying jobs as dishwashers, janitors, maids, car washers, and handymen that native-born workers often spurned, particularly when boom times made better-paying jobs plentiful. As a woman in Galveston, Texas, observed: "We may vote against immigration, but we still want a cheap gardener." Noting this paradox, the *Economist* of London commented in 1997: "Americans' bouts of anti-immigrant fervor tend to be ambivalent, hypocritical . . . and futile."

The 1990s also saw a reaction against affirmative-action programs that included special preferences for minorities. The Supreme Court in 1995 restricted the use of race as a consideration in awarding federal contracts, and in 1996 California voters passed Proposition 209, ending racial or ethnic preferences in any state agency, including the University of California. Though it faced a test in the courts, Proposition 209 had immediate and dramatic results. Minority enrollment at the University of California Law School at Berkeley fell sharply, and set-asides for minority businesses in state-contract competitions were ended. Similar initiatives were proposed in other states. Critics of affirmative action such as Ward Connerly of the University of California Board of Regents (himself an African American), and the historians Stephen and Abigail Thernstrom, authors of *Black and White in America* (1997), insisted that they were simply affirming the principle of equality for all. Others, however, including Andrew Hacker in *Two Nations Black and White: Separate, Hostile and Unequal* (1995) and Jim Sleeper in *Liberal Racism* (1997), saw subtle racism in some of the attacks on affirmative action. A 1997 opinion poll found that while most whites opposed legally mandated racial or ethnic preferences in academia or the workplace, they did support other programs designed to increase minority access. The poll also revealed more support for means-tested affirmative-action programs (that is, programs favoring the poor) than those benefiting entire racial or ethnic groups.

As debates over immigration and affirmative action unfolded, social and cultural observers wrestled with the question of how to preserve a common sense of civic loyalty within a context of multiculturalism and interest-group politics. In *Democracy's Discontent: America in Search of a Public Philosophy* (1996), government professor Michael Sandel discussed the erosion of America's political culture, which he called

Grassroots Philanthropy. *Despite worries about selfishness and materialism in the booming 1990s, the volunteer impulse remained strong, as illustrated by these volunteers with Habitat for Humanity, a program to help the poor acquire their own houses. One high-visibility Habitat for Humanity volunteer was former president Jimmy Carter.* (Bob Daemmrich/The Image Works)

"civic republicanism," and proposed remedies. Political scientist Robert Putnam, in a 1995 essay called "Bowling Alone," cited the decline of bowling leagues, together with falling voter turnout and a drop in volunteers for such organizations as the Red Cross and the Boy Scouts, as symptomatic of the deterioration of social consciousness in favor of privatized, self-centered pursuits. (Some challenged Putnam's evidence, arguing that many forms of voluntarism were thriving.)

The cultural wars that erupted in the 1970s and gained momentum in the 1980s (see chapters 13 and 14), featuring a conservative backlash against multiculturalism, "political correctness," and the alleged decline of academic standards, continued in the 1990s. Conservative critics like William Bennett and Lynne Cheney, Republican officials in the Reagan and Bush administrations, lamented the erosion of intellectual rigor in the schools and the decline of a common culture as society splintered into many separate camps, each asserting its own identity and pursuing its own objectives. The historian Gertrude Himmelfarb summed up the apocalyptic mood of cultural conservatives in her 1994 book *On Looking into the Abyss.*

But other observers took a more constructive and hopeful view. In *Post-Ethnic America: Beyond Multiculturalism* (1995), historian David Hollinger argued for a cosmopolitan society in which individuals could choose their affinity group on the basis of their interests, talents, and individual preference, rather than being locked into a fixed cultural-political identity determined by gender, ethnicity, race, or socioeconomic background. Such a vision, Hollinger contended, reflected the American tradition of openness and possibility. Historian Lawrence Levine, in *The Opening of the American Mind* (1996), rejected the conservatives' romantic idea of a lost Eden of social homogeneity and cultural consensus. Cultural diversity and contentious disagreements, Levine insisted, have characterized America from the beginning.

The evangelical revival of the 1970s and 1980s also remained strong at century's end. Evangelical churches flourished, the nation's 2,500 Christian bookstores racked up $3 billion in annual sales, Christian music groups proliferated, and bumper sticks proclaimed "Praise the Lord" and "Real Men Love Jesus." From the evangelical perspective, modern America was a degenerate society where academic postmodernists dismissed timeless verities as nothing but social constructs; where a secular mass culture denigrated religion, marketed indecency, and celebrated homosexuality; and where the government upheld abortion, defended pornography, and banned prayer in the schools. In such a situation, millions of troubled believers found comfort and assurance in traditional religion, a strict moral code, and the clarity of a "Bible-based" faith. Evangelicalism's quarrel with contemporary America was highlighted in 1997 when leaders of the Southern Baptist Convention urged the church's 15 million members to boycott the Disney Corporation for sponsoring "Gay Pride" days at its theme parks and granting benefits to the partners of homosexual employees.

In 1991, a former football coach at the University of Colorado, Bill McCartney, founded Promise Keepers, a men's religious movement that called upon American males to love Jesus, live pure sex lives, and fulfill their divinely ordained role as strong husbands and attentive fathers. Featuring mass rallies at football stadiums, the movement grew steadily through the decade, attracting mostly white, middle-class, thirty-something males of evangelical religious backgrounds. In October 1997, some seven hundred thousand Promise Keepers rallied on the Mall in Washington, D.C., for a day of preaching, hymn singing, male bonding, and tearful group prayer. Some feminist groups criticized the movement as a reactionary reassertion of patriarchal authority, but Promise Keeper leaders denied the charge.

Evangelical Christians continued to make their voices heard in politics. Jerry Falwell disbanded the Moral Majority, but Pat Robertson's Christian Coalition, founded in 1989, continued to thrive. Under executive director Ralph Reed, a savvy young political operative (and history Ph.D. from Emory University), the Christian Coalition perfected its "stealth" strategy of electing conservative Christians to local committees and boards, where they pushed the conservative agenda. *U.S. News and World Report,* praising Reed's organizing skills, said: "He looks like a choir boy and acts like a ward boss." Calling for a return to traditional morality and "family values," the Religious Right stressed such emotional "hot button" issues as abortion, creationism, school prayer, suggestive pop-music lyrics, Internet pornography, sex education in the schools, and explicit or suggestive sex on TV and movie screens. Anathematizing Bill and Hillary Clinton, they overwhelmingly backed conservative Republican candidates. Some evangelicals found this politicized religion troubling. The Reverend Richard John Neuhaus, a conservative Christian editor, commented: "The conflation of Christian faith with a specific political agenda inevitably leads to a distortion of faith."

The rapid pace of change triggered a wave of nostalgia for simpler times. Often this took a benign form: Civil War battle reenactments; the revivals of old Broadway musicals in the later 1990s; a Hollywood vogue for making movies of the novels of Jane Austen or Henry James—even of the *Titanic* disaster. Sometimes, however, the reaction against modernity took a more unsettling turn. For many citizens, Washington, D.C., came to embody all that had gone wrong in America. Right-wing radio commentators like Rush Limbaugh and G. Gordon Liddy tirelessly ridiculed the idiocies of government. A freshly hatched Republican congresswoman from Wyoming in 1995 denounced the Internal Revenue Service as "the Gestapo." In 1964, 76 percent of Americans had told pollsters that the government could be trusted "always" or "most of the time." By 1994, the figure had fallen to 19 percent. (Interestingly, however, most respondents saw their own legislators as exceptions to the general rule.)

The paranoia seeped into the mass culture as well. The popular 1990s TV series *The X-Files* featured two lone FBI agents, Scully and Mulder, battling weird, sometimes paranormal conspiracies hatched by government agencies and other shadowy powers. The series' motto "Trust No One" summed up the mood. Cultural historian Ruth Rosen, writing in the *Chronicle of Higher Education* in 1997, described the program's appeal for both younger and older viewers linked by "a deep and abiding distrust of our government ... that has been powerfully reinforced during the past three decades." A 1998 Hollywood film, *Wag the Dog,* offered a profoundly cynical view of politics.

Some cultural observers saw this distrust of government as a legacy of the Cold War. For decades, Americans had been taught to view the world in black-and-white terms, with the Soviet Union as the embodiment of evil, and America as wholly virtuous. With the end of the Cold War, they suggested, many people simply transferred this black-and-white worldview to the domestic sphere, with Washington, D.C., replacing Moscow as the heart of darkness.

When combined with religious fundamentalism, this outlook could lead to the conclusion that the federal government was, quite literally, satanic. Paul Robertson's best-selling paperback *The New World Order* (1991) portrayed all of U.S. history as a vast conspiracy that will culminate in the rule of the Antichrist. Another Bible-prophecy believer with a conspiratorial turn of mind, David Koresh, isolated his followers in a compound near Waco, Texas, warning them that satanic powers, in the form of government authorities, were arrayed against them. When local and federal officials sought to arrest Koresh on charges of child abuse, statutory rape, and gun-law violations, his prophecies were tragically fullfilled. Ten persons died in February 1993 when federal agents stormed the Waco compound. On April 19, after a two-month standoff (and an orgy of media publicity), the FBI launched a second assault. As the tanks rumbled in, fires broke out within the compound; Koresh and some eighty of his followers, including seventeen children, perished in the flames.

In its most extreme form, the antigovernment ideology led some Americans to form heavily armed "militias" or retreat to survivalist communes in remote corners of the Great Plains or the Pacific Northwest, preparing for the final battle against the forces of evil. In 1997, estimates of the number of right-wing militia members in some thirty states ranged from ten thousand to sixty thousand. Often racist, anti-

Semitic, and obsessed with conspiracy theories, these groups used the latest communications technologies, including faxes and the Internet, to spread their message of hatred and fear.

Some unstable individuals took matters into their own hands. On April 19, 1995, the second anniversary of the Waco disaster, a powerful bomb hidden in a parked truck destroyed the Murrah Federal Building in Oklahoma City, killing 168 men, women, and children. (A daycare center in the building was hard hit.) Police soon arrested Timothy McVeigh, a decorated Gulf War veteran who had developed an abiding hatred of government. In 1997, McVeigh was convicted of murder and sentenced to death. A co-conspirator, Terry Nichols, McVeigh's former army buddy, was convicted of involuntary manslaughter, but escaped the death penalty. Both had tenuous links to the militia movement. What was America coming to? many wondered.

In another disturbing instance of an alienated loner resorting to ideologically motivated violence, a series of package bombs were mailed from 1978 to 1995 to individuals engaged in corporate activities that could be interpreted as promoting technology or jeopardizing the environment. Three people died and twenty-eight others were injured when they opened the packages. The perpetrator, dubbed the "Unabomber," sent long manifestoes to the press denouncing the modern technological order as inhumane and destructive. In 1996, authorities arrested Theodore Kaczynski, a mathematician and Harvard graduate, in his remote Montana cabin and charged him with the bombings. Although these isolated acts of antisocial violence were clearly the work of a few disturbed individuals, they contributed to the nagging sense of unease, suggesting the psychic toll that rapid social and technological change can take on a society, particularly on those who feel marginalized, disinherited, and powerless.

Conclusion

And so we come to the end of a history that began with an American nation united in its focus on fighting a global war, and ends with a far less cohesive U.S. citizenry engaged in the more diffuse but no less urgent task of redefining the nation's goals and purposes in a post–Cold War society and culture radically different from that of the 1940s. But continuities as well as discontinuities can be discerned. Despite troubling evidences of anxiety and alienation in the body politic, and the debased level of political campaigning, the democratic process still functions, demonstrating its resilience and its capacity for renewal. At the vital centers of U.S. political life—from Washington, D.C., to state capitals to local town meetings, community forums, activist gatherings, class discussions, and letters-to-the editor columns—Americans continue to address the nation's problems in a creative, lively process sometimes marked by the clash of differing economic interests, ethical perspectives, and ideological commitments.

Such clashes—and their peaceful if not always amicable resolution—are what democracy is all about. As the new century and the new millennium dawned, Americans, particularly the young who would soon assume the mantle of leadership in all realms of the national life, had cause for confidence as well as reasons for apprehension. With the commitment of a socially engaged citizenry, a form of government that had served the United States well for more than two hundred years would surely continue to do so, as the nation confronted the challenges of an unknown future.

SELECTED READINGS

For contemporary trends and issues, the *New York Times, Los Angeles Times, Boston Globe, Washington Post,* and other major newspapers can provide valuable background and perspective. So, too, can the leading news magazines, journals of opinion, and special-topic periodicals. See, for example, *Atlantic, Business Week, Christian Century, Christianity Today, Economist* (London), *Foreign Affairs, Fortune, Harper's, Ms., Nation, National Review, New Republic, New York Review of Books, New York Times Magazine, Newsweek, Progressive, Public Interest, Science, Time, Variety,* and *U.S. News and World Report.*

Clinton-Era Politics, Domestic Issues, and Political Discourse

Charles F. Allen, *The Comeback Kid: The Life and Career of Bill Clinton* (1992); E. J. Dionne, *They Only Look Dead: Why Progressives Will Dominate the Next Political Era* (1996); Elizabeth Drew, *Whatever It Takes: The Real Struggle for Political Power in America* (1997); Jack W. Germond and Jules Witcover, *Mad as Hell: Revolt at the Ballot Box: 1992* (1993); Mark Gerson, *The Neoconservative Vision* (1996); Stanley B. Greenberg and Theda Skocpol, eds., *The New Majority: Toward a Popular Progressive Politics* (1997); Ken Gross, *Ross Perot: The Man Behind the Myth* (1992); Jacob S. Hacker, *The Road to Nowhere: The Genesis of President Clinton's Plan for Health Security* (1997); Webb Hubbell, *Friends in High Places: Our Journey from Little Rock to Washington, D.C.* (1997); Peter Irons, *Brennan vs. Rehnquist: The Battle for the Constitution* (1994); Kathleen Hall Jamieson, *Packaging the Presidency: . . . Presidential Campaign Advertising* (3d ed., 1996); Michael Lind, *The Next American Nation: The New Nationalism and the Fourth American Revolution* (1995); David Maraniss, *First in His Class: A Biography of Bill Clinton* (1995); Carrick Mollenkamp et al., *The People* v. *Big Tobacco* (1998); Charles Noble, *Welfare as We Knew It: A Political History of the American Welfare State* (1997); Robert B. Reich, *Locked in the Cabinet* (1997); Tom Rosenstiel, *Strange Bedfellows: How Television and the Presidential Candidates Changed American Politics, 1992* (1993); Larry J. Sabato, ed., *Toward the Millennium: The Elections of 1996* (1997); Michael J. Sandel, *Democracy's Discontent: America in Search of a Public Philosophy* (1996); Judith N. Shklar, *Redeeming American Political Thought* (1997); James B. Stewart, *Blood Sport: The President and His Adversaries* (1996); Jacob Weisberg, *In Defense of Government: The Fall and Rise of Public Trust* (1996); Bob Woodward, *The Choice: How Clinton Won* (1996).

America in the World at Century's End

Benjamin R. Barber, *Jihad vs. McWorld* (1996); Henry Brandon, ed., *U.S.-European Relations* (1992); John Lewis Gaddis, *Now We Know: Rethinking Cold War History* (1997); David C. Gompert and F. Stephen Larrabee, *America and Europe: a Partnership for a New Era* (1997); Samuel P. Huntington, *The Clash of Civilizations and the Remaking of World Order* (1996); Paul Kennedy, *Preparing for the Twenty-First Century* (1993); Joseph S. Nye, *Bound to Lead: The Changing Nature of American Power* (1990); Robert W. Tucker and David C. Hendrickson, *The Imperial Temptation: The New World Order and America's Pur-*

poses (1992); Stansfield Turner, *Caging the Nuclear Genie* (1997); William B. Vogele, *Stepping Back: Nuclear Arms Control and the End of the Cold War* (1994); Daniel Yergin and Thane Gustafson, *Russia 2010* (1993).

Social Issues and Trends in the 1990s

Karen Anderson, *Changing Woman: A History of Racial Ethnic Women in Modern America* (1996); Peter Arno, *Against the Odds* (1992) [AIDS research and politics]; Mary Jo Bane and David T. Ellwood, *Welfare Realities: From Rhetoric to Reform* (1994); Francis J. Beckwith and Todd E. Jones, eds., *Affirmative Action: Social Justice or Reverse Discrimination?* (1997); Fergus M. Bordewich, *Killing the White Man's Indian: Reinventing Native-Americans at the End of the 20th Century* (1996); Thomas D. Boston and Catherine L. Ross, eds., *The Inner City: Urban Poverty and Economic Development in the Next Century* (1997); Arthur L. Caplan, *Am I My Brother's Keeper? The Ethical Frontiers of Biomedicine* (1997); Ellis Cose, *The Rage of a Privileged Class: Why Are Middle-Class Blacks Angry?* (1993); Elizabeth Fee and Daniel M. Fox, eds., *AIDS: The Making of a Chronic Disease* (1992); Neil Foley, *The White Scourge: Mexicans, Blacks, and Poor Whites in Texas Cotton Culture* (1997); Geoffrey Fox, *Hispanic Nation: Culture, Politics, and the Constructing of Identity* (1996); Cynthia Gorney, *Articles of Faith: A Frontline History of the Abortion Wars* (1998); Denis Lynn Daly Heyck, ed., *Barrios and Borderlands: Cultures of Latinos and Latinas in the United States* (1993); Bill Ong Hing, *Making and Remaking Asian America Through Immigration Policy, 1950–1990* (1993); Jong-deuk Jung, *A Study of Korean Immigration in America* (1991); Richard Kluger, *Ashes to Ashes* (1996) [cigarettes and public health]; Gina Kolata, *Clone: The Road to Dolly, and the Path Ahead* (1997); Alex Kotlowitz, *There Are No Children Here: The Story of Two Boys Growing Up in the Other America* (1991); Jonathan Kozol, *Amazing Grace: The Lives of Children and the Conscience of a Nation* (1995); Robert Kuttner, *Everything for Sale: The Virtues and Limits of Markets* (1996); Walter Benn Michaels, *Our America: Nativism, Modernism, and Pluralism* (1995); Joel Millman, *The Other Americans: How Immigrants Renew Our Country, Our Economy, and Our Values* (1997); Richard Moe and Carter Wilkie, *Changing Places: Rebuilding Community in the Age of Sprawl* (1997); Joan K. Peters, *When Mothers Work: Loving Our Children Without Sacrificing Ourselves* (1997); James Risen and Judy Thomas, *Wrath of Angels: The American Abortion Wars* (1998); Roger Rosenblatt, *Life Itself: Abortion in the American Mind* (1992); Philip Shabecoff, *A Fierce Green Fire: The American Environmental Movement* (1994); Randy Shilts, *And the Band Played On: Politics, People, and the AIDS Epidemic* (1987); Peter Skerry, *Mexican Americans: The Ambivalent Minority* (1993); Arlene S. Skolnick, *Embattled Paradise: The American Family in an Age of Uncertainty* (1991); Robert C. Smith, *Racism in the Post-Civil Rights Era: Now You See It, Now You Don't* (1995); Rickie Solinger, *Abortion Wars: A Half Century of Struggle, 1950–2000* (1997); Catherine McNicol Stock, *Rural Radicals: Righteous Rage in the American Grain* (1996); William Wei, *The Asian American Movement* (1993); Tom Wicker, *Tragic Failure: Racial Integration in America* (1996); William Julius Wilson, *When Work Disappears: The World of the New Urban Poor* (1996).

Cultural Discourse, Religious Trends, the Computer Revolution

Steven Barboza, *American Jihad: Islam After Malcolm X* (1994); William J. Bennett, *The De-Valuing of America: How to Win the Fight for Our Culture and Our Children* (1992); Francis Cairncross, *The Death of Distance: How the Communications Revolution Will Change Our Lives* (1997); Joel A. Carpenter, *Revive Us Again: The Reawakening of American Fundamentalism* (1997); Stephen L. Carter, *The Culture of Disbelief: How American Law and Politics Trivialize Religious Devotion* (1993); Dinesh D'Souza, *The End of Racism* (1995); James L. Guth, et al., *The Bully Pulpit: The Politics of Protestant Clergy* (1997); Robert Hughes, *Cul-*

ture of Complaint: The Fraying of America (1993); Martin Harwit, *An Exhibit Denied* (1996) [the *Enola Gay* controversy]; Gilles Kepel, *Allah in the West: Islamic Movements in America and Europe* (1997); Philip Lamy, *Millennium Rage: Survivalists, White Supremacists, and the Doomsday Prophecy* (1996); Christopher Lasch, *The Revolt of the Elites and the Betrayal of Democracy* (1995); Edward T. Linenthal and Tom Engelhardt, eds., *History Wars: The* Enola Gay *and Other Battles for the American Past* (1996); Edward N. Luttwack, *The Endangered American Dream* (1993); William Martin, *With God on Our Side: The Rise of the Religious Right in America* (1996); Hamish McRae, *The World in 2020: Power, Culture, and Prosperity* (1994); Joseph S. Nye et al., *Why People Don't Trust Government* (1997); Ralph Reed, *Active Faith: How Christians Are Changing the Soul of American Politics* (1996); Robert J. Samuelson, *The Good Life and Its Discontents: The American Dream in an Age of Entitlement, 1945–1995* (1995); James D. Tabor and Eugene V. Gallagher, *Why Waco? Cults and the Battle for Religious Freedom in America* (1995); Don Tapscott, *Growing Up Digital: The Rise of the Net Generation* (1998); James Wallace, *Overdrive: Bill Gates and the Race to Control Cyberspace* (1997); Justin Watson, *The Christian Coalition: Dreams of Restoration, Demands for Recognition* (1997).

Index

CREDITS

Photographs
Part One: Archive Photos. Part Two: Movie Stills Archive. Part Three: Roger Malloch/ Magnum Photos, Inc. Part Four: AP/Wide World Photos.

Text Credits